Soldier Creek Music Series

Number 1

Richard P. Smiraglia

General Editor

Music Subject Headings

Compiled from *Library of Congress Subject Headings*

by

Perry Bratcher and Jennifer Smith

Edited and with a foreword by
Richard P. Smiraglia

Soldier Creek Press
Lake Crystal, Minnesota
1988

ISBN 0-936996-31-5

Soldier Creek Press
Postal Drawer U
Lake Crystal, Minnesota 56055

This book was produced using an Apple Macintosh II computer, Apple LaserWriter,
Aldus PageMaker 3.0 desktop publishing program, and Microsoft Word 3.0
word processing program.
Typesetting provided by Apple Blossom Books, Belle Plaine, Minnesota.

CONTENTS

FOREWORD

Library of Congress (LC) subject headings for music have an interesting history.[1] Music librarians (who had organized their own professional association, the Music Library Association (MLA), in 1931) began to tackle the problem of subject access to music in card catalogs right away. In 1935 MLA produced the first of two provisional lists of music subject headings; one list was for books about music and the other was for music scores. Both lists were developed following guidelines that were based on the practice of the Library of Congress at that time. While the headings for books about music were drawn from LC's own cataloging, the list of headings for scores was a proposed list. An important fact to remember about the development of LC subject headings for music is that from 1943 until 1981 LC's Music Division used a classified catalog for subject access. Although LC music subject headings were applied on printed catalog cards, they were not in use internally at LC.

In 1952, as a service to card subscribers, LC published a formal separate list of music subject headings.[2] A year later, after consultation with music librarians, LC began using these headings for sound recordings as well. Few major changes in the structure of the list were made over the next three decades. In 1981 broad changes were made in the application of headings for music of ethnic and national groups. Since 1981, when LC closed its card catalogs and began maintaining verbal subject access in an on-line system, changes have been both more far-reaching and more rapid. Two notable examples are the 1984 introduction of free-floating period subdivision, and the sweeping modernization of headings for music in popular idioms that took place in 1987.

The production of a separate, unified list of LC music subject headings often has been rumored. This volume is the first such effort to appear in print. This book began as an attempt to cumulate all changes and additions to LC music headings, as well as special operational decisions of the Music Section of the LC Special Materials Cataloging Division following the publication of the ninth edition of *Library of Congress Subject Headings* (LCSH). These changes are issued monthly in the *Music Cataloging Bulletin* (MCB) published by MLA. As part of the process of considering publication of this cumulation of music subject heading practice, the authors were encouraged to compile a complete list of LC music subject headings. They produced a cut-and-paste version of the applicable headings from the tenth edition of LCSH. These headings were converted to machine-readable form by Soldier Creek Press, then checked for accuracy against the quarterly microfiche. This list is complete through the September 1987 issue. As part of the editorial process, the completed list has been compared to all changes to the tenth edition of LCSH announced in the MCB through December 1987. Additionally, editors have spot-checked the list against the online subject authority file.

Because the present list is a reflection of the LC list for music subject headings, users might notice a few inconsistencies. For example, many free-floating subdivisions such as "--Scores" appear in the list, because these subdivisions appeared in the microfiche edition of the main list and/or the online subject authority records. Pattern headings for names of persons have been removed from the list, because all subdivisions appear in the *Subject Cataloging Manual*[3] (SCM) directive no. H1110, which is reproduced in the introduction to this volume.

Of course, the authors hope this publication will be useful for regular, everyday cataloging of music materials, providing music catalogers with a handy desk-reference set of subject headings that can be used in bibliographic records for scores, recordings, and books about music. The Introduction contains all LC policy statements from the *SCM* that apply to music headings, as well as simple instructions for the formulation of headings for musical works. The section of the Introduction entitled "Significant Changes and Revisions" should be of use to those planning and implementing retrospective conversion projects that include music records.

Soldier Creek Press also hopes that this volume will help to spur study of the LC music headings. This volume provides a convenient context for studying music headings, and, because the music headings are isolated from other subject headings, this list could provide a more easily scrutinized record of the hierarchy, syndetic structure, and vocabulary control of music headings in LCSII.

With this volume we launch the *Soldier Creek Music Series*. These volumes, which will appear at irregular intervals, have been written with the intention of providing handy, affordable desk references for working music catalogers as well as useful, practical tools for students of music cataloging.

Richard P. Smiraglia
Editor, *Soldier Creek Music Series*

NOTES

1. For a brief historical sketch, see Smiraglia, Richard P. "Chapter 6: Verbal Subject Analysis." In *Music Cataloging: The Bibliographic Control of Music and Sound Recordings*. Englewood, Colo.: Libraries Unlimited, in press.

2. Library of Congress. Subject Cataloging Division. *Music Subject Headings Used on Printed Catalog Cards of the Library of Congress*. Washington, D.C.: Govt. Printing Office, 1952.

3. Library of Congress. Subject Cataloging Division. *Subject Cataloging Manual: Subject Headings*. Rev. ed. Washington: Library of Congress, 1985-

INTRODUCTION

This manual brings together pertinent music subject heading information from several sources. The introduction includes basic instructions for using LC music subject headings. This is followed by a list of all the music subject headings that have been established by the Library of Congress as of September 1987. This manual should prove especially useful to the novice cataloger as well as the seasoned professional who must work with music. It should also be a valuable guide to those engaged in retrospective conversion projects.

Many libraries implementing retrospective conversion projects find outdated subject headings on their old cards. This manual can be used to verify any headings in question, and catalogers can update their records accordingly. Close attention should be given to the following aspects not included elsewhere in this narrative:

1) Headings with invalid qualifiers for accompanying medium have been replaced. The general term "with instrumental ensemble" has replaced terms listing specific instruments.

2) The subdivision "Repairing" has been replaced by the subdivision "Maintenance and repair."

3) Invalid subdivisions for musical format (i.e. those not found in the list of free-floating subdivisions for music headings) have been deleted. See the section SUBDIVISIONS (pg. 22) for the current list.

GENERAL PRINCIPLES

The two principles known as specificity and coextensivity govern the establishment and use of LC subject headings for all materials. These concepts find special application for music materials. The principle of specificity requires the cataloger to assign the most specific heading possible to each work. The principle of coextensivity[1] requires that one or more headings be used to completely describe the subject of the work. Two musical concepts, form of composition and medium of performance, commonly are brought out in subject analysis of musical works. Many music headings incorporate terms denoting both concepts (e.g., **Sonatas (Piano)** or **Concertos (Violin)**). Occasionally because of the structure of the list, two or more headings will be required to achieve coextensitvity (e.g., **Allemandes and Piano music**).

A third general principle governs the selection of terms used in music subject headings. That is that subject headings for musical works are in essence *form* headings rather than *subject* headings, and so they are given in the plural form. Thus **Sonatas** is used for a musical work that is a sonata, whereas **Sonata** is used for a book about the sonata as a musical form.

COMPOSITIONS

The Library of Congress classification approaches music by addressing the medium of performance, subarranged in some instances by type of composition (e.g., concertos, sonatas, etc.) or the topic of music (e.g., sea songs, etc.). In the subject catalog it is necessary to differentiate between the two approaches in order to retrieve the relevant works.

Largely, the differentiation is determined by qualifying the forms of composition with the medium of performance.

> **Quintets (Bassoon, clarinet, flute, horn, oboe)**
> **Concertos (Flute with string orchestra)**
> **Variations (Organ)**

When the medium of performance is implied by the name of the type of composition, no qualifier is necessary.

> **Symphonies**
>> (for orchestra)
>
> **Symphonic poems**
>> (for orchestra)
>
> **Overtures**
>> (for orchestra)
>
> **Chorale preludes**
>> (for organ)

However, if the work is for another medium the heading is qualified.

> **Symphonies (Band)**
> **Symphonic poems (String orchestra)**
> **Overtures (Band)**
> **Chorale preludes (Piano)**

Headings that are not qualified by a medium, including headings for most dance forms, are assigned in conjunction with a second heading for the medium.

> Allemandes *and* Piano music
> Jigs *and* Orchestral music

INSTRUMENTAL MUSIC

These headings include terms indicating musical form (concerto, mass, etc.) and medium of performance (clarinet, flute, etc.). When no musical form is specified, headings indicating performing ensemble (quartets, wind music, etc.) are used.

Order of instruments

The order of precedence for specifying musical instruments has been established as follows:

1) Keyboard instruments
2) Wind instruments (includes woodwinds and brasses)
3) Plectral instruments
4) Percussion and other instruments
5) Bowed stringed instruments
6) Unspecified instruments
7) Continuo

To determine into which category the instruments fall, refer to Class M (M6-M175.5) of the LC classification schedules.[2]

Order within categories

The instruments within each category are given in alphabetical order with the exception of string instruments, which are given in score order (violin, viola, violoncello, double bass). The number of instruments (if more than one) is given in parentheses.

> **Sextets (Piano, clarinet, flute, oboe, violin, violoncello)**
> **Quartets (Bassoon, clarinet, trumpet, tuba)**
> **Quartets (Flute, violins (2), violoncello)**

Two Instruments

The instruments are given in alphabetical order, except for string instruments, which are given in score order. If one instrument is chordal (usually a keyboard instrument) or serves as an accompaniment for the other, the accompanying or chordal instrument is given in second position. **Duets** is used for two unspecified instruments. Compositions for two voices are entered under **Sacred duets or Vocal duets** as deemed appropriate.[3]

> **Clarinet and oboe music**
> **Trumpet and piano music**
> **Violin and viola music**
> **Violin and guitar music**
> (The guitar is considered a chordal instrument here)

VOCAL MUSIC

Headings for vocal music bring out voice range, number of parts, and type of accompaniment, as appropriate. Voice ranges can be determined by comparing the printed score to the example below. While these ranges are not exact and might vary slightly from individual to individual, they represent the accepted standards.

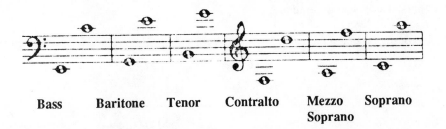

| Bass | Baritone | Tenor | Contralto | Mezzo Soprano | Soprano |

The headings **Songs** and **Sacred songs** are qualified by voice range and accompaniment.

> **Songs (Low voice) with guitar**
> **Sacred songs (High voice) with piano**
> **Songs, Unaccompanied**

Headings for ensembles of solo vocalists (i.e., **Sacred duets [trios, etc.]** and **Vocal duets [trios, etc.]**) are qualified similarly.

> **Vocal quartets with piano**
> **Vocal quintets with organ**
> **Sacred duets with guitar**

Headings for larger vocal forms (i.e. **Cantatas; Cantatas, Sacred; Cantatas, Secular; Masses;** and **Requiems**) are qualified by the type of chorus, but not by type of accompaniment. The qualifier "(Mixed voices)" is not used, but is assumed if the heading is not qualified.

> **Cantatas, Sacred (Equal voices)**
> **Masses (Men's voices)**
> **Requiems (Women's voices)**

Headings for solo cantatas are qualified by solo voice range only and not by type of chorus or type of accompaniment.

> **Solo cantatas (Medium voice)**
> **Solo cantatas, Sacred (Low voice)**

Chorus headings are qualified by type of chorus, number of vocal parts, and type of accompaniment.

> **Choruses, Sacred (Mixed voices, 4 parts) with piano**
> **Choruses, Secular (Men's voices) with orchestra**
> **Choruses with band**
> **Choruses, Secular (Women's voices), Unaccompanied**

TOPICAL, ETC., HEADINGS

In addition to those headings assigned for medium or musical form, the following musical aspects relating to the work in hand are brought out by assigning one or more of the following headings:

1. For seasons, holidays, religious festivals, etc., the heading for the type of music, e.g.,

> **Christmas music**

2. For music about a topic or person, the topic or name with the subdivision "Songs and music"

> **[Topic or Name of person]—Songs and music**

However, for certain types of music, one should consult the subject headings list to identify specific headings for songs about these topics:

> **Sea songs**
> **Work-songs**

3. For liturgical texts:

> **Magnificat (Music)**
> **Psalms (Music)—22nd Psalm**

4. For musical settings of a pre-existing literary text, see the subdivision "Musical settings" under headings for authors and also under headings for literature, poetry, drama, etc.:

> **[Headings for author]—Musical settings.**
> **Shakespeare, William, 1564-1616—Musical settings.**
> **English literature—Musical settings.**[4]

ARRANGED

The free floating term "Arranged" is assigned to headings for the ensembles arranged *for*, not to the headings for the ensembles arranged *from*.

> **Clarinet and piano music, Arranged**
> (work originally written for flute and piano, arranged for clarinet and piano)

not   **Flute and piano music, Arranged**
> (work originally written for flute and piano, arranged for clarinet and piano)

The qualifier is free-floating when used after medium and form headings. However, certain headings for forms include an alternative structure that is printed under each heading involved: **[Form] arranged for [medium]**.

> **Operas arranged for string quartet**

PATTERN HEADINGS

Pattern headings are used to avoid redundancy in the list by providing a model that can be used to form subject headings for similar materials. There are currently two types of pattern headings in music, pattern headings for compositions and pattern headings for musical instruments.

Formerly a pattern heading existed for composers (Wagner). This pattern heading has been discontinued, and a list of subdivisions for use under names of persons has been established instead.

Guidance for the use of these headings is provided in the Library of Congress *Subject Cataloging Manual : Subject Headings.*

PATTERN HEADINGS FOR MUSIC COMPOSITIONS

Pattern: Operas

Types of headings designated by the category: Headings for music compositions, including headings for form, medium, style, music for special seasons or occasions, musical settings of special texts, etc. Examples; **Concertos (Oboe)**; **Trios (Piano, flute, violin)**; **Rock music**; **Easter music**; **Magnificat (Music)**. They may be assigned to music compositions published as collections or as separate works, or to textual works about music compositions, as appropriate, according to the instructions given below.

Topical and form subdivisions for music compositions:

—**Analysis, appreciation**
—**Bibliography**
—**Bibliography—Catalogs**
—**Bibliography—Graded lists**
—**Cadenzas**
—**Discography**
—**Discography—Methodology**
—**Excerpts***
—**Excerpts, Arranged***
—**First performances** (May subdivide geographically)
—**History and criticism****
—**Instructive editions**
—**Instrumental settings**
—**Interpretation (Phrasing, dynamics, etc.)**
—**Juvenile**
—**Librettos**
—**Programs**
—**Scenarios**
—**Simplified editions**
—**Stage guides**
—**Stories, plots, etc.**
—**Teaching pieces**
—**Thematic catalogs**
—**Themes, motives, Literary**

* Use only under form headings. May be further subdivided by musical format subdivisions.
** Not valid under the heading **Operas**; Do not use the subdivision "History and criticism" under the pattern heading "Operas" since a separate heading "Opera" is assigned to works about the topic. The same provision applies in other cases where separate headings exist for topic in the singular and form in the plural, e.g. **Symphony** and **Symphonies**; **Suite (Music)** and **Suites**; **Sonata** and **Sonatas**; **Sonata (Piano)** and **Sonatas (Piano)**; etc.[5]

PATTERN HEADINGS FOR MUSICAL INSTRUMENTS

Pattern: Piano

Types of headings designated by the category: Headings for specific instruments or groups of instruments. Examples: **Flute; Wind instruments**. The category does not include the general heading **Musical instruments**.

—**Catalogs, Manufacturers'**
—**Catalogs and collections** (May subdivide geographically)
—**Chord diagrams**
—**Construction**
—**Dictionaries**
—**History**
—**Instruction and study** (May subdivide geographically)
—**Instruction and study—Fingering**
—**Instruction and study—Juvenile**
—**Instruction and study—Pedaling**
—**Keys**
—**Maintenance and repair**
—**Methods**
—**Methods—Group instruction**
—**Methods—Juvenile**
—**Methods—Self-instruction**
—**Methods (Jazz, [Rock, Bluegrass, etc.])***
—**Orchestra studies**
—**Performance**
—**Practicing**
—**Strings**
—**Studies and exercises**
—**Studies and exercises—Fingering**
—**Studies and exercises—Juvenile**
—**Studies and exercises—Pedaling**
—**Studies and exercises—(Jazz, [Rock, Bluegrass, etc.])***
—**Tuning**

* When assigning the subdivision "Methods" or "Studies and exercises" qualified by a particular style of popular music, always assign as a second heading the style of music subdivided by "Instruction and study". Examples:

1. **Banjo—Methods (Bluegrass)**
2. **Bluegrass music—Instruction and study**

1. **Guitar—Studies and excercises (Rock)**
2. **Rock music—Instruction and study**[6]

PATTERN HEADINGS FOR PERSONS

Subdivisions to be used under names of persons are outlined below.

General principle: When assigning a name heading for any person except literary authors, subdivide the name on a free-floating basis by the appropriate form and topical subdivisions listed below. If a topical subdivision is assigned which represents an important approach to the work, also provide direct subject access to that topic by assigning an additional heading to the work.

Procedures:

1. Assign an unsubdivided personal name heading for the complete biography of a person or for general criticism of his life and/or work. Also use unsubdivided personal name headings for works dealing with more than three separate aspects of an individual's life or work, or discussing one or more specific minor topics not covered by subdivisions on this list. Consult H 1330 for guidelines and instructions on assigning subject headings to biographical works.

2. As needed, subdivide personal name headings by appropriate form and topical subdivisions from this list on a free-floating basis. Assign the subdivisions according to the guidelines and scope notes provided. If a specific subdivision is applicable to the topic of the work being cataloged, use it without regard to the size of the file already accumulated or anticipated about the person in the data base.

3. Varying or conflicting and additional subdivisions have been established and printed in *Library of Congress Subject Headings* under a few unique and highly significant individuals, e.g. **Gautama Buddha**; **Muhammad, d.632**; and **Jesus Christ**. In those cases, the printed subdivisions take precedence over this list and should continue to be used.

4. For works discussing subtopics or aspects of topical subdivisions on the list that are too specific to be separately established, assign the broader subdivision under which the topic is subsumed. Make an additional entry under the specific topic.

5. Persons with multifaceted careers.

   a. Treat persons with multifaceted careers according to the emphasis of the work at hand unless a direct conflict exists between this list and the list of subdivisions used under individual literary authors.

   b. Direct conflicts with the literary authors list. In situations where there is a direct conflict between subdivisions on this list and the literary authors list, assign subdivisions from the field in which the person is better known. If the person is better known as a literary author, assign subdivisions according to H 1155.4. Subdivisions in direct conflict with subdivisions on H 1155.4 are noted in this list by the statement "Do not use under persons also known as literary authors." Consult H 1155.4 for the subdivisions used under individual literary authors in those cases.

   c. Once it has been determined that a person is better known as a literary author and a conflicting subdivision has been assigned under that person, continue to use that subdivision for the concept in question, regardless of the particular orientation of the work in hand.

6. Assignment of additional headings. Bring out by means of an additional heading the topic of a subdivision representing an important aspect by which the work should be retrieved. Many subdivisions are not important topics in their own right, e.g. form subdivisions and subdivisions such as **—Childhood and youth**, which express personal aspects of an individual's life. Other subdivisions, however, do represent significant concepts which should be brought out by both a topical subdivision under the person's name and a subject heading for the topic itself. Situations requiring additional headings are noted in the list.

7. [name of person], in fiction, drama, poetry, etc. Assign this phrase heading as a topical heading for works which discuss the person as a theme in belles lettres in general, in specific literary genres, or in musical dramatic works such as operas, ballets, musical comedies, etc.

Subdivisions

—Abdication, [date]

—Abstracts

—Adaptations
   Use under individuals such as artists or composers for discussions of adaptations by others of their creative works. For discussions of an individual's adaptations of themes from others, see **—Sources**.

—Adversaries
Use for discussions of contemporaries who opposed the person's point of view or work.

—Aesthetics
Use for discussions of the individual's philosophy of art or beauty, whether explicitly stated or inferred from his creative works

—Alcohol use
Use for works about the person's use or abuse of alcohol.
See also **—Drug use**

Allegory, see **—Symbolism**

Ancestry, see **—Family**

—Anecdotes
Use for collections of brief narratives of true incidents from the individual's life.

—Anniversaries, etc.

—Anniversaries, etc., [date]
Use for works dealing with the anniversary celebration itself. Do not use for works merely published on the occasion of an anniversary.

—Appreciation (May be subdivided geographically)
Use for works on public response and reception, praise, etc. of the person's artistic works. Use under persons active in the fine arts, music and performing arts. For works consisting of critical analysis or interpretation of artistic works without biographical details, see **—Criticism and interpretation**. For works on public opinion about the person, see **—Public opinion**. For works on the person's impact on other persons, groups, movements, etc., see **—Influence**. For works on systems of beliefs and rituals connected with divine persons or saints, see **—Cult**.

—Archaeological collections
Use according to H1427 for works about the person's collections of archaeological items or artifacts.

—Archives
Use for collections or discussions of documentary materials or records relating to the person's public or private activities, including manuscripts, diaries, correspondence, photographs, or other items of historical interest.
See also **—Correspondence; —Diaries; —Iconography; —Manuscripts; — Notebooks, sketchbooks, etc.**

—Archives—Catalogs

—Art
Use under persons living before 1400 A.D. for works consisting of reproductions of works of art depicting the person, or works discussing such art. For persons living after 1400, see **—Portraits**.

—Art collections
Use according to H 1427 for works about the person's own art collection

—Assassination

—Assassination attempt, [date]

—Assassination attempts

Associates, see **—Friends and associates**

Attitude towards [specific topic], see **—Views on [specific topic]**

—Authorship
Use for discussions of the validity of attributing authorship of works to the person. For discussions of the person's literary ability and accomplishments, see **—Literary art**.

Autobiography, use [name of person]

—Autographs
Use for collections or discussions of the person's autographs or handwriting.

—Autographs—Facsimiles

Autographs, Spurious, see **—Forgeries**

—Bibliography
Use for lists of publications by or about the person.

—Bibliography—Catalogs

—Bibliography—Microform catalogs.

Biography, use [name of person]

—Birthplace

Bones, see **—Museums, relics, etc.; —Tomb**

—Bonsai collections
Use according to H 1427 for works about the person's collection of bonsai.

—Books and reading
Use for works dealing with written material known to have been read by the person, his reading habits and interests, books borrowed from friends or libraries, etc.
See also **—Library**

Burial, see **—Death and burial**

—Captivity, [dates]
Use for works discussing periods in which the person was held captive in bondage or confinement, especially under house arrest, as a hostage, or in battle. Do not use under persons also known as literary authors. For works discussing periods in which the person was actually imprisoned in a correctional institution or prisoner of war camp, see **—Imprisonment, [dates]**.
See also **—Exile, [dates]; —Kidnapping, [date]**

—Career in [specific field or discipline]
Use for works limited to describing events in the person's occupational life or participation in a profession or vocation. Assign an additional heading for the field. Do not use under persons also known as literary authors. For works discussing the person's actual substantive contributions or accomplishments in a specific field or topic, whether made as a result of a vocation or an avocation, see **—Contributions in [specific field or topic]**.
See also **—Resignation from office**

—Caricatures and cartoons
Use for collections or discussions of caricatures or pictorial humor about the person.

Cartoons, satire, etc., see **—Caricatures and cartoons; —Humor**

—Catalogs

Use under artists and craftspersons for works listing their art works or crafts which are available or located in particular institutions or places.

See also —**Archives—Catalogs**; —**Bibliography—Microform catalogs**; —**Catalogues raisonnes**; —**Discography**; —**Exhibitions**; —**Film catalogs**; —**Library—Catalogs**; —**Manuscripts—Catalogs**; —**Manuscripts—Microform catalogs**; —**Phonotape catalogs**; —**Slides—Catalogs**; —**Thematic catalogs**; —**Video tape catalogs**

—Catalogs raisonnes

Use for comprehensive listings of an artist's or craftperson's works in one medium or all media, usually chronologically or systematically arranged, and accompanied by descriptive or critical notes.

Centennial celebrations, etc., see —**Anniversaries, etc.**

Character, see —**Ethics**; —**Psychology**; —**Religion**

—Childhood and youth

Do not use under persons also known as literary authors

—Chronology

Use for works which list by date the events in the life of the person

—Circus collections

Use according to H 1427 for works about the person's collections of circus items.

—Claims vs. ...

Use for works about the legal claims filed by the person. Complete the subdivision with the name of the jurisdiction against which the claim was brought.

—Clothing

—Coin collections

Use according to H 1427 for works about the person's coin collections

—Collected works

Use for collected works about the person. Do not use for the published collected works of the person.

Commentaries, see —**Criticism and interpretation**

Companions, see —**Friends and associates**

—Concordances

Use as a form subdivision for indexes to the principal words found in the writings of the person.

—Congresses

—Contributions in [specific field or topic]

Use for works discussing the person's actual substantive contributions or accomplishments in a specific field or topic, whether made as a result of a vocation or an avocation. Also use for discussions of the person's philosophy or system of thought on a particular topic which he propounded or imparted to others. Use this subdivision to bring out one specific field or topic for a person active in more than one field, or to bring out subtopics or aspects of a particular field to which an individual contributed. Assign an additional heading for the field or topic. Do not use this subdivision for a work discussing the person's general contributions in the discipline or field with which he is solely or primarily identified. Assign the person's name without subdivision in such cases. Do not use under persons also known as literary authors. For works limited to describing events in the person's occupational life or participation in a profession or vocation, see —**Career in [specific field or discipline]**.

—Coronation

—Correspondence
  Use as a form or topical subdivision for the letters from and/or to the person. Assign an additional heading for indivdual correspondents.

  Costume, see **—Clothing**

—Criticism and interpretation
  Use for works consisting of critical analysis or interpretation of the person's artistic works or endeavors without biographical details. Use this subdivision only under persons active in the fine arts, music, and performing arts. For works on public response and reception, praise, etc. of the person's artistic works, see **—Appreciation**.

  Crowning, see **—Coronation**

—Cult (May subdivide geographically)
  Use under divine persons, saints, or persons worshipped for systems of beliefs or rituals associated with the person.

—Death and burial
  Use for works on the person's death, funeral, and burial, including his last illness. Do not use under persons also known as literary authors.
  See also **—Assassination; —Tomb**

—Death mask

  Devotional literature, see **—Prayer-books and devotions**

—Diaries
  Use for collections or discussions of the person's diaries. Also use for individual diaries.

—Dictionaries, indexes, etc.
  See also **—Concordances**.

—Disciples
  Use for works discussing persons who received instruction from the individual or accepted his doctrines or teachings and assisted in spreading or implementing them.

—Discography
  Use for lists or catalogs of sound recordings by or about the person.
  See also **—Phonotape catalogs**.

  Diseases, see **—Health**

—Drama
  Use as a form subdivision for plays and musical dramatic works, including operas, ballets, musical comedies, etc., about the person. Do not use under persons also known as literary authors. For criticism or discussions of plays, etc. about an individual, assign **[name of person], in fiction, drama, poetry, etc.** as a topical heading.

—Dramaturgy
  Use under composers for discussions of their technique in writing operas and other dramatic works. Do not use under persons also known as literary authors.

—Drug use
  Use for works about the person's use or abuse of drugs.
  See also **—Alcohol use**

  Dwellings, see **—Homes and haunts**

  Early life, see **—Childhood and youth**

Education, see —**Knowledge and learning**

—**Employees**
Use for works discussing persons employed by the individual, including household servants, etc.

Enemies, see —**Adversaries**

—**Estate**
Use for discussions of the aggregate of property or liabilities of all kinds that a person leaves for disposal at his death.
See also —**Will**

—**Ethics**
Use for discussions of the individual's ethical system and values.
See also —**Religion.**

—**Ethnological collections**
Use according to H 1427 for works about the person's ethnological collections.

—**Ethnomusicological collections**
Use according to H 1427 for works about the person's ethnomusicological collections

—**Exhibitions**
Use for works about exhibitions on the life or work of the person, including catalogs of single exhibitions.

—**Exile, [dates]** (May subdivide geographically)
Do not use under persons also known as literary authors

—**Family**
Use for discussions of the person's family or relations with family members. Also use for genealogical works.
Assign an additional heading for the name of the family. Do not use under persons also known as literary authors.

—**Fiction**
Use as a form subdivision for works of fiction about the person. Do not use under persons also known as literary authors. For criticism or discussions of fiction about a person, assign **[name of person], in fiction, drama, poetry, etc.** as a topical heading.

—**Film catalogs**

—**Finance, Personal**
Use for discussions of the person's financial affairs.
See also —**Estate**; —**Will.**

Folktales, see —**Legends**

—**Forgeries**
Use for discussions of forgeries of the person's creative works or signature. In the case of individual forgeries, assign an additional heading for the name of the forger.

—**Freemasonry**
Use for works discussing the person's membership or participation in the Freemasons.

Frequented places, see —**Homes and haunts**

—**Friends and associates**
Use for discussions of the person's close and immediate contacts such as companions, co-workers, etc.
See also —**Adversaries**; —**Disciples**; —**Employees**; —**Relations with [specific class of persons or ethnic group]**

Funeral, see —**Death and burial**

Genealogy, see —**Family**

Grave, see —**Tomb**

Handwriting, see —**Autographs**

—**Harmony**
Use under composers for works discussing their uses of harmony

Haunts, see —**Homes and haunts**

—**Health**
Use for works about the person's state of health, including diseases suffered and accounts of specific diseases. Do not use under persons also known as literary authors. For accounts of specific diseases assign an additional heading of the type: [disease]—**Patients**—[place]—**Biography**.
See also —**Alcohol use**; —**Drug use**; —**Mental health**.

—**Herbarium**

—**Homes and haunts**
Use for works discussing the person's home or dwellings, favorite places, or places he habitually frequented.
See also —**Birthplace**; —**Journeys**; —**Palaces**.

—**Humor**
Use as a form subdivision for humorous writings about the person. Do not use under persons also known as literary authors. For pictorial humor, see —**Caricatures and cartoons**.

—**Iconography**
Use for works consisting of pictures or other visual images relating to the person, including portraits, portraits of family and friends, views of birthplace, etc.
See also —**Art**; —**Caricatures and cartoons**; —**Numismatics**; —**Portraits**.

Imitations, see —**Parodies, imitations, etc.**

—**Impeachment**

—**Imprisonment, [dates]**
Use for works discussing periods in which the person was actually imprisoned in a correctional institution or a prisoner of war camp. Do not use under persons also known as literary authors. For works discussing periods in which the person was held captive in bondage or confinement, especially under house arrest, as a hostage, or in battle, see —**Captivity, [dates]**.
See also —**Exile, [dates]**

—**Inauguration, [date]**

Indexes, see —**Concordances**; —**Dictionaries, indexes, etc.**

—**Influence**
Use for works discussing the person's impact on other persons, groups, movements, etc. Assign an additional heading for the person or group influenced. For works on public response and reception, praise, etc. of the person's artistic works, see —**Appreciation**.

—**Information services** (May subdvide geographically)

Interment, see —**Death and burial**

Interpretation, see —**Criticism and interpretation**

—Interviews
Use for works consisting of transcripts of what was said during the course of interviews or conversations with the person on one or more occasions.

Journals, see —**Diaries**

—Journeys (May subdivide geographically)
Use for works about voyages and travels undertaken by the person. When the subdivision is further subdivided by place, assign an additional heading of the type: [place]—**Description** or [place]—**Description and travel**, as appropriate.
See also —**Exile, [dates]**

—Juvenile drama
Do not use under persons also known as literary authors.

—Juvenile fiction
Do not use under persons also known as literary authors.

—Juvenile films

—Juvenile humor
Do not use under persons also known as literary authors.

—Juvenile literature

—Juvenile poetry
Do not use under persons also known as literary authors.

—Juvenile sound recordings

—Kidnapping, [date]

—Knowledge—[topic]
Use for works discussing the person's knowledge of a specific topic, whether explicitly stated or inferred from his life and work. Also use for discussions of the person's educational background in a specific topic. Assign an additional heading for the specific topic. Under literary authors, further subdivision of —**Knowledge** is restricted to subdivisions listed in H 1155.4. For works on the person's opinions or attitudes on a specific topic, whether explicitly stated or inferred, see —**Views on [specific topic]**.

—Knowledge and learning
Use for works about the person's formal or informal learning or scholarship in general. For knowledge of learning of specific topics, see —**Knowledge—[topic]**.

—Language
See also —**Literary art;** —**Oratory**

Last illness, see —**Death and burial**

Leadership, Military, see —**Military leadership**

Learning, see —**Knowledge and learning**

—Legends
Use as a form subdivision for stories about the person which have come down from the past and which are popularly taken as historical though not verifiable. Do not use under persons also known as literary authors.
See also —**Romances**

Letters, see **—Correspondence**

—Library
> Use for works discussing the person's own library.
> See also **—Books and reading**

—Library—Catalogs

—Library resources (May subdivide geographically)
> Use for works describing the resources or special collections available in libraries for research or study about the person.

—Literary art
> Use for discussions of the person's literary ability and accomplishments. Do not use under multi-career persons who are also recognized literary authors. Under persons who are also recognized as literary authors, use appropriate subdivisions from H 1155.4. For discussions of the validity of attributing authorship of specific works to the person, see **—Authorship.**

—Literary collections
> Use for literary anthologies about the person which involve two or more literary forms. Do not use under persons also known as literary authors. For anthologies in one literary form, see the form, e.g. **—Drama; —Fiction; —Poetry.**

Litigation, see **—Trials, litigation, etc.**

—Manuscripts
> Use for works discussing writings made by hand, typewriter, etc., by or about the person. Do not use for individual works in manuscript form.
> See also **—Archives; —Autographs; —Correspondence; —Diaries**

—Manuscripts—Catalogs

—Manuscripts—Facsimiles

—Manuscripts—Indexes

—Manuscripts—Microform catalogs

—Map collections
> Use according to H 1427 for works about the person's collections of maps.

—Medals
> Use for works about medals issued to commemorate the person.

—Meditations
> Use as a form subdivision for works containing descriptions of thoughts or reflections on the spiritual significance of the person's life or deeds.

—Mental health
> Use for works discussing the person's state of mental health, including mental illness and accounts of specific mental disorders. Do not use under persons also known as literary authors. For accounts of specific disorders or situations, assign an additional heading of the type: [disease]**—Patients—**[place]**—Biography; Psychotherapy patients—**[place]**—Biography;** etc.

—Military leadership

—Miscellanea
> Use for collections of curiosa relating to the person as well as for texts about the person in question and answer format.

—Monuments (May subdivide geographically)
>Use for works about monuments erected in honor of the person.
>See also **—Museums, relics, etc.; —Shrines; —Tomb**

Motives, themes, see **—Themes, motives**

—Museums, relics, etc. (May subdivide geographically)
>Use for works on museums devoted to the person. Also includes works on disinterred bones.
>See also **—Archives; —Death mask; —Shrines; —Tomb**

Music, see **—Songs and music**

—Musical instrument collections
>Use according to H 1427 for works about the person's collections of musical instruments.

—Musical settings
>Use as a form subdivision for musical scores or sound recordings in which writings or words of the person have been set to music.

—Name
>Use for discussions of the history, orthography, etymology, etc. of the person's name.

—Natural history collections
>Use according to H 1427 for works about the person's collections of natural history items or specimens.

—Notebooks, sketchbooks, etc.
>Use for collections or discussions of the person's notebooks, sketchbooks, etc. Also use for individual works.

—Notebooks, sketchbooks, etc.—Facsimiles

—Numismatic collections
>Use according to H 1427 for works about the person's numismatics collections.
>See also **—Coin collections**

—Numismatics
>Use for works discussing the representation of the person on coins, tokens, medals, paper money, etc.
>See also **—Medals**

Opponents, see **—Adversaries**

—Oratory
>Use for works discussing the person's public speaking ability.

—Outlines, syllabi, etc.

—Palaces (May subdivide geographically)

—Pardon
>Use for works about the person's legal release from the penalty of an offense.

—Parodies, imitations, etc.
>Use as both a form and topical subdivision for imitations, either comic or distorted, of the person's creative works.

Patronage of the arts, see **—Art patronage**

—Performances (May subdivide geographically)
Use under performing artists or performers of all types for works about their performances. Also use under composers, choreographers, etc. for works about performances of their compositions or works.

—**Periodicals**

Personal finance, see —**Finance, Personal**

Personality, see —**Psychology**

—**Philosophy**
Use for discussions of the individual's personal philosophy. Do not use under names of philosophers.
See also —**Aesthetics**; —**Ethics**; —**Religion**

—**Phonotape catalogs**

—**Photograph collections**
Use according to H 1427 for works about the person's collections of photographs.

Pictorial humor, see —**Caricatures and cartoons**

Pictorial works, see —**Iconography**; —**Art**; —**Portraits**

Place of birth, see —**Birthplace**

Places frequented, see —**Homes and haunts**

—**Poetry**
Use as a form subdivision for works of poetry about the person. Do not use under persons also known as literary authors. For criticism or discussions of poetry about a person, assign **[name of person], in fiction, drama, poetry, etc.** as a topical heading.

—**Political and social views**
Use for works discussing the person's political and/or social views in general. For works on specific topics, see —**Views on [specific topic]**.

—**Portraits**
Use for collections or discussions of portraits of persons living after 1400 A.D., including potrait sculpture. For persons living before 1400, see —**Art**.
See also —**Caricatures and cartoons**; —**Death mask**; —**Numismatics**; —**Posters**; —**Self-portraits**

—**Poster collections**
Use according to H 1427 for works about the person's collections of posters.

—**Posters**
Use for collections or discussions of posters depicting the person.

—**Prayer-books and devotions**
Use as a form subdivision, particularly under divine persons or saints, for works of devotions directed to those persons whose help or prayers are requested.

—**Prayer-books and devotions—English, [French, German, etc.]**

—**Pre-existence**
Use for works discussing the person's existence in a previous state or life.

Professional life, see —**Career in [specific field or discipline]**

—**Prophecies**
Use for works about the prophecies made by the person

—Psychology
> Use for discussions or interpretations of the person's psychological traits, personality, character, etc. Do not use under persons also known as literary authors.

—Public opinion
> Use for works about public opinion about the person. Do not use under persons also known as literary authors. For works on public response and reception, praise, etc. of the person's artistic works, see **—Appreciation**.

Public speaking, see **—Oratory**

—Quotations
> Use for collections or discussions of the person's quotations.

Reading habits, see **—Books and reading**

—Relations with [specific class of persons or ethnic group]
> Assign an additional heading for the specific group with appropriate subdivision if necessary. Specific subdivisions are established under literary authors. See H 1155.4.

Relations with employees, see **—Employees**

Relations with family, see **—Family**

Relations with friends and associates, see **—Friends and associates**

Relics, see **—Museums, relics, etc.**

—Religion
> Use for discussions of the person's religious beliefs and practices. Do not use under names of theologians.
> See also **—Ethics**

Residences, see **—Homes and haunts**

—Resignation from office
> See also **—Abdication, [date]; —Impeachment**

Rhetoric, see **—Literary art; —Oratory**

—Romances
> Use as a form subdivision under names of historical or legendary figures for medieval tales based chiefly on legends of chivalric love and adventure. Do not use under persons also known as literary authors.

Satire, see **—Humor**

Sayings, see **—Quotations**

Scholarship, see **—Knowledge and learning**

—Scientific apparatus collections
> Use according to H 1427 for works about the person's collections of scientific apparatus.

—Seal
> Use for works discussing the devices, such as emblems, symbols or words, used by an individual to authenticate his writing or documents.

—Self-portraits
> Use for reproductions or discusions of self-portraits by the person.

Sepulchral monument, see —**Tomb**

—**Sermons**
Use as a form subdivision, particularly under divine persons or saints, for single sermons or collections of sermons about the person.

Servants, see —**Employees**

—**Sexual behavior**

—**Shrines** (May subdivide geographically)
Use for works discussing structures or places consecrated or devoted to the person and serving as places of religious veneration or pilgrimage.
See also —**Museums, relics, etc.**

Sketchbooks, see —**Notebooks, sketchbooks, etc.**

—**Slide collections**
Use according to H 1427 for works about the person's collections of slides.

—**Slides**

—**Slides—Catalogs**

Social views, see —**Political and social views**

—**Societies, etc.**
Use for works discussing organizations devoted to or specializing in the person's life or work.

—**Songs and music**
Use as a form subdivision for collections or single works of vocal or instrumental music about the person. For collections or single works in musical dramatic forms such as operas, ballets, musical comedies, etc., see —**Drama**.

—**Sources**
Use for discussions of the person's sources of ideas or inspiration for his endeavors or creative works. For discussions of adaptations by others of an individual's creative works, see —**Adaptations**.

Spiritual life, see —**Religion**

—**Stories of operas**
Use under composers for works discussing or summarizing the stories or plots of their operas.

—**Study and teaching** (May subdivide geographically)
Use for works on methods of studying and teaching about the person.

Style, Literary, see —**Literary art**

—**Symbolism**
Use for discussions of the symbols employed by the person in his creative works.

Tales, see —**Legends;** —**Romances**

—**Teachings**
Use for works discussing in general the body of knowledge, precepts, or doctrines the person taught to others.

—**Thematic catalogs**
Use under composers for listings of the themes of their musical compositions. Do not use under persons also known as literary authors.

—Themes, motives

Use for discussions of the themes and motives in the person's creative works. Do not use under persons also known as literary authors.

—Tomb

Use for works about the person's grave, interred bones, etc. For works on disinterred bones, see **—Museums, relics, etc.**
See also **—Death and burial.**

Travels, see **—Journeys**

—Trials, litigation, etc.

Use for proceedings or discussions of proceedings of civil or criminal actions to which the person is a party.

—Video tape catalogs

—Views on [specific topic]

Use for works on the person's opinions or attitudes on a specific topic, whether explicitly stated or inferred. Assign an additional heading for the specific topic. Do not use under persons also known as literary authors. For works on the person's knowledge of a specific topic, whether explicitly stated or inferred from his life and works, see **—Knowledge—[specific topic].**

Views on aesthetics, see **—Aesthetics**

Views on ethics, see **—Ethics**

Views on politics and society, see **—Political and social views**

Views on society, see **—Political and social views**

Voyages, see **—Journeys**

—Will

Use for discussions of the person's legal declaration regarding the disposition of his property or estate.
See also **—Estate.**

Writing skill, see **—Literary art**

—Written works

Use under persons active in the fine arts, music, and performing arts for discussions, listings, etc., of their non-literary textual works. Do not use under persons also known as literary authors.

—Yearbooks, see **—Periodicals.**

Youth, see **—Childhood and youth**[7]

SUBDIVISIONS

Musical format

Do not use subdivisions for musical format under headings for music of special seasons, occasions, styles, etc., where the medium is not directly stated or implied, e.g. **Christmas music; Country music; Te Deum laudamus (Music);** etc. These subdivisions are also not used under headings for categories of works which are generally published in only one format, e.g. hymns, compositions for one instrument, and songs and choruses without accompaniment or with the accompaniment of only one instrument or two keyboard instruments.

—Chorus scores with piano
—Chorus scores without accompaniment
—Parts
—Parts (solo)
—Piano scores
—Piano scores (4 hands)
—Scores
—Scores and parts
—Scores and parts (solo)
—Vocal scores with accordion
—Vocal scores with continuo
—Vocal scores with guitar
—Vocal scores with harpsichord
—Vocal scores with organ
—Vocal scores with piano
—Vocal scores with piano (4 hands)
—Vocal scores with piano and organ
—Vocal scores with pianos (2)[8]

Solo with piano

The subdivisions "Solo with piano" and "Solos with piano" are used under headings for solo instrument(s) and an accompanying ensemble when the accompaniment is arranged for piano.

Concertos (Flute)—Solo with piano
BT Flute and piano music, Arranged

Subdivisions under headings for musical instruments that are qualified by genre

When the subdivisions "Methods" or "Studies and exercises" qualified by a particular style of popular music are used, a second heading for the style of music subdivided by "Instruction and study" is added.

Piano—Methods (Jazz)
Jazz music—Instruction and study

Piano—Studies and exercises (Rock)
Rock music—Instruction and study

Period Subdivisions for Music

The following subdivisions are used as free-floating subdivisions for headings for music compositions:

—To 500
—500-1400
—15th century
—16th century
—17th century
—18th century
—19th century
—20th century

Assign period subdivisions to textual works about music, including under headings used solely for such works, e.g. **Choral music; Symphony; Concerto;** etc. They may also be assigned to collections of Western art music by two or more composers emphasizing a period. Do not assign them to works where a period is emphasized only in a series statement. When assigning multiple headings to a collection, assign period subdivisions only under those headings which refer to works of two or more composers in the collection. Period subdivisions are not used for collections or compositions by only one composer or for separate music compositions. They are also not used under headings for folk, popular, and non-Western music.[9]

These subdivisions may be assigned after any music heading for collections of western art music and for works which discuss the music where period is emphasized in the work. They are assigned after local subdivisions and before other free-floating subdivisions, e.g.:

> **Music—England—19th century—History and criticism**
> **Songs—Germany—20th century—History and criticism**
> **Symphonies—20th century—Scores**

Note especially that the headings **Music—History and criticism—[period]** are cancelled in favor of **Music—[period]—History and criticism**. In addition, LC's policy of assigning multiple headings to bring out period and locality has been discontinued in favor of single headings, e.g., for a work on French baroque music:

Former headings:

> **Music—History and criticism—17th century**
> **Music—History and criticism—18th century**
> **Music—France—History and criticism**[10]

New headings:

> **Music—France—17th century—History and criticism**
> **Music—France—18th century—History and criticism**

All occurrences of the subdivision "To 1800" have been deleted. In addition, the standard subdivision "Early works to 1800" is now to be assigned where appropriate to headings for music literature and instruction if other provision for subdivision has not been made in the list (as under **Music—History and criticism** and **Music—Theory**).[11]

Topical Headings

Songs and music — Use as a free floating subdivision under topical headings, as well as under names of corporate bodies, persons (except religious persons), or places (except names of countries) for collections or single works of vocal or instrumental music about the topic or entity named. For works that discuss songs or music encompassing particular subjects, further subdivide the subdivision "History and criticism." For songs or music about particular religious persons or deities assign the phrase heading **[person] in music**, e.g. **Jean d'Arc, Saint, 1412-1431, in music.**[12]

MUSIC OF ETHNIC AND NATIONAL GROUPS[13]

The purpose of these subject headings is to provide guidelines for assigning subject headings to works which consist of or discuss the music of ethnic groups, music with national emphasis, and non-western art music, including works about the musical instruments of these groups. These instructions do not apply to works that consist of song texts as poetry without indications of the music.

ASSIGNMENT OF HEADINGS

1. General rule. Assign as appropriate a combination of the following headings to the type of works described above:

> a. **[ethnic or national group]—[local subdivision]—Music.**
>   (replaces all headings of Music, [ethnic or national group qualifier])
> b. [heading(s) for musical genre or style, or for ballads and songs with national emphasis]
> c. [heading(s) for language, i.e. **Ballads, Folk-songs,** or **Songs** with language qualifier]
> d. **Musical instruments—[local subdivision]**
> e. [other topics, as applicable]

2. Special provisions

> a. Assign to any work of music the first two categories of headings listed above. Assign the remaining headings as appropriate for the work. For works that consist of the texts of ballads, folk songs, or songs of ethnic groups, assign only headings in the third category above with the subdivision **—Texts.**

> b. Works about the music of ethnic and national groups. To such works, assign headings from the above categories, as applicable, with appropriate subdivisions such as **—History and criticism, —Bibliography, —Discography,** etc.

Works solely about the musical instruments of a people are assigned the headings specified in paragraph 4, below. Although some discussion of musical instruments as well, do not assign the subject heading **Musical instruments** unless the work devotes at least 20% of the text to a discussion of the musical instruments themselves.

EXPLANATION OF HEADINGS

1. *Ethnic or national group.*

> a. These headings are generally in the form **[ethnic or national group]—[local subdivision, if appropriate]— Music,** e.g.,

> > **Kabre (African people)—Music**
> > **Germans—Hungary—Music**
> > **Afro-Americans—Louisiana—Music**
> > **Jews—Music**

> b. Do not assign this type of heading for an individual nationality with its own country. Headings in the second category, below, with local subdivision, are generally sufficient for this purpose.

> c. For American Indian music, assign two headings, one designating the major group and one designating the specific tribe, if any, i.e.

> > **Indians of North America [Mexico, the West Indies, Central America, or South America]—[local subdivision]—Music**
> > **[Name of tribe]—Music**

> d. Assign headings such as Music, Buddhist, [Islamic, etc.] for music of religious groups.
> Note: The heading **Music, Jewish** has been cancelled and replaced by the heading **Jews—Music.**

2. *Type or style of music*

    a. Assign, with local subdivision, a heading of the following type:

> **Music** [use for comprehensive works containing music of various genres]
> **Folk music**
> **Music, Popular (Songs, etc.)**
> **Dance music**
> **Folk dance music**
> **Patriotic music**

Included in this category are headings for songs with national emphasis, e.g. **National songs; Political ballads and songs; Revolutionary ballads and songs; War-songs;** etc. These headings are not qualified by language.

Note: The various headings for folk music may be used for the music of cultures in which musical types and styles, such as art music, popular music, or folk music, are not differentiated.

    b. For national groups in countries other than their own, assign headings to bring out both localities, e.g.

> **1. Italians—Hungary—Music**
> **2. Folk music—Hungary**
> **3. Folk music—Italy**

    3. *Headings for language.* If the work is composed entirely or primarily of ballads, folk songs, or songs, assign one or more of the following headings in order to designate the original language of the text:

> **Ballads, [language]** (May subdivide geographically)
> **Folk-songs, [language]** (May subdivide geographically)
> **Songs, [language]** (May subdivide geographically)

Note: Do not bring out the language into which the original texts may be translated; do not use the subdivisions **—Translations into [language]** and **—Translations from [language]** after these headings.

Subdivide by place when appropriate, even if the name of the language corresponds with the name of the country, e.g.:

> **Ballads, Irish—Ireland**
> **Folk-songs, Swedish—Sweden**

When three or more languages are represented, assign the headings without language qualifier:

> **Ballads** (May subdivide geographically)
> **Folk-songs** (May subdivide geographically)
> **Songs** (May subdivide geographically)

4. *Musical instruments.*

    a. Assign the following combination of headings to works solely about the musical instruments of a people:

> **[ethnic or national group]—[local subdivision]—Music—History and criticism**
> **Musical instruments—[local subdivision]**
> **[specific musical instruments, if applicable]**

Note: Do not use the subdivision **—History and criticism** under the heading **Musical instruments** or under headings for specific musical instruments.

b. For national groups in countries other than their own, assign the heading **Musical instruments—[place]** for each of the two localities involved, e.g.

> **1. Irish—Australia—Music—History and criticism**
> **2. Musical instruments—Australia**
> **3. Musical instruments—Ireland**

5. Assign other headings as needed, e.g.:

Kumiuta	**Flamenco music**
Koto music	**Sarod music**
Bagpipe music	**Hunting songs**
Buddhist hymns	**Erotic songs**
Raga	**Satirical songs**

EXAMPLES:

Title: Quechua songs of Peru.

> **1. Indians of South America—Peru—Music.**
> **2. Quechua Indians—Music.**
> **3. Folk-songs, Quechua—Peru.**

Title: Black American music.

> **1. Afro-Americans—Music—History and criticism.**
> **2. Music—United States—History and criticism.**

Title: Songs and dances of Quebec.

> **1. French-Canadians—Music.**
> **2. Folk music—Quebec (Province)**
> **3. Folk dance music—Quebec (Province)**
> **4. Folk-songs, French—Quebec (Province)**

Title: Misique kabiye, Togo.

> **1. Kabre (African people)—Music.**
> **2. Folk music—Togo.**

Title: Traditional and modern music of the Maori.

> **1. Maoris—Music—History and criticism.**
> **2. Folk music—New Zealand—History and criticism.**
> **3. Music—New Zealand—History and criticism.**

Title: Spinnstubenlieder; Lieder der Frauengemeinschaften in den magyarischen Sprachinseln im Burgenland.

> **1. Hungarians—Austria—Burgenland—Music—History and criticism.**
> **2. Folk music—Austria—Burgenland—History and criticism.**
> **3. Folk music—Hungary—History and criticism.**
> **4. Folk-songs, Hungarian—Austria—Burgenland—History and criticism.**

Title: Introduction to shamisen kumiuta.

    1. Kumiuta—History and criticism.
    2. Music—Japan—History and criticism.
    3. Songs, Japanese—Japan—History and criticism.

Title: The art of Portuguese fado.

    1. Fados.
    2. Music—Portugal.
    3. Folk-songs, Portuguese—Portugal.

Title: Classical Japanese koto music.

    1. Koto music.
    2. Music—Japan.

Title: The music, songs, and instruments of the Acoli people of Uganda.

    1. Acoli (African people)—Music—History and criticism.
    2. Folk music—Uganda—History and criticism.
    3. Folk-songs, Acoli—Uganda—History and criticism.
    4. Musical instruments—Uganda.

SIGNIFICANT CHANGES AND REVISIONS

In this section, significant changes or revisions to music headings since 1982 are identified:

FACSIMILES OF MUSIC MANUSCRIPTS

In addition to headings for the music itself, assign to these works (either collections or single works) the following heading: **Music—Manuscripts—Facsimiles**

If the work is by a single composer and in the composer's hand, also assign the following as an additonal heading: **[Name of composer]—Manuscripts—Facsimiles**[14]

GENERAL COLLECTIONS OF MUSIC

For general collections of music (scores or sound recordings), like the complete works of a composer only one heading, **Music**, will now be assigned.[15]

MUSICAL ANALYSIS; MUSIC APPRECIATION

Two new headings **Musical analysis** and **Music appreciation** have been established to replace the heading **Music—Analysis, appreciation**. They were established in order to separate scholarly works on analysis from the much more numerous works on music appreciation. The subdivision "Analysis, appreciation" is retained under other music headings as a free-floating subdivision.[16]

ANALYTICAL GUIDES

This term has been cancelled and replaced by **Music appreciation** or **Musical analysis**, whichever is deemed appropriate.

SPECIAL MUSIC EDUCATION

Revisions have been made to improve access to material on special music education. These headings make use of the term "Music" as a free floating subdivision under the term **[Class of exceptional person]—Education** .

> **Physically handicapped children—Education—Music**
> **Gifted children—Education—Music**
> **Mentally handicapped children—Music**

Other terms that might be of use are:

> **Music—Instruction and study**
> **Music—Instruction and study—Juvenile**
> **Music therapy**

EXPLANATION OF NEW FORMAT OF MUSIC SUBJECT HEADINGS

Several changes have occurred in the format of subject headings in LCSH since the publication of the 10th edition. These changes have taken place because the LCSH in microfiche (published quarterly) is now a byproduct of the online system used to input and update authority records. The new features, which also are used in this publication's list, are summarized as follows:

1) New codes have been used to show the cross reference structure
2) The order of display of the references has changed, with see also references (now narrower terms) printed last

> USE = Use the heading referred to (formerly *see*)
> UF = Used For (formerly *x*)
> BT = Broader Term (formerly *xx*)
> RT = Related Term (formerly *xx* and *sa*)
> SA = See Also (used to introduce general *see also* references)
> NT = Narrower term (formerly *see*)

3) The term (May Subd Geog) has replaced the term (Indirect) for geographic subdivision practice.[17]

NOTES

1. A heading (or a complex of headings) is said to be coextensive when it "defines precisely the complete [subject] contents, but no more than the contents, of an item." Cf. Wynar, Bohdan S. *Introduction to Cataloging and Classification.* 7th ed. by Arlene G. Taylor. Littleton, Colo.: Libraries Unlimited, 1985, p. 604.

2. Library of Congress. Subject Cataloging Division. *Library of Congress Classification. Class M; Music and Books On Music,* 3rd ed. (Washington, D.C.: Library of Congress, 1978), 3-10.

3. Library of Congress. Subject Cataloging Division. *Library of Congress Subject Headings,* 10th ed., 2 vol. (Washington, D.C.: Library of Congress, 1986), xvi.

4. Music Library Association. *Music Cataloging Bulletin* 11, no. 1 (Jan. 1984): 2.

5. Library of Congress. Subject Cataloging Division. *Subject Cataloging Manual: Subject Headings.* Rev. ed. (Washington, D.C.: Library of Congress, 1985), H1160(1-2).

6. *Subject Cataloging Manual,* H1161(1).

7. *Subject Cataloging Manual,* H1110(1-9).

8. *Subject Cataloging Manual,* H1160(2).

9. *Subject Cataloging Manual,* H1160(1).

10. *Music Cataloging Bulletin* 14, no. 1 (Jan. 1983): 1.

11. *Music Cataloging Bulletin* 11, no. 2 (Feb. 1980): 1.

12. Library of Congress. Subject Cataloging Division. *Library of Congress Subject Headings.* 8th ed.(Washington, D.C.: Library of Congress, 1975), p. lxv.

13. *Subject Cataloging Manual,* H1917(1-5).

14. *Music Cataloging Bulletin* 15, no. 8 (Aug. 1984): 1.

15. *Music Cataloging Bulletin* 15, no. 11 (Nov. 1984): 1.

16. *Music Cataloging Bulletin* 13, no. 10 (Oct. 1982): 2.

17. Library of Congress. Processing Services. *Cataloging Service Bulletin* 37 (Summer 1987): 54-55.

Abbey Road Studios (London, England)
    UF EMI Abbey Road Studios (London, England)
        EMI Recording Studios (London, England)
        EMI Studios (London, England)
    BT Sound studios—England

Ability, Musical
    USE Musical ability

Abkhaz folk-songs
    USE Folk-songs, Abkhaz

Abkhaz songs
    USE Songs, Abkhaz

Accentuation (Music)
    USE Musical accentuation

Accompaniment, Musical
    USE Musical accompaniment

Accordeon
    USE Accordion

Accordion *(History, ML1083; Instruction, MT680)*
    UF Accordeon
        Piano accordion
    RT Bandonion
        Concertina
    NT Button-key accordions
    —Construction *(ML990.A4)*
    —Instruction and study *(MT680)*
        NT Accordion music—Teaching pieces
    —Methods
    — —Juvenile *(MT801.A3)*
    — —Self-instruction *(MT680)*
        UF Accordion—Self-instruction
    —Self-instruction
        USE Accordion—Methods—Self-instruction

Accordion and flute music
    USE Flute and accordion music

Accordion and guitar music *(M298)*
    UF Guitar and accordion music

Accordion and percussion music *(M298)*
    UF Percussion and accordion music

Accordion and piano music *(M284.A3; M285.A3)*
    UF Piano and accordion music

Accordion and piano music, Arranged *(M284.A3; M285.A3)*
    NT Concertos (Accordion)—Solo with piano
        Concertos (Accordion with chamber orchestra)—Solo with piano
        Suites (Accordion with orchestra)—Solo with piano

Accordion and piano music (Jazz) *(M284.A3; M285.A3)*

Accordion and recorder music
    USE Recorder and accordion music

Accordion and vibraphone music
    USE Vibraphone and accordion music

Accordion and violin music
    USE Violin and accordion music

Accordion and zither music
    USE Zither and accordion music

Accordion band
    USE Accordion ensembles

Accordion ensembles
    Here are entered compositions for two or more accordions.
    UF Accordion band
    BT Accordion music
        Instrumental music
    SA Suites, Variations, Waltzes, *and similar headings with specification of instruments which include the specification Accordion ensemble*
    NT Canons, fugues, etc. (Accordion ensemble)
        Concertos (Flute with accordion ensemble)
        Flute with accordion ensemble
        Minuets (Accordion ensemble)
        Polonaises (Accordion ensemble)
        Waltzes (Accordion ensemble)

Accordion music *(M175.A4)*
    SA Concertos, Polkas, Sonatas, Suites, *and similar headings with specification of instruments;* Trios [Quartets, etc.] *followed by specifications which include the accordion; also* Accordion ensembles *and headings that begin with the words accordion or accordions*
    NT Accordion ensembles
        Canons, fugues, etc. (Accordion)
        Marches (Accordion)
        Overtures arranged for accordion
        Polkas (Accordion)
        Rondos (Accordion)
        Sonatas (Accordion)
        Suites (Accordion)
        Waltzes (Accordion)
    —Teaching pieces *(MT680)*
        BT Accordion—Instruction and study

Accordion music (Jazz) *(M175.A4)*

Accordion with chamber orchestra *(M1039.4.A3)*
    RT Concertos (Accordion with chamber orchestra)
    NT Suites (Accordion with chamber orchestra)

Accordion with orchestra *(M1039.4.A3)*
    BT Orchestral music
    RT Concertos (Accordion)
    NT Suites (Accordion with orchestra)

Accordion with plectral ensemble *(M1360)*
    BT Plectral ensembles
    RT Concertos (Accordion with plectral ensemble)

Accordion with string ensemble
    NT Concertos (Accordion with string ensemble)

Accordion with string orchestra *(M1105-M1106)*
    RT Concertos (Accordion with string orchestra)

Accordionists [May Subd Geog]

Acoli folk-songs
   USE Folk-songs, Acoli
Acoustics
   USE Architectural acoustics
       Hearing
       Molecular acoustics
       Music—Acoustics and physics
       Psychoacoustics
       Sound
       Underwater acoustics
Acrobats of God (Ballet)
   BT Ballets
Act-tune
   USE Entr'acte music
Acting in opera (MT955)
   BT Opera
Action songs
   USE Games with music
Ad Dominum (Music)
   USE Psalms (Music)—120th Psalm
Ad te, Domine, clamabo (Music)
   USE Psalms (Music)—28th Psalm
Adaptation (Music)
   USE Arrangement (Music)
Advent
   BT Church year
       Fasts and feasts
   NT Advent sermons
   —Songs and music
      USE Advent music
Advent hymns
   BT Hymns
Advent music
   UF Advent—Songs and music
   BT Church music
       Music
       Sacred vocal music
Advertising [May Subd Geog]
   NT Music in advertising
Adyghe folk-songs
   USE Folk-songs, Adyghe
Adyghe songs
   USE Songs, Adyghe
Adzhar folk-songs
   USE Folk-songs, Adzhar
Aeolian harp *(ML1005-ML1106)*
   UF Eolian harp
   BT Harp
Aeolian pipe-organ
   USE Player-organ
Aeolian-vocalion *(ML1055.A3)*
   UF Vocalion, Aeolian
   BT Musical instruments (Mechanical)
       Phonograph
Aeronautics [May Subd Geog]
   —Music
      USE Aeronautics—Songs and music
   —Songs and music *(M1977.A; M1978.A;*
       History and criticism, ML3780)
      UF Aeronautics—Music
         Aeronautics in music
Aeronautics in music
   USE Aeronautics—Songs and music

Aesthetics
   NT Music—Philosophy and aesthetics
       Music and architecture
Afrikaner song-books
   USE Song-books, Afrikaner
Afro-American composers [May Subd Geog]
   UF Composers, Afro-American
   NT Afro-American women composers
Afro-American minstrel shows
   USE Minstrel shows
Afro-American musicians [May Subd Geog]
   UF Musicians, Afro-American
   BT Afro-American entertainers
       Afro-Americans in the performing arts
   NT Afro-American singers
       Afro-American women musicians
Afro-American singers [May Subd Geog]
   UF Singers, Afro-American
   BT Afro-American musicians
Afro-American spirituals
   USE Spirituals (Songs)
Afro-American women composers [May Subd Geog]
   UF Women composers, Afro-American
   BT Afro-American composers
Afro-American women musicians [May Subd Geog]
   UF Women musicians, Afro-American
   BT Afro-American musicians
Afro-Americans [May Subd Geog]
   —Music *(History, ML3556; Music,*
       M1670-1671)
   NT Blues (Music)
       Gospel music
       Jazz music
       Rhythm and blues music
       Soul music
       Spirituals (Songs)
   —Songs and music
Afternoon of a faun (Ballet)
   UF Après-midi d'un faune (Ballet)
   BT Ballets
Aged musicians [May Subd Geog]
   BT Musicians
Agnus Dei *(Music)*
   BT Masses
Agri folk-songs
   USE Folk-songs, Agri
Alabados *(ML3086)*
   BT Hispanic Americans—Music
       Hymns, Spanish
Albanian folk-songs
   USE Folk-songs, Albanian
Alboka *(ML990.A5)*
   BT Musical instruments—Spain
       Pipe (Musical instrument)
       Wind instruments
Aleatory music
   USE Chance composition
       Chance compositions
All Saints' Day *(BV67)*
   —Songs and music
   USE All Saints' Day music

All Saints' Day music *(M2088.A5;*
        M2098.A5)
  UF All Saints' Day—Songs and music
  BT Church music
        Sacred vocal music
Alleluia (Music)
  UF Alleluja (Music)
  BT Chants (Plain, Gregorian, etc)—
        History and criticism
Alleluja (Music)
  USE Alleluia (Music)
Allemande
  UF Allmayne
        Almain
        Almand
Allemandes
  BT Dance music
Allen organ *(ML597)*
  BT Electronic organ
Allmayne
  USE Allemande
Almain
  USE Allemande
Almand
  USE Allemande
Alpenhorn *(History and construction,*
        ML980)
  UF Alpine horn
  BT Brass instruments
        Horn (Musical instrument)
  RT Lur
Alpenhorn and organ music *(M182-186)*
  UF Organ and alpenhorn music
Alpenhorn music *(M110)*
Alpine horn
  USE Alpenhorn
Alteration, Chromatic
  USE Chromatic alteration (Music)
Althorn
  USE Alto horn
Alto cornet
  USE Alto horn
Alto horn *(ML975-ML976)*
  UF Althorn
        Alto cornet
        Alto saxhorn
        Mellophone
  BT Brass instruments
        Fluegelhorn
        Horn (Musical instrument)
Alto horn and piano music *(M270-M271)*
  UF Piano and alto horn music
  NT Sonatas (Alto horn and piano)
Alto horn music *(M110)*
  NT Brass quintets (Alto horn, baritone,
        cornets (2), tuba)
Alto saxhorn
  USE Alto horn
Ambo (Zambia) folk-songs
  USE Folk-songs, Ambo (Zambia)
Amen (Liturgy)
  BT Amens (Music)
        Liturgies

Amens (Music)
  BT Sacred vocal music
  NT Amen (Liturgy)
American hymns
  USE Hymns, English
American lullabies
  USE Lullabies, American
Amusements [May Subd Geog]
  NT Musical recreations
Amusia
  BT Music—Physiological aspects
        Music—Psychology
Analog-to-digital converters—Standards
        [May Subd Geog]
  NT MIDI (Standard)
Analysis, Melodic
  USE Melodic analysis
Analysis, Musical
  USE Musical analysis
Analytical guides (Music)
  USE *subdivision* Analysis, appreciation *under*
          headings for music compositions
        Music appreciation
        Musical analysis
Ancient music
  USE *subdivision* To 500 *under music*
          headings
        Music—To 500
Ancient musical instruments
  USE Musical instruments. Ancient
Anecdotes, Musical
  USE Music—Anecdotes, facetiae, satire, etc.
Angk Lung *(ML1040)*
  UF Kechruk
  BT Musical instruments—Indonesia
        Xylophone
Anglo-Saxon songs
  USE Songs, Anglo-Saxon
Annual Gathering of Traditional Indiana
        Fiddlers and Other Folks
  USE Battle Ground Fiddlers' Gathering,
        Battle Ground, Ind.
Anthem
        Here are entered works on the anthem as
          a musical form. Works composed in
          the form are entered under Anthems.
  BT Church music
        Part-songs, Sacred
  Note under Anthems
Anthems *(M2038-M2099)*
        Here are entered works composed in the
          form of the anthem.
        A second heading for medium is assigned
          if a specific medium of performance is
          given, or if a general medium is im-
          plied in the work, *e.g.*: 1. Anthems. 2.
          Choruses, Sacred (Mixed voices, 4
          parts), Unaccompanied. Or, 1. An-
          thems. 2. Choruses, Sacred, with or-
          gan.
        Works on the anthem as a musical form
          are entered under Anthem.

Anthems *(M2038-M2099)*
  (Continued)
    BT Choruses, Sacred
        Motets
        Part-songs, English
        Part-songs, Sacred
        Sacred duets
        Sacred nonets
        Sacred octets
        Sacred quartets
        Sacred quintets
        Sacred septets
        Sacred sextets
        Sacred trios
    Notes under Anthem; Part-songs, Sacred
Anthems, National
  USE National songs
Antiphonaries (Music)
    BT Sacred vocal music
        Service books (Music)
    NT Antiphons (Music)
Antiphons (Music)
    BT Antiphonaries (Music)
        Sacred vocal music
    NT Regina Caeli Laetare (Music)
        Salve Regina (Music)
Apollo lyre
  USE Lyre-guitar
Appalachian dulcimer *(ML1015-ML1018)*
    UF American dulcimer
        Mountain dulcimer
        Plucked dulcimer
    BT Dulcimer
        Zither
Appalachian dulcimer and guitar music
        (M292-M293)
    UF Guitar and Appalachian dulcimer music
Appalachian dulcimer music *(M142.A7)*
Appalachian dulcimer music (Appalachian
        dulcimers (2)) *(M292-M293)*
Appreciation of music
  USE Music appreciation
Après-midi d'un faune (Ballet)
  USE Afternoon of a faun (Ballet)
Arabic songs
  USE Songs, Arabic
Arabs [May Subd Geog]
  —Music
        NT Belly dance music
Archicembalo *(ML653-ML655)*
    BT Piano
Archiluth
  USE Archlute
Archiphone
    BT Organ
Archiphone music *(M6-M14.6)*
    NT Suites (Archiphone, violins (2))
Archlute *(ML1015.A)*
    UF Archiluth
        Arcileuto
        Arciliuto
        Erzlaute

Archlute *(ML1015.A)*
  (Continued)
    UF Liuto attiorbato
    BT Lute
Archlute music *(M142.A8)*
Arcileuto
  USE Archlute
Arciliuto
  USE Archlute
Arias
  USE *subdivision* Excerpts *under* Cantatas;
            Masses; Operas; Oratorios
        Sacred songs
        Solo cantatas
        Songs
Armenian songs
  USE Songs, Armenian
Armies [May Subd Geog]
  —Music
        USE Military music
            Music in the army
            War-songs
Aromanian folk-songs
  USE Folk-songs, Aromanian
Arpeggione *(ML760)*
    UF Guitar violoncello
        Guitare d'amour
    BT Violoncello
Arpeggione and piano music *(M239)*
    UF Piano and arpeggione music
    NT Sonatas (Arpeggione and piano)
Arrangement (Music)
    UF Adaption (Music)
        Transcription (Music)
    BT Music
    RT Instrumentation and orchestration
  —Copyright
        USE Copyright—Adaptations
Art and music
    UF Music and art
    RT Music in art
Art songs
    USE Sacred songs
        Songs
Ascension Day music
    BT Church music
        Music
        Sacred vocal music
Atonality
        ML3811 (Acoustics and physics)
        MT46 (Instruction)
    BT Tonality
Attendite, popule (Music)
    USE Psalms (Music)—78th Psalm
Audio-visual materials
    UF AV materials
Audio visual
  USE subject headings beginning with
            the words Audio-visual
Audiocassettes
    UF Audio cassettes
        Audiocassette recordings
        Audiocassette tapes

Audiocassettes
(Continued)
> Audiotape cassettes
> Cassettes, Audio
> Compact audiocassettes
BT Phonotapes

Audiocassettes for children [May Subd Geog]
BT Children's mass media

Aulos *(ML990.A)*
BT Musical instruments, Ancient—Greece
> Woodwind instruments

Australian (Aboriginal) folk-songs
USE Folk-songs, Australian (Aboriginal)

Australian songs
USE Songs, Australian (Aboriginal)

Authors
NT Musicians as authors

Authorship
NT Popular music—Writing
> and publishing

Autoharp *(ML1015)*
BT Zither

Autoharp music *(M175.A8)*

Ave Maria (Music)
BT Mary, Blessed Virgin, Saint—Songs and
> music

Ave Maris Stella (Music)
BT Mary, Blessed Virgin, Saint—Songs and
> music

Ave Regina coelorum (Music)
BT Mary, Blessed Virgin, Saint—Songs and
> music

Azerbaijani songs
USE Songs, Azerbaijani

Aztec music
USE Aztecs—Music

Aztecs
—Music *(ML3575)*
> UF Aztec music

Baǧlama
BT Lute
> Mandolin

Bagpipe *(ML980)*
UF Cornemuse
> Musette
BT Music—Scotland
> Woodwind instruments
NT Duda
> Gaita
—Reeds

Bagpipe and continuo music
UF Continuo and bagpipe music
NT Suites (Bagpipe and continuo)

Bagpipe and drum music *(M298)*
UF Drum and bagpipe music
BT Bagpipe music
> Percussion music
NT Pipe band music

Bagpipe and hurdy-gurdy music *(M298)*
UF Hurdy-gurdy and bagpipe music

Bagpipe band music
USE Pipe band music

Bagpipe bands
USE Pipe bands

Bagpipe music *(M145)*
RT Pipe music
SA *Concertos, Minuets, Sonatas, Suites,* and similar
> headings with specification of instruments;
> *Trios [Quartets, etc.], Wind trios [quartets,
> etc.],* and *Woodwind trios [quartets, etc.]*
> followed by specifications which include the
> bagpipe; also *Wind ensembles, Woodwind
> ensembles,* and headings that begin with the
> words Bagpipe or Bagpipes
NT Bagpipe and drum music
> Pibroch
> Pibrochs
> Pipe band music

Bagpipe music (Bagpipes (2)) *(M288-M289)*
NT Suites (Bagpipes (2))

Bagpipe with band *(M1205; M1257)*
RT Concertos (Bagpipe with band)

Bagpipers [May Subd Geog]
UF Pipers (Bagpipes)
BT Musicians

Bajans
USE Bhajans

Bajjika songs
USE Songs, Bajjika

Bala
USE Balo

Balafo
USE Balo

Balafon
USE Balo

Balafou
USE Balo

Balalaika *(ML1015-ML1018)*
BT Guitar
NT Domra
> Tambura

Balalaika and bandonion music *(M298)*
UF Bandonion and balalaika music

Balalaika and piano music *(M282-M283)*
UF Piano and balalaika music
NT Rondos (Balalaika and piano)
> Sonatas (Balalaika and piano)
> Suites (Balalaika and piano)
> Waltzes (Balalaika and piano)

Balalaika and piano music, Arranged
(M282.B3; M283.B3)
NT Concertos (Balalaika)—Solo with piano

Balalaika music *(M142.B2)*
NT Balalaika with chamber orchestra
> Concertos (Balalaika with chamber
> orchestra)
> Domra music

Balalaika players [May Subd Geog]

Balalaika with chamber orchestra
(M1037.4.B3)
BT Balalaika music
RT Concertos (Balalaika with chamber
> orchestra)

Balalaika with chamber orchestra, Arranged
(M1037.4.B3)

Balalaika with orchestra *(M1037.4.B3)*
　　RT　Concertos (Balalaika)
Balaphon
　　USE　Balo
Baldwin organ *(ML579)*
　　UF　Orga-sonic organ
　　BT　Electronic organ
Ballad opera *(History, ML1950)*
　　BT　Ballads, English
　　　　English drama
　　　　English drama (Comedy)
　　　　Opera
　　RT　Singspiel
Ballad operas *(M1500-M1503.5)*
　　BT　Operas
Ballads [May Subd Geog] *(History and criticism, PN1376; Music, M1627; Music Literature, ML3545)*
　　　　Here are entered collections of ballads in various unrelated languages. Works in a single language or group of languages are entered under this heading with language qualifier, *e.g.* Ballads, English; Ballads, Germanic. For works consisting of ballads of an individual ethnic group, additional subject entries are made under the heading [ethnic group]—Music and under the heading Folk music—[place] or Music—[place].
　　BT　Lyric poetry
　　　　Poetry
　　　　Songs
　　　　Vocal music
　　RT　Folk-songs
　　NT　Political ballads and songs
　　　　Revolutionary ballads and songs
Ballads, Basque [May Subd Geog]
　　UF　Basque ballads
Ballads, Bengali [May Subd Geog]
　　UF　Bengali ballads
Ballads, Byelorussian [May Subd Geog]
　　UF　Byelorussian ballads
Ballads, Catalan [May Subd Geog]
　　UF　Catalan ballads
Ballads, Chinese [May Subd Geog]
　　UF　Chinese ballads
Ballads, Danish [May Subd Geog]
　　UF　Danish ballads
　　NT　Grimilds hævn (Ballad)
Ballads, English [May Subd Geog]
　　UF　English ballads
　　NT　Ballad opera
　　Note under ballads
Ballads, Estonian [May Subd Geog]
　　UF　Estonian ballads
Ballads, Fang [May Subd Geog]
　　UF　Fang ballads
Ballads, French [May Subd Geog]
　　UF　French ballads
Ballads, Friesian [May Subd Geog]
　　UF　Friesian ballads

Ballads, Gallegan [May Subd Geog]
　　UF　Gallegan ballads
Ballads, German [May Subd Geog]
　　UF　German ballads
Ballads, Germanic [May Subd Geog]
　　UF　Germanic ballads
　　Note under Ballads
Ballads, Hebrew [May Subd Geog]
　　UF　Hebrew ballads
Ballads, Hungarian [May Subd Geog]
　　UF　Hungarian ballads
Ballads, Irish [May Subd Geog]
　　UF　Irish ballads
Ballads, Italian [May Subd Geog]
　　UF　Italian ballads
Ballads, Japanese [May Subd Geog]
　　UF　Japanese ballads
　　NT　Kouta
　　　　Nagauta
Ballads, Kalinga [May Subd Geog]
　　UF　Kalinga ballads
Ballads, Kannada [May Subd Geog]
　　UF　Kannada ballads
Ballads, Korean [May Subd Geog]
　　UF　Korean ballads
　　NT　P'ansori
Ballads, Ladino [May Subd Geog] *(PC4813.8)*
　　UF　Ladino ballads
Ballads, Lithuanian [May Subd Geog]
　　UF　Lithuanian ballads
Ballads, Manx [May Subd Geog]
　　UF　Manx ballads
Ballads, Mongolian [May Subd Geog]
　　UF　Mongolian ballads
Ballads, Norwegian [May Subd Geog]
　　UF　Norwegian ballads
Ballads, Old Norse [May Subd Geog]
　　UF　Old Norse ballads
Ballads, Oriya [May Subd Geog]
　　UF　Oriya ballads
Ballads, Portuguese [May Subd Geog]
　　UF　Portuguese ballads
Ballads, Romanian [May Subd Geog]
　　UF　Cîntece Batrînesti ballads
　　　　Romanian ballads
Ballads, Russian [May Subd Geog]
　　UF　Russian ballads
Ballads, Ryukyu [May Subd Geog]
　　UF　Ryukyu ballads
Ballads, Serbo-Croatian [May Subd Geog]
　　UF　Serbo-Croatian ballads
Ballads, Spanish [May Subd Geog]
　　　　Here are entered collections of Spanish ballads, including those called in Spanish "romances". Collections of Spanish medieval metrical romances and their prose versions are entered under Romances, Spanish.
　　UF　Spanish ballads
Ballads, Tamil [May Subd Geog]
　　UF　Tamil ballads
Ballads, Telugu [May Subd Geog]
　　UF　Telugu ballads

Ballads, Twi [May Subd Geog]
  UF Twi ballads
Ballads, Ukrainian [May Subd Geog]
  UF Ukrainian ballads
Ballate
  BT Part-songs, Italian
Ballet dance music
      Here are entered works intended for use
        with ballet dance instruction. Ballet
        scores are entered under Ballets.
  BT Ballets
      Dance music
  Note under Ballets
Ballets *(M1520-M1526)*
      Here are entered musical works composed for
        ballet. Works on the ballet are entered under
        Ballet. Works intended for use with ballet
        dance instruction are entered under Ballet
        dance music.
  BT Dramatic music
  RT Pantomimes with music
  NT Acrobats of God (Ballet)
      Afternoon of a faun (Ballet)
      Ballet dance music
      Black angels (Ballet)
      Bolero (Ballet)
      Buffalo soldier (Ballet)
      Coppélia (Ballet)
      Cortege of eagles (Ballet)
      Don Quixote (Ballet)
      Emperor's new clothes (Ballet)
      Firebird (Ballet)
      Flower Festival in Genzano (Ballet)
      Giselle (Ballet)
      Isadora (Ballet)
      Legend of Joseph (Ballet)
      Magic flute (Ballet)
      Medea (Ballet)
      Midsummer night's dream (Ballet)
      Mozartiana (Ballet)
      Nutcracker (Ballet)
      Petroushka (Ballet)
      Rite of spring (Ballet)
      Romeo and Juliet (Ballet)
      Saint Matthew Passion (Ballet)
      Scheherazade (Ballet)
      Seraphic dialogue (Ballet)
      Steadfast tin soldier (Ballet)
      Sue's Leg (Ballet)
      Swan lake (Ballet)
      Tealia (Ballet)
      Union Jack (Ballet)
  Note under Ballet dance music
  —2-piano scores *(M1523)*
      UF Ballets arranged for piano (Pianos
            (2))
      BT Piano music (Pianos (2)), Arranged
  —Excerpts
      NT Overtures
          Suites (Orchestra)
  — —Scores *(M1524-M1525)*
      UF Ballets—Scores—Excerpts
  —Piano scores *(M1523)*

Ballets *(M1520-M1526)*
  (Continued)
  —Piano scores (4 hands) *(M1523)*
      UF Ballets arranged for piano (4 hands)
      BT Piano music (4 hands), Arranged
  —Scores *(M1520)*
  — —Excerpts
      USE Ballets—Excerpts—Scores
  —Stories, plots, etc. *(MT95-MT100)*
      BT Plots (Drama, novel, etc.)
Ballets arranged for flute and piano
        (M243-M244)
  BT Flute and piano music, Arranged
Ballets arranged for piano (4 hands)
  USE Ballets—Piano scores (4 hands)
Ballets arranged for piano (Pianos (2))
  USE Ballets—2-piano scores
Balo *(ML1048)*
  UF Bala
      Balafo
      Balafon
      Balafou
      Balaphon
  BT Musical instruments—Africa,
          French-speaking West
      Xylophone
Bamboo pipe
  USE Pipe (Musical instrument)
Bamileke folk-songs
  USE Folk-songs, Bamileke
Bāmsurī
  USE Bānsurī
Band music *(M1200-1268)*
  BT Instrumental music
      Orchestral music
  RT Military music
  SA Concertos ([Solo instrument(s)] with band);
        [Solo instrument(s)] with band; Suites,
        Variations, Waltzes, *and similar headings*
        with specification of instruments which
        include the specification Band
  NT Big band music
      Brass band music
      Canons, fugues, etc. (Band)
      Chorale preludes (Band)
      Clarinet choir music
      Clarinet with band
      Concertos (Band)
      Concertos (Bassoon, clarinet, flute,
          horn, oboe with band)
      Concertos (Cornet with band)
      Concertos (Flutes (4) with band)
      Concertos (Horns (4) with band)
      Concertos (Organ with band)
      Concertos (Piano with band)
      Concertos (Trombone with band)
      Dance-orchestra music
      Fanfares
      Flutes (4) with band
      Horn with band
      Marches (Band)
      Military music
      Minuets (Band)

Band music *(M1200-1268)*
   (Continued)
    NT Oboe with band
        Overtures (Band)
        Passacaglias (Band)
        Pipe band music
        Polkas (Band)
        Polonaises (Band)
        Potpourris (Band)
        Rondos (Band)
        Suites (Band)
        Symphonic poems (Band)
        Symphonies (Band)
        Trombone with band
        Trombones (3) with band
        Variations (Band)
        Vocal ensembles with band
        Waltzes (Band)
        Wind ensembles
    —Analysis, appreciation *(MT125; MT130)*
Band music, Arranged
    NT Concerti grossi arranged for band
Band organ *(History, ML1058)*
    UF Fair organ
        Fairground organ
    BT Mechanical organs
Bandmasters
    USE United States. Army—Bandmasters;
        and similar headings
        Bandsmen
        Conductors (Music)
        United States. Army—Bandmasters
Bandmen
    USE Bandsmen
Bandoneon
    USE Bandonion
Bandonion *(History, ML1083; Instruction,*
    MT681)
    UF Bandoneon
    BT Button-key accordions
    RT Accordion
        Concertina
Bandonion and balalaika music
    USE Balalaika and bandonion music
Bandonion and piano music *(M284.B33;*
    M285.B33)
    UF Piano and bandonion music
Bandonion and piano music, Arranged
    (M284.B33; M285.B33)
    NT Concertos (Bandonion)—Solo with
        piano
        Concertos (Bandonion with chamber
        orchestra)—Solo with piano
Bandonion music *(M175.B2)*
Bandonion with chamber orchestra
    (M1039.4.B3)
    RT Concertos (Bandonion with chamber
        orchestra)
Bandonion with orchestra *(M1039.4.B3)*
    RT Concertos (Bandonion)
Bandora
    USE Pandora (Musical instrument)

Bandoura
    USE Bandura
Bands, Rock
    USE Rock groups
Bands (Music) [May Subd Geog] *(ML1300-1354;*
    MT733)
    BT Instrumental music—History and
        criticism
        Military music—History and criticism
        Music
        Musical groups
    RT Conducting
        Orchestra
        Wind instruments
    NT Big bands
        Brass bands
        Bugle and drum corps
        Dance orchestras
        Drum majors
        Fife and drum corps
        Instrumentation and orchestration
        (Band)
        Mandolin orchestras
        Marching bands
        Mariachi
        Pipe bands
        Rhythm bands and orchestras
        Steel band (Musical ensemble)
        United States. Army—Bandmasters
Bandsmen *(ML399; ML419)*
    UF Bandmasters
        Bandmen
    BT Musicians
Bandstands [May Subd Geog]
    BT Pavilions
Bandura *(ML1015.B25)*
    UF Bandoura
    BT Lute
Bandurria *(ML1015-ML1018)*
    BT Guitar
        Lute
Bandurria music *(M142.B3)*
Banjarese folk-songs
    USE Folk-songs, Banjarese
Banjo *(ML1015-ML1018)*
    —Group instruction
        USE Banjo—Methods—Group
            instruction
    —Methods *(MT562)*
    — —Group instruction *(MT562)*
        UF Banjo—Group instruction
    — —Self-instruction *(MT568)*
        UF Banjo—Self-instruction
    —Methods (Bluegrass) *(MT562; MT568)*
    —Self-instruction
        USE Banjo—Methods—Self-instruction
Banjo and flute music
    USE Flute and banjo music
Banjo and guitar music *(M292-M293)*
    UF Guitar and banjo music
Banjo and percussion music
    USE Percussion and banjo music

Banjo band
USE Plectral ensembles
Banjo makers [May Subd Geog]
BT Stringed instrument makers
Banjo music *(M120-M122)*
NT Banjo with instrumental ensemble
Plectral ensembles
Banjo with instrumental ensemble
BT Banjo music
Bānsurī *(ML990.B32)*
UF Bāmsurī
Halur
Husor
Solor
BT Flute
Musical instruments—India
Musical instruments—Pakistan
Bantu folk-songs
USE Folk-songs, Bantu
Barbershop quartets *(M1580.4; M1581.4;*
M1594; M1604)
UF Quartets, Barbershop
BT Choruses, Secular (Men's voices, 4
parts), Unaccompanied
Choruses, Secular (Women's voices, 4
parts), Unaccompanied
Vocal quartets, Unaccompanied
RT Barbershop singing
Barbershop singing [May Subd Geog] *(ML3516)*
UF Barbershopping
Singing, Barbershop
BT Choral singing
Ensemble singing
RT Barbershop quartets
Bards and bardism *(ML287-ML289;*
ML3653-ML3656)
UF Scops
BT Druids and Druidism
Poetry
Poets
RT Minstrels
Scalds and scaldic poetry
NT Meistersinger
Minnesingers
Troubadours
Trouvères
Baritone (Musical instrument) *(History and*
construction, ML975-ML978)
BT Brass instruments
RT Euphonium
Trombone
—Orchestra studies *(MT496)*
BT Baritone (Musical instrument)—
Studies and exercises
—Studies and exercises *(MT496)*
NT Baritone (Musical instrument)—
Orchestra studies
Baritone and cornet music *(M288-9)*
UF Cornet and baritone music
NT Suites (Baritone and cornet)
Baritone and piano music *(M262-M263)*
UF Piano and baritone music
NT Rondos (Baritone and piano)
Sonatas (Baritone and piano)

Baritone and piano music, Arranged
(M262-M263)
Baritone music *(M90-M94)*
SA Concertos, Minuets, Sonatas, Suites,
and similar headings with
specification of instruments; Brass
trios [quartets, etc.], Trios [Quartets,
etc.] *and* Wind trios [quartets, etc.]
followed by specifications which
include the baritone; also Brass
ensembles, Wind ensembles, *and*
headings that begin with the words
baritone or baritones
Baritone with string orchestra *(M1134.B37;*
M1135.B37)
RT Concertos (Baritone with string
orchestra)
Baroque music
USE *subdivisions* 17th century and 18th
century *under music headings*
Music—17th century
Music—18th century
Barrel organ
UF Hand-organ
BT Mechanical organs
Barrel organ, Hydraulic
BT Hydraulic organ
Barrel-organ music
Barrel-organ players
USE Organ grinders
Barrel organists [May Subd Geog]
USE Organ grinders
Baryton *(ML760)*
UF Viola di bordone
Viola paredon
BT Viol
Viola da gamba
Baryton music *(M59)*
NT String trios (Baryton, viola, violoncello)
String trios (Baryton, violin,
violoncello)
Suites (Horns (2), baryton, violins (2),
viola, violoncello, violone)
Basque folk-songs
USE Folk-songs, Basque
Basque musicians
USE Musicians, Basque
Bass, Electric
USE Bass guitar
Bass clarinet *(ML945-ML948)*
BT Clarinet
Bass clarinet and clarinet music
(M288-M289)
UF Clarinet and bass clarinet music
Bass clarinet and percussion music *(M298)*
UF Percussion and bass clarinet music
Bass clarinet and piano music *(M248-M252)*
UF Piano and bass clarinet music
NT Sonatas (Bass clarinet and piano)
Bass clarinet music *(M70-M74)*
Specification of bass clarinet in music
headings is limited to headings with
specifications for one or two solo in-
struments. In other music headings the

Bass clarinet music *(M70-M74)*
(Continued)
> bass clarinet is included in general specifications for clarinet.

SA Concertos, Minuets, Sonatas, Suites, *and similar headings with specification of instruments which include specifications for bass clarinet or clarinet;* Trios [quartets, etc.], Wind trios [quartets, etc.] *and* Woodwind trios [quartets, etc.] *followed by specifications which include clarinet; also* Wind ensembles, Woodwind ensembles, *and headings that begin with the words bass clarinet or bass clarinets*

Bass clarinet with chamber orchestra *(M1024-M1025)*
RT Concertos (Bass clarinet with chamber orchestra)

Bass clarinet with instrumental ensemble
RT Concertos (Bass clarinet with instrumental ensemble)

Bass clarinet with orchestra *(M1024-M1025)*
RT Concertos (Bass clarinet)

Bass clarinet with string ensemble
RT Concertos (Bass clarinet with string ensemble)
NT Concertos (Bass clarinet with string orchestra)

Bass clarinet with string orchestra *(M1124-M1125)*
BT Concertos (Bass clarinet with string orchestra)

Bass drum
USE Drum

Bass guitar *(ML1015)*
UF Bass, electric
Electric bass
BT Electric Guitar
—Instruction and study
— —Harmonics
BT Harmonics (Music)

Bass horn
USE Tuba

Bass players
USE Double-bassists

Bass trombone *(ML965-ML968)*
BT Trombone

Bass trombone and organ music *(M182-M186)*
UF Organ and bass trombone music

Bass trombone and piano music *(M262-M263)*
UF Piano and bass trombone music
NT Sonatas (Bass trombone and piano)

Bass trombone and piano music, Arranged *(M262-M263)*
NT Bass trombone with band—Solo with piano

Bass trombone music *(M90-M94)*
> Specification of bass trombone in music headings is limited to headings with specifications for one or two solo instruments. In other music headings the

Bass trombone music *(M90-M94)*
(Continued)
> bass trombone is included in the general specifications for trombone.

SA Concertos, Minuets, Sonatas, Suites, *and similar headings with specification of instruments which include specifications for bass trombone or trombone; also* Trios [Quartets, etc.], Wind trios [quartets, etc.] *and* Brass trios [quartets, etc.] *followed by specifications which include trombone; also* Wind ensembles, Brass ensembles, *and headings beginning with the words Bass trombone or Bass trombones*

Bass trombone with band *(M1205-M1206; M1257)*
RT Concertos (Bass trombone with band)
—Solo with piano *(M1206; M1257)*
BT Bass trombone and piano music, Arranged

Bass trombone with instrumental ensemble
RT Concertos (Bass trombone with instrumental ensemble)

Bass trombone with orchestra *(M1032-M1033)*
RT Concertos (Bass trombone)

Bass viol
USE Double bass
Viola da gamba

Bassari folk-songs
USE Folk-songs, Bassari

Basset clarinet *(History, ML945-ML948)*
BT Clarinet

Basset clarinet with orchestra *(M1024-M1025)*
NT Concertos (Basset clarinet)

Basset horn *(ML990.B35)*
BT Clarinet
Woodwind instruments

Basset horn and clarinet music *(M288-M289)*
UF Clarinet and basset-horn music

Basset horn and clarinet with orchestra *(M1040-M1041)*
RT Concertos (Basset horn and clarinet)

Basset horn and piano music *(M270.B4; M271.B4)*
UF Piano and basset-horn music
BT Piano music
NT Sonatas (Basset horn and piano)

Basset horn and piano music, Arranged *(M271.B4)*
NT Concertos (Basset horn)—Solo with piano

Basset horn music *(M110.B35)*
SA Concertos, Minuets, Sonatas, Suites *and similar headings with specification of instruments;* Trios [Quartets, etc.], Wind trios [quartets, etc.], and Woodwind trios [quartets, etc.] *followed by specifications which include the basset horn; also* Wind

Basset horn music *(M110.B35)*
(Continued)
  ensembles, Woodwind ensembles,
  and headings that begin with the
  words Basset horn or Basset horns
 NT Trios (Basset horn, viola, violoncello)
Basset horn with chamber orchestra
  (M1034.B38; M1035.B38)
 RT Concertos (Basset horn with chamber
   orchestra)
Basset horn with orchestra *(M1034.B38;*
  M1035.B38)
 RT Concertos (Basset horn)
Basso continuo
 USE Continuo *used as part of the*
   specification of medium in headings,
   e.g. Trio-sonatas (Violins (2),
   continuo)
  Thorough bass
Basso ostinato
 USE Ground bass
Bassoon *(History, ML953)*
 UF Curtall
 BT Woodwind instruments
 NT Contrabassoon
  Dulcian
  Pommer
  Sarrusophone
 —Construction *(ML951)*
 —Orchestra studies *(MT406)*
  BT Bassoon—Studies and exercises
 —Reeds
 —Studies and exercises *(MT405)*
  NT Bassoon—Orchestra studies
Bassoon and clarinet music
 UF Clarinet and bassoon music
Basque folk-songs
 USE Folk-songs, Basque
Basque musicians
 USE Musicians, Basque
Bass, Electric
 USE Bass guitar
Bass clarinet *(ML945-ML948)*
 BT Clarinet
Bass clarinet and clarinet music
  (M288-M289)
 UF Clarinet and bass clarinet music
Bass clarinet and percussion music *(M298)*
 UF Percussion and bass clarinet music
Bass clarinet and piano music *(M248-M252)*
 UF Piano and bass clarinet music
 NT Sonatas (Bass clarinet and piano)
Bass clarinet music *(M70-M74)*
  Specification of bass clarinet in music
   headings is limited to headings with
   specifications for one or two solo in-
   struments. In other music headings the
   bass clarinet is included in general
   specifications for clarinet.
 SA Concertos, Minuets, Sonatas, Suites,
   and similar headings with
   specification of instruments which
   include specifications for bass

Bass clarinet music *(M70-M74)*
(Continued)
 SA *clarinet or clarinet;* Trios [quartets,
   etc.], Wind trios [quartets, etc.] *and*
   Woodwind trios [quartets, etc.]
   followed by specifications which
   include clarinet; also Wind
   ensembles, Woodwind ensembles,
   and headings that begin with the
   words bass clarinet or bass clarinets
Bass clarinet with chamber orchestra
  (M1024-M1025)
 RT Concertos (Bass clarinet with
   chamber orchestra)
Bass clarinet with instrumental ensemble
 RT Concertos (Bass clarinet with instrumental
   ensemble)
Bass clarinet with orchestra *(M1024-M1025)*
 RT Concertos (Bass clarinet)
Bass clarinet with string ensemble
 RT Concertos (Bass clarinet with string
   ensemble)
 NT Concertos (Bass clarinet with string
   orchestra)
Bass clarinet with string orchestra
  (M1124-M1125)
 BT Concertos (Bass clarinet with string
   orchestra)
Bass drum
 USE Drum
Bass guitar *(ML1015)*
 UF Bass, electric
  Electric bass
 BT Electric Guitar
 —Instruction and study
 — —Harmonics
  BT Harmonics (Music)
Bass horn
 USE Tuba
Bass players
 USE Double-bassists
Bass trombone *(ML965-ML968)*
 BT Trombone
Bass trombone and organ music *(M182-M186)*
 UF Organ and bass trombone music
Bass trombone and piano music *(M262-M263)*
 UF Piano and bass trombone music
 NT Sonatas (Bass trombone and piano)
Bass trombone and piano music, Arranged
  (M262-M263)
 NT Bass trombone with band—Solo with piano
Bass trombone music *(M90-M94)*
  Specification of bass trombone in music
   headings is limited to headings with
   specifications for one or two solo in-
   struments. In other music headings the
   bass trombone is included in the general specifications for trombone.
 SA Concertos, Minuets, Sonatas, Suites,
   and similar headings with
   specification of instruments which
   include specifications for bass
   trombone or trombone; also Trios

Bass trombone music *(M90-M94)*
(Continued)
    SA [Quartets, etc.], Wind trios [quartets, etc.]
        and Brass trios [quartets, etc.]
        followed by specifications which
        include trombone; also Wind
        ensembles, Brass ensembles, *and*
        headings beginning with the words
        Bass trombone or Bass trombones
Bass trombone with band *(M1205-M1206;*
        M1257)
    RT Concertos (Bass trombone with band)
  —Solo with piano *(M1206; M1257)*
      BT Bass trombone and piano music,
          Arranged
Bass trombone with instrumental ensemble
    RT Concertos (Bass trombone with
        instrumental ensemble)
Bass trombone with orchestra *(M1032-M1033)*
    RT Concertos (Bass trombone)
Bass viol
  USE Double bass
        Viola da gamba
Bassari folk-songs
  USE Folk-songs, Bassari
Basset clarinet *(History, ML945-ML948)*
    BT Clarinet
Basset clarinet with orchestra
        (M1024-M1025)
    NT Concertos (Basset clarinet)
Basset horn *(ML990.B35)*
    BT Clarinet
        Woodwind instruments
Basset horn and clarinet music *(M288-M289)*
    UF Clarinet and basset-horn music
Basset horn and clarinet with orchestra
        (M1040-M1041)
    RT Concertos (Basset horn and clarinet)
Basset horn and piano music *(M270.B4;*
        M271.B4)
    UF Piano and basset-horn music
    BT Piano music
    NT Sonatas (Basset horn and piano)
Basset horn and piano music, Arranged
        (M271.B4)
    NT Concertos (Basset horn)—Solo with
        piano
Basset horn music *(M110.B35)*
    SA Concertos, Minuets, Sonatas, Suites
        and similar headings with
        specification of instruments; Trios
        [Quartets, etc.], Wind trios [quartets,
        etc.], and Woodwind trios [quartets,
        etc.] *followed by specifications which*
        include the basset horn; also Wind
        ensembles, Woodwind ensembles,
        and headings that begin with the
        words Basset horn or Basset horns
    NT Trios (Basset horn, viola, violoncello)
Basset horn with chamber orchestra
        (M1034.B38; M1035.B38)
    RT Concertos (Basset horn with chamber
        orchestra)

Basset horn with orchestra *(M1034.B38;*
        M1035.B38)
    RT Concertos (Basset horn)
Basso continuo
  USE Continuo *used as part of the*
        specification of medium in headings,
        e.g. Trio-sonatas (Violins (2),
        continuo)
      Thorough bass
Basso ostinato
  USE Ground bass
Bassoon *(History, ML953)*
    UF Curtall
    BT Woodwind instruments
    NT Contrabassoon
        Dulcian
        Pommer
        Sarrusophone
  —Construction *(ML951)*
  —Orchestra studies *(MT406)*
      BT Bassoon—Studies and exercises
  —Reeds
  —Studies and exercises *(MT405)*
      NT Bassoon—Orchestra studies
Bassoon and clarinet music
    UF Clarinet and bassoon music
    NT Bassoon and clarinet with
        orchestra
        Bassoon and clarinet with string
        orchestra
        Concertos (Bassoon and clarinet)
        Concertos (Bassoon and clarinet with
        string orchestra)
        Sonatas (Bassoon and clarinet)
Bassoon and clarinet with orchestra
        (M1040-M1041)
    BT Bassoon and clarinet music
    RT Concertos (Bassoon and clarinet)
Bassoon and clarinet with string orchestra
        (M1105-M1106)
    BT Bassoon and clarinet music
    RT Concertos (Bassoon and clarinet with
        string orchestra)
  —Solos with piano *(M1106)*
      BT Trios (Piano, bassoon, clarinet),
          Arranged
Bassoon and continuo music
    UF Continuo and bassoon music
    NT Rondos (Bassoon and continuo)
        Sonatas (Bassoon and continuo)
        Suites (Bassoon and continuo)
Bassoon and double-bass music *(M290-M291)*
    UF Double-bass and bassoon music
Bassoon and English-horn music *(M288-M289)*
    UF English-horn and bassoon music
    BT Bassoon music
        English-horn music
    NT Suites (Bassoon and English horn)
Bassoon and flute music *(M288-M289)*
    UF Flute and bassoon music
    NT Bassoon and flute with string orchestra
        Canons, fugues, etc. (Bassoon and flute)
        Concertos (Bassoon and flute with
        string orchestra)

Bassoon and flute music *(M288-M289)*
(Continued)
NT Sonatas (Bassoon and flute)
Suites (Bassoon and flute)
Bassoon and flute with string orchestra
(M1140-M1141)
BT Bassoon and flute music
RT Concertos (Bassoon and flute with
string orchestra)
Bassoon and guitar music *(M296-M297)*
UF Guitar and bassoon music
NT Sonatas (Bassoon and guitar)
Bassoon and harpsichord music *(M253-M254)*
UF Harpsichord and bassoon music
NT Sonatas (Bassoon and harpsichord)
Bassoon and horn music *(M288-M289)*
UF Horn and bassoon music
Bassoon and oboe music *(M288-M289)*
UF Oboe and bassoon music
NT Bassoon and oboe with orchestra
Bassoon and oboe with string orchestra
Canons, fugues, etc. (Bassoon and oboe)
Concertos (Bassoon and oboe)
Concertos (Bassoon and oboe with
string orchestra)
Sonatas (Bassoon and oboe)
Suites (Bassoon and oboe)
Bassoon and oboe with orchestra
(M1040-M1041)
BT Bassoon and oboe music
RT Concertos (Bassoon and oboe)
Bassoon and oboe with string orchestra
(M1105-M1106)
BT Bassoon and oboe music
RT Concertos (Bassoon and oboe with
string orchestra)
Bassoon and organ music *(M182-M186)*
UF Organ and bassoon music
NT Chorale preludes (Bassoon and organ)
Sonatas (Bassoon and organ)
Suites (Bassoon and organ)
Bassoon and percussion music *(M298)*
UF Percussion and bassoon music
Bassoon and piano music *(M253-M254)*
UF Piano and bassoon music
NT Canons, fugues, etc. (Bassoon and
piano)
Passacaglias (Bassoon and piano)
Polonaises (Bassoon and piano)
Potpourris (Bassoon and piano)
Sonatas (Bassoon and piano)
Suites (Bassoon and piano)
Note under Duets
Bassoon and piano music, Arranged
(M253-M254)
NT Bassoon with chamber orchestra—Solo
with piano
Bassoon with orchestra—Solo with
piano
Bassoon with orchestra, Arranged—
Solo with piano
Bassoon with string orchestra—Solo
with piano

Bassoon and piano music, Arranged
(M253-M254)
(Continued)
NT Concertos (Bassoon)—Solo with piano
Concertos (Bassoon with band), Arranged—
Solo with piano
Concertos (Bassoon with chamber
orchestra)—Solo with piano
Concertos (Bassoon with string
ensemble)—Solo with piano
Concertos (Bassoon with string
orchestra)—Solo with piano
Concertos (Bassoon with string
orchestra), Arranged—Solo with
piano
Rondos (Bassoon with orchestra)—Solo
with piano
Suites (Bassoon with orchestra)—Solo
with piano
Suites (Bassoon with string orchestra)—
Solo with piano
Variations (Bassoon with orchestra)—
Solo with piano
Bassoon and piccolo music *(M288-M289)*
UF Piccolo and bassoon music.
NT Bassoon and piccolo with string
orchestra
Concertos (Bassoon and piccolo with
string orchestra)
Bassoon and piccolo with string orchestra
(M1105-M1106)
BT Bassoon and piccolo music
RT Concertos (Bassoon and piccolo with
string orchestra)
Bassoon and recorder music *(M288-M289)*
UF Recorder and bassoon music
NT Bassoon and recorder with string
orchestra
Concertos (Bassoon and recorder with
string orchestra)
Bassoon and recorder with string orchestra
(M1105-M1106)
BT Bassoon and recorder music
RT Concertos (Bassoon and recorder with
string orchestra)
Bassoon and trumpet music *(M288-M289)*
UF Trumpet and bassoon music
NT Bassoon and trumpet with string
orchestra
Concertos (Bassoon and trumpet with
string orchestra)
Bassoon and trumpet with string orchestra
(M1105-M1106)
BT Bassoon and trumpet music
RT Concertos (Bassoon and trumpet with
string orchestra)
Bassoon and tuba music *(M288-M289)*
UF Tuba and bassoon music
NT Suites (Bassoon and tuba)
Bassoon and vibraphone music
(M298)
UF Vibraphone and bassoon music

Bassoon and viola music *(M290-M291)*
UF   Viola and bassoon music
NT   Suites (Bassoon and viola)
Bassoon and violin music *(M290-M291)*
UF   Violin and bassoon music
NT   Bassoon and violin with string orchestra
     Concertos (Bassoon and violin with
        string orchestra)
     Suites (Bassoon and violin)
Bassoon and violin with chamber orchestra
     (M1040-M1041)
NT   Concertos (Bassoon and violin with
        chamber orchestra)
**Bassoon and violin with instrumental
     ensemble**
RT   Concertos (Bassoon and violin with
        instrumental ensemble)
NT   Rondos (Bassoon and violin with
        instrumental ensemble)
Bassoon and violin with string orchestra
     (M1105-M1106)
BT   Bassoon and violin music
RT   Concertos (Bassoon and violin with
        string orchestra)
Bassoon and violoncello music *(M290-M291)*
UF   Violoncello and bassoon music
NT   Sonatas (Bassoon and violoncello)
     Suites (Bassoon and violoncello)
Bassoon and violoncello with orchestra
     (M1040-M1041)
RT   Concertos (Bassoon and violoncello)
**Bassoon, clarinet, English horn, flute with
     orchestra** *(M1040-M1041)*
BT   Woodwind quartets (Bassoon, clarinet,
        English horn, flute)
RT   Concertos (Bassoon, clarinet, English
        horn, flute)
Bassoon, clarinet, flute, horn, oboe with band
     (M1205-6)
BT   Wind quintets (Bassoon, clarinet, flute,
        horn, oboe)
RT   Concertos (Bassoon, clarinet, flute,
        horn, oboe with band)
**Bassoon, clarinet, flute, horn, oboe with
     chamber orchestra** *(M1040-1041)*
BT   Wind quintets (Bassoon, clarinet, flute,
        horn, oboe)
RT   Concertos (Bassoon, clarinet, flute,
        horn, oboe with chamber orchestra)
—Scores *(M1040)*
**Bassoon, clarinet, flute, horn, oboe with
     orchestra** *(M1040-1041)*
BT   Orchestral music
     Wind quintets (Bassoon, clarinet, flute,
        horn, oboe)
RT   Concertos (Bassoon, clarinet, flute,
        horn, oboe)
**Bassoon, clarinet, flute, horn, oboe with string
     orchestra** *(M1105-6)*
BT   Wind quintets (Bassoon, clarinet, flute,
RT   Concertos (Bassoon, clarinet, flute,
        horn, oboe with string orchestra)

**Bassoon, clarinet, flute, horn, oboe with string
     orchestra** *(M1105-6)*
(Continued)
NT   Suites (Bassoon, clarinet, flute, horn,
        oboe with string orchestra)
—Scores *(M1105)*
**Bassoon, clarinet, flute, horn, violoncello with
     string orchestra** *(M1105-6)*
BT   Quintets (Bassoon, clarinet, flute, horn,
        violoncello)
     String-orchestra music
RT   Concertos (Bassoon, clarinet, flute,
        horn, violoncello with string
        orchestra)
Bassoon, clarinet, flute, horn with orchestra
     (M1040-1041)
BT   Wind quartets (Bassoon, clarinet, flute,
        horn)
RT   Concertos (Bassoon, clarinet, flute,
        horn)
**Bassoon, clarinet, flute, horn, harp with
     orchestra** *(M1040-1041)*
BT   Orchestral music
     Quintets (Bassoon, clarinet, flute, oboe,
        harp)
RT   Concertos (Bassoon, clarinet, flute,
        oboe, harp)
**Bassoon, clarinet, flute, oboe, violins (2),
     viola, violoncello with orchestra**
     (M1105-M1106)
**Bassoon, clarinet, flute, oboe, violins (2),
     viola, violoncello with string
     orchestra**
BT   Octets (Bassoon, clarinet, flute, oboe,
        violins (2), viola, violoncello)
     String-orchestra music
RT   Concertos (Bassoon, clarinet, flute,
        oboe, violins (2), viola, violoncello
        with string orchestra)
NT   Concertos (Bassoon, clarinet, flute,
        oboe, violins (2), viola, violoncello
        with string orchestra)
—Scores *(M1105)*
**Bassoon, clarinet, flute, oboe with chamber
     orchestra** *(M1040-1041)*
BT   Chamber-orchestra music
     Woodwind quartets (Bassoon, clarinet,
        flute, oboe)
RT   Concertos (Bassoon, clarinet, flute,
        oboe with chamber orchestra)
NT   Variations (Bassoon, clarinet, flute,
        oboe with chamber orchestra)
Bassoon, clarinet, flute, oboe with orchestra
     (M1040-1041)
BT   Woodwind quartets (Bassoon, clarinet,
        flute, oboe)
RT   Concertos (Bassoon, clarinet, flute,
        oboe)
**Bassoon, clarinet, flute, oboe with string
     orchestra** *(M1105-6)*
BT   String-orchestra music
     Woodwind quartets (Bassoon, clarinet,
        flute, oboe)

Bassoon, clarinet, flute, oboe with string orchestra (*M1105-6*)

(*Continued*)

RT Concertos (Bassoon, clarinet, flute, oboe with string orchestra)

Bassoon, clarinet, flute, trumpet with string orchestra (*M1105-6*)

BT Wind quartets (Bassoon, clarinet, flute, trumpet)

RT Concertos (Bassoon, clarinet, flute, trumpet with string orchestra)

BT Concertos (Bassoon, clarinet, flute, trumpet with string orchestra)

—Scores (*M1105*)

Bassoon, clarinet, flute with string orchestra (*M1105-6*)

BT String-orchestra music
Woodwind trios (Bassoon, clarinet, flute)

RT Concertos (Bassoon, clarinet, flute with string orchestra)

Bassoon, clarinet, horn, oboe with orchestra (*M1040-1041*)

BT Wind quartets (Bassoon, clarinet, horn, oboe)

RT Concertos (Bassoon, clarinet, horn, oboe)

Bassoon, clarinet, horn, oboe with string orchestra (*M1105-6*)

BT Wind quartets (Bassoon, clarinet, horn, oboe)

RT Concertos (Bassoon, clarinet, horn, oboe with string orchestra)

Bassoon, clarinet, oboe, violin, viola, violoncello with orchestra (*M1040-1041*)

BT Sextets (Bassoon, clarinet, oboe, violin, viola, violoncello)

RT Concertos (Bassoon, clarinet, oboe, violin, viola, violoncello)

Bassoon, clarinet, oboe with string orchestra (*M1105-6*)

BT String-orchestra music
Woodwind trios (Bassoon, clarinet, oboe)

RT Concertos (Bassoon, clarinet, oboe with string orchestra)

NT Suites (Bassoon, clarinet, oboe with string orchestra)

Bassoon, clarinet, trumpet with orchestra (*M1040-1041*)

BT Wind trios (Bassoon, clarinet, trumpet)

RT Concertos (Bassoon, clarinet, trumpet)

Bassoon, clarinet, trumpet with string orchestra (*M1140-1141*)

BT Wind trios (Bassoon, clarinet, trumpet)

RT Concertos (Bassoon, clarinet, trumpet with string orchestra)

Bassoon, clarinets (2), oboe with orchestra (*M1040-1041*)

BT Woodwind quartets (Bassoon, clarinets (2), oboe)

RT Concertos (Bassoon, clarinets (2), oboe)

Bassoon, flute, horn, oboe, trumpet with string orchestra (*M1140-1141*)

BT Wind quintets (Bassoon, flute, horn, oboe, trumpet)

RT Concertos (Bassoon, flute, horn, oboe, trumpet with string orchestra)

NT Suites (Bassoon, flute, horn, oboe, trumpet with string orchestra)

Bassoon, flute, horn, oboe with chamber orchestra (*M1040-1041*)

BT Wind quartets (Bassoon, flute, horn, oboe)

RT Concertos (Bassoon, flute, horn, oboe, with chamber orchestra)

Bassoon, flute, horn, oboe with orchestra (*M1040-1041*)

BT Wind quartets (Bassoon, flute, horn, oboe)

RT Concertos (Bassoon, flute, horn, oboe,)

Bassoon, flute, horn, oboe with string orchestra (*M1105-6*)

BT Wind quartets (Bassoon, flute, horn, oboe)

RT Concertos (Bassoon, flute, horn, oboe with string orchestra)

—Scores (*M1105*)

Bassoon, flute, oboe with orchestra (*M1040-1041*)

BT Woodwind trios (Bassoon, flute, oboe)

RT Concertos (Bassoon, flute, oboe)

Bassoon, flute, violin, violoncello with orchestra (*M1040-1041*)

BT Quartets (Bassoon, flute, violin, violoncello)

RT Concertos (Bassoon, flute, violin, violoncello)

Bassoon, flutes (2) with string orchestra (*M1140-1141*)

BT Woodwind trios (Bassoon, flutes (2))

RT Concertos (Bassoon, flutes (2) with string orchestra)

Bassoon, horn, trumpet, double bass with orchestra (*M1040-1041*)

BT Quartets (Bassoon, horn, trumpet, double bass)

RT Concertos (Bassoon, horn, trumpet, double bass)

—Scores (*M1040*)

Bassoon music (*M75-M79*)

SA Concertos, Minuets, Sonatas, Suites *and similar headings with specification of instruments;* Trios [Quartets, etc.], Wind trios [quartets, etc.] *and* Woodwind trios [quartets, etc.] *followed by specifications which include the bassoon; also* Wind ensembles, Woodwind ensembles, *and headings that begin with the words bassoon or bassoons*

NT Bassoon and English-horn music
Recorded accompaniments (Bassoon)
Sonatas (Bassoon)

Bassoon music *(M75-M79)*
　(Continued)
　NT　Suites (Bassoon)
　Notes under Wind instrument music; Wood-
　　　wind instrument music
Bassoon music (Bassoons (2)) *(M288-M289)*
　NT　Canons, fugues, etc. (Bassoons (2))
　　　Sonatas (Bassoons (2))
　　　Suites (Bassoons (2))
Bassoon music (Bassoons (2)), Arranged
　　　(M288-M289)
Bassoon music (Bassoons (4))
　USE　Woodwind quartets (Bassoons (4))
Bassoon, oboe, trumpet with string orchestra
　　　(M1105-6)
　BT　Wind trios (Bassoon, oboe, trumpet)
　RT　Concertos (Bassoon, oboe, trumpet with
　　　string orchestra)
Bassoon, oboe, violin, viola with orchestra
　　　(M1040-1041)
　BT　Quartets (Bassoon, oboe, violin, viola)
　RT　Concertos (Bassoon, oboe, violin, viola)
Bassoon, oboe, violin, violoncello with
　　　chamber orchestra *(M1040-1041)*
　BT　Chamber-orchestra music
　　　Quartets (Bassoon, oboe, violin, violoncello)
　RT　Concertos (Bassoon, oboe, violin,
　　　violoncello with chamber orchestra)
　—Scores *(M1040)*
Bassoon, oboe, violin, violoncello with
　　　orchestra *(M1040-1041)*
　BT　Quartets (Bassoon, oboe, violin,
　　　violoncello)
　RT　Concertos (Bassoon, oboe, violin,
　　　violoncello)
　—Solos with piano *(M1041)*
　　　BT　Quintets (Piano, bassoon, oboe,
　　　　　violin, violoncello), Arranged
Bassoon players
　USE　Bassoonists
Bassoon, violins (2) with string orchestra
　　　(M1140-1141)
　BT　Trios (Bassoon, violins (2))
　RT　Concertos (Bassoon, violins (2) with
　　　string orchestra)
Bassoon with band *(M1205-M1206)*
　RT　Concertos (Bassoon with band)
Bassoon with band, Arranged *(M1257)*
　—Scores and parts *(M1257)*
Bassoon with chamber orchestra *(M1026-M1207)*
　RT　Concertos (Bassoon with chamber
　　　orchestra)
　—Solo with piano *(M1027)*
　　　BT　Bassoon and piano music, Arranged
Bassoon with instrumental ensemble
　BT　Concertos (Bassoon with instrumental
　　　ensemble)
Bassoon with orchestra *(M1026-M1027)*
　RT　Concertos (Bassoon)
　NT　Rondos (Bassoon with orchestra)
　　　Suites (Bassoon with orchestra)
　　　Variations (Bassoon with orchestra)

Bassoon with orchestra *(M1026-M1027)*
　(Continued)
　—Solo with piano *(M1027)*
　　　BT　Bassoon and piano music, Arranged
Bassoon with orchestra, Arranged *(M1026-M1027)*
　—Solo with piano *(M1027)*
　　　BT　Bassoon and piano music, Arranged
Bassoon with string ensemble
　RT　Concertos (Bassoon with string
　　　ensemble)
Bassoon with string orchestra *(M1105-M1106)*
　RT　Concertos (Bassoon with string
　　　orchestra)
　NT　Suites (Bassoon with string orchestra)
　—Solo with piano *(M1106)*
　　　BT　Bassoon and piano music, Arranged
Bassoon with wind ensemble
　NT　Concertos (Bassoon with wind ensemble)
Bassoonists *(ML399)*
　UF　Bassoon players
Bassoons (2) with orchestra
　　　(M1026-M1027)
　NT　Concertos (Bassoons (2))
Bassoons (2) with string orchestra
　　　(M1126-M1127)
　RT　Concertos (Bassoons (2) with string orchestra)
Baton twirling *(MT733.6)*
　BT　Drill (not military)
　RT　Drum majoring
Battle Ground Fiddlers' Gathering, Battle
　　　Ground, Ind.
　UF　Annual Gathering of Traditional Indiana
　　　Fiddlers and Other Folks
　　　Gathering of Traditional Indiana Fiddlers
　　　and Other Folks
　BT　Music festivals—Indiana
Battle-songs
　USE　War-songs
Bawdy songs [May Subd Geog] *(M1977.B38;*
　　　M1978.B38)
　UF　Dirty songs
　　　Ribald songs
　BT　Humorous songs
　　　Songs
　RT　Erotic songs
Bayan *(History, ML1083; Instruction,*
　　　MT681)
　BT　Button-key accordions
　　　Musical instruments—Soviet Union
Bazoo
　USE　Kazoo
Be bop music
　USE　Jazz music
Beati immaculati (Music)
　USE　Psalms (Music)—119th Psalm
Beati omnes (Music)
　USE　Psalms (Music)—128th Psalm
Beati quorum (Music)
　USE　Psalms (Music)—32d Psalm
Beatitudes (Music)
Beatus qui intelligit (Music)
　USE　Psalms (Music)—41st Psalm

Beatus vir, qui non abiit (Music)
USE Psalms (Music)—1st Psalm
Beatus vir, qui timet Dominum (Music)
USE Psalms (Music)—112th Psalm
Bebop music
USE Jazz music
Bel canto *(MT845)*
BT Singing—Methods
Bell-lyra
USE Glockenspiel
Bell ringing
USE Change ringing
Handbell ringing
Bella Coola folk-songs
USE Folk-songs, Bella Coola
Bells [May Subd Geog]
NT Carillons
Change ringing
Handbell ringing
Handbells
Belly dance music [May Subd Geog]
BT Arabs—Music
Dance music
Benedic, anima mea Domino, Domine Deus
(Music)
USE Psalms (Music)—104th Psalm
Benedic, anima mea Domino et omnia (Music)
USE Psalms (Music)—103d Psalm
Benedicam Dominum (Music)
USE Psalms (Music)—34th Psalm
Benediction of the Blessed Sacrament (Music)
(M2150.4.B45)
Benedictus Dominus (Music)
USE Psalms (Music)—144th Psalm
Benedixisti, Domine (Music)
USE Psalms (Music)—85th Psalm
Bengali ballads
USE Ballads, Bengali
Bengali folk-songs
USE Folk-songs, Bengali
Bengali songs
USE Songs, Bengali
Berimbao
USE Berimbau
Berimbau *(ML1015.B4)*
UF Berimbao
BT Musical instruments—Brazil
Berimbau and piccolo music
USE Piccolo and berimbau music
Bhajans *(M1808-M1809)*
UF Bajans
BT Poetry
Sacred songs
Bhili folk-songs
USE Folk-songs, Bhili
Bhojpuri folk-songs
USE Folk-songs, Bhojpuri
Bible [May Subd Geog]
—Hymnological use
USE Bible—Use in hymns
—Music
USE Music in the Bible

Bible [May Subd Geog]
(Continued)
—Musical instruments
USE Music in the Bible
—Use in hymns
UF Bible—Hymnological use
BT Bible—Use
Hymns
Bible. O.T. Psalms—Music
USE Music in the Bible
Psalms (Music)
Bichromatic harmonium *(ML597)*
UF Harmonium, Bichromatic
BT Microtones
Reed-organ
Big band music *(M1356; M1366)*
UF Dance band music
Jazz band music
Stage band music
BT Band music
Dance-orchestra music
Jazz ensembles
Jazz music
Music
NT Jazz vocals
Big bands [May Subd Geog]
UF Dance bands
Jazz bands
Stage bands
BT Bands (Music)
Dance orchestras
Jazz music
Music
Bîn
USE Vina
Biwa *(ML1015.B55; ML1018.B55)*
BT Lute
Musical instruments—Japan
Biwa and shakuhachi music
USE Shakuhachi and biwa music
Biwa music *(M142.B)*
NT Quartets (Flute, shakuhachi, biwa, harp)
Sextets (Shakuhachi, biwa, kotos (2),
shamisen, percussion)
Biwa players [May Subd Geog]
BT Musicians
Black angels (Ballet)
BT Ballets
Black hymns
USE Hymns, Black
Black musicians
USE Musicians, Black
Blackface entertainers [May Subd Geog]
(PN2071.B58)
UF Black-face entertainers
Entertainers, Blackface
BT Entertainers
RT Minstrel shows
Blackfaced minstrel shows
USE Minstrel shows
Blacks in the performing arts
NT Musicians, Black

Blind, Music for the *(HV1695; MT38)*
    UF Music for the blind
    BT Music
        Music for the visually handicapped
    NT Braille music-notation
Blind musicians [May Subd Geog]
    UF Musicians, Blind
    BT Blind
        Physically handicapped musicians
    —Japan
        NT Goze
Blockflute
   USE Recorder (Musical instrument)
Bluegrass music [May Subd Geog]
        ML3519-ML3520 (History and criticism)
    BT Country music
    SA *subdivisions* Methods (Bluegrass) *and*
        Studies and exercises (Bluegrass) *under*
        names of musical instruments
    NT Piano—Methods (Bluegrass)
        Piano—Studies and exercises
        (Bluegrass)
    —To 1951
    —1951-1960
    —1961-1970
    —1971-1980
    —1981-
Bluegrass musicians [May Subd Geog]
    BT Country musicians
Blues (Music) [May Subd Geog]
        ML3521 (History and criticism)
    UF Blues (Songs, etc.)
    BT Afro-Americans—Music
        Folk music—United States
        Popular music
    SA subdivision *Methods (Blues) and Studies*
        and exercises (Blues) under names of
        instruments
    NT Guitar—Methods (Blues)
        Piano music (Blues)
    —To 1931
    —1931-1940
    —1941-1950
    —1951-1960
    —1961-1970
    —1971-1980
    —1981-
Boatmen's songs
   USE Sea songs
Bodhran
    BT Drum
        Musical instruments—Ireland
Boehm flute
   USE Flute
Bolero (Ballet)
    BT Ballets
Boleros
    BT Dance music
Bones (Musical instrument) *(ML1040)*
    BT Percussion instruments
Bongo *(ML1035)*
    BT Percussion instruments

Bongo *(ML1035)*
    (Continued)
    —Methods
    — —Self-instruction *(MT662)*
Boogie-woogie music
   USE Piano music (Boogie woogie)
Bordun
   USE Bourdon
Bosavi folk-songs
   USE Folk-songs, Bosavi
Bouffons, Guerre des
   USE Guerre des Bouffons
Bourdon
    UF Bordun
        Drone bass
    BT Harmony
    RT Organ-point
    NT Fauxbourdon
Bourrées
    BT Dance music
Bouzoukee
   USE Bouzouki
Bouzouki *(History and criticism, ML1015.B;*
        Instruction, MT654.B69)
    UF Bouzoukee
        Buzuki
    BT Lute
        Musical instruments—Greece
        Stringed instruments
Bow (Music)
   USE Stringed instruments, Bowed—Bow
Boy choir training
   USE Choirboy training
Braille music-notation *(MT38)*
    BT Blind, Music for the
        Musical notation
Brass band music *(M1200-1269)*
    UF Brass choir music
    BT Band music
    SA Concertos ([Solo instrument(s)] with
        brass band); [Solo instrument(s)]
        with brass band; Suites, Variations,
        Waltzes, *and similar headings with*
        specification of instruments which
        include the specification Brass band
    NT Fanfares
Brass bands [May Subd Geog] *(History and*
        criticism, ML1300-1354; Instruction
        and study, MT733)
    UF Brass choirs
    BT Bands (Music)
        Musical groups
    NT Instrumentation and orchestration
        (Brass band)
Brass choir music
   USE Brass band music
        Brass ensembles
        Instrumental ensembles
Brass choirs
   USE Brass bands
Brass ensemble with orchestra
    RT Concertos (Brass ensemble)

Brass ensembles

M955-M959

Here are entered compositions for ten or more different solo brass instruments and collections of compositions for a varying number or combination of different solo brass instruments. Compositions for ten or more like brass instruments and collections of compositions for a varying number of like brass instruments are entered under Horn ensembles, Tuba ensembles, and similar headings.

When used in conjunction with specific solo instrument(s), the qualifier brass ensemble may stand for any number and combination of solo instruments.

UF Brass choir music

BT Wind ensembles

SA Concertos [Solo instrument(s)] with brass ensemble); [Solo instrument(s)] with brass ensemble; Suites, Variations, Waltzes, *and similar headings with specification of instruments which include the specification: Brass ensemble*

NT Symphonies (Brass ensemble)

Notes under Instrumental ensembles; Wind ensembles

Brass instrument makers [May Subd Geog]

BT Wind instrument makers

Brass instrument music *(M111)*

Here are entered musical compositions for an unspecified solo brass instrument. Works for a specified instrument are entered under Horn music, Trumpet music, and similar headings

UF Melody instrument music

Unspecified instrument music

BT Solo instrument music

Wind instrument music

Brass instruments *(History and construction, ML933; Instruction, MT339)*

BT Wind instruments

NT Alpenhorn

Alto horn

Baritone (Musical instrument)

Bugle

Cornet

Cornett

Euphonium

Fluegelhorn

Horn (Musical instrument)

Instrumentation and orchestration (Brass band)

Lur

Ophicleide

Russian horn

Sarrusophone

Serpent (Musical instrument)

Trombone

Trumpet

Tuba

Brass instruments *(History and construction, ML933; Instruction, MT339)*

(Continued)

—Mouthpieces

UF Mouthpieces (Music)

—Tuning

Example under Tuning

Brass nonets *(M955-M956; M957.4; M958-M959)*

Collections of compositions for various combinations of nine brass instruments are entered under this heading without specification of instruments.

Separate compositions and collections of compositions for nine specific brass instruments are entered under this heading followed by specification of instruments in alphabetical order.

Headings with specification of instruments are printed below only if specific cross references are needed.

UF Nonets, Brass

SA Suites, Variations, Waltzes, *and similar headings with specification of instruments*

Note under Wind nonets

Brass octets *(M855-M856; M857.4; M858-M859)*

Collections of compositions for various combinations of eight brass instruments are entered under this heading without specification of instruments. Separate compositions and collections of compositions for eight specific brass instruments are entered under this heading followed by specification of instruments in alphabetical order.

Headings with specification of instruments are printed below only if specific cross references are needed.

UF Octets, Brass

SA Suites, Variations, Waltzes, *and similar headings with specification of instruments*

Note under Wind octets

Brass octets (Horns (8)) *(M855-M856; M857.4; M858-M859)*

UF Horn music (Horns (8))

Brass octets (Trombones (8)) *(M855-M856; M857.4; M858-M859)*

UF Trombone music (Trombones (8))

Brass octets (Trumpets (8)) *(M855-856; M857.4; M858-M859)*

UF Trumpet music (Trumpets (8))

NT Concertos (Trumpets (8) with string orchestra)

Trumpets (8) with string orchestra

Brass quartets *(M455-M456; M457.4; M458-M459)*

Collections of compositions for various combinations of four brass instruments are entered under this heading without specification of instruments.

Separate compositions and collections

Brass quartets *(M455-M456; M457.4; M458-M459)*

(*Continued*)

of compositions for four specific brass instruments are entered under this heading followed by specification of instruments in alphabetical order.

Headings with specification of instruments are printed below only if specific cross references are needed.

UF Quartets, Brass

SA Suites, Variations, Waltzes, *and similar headings with specification of instruments*

Note under Wind quartets

Brass quartets (Baritone, fluegelhorn, horn, trumpet) *(M455-M456; M457.4; M458-M459)*

BT Fluegelhorn music

Brass quartets (Cornets (4)) *(M455-M456; M457.4; M458-M459)*

UF Cornet music (Cornets (4))

NT Concertos (Cornets (4) with band)
Cornets (4) with band

Brass quartets (Horns (4)) *(M455-M456; M457.4; M458-M459)*

UF Horn music (Horns (4))

NT Concertos (Horns (4))
Concertos (Horns (4) with band)
Horns (4) with band
Horns (4) with orchestra

Brass quartets (Trombones (4)) *(M455-M456; M457.4; M458-M459)*

UF Trombone music (Trombones (4))

NT Concertos (Trombones (4) with band)
Trombones (4) with band

Brass quartets (Trumpets (4)) *(M455-M456; M457.4; M458-M459)*

UF Trumpet music (Trumpets(4))

NT Concertos (Trumpets (4) with string orchestra)
Trumpets (4) with string orchestra

Brass quartets (Tubas (4)) *(M455-M456; M457.4; M458-M459)*

UF Tuba music (Tubas (4))

Brass quintets *(M555-M556; M557.4; M558-M559)*

Collections of compositions for various combinations of five brass instruments are entered under this heading without specification of instruments. Separate compositions and collections of compositions for five specific brass instruments are entered under this heading followed by specification of instruments in alphabetical order.

Headings with specification of instruments are printed below only if specific cross references are needed.

UF Quintets, Brass

SA Suites, Variations, Waltzes, *and similar headings with specification of instruments*

Note under Wind quintets

Brass quintets (Alto horn, baritone, cornets (2), tuba)

BT Alto horn music

Brass quintets (Euphonium, horns (4)) *(M555-M556; M557.4; M558-M559)*

NT Concertos (Euphonium, horns (4) with band)
Euphonium, horns (4) with band

Brass quintets (Horn, trombone, trumpets (2), tuba) *(M555-M556; M557.4; M558-M559)*

NT Concertos (Horn, trombone, trumpets (2), tuba)
Concertos (Horn, trombone, trumpets (2), tuba with instrumental ensemble)
Concertos (Horn, trombone, trumpets (2), tuba with string orchestra)
Horn, trombone, trumpets (2), tuba with instrumental ensemble
Horn, trombone, trumpets (2), tuba with orchestra
Horn, trombone, trumpets (2), tuba with string orchestra

Brass quintets (Horn, trombones (2), trumpets (2)) *(M555-M556; M557.4; M558-M559)*

NT Concertos (Horn, trombones (2), trumpets (2))
Concertos (Horn, trombones (2), trumpets (2) with chamber orchestra)
Concertos (Horn, trombones (2), trumpets (2) with string orchestra)
Horn, trombones (2), trumpets (2) with chamber orchestra
Horn, trombones (2), trumpets (2) with orchestra
Horn, trombones (2), trumpets (2) with string orchestra

Brass quintets (Horns (5)) *(M555-M556; M557.4; M558-M559)*

UF Horn music (Horns (5))

Brass quintets (Trombones (5)) *(M555-M556; M557.4; M558-M559)*

UF Trombone music (Trombones (5))

Brass quintets (Trumpets (5)) *(M555-M556; M557.4; M558-M559)*

UF Trumpet music (Trumpets (5))

Brass septets *(M755-M756; M757.4; M758-M759)*

Collections of compositions for various combinations of seven brass instruments are entered under this heading without specification of instruments. Separate compositions and collections of compositions for seven specific brass instruments are entered under this heading followed by specification of instruments in alphabetical order.

Headings with specification of instruments are printed below only if specific cross references are needed.

UF Septets, Brass

SA Suites, Variations, Waltzes, *and similar headings with specification of instruments*

Brass septets *(M755-M756; M757.4; M758-M759)*
(Continued)
Note under Wind septets
Brass septets (Horns (2), trombones (2), trumpets (2), tuba)
  NT Concertos (Horns (2), trombones (2), trumpets (2), tuba)
     Horns (2), trombones (2), trumpets (2), tuba with orchestra
Brass septets (Horns (7)) *(M755-M756; M757.4; M758-M759)*
  UF Horn music (Horns (7))
Brass septets (Trombones (7)) *(M755-M756; M757.4; M758-M759)*
  UF Trombone music (Trombones (7))
Brass septets (Trumpets (7)) *(M755-M756; M757.4; M758-M759)*
  UF Trumpet music (Trumpets (7))
Brass sextets *(M655-M656; M657.4; M658-M659)*
     Collections of compositions for various combinations of six brass instruments are entered under this heading without specification of instruments. Separate compositions and collections of compositions for six specific brass instruments are entered under this heading followed by specification of instruments in alphabetical order.
     Headings with specification of instruments are printed below only if specific cross references are needed.
  UF Sextets, Brass
  SA Suites, Variations, Waltzes, *and similar headings with specification of instruments*
Note under Wind sextets
Brass sextets (Horns (6)) *(M655-M656; M657.4; M658-M659)*
  UF Horn music (Horns (6))
Brass sextets (Trombones (3), trumpets (3)) *(M655-M656; M657.4; M658-M659)*
  NT Concertos (Trombones (3), trumpets (3) with band)
     Trombones (3), trumpets (3) with band
Brass sextets (Trumpets (6)) *(M655-M656; M657.4; M658-M659)*
  UF Trumpet music (Trumpets (6))
Brass sextets (Tubas (6)) *(M655-M656; M657.4; M658-M659)*
  UF Tuba music (Tubas (6))
Brass trios *(M355-M356; M357.4; M358-M359)*
     Collections of compositions for various combinations of three brass instruments are entered under this heading without specification of instruments. Separate compositions and collections of compositions for three specific brass instruments are entered under this heading followed by specification of instruments in alphabetical order.
     Headings with specification of instruments are printed below only if specific cross references are needed.

Brass trios *(M355-M356; M357.4; M358-M359)*
(Continued)
  UF Trios, Brass
  SA Suites, Variations, Waltzes, *and similar headings with specification of instruments*
Note under Chamber music; Wind trios
Brass trios (Cornets (3)) *(M355-M359)*
  UF Cornet music (Cornets (3))
Brass trios (Horns (3)) *(M355-M356; M357.4; M358-M359)*
  UF Horn music (Horns (3))
  NT Concertos (Horns (3))
     Concertos (Horns (3) with band)
     Concertos (Horns (3) with string orchestra)
     Horns (3) with band
     Horns (3) with orchestra
     Horns (3) with string orchestra
Brass trios (Trombones (3)) *(M355-M356; M357.4; M358-M359)*
  UF Trombone music (Trombones (3))
  NT Concertos (Trombones (3) with band)
     Trombones (3) with band
Brass trios (Trumpets (3)) *(M355-M356; M357.4; M358-M359)*
  UF Trumpet music (Trumpets (3))
  NT Concertos (Trumpets (3))
     Concertos (Trumpets (3) with band)
     Concertos (Trumpets (3) with string orchestra)
     Trumpets (3) with band
     Trumpets (3) with orchestra
     Trumpets (3) with string orchestra
Brazilian lullabies
  USE Lullabies, Brazilian
Breathing exercises
  NT Singing—Breathing exercises
Breton folk-songs
  USE Folk-songs, Breton
Breton songs
  USE Songs, Breton
Brettingham, Matthew, 1699-1769. Norfolk House Music Room *(NK2047.6.B)*
  UF Music Room from Norfolk House (Interior decoration)
     Norfolk House Music Room (Interior decoration)
Buddhism [May Subd Geog]
  —Hymns
     USE Buddhist hymns
Buddhism and music
  USE Music—Religious aspects—Buddhism
Buddhist hymns
  UF Buddhism—Hymns
     Hymns, Buddhist
Buddhist hymns, English, [Japanese, etc.]
Buddhist hymns, Japanese [May Subd Geog]
  UF Japanese Buddhist hymns
Buddhist hymns, Korean [May Subd Geog]
  UF Korean Buddhist hymns
Buddhist music
  USE Music, Buddhist

Buddhists [May Subd Geog]
—Music
   USE Music, Buddhist
Buffalo soldier (Ballet)
  BT Ballets
Bugaku
  BT Gagaku
Bugle *(ML960-961)*
  BT Brass instruments
  NT Trumpet
Bugle and drum corps [May Subd Geog]
  UF Drum and bugle corps
      Drum corps
  BT Bands (Music)
Bugle and drum music *(M1270)*
  UF Drum and bugle music
  BT Percussion music
      Trumpet music
Bugle and organ music *(M182-186)*
  UF Organ and bugle music
Bugle-calls
  BT Fanfares
      Hunting music
      Military music
      Signals and signaling
  RT Military calls
      Trumpet-calls
Bugle music *(M110.B)*
  NT Sextets (Piano (4 hands), bugle,
        clarinet, percussion, violin)
Buin folk-songs
  USE Folk-songs, Buin
Bulgarian folk-songs
  USE Folk-songs, Bulgarian
Bundeli folk-songs
  USE Folk-songs, Bundeli
Burgundian folk-songs
  USE Folk-songs, Burgundian
Burmese folk-songs
  USE Folk-songs, Burmese
Button accordions
  USE Button-key accordions
Button-key accordions *(History, ML1083;*
       Instruction, MT681)
  UF Button accordions
  BT Accordion
  NT Bandonion
      Bayan
      Melodeon (Button-key accordion)
Buzuki
  USE Bouzouki
Byelorussian ballads
  USE Ballads, Byelorussian
Byelorussian folk-songs
  USE Folk-songs, Byelorussian
Byzantine music
  USE Music, Byzantine
Cabarets
  USE Music-halls (Variety-theaters, cabarets,
      etc.)
Cabinet organ
  USE Reed-organ

Cadence (Music) *(Harmony, ML44, MT50)*
  UF Clausulae (Cadences)
  BT Harmony
      Musical form
Cadence calls
  USE Jody calls
Cadences (Soldiers' songs)
  USE Jody calls
Cadenzas
  USE *subdivision* Cadenzas *under music*
        headings, e.g. Concertos—Cadenzas;
        Operas—Cadenzas
Cajun French songs
  USE Songs, Cajun French
Calliope *(ML597)*
  BT Mechanical organs
Calliope music *(M175.C3)*
  UF Merry-go-round music
  BT Organ music
Calliope music (4 hands) *(M175.C3)*
  NT Suites (Calliope, 4 hands)
Calls, Cadence
  USE Jody calls
Calls, Jody
  USE Jody calls
Calls, Military
  USE Military calls
Calypso (Music) [May Subd Geog]
  UF Calypso (Songs, etc.)
  BT Popular music
Calypso musicians [May Subd Geog]
  BT Musicians
Camp-meeting hymns
  USE Revivals—Hymns
Campaign songs
      M1659.7-M1665 (Music)
      This heading may be qualified by date
        and subdivided by party, *e.g.* Campaign
        songs, 1840—Whig.
  BT Songs—United States
      Songs, English—United States
  NT Revolutionary ballads and songs
Campaign songs, 1840
—Whig
    Note under Campaign songs
Camping [May Subd Geog]
—Songs and music *(M1977.C3;*
    M1978.C3)
  BT Children's songs
Cancans
  BT Dance music
Candlemas music *(M2078.C2)*
  BT Sacred vocal music
Canons, fugues, etc.
      Here are entered collections of miscel-
        laneous canons, fugues and similar
        compositions. Separate canons,
        fugues, etc. and collections of canons,
        fugues, etc. for a specific medium are
        entered under the heading followed by
        specification of medium.
  UF Fugues

Canons, fugues, etc.
> *(Continued)*
> UF Preludes and fugues
> > Toccatas and fugues
> *Notes under* Canon (Music); Fugue

Canons, fugues, etc. (Accordion) *(M175.A4)*
> BT Accordion music

Canons, fugues, etc. (Accordion), Arranged
> *(M175.A4)*

Canons, fugues, etc. (Accordion ensemble)
> BT Accordion ensembles

Canons, fugues, etc. (Band) *(M1245)*
> BT Band music

Canons, fugues, etc. (Band), Arranged
> *(M1258)*

Canons, fugues, etc. (Bassoon and flute)
> *(M288-M289)*
> BT Bassoon and flute music

Canons, fugues, etc. (Bassoon and oboe)
> *(M288-9)*
> BT Bassoon and oboe music

Canons, fugues, etc. (Bassoon and piano)
> *(M253-M254)*
> BT Bassoon and piano music

Canons, fugues, etc. (Bassoons (2))
> *(M288-M289)*
> BT Bassoon music (Bassoons (2))

Canons, fugues, etc. (Chamber orchestra)
> *(M1045)*
> BT Chamber-orchestra music
> —Scores *(M1045)*

Canons, fugues, etc. (Chamber orchestra),
> Arranged *(M1060)*

Canons, fugues, etc. (Clarinet and flute)
> *(M288-9)*
> BT Clarinet and flute music

Canons, fugues, etc. (Clarinet and percussion)
> *(M298)*
> BT Clarinet and percussion music

Canons, fugues, etc. (Clarinet and piano)
> *(M248-250)*
> BT Clarinet and piano music

Canons, fugues, etc. (Clarinet, violins (2),
> viola, violoncello) *(M560-M562)*
> BT Quintets (Clarinet, violins (2), viola,
> > violoncello)

Canons, fugues, etc. (Clavichord) *(M25)*

Canons, fugues, etc. (Electronic music)
> *(M1473)*
> BT Electronic music

Canons, fugues, etc. (Flute and piano)
> *(M240-M242)*
> BT Flute and piano music

Canons, fugues, etc. (Flute and trumpet with
> string orchestra) *(M1140-M1141)*
> BT Flute and trumpet with string orchestra

Canons, fugues, etc. (Flute and violin)
> M290-M291
> BT Flute and violin music

Canons, fugues, etc. (Flute and violoncello)
> *(M290-M291)*
> BT Flute and violoncello music

Canons, fugues, etc. (Flute with string
> orchestra) *(M1105-M1106)*
> BT Flute with string orchestra

Canons, fugues, etc. (Flutes (2)) *(M288-M289)*
> BT Flute music (Flutes (2))

Canons, fugues, etc. (Flutes (2) with string
> orchestra) *(M1105-M1106)*
> BT Flutes (2) with string orchestra
> —Scores *(M1105)*

Canons, fugues, etc. (Glass harmonica) *(M165)*

Canons, fugues, etc. (Guitar) *(M125-M127)*
> BT Guitar music

Canons, fugues, etc. (Harpsichord) *(M25)*
> BT Harpsichord music

Canons, fugues, etc. (Harpsichord), Arranged
> *(M32.8.M38)*

Canons, fugues, etc. (Harpsichord, violins (3))
> *(M410-M411; M412.2)*
> BT Canons, fugues, etc. (Piano, violins (3))
> Quartets (Harpsichord, violins (3))

Canons, fugues, etc. (Harpsichord, violins (3),
> viola da gamba) *(M510-M512)*
> BT Canons, fugues, etc. (Piano, violins (3),
> > violoncello)
> Quintets (Harpsichord, violins (3), viola
> da gamba)

Canons, fugues, etc. (Harpsichords (2))
> *(M214)*
> BT Harpsichord music (Harpsichords (2))

Canons, fugues, etc. (Horns (2)) *(M288-M289)*
> BT Horn music (Horns (2))

Canons, fugues, etc. (Instrumental ensemble)
> BT Instrumental ensembles

Canons, fugues, etc. (Instrumental ensemble),
> Arranged

Canons, fugues, etc. (Lute) *(M140-M141)*
> BT Lute music

Canons, fugues, etc. (Oboe with string
> orchestra) *(M1105-M1106)*
> BT Oboe with string orchestra

Canons, fugues, etc. (Orchestra) *(M1045; M1060)*
> BT Orchestral music

Canons, fugues, etc. (Orchestra), Arranged
> —Scores *(M1060)*

Canons, fugues, etc. (Organ) *(M10)*
> BT Organ music

Canons, fugues, etc. (Organ, 4 hands)
> *(M181)*
> BT Organ music (4 hands)

Canons, fugues, etc. (Organ), Arranged
> *(M12-M13)*

Canons, fugues, etc. (Organ, baritone, cornets
> (2), trombone) *(M500-M502)*
> BT Quintets (Organ, baritone, cornets (2),
> > trombone)

Canons, fugues, etc. (Organ, violin, viola da
> gamba) *(M300-M302)*
> BT Trios (Organ, violin, viola da gamba)

Canons, fugues, etc. (Organ, violins (2), viola
> da gamba) *(M400-M402)*
> BT Quartets (Organ, violins (2), viola da
> > gamba)

Canons, fugues, etc. (Organ, viols (3))
(M990)
BT   Quartets (Organ, viols (3))
Canons, fugues, etc. (Organs (2))
(M180-M181)
BT   Organ music (Organs (2))
Canons, fugues, etc. (Piano) (M20-22; M25)
BT   Piano music
Canons, fugues, etc. (Piano, 1 hand) (M26;
M26.2)
BT   Piano music (1 hand)
Canons, fugues, etc. (Piano, 4 hands)
(M200-201; M204)
BT   Piano music (4 hands)
**Canons, fugues, etc. (Piano, 4 hands),
Arranged** (M211)
Canons, fugues, etc. (Piano, 6 hands) (M213)
BT   Piano music (6 hands)
Canons, fugues, etc. (Piano), Arranged
Canons, fugues, etc. (Piano quartet)
(M410-412)
BT   Piano quartets
Canons, fugues, etc. (Piano, violins (2))
(M310-M311; M312.4)
BT   Trios (Piano, violins (2))
Canons, fugues, etc. (Piano, violins (3))
(M410-411; M412.2)
BT   Quartets (Piano, violins (3))
NT   Canons, fugues, etc. (Harpsichord,
violins (3))
**Canons, fugues, etc. (Piano, violins (3),
violoncello)** (M510-512)
BT   Quintets (Piano, violins (3), violoncello)
NT   Canons, fugues, etc. (Harpsichord,
violins (3), viola da gamba)
Canons, fugues, etc. (Piano with orchestra)
(M1010-1011)
BT   Piano with orchestra
Canons, fugues, etc. (Pianos (2)) (M214)
BT   Piano music (Pianos (2))
Canons, fugues, etc. (Pianos (2)), Arranged
(M215)
Canons, fugues, etc. (Recorder and piano)
(M240-M242)
BT   Recorder and piano music
**Canons, fugues, etc. (Recorder and piano),
Arranged** (M243-M244)
**Canons, fugues, etc. (Recorder, violin,
violoncello)** (M360-M362)
BT   Trios (Recorder, violin, violoncello)
Canons, fugues, etc. (Recorders (2))
(M288-M289)
BT   Recorder music (Recorders (2))
Canons, fugues, etc. (String ensemble)
(M950-M952)
BT   String ensembles
Canons, fugues, etc. (String orchestra)
(M1145)
BT   String-orchestra music
**Canons, fugues, etc. (String orchestra),
Arranged** (M1160)
Canons, fugues, etc. (String quartet) (M450-M452)
BT   String quartets

Canons, fugues, etc. (String quartet), Arranged
(M453-M454)
Canons, fugues, etc. (String trio) (M349-M351)
BT   String trios
Canons, fugues, etc. (String trio), Arranged
(M352-M353)
**Canons, fugues, etc. (String trio with string
orchestra)** (M1105-M1106)
BT   String trio with string orchestra
—Scores (M1105)
Canons, fugues, etc. (Trombones (2))
(M288-M289)
BT   Trombone music (Trombones (2))
Canons, fugues, etc. (Trumpet and organ)
(M182-M186)
BT   Trumpet and organ music
**Canons, fugues, etc. (Trumpet with string
orchestra)** (M1105-M1106)
BT   Trumpet with string orchestra
—Scores and parts (M1105)
Canons, fugues, etc. (Tuba and percussion)
(M297-M298)
BT   Tuba and percussion music
Canons, fugues, etc. (Tubas (2))
(M288-M289)
BT   Tuba music (Tubas (2))
Canons, fugues, etc. (Vihuela) (M142.V53)
BT   Vihuela music
Canons, fugues, etc. (Viola) (M47)
BT   Viola music
Canons, fugues, etc. (Violas (2)) (M286-M287)
BT   Viola music (Violas (2))
**Canons, fugues, etc. (Violas (2), violoncellos
(2))** (M450-M451; M452.4)
BT   String quartets (Violas (2), violoncellos
(2))
Canons, fugues, etc. (Violin)
BT   Violin music
Canons, fugues, etc. (Violin and harpsichord)
(M217-M218; M221)
BT   Violin and harpsichord music
Canons, fugues, etc. (Violin and organ) (M182-M184)
BT   Violin and organ music
Canons, fugues, etc. (Violin and piano)
(M217-M218; M221)
BT   Violin and piano music
Canons, fugues, etc. (Violin and violoncello)
(M286-M287)
BT   Violin and violoncello music
**Canons, fugues, etc. (Violin, viola, viola da
gamba)** (M349-M351)
BT   String trios (Violin, viola, viola da
gamba)
Canons, fugues, etc. (Violins (2)) (M286-M287)
BT   Violin music (Violins (2))
**Canons, fugues, etc. (Violins (2), viola,
violoncello, double bass)** (M550-552)
BT   String quintets (Violins (2), viola,
violoncello, double bass)
**Canons, fugues, etc. (Violins (2), violas (2),
violoncello)** (M550-M552)
BT   String quintets (Violins (2), violas (2),
violoncello)

Canons, fugues, etc. (Violins (3)) *(M349-M351)*
  BT String trios (Violins (3))
Canons, fugues, etc. (Violins (3), viola, violoncello) *(M550-M552)*
  BT String quintets (Violins (3), viola, violoncello)
Canons, fugues, etc. (Violins (4), violas (2), violoncellos (2)) *(M850-M852)*
  BT String octets (Violins (4), violas (2), violoncellos (2))
Canons, fugues, etc. (Violoncello and piano) *(M229-M230; M233)*
  BT Violoncello and piano music
Canons, fugues, etc. (Violoncello and piano), Arranged *(M235-M236)*
Canons, fugues, etc. (Violoncello with band) *(M1205-M1206)*
  BT Violoncello with band
Canons, fugues, etc. (Violoncellos (2)) *(M286-M287)*
  BT Violoncello music (Violoncellos (2))
Canons, fugues, etc. (Violoncellos (4))
  BT String quartets (Violoncellos (4))
Canons, fugues, etc. (Viols (2)) *(M990)*
  BT Viol music (Viols (2))
Canons, fugues, etc. (Viols (3)) *(M990)*
  BT String trios (Viols (3))
Canons, fugues, etc. (Viols (4)) *(M990)*
  BT String quartets (Viols (4))
Canons, fugues, etc. (Viols (5)) *(M990)*
  BT String quintets (Viols (5))
Canons, fugues, etc. (Viols (6)) *(M990)*
  BT String sextets (Viols (6))
Canons, fugues, etc. (Viols (7)) *(M990)*
  BT String septets (Viols (7))
Canons, fugues, etc. (Vocal)
  BT Choruses
      Part-songs
      Vocal music
  RT Glees, catches, rounds, etc.
Canons, fugues, etc. (Wind ensemble)
  BT Wind ensembles
Cantata *(ML1500-ML1554; ML2400; ML3260)*
  BT Choral music
      Church music
      Oratorio
  Example under Vocal music—History and criticism
Cantatas
      Here are entered collections of sacred and secular cantatas for mixed voices or for various groups of voices (men's, mixed, women's).
  BT Choruses
  NT Solo cantatas
  Example under reference from Arias
Cantatas, Sacred *(M2020-M2036)*
      Here are entered, with appropriate subdivisions, sacred cantatas for mixed voices or collections of sacred cantatas for various groups of voices (men's, mixed, women's)
  UF Sacred cantatas

Cantatas, Sacred *(M2020-M2036)*
(Continued)
  BT Sacred vocal music
  NT Pantomimes with music, Sacred
      Solo cantatas, Sacred
  —Excerpts
  — —Vocal scores with piano *(M2027-8)*
      UF Cantatas, Sacred—Vocal scores with piano—Excerpts
  —Excerpts, Arranged
  —Vocal scores with piano
  — —Excerpts
      USE Cantatas, Sacred—Excerpts—Vocal scores with piano
  —Vocal scores with pianos (2) *(M2023)*
Cantatas, Sacred (Equal voices)
  —Vocal scores with organ
Cantatas, Sacred (Men's voices) *(M2029-2032)*
Cantatas, Sacred (Unison) *(M2101.5)*
Cantatas, Sacred (Women's voices) *(M2033-6)*
Cantatas, Secular *(M1530-M1546)*
      Cf. note under Cantatas, Sacred
  UF Secular cantatas
  NT Pantomimes with music
      Solo cantatas, Secular
  —Excerpts, Arranged
Cantatas, Secular (Equal voices)
Cantatas, Secular (Men's voices) *(M1538-1542)*
Cantatas, Secular (Unison) *(M1609)*
Cantatas, Secular (Women's voices) *(M1543-6)*
Cantate Domino canticum novum, cantate Domino (Music)
  USE Psalms (Music)—96th Psalm
Cantate Domino canticum novum, laus eius (Music)
  USE Psalms (Music)—149th Psalm
Cantate Domino canticum novum, quia mirabilia fecit (Music)
  USE Psalms (Music)—98th Psalm
Cante flamenco
  USE Flamenco music
Cante hondo
  USE Flamenco
      Flamenco music
Canticles
  BT Liturgies
  RT Hymns
  NT Benedictus Dominus Deus Israel
      Nunc dimittis (Music)
Cantors, Jewish
  BT Musicians, Jewish
Cāranō
  USE Charans
Carillon music *(M172)*
  NT Carillon with band
      Carillon with orchestra
      Concertos (Carillon with band)
      Sonatas (Carillon)
      Suites (Carillon)

Carillon with band *(M1205-6)*
    BT Carillon music
    RT Concertos (Carillon with band)
Carillon with instrumental ensemble
    RT Concertos (Carillon with instrumental
            ensemble)
Carillon with orchestra *(M1038-9)*
    BT Carillon music
    RT Concertos (Carillon)
Carillons [May Subd Geog]
    BT Bells
        Church music
        Music
    NT Change ringing
        Handbell ringing
    —England
        NT Loughborough War Memorial Tower
                and Carillon (Loughborough,
                Leicestershire)
Carnatic music
    USE Music, Karnatic
Carnival songs *(Italian literature, PQ4222.C4)*
    BT Songs
Carols [May Subd Geog]
                Here and with local subdivision are en-
                tered collections of carols in various
                languages. Works in a single language
                are entered under this heading quali-
                fied by the name of the language, *e.g.*
                Carols, English; Carols, Czech.
    UF Christmas carols
        Easter carols
    BT Christian poetry
        Christmas—Poetry
        Christmas music
        Church music
        Easter—Poetry
        Easter music
        Folk-songs
        Hymns
        Sacred vocal music
        Songs
    NT Villancicos (Poetry)
Carols, Czech [May Subd Geog]
    UF Czech carols
    Note under Carols
Carols, Dutch [May Subd Geog]
    UF Dutch carols
Carols, English [May Subd Geog]
    UF English carols
    Note under Carols
Carols, French [May Subd Geog]
    UF Noels
Carols, Polish [May Subd Geog]
    UF Polish carols
Carols, Romanian [May Subd Geog]
    UF Romanian carols
Castanet music *(M175.C35)*
    NT Quartets (Electronic harpsichord,
            castanets, percussion, violoncello)
Castanets *(MT720)*
Castanets with chamber orchestra *(M1038-
        M1039)*

Castanets with chamber orchestra *(M1038-M1039)*
    (Continued)
    RT Concertos (Castanets with chamber
            orchestra)
Castanets with string orchestra *(M1138-M1139)*
Castrati *(History of vocal technique,*
            ML1460; Voice culture, MT821)
    BT Singers
Catalan ballads
    USE Ballads, Catalan
Catalan folk-songs
    USE Folk-songs, Catalan
Cataloging of music *(ML111)*
    UF Music—Cataloging
    BT Music librarianship
Cataloging of sound recordings *(Z695.715)*
    UF Sound recordings—Cataloging
    BT Music librarianship
Catches
    USE Glees, catches, rounds, etc.
Catholic Church *(Indirect)*
    —Music
        USE Church music—Catholic Church
Catholic Church music
    USE Church music—Catholic Church
Catholic song-books
    USE Song-books, Catholic
Celesta *(ML1040)*
    BT Keyboard instruments
        Percussion instruments
Celesta and flute music
    USE Flute and celesta music
Celesta and glockenspiel music
    USE Glockenspiel and celesta music
Celesta and harpsichord music *(M284.C4;*
            M285.C4)
    UF Harpsichord and celesta music
Celesta and percussion music
    USE Percussion and celesta music
Celesta and recorder music
    USE Recorder and celesta music
Celesta and violin music
    USE Violin and celesta music
Celesta music *(M175.C44)*
    SA Concertos, Minuets, Sonatas, Suites,
            and similar headings with
            specification of instruments; Trios
            [Quartets, etc.] *followed by*
            specifications which include the
            celesta; also headings that begin with
            the words celesta or celestas
Celtic musicians
    USE Musicians, Celtic
Cembalo
    USE Dulcimer
        Harpsichord
Centers for the performing arts *(Indirect)*
            (PN1585-PN1589)
    UF Performing arts centers
    BT Art centers
        Arts facilities
        Performing arts
    SA names of individual centers

Centers for the performing arts *(Indirect)*
    (PN1585-PN1589)
  (Continued)
    NT   Auditoriums
         Music-halls
         Theaters
Cetra
   USE   English guitar
Cha-chas
   BT   Dance music
Chaconne
Chaconnes
      Here are entered collections of chaconne
         music for various mediums. Individual
         chaconnes and collections of chaconnes
         for a specific medium are entered under the
         heading followed by specification of medium.
   UF   Ciacone
Chaconnes (Harp) *(M115-117)*
   BT   Harp music
Chaconnes (Harp with string orchestra)
      (M1136-1137)
   BT   Harp with string orchestra
   —Solo with piano *(M1137)*
      BT   Harp and piano music, Arranged
Chaconnes (Harpsichord) *(M24)*
   BT   Harpsichord music
Chaconnes (Harpsichord), Arranged *(M38)*
   BT   Harpsichord music, Arranged
Chaconnes (Harpsichord, recorders (3))
      (M415-417)
   BT   Quartets (Harpsichord, recorders (3))
Chaconnes (Organ) *(M6-M7; M11)*
   BT   Organ music
Chaconnes (Piano) *(M25)*
   BT   Piano music
Chaconnes (String orchestra) *(M1145)*
   BT   String-orchestra music
Chaconnes (Theorbo) *(M142.T)*
   BT   Theorbo music
Chaconnes (Tuba and piano) *(M264-M265)*
   BT   Tuba and piano music
Chaconnes (Unspecified instrument and organ)
      (M298.5)
   BT   Duets (Unspecified instrument and organ)
Chaconnes (Unspecified instrument and piano)
      (M285.5-285.6)
   BT   Duets (Unspecified instrument and piano)
Chaconnes (Viola and piano) *(M224-6)*
   BT   Viola and piano music
Chaconnes (Viola da gamba and continuo)
   BT   Viola da gamba and continuo music
Chaconnes (Violin) *(M40-42)*
   BT   Violin music
Chaconnes (Violin and continuo)
   BT   Violin and continuo music
Chaconnes (Violin and harpsichord)
      (M217-M218; M221)
   BT   Violin and harpsichord music
Chaconnes (Violin and organ) *(M182-4)*
   BT   Violin and organ music
Chaconnes (Violin and organ), Arranged
      (M185-6)

Chaconnes (Violin and piano) *(M217-M218;*
      M221)
   BT   Violin and piano music
Chaconnes (Violin with string orchestra)
      (M1105-6)
   BT   Violin with string orchestra
Chaconnes (Violin with string orchestra),
      Arranged *(M1105-6)*
   —Scores *(M1105)*
Chaconnes (Violoncello and piano)
      (M229-M230; M233-M236)
   BT   Violoncello and piano music
Chaconnes (Violoncello with chamber
      orchestra) *(M1016-1017)*
   BT   Violoncello with chamber orchestra
   —Scores *(M1016)*
   —Solo with piano *(M1017)*
      BT   Violoncello and piano music,
          Arranged
Chalumeau (Double-reed musical instrument)
   USE   Shawm
Chalumeau (Single-reed musical instrument)
      (ML990.C5)
   UF   Mock trumpet
   BT   Clarinet
        Woodwind instruments
Chalumeau music *(M110.C)*
   SA   Concerto; Minuets; Sonatas; Suites;
      and similar headings with specification
      of instruments; Trios [Quartets, etc.];
      Wind trios [quartets, etc.], *and* Woodwind
      trios [quartets, etc.] *followed by specifications*
      which include the chalumeau; also Wind
      ensembles; Woodwind ensembles *and*
      headings that begin with the words
      chalumeau or chalumeaux
Chamber music *(Indirect) (M177-M990)*
      Here are entered miscellaneous collec-
         tions of chamber music for various com-
         binations of two or more solo instruments.
      Compositions for two specified solo
         instruments are entered under headings
         specifying the instruments, *e.g.* Flute
         music (Flutes (2)); Oboe and harpsi-
         chord music; Violin and viola music,
         etc., and under names of forms, followed
         by instrumental specifications, *e.g.*, Sonatas
         (Violin and piano); Suites (Flute and piano);
         etc.
      Compositions for two unspecified instru-
         ments, or for one specified and one un-
         specified instrument are entered under
         Duets or names of forms followed by
         instrumental specification, *e.g.* Duets
         (Unspecified instruments (2)); Duets
         (Unspecified instrument and guitar
         [piano, etc]); Sonatas (Unspecified in-
         struments (2)).
      Compositions for three or more solo in-
         struments are entered under appropriate
         headings for the medium or form,
         e.g. Trios, Quartets, etc.; Piano trios,
         etc.; String trios, etc.; Wind trios, etc.;

Chamber music *(Indirect) (M177-M990)*
    (Continued)

              Brass trios, etc.; Woodwind trios, etc.;
              Instrumental [Piano, String, etc.] en-
              sembles; Suites, Variations, Waltzes,
              etc.
    BT Instrumental music
        Music
    NT Chamber music groups
    —Dictionaries *(ML102)*
        Example under Music—Dictionaries
    —History and criticism *(ML1100-ML1165)*
        Example under Criticism
        RT Chamber orchestra
        NT Ensemble playing
            Music in the home
            Orchestra
            String quartet
            String trio

Chamber music ensembles
  USE Chamber music groups

Chamber music groups *(Indirect)*
    UF Chamber music ensembles
        Ensembles, Chamber music
        Groups, Chamber music
        String quartets (Musical groups)
    BT Chamber music
        Musical groups
    RT Chamber orchestra

Chamber orchestra *(ML1200-1251)*
    BT Musical groups
        Orchestra
    RT Chamber music—History and criticism
        Chamber music groups
    NT Chamber-orchestra music
        Instrumentation and orchestration

Chamber-orchestra music *(M1000-1049)*
    BT Chamber orchestra
        Instrumental music
        Orchestral music
    RT Salon-orchestra music
    SA Concertos ([Solo instrument(s)] with
        chamber orchestra); [Solo
        instrument(s)] with chamber
        orchestra; Suites, Variations,
        Waltzes, *and similar headings with
        specification of instruments which
        include the specification Chamber
        orchestra*
    NT Bassoon, clarinet, flute, oboe with
        chamber orchestra
        Bassoon, oboe, violin, violoncello with
        chamber orchestra
        Canon, fugues, etc. (Chamber
        orchestra)
        Clarinet and flute with chamber
        orchestra
        Concertos (Bassoon, clarinet, flute,
        horn, oboe with chamber orchestra)
        Concertos (Bassoon, clarinet, flute,
        oboe with chamber orchestra)
        Concertos (Bassoon, flute, horn, oboe
        with chamber orchestra)

Chamber-orchestra music *(M1000-1049)*
    (Continued)
    NT Concertos (Bassoon, oboe, violin,
        violoncello with chamber orchestra)
        Concertos (Chamber orchestra)
        Concertos (Clarinet and flute with
        chamber orchestra)
        Concertos (Double bass with chamber
        orchestra)
        Concertos (Flute with chamber
        orchestra)
        Concertos (Oboe and violin with
        chamber orchestra)
        Concertos (Oboe with chamber
        orchestra)
        Concertos (Piano with chamber
        orchestra)
        Concertos (Saxophone with chamber
        orchestra)
        Concertos (Violin with chamber
        orchestra)
        Flutes (2) with chamber orchestra
        Guitar with chamber orchestra
        Jazz quartet with chamber orchestra
        Marches (Chamber orchestra)
        Oboe and violin with chamber
        orchestra
        Oboe with chamber orchestra
        Overtures (Chamber orchestra)
        Percussion with chamber orchestra
        Polkas (Chamber orchestra)
        Polonaises (Chamber orchestra)
        String-orchestra music
        Suites (Chamber orchestra)
        Symphonic poems (Chamber orchestra)
        Symphonies (Chamber orchestra)
        Variations (Chamber orchestra)
        Viola d'amore with chamber orchestra
        Violin and piano with chamber
        orchestra
        Violin and viola with chamber orchestra
        Waltzes (Chamber orchestra)

Chamber-orchestra music, Arranged *(M1060-1075)*

Chance composition
    Here are entered works dealing with
        compositions which have been created by
        chance methods or which may be performed
        in random or indeterminate style.
    UF Aleatory music
        Chance music
        Music, Aleatory
        Music, Chance
    BT Composition (Music)
        Improvisation (Music)

Chance compositions
    Here are entered works which have
        been composed by chance methods or
        which may be performed in random or
        indeterminate style. The heading is used
        as a second heading for those works
        having a specifically named medium of
        performance, *e.g.* 1. Piano music.
        2. Chance compositions.

Chance compositions
  (Continued)
  UF Aleatory music
      Chance music
      Music, Aleatory
      Music, Chance
  BT Music
Chance music
  USE Chance composition
      Chance compositions
Chang go
  USE Changgo
Change ringing *(MT710)*
  UF Bell ringing
      Chiming
  BT Bells
      Carillons
Changgo *(Instruction, MT725.C45)*
  UF Chang go
  BT Hourglass drum
      Musical instruments—Korea
Ch'anggŭk
  BT Opera—Korea
Chanting
  USE Chants (Plain, Gregorian, etc.)
Chants (Armenian)
  BT Armenian Church—Liturgy
Chants (Plain, Gregorian, etc.)
  UF Chanting
      Gregorian chant
      Plain chant
      Plain song
      Plainsong
  BT Church music—Catholic Church
      Liturgics
      Music—500-1400
      Oral interpretation
      Sacred vocal music
  —Accompaniment *(M14; MT190)*
    BT Musical accompaniment
        Organ—Instruction and study
    RT Hymns—Accompaniment
  —History and criticism *(ML3082)*
    NT Alleluia (Music)
  —Instruction and study *(MT860)*
    BT Music—Theory
        Musical meter and rhythm
        Singing—Instruction and study
  NT Neumes
Chants (Sufi) *(BP189.58)*
  UF Dhikr'
      Sufi chants
  BT Sufism—Liturgy
Chantys
  USE Sea songs
Chapels (Music) [May Subd Geog]
  UF Chapels royal
      Music chapels
  BT Church music
      Orchestra
  RT Choirs (Music)
  NT Maîtrises

Chapels royal
  USE Chapels, Court
      Chapels (Music)
Charango
      MT599.C45 (Instruction)
  BT Guitar
      Musical instruments—Andes Region
Charans
  UF Cáranó
  BT Minstrels
Chastushkas
  USE Chastushki
Chastushki [May Subd Geog]
  UF Chastushkas
  BT Folk-songs, Russian
Chechen folk-songs
  USE Folk-songs, Chechen
Chechen songs
  USE Songs, Chechen
Cheng (Musical instrument)
      ML1015.C47 (History)
      MT654.C47 (Instruction)
  BT Musical instruments—China
      Zither
Cheng music *(M142.C49)*
  BT Zither music
Cheyenne hymns
  USE Hymns, Cheyenne
Chhattisgarhi folk-songs
  USE Folk-songs, Chhattisgarhi
Chi na
  USE So na
Chicken scratch music
  BT Indians of North America—Arizona—
        Music
      Papago Indians—Music
      Pima Indians—Music
      Popular music—Arizona
Children as musicians *(ML83)*
  BT Gifted children
      Musicians
  NT Rhythm bands and orchestras
Children's music
  USE Music—Juvenile
Children's opera
  USE Opera—Juvenile
Children's songs [May Subd Geog] *(Music,*
     M1990-M1998; Singing games,
     GV1215)
  UF Songs—Juvenile
  BT Children's poetry
      Music—Juvenile
      School song-books
      Songs
  NT Camping—Songs and music
      Games with music
      Kindergarten—Music
      Lullabies
      Nursery rhymes
      Nursery schools—Music
      Sunday-schools—Hymns
Chime and flute music
  USE Flute and chime music

Chime and piano music *(M284.C; M285.C)*
  UF Piano and chime music
Chime music *(M172)*
  NT Sextets (Chimes, xylophone, violins (2),
        viola, violoncello)
Chimes
  BT Bells
      Music
  NT Chiming clock music
      Windchimes
**Chimes, xylophone, violins (2), viola,
      violoncello with string orchestra**
      (M1140-1141)
  BT Sextets (Chimes, xylophone, violins (2),
        viola, violoncello)
  RT Concertos (Chimes, xylophone, violins
        (2), viola, violoncello with string
        orchestra)
Chiming
  USE Change ringing
Chiming clock music
  UF Chiming clock selections
      Clock chimes selections
      Clock music
      Music, Chiming clock
  BT Chimes
Chiming clock selections
  USE Chiming clock music
Chiming clocks [May Subd Geog]
        Here are entered works about clocks
        equipped with carillons or other
        chiming mechanisms. Works about
        clocks equipped with mechanical
        organs are entered under the heading
        Musical clock.
  UF Clocks, Chiming
  BT Clocks and watches
  Note under Musical clock
Chimney flute
  USE Rohrflöte
Ch'in (Musical instrument) *(ML1015.C5)*
  BT Musical instruments—China
      Zither
Ch'in music *(ML142.C5)*
  NT Quintets (Ch'in, violin, viola
        violoncello, double bass)
Chinese ballads
  USE Ballads, Chinese
Chinese drama
  NT Operas, Chinese
Chinese folk-songs
  USE Folk-songs, Chinese
Chinese hymns
  USE Hymns, Chinese
Chinese lute
  USE P'i p'a
Chinese operas
  USE Operas, Chinese
Chinese songs
  USE Songs, Chinese
Chiroplast *(MT221)*
  BT Piano—Instruction and study

Chitarrone
        ML1015.C (History)
  BT Lute
Chitarrone music
        M142.C
Choir books
  USE Service books (Music)
Choir boy training
  USE Choirboy training
Choir boys
  USE Choirboys
Choirboy training *(MT915)*
  UF Boy choir training
      Choir boy training
  BT Choirs (Music)
      Choral singing—Juvenile
  —Handbooks, manuals, etc.
      UF Choirboy training—Manuals,
            text-books, etc.
  —Text-books
      UF Choirboy training—Manuals,
            text-books, etc.
Choirboys
  UF Choir boys
  BT Church musicians
      Singers
  NT Seises
Choirs (Music) [May Subd Geog] *(Instruction,
        MT88)*
  BT Church music
      Musical groups
  RT Chapels (Music)
      Choral music
      Choral singing
      Choral societies
      Conducting, Choral
  NT Choirboy training
      Maîtrises
Choral conducting
  USE Conducting, Choral
Choral music [May Subd Geog] *(History: general,
        ML1500-ML1554; sacred
        ML2900-ML3275; secular,
        ML2400-ML2770)*
        Here are entered works on choral music.
        Collections of sacred and secular
        choral compositions are entered under
        the heading Choruses.
  UF Music, Choral
  BT Church music
      Music
      Vocal music—History and criticism
  RT Choirs (Music)
      Choral societies
  NT Cantata
      Choral singing
      Conducting, Choral
      Madrigal
      Motet
      Part-songs
      Part-songs, Sacred
  Note under Choruses

Choral singing [May Subd Geog] *(MT875)*
  UF Singing, Choral
  BT Choral music
       Singing
  RT Choirs (Music)
       Conducting, Choral
  NT Barbershop singing
       Choral societies
  —Diction *(MT875)*
     BT Singing—Diction
  —Interpretation (Phrasing, dynamics, etc.)
     (MT875)
  —Juvenile
     UF Choral singing, Juvenile
     BT School song-books
     NT Choirboy training
Choral societies [May Subd Geog] *(ML25-ML28;*
     MT88)
  UF Singing societies
  BT Choral singing
       Music—Societies, etc.
       Musical groups
  RT Choirs (Music)
       Choral music
  NT Community music
Choral societies, German *(ML26-28)*
Chorale *(Catholic, ML3084;*
      Nondenominational, ML3265;
      Protestant, ML3184)
  BT Church music
       Church music—Lutheran Church
       Hymn tunes
       Hymns, German
       Lutheran Church—Hymns
  RT Chorale prelude
Chorale prelude
  BT Hymns, German
  RT Chorale
Chorale preludes
     Here are entered compositions originally
        written or arranged for organ. Similar
        compositions written for media other
        than organ receive the heading Chorale
        preludes, followed by specification of
        medium, *e.g.* Chorale preludes (Orchestra)
  BT Organ music
  RT Chorales
Chorale preludes (Band) *(M1245; M1258)*
  BT Band music
Chorale preludes (Bassoon and organ)
     (M182-186)
  BT Bassoon and organ music
Chorale preludes (Clarinet and organ)
     (M182-186)
  BT Clarinet and organ music
Chorale preludes (Fluegelhorn and organ)
  BT Fluegelhorn and organ music
Chorale preludes (Flute and organ)
     (M182-186)
  BT Flute and organ music
Chorale preludes (Harpsichord)
  BT Harpsichord music

Chorale preludes (Horn and organ)
     (M182-186)
  BT Horn and organ music
Chorale preludes (Instrumental ensemble)
  BT Instrumental ensembles
Chorale preludes (Oboe and organ)
     (M182-6)
  BT Oboe and organ music
Chorale preludes (Orchestra) *(M1045;*
     M1060)
  BT Orchestral music
  Note under Chorale preludes
Chorale preludes (Piano)
  BT Piano music
Chorale preludes (Piano and organ)
     (M182-6)
  BT Piano and organ music
Chorale preludes (Pianos (2)) *(M214-215)*
  BT Piano music (Pianos (2))
Chorale preludes (String orchestra) *(M1145;*
     M1160)
  BT String-orchestra music
  —Scores and parts *(M1145; M1160)*
Chorale preludes (Trombone and organ)
     (M182-186)
  BT Trombone and organ music
Chorale preludes (Trumpet and organ)
     (M182-186)
  BT Trumpet and organ music
Chorale preludes (Viola and organ)
     (M182-186)
  BT Viola and organ music
Chorale preludes (Viola da gamba and organ)
     (M239)
  BT Viola da gamba and organ music
Chorale preludes (Violin and organ)
     (M182-186)
  BT Violin and organ music
Chorale preludes (Violin and piano)
     (M217-M218; M221-M223)
  BT Violin and piano music
Chorale preludes (Violoncello and organ)
     (M182-186)
  BT Violoncello and organ music
Chorale preludes (Violoncello and piano)
     (M229-M230; M233-M236)
  BT Violoncello and piano music
Chorales
  BT Choruses, Sacred
       Hymns, German
       Lutheran Church—Hymns
       Sacred vocal music
       Tune-books
  RT Chorale preludes
  —Analysis, appreciation
     UF Chorales—Analytical guides
  —Analytical guides
     USE Chorales—Analysis, appreciation
Choruses *(M1495)*
     Here are entered collections of sacred
        and secular choral compositions for
        various groups of voices (men's,

Choruses *(M1495)*
(Continued)

> mixed, women's, etc.) both accompanied and unaccompanied. The heading is also qualified as appropriate in the following order: 1) voice grouping; 2) number of vocal parts when 8 or less (included only in headings without specification of accompaniment, with specification of accompaniment for a solo instrument or for 2 keyboard instruments, and with the specification, Unaccompanied); and 3) specification of accompaniment or the specification, Unaccompanied. Textual works about choruses are entered under the heading Choral music.

BT   Vocal music

NT   Canons, fugues, etc. (Vocal)
     Cantatas
     Choruses, Sacred
     Choruses, Secular
     Rondos (Vocal)
     Song-books

Note under Choral music

Choruses, Sacred *(M2060-2101.5)*

> Here are entered collections of sacred choral compositions for various groups of voices (men's, mixed, women's, etc.) both accompanied and unaccompanied. The heading is also qualified as appropriate in the following order: 1) voice grouping; 2) number of vocal parts when 8 or less (included only in headings without specification of accompaniment, with specification of accompaniment for a solo instrument or for 2 keyboard instruments, and with the specification, Unaccompanied); and 3) specification of accompaniment or the specification, Unaccompanied.

UF   Sacred choruses

BT   Choruses

NT   Anthems
     Chorales
     Part-songs, Sacred
     Sacred duets
     Sacred nonets
     Sacred octets
     Sacred quartets
     Sacred quintets
     Sacred septets
     Sacred sextets
     Sacred trios
     Service books (Music)

Choruses, Sacred (Changing voices)

Choruses, Sacred (Equal voices) *(M2060)*

Choruses, Sacred (Equal voices, 3 parts)

Choruses, Sacred (Equal voices, 3 parts), Unaccompanied

Choruses, Sacred (Equal voices, 3 parts) with piano

Choruses, Sacred (Equal voices), Unaccompanied *(M2084)*

Choruses, Sacred (Equal voices) with instrumental ensemble *(M2021; M2023-2028)*

Choruses, Sacred (Men's voices) *(M2060)*

Choruses, Sacred (Men's voices, 4 parts)

Choruses, Sacred (Men's voices, 4 parts), Unaccompanied *(M2083; M2093)*

Choruses, Sacred (Men's voices, 4 parts) with piano, 4 hands *(M2063; M2073)*

Choruses, Sacred (Men's voices), Unaccompanied *(M2083)*

Choruses, Sacred (Men's voices) with band *(M2029-2032)*

Choruses, Sacred (Men's voices) with instrumental ensemble *(M2029)*
—Vocal scores with piano *(M2030)*
>   BT   Choruses, Sacred (Men's voices)
>   with piano

Choruses, Sacred (Men's voices) with orchestra *(M2029-2032)*
—Vocal scores with organ *(M2030)*
>   BT   Choruses, Sacred (Men's voices)
>   with organ
—Vocal scores with piano *(M2030)*
>   BT   Choruses, Sacred (Men's voices)
>   with piano

Choruses, Sacred (Men's voices) with organ *(M2063; M2073)*

NT   Choruses, Sacred (Men's voices) with
     orchestra—Vocal scores with organ

Choruses, Sacred (Men's voices) with piano *(M2063; M2073)*

NT   Choruses, Sacred (Men's voices) with
     instrumental ensemble—Vocal scores
     with piano
     Choruses, Sacred (Men's voices) with
     orchestra—Vocal scores with piano

Choruses, Sacred (Mixed voices) *(M2060)*

Choruses, Sacred (Mixed voices, 2 parts) with handbells *(M2080.5)*

Choruses, Sacred (Mixed voices, 3 parts) with harpsichord *(M2060; M2072)*

Choruses, Sacred (Mixed voices, 4 parts)

Choruses, Sacred (Mixed voices, 4 parts), Unaccompanied *(M2082; M2092)*

Choruses, Sacred (Mixed voices, 4 parts) with continuo

Choruses, Sacred (Mixed voices, 4 parts) with guitar *(M2080.5)*

Choruses, Sacred (Mixed voices, 4 parts) with organ *(M2062; M2072)*

Choruses, Sacred (Mixed voices, 4 parts) with piano *(M2062; M2072)*

Choruses, Sacred (Mixed voices, 4 parts) with piano and organ *(M2062; M2072)*

Choruses, Sacred (Mixed voices, 4 parts) with pianos (2) *(M2062; M2072)*

Choruses, Sacred (Mixed voices, 8 parts), Unaccompanied *(M2082; M2092)*

Choruses, Sacred (Mixed voices),
    Unaccompanied *(M2082)*
Choruses, Sacred (Mixed voices) with band
    (M2021)
—Vocal scores with piano *(M2023)*
    BT Choruses, Sacred (Mixed voices)
        with piano
Choruses, Sacred (Mixed voices) with chamber
    orchestra *(M2021-2028)*
—Vocal scores with organ *(M2023)*
    BT Choruses, Sacred (Mixed voices)
        with organ
—Vocal scores with piano *(M2023)*
    BT Choruses, Sacred (Mixed voices)
        with piano
Choruses, Sacred (Mixed voices) with
    electronic music *(M2021)*
    BT Electronic music
Choruses, Sacred (Mixed voices) with
    instrumental ensemble *(M2021)*
—Vocal scores with organ *(M2023)*
    BT Choruses, Sacred (Mixed voices)
        with organ
—Vocal scores with piano *(M2023)*
    BT Choruses, Sacred (Mixed voices)
        with piano
Choruses, Sacred (Mixed voices) with jazz
    ensemble *(M2021)*
    BT Jazz ensembles
Choruses, Sacred (Mixed voices) with
    orchestra
—Vocal scores with organ *(M2023)*
    BT Choruses, Sacred (Mixed voices)
        with organ
—Vocal scores with piano *(M2023)*
    BT Choruses, Sacred (Mixed voices)
        with piano
Choruses, Sacred (Mixed voices) with organ
    (M2062)
    NT Choruses, Sacred (Mixed voices) with
        chamber orchestra—Vocal scores
        with organ
        Choruses, Sacred (Mixed voices) with
        instrumental ensemble—Vocal scores
        with organ
        Choruses, Sacred (Mixed voices) with
        orchestra—Vocal scores with organ
        Choruses, Sacred (Mixed voices) with
        string orchestra—Vocal scores with
        organ
Choruses, Sacred (Mixed voices) with piano
    (M2062)
    NT Choruses, Sacred (Mixed voices) with
        band—Vocal scores with piano
        Choruses, Sacred (Mixed voices) with
        chamber orchestra—Vocal scores
        with piano
        Choruses, Sacred (Mixed voices) with
        instrumental ensemble—Vocal scores
        with piano
        Choruses, Sacred (Mixed voices) with
        orchestra—Vocal scores with piano

Choruses, Sacred (Mixed voices) with piano
    (M2062) (Continued)
    NT Choruses, Sacred (Mixed voices) with
        string orchestra—Vocal scores with
        piano
Choruses, Sacred (Mixed voices) with string
    orchestra
—Vocal scores with organ *(M2023)*
    BT Choruses, Sacred (Mixed voices)
        with organ
—Vocal scores with piano *(M2023)*
    BT Choruses, Sacred (Mixed voices)
        with piano
Choruses, Sacred, Unaccompanied *(M2081)*
Choruses, Sacred, (Unison) *(M2101.5)*
Choruses, Sacred, (Unison) with guitar
    (M2101.5)
Choruses, Sacred, (Unison) with instrumental
    ensemble *(M2101.5)*
Choruses, Sacred (Unison) with orchestra
—Scores *(M2101.5)*
Choruses, Sacred (Unison) with organ
    (M2101.5)
    NT Choruses, Sacred (Unison) with string
        orchestra—Vocal scores with organ
Choruses, Sacred (Unison) with piano
    (M2101.5)
    NT Choruses, Sacred (Unison) with string
        orchestra—Vocal scores with piano
Choruses, Sacred (Unison) with string
    ensemble *(M2101.5)*
Choruses, Sacred (Unison) with string
    orchestra
—Vocal scores with organ *(M2101.5)*
    BT Choruses, Sacred (Unison) with
        organ
—Vocal scores with piano *(M2101.5)*
    BT Choruses, Sacred (Unison) with
        piano
Choruses, Sacred, with instrumental ensemble
    NT Sacred monologues with music (Chorus
        with instrumental ensemble)
Choruses, Sacred, with orchestra
    NT Sacred monologues with music (Chorus
        with orchestra)
Choruses, Sacred, with organ *(M2061)*
    NT Sacred monologues with music (Chorus
        with orchestra)—Vocal scores with
        organ
Choruses, Sacred, with piano *(M2061)*
    NT Sacred monologues with music (Chorus
        with orchestra)—Vocal scores with
        piano
Choruses, Sacred (Women's voices) *(M2060)*
Choruses, Sacred (Women's voices, 3 parts)
    with harp *(M2080.7)*
Choruses, Sacred (Women's voices, 4 parts)
Choruses, Sacred (Women's voices, 4 parts),
    Unaccompanied *(M2084; M2094)*
Choruses, Sacred (Women's voices, 4 parts)
    with piano *(M2064; M2074)*
Choruses, Sacred (Women's voices, 8 parts),
    Unaccompanied *(M2084; M2094)*

Choruses, Sacred (Women's voices), Unaccompanied *(M2084)*

Choruses, Sacred (Women's voices) with chamber orchestra *(M2033-2036)*
—Vocal scores with piano *(M2034)*
    BT Choruses, Sacred (Women's voices) with piano

Choruses, Sacred (Women's voices) with instrumental ensemble *(M2033)*
—Vocal scores with piano *(M2034)*
    BT Choruses, Sacred (Women's voices) with piano

Choruses, Sacred (Women's voices) with orchestra *(M2033-2036)*
—Vocal scores with organ *(M2034)*
    BT Choruses, Sacred (Women's voices) with organ

Choruses, Sacred (Women's voices) with organ *(M2064)*
  NT Choruses, Sacred (Women's voices) with orchestra—Vocal scores with organ

Choruses, Sacred (Women's voices) with piano *(M2064)*
  NT Choruses, Sacred (Women's voices) with chamber orchestra—Vocal scores with piano
      Choruses, Sacred (Women's voices) with instrumental ensemble—Vocal scores with piano
      Choruses, Sacred (Women's voices) with string orchestra—Vocal scores with piano

Choruses, Sacred (Women's voices) with string orchestra *(M2033-2036)*
—Vocal scores with piano *(M2034)*
    BT Choruses, Sacred (Women's voices) with piano

Choruses, Secular *(M1547-M1610)*
      Here are entered collections of secular choral compositions for various groups of voices (men's, mixed, women's, etc.) both accompanied and unaccompanied. The heading is also qualified as appropriate in the following order: 1) voice grouping; 2) number of vocal parts when 8 or less (included only in headings without specification of accompaniment, with specification of accompaniment for a solo instrument or for 2 keyboard instruments, and with the specification, Unaccompanied); and 3) specification of accompaniment or the specification, Unaccompanied.
  UF Secular choruses
  BT Choruses
  RT Part-songs
  NT Song-books
      Vocal duets
      Vocal nonets
      Vocal octets
      Vocal quartets
      Vocal quintets

Choruses, Secular *(M1547-M1610)*
(Continued)
  NT Vocal septets
      Vocal sextets
      Vocal trios

Choruses, Secular (Children's voices) *(M1546.5; M1997-M1998)*

Choruses, Secular (Children's voices) with instrumental ensemble *(M1546.5; M1997-M1998)*

Choruses, Secular (Children's voices) with orchestra *(M1546.5)*
—Vocal scores with piano *(M1546.5)*
    BT Choruses, Secular (Children's voices) with piano

Choruses, Secular (Children's voices) with piano *(M1997-1998)*
  NT Choruses, Secular (Children's voices) with orchestra—Vocal scores with piano

Choruses, Secular (Equal voices, 3 parts), Unaccompanied

Choruses, Secular (Equal voices, 3 parts) with piano

Choruses, Secular (Equal voices), Unaccompanied *(M1581)*

Choruses, Secular (Equal voices) with chamber orchestra

Choruses, Secular (Equal voices) with instrumental ensemble

Choruses, Secular (Equal voices) with orchestra
—Vocal scores with piano
    BT Choruses, Secular (Equal voices) with piano

Choruses, Secular (Equal voices) with piano
  NT Choruses, Secular (Equal voices) with orchestra—Vocal scores with piano

Choruses, Secular (Men's voices) *(M1547)*

Choruses, Secular (Men's voices, 3 parts) with percussion *(M1576)*

Choruses, Secular (Men's voices, 3 parts) with violin *(M1576)*

Choruses, Secular (Men's voices, 4 parts)

Choruses, Secular (Men's voices, 4 parts), Unaccompanied *(M1580; M1590)*
  NT Barbershop quartets

Choruses, Secular (Men's voices, 4 parts) with piano and reed-organ *(M1550; M1560)*

Choruses, Secular (Men's voices, 8 parts), Unaccompanied *(M1580; M1590)*

Choruses, Secular (Men's voices), Unaccompanied *(M1580)*

Choruses, Secular (Men's voices) with accordion *(M1550)*

Choruses, Secular (Men's voices) with band *(M1539)*
—Vocal scores with piano *(M1540)*
    BT Choruses, Secular (Men's voices) with piano

Choruses, Secular (Men's voices) with electronic music *(M1539)*
  BT Electronic music

Choruses, Secular (Men's voices) with instrumental ensemble *(M1539-1542)*
—Vocal scores with piano *(M1540)*
   BT Choruses, Secular (Men's voices) with piano

Choruses, Secular (Men's voices) with orchestra *(M1538-1542)*
—Vocal scores with piano *(M1540)*
   BT Choruses, Secular (Men's voices) with piano

Choruses, Secular (Men's voices) with piano *(M1550)*
  NT Choruses, Secular (Men's voices) with band—Vocal scores with piano
    Choruses, Secular (Men's voices) with instrumental ensemble—Vocal scores with piano
    Choruses, Secular (Men's voices) with orchestra—Vocal scores with piano
    Choruses, Secular (Men's voices) with string orchestra—Vocal scores with piano

Choruses, Secular (Men's voices) with piano, 4 hands *(M1550)*

Choruses, Secular (Men's voices) with string orchestra *(M1539-1542)*
—Vocal scores with piano *(M1540)*
   BT Choruses, Secular (Men's voices) with piano

Choruses, Secular (Mixed voices) *(M1547)*

Choruses, Secular (Mixed voices, 4 parts)

Choruses, Secular (Mixed voices, 4 parts), Unaccompanied *(Collections, M1579; Separate works, M1582)*

Choruses, Secular (Mixed voices, 4 parts) with continuo

Choruses, Secular (Mixed voices, 4 parts) with guitar *(M1575)*

Choruses, Secular (Mixed voices, 4 parts) with organ *(M1549; M1552)*

Choruses, Secular (Mixed voices, 4 parts) with piano *(M1549; M1552)*

Choruses, Secular (Mixed voices, 4 parts) with piano, 4 hands *(M1549; M1552)*

Choruses, Secular (Mixed voices, 4 parts) with pianos (2) *(M1549; M1552)*

Choruses, Secular (Mixed voices, 5 parts) with flute *(M1575)*

Choruses, Secular (Mixed voices, 8 parts) with horn *(M1575)*

Choruses, Secular (Mixed voices, 16 parts), Unaccompanied *(M1579.6; M1586)*

Choruses, Secular (Mixed voices), Unaccompanied *(M1579)*

Choruses, Secular (Mixed voices) with band *(M1531-1537)*
—Vocal scores with piano *(M1533)*
   BT Choruses, Secular (Mixed voices) with piano

Choruses, Secular (Mixed voices) with chamber orchestra *(M1531-1537)*
—Vocal scores with piano *(M1533)*
   BT Choruses, Secular (Mixed voices) with piano

Choruses, Secular (Mixed voices) with clarinet *(M1531)*

Choruses, Secular (Mixed voices) with dance orchestra *(M1531-1537)*

Choruses, Secular (Mixed voices) with electronic music *(M1531)*
  BT Electronic music

Choruses, Secular (Mixed voices) with instrumental ensemble *(M1531)*
—Vocal scores with piano *(M1533)*
   BT Choruses, Secular (Mixed voices) with piano

Choruses, Secular (Mixed voices) with kayakeum *(M1549)*

Choruses, Secular (Mixed voices) with orchestra *(M1530)*
—Vocal scores with organ *(M1533)*
   BT Choruses, Secular (Mixed voices) with organ
—Vocal scores with piano *(M1533)*
   BT Choruses, Secular (Mixed voices) with piano
—Vocal scores with piano (4 hands) *(M1533)*
   BT Choruses, Secular (Mixed voices) with piano, 4 hands

Choruses, Secular (Mixed voices) with organ *(Collections, M1549; Separate works, M1552)*
  NT Choruses, Secular (Mixed voices) with orchestra—Vocal scores with organ

Choruses, Secular (Mixed voices) with percussion *(M1531)*
Note under Percussion music

Choruses, Secular (Mixed voices) with piano *(M1549)*
  NT Choruses, Secular (Mixed voices) with band—Vocal scores with piano
    Choruses, Secular (Mixed voices) with chamber orchestra—Vocal scores with piano
    Choruses, Secular (Mixed voices) with instrumental ensemble—Vocal scores with piano
    Choruses, Secular (Mixed voices) with orchestra—Vocal scores with piano
    Choruses, Secular (Mixed voices) with string orchestra—Vocal scores with piano

Choruses, Secular (Mixed voices) with piano, 4 hands *(M1549; 1552)*
  NT Choruses, Secular (Mixed voices) with orchestra—Vocal scores with piano (4 hands)

Choruses, Secular (Mixed voices) with string orchestra
—Vocal scores with piano *(M1533)*
   BT Choruses, Secular (Mixed voices) with piano

Choruses, Secular, Unaccompanied *(M1578)*

Choruses, Secular (Unison) *(M1609)*

Choruses, Secular (Unison) with band
—Vocal scores with piano *(M1609)*
   BT Choruses, Secular (Unison) with piano

Choruses, Secular (Unison) with chamber orchestra *(M1609)*

Choruses, Secular (Unison) with instrumental ensemble *(M1609)*

Choruses, Secular (Unison) with orchestra
—Vocal scores with piano *(M1609)*
    BT Choruses, Secular (Unison) with piano

Choruses, Secular (Unison) with piano *(M1609)*
  NT Choruses, Secular (Unison) with band—Vocal scores with piano
      Choruses, Secular (Unison) with orchestra—Vocal scores with piano
      Choruses, Secular (Unison) with string orchestra—Vocal scores with piano

Choruses, Secular (Unison) with string orchestra
—Vocal scores with piano *(M1609)*
    BT Choruses, Secular (Unison) with piano

Choruses, Secular (Unison) with ti tzŭ *(M1609)*

Choruses, Secular, with accordion *(M1548)*

Choruses, Secular, with band *(M1531)*
—Scores and parts *(M1531)*

Choruses, Secular, with piano *(M1548)*
  NT Waltzes (Chorus with piano)

Choruses, Secular, with piano, 4 hands *(M1548)*
  NT Waltzes (Chorus with piano, 4 hands)

Choruses, Secular (Women's voices) *(M1547)*

Choruses, Secular (Women's voices, 2 parts) with violoncello *(M1577)*

Choruses, Secular (Women's voices, 3 parts) with harp *(M1577)*

Choruses, Secular (Women's voices, 4 parts), Unaccompanied *(M1581; M1600)*
  NT Barbershop quartets

Choruses, Secular (Women's voices, 4 parts) with piano *(M1551; M1570)*

Choruses, Secular (Women's voices, 7 parts) with orchestra *(M1543-4)*

Choruses, Secular (Women's voices, 8 parts) with piano *(M1551; M1570)*

Choruses, Secular (Women's voices), Unaccompanied *(M1581)*

Choruses, Secular (Women's voices) with band *(M1543.5)*

Choruses, Secular (Women's voices) with chamber orchestra *(M1543-6)*
—Scores *(M1543)*

Choruses, Secular (Women's voices) with electronic music *(M1543.5)*
  BT Electronic music

Choruses, Secular (Women's voices) with instrumental ensemble *(M1543.5)*

Choruses, Secular (Women's voices) with orchestra *(M1543-1546)*
—Vocal scores with piano *(M1544)*
    BT Choruses, Secular (Women's voices) with piano

Choruses, Secular (Women's voices) with piano *(M1551)*
  NT Choruses, Secular (Women's voices) with orchestra—Vocal scores with piano
      Choruses, Secular (Women's voices) with string orchestra—Vocal scores with piano

Choruses, Secular (Women's voices) with string orchestra
—Vocal scores with piano *(M1544)*
    BT Choruses, Secular (Women's voices) with piano

Choruses, Unaccompanied *(M1495)*

Choruses (Equal voices) *(M1495)*

Choruses (Men's voices) *(M1495)*

Choruses (Men's voices, 4 parts)

Choruses (Men's voices, 4 parts), Unaccompanied

Choruses (Men's voices, 4 parts) with piano

Choruses (Men's voices), Unaccompanied *(M1495)*

Choruses (Men's voices) with piano *(M1495)*

Choruses (Mixed voices) *(M1495)*

Choruses (Mixed voices, 4 parts)

Choruses (Mixed voices, 4 parts), Unaccompanied

Choruses (Mixed voices, 4 parts) with piano

Choruses (Mixed voices), Unaccompanied *(M1495)*

Choruses (Mixed voices) with piano *(M1495)*

Choruses (Unison) *(M1495)*

Choruses (Unison) with piano *(M1495)*

Choruses (Women's voices) *(M1495)*

Choruses (Women's voices, 3 parts), Unaccompanied

Choruses (Women's voices, 3 parts) with piano

Choruses (Women's voices), Unaccompanied *(M1495)*

Choruses (Women's voices) with piano *(M1495)*

Choruses with band
  NT Monologues with music (Chorus with band)

Choruses with chamber orchestra
  NT Monologues with music (Chorus with chamber orchestra)

Choruses with electronic music
  NT Monologues with music (Chorus with electronic music)

Choruses with instrumental ensemble
  NT Monologues with music (Chorus with instrumental ensemble)

Choruses with orchestra
  NT Monologues with music (Chorus with orchestra)
      Polkas (Chorus with orchestra)
      Waltzes (Chorus with orchestra)

Choruses with piano *(M1495)*
  NT Monologues with music (Chorus with piano)

Choruses with piano, 4 hands *(M1495)*
  NT Monologues with music (Chorus with piano, 4 hands)

Chŏttae
  USE Taegŭm
Christian hymns
  USE Hymns
Christian rock music [May Subd Geog] *(History,
    ML3187.5)*
  UF Jesus rock music
      Rock music, Christian
  BT Contemporary Christian music
      Rock music
Christmas [May Subd Geog]
  —Songs and music
      USE Christmas music
Christmas carols
  USE Carols
Christmas music
  UF Christmas—Songs and music
      Christmas songs
  BT Church music
      Holidays—Songs and music
      Music
      Sacred vocal music
  NT Carols
Christmas pantomime
  USE Pantomime (Christmas entertainment)
Christmas songs
  USE Christmas music
Chromatic alteration (Music)
  UF Alteration, Chromatic
  BT Harmony
      Music—Instruction and study
      Music—Theory
Chromophone
  USE Harmony—Mechanical aids
Chronometer (Music)
  USE Metronome
Church music [May Subd Geog] *(Aesthetics,
    ML3869; History, ML178,
    ML3000-3190, ML3270; Instruction
    and study, MT88, MT860-865,
    MT915)*
      Here are entered works on church music
      and on sacred vocal music in general.
      Sacred vocal compositions are entered
      under the heading Sacred vocal music
      and headings referred to under that
      heading.
      Subdivided, when desirable, by denomi-
      nation as well as by locality, e.g.
        1. Church music—Church of England.
        2. Church music—England.
  UF Church music—History and criticism
      Music, Religious
      Music, Sacred
      Pastoral music (Sacred)
      Religious music
      Sacred music
  BT Devotional exercises
      Liturgics
      Music
      Music—Religious aspects—Christianity
  RT Music in churches
      Psalmody

Church music [May Subd Geog] *(Aesthetics,
    ML3869; History, ML178,
    ML3000-3190, ML3270; Instruction
    and study, MT88, MT860-865,
    MT915) (Continued)*
  NT Advent music
      All Saints' Day music
      Anthem
      Ascension Day music
      Cantata
      Carillons
      Carols
      Chapels (Music)
      Choirs (Music)
      Choral music
      Chorale
      Christmas music
      Conducting, Choral
      Corpus Christi festival music
      Easter music
      Epiphany music
      Funeral music
      Holy-Week music
      Hymns
      Lenten music
      Mary, Blessed Virgin, Saint—Songs and
        music
      Mass (Music)
      Memorial music
      Motet
      Music in Christian education
      Music in monasteries
      Oratorio
      Organ—History
      Organ music
      Part-songs, Sacred
      Passion-music—History and criticism
      Sequences (Liturgy)
      Wedding music
  Note under Sacred vocal music
  —Almanacs, yearbooks, etc. *(ML13-21)*
      UF Church music—Yearbooks
  —Anglican Communion
      NT Church music—Church of England
          Church music—Episcopal Church
  —Catholic Church
      UF Catholic Church—Music
          Catholic Church music
          Church music—Catholic Church—
            History and criticism
      NT Chants (Plain, Gregorian, etc.)
          Maîtrises
          Mass (Music)
          Motet
          Tonarius
  ——History and criticism
      USE Church music—Catholic Church
  —Catholic Church (Byzantine rite)
        (ML3060)
      BT Church music—Orthodox Eastern
            Church
  —Choruses and choir books
      USE Service books (Music)

Church music [May Subd Geog] *(Aesthetics, ML3869; History, ML178, ML3000-3190, ML3270; Instruction and study, MT88, MT860-865, MT915) (Continued)*
  —Church of England *(ML3166)*
    BT Church music—Anglican Communion
    Note under Church music
  —Episcopal Church *(ML3166)*
    UF Church music—Protestant Episcopal Church in the U.S.A.
    BT Church music—Anglican Communion
  —Greek Church
    USE Church music—Orthodox Eastern Church
  —History and criticism
    USE Church music
  —Lutheran Church *(ML3168)*
    NT Chorale
  —Orthodox Eastern Church *(ML3060)*
    UF Church music—Greek Church
    NT Chants (Byzantine)
        Church music—Catholic Church (Byzantine rite)
  —Protestant churches *(ML3100-3188)*
    NT Chants (Anglican)
  —Protestant Episcopal Church in the U.S.A.
    USE Church music—Episcopal Church
  —Service books
    USE Service books (Music)
  —Societies, etc. *(ML128)*
    Here are entered works about societies for the cultivation of church music and the publications of such societies.
    BT Music—Societies, etc.
  —Yearbooks
    USE Church music—Almanacs, yearbooks, etc.

GEOGRAPHIC SUBDIVISIONS

  —England *(ML2931)*
    Note under Church music
  —France *(ML2927)*
    NT Maîtrises
Church music (Canon law)
Church musicians [May Subd Geog]
  UF Liturgical musicians
      Parish musicians
      Pastoral musicians
  BT Musicians
  NT Choirboys
      Organists
  —Catholic Church, [Presbyterian Church, etc.]
Chuvash folk-songs
  USE Folk-songs, Chuvash
Cimbalom *(ML1040)*
  UF Cymbalom
  BT Dulcimer
Cimbalom and flute music
  USE Flute and cimbalom music

Cimbalom and horn music
  USE Horn and cimbalom music
Cimbalom and piano music *(M284.C45; M285.C45)*
  UF Piano and cimbalom music
Cimbalom and violin music
  USE Violin and cimbalom music
Cimbalom and zither music *(M298)*
  UF Zither and cimbalom music
Cimbalom music *(M175.C5)*
  SA Concertos, Minuets, Sonatas, Suites, *and similar headings with specification of instruments;* Trios, Quartets, etc. *followed by specifications which include the cimbalom; also* Instrumental ensembles *and headings that begin with the words* Cimbalom *or* Cimbaloms
  NT Quartets (Cimbalom, violin, viola, double bass)
      Quintets (Cimbalom, violins (2), viola, violoncello)
      Suites (Cimbalom)
Cimbalom music (Cimbaloms (2)) *(M298)*
Cimbalom players [May Subd Geog]
Cimbalom with chamber orchestra *(M1039.4.C55)*
  RT Concertos (Cimbalom with chamber orchestra)
Cimbalom with instrumental ensemble
  RT Concertos (Cimbalom with instrumental ensemble)
Cimbalom with orchestra *(M1039.4.C55)*
  RT Concertos (Cimbalom)
Cimbaloms (2) with orchestra *(M1039.4.C55)*
Cîntece batrîneşti
  USE Ballads, Romanian
Citara
  USE Cithara
      Sitar
Cithara *(ML760)*
  UF Citara
      Kithara
  BT Cithern
      Musical instruments, Ancient
        —Greece
  NT Lyre-guitar
Cithara with orchestra *(M1037.4.C58)*
  RT Concertos (Cithara)
Cithern *(ML760)*
  UF Cittharn
  BT Guitar
  RT Zither
  NT Cithara
      English guitar
      Pandora (Musical instrument)
  —Methods *(MT599.C5)*
Cithern and lute music *(M292-293)*
  UF Lute and cithern music
Cithern and unspecified instrument music
  USE Duets (Unspecified instrument and cithern)
Cithern and vihuela music *(M292-293)*
  UF Vihuela and cithern music

Cithern music *(M142.C5)*
SA Concertos, Minuets, Sonatas, Suites, *and similar headings with specification of instruments; also* Trios [Quartets, etc.] *followed by specifications which include the cithern; also* Plectral ensembles; *and headings beginning with the words Cithern or Citherns*

Cittharn
USE Cithern

Clapper (Musical instrument)
BT Rattle

Clarinet *(History and construction, ML945-8)*
UF Clarionet
Primer clarinet
BT Woodwind instruments
NT Bass clarinet
Basset horn
Chalumeau (Single-reed musical instrument)
Clarinette d'amour
Tárogató
—Fingering charts
—Methods *(MT382)*
——Self-instruction *(MT388)*
UF Clarinet—Self-instruction
—Methods (Jazz) *(MT382)*
—Orchestra studies *(MT386)*
BT Clarinet—Studies and exercises
—Reeds
—Self-instruction
USE Clarinet—Methods—Self-instruction
—Studies and exercises *(MT385)*
NT Clarinet—Orchestra studies

Clarinet, English horn, flute, oboe with string orchestra *(M1105-6)*
BT Woodwind quartets (Clarinet, English horn, flute, oboe)
RT Concertos (Clarinet, English horn, flute, oboe with string orchestra)
NT Suites (Clarinet, English horn, flute, oboe with string orchestra)

Clarinet and bass clarinet music
USE Bass clarinet and clarinet music

Clarinet and basset-horn music
USE Basset-horn and clarinet music

Clarinet and bassoon music
USE Bassoon and clarinet music

Clarinet and continuo music
NT Sonatas (Clarinet and continuo)

Clarinet and double-bass music *(M290-291)*
UF Double-bass and clarinet music

Clarinet and English-horn music *(M288-289)*
UF English-horn and clarinet music

Clarinet and English horn with orchestra *(M1040-1041)*
RT Concertos (Clarinet and English horn)

Clarinet and flute music *(M288-9)*
UF Flute and clarinet music
NT Canons, fugues, etc. (Clarinet and flute)

Clarinet and flute music *(M288-9)*
(Continued)
NT Clarinet and flute with chamber orchestra
Clarinet and flute with string orchestra
Concertos (Clarinet and flute with chamber orchestra)
Concertos (Clarinet and flute with string orchestra)
Sonatas (Clarinet and flute)
Suites (Clarinet and flute)
Variations (Clarinet and flute)

Clarinet and flute with band *(M1205-1206)*
RT Concertos (Clarinet and flute with band)

Clarinet and flute with chamber orchestra *(M1040-1041)*
BT Chamber-orchestra music
Clarinet and flute music
RT Concertos (Clarinet and flute with chamber orchestra)
NT Suites (Clarinet and flute with chamber orchestra)

Clarinet and flute with orchestra *(M1040-1041)*
RT Concertos (Clarinet and flute)
—Solos with piano *(M1041)*
BT Trios (Piano, clarinet, flute), Arranged

Clarinet and flute with string orchestra *(M1105-6)*
BT Clarinet and flute music
RT Concertos (Clarinet and flute with string orchestra)
NT Suites (Clarinet and flute with string orchestra)
—Scores *(M1105)*

Clarinet and guitar music *(M296-7)*
UF Guitar and clarinet music

Clarinet and guitar music, Arranged *(M296-7)*

Clarinet and harp music *(M296-7)*
UF Harp and clarinet music
NT Clarinet and harp with string orchestra
Concertos (Clarinet and harp with string orchestra)
Sonatas (Clarinet and harp)
Variations (Clarinet and harp)

Clarinet and harp with string orchestra *(M1105-6)*
UF Harp and clarinet with string orchestra
BT Clarinet and harp music
RT Concertos (Clarinet and harp with string orchestra)

Clarinet and harpsichord music *(M248-252)*
UF Harpsichord and clarinet music

Clarinet and horn music *(M288-9)*
UF Horn and clarinet music
NT Variations (Clarinet and horn)

Clarinet and horn with orchestra *(M1040-1041)*
RT Concertos (Clarinet and horn)

Clarinet and koto music *(M296-297)*
UF Koto and clarinet music
NT Variations (Clarinet and koto)

Clarinet and marimba music *(M298)*
UF Marimba and clarinet music
Clarinet and oboe music *(M288-9)*
UF Oboe and clarinet music
NT Clarinet and oboe with orchestra
Concertos (Clarinet and oboe)
Suites (Clarinet and oboe)
Clarinet and oboe with orchestra *(M1040-1041)*
BT Clarinet and oboe music
RT Concertos (Clarinet and oboe)
—Scores *(M1040-1041)*
Clarinet and organ music *(M182-186)*
UF Organ and clarinet music
NT Chorale preludes(Clarinet and organ)
Clarinet and percussion music *(M298)*
UF Percussion and clarinet music
NT Canons, fugues, etc. (Clarinet and percussion)
Sonatas (Clarinet and percussion)
Clarinet and piano music *(M248-250)*
UF Piano and clarinet music
NT Canons, fugues, etc. (Clarinet and piano)
Marches (Clarinet and piano)
Minuets (Clarinet and piano)
Overtures (Clarinet and piano)
Rondos (Clarinet and piano)
Sonatas (Clarinet and piano)
Suites (Clarinet and piano)
Variations (Clarinet and piano)
Waltzes (Clarinet and piano)
Clarinet and piano music, Arranged *(M251-2)*
NT Clarinet with band—Solo with piano
Clarinet with chamber orchestra—Solo with piano
Clarinet with orchestra—Solo with piano
Clarinet with string orchestra—Solo with piano
Concertos (Clarinet)—Solo with piano
Concertos (Clarinet with band)—Solo with piano
Concertos (Clarinet with chamber orchestra)—Solo with piano
Concertos (Clarinet with string ensemble)—Solo with piano
Concertos (Clarinet with string orchestra)—Solo with piano
Concertos (Clarinet with string orchestra), Arranged—Solo with piano
Suites (Clarinet with orchestra)—Solo with piano
Suites (Clarinet with string orchestra)—Solo with piano
Variations (Clarinet with orchestra)—Solo with piano
Variations (Clarinet with string ensemble)—Solo with piano
Clarinet and piano music, Arranged (Jazz)
USE Clarinet and piano music (Jazz)

Clarinet and piano music (Jazz) *(M248-252)*
UF Clarinet and piano music, Arranged (Jazz)
Clarinet and piano with orchestra *(M1040-1041)*
RT Concertos (Clarinet and piano)
Clarinet and piccolo music *(M288-289)*
UF Piccolo and clarinet music
Clarinet and saxophone music *(M288-289)*
UF Saxophone and clarinet music
Clarinet and trombone music *(M288-289)*
UF Trombone and clarinet music
Clarinet and trumpet music *(M288-289)*
UF Trumpet and clarinet music
Clarinet and trumpet with band *(M1205-1206)*
RT Concertos (Clarinet and trumpet with band)
Clarinet and trumpet with string orchestra *(M1105-1106)*
RT Concertos (Clarinet and trumpet with string orchestra)
Clarinet and tuba music *(M288-9)*
UF Tuba and clarinet music
NT Suites (Clarinet and tuba)
Clarinet and vibraphone music *(M298)*
UF Vibraphone and clarinet music
NT Clarinet and vibraphone with string orchestra
Concertos (Clarinet and vibraphone with string orchestra)
Clarinet and vibraphone with string orchestra *(M1105-6)*
BT Clarinet and vibraphone music
RT Concertos (Clarinet and vibraphone with string orchestra)
Clarinet and viola music *(M290-291)*
UF Viola and clarinet music
Clarinet and viola with orchestra *(M1040-1041)*
RT Concertos (Clarinet and viola)
Clarinet and violin music *(M290-291)*
UF Violin and clarinet music
NT Clarinet and violin with orchestra
Clarinet and violin with string orchestra
Concertos (Clarinet and violin)
Concertos (Clarinet and violin with string orchestra)
Suites (Clarinet and violin)
Clarinet and violin music, Arranged *(M290-291)*
Clarinet and violin with orchestra *(M1040-1041)*
BT Clarinet and violin music
RT Concertos (Clarinet and violin)
Clarinet and violin with string orchestra *(M1105-6)*
BT Clarinet and violin music
RT Concertos (Clarinet and violin with string orchestra)
—Scores *(M1105)*

Clarinet and violoncello music
  UF Violoncello and clarinet music
  NT Clarinet and violoncello with orchestra
      Concertos (Clarinet and violoncello)
      Sonatas (Clarinet and violoncello)
      Suites (Clarinet and violoncello)
Clarinet and violoncello with orchestra
      (M1040-1041)
  BT Clarinet and violoncello music
  RT Concertos (Clarinet and violoncello)
Clarinet choir music
      Here are entered compositions for clari-
      nets, two or more to a part.
  BT Band music
  SA Concertos ([Solo instrument(s)] with clari-
      net choir); [Solo instrument(s)] with clari-
      net choir; Suites, Variations, Waltzes, *and
      similar headings with specification of instru-
      ments which include the specification Clari-
      net choir*
Clarinet d'amour
 · USE Clarinette d'amour
Clarinet ensembles *(M955-M956; M957.2;
      M958-M959)*
      Here are entered compositions for ten or
      more clarinets, one player to a part,
      and collections for a varying number of
      clarinets, one player to a part.
Clarinet, flute, harp with string orchestra
      (M1105-6)
  BT Trios (Clarinet, flute, harp)
  RT Concertos (Clarinet, flute, harp with
      string orchestra)
  —Scores and parts *(M1105)*
Clarinet, flute, oboe, harp, percussion with
      orchestra *(M1040-1041)*
  BT Quintets (Clarinet, flute, oboe, harp,
      percussion)
  RT Concertos (Clarinet, flute, oboe, harp,
      percussion)
Clarinet, flute, oboe with instrumental
      ensemble
  BT Woodwind trios (Clarinet, flute, oboe)
  RT Concertos (Clarinet, flute, oboe with
      instrumental ensemble)
Clarinet, flute, oboe with string orchestra
      (M1105-6)
  BT Woodwind trios (Clarinet, flute, oboe)
  RT Concertos (Clarinet, flute, oboe with
      string orchestra)
  —Scores *(M1105)*
Clarinet, flute, trumpet with string orchestra
      (M1105-6)
  BT String-orchestra music
      Wind trios (Clarinet, flute, trumpet)
  RT Concertos (Clarinet, flute, trumpet with
      string orchestra)
  NT Suites (Clarinet, flute, trumpet with
      string orchestra)
Clarinet, flute, violin, violoncello with
      chamber orchestra *(M1040-1041)*
  BT Quartets (Clarinet, flute, violin,
      violoncello)

Clarinet, flute, violin, violoncello with
      chamber orchestra *(M1040-1041)*
  (Continued)
  RT Concertos (Clarinet, flute, violin,
      violoncello with chamber orchestra)
Clarinet, harp, celesta, violin with string
      orchestra *(M1140-1141)*
  BT Quartets (Clarinet, harp, celesta, violin)
  RT Concertos (Clarinet, harp, celesta,
      violin with string orchestra)
Clarinet, harp, celesta with string orchestra
      (M1140-1141)
  BT Trios (Clarinet, harp, celesta)
  RT Concertos (Clarinet, harp, celesta
      with string orchestra)
Clarinet, harp, violin, violoncello with string
      orchestra *(M1105)*
  BT Quartets (Clarinet, harp, violin,
      violoncello)
      String-orchestra music
  RT Concertos (Clarinet, harp, violin,
      violoncello with string orchestra)
  —Scores *(M1105)*
Clarinet music *(M70-74)*
      Specification of clarinet in music head-
      ings includes all ranges of the instru-
      ment, except for bass clarinet, which is
      specified individually in headings with
      specifications for one or two solo in-
      struments.
  SA Concertos, Minuets, Sonatas, Suites,
      *and similar headings with
      specification of instruments;* Trios
      [Quartets, etc.], Wind trios [quartets,
      etc.], *and* Woodwind trios [quartets,
      etc.] *followed by specifications which
      include the clarinet; also* Wind
      ensembles, Woodwind ensembles,
      *and headings that begin with the
      words clarinet or clarinets*
  NT Recorded accompaniments (Clarinet)
      Sonatas (Clarinet)
      Suites (Clarinet)
  Notes under Wind instrument music; Wood-
      instrument music
Clarinet music (Clarinets (2)) *(M288-9)*
  NT Clarinets (2) with orchestra
      Clarinets (2) with string orchestra
      Concertos (Clarinets (2))
      Sonatas (Clarinets (2))
      Suites (Clarinets (2))
Clarinet music (Clarinets (2)), Arranged
      (M288-9)
Clarinet music (Clarinets (3))
  USE Woodwind trios (Clarinets (3))
Clarinet music (Clarinets (4))
  USE Woodwind quartets (Clarinets (4))
Clarinet music (Clarinets (5))
  USE Woodwind quintets (Clarinets (5))
Clarinet music (Clarinets (6))
  USE Woodwind sextets (Clarinets (6))
Clarinet music (Clarinets (7))
  USE Woodwind septets (Clarinets (7))

Clarinet music (Clarinets (8))
  USE Woodwind octets (Clarinets (8))
Clarinet music (Clarinets (9))
  USE Woodwind nonets (Clarinets (9))
Clarinet, oboe, violin with orchestra
      (M1040-1041)
  BT Trios (Clarinet, oboe, violin)
  RT Concertos (Clarinet, oboe, violin)
Clarinet players
  USE Clarinetists
Clarinet, trombone, trumpet with string
      orchestra *(M1105-6)*
  BT Wind trios (Clarinet, trombone,
      trumpet)
  RT Concertos (Clarinet, trombone, trumpet
      with string orchestra)
Clarinet with band *(M1205)*
  BT Band music
  RT Concertos (Clarinet with band)
  NT Variations (Clarinet with band)
  —Solo with piano *(M1206)*
      BT Clarinet and piano music, Arranged
Clarinet with brass ensemble *(M955-9)*
Clarinet with chamber orchestra *(M1024-5)*
  RT Concertos (Clarinet with chamber
      orchestra)
  NT Rondos (Clarinet with chamber
      orchestra)
  —Solo with piano *(M1025)*
      BT Clarinet and piano music, Arranged
Clarinet with chamber orchestra, Arranged
      (M1024-5)
  —Scores *(M1024)*
Clarinet with dance orchestra *(M1353)*
  RT Concertos (Clarinet with dance
      orchestra)
Clarinet with instrumental ensemble
  RT Concertos (Clarinet with instrumental
      ensemble)
Clarinet with jazz ensemble *(M955-7)*
  RT Concertos (Clarinet with jazz ensemble)
Clarinet with orchestra *(M1024-5)*
  RT Concertos (Clarinet)
  NT Suites (Clarinet with orchestra)
      Variations (Clarinet with orchestra)
  BT Concertos (Clarinet)
  —Solo with piano *(M1025)*
      BT Clarinet and piano music, Arranged
Clarinet with percussion ensemble
  RT Concertos (Clarinet with percussion
      ensemble)
Clarinet with string ensemble
  RT Concertos (Clarinet with string
      ensemble)
  NT Variations (Clarinet with string
      ensemble)
Clarinet with string orchestra *(M1105-6)*
  RT Concertos (Clarinet with string
      orchestra)
  NT Suites (Clarinet with string orchestra)
      Variations (Clarinet with string orchestra)
  —Solo with piano *(M1106)*
      BT Clarinet and piano music, Arranged

Clarinet with wind ensemble
  RT Concertos (Clarinet with wind ensemble)
Clarinetists
  UF Clarinet players
Clarinets (2), oboes (2) with string orchestra
      (M1140-1141)
  BT Woodwind quartets (Clarinets (2),
      oboes (2))
  RT Concertos (Clarinets (2), oboes (2) with
      string orchestra)
Clarinets (2) with orchestra *(M1024-5)*
  UF Two clarinets with orchestra
  BT Clarinet music (Clarinets (2))
  RT Concertos (Clarinets (2))
  —Scores *(M1024)*
Clarinets (2) with string orchestra
      (M1024-5)
  BT Clarinet music (Clarinets (2))
  RT Concertos (Clarinets (2) with string
      orchestra)
  NT Suites (Clarinets (2) with string
      orchestra)
Clarinets (3) with string orchestra
      (M1124-5)
  BT Woodwind trios (Clarinets (3))
  RT Concertos (Clarinets (3) with string
      orchestra)
Clarinets (4) with orchestra *(M1024-1025)*
  BT Woodwind quartets (Clarinets (4))
  RT Concertos (Clarinets (4))
  —Solos with piano *(M1025)*
      BT Quintets (Piano, clarinets (4)),
        Arranged
Clarinets (4) with string orchestra
      (M1124-1125)
  BT Woodwind quartets (Clarinets (4))
  RT Concertos (Clarinets (4) with string
      orchestra)
      Suites (Clarinets (4) with string
      orchestra)
  —Scores *(M1105)*
Clarinets (6) with band *(M1205-1206)*
  BT Woodwind sextets (Clarinets (6))
  RT Concertos (Clarinets (6) with band)
Clarinette d'amour
  UF Clarinet d'amour
      Clarinetto d'amore
  BT Clarinet
Clarinetto d'amore
  USE Clarinette d'amour
Clarionet
  USE Clarinet
Classical music
  USE Music
Classical period music
  USE *subdivisions* 18th century *and* 19th
      century *under music headings*
      Music—18th century
      Music—19th century
Classicism in music
  BT Music—Philosophy and aesthetics
      Style, Musical

Classification
  —Music *(ML111)*
    UF Music—Classification
    BT Music librarianship
  —Sound recordings *(Z697.P545)*
    UF Sound recordings—Classification
    BT Music librarianship
Clausulae (Cadences)
  USE Cadence (Music)
Clausulae (Part-songs)
  BT Part-songs
    Part-songs, Sacred
Clavecin
  USE Harpsichord
Claves
  BT Percussion instruments
Claves and oboe music
  USE Oboe and claves music
Claves music
Clavi-harp *(ML1091)*
  UF Claviharpe
    Keyed harp
  BT Harp
    Keyboard instruments
Clavi-harp music *(M175.C)*
Clavicembalo
  USE Harpsichord
Clavichord *(ML651; Tuning, MT165)*
  BT Piano
Clavichord makers [May Subd Geog]
  BT Musical instrument makers
Clavichord music *(M20-39)*
  BT Keyboard instrument music
    Piano music
  SA Concertos, Minuets, Sonatas, Suites
    and similar headings with
    specification of instruments;
    Trios, [Quartets, etc.] *followed by*
    specifications which include the
    clavichord; also headings that
    begin with the words Clavichord or
    Clavichords
Clavichord music, Arranged *(M32.8-38.5)*
Clavichord music (4 hands) *(M200-M204;*
    M207-M211)
  BT Piano music (4 hands)
Clavicylinder *(ML1055)*
  UF Euphonium (Chladni's)
Claviharpe
  USE Clavi-harp
Clavioline *(ML1092)*
  BT Musical instruments, Electronic
Clavioline music *(M175.C54)*
  NT Septets (Piano, guitar, clavioline,
    musical saw, percussion, vibraphone,
    xylophone)
Claviorganum *(ML651)*
  BT Harpsichord
    Organ
Claviorganum music *(M6-13)*
  BT Harpsichord music
    Organ music

Clock, Musical
  USE Musical clock
Clock chimes selections
  USE Chiming clock music
Clock music
  USE Chiming clock music
Clubs, Musical
  USE Music—Societies, etc.
Coda (Music)
  BT Musical form
Coeli enarrant (Music)
  USE Psalms (Music)—19th Psalm
Colascione
  USE Lute
College operas, revues, etc. *(M1504)*
    Subdivided by college or university.
  UF College revues
    Collegiate shows
  BT College theater
    Musical revues, comedies, etc.
    Operas
  RT Operatic scenes
College revues
  USE College operas, revues, etc.
College songs
  USE Students' songs
Collegiate shows
  USE College operas, revues, etc.
Color and music
  USE Music and color
Color-music
  USE Music and color
Comic opera
  USE Opera
    Operetta
    Zarzuela
Comic songs
  USE Humorous songs
Commercials, Singing
  USE Singing commercials
Communion-service music *(M2016.5; M2017;*
    M2017.2)
  BT Lord's Supper (Liturgy)
    Sacred vocal music
  RT Masses
Communism and music
  UF Music and communism
Community music [May Subd Geog] *(M1997.C5;*
    History and criticism, ML2500-ML2770;
    Instruction, MT875)
  UF Music, Community
    Singing, Community
  BT Choral societies
    Community art projects
  RT Music Week
  NT Music as recreation
    Music in the army
    Playground music
Community song-books
  USE Song-books
Compact disc industry [May Subd Geog]
    HD9697.P56-HD9697.P564

Compact disc players *(TK7881.75)*
  UF Audiodisc players
       CD players
       Digital audio disc players
       Disc players, Compact
       Players, Compact disc
  BT Phonograph
Compact discs
       TK7882.C56 (Technology)
  UF CDs (Compact discs)
       Compact disks
       Digital compact discs
       Discs, Compact
       Disks, Compact
  BT Optical storage devices
       Sound recordings
  NT CD-I technology
       CD-ROM
Compact disks
  USE Compact discs
Companies, Opera
  USE Opera companies
Complancha
  USE Laments
Compline music *(Catholic liturgical music, M2149.5.C6)*
Composers [May Subd Geog] *(Biography: collective, ML390; individual, ML410)*
  UF Music—Biography
       Songwriters
  BT Musicians
  NT Women composers
  —Autographs *(ML93-98)*
  —Dictionaries
     USE Music—Bio-bibliography
  —Czechoslovakia
  — —Slovak Socialist Republic
     UF Composers, Slovak
Composers, Afro-American
  USE Afro-American composers
Composers, Jewish [May Subd Geog]
  UF Composers, Yiddish
       Jewish composers
       Yiddish composers
Composers, Slovak
  USE Composers—Czechoslovakia—
       Slovak Socialist Republic
Composers, Women
  USE Women composers
Composers, Yiddish
  USE Composers, Jewish
Composers' sketches
  USE Musical sketches
Composition (Music) *(History, ML430-ML55; Instruction, MT40-MT67)*
  UF Music—Composition
       Musical composition
  BT Music
       Music—Instruction and study
       Music—Theory
  NT Chance composition
       Counterpoint
       Ground bass

Composition (Music) *(History, ML430-ML55; Instruction, MT40-MT67)*
  (Continued)
  NT Harmony
       Imitation (in music)
       Instrumentation and orchestration
       Melody
       Musical accompaniment
       Musical form
       Musical revue, comedy, etc.—Writing and publishing
       Popular music—Writing and publishing
       Symmetrical inversion (Music)
  —Mechanical aids
     NT Electronic composition
Compound stops
  USE Mixture stops
Computer composition
  BT Computer sound processing
       Electronic composition
  RT Computer music
Computer music
  UF Music, Computer
       Tape-recorder music
  BT Electronic music
       Music
       Technology and the arts
  RT Computer composition
Concert agents
  UF Concerts—Agents
  BT Commercial agents
  RT Impresarios
Concert halls
  USE Music-halls
Concerti grossi *(Orchestral accompaniment, M1040-M1041; String-orchestra accompaniment, M1140-M1141)*
  BT Concertos
  —Analytical guides *(MT125; MT130)*
  —Solos with piano *(M1041; M1106)*
Concerti grossi, Arranged *(M1040-1041)*
Concerti grossi arranged for band *(M1257)*
  BT Band music, Arranged
Concerti grossi arranged for organ *(M12-13)*
  BT Organ music, Arranged
Concerti grossi arranged for piano *(M37)*
  BT Piano music, Arranged
Concerti grossi arranged for piano (4 hands) *(M210)*
  BT Piano music (4 hands), Arranged
Concerti grossi arranged for piano (Pianos (2)) *(M215)*
  BT Piano music (Pianos (2)), Arranged
Concerti grossi arranged for string orchestra *(M1160)*
  BT String-orchestra music, Arranged
  —Scores *(M1160)*
Concertina *(History, ML1083; Instruction, MT681)*
  RT Accordion
       Bandonion
Concertina and guitar music
  UF Guitar and concertina music
  NT Potpourris (Concertina and guitar)

Concertina band
  USE Concertina ensembles
Concertina ensembles *(M1362)*
        Here are entered compositions for two or
          more concertinas.
  UF Concertina band
      Concertina orchestra
  BT Concertina music
      Instrumental music
Concertina music *(M154)*
  NT Concertina ensembles
Concertina orchestra
  USE Concertina ensembles
Concertina players [May Subd Geog]
Concerto [May Subd Geog] *(History, ML1263)*
Concerto grosso *(ML448)*
Concertos *(M1004.5-1041)*
        Here are entered collections of concertos
          for various instruments. Concertos for
          particular instruments or for full in-
          strumental ensemble (more performers
          than there are musical parts), are en-
          tered under the heading followed by
          the qualifier for the solo instrument(s)
          or the ensemble, *e.g.* Concertos
          (Piano); Concertos (Bassoon and clari-
          net); Concertos (Orchestra). For
          works for solo instrument(s) and ac-
          companiment other than orchestra,
          the full medium is expressed in the
          qualifier, *e.g.* Concertos (Flute with
          string orchestra); Concertos (Trumpet
          with band)
  BT Orchestral music
  NT Concerti grossi
  —Cadenzas *(M1004.6)*
        The subdivision is also used after the
          heading with a medium qualifier,
          e.g. Concertos (Piano)—Cadenzas.
      Example under reference from Cadenzas
Concertos (Accordion) *(M1039.4.A)*
  RT Accordion with orchestra
  —Solo with piano *(M1039.4.A3)*
      BT Accordion and piano music,
          Arranged
Concertos (Accordion with chamber orchestra)
        (M1039.4.A3)
  RT Accordion with chamber orchestra
  —Solo with piano *(M1039.4.A3)*
      BT Accordion and piano music,
          Arranged
Concertos (Accordion with plectral ensemble)
        (M1360)
  BT Plectral ensembles
  RT Accordion with plectral ensemble
  —Scores *(M1360)*
Concertos (Accordion with string ensemble)
  BT Accordion with string ensemble
Concertos (Accordion with string orchestra)
        (M1040-1041)
  RT Accordion with string orchestra
  —Scores *(M1105)*

Concertos (Bagpipe with band) *(M1205;*
        M1257)
  RT Bagpipe with band
Concertos (Balalaika) *(M1037.4.B3)*
  RT Balalaika with orchestra
  —Solo with piano *(M1037.4.B3)*
      BT Balalaika and piano music, Arranged
Concertos (Balalaika with chamber orchestra)
        (M1037.4.B3)
  BT Balalaika music
  RT Balalaika with chamber orchestra
  —Scores *(M1037.4.B3)*
Concertos (Band) *(M1203)*
  BT Band music
Concertos (Bandonion) *(M1039.4.B3)*
  RT Bandonion with orchestra
  —Solo with piano *(M1039.4.B3)*
      BT Bandonion and piano music,
          Arranged
**Concertos (Bandonion with chamber
        orchestra)** *(M1039.4.B3)*
  RT Bandonion with chamber orchestra
  —Solo with piano *(M1039.4.B3)*
      BT Bandonion and piano music,
          Arranged
Concertos (Baritone with string orchestra)
        (M1134.B37; M1135.B37)
  RT Baritone with string orchestra
Concertos (Bass clarinet) *(M1024-1025)*
  RT Bass clarinet with orchestra
**Concertos (Bass clarinet with chamber
        orchestra)** *(M1024-1025)*
  RT Bass clarinet with chamber orchestra
**Concertos (Bass clarinet with instrumental
        ensemble)**
  RT Bass clarinet with instrumental ensemble
Concertos (Bass clarinet with string ensemble)
  RT Bass clarinet with string ensemble
**Concertos (Bass clarinet with string
        orchestra)** *(M1124-1125)*
  BT Bass clarinet with string ensemble
  NT Bass clarinet with string orchestra
Concertos (Bass trombone) *(M1032-1033)*
  RT Bass trombone with orchestra
Concertos (Bass trombone with band)
        (M1205-M1206; M1257)
  RT Bass trombone with band
**Concertos (Bass trombone with instrumental
        ensemble)**
  RT Bass trombone with instrumental
      ensemble
Concertos (Basset clarinet) *(M1024-M1025)*
  BT Basset clarinet with orchestra
Concertos (Basset horn) *(M1034.B38;*
        M1035.B38)
  RT Basset horn with orchestra
  —Solo with piano *(M1035.B38)*
      BT Basset horn and piano music,
          Arranged
Concertos (Basset horn and clarinet)
        (M1040-1041)
  RT Basset horn and clarinet with orchestra

Concertos (Basset horn with chamber orchestra) *(M1034.B38; M1035.B38)*
RT   Basset horn with chamber orchestra

Concertos (Bassoon) *(M1026-7)*
RT   Bassoon with orchestra
—Cadenzas *(M1004.7; M1026.5)*
—Solo with piano *(M1027)*
BT   Bassoon and piano music, Arranged

Concertos (Bassoon and clarinet) *(M1040-1041)*
BT   Bassoon and clarinet music
RT   Bassoon and clarinet with orchestra
—Solos with piano *(M1041)*
BT   Trios (Piano, bassoon, clarinet), Arranged
Note under Concertos

Concertos (Bassoon and clarinet with string orchestra) *(M1105-6)*
BT   Bassoon and clarinet music
String-orchestra music
RT   Bassoon and clarinet with string orchestra

Concertos (Bassoon and flute with string orchestra) *(M1140-1141)*
BT   Bassoon and flute music
RT   Bassoon and flute with string orchestra

Concertos (Bassoon and oboe) *(M1040-1041)*
BT   Bassoon and oboe music
RT   Bassoon and oboe with orchestra

Concertos (Bassoon and oboe with string orchestra) *(M1105-6)*
BT   Bassoon and oboe music
RT   Bassoon and oboe with string orchestra
—Solos with piano *(M1106)*
BT   Trios (Piano, bassoon, oboe), Arranged

Concertos (Bassoon and piccolo with string orchestra) *(M1105-6)*
BT   Bassoon and piccolo music
RT   Bassoon and piccolo with string orchestra
—Scores *(M1105)*

Concertos (Bassoon and recorder with string orchestra) *(M1105-6)*
BT   Bassoon and recorder music
RT   Bassoon and recorder with string orchestra

Concertos (Bassoon and trumpet with string orchestra) *(M1105-6)*
BT   Bassoon and trumpet music
RT   Bassoon and trumpet with string orchestra
—Solos with piano *(M1106)*
BT   Trios (Piano, bassoon, trumpet), Arranged

Concertos (Bassoon and violin with chamber orchestra) *(M1040-M1041)*
BT   Bassoon and violin with chamber orchestra

Concertos (Bassoon and violin with instrumental ensemble)
RT   Bassoon and violin with instrumental ensemble

Concertos (Bassoon and violin with string orchestra) *(M1105-6)*
BT   Bassoon and violin music
RT   Bassoon and violin with string orchestra
—Solos with piano *(M1106)*
BT   Trios (Piano, bassoon, violin), Arranged

Concertos (Bassoon and violoncello) *(M1040-1041)*
RT   Bassoon and violoncello with orchestra

Concertos (Bassoon, clarinet, English horn, flute) *(M1040-1041)*
BT   Orchestral music
Woodwind quartets (Bassoon, clarinet, English horn, flute)
RT   Bassoon, clarinet, English horn, flute with orchestra
—Solos with piano *(M1041)*
BT   Quintets (Piano, bassoon, clarinet, English horn, flute), Arranged

Concertos (Bassoon, clarinet, flute, horn) *(M1040-1041)*
BT   Wind quartets (Bassoon, clarinet, flute, horn)
RT   Bassoon, clarinet, flute, horn with orchestra

Concertos (Bassoon, clarinet, flute, horn, oboe) *(M1040-1041)*
BT   Wind quintets (Bassoon, clarinet, flute, horn, oboe)
RT   Bassoon, clarinet, flute, horn, oboe with orchestra
—Scores *(M1040)*

Concertos (Bassoon, clarinet, flute, horn, oboe with band) *(M1205-6)*
BT   Band music
Wind quintets (Bassoon, clarinet, flute, horn, oboe)
RT   Bassoon, clarinet, flute, horn, oboe with band
—Scores and parts *(M1205)*

Concertos (Bassoon, clarinet, flute, horn, oboe with chamber orchestra) *(M1040-1041)*
BT   Chamber-orchestra music
Wind quintets (Bassoon, clarinet, flute, horn, oboe)
RT   Bassoon, clarinet, flute, horn, oboe with chamber orchestra

Concertos (Bassoon, clarinet, flute, horn, oboe with string orchestra) *(M1105-6)*
BT   Wind quintets (Bassoon, clarinet, flute, horn, oboe)
RT   Bassoon, clarinet, flute, horn, oboe with string orchestra
—Solos with piano *(M1106)*
BT   Sextets (Piano, bassoon, clarinet, flute, horn, oboe), Arranged

Concertos (Bassoon, clarinet, flute, horn, violoncello with string orchestra) *(M1105-6)*
BT   Quintets (Bassoon, clarinet, flute, horn, violoncello)

Concertos (Bassoon, clarinet, flute, horn, violoncello with string orchestra) *(M1105-6) (Continued)*

RT Bassoon, clarinet, flute, horn, violoncello with string orchestra

Concertos (Bassoon, clarinet, flute, oboe) *(M1040-1041)*

BT Woodwind quartets (Bassoon, clarinet, flute, oboe)

RT Bassoon, clarinet, flute, oboe with orchestra

—Solos with piano *(M1041)*

BT Quintets (Piano, bassoon, clarinet, flute, oboe), Arranged

Concertos (Bassoon, clarinet, flute, oboe, harp) *(M1040-1041)*

BT Quintets (Bassoon, clarinet, flute, oboe, harp)

RT Bassoon, clarinet, flute, oboe, harp with orchestra

—Scores *(M1040)*

Concertos (Bassoon, clarinet, flute, oboe, violins (2), viola, violoncello with string orchestra)

BT Bassoon, clarinet, flute, oboe, violins (2), viola, violoncello with string orchestra

Octets (Bassoon, clarinet, flute, oboe, violins (2), viola, violoncello)

String-orchestra music

Concertos (Bassoon, clarinet, flute, oboe with chamber orchestra) *(M1040-1041)*

BT Chamber-orchestra music

Woodwind quartets (Bassoon, clarinet, flute, oboe)

RT Bassoon, clarinet, flute, oboe with chamber orchestra

Concertos (Bassoon, clarinet, flute, oboe with string orchestra) *(M1105-6)*

BT Woodwind quartets (Bassoon, clarinet, flute, oboe)

RT Bassoon, clarinet, flute, oboe with string orchestra

—Scores *(M1105-6)*

Concertos (Bassoon, clarinet, flute, trumpet with string orchestra) *(M1105-6)*

BT Wind quartets (Bassoon, clarinet, flute, trumpet)

RT Bassoon, clarinet, flute, trumpet with string orchestra

Concertos (Bassoon, clarinet, flute with string orchestra) *(M1105-6)*

BT Woodwind trios (Bassoon, clarinet, flute)

RT Bassoon, clarinet, flute with string orchestra

Concertos (Bassoon, clarinet, horn, oboe) *(M1040-1041)*

BT Wind quartets (Bassoon, clarinet, horn, oboe)

RT Bassoon, clarinet, horn, oboe with orchestra

Concertos (Bassoon, clarinet, horn, oboe) *(M1040-1041)* *(Continued)*

—Solos with piano *(M1041)*

BT Quintets (Piano, bassoon, clarinet, horn, oboe), Arranged

Concertos (Bassoon, clarinet, horn, oboe with string orchestra) *(M1140-1)*

BT Wind quartets (Bassoon, clarinet, horn, oboe)

RT Bassoon, clarinet, horn, oboe with string orchestra

—Scores *(M1105-6)*

Concertos (Bassoon, clarinet, oboe, violin, viola, violoncello) *(M1040-1041)*

BT Sextets (Bassoon, clarinet, oboe, violin, viola, violoncello)

RT Bassoon, clarinet, oboe, violin, viola, violoncello with orchestra

Concertos (Bassoon, clarinet, oboe with string orchestra) *(M1105-6)*

BT Woodwind trios (Bassoon, clarinet, oboe)

RT Bassoon, clarinet, oboe with string orchestra

Concertos (Bassoon, clarinet, trumpet) *(M1040-1041)*

BT Wind trios (Bassoon, clarinet, trumpet)

RT Bassoon, clarinet, trumpet with orchestra

—Scores *(M1040)*

Concertos (Bassoon, clarinet, trumpet with string orchestra) *(M1140-1141)*

BT Wind trios (Bassoon, clarinet, trumpet)

RT Bassoon, clarinet, trumpet with string orchestra

Concertos (Bassoon, clarinets (2), oboe) *(M1040-1041)*

BT Woodwind quartets (Bassoon, clarinets (2), oboe)

RT Bassoon, clarinets (2), oboe with orchestra

Concertos (Bassoon, flute, horn, oboe) *(M1040-1041)*

BT Wind quartets (Bassoon, flute, horn, oboe)

RT Bassoon, flute, horn, oboe with orchestra

—Solos with piano *(M1041)*

BT Quintets (Piano, bassoon, flute, horn, oboe), Arranged

Concertos (Bassoon, flute, horn, oboe), Arranged *(M1040-1041)*

Concertos (Bassoon, flute, horn, oboe, trumpet with string orchestra) *(M1140-1141)*

BT Wind quintets (Bassoon, flute, horn, oboe, trumpet)

RT Bassoon, flute, horn, oboe, trumpet with string orchestra

Concertos (Bassoon, flute, horn, oboe with chamber orchestra) *(M1040-1041)*
- BT Chamber-orchestra music
  Wind quartets (Bassoon, flute, horn, oboe)
- RT Bassoon, flute, horn, oboe with chamber orchestra

Concertos (Bassoon, flute, horn, oboe with string orchestra) *(M1105-6)*
- BT Wind quartets (Bassoon, flute, horn, oboe)
- RT Bassoon, flute, horn, oboe with string orchestra

Concertos (Bassoon, flute, oboe) *(M1040-1041)*
- BT Woodwind trios (Bassoon, flute, oboe)
- RT Bassoon, flute, oboe with orchestra

Concertos (Bassoon, flute, violin, violoncello) *(M1040-1041)*
- BT Quartets (Bassoon, flute, violin, violoncello)
- RT Bassoon, flute, violin, violoncello with orchestra

Concertos (Bassoon, flutes (2) with string orchestra) *(M1140-1141)*
- BT Woodwind trios (Bassoon, flutes (2))
- RT Bassoon, flutes (2) with string orchestra

Concertos (Bassoon, horn, trumpet, double bass) *(M1040-1041)*
- BT Quartets (Bassoon, horn, trumpet, double bass)
- RT Bassoon, horn, trumpet, double bass with orchestra

Concertos (Bassoon, oboe, trumpet with string orchestra) *(M1105-6)*
- BT Wind trios (Bassoon, oboe, trumpet)
- RT Bassoon, oboe, trumpet with string orchestra

Concertos (Bassoon, oboe, violin, viola) *(M1040-1041)*
- BT Quartets (Bassoon, oboe, violin, viola)
- RT Bassoon, oboe, violin, viola with orchestra

Concertos (Bassoon, oboe, violin, violoncello) *(M1040-1041)*
- BT Quartets (Bassoon, oboe, violin, violoncello)
- RT Bassoon, oboe, violin, violoncello with orchestra

Concertos (Bassoon, oboe, violin, violoncello with chamber orchestra) *(M1040-1041)*
- BT Chamber-orchestra music
  Quartets (Bassoon, oboe, violin, violoncello)
- RT Bassoon, oboe, violin, violoncello with chamber orchestra

Concertos (Bassoon, violins (2) with string orchestra) *(M1140-1141)*
- BT Trios (Bassoon, violins (2))
- RT Bassoon, violins (2) with string orchestra

Concertos (Bassoon with band) *(M1205-6)*
- RT Bassoon with band

Concertos (Bassoon with band), Arranged *(M1205-M1206)*
- —Solo with piano *(M1206)*
  - BT Bassoon and piano music, Arranged

Concertos (Bassoon with chamber orchestra) *(M1026-7)*
- RT Bassoon with chamber orchestra
- —Scores *(M1026)*
- —Solo with piano *(M1027)*
  - BT Bassoon and piano music, Arranged

Concertos (Bassoon with instrumental ensemble)
- NT Bassoon with instrumental ensemble

Concertos (Bassoon with string ensemble)
- RT Bassoon with string ensemble
- —Solo with piano *(M253-254)*
  - BT Bassoon and piano music, Arranged

Concertos (Bassoon with string orchestra) *(M1105-6)*
- RT Bassoon with string orchestra
- —Solo with piano *(M1106)*
  - BT Bassoon and piano music, Arranged

Concertos (Bassoon with string orchestra), Arranged *(M1105-6)*
- —Solo with piano *(M1106)*
  - BT Bassoon and piano music, Arranged

Concertos (Bassoon with wind ensemble)
- BT Bassoon with wind ensemble

Concertos (Bassoons (2))
  M1026-M1027
- BT Bassoons (2) with orchestra

Concertos (Bassoons (2) with string orchestra) *(M1126-1127)*
- RT Bassoons (2) with string orchestra
- —Solos with piano *(M1127)*
  - BT Trios (Piano, bassoons (2)), Arranged

Concertos (Brass ensemble)
- RT Brass ensemble with orchestra

Concertos (Carillon) *(M1038-1039)*
- RT Carillon with orchestra

Concertos (Carillon with band) *(M1205-6)*
- BT Carillon music
- RT Carillon with band

Concertos (Carillon with instrumental ensemble)
- RT Carillon with instrumental ensemble

Concertos (Castanets with chamber orchestra) *(M1038-1039)*
- RT Castanets with chamber orchestra

Concertos (Chamber orchestra) *(M1042)*
- BT Chamber-orchestra music

Concertos (Chimes, xylophone, violins (2), viola, violoncello with string orchestra) *(M1140-1141)*
- BT Sextets (Chimes, xylophone, violins (2), viola, violoncello)
- RT Chimes, xylophone, violins (2), viola, violoncello with string orchestra

Concertos (Cimbalom) *(M1039.C55)*
- RT Cimbalom with orchestra

Concertos (Cimbalom with chamber orchestra) *(M1039.4.C55)*
- RT Cimbalom with chamber orchestra

Concertos (Cimbalom with instrumental
       ensemble)
RT Cimbalom with instrumental ensemble
Concertos (Cithara) *(M1037.4.C58)*
RT Cithara with orchestra
Concertos (Clarinet) *(M1024-5)*
RT Clarinet with orchestra
—Solo with piano *(M1025)*
    BT Clarinet and piano music, Arranged
Concertos (Clarinet and English horn) *(M1040-1041)*
RT Clarinet and English horn with orchestra
—Solos with piano *(M1041)*
    BT Trios (Piano, clarinet, English horn),
          Arranged
Concertos (Clarinet and flute) *(M1040-1041)*
RT Clarinet and flute with orchestra
Concertos (Clarinet and flute with band)
       (M1205-1206)
RT Clarinet and flute with band
Concertos (Clarinet and flute with chamber
       orchestra) *(M1040-1041)*
BT Chamber-orchestra music
     Clarinet and flute music
RT Clarinet and flute with chamber
     orchestra
Concertos (Clarinet and flute with string
       orchestra)
BT Clarinet and flute music
RT Clarinet and flute with string orchestra
Concertos (Clarinet and harp with string
       orchestra) *(M1105-6)*
BT Clarinet and harp music
     String-orchestra music
RT Clarinet and harp with string orchestra
Concertos (Clarinet and horn) *(M1040-1041)*
RT Clarinet and horn with orchestra
Concertos (Clarinet and oboe) *(M1040-1041)*
BT Clarinet and oboe music
RT Clarinet and oboe with orchestra
Concertos (Clarinet and piano)
       (M1040-1041)
RT Clarinet and piano with orchestra
Concertos (Clarinet and trumpet with band)
       (M1205-1206)
RT Clarinet and trumpet with band
—Solos with piano *(M1206)*
    BT Trios (Piano, clarinet, trumpet),
          Arranged
Concertos (Clarinet and trumpet with string
       orchestra) *(M1105-1106)*
RT Clarinet and trumpet with string
     orchestra
Concertos (Clarinet and vibraphone with
       string orchestra) *(M1105-6)*
BT Clarinet and vibraphone music
RT Clarinet and vibraphone with string
     orchestra
—Scores *(M1105)*
Concertos (Clarinet and viola) *(M1040-1041)*
RT Clarinet and viola with orchestra
—Solos with piano *(M1041)*
    BT Trios (Piano, clarinet, viola),
          Arranged

Concertos (Clarinet and violin)
       (M1040-1041)
BT Clarinet and violin music
RT Clarinet and violin with orchestra
—Solos with piano *(M1041)*
    BT Trios (Piano, clarinet, violin),
          Arranged
Concertos (Clarinet and violin with string
       orchestra) *(M1105-6)*
BT Clarinet and violin music
RT Clarinet and violin with string orchestra
—Solos with piano *(M1141)*
    BT Trios (Piano, clarinet, violin),
          Arranged
Concertos (Clarinet and violoncello) *(M1040-1041)*
BT Clarinet and violoncello music
RT Clarinet and violoncello with orchestra
—Solos with piano *(M1041)*
    BT Trios (Piano, clarinet, violoncello),
          Arranged
Concertos (Clarinet, English horn, flute, oboe
       with string orchestra) *(M1105-6)*
BT Woodwind quartets (Clarinet, English
     horn, flute, oboe)
RT Clarinet, English horn, flute, oboe with
     string orchestra
Concertos (Clarinet, flute, harp with string
       orchestra) *(M1105-6)*
BT Trios (Clarinet, flute, harp)
RT Clarinet, flute, harp with string
     orchestra
Concertos (Clarinet, flute, oboe, harp,
       percussion) *(M1040-1041)*
BT Quintets (Clarinet, flute, oboe, harp,
     percussion)
RT Clarinet, flute, oboe, harp, percussion
     with orchestra
Concertos (Clarinet, flute, oboe with
       instrumental ensemble)
BT Woodwind trios (Clarinet, flute, oboe)
RT Clarinet, flute, oboe with instrumental
     ensemble
Concertos (Clarinet, flute, oboe with string
       orchestra) *(M1105-6)*
BT Woodwind trios (Clarinet, flute, oboe)
RT Clarinet, flute, oboe with string orchestra
Concertos (Clarinet, flute, trumpet with string
       orchestra) *(M1105-6)*
BT String-orchestra music
     Wind trios (Clarinet, flute, trumpet)
RT Clarinet, flute, trumpet with string
     orchestra
Concertos (Clarinet, flute, violin, violoncello
       with chamber orchestra) *(M1040-1041)*
BT Quartets (Clarinet, flute, violin,
     violoncello)
RT Clarinet, flute, violin, violoncello with
     chamber orchestra
Concertos (Clarinet, harp, celesta, violin with
       string orchestra)
BT Quartets (Clarinet, harp, celesta, violin)
RT Clarinet, harp, celesta, violin with string
     orchestra

Concertos (Clarinet, harp, celesta with string orchestra) *(M1140-1141)*
  BT Trios (Clarinet, harp, celesta)
  RT Clarinet, harp, celesta with string orchestra

Concertos (Clarinet, harp, violin, violoncello with string orchestra) *(M1105)*
  BT Quartets (Clarinet, harp, violin, violoncello)
  RT Clarinet, harp, violin, violoncello with string orchestra

Concertos (Clarinet, oboe, violin) *(M1040-1041)*
  BT Trios (Clarinet, oboe, violin)
  RT Clarinet, oboe, violin with orchestra

Concertos (Clarinet, trombone, trumpet with string orchestra) *(M1105-6)*
  BT Wind trios (Clarinet, trombone, trumpet)
  RT Clarinet, trombone, trumpet with string orchestra
  —Scores *(M1105)*
  —Solos with piano *(M1106)*
      BT Quartets (Piano, clarinet, trombone, trumpet), Arranged

Concertos (Clarinet with band) *(M1205)*
  RT Clarinet with band
  —Solo with piano *(M1205)*
      BT Clarinet and piano music, Arranged

Concertos (Clarinet with chamber orchestra) *(M1024-5)*
  RT Clarinet with chamber orchestra
  —Solo with piano *(M1025)*
      BT Clarinet and piano music, Arranged

Concertos (Clarinet with dance orchestra) *(M1353)*
  RT Clarinet with dance orchestra
  —Scores *(M1353)*

Concertos (Clarinet with instrumental ensemble)
  RT Clarinet with instrumental ensemble

Concertos (Clarinet with jazz ensemble) *(M955-7)*
  RT Clarinet with jazz ensemble

Concertos (Clarinet with percussion ensemble)
  RT Clarinet with percussion ensemble

Concertos (Clarinet with string ensemble)
  RT Clarinet with string ensemble
  —Solo with piano
      BT Clarinet and piano music, Arranged

Concertos (Clarinet with string orchestra) *(M1105-6)*
  RT Clarinet with string orchestra
  —Solo with piano *(M1106)*
      BT Clarinet and piano music, Arranged

Concertos (Clarinet with string orchestra), Arranged *(M1105-6)*
  —Solo with piano *(M1106)*
      BT Clarinet and piano music, Arranged

Concertos (Clarinet with wind ensemble)
  RT Clarinet with wind ensemble

Concertos (Clarinets (2)) *(M1024-5)*
  BT Clarinet music (Clarinets (2))
      Orchestral music
  RT Clarinets (2) with orchestra

Concertos (Clarinets (2), oboes (2) with string orchestra) *(M1140-1141)*
  BT Woodwind quartets (Clarinets (2), oboes (2))
  RT Clarinets (2), oboes (2) with string orchestra

Concertos (Clarinets (2) with string orchestra) *(M1124-1125)*
  RT Clarinets (2) with string orchestra
  —Solos with piano *(M1125)*
      BT Trios (Piano, clarinets (2)), Arranged

Concertos (Clarinets (3) with string orchestra) *(M1124-1125)*
  BT Woodwind trios (Clarinets (3))
  RT Clarinets (3) with string orchestra

Concertos (Clarinets (4)) *(M1024-1025)*
  BT Woodwind quartets (Clarinets (4))
  RT Clarinets (4) with orchestra

Concertos (Clarinets (4) with string orchestra) *(M1124-1125)*
  BT Woodwind quartets (Clarinets (4))
  RT Clarinets (4) with string orchestra

Concertos (Clarinets (6) with band) *(M1205-1206)*
  BT Woodwind sextets (Clarinets (6))
  RT Clarinets (6) with band

Concertos (Contrabassoon with string ensemble)
  RT Contrabassoon with string ensemble

Concertos (Cornet) *(M1030-1031)*
  BT Cornet music
  RT Concertos (Trumpet)
      Cornet with orchestra

Concertos (Cornet and euphonium with brass band) *(M1205-1206; 1257)*
  RT Cornet and euphonium with brass band

Concertos (Cornet and trumpet) *(M1040-1041)*
  BT Cornet and trumpet music
  RT Cornet and trumpet with orchestra

Concertos (Cornet with band) *(M1205)*
  BT Band music
  RT Cornet with band

Concertos (Cornet with brass band) *(M1205-M1206; M1257)*
  RT Cornet with brass band

Concertos (Cornet with instrumental ensemble)
  RT Cornet with instrumental ensemble

Concertos (Cornet with string orchestra) *(M1130-1131)*
  RT Cornet with string orchestra
  —Solo with piano *(M1131)*
      BT Cornet and piano music, Arranged

Concertos (Cornets (4) with band) *(M1205-1206)*
  BT Brass quartets (Cornets (4))
  RT Cornets (4) with band

Concertos (Dance orchestra) *(M1356)*
  BT Dance-orchestra music

Concertos (Dobro with instrumental ensemble)
  RT Dobro with instrumental ensemble

Concertos (Domra) *(M1037.4.D64)*
  BT Domra music
  RT Domra with orchestra
  —Solo with piano *(M1037.4.D64)*
      BT Domra and piano music, Arranged
Concertos (Domra with chamber orchestra)
      (M1037.4.D64)
  BT Domra music
  RT Domra with chamber orchestra
  —Solo with piano *(M1037.4.D64)*
      BT Domra and piano music, Arranged
Concertos (Double bass) *(M1018)*
  RT Double bass with orchestra
  —Solo with piano *(M1018)*
      BT Double-bass and piano music,
         Arranged
Concertos (Double bass), Arranged *(M1018)*
  —Solo with piano *(M1018)*
      BT Double-bass and piano music,
         Arranged
Concertos (Double bass with band)
      (M1205-6)
  RT Double bass with band
  —Solo with piano *(M1206)*
      BT Double-bass and piano music,
         Arranged
Concertos (Double bass with chamber
      orchestra) *(M1018)*
  BT Chamber-orchestra music
  RT Double bass with chamber orchestra
Concertos (Double bass with instrumental
      ensemble)
  RT Double bass with instrumental
      ensemble
Concertos (Double bass with string orchestra)
      (M1118)
  BT String-orchestra music
  RT Double bass with string orchestra
  —Solo with piano *(M1118)*
      BT Double-bass and piano music,
         Arranged
Concertos (Double basses (2)) *(M1018)*
  RT Double basses (2) with orchestra
  —Solos with piano *(M1018)*
      BT Trios (Piano, double basses (2)),
         Arranged
Concertos (Dulcimer with string orchestra)
  RT Dulcimer with string orchestra
Concertos (Electronic organ)
      (M1005-M1006)
  BT Electronic organ with orchestra
Concertos (English horn) *(M1034.E5;*
      M1035.E5)
  RT English horn with orchestra
Concertos (English horn and flute with string
      orchestra) *(M1105-6)*
  BT English horn and flute music
  RT English horn and flute with string
      orchestra
  —Solos with piano *(M1106)*
      BT Trios (Piano, English horn, flute),
         Arranged

Concertos (English horn and harp with string
      orchestra) *(M1105-6)*
  BT English horn and harp music
  RT English horn and harp with string
      orchestra
Concertos (English horn and harpsichord
      with string orchestra) *(M1140-M1141)*
  BT English horn and harpsichord music
Concertos (English horn and oboe with string
      orchestra) *(M1105-6)*
  BT English horn and oboe music
  RT English horn and oboe with string
      orchestra
Concertos (English horn and trumpet with
      string orchestra) *(M1105-6)*
  BT English horn and trumpet music
  RT English horn and trumpet with string
      orchestra
Concertos (English horn and violoncello)
      (M1040-1041)
  RT English horn and violoncello with
      orchestra
Concertos (English horn, flute, viola,
      violoncello with string orchestra)
      (M1140-1141)
  BT Quartets (English horn, flute, viola,
      violoncello)
  RT English horn, flute, viola, violoncello
      with string orchestra
Concertos (English horn with chamber
      orchestra) *(M1034-5)*
  RT English horn with chamber orchestra
  —Scores *(M1034)*
  —Solo with piano *(M1035.E5)*
      BT English horn and piano music,
         Arranged
Concertos (English horn with string orchestra)
      (M1105-6)
  RT English horn with string orchestra
  —Scores *(M1105)*
  —Solo with piano *(M1106)*
      BT English horn and piano music,
         Arranged
Concertos (English horns (2)) *(M1134.E5;*
      M1135.E5)
  BT English-horn music (English horns (2))
      with string orchestra
Concertos (English horns (2) with string
      orchestra) *(M1134.E5; M1135.E5)*
  BT English-horn music (English horns (2))
  RT English horns (2) with string orchestra
Concertos (Euphonium, horns (4) with band)
      (M1205-1206)
  BT Brass quintets (Euphonium, horns (4))
  RT Euphonium, horns (4) with band
Concertos (Euphonium with band)
      (M1205-M1206; M1257)
  RT Euphonium with band
Concertos (Euphonium with wind ensemble)
  RT Euphonium with wind ensemble
Concertos (Euphoniums (2) with band)
      (M1205-M1206; M1257)
  RT Euphoniums (2) with band

Concertos (Fluegelhorn with string orchestra)
    (M1134.F7; M1135.F7)
  RT Fluegelhorn with string orchestra
Concertos (Flute) *(M1020-1021)*
  RT Flute with orchestra
  NT Concertos (Recorder)
  —Cadenzas *(M1004.7; M1020.5)*
  —Solo with piano *(M1021)*
      BT Flute and piano music, Arranged
Concertos (Flute and guitar) *(M1040-1041)*
  RT Flute and guitar with orchestra
Concertos (Flute and guitar with string orchestra) *(M1140-1141)*
  RT Flute and guitar with string orchestra
Concertos (Flute and harp) *(M1040-1041)*
  BT Flute and harp music
  RT Flute and harp with orchestra
  —Solos with piano *(M1041)*
      BT Trios (Piano, flute, harp), Arranged
Concertos (Flute and harp with string ensemble)
  RT Flute and harp with string ensemble
Concertos (Flute and harp with string orchestra) *(M1105-6)*
  BT Flute and harp music
      String-orchestra music
  RT Flute and harp with string orchestra
Concertos (Flute and harpsichord with string ensemble)
  BT Flute and harpsichord with string ensemble
Concertos (Flute and harpsichord with string orchestra) *(M1105-6)*
  BT Flute and harpsichord music
  RT Flute and harpsichord with string orchestra
  —Scores *(M1105)*
Concertos (Flute and horn with string orchestra) *(M1105-6)*
  BT Flute and horn music
      String-orchestra music
  RT Flute and horn with string orchestra
  —Solos with piano *(M1106)*
      BT Trios (Piano, flute, horn),
          Arranged
Concertos (Flute and oboe) *(M1040-1041)*
  BT Flute and oboe music
  RT Flute and oboe with orchestra
  —Solos with piano *(M1041)*
      BT Trios (Piano, flute, oboe),
          Arranged
Concertos (Flute and oboe d'amore with string orchestra) *(M1140-1141)*
  RT Flute and oboe d'amore with string orchestra
Concertos (Flute and oboe with chamber orchestra) *(M1040-1041)*
  BT Flute and oboe music
  RT Flute and oboe with chamber orchestra
Concertos (Flute and oboe with chamber orchestra), Arranged
    (M1040-1041)

Concertos (Flute and oboe with string orchestra) *(M1105-6)*
  BT Flute and oboe music
      String-orchestra music
  RT Flute and oboe with string orchestra
Concertos (Flute and percussion with string orchestra) *(M1105-6)*
  BT Flute and percussion music
  RT Flute and percussion with string orchestra
  —Scores *(M1105)*
Concertos (Flute and piano) *(M1040-1041)*
  RT Flute and piano with orchestra
Concertos (Flute and piano with string ensemble)
  BT Flute and piano with string ensemble
Concertos (Flute and piano with string orchestra) *(M1105-6)*
  BT Flute and piano music
  RT Flute and piano with string orchestra
Concertos (Flute and recorder with string orchestra) *(M1105-6)*
  BT Flute and recorder music
  RT Flute and recorder with string orchestra
Concertos (Flute and trombone with chamber orchestra) *(M1040-1041)*
  BT Flute and trombone music
  RT Flute and trombone with chamber orchestra
Concertos (Flute and trumpet with string orchestra) *(M1105-6)*
  BT Flute and trumpet music
  RT Flute and trumpet with string orchestra
Concertos (Flute and viola d'amore with string orchestra) *(M1105-6)*
  BT Flute and viola d'amore music
      String-orchestra music
  RT Flute and viola d'amore with string orchestra
Concertos (Flute and viola d'amore with string orchestra), Arranged *(M1105-6)*
  —Solos with piano *(M1106)*
      BT Trios (Piano, flute, viola d'amore),
          Arranged
Concertos (Flute and viola with instrumental ensemble)
  RT Flute and viola with instrumental ensemble
Concertos (Flute and viola with string ensemble)
  RT Flute and viola with string ensemble
Concertos (Flute and violin) *(M1040-1041)*
  BT Flute and violin music
  RT Flute and violin with orchestra
  —Solos with piano *(M1041)*
      BT Trios (Piano, flute, violin),
          Arranged
Concertos (Flute and violin with string orchestra) *(M1105-6)*
  BT Flute and violin music
      String-orchestra music
  RT Flute and violin with string orchestra

Concertos (Flute and violoncello with string orchestra) *(M1105-6)*
- BT   Flute and violoncello music
- RT   Flute and violoncello with string orchestra

Concertos (Flute), Arranged *(M1020-1021)*
- —Parts *(M1020)*

Concertos (Flute, horn, harp with string orchestra) *(M1105-6)*
- BT   Trios (Flute, horn, harp)
- RT   Flute, horn, harp with string orchestra
- —Scores *(M1105)*

Concertos (Flute, oboe d'amore, viola d'amore with string orchestra) *(M1105-6)*
- BT   Trios (Flute, oboe d'amore, viola d'amore)
- RT   Flute, oboe d'amore, viola d'amore with string orchestra

Concertos (Flute, oboe d'amore, violin with string orchestra) *(M1140-1141)*
- BT   Trios (Flute, oboe d'amore, violin)
- RT   Flute, oboe d'amore, violin with string orchestra

Concertos (Flute, oboe, trumpet with string orchestra) *(M1105-6)*
- BT   String-orchestra music
     Wind trios (Flute, oboe, trumpet)
- RT   Flute, oboe, trumpet with string orchestra

Concertos (Flute, oboe, violin, violoncello) *(M1105-6)*
- BT   Quartets (Flute, oboe, violin, violoncello)
- RT   Flute, oboe, violin, violoncello with orchestra

Concertos (Flute, oboe, violin with string orchestra) *(M1140-1141)*
- BT   Trios (Flute, oboe, violin)
- RT   Flute, oboe, violin with string orchestra

Concertos (Flute, saxophone, harp with string orchestra) *(M1105-6)*
- BT   Trios (Flute, saxophone, harp)
- RT   Flute, saxophone, harp with string orchestra

Concertos (Flute, timpani, violin with string orchestra) *(M1140-1141)*
- BT   Trios (Flute, timpani, violin)
- RT   Flute, timpani, violin with string orchestra

Concertos (Flute, viola, violoncello with string orchestra) *(M1105-6)*
- BT   Trios (Flute, viola, violoncello)
- RT   Flute, viola, violoncello with string orchestra
- —Scores *(M1105)*

Concertos (Flute with accordion ensemble)
- BT   Accordion ensembles
- RT   Flute with accordion ensemble

Concertos (Flute with band) *(M1205-6)*
- RT   Flute with band

Concertos (Flute with brass ensemble)
- RT   Flute with brass ensemble

Concertos (Flute with chamber orchestra) *(M1020-1021)*
- BT   Chamber-orchestra music
- RT   Flute with chamber orchestra
- —Solo with piano *(M1021)*
  - BT   Flute and piano music, Arranged

Concertos (Flute with flute ensemble)
- RT   Flute with flute ensemble

Concertos (Flute with instrumental ensemble)
- RT   Flute with instrumental ensemble

Concertos (Flute with jazz ensemble) *(M1366)*
- RT   Flute with jazz ensemble

Concertos (Flute with percussion ensemble)
- RT   Flute with percussion ensemble

Concertos (Flute with string ensemble)
- RT   Flute with string ensemble

Concertos (Flute with string orchestra) *(M1105-6)*
- RT   Flute with string orchestra
- —Solo with piano *(M1106)*
  - BT   Flute and piano music, Arranged
- *Note under* Concertos

Concertos (Flute with string orchestra), Arranged *(M1105-6)*
- —Solo with piano *(M1106)*
  - BT   Flute and piano music, Arranged

Concertos (Flute with wind ensemble) *(M955-7)*
- RT   Flute with wind ensemble

Concertos (Flute with woodwind ensemble)
- RT   Flute with woodwind ensemble

Concertos (Flutes (2)) *(M1020-1021)*
- BT   Flute music (Flutes (2))
- RT   Flutes (2) with orchestra
- —Solos with piano *(M1021)*
  - BT   Trios (Piano, flutes (2)), Arranged

Concertos (Flutes (2), glockenspiel with string orchestra) *(M1105-6)*
- BT   String-orchestra music
     Trios (Flutes (2), glockenspiel)
- RT   Flutes (2), glockenspiel with string orchestra
- —Scores *(M1105)*

Concertos (Flutes (2), marimba with string orchestra) *(M1105-6)*
- BT   String-orchestra music
     Trios (Flutes (2), marimba)
- RT   Flutes (2), marimba with string orchestra

Concertos (Flutes (2), viola, violoncello with string orchestra) *(M1140-1141)*
- BT   Quartets (Flutes (2), viola, violoncello)
- RT   Flutes (2), viola, violoncello with string orchestra

Concertos (Flutes (2), violin, violoncello with string orchestra) *(M1140-1141)*
- BT   Quartets (Flutes (2), violin, violoncello)
- RT   Flutes (2), violin, violoncello with string orchestra

Concertos (Flutes (2), violin with string orchestra) *(M1140-1141)*
- BT   Trios (Flutes (2), violin)
- RT   Flutes (2), violin with string orchestra

Concertos (Flutes (2), violoncello with string orchestra) *(M1140-1141)*
BT	Trios (Flutes (2), violoncello)
RT	Flutes (2), violoncello with string orchestra
Concertos (Flutes (2) with chamber orchestra) *(M1020-1021)*
BT	Flute music (Flutes (2))
RT	Flutes (2) with chamber orchestra
Concertos (Flutes (2) with chamber orchestra), Arranged *(M1020-1021)*
—Parts *(M1020-1021)*
Concertos (Flutes (2) with flute ensemble)
RT	Flutes (2) with flute ensemble
Concertos (Flutes (2) with string orchestra) *(M1105-6)*
BT	Flute music (Flutes (2))
RT	Flutes (2) with string orchestra
—Solos with piano *(M1121)*
BT	Trios (Piano, flutes (2)), Arranged
Concertos (Flutes (3) and harp) *(M1040-1041)*
BT	Quartets (Flutes (3), harp)
RT	Flutes (3) and harp with orchestra
Concertos (Flutes (3) with band) *(M1205-1206)*
BT	Woodwind trios (Flutes (3))
RT	Flutes (3) with band
Concertos (Flutes (3) with string orchestra) *(M1120-1121)*
BT	Woodwind trios (Flutes (3))
RT	Flutes (3) with string orchestra
Concertos (Flutes (4) with band) *(M1205-1206)*
BT	Woodwind quartets (Flutes (4))
RT	Flutes (4) with band
Concertos (Flutes (4) with chamber orchestra) *(M1020-1021)*
BT	Woodwind quartets (Flutes (4))
RT	Flutes (4) with chamber orchestra
Concertos (Glockenspiel with string orchestra) *(M1105-6)*
RT	Glockenspiel with string orchestra
—Scores *(M1105)*
Concertos (Guitar) *(M1037.4.G8)*
RT	Guitar with orchestra
—Parts
—Solo with piano *(M1037.4.G8)*
BT	Guitar and piano music, Arranged
Concertos (Guitar and harp with chamber orchestra) *(M1040-1041)*
RT	Guitar and harp with chamber orchestra
Concertos (Guitar and harpsichord with string orchestra) *(M1140-1141)*
BT	Guitar and harpsichord music
RT	Guitar and harpsichord with string orchestra
Concertos (Guitar and piano with jazz ensemble)
RT	Guitar and piano with jazz ensemble

Concertos (Guitar and piano with string orchestra) *(M1140-1141)*
BT	Guitar and piano music
RT	Guitar and piano with string orchestra
Concertos (Guitar), Arranged *(M1037.4.G8)*
—Solo with piano *(M1037.4.G8)*
BT	Guitar and piano music, Arranged
Concertos (Guitar with chamber orchestra) *(M1037.4.G8)*
RT	Guitar with chamber orchestra
—Solo with piano *(M1037.4.G8)*
BT	Guitar and piano music, Arranged
Concertos (Guitar with instrumental ensemble)
RT	Guitar with instrumental ensemble
Concertos (Guitar with plectral ensemble)
BT	Guitar with plectral ensemble
Concertos (Guitar with string ensemble)
RT	Guitar with string ensemble
Concertos (Guitar with string orchestra) *(M1105-6)*
RT	Guitar with string orchestra
BT	Guitar with string orchestra
—Solo with piano *(M1137.4.G8)*
BT	Guitar and piano music, Arranged
Concertos (Guitar with string orchestra), Arranged *(M1105-6)*
Concertos (Guitars (2)) *(M1037.4.G8)*
BT	Guitar music (Guitars (2))
RT	Guitars (2) with orchestra
—Solos with piano *(M1037.4.G8)*
BT	Trios (Piano, guitars (2)), Arranged
Concertos (Guitars (2) with chamber orchestra) *(M1037.4.G8)*
BT	Guitar music (Guitars (2))
RT	Guitars (2) with chamber orchestra
Concertos (Guitars (2) with chamber orchestra), Arranged *(M1037.4.G8)*
Concertos (Guitars (2) with jazz ensemble) *(M1366)*
RT	Guitars (2) with jazz ensemble
Concertos (Guitars (3) with chamber orchestra) *(M1037.4.G8)*
BT	Trios (Guitars (3))
RT	Guitars (3) with chamber orchestra
Concertos (Guitars (4)) *(M1037.4.G8)*
BT	Quartets (Guitars (4))
RT	Guitars (4) with orchestra
Concertos (Guslis (2) with chamber orchestra) *(M1037.4.G85)*
RT	Guslis (2) with chamber orchestra
Concertos (Hardanger fiddle with string orchestra) *(M1119.H37)*
RT	Hardanger fiddle with string orchestra
Concertos (Harmonica) *(M1039.4.M6)*
RT	Harmonica with orchestra
—Solo with piano *(M1039.4.M6)*
BT	Harmonica and piano music, Arranged
Concertos (Harmonica with chamber orchestra) *(M1039.4.M6)*
RT	Harmonica with chamber orchestra

Concertos (Harmonica with string orchestra)
    (M1139.4.M6)
  RT Harmonica with string orchestra
Concertos (Harp) *(M1036-7)*
  RT Harp with orchestra
  —Solo with piano *(M1037)*
      BT Harp and piano music, Arranged
Concertos (Harp and lute) *(M1040-1041)*
  BT Harp and lute music
  RT Harp and lute with orchestra
Concertos (Harp and organ with string
     orchestra) *(M1105-6)*
  RT Harp and organ with string orchestra
Concertos (Harp and piano) *(M1040-1041)*
  BT Harp and piano music
  RT Harp and piano with orchestra
Concertos (Harp), Arranged *(M1036-7)*
Concertos (Harp, violin, violoncello)
    (M1040-1041)
  BT Trios (Harp, violin, violoncello)
  RT Harp, violin, violoncello with orchestra
Concertos (Harp with band) *(M1205-1206)*
  RT Harp with band
Concertos (Harp with brass ensemble)
  RT Harp with brass ensemble
Concertos (Harp with chamber orchestra)
    (M1036-7)
  RT Harp with chamber orchestra
  —Scores *(M1036)*
Concertos (Harp with instrumental ensemble)
  RT Harp with instrumental ensemble
Concertos (Harp with string orchestra)
    (M1105-6)
  BT String-orchestra music
  RT Harp with string orchestra
  —Solo with piano *(M1137)*
      BT Harp and piano music, Arranged
Concertos (Harp with string orchestra),
     Arranged *(M1105-6)*
  —Solo with piano *(M1106)*
      BT Harp and piano music, Arranged
Concertos (Harps (2)) *(M1036-7)*
  BT Harp music (Harps (2))
  RT Harps (2) with orchestra
Concertos (Harps (2), percussion with string
     orchestra) *(M1140-1141)*
  BT Sextets (Harps (2), percussion)
  RT Harps (2), percussion with string
      orchestra
Concertos (Harps (2) with chamber orchestra)
    (M1036-1037)
  RT Harps (2) with chamber orchestra
Concertos (Harps (2) with string ensemble)
  RT Harps (2) with string ensemble
Concertos (Harps (2) with string orchestra)
    (M1105-6)
  BT Harp music (Harps (2))
  RT Harps (2) with string orchestra
Concertos (Harps (4) with string orchestra)
    (M1136-1137)
  BT Quartets (Harps (4))
  RT Harps (4) with string orchestra

Concertos (Harpsichord) *(M1010-1011)*
  BT Concertos (Piano)
  RT Harpsichord with orchestra
  —2-harpsichord scores *(M1011)*
      BT Harpsichord music (Harpsichords
        (2)), Arranged
  —2-piano scores *(M1011)*
      BT Piano music (Pianos (2)), Arranged
  —Solo with piano *(M1011)*
      BT Harpsichord and piano music,
        Arranged
Concertos (Harpsichord and organ with
     chamber orchestra) *(M1040-1041)*
  RT Harpsichord and organ with chamber
      orchestra
Concertos (Harpsichord and piano)
    (M1010-1011)
  BT Harpsichord and piano music
  RT Harpsichord and piano with orchestra
Concertos (Harpsichord and piano with dance
     orchestra) *(M1353)*
  BT Harpsichord and piano music
  RT Harpsichord and piano with dance
      orchestra
Concertos (Harpsichord and piano with wind
     ensemble)
  RT Harpsichord and piano with wind
      ensemble
Concertos (Harpsichord), Arranged
    (M1010-1011)
Concertos (Harpsichord, flute, harp with
     string orchestra) *(M1105-1106)*
  BT Trios (Harpsichord, flute, harp)
  RT Harpsichord, flute, harp with string
      orchestra
Concertos (Harpsichord, flute, oboe with
     string orchestra) *(M1105-6)*
  BT Trios (Harpsichord, flute, oboe)
  RT Harpsichord, flute, oboe with string
      orchestra
Concertos (Harpsichord, flute, violin with
     string orchestra) *(M1105-6)*
  BT Trios (Harpsichord, flute, violin)
  RT Harpsichord, flute, violin with string
      orchestra
Concertos (Harpsichord, flutes (2) with
     string orchestra) *(M1105-6)*
  BT String-orchestra music
      Trios (Harpsichord, flutes (2))
  RT Harpsichord, flutes (2) with string
      orchestra
  —Scores
Concertos (Harpsichord, guitars (2), harp,
     double bass) *(M1040-1041)*
  BT Quintets (Harpsichord, guitars (2),
      harp, double bass)
  RT Harpsichord, guitars (2), harp, double
      bass with orchestra
Concertos (Harpsichord, piano, harp with
     string orchestra) *(M1140-1141)*
  BT Trios (Harpsichord, piano, harp)
  RT Harpsichord, piano, harp with string
      orchestra

Concertos (Harpsichord, piano, violin)
    (M1040-1041)
  BT Trios (Harpsichord, piano, violin)
  RT Harpsichord, piano, violin with
      orchestra
Concertos (Harpsichord, violin, violoncello
    with string orchestra) *(M1140-1141)*
  BT Trios (Harpsichord, violin, violoncello)
  RT Harpsichord, violin, violoncello with
      string orchestra
Concertos (Harpsichord, violins (2),
    violoncello) *(M1040-M1041)*
  BT Harpsichord, violins (2), violoncello
      with orchestra
      Quartets (Harpsichord, violins (2),
      violoncello)
Concertos (Harpsichord with chamber
    orchestra) *(M1010-1011)*
  BT Harpsichord with instrumental
      ensemble
  RT Harpsichord with chamber orchestra
  —Scores *(M1010)*
  —Solo with piano *(M1011)*
      BT Harpsichord and piano music,
        Arranged
Concertos (Harpsichord with instrumental
    ensemble)
  —Solo with piano *(M215)*
      BT Harpsichord and piano music,
        Arranged
Concertos (Harpsichord with string ensemble)
  RT Harpsichord with string ensemble
Concertos (Harpsichord with string orchestra)
    (M1105-6)
  RT Harpsichord with string orchestra
  —2-piano scores *(M1111)*
      BT Piano music (Pianos (2)), Arranged
  —Solo with piano *(M1111)*
      BT Harpsichord and piano music,
        Arranged
Concertos (Harpsichord with string
    orchestra), Arranged *(M1105-6)*
Concertos (Harpsichords (2)) *(M1010-1011)*
  BT Harpsichord music (Harpsichords (2))
  RT Harpsichords (2) with orchestra
Concertos (Harpsichords (2) with string
    orchestra) *(M1105-6)*
  BT Harpsichord music (Harpsichords (2))
  RT Harpsichords (2) with string orchestra
Concertos (Harpsichords (2) with string
    orchestra), Arranged *(M1105-6)*
Concertos (Harpsichords (3) with string
    orchestra) *(M1105-6)*
  BT Harpsichord music (Harpsichords (3))
  RT Harpsichords (3) with string orchestra
Concertos (Harpsichords (4)) *(M1010-1011)*
  BT Harpsichord music (Harpsichords (4))
  RT Harpsichords (4) with orchestra
Concertos (Harpsichords (4)), Arranged
    (M1010-1011)
Concertos (Harpsichords (4) with string
    orchestra) *(M1105-6)*
  BT Harpsichord music (Harpsichords (4))
  RT Harpsichords (4) with string orchestra

Concertos (Horn) *(M1028-9)*
  RT Horn with orchestra
  —Solo with piano *(M1029)*
      BT Horn and piano music, Arranged
Concertos (Horn and harp) *(M1040-1041)*
  RT Horn and harp with orchestra
Concertos (Horn and trombone)
    (M1040-1041)
  RT Horn and trombone with orchestra
Concertos (Horn, trombone, trumpets (2),
    tuba) *(M1040-1041)*
  BT Brass quintets (Horn, trombone,
      trumpets (2), tuba)
  RT Horn, trombone, trumpets (2), tuba
      with orchestra
  —Solos with piano *(M1041)*
      BT Sextets (Piano, horn, trombone,
        trumpets (2), tuba), Arranged
Concertos (Horn, trombone, trumpets (2),
    tuba with instrumental ensemble)
  BT Brass quintets (Horn, trombone,
      trumpets (2), tuba)
  RT Horn, trombone, trumpets (2), tuba
      with instrumental ensemble
Concertos (Horn, trombone, trumpets (2),
    tuba with string orchestra)
    (M1140-1141)
  BT Brass quintets (Horn, trombone,
      trumpets (2), tuba)
  RT Horn, trombone, trumpets (2), tuba
      with string orchestra
      Horn, trombone, trumpets (2), tuba
      with string orchestra
Concertos (Horn, trombones (2), trumpets
    (2)) *(M1040-1041)*
  BT Brass quintets (Horn, trombones (2),
      trumpets (2))
  RT Horn, trombones (2), trumpets (2) with
      orchestra
Concertos (Horn, trombones (2), trumpets (2)
    with chamber orchestra)
    (M1040-1041)
  BT Brass quintets (Horn, trombones (2),
      trumpets (2))
  RT Horn, trombones (2), trumpets (2) with
      chamber orchestra
Concertos (Horn, trombones (2), trumpets (2)
    with string orchestra)
    (M1140-1141)
  BT Brass quintets (Horn, trombones (2),
      trumpets (2))
  RT Horn, trombones (2), trumpets (2) with
      string orchestra
Concertos (Horn with band) *(M1205)*
  RT Horn with band
  —Scores *(M1205)*
Concertos (Horn with band), Arranged
    (M1257)
  —Scores *(M1257)*
Concertos (Horn with chamber orchestra)
    (M1028-9)
  RT Horn with chamber orchestra
Concertos (Horn with horn ensemble)
  RT Horn with horn ensemble

Concertos (Horn with instrumental ensemble)
  RT Horn with instrumental ensemble
Concertos (Horn with percussion ensemble)
  RT Horn with percussion ensemble
Concertos (Horn with string ensemble)
  RT Horn with string ensemble
  —Solo with piano
      BT Horn and piano music, Arranged
Concertos (Horn with string orchestra)
    (M1105-6)
  RT Horn with string orchestra
  —Scores *(M1105)*
  —Solo with piano *(M1106)*
      BT Horn and piano music, Arranged
Concertos (Horn with string orchestra),
    Arranged *(M1105-6)*
  —Scores *(M1105)*
Concertos (Horns (2)) *(M1028-9)*
  BT Horn music (Horns (2))
  RT Horns (2) with orchestra
  —Solos with piano *(M1029)*
      BT Trios (Piano, horns (2)), Arranged
Concertos (Horns (2), oboes (2) with string
    orchestra) *(M1140-1141)*
  BT Wind quartets (Horns (2), oboes (2))
  RT Horns (2), oboes (2) with string
      orchestra
Concertos (Horns (2), trombones (2),
    trumpets (2), tuba) *(M1040-1041)*
  BT Brass septets (Horns (2), trombones (2),
      trumpets (2), tuba)
  RT Horns (2), trombones (2), trumpets (2),
      tuba with orchestra
Concertos (Horns (2) with string orchestra)
    (M1128-1129)
  BT Horn music (Horns (2))
      String-orchestra music
  RT Horns (2) with string orchestra
  —Solos with piano *(M1129)*
      BT Trios (Piano, horns (2)), Arranged
Concertos (Horns (3)) *(M1028-9)*
  BT Brass trios (Horns (3))
  RT Horns (3) with orchestra
Concertos (Horns (3) with band)
    (M1205-1206)
  BT Brass trios (Horns (3))
  RT Horns (3) with band
Concertos (Horns (3) with string orchestra)
    (M1128-1129)
  BT Brass trios (Horns (3))
  RT Horns (3) with string orchestra
Concertos (Horns (4)) *(M1028-1029)*
  BT Brass quartets (Horns (4))
  RT Horns (4) with orchestra
  —Solos with piano *(M1029)*
      BT Quintets (Piano, horns (4)),
        Arranged
Concertos (Horns (4) with band)
    (M1205-1206)
  BT Band music
      Brass quartets (Horns (4))
      Horns (4) with band
Concertos (Hu ch'in) *(M1039.4.H83)*
  RT Hu ch'in with orchestra

Concertos (Hu ch'in with instrumental
    ensemble)
  RT Hu ch'in with instrumental ensemble
Concertos (Hurdy-gurdies (2)) *(M1039.4.H87)*
  BT Hurdy-gurdy music (Hurdy-gurdies (2))
  RT Hurdy-gurdies (2) with orchestra
Concertos (Hurdy-gurdies (2) with instrumental
    ensemble)
  RT Hurdy-gurdies (2) with instrumental
      ensemble
Concertos (Hurdy-gurdy) *(M1039.4.H87)*
  RT Hurdy-gurdy with orchestra
Concertos (Hurdy-gurdy with chamber
    orchestra) *(M1039.4.H87)*
  BT Hurdy-gurdy with chamber orchestra
Concertos (Hurdy-gurdy with chamber
    orchestra), Arranged
    (M1039.4.H87)
Concertos (Hurdy-gurdy with instrumental
    ensemble)
  RT Hurdy-gurdy with instrumental
      ensemble
Concertos (Jazz ensemble) *(M1040-1041)*
  BT Jazz ensembles
  RT Jazz ensemble with orchestra
Concertos (Jazz ensemble with chamber
    orchestra) *(M1040-1041)*
  BT Jazz ensembles
  RT Jazz ensemble with chamber orchestra
Concertos (Jazz ensemble with string
    orchestra) *(M1140-1141)*
  BT Jazz ensembles
  RT Jazz ensemble with string orchestra
Concertos (Jazz octet) *(M1040-1041)*
  BT Orchestral music
  RT Jazz octet with orchestra
      Jazz octets
Concertos (Jazz quartet) *(M1040-1041)*
  BT Jazz quartets
      Orchestral music
  RT Jazz quartet with orchestra
Concertos (Jazz quintet) *(M1040-1041)*
  BT Jazz quintets
  RT Jazz quintet with orchestra
Concertos (Jazz quintet with band) *(M1205-1206)*
  RT Jazz quintet with band
Concertos (Jazz quintet with string orchestra)
    (M1140-1141)
  BT Jazz quintets
  RT Jazz quintet with string orchestra
Concertos (Jazz trio) *(M1040-1041)*
  BT Jazz trios
  RT Jazz trio with orchestra
Concertos (Jazz trio with chamber orchestra)
    (M1040-1041)
  RT Jazz trio with chamber orchestra
Concertos (Keyed fiddle)
    (M1019.K)
  BT Keyed fiddle with orchestra
Concertos (Koto) *(M1037.4.K68)*
  BT Koto music
  RT Koto with orchestra
  —Scores *(M1037.4.K68)*

Concertos (Lute and viola d'amore with string
      orchestra) *(M1140-1141)*
  RT Lute and viola d'amore with string
      orchestra
Concertos (Lute with string orchestra)
      (M1105-6)
  RT Lute with string orchestra
Concertos (Lutes (2) with string orchestra)
      (M1137.4.L88)
  RT Lutes (2) with string orchestra
Concertos (Mandola and Jew's harp with
      string orchestra) *(M1140-M1141)*
  BT Mandola and Jew's harp with string
      orchestra
Concertos (Mandolin) *(M1037.4.M3)*
  RT Mandolin with orchestra
  —Solo with piano *(M1037.4.M3)*
      BT Mandolin and piano music,
      Arranged
Concertos (Mandolin), Arranged
      (M1037.4.M3)
Concertos (Mandolin with string orchestra)
      (M1105-6)
  RT Mandolin with string orchestra
  —Solo with piano *(M1137.4.M3)*
      BT Mandolin and piano music,
      Arranged
Concertos (Mandolins (2) with string
      orchestra) *(M1105-6)*
  BT Mandolin music (Mandolins (2))
      String-orchestra music
  RT Mandolins (2) with string orchestra
  —Solos with piano *(M1137.4.M3)*
      BT Trios (Piano, mandolins (2)),
      Arranged
Concertos (Marimba) *(M1039.4.M3)*
  RT Marimba with orchestra
  —Solo with piano *(M1039.4)*
      BT Marimba and piano music, Arranged
Concertos (Marimba and piano with string
      orchestra) *(M1140-1141)*
  RT Marimba and piano with string orchestra
Concertos (Marimba with band)
      (M1205-M1206; M1257)
  RT Marimba with band
Concertos (Marimba with string orchestra)
      (M1138-1139)
  RT Marimba with string orchestra
Concertos (Oboe) *(M1022-3)*
  RT Oboe with orchestra
  —Solo with piano *(M1023)*
      BT Oboe and piano music, Arranged
Concertos (Oboe and harp) *(M1040-1041)*
  BT Oboe and harp music
  RT Oboe and harp with orchestra
  —Scores *(M1040)*
Concertos (Oboe and harp with chamber
      orchestra) *(M1040-1041)*
  RT Oboe and harp with chamber orchestra
Concertos (Oboe and harp with string
      orchestra) *(M1105-6)*
  BT Oboe and harp music
  RT Oboe and harp with string orchestra

Concertos (Oboe and harpsichord with string
      orchestra) *(M1140-1141)*
  BT Oboe and harpsichord music
      String-orchestra music
  RT Oboe and harpsichord with string
      orchestra
Concertos (Oboe and percussion with string
      orchestra) *(M1140-1141)*
  RT Oboe and percussion with string
      orchestra
Concertos (Oboe and piano with string
      ensemble)
  BT Oboe and piano with string ensemble
Concertos (Oboe and recorder with string
      orchestra) *(M1105-6)*
  BT Oboe and recorder music
  RT Oboe and recorder with string orchestra
Concertos (Oboe and trumpet with string
      orchestra) *(M1105-6)*
  BT Oboe and trumpet music
      String-orchestra music
  RT Oboe and trumpet with string orchestra
Concertos (Oboe and trumpet with string
      orchestra), Arranged *(M1105-6)*
Concertos (Oboe and viola with string
      orchestra) *(M1105-6)*
  BT Oboe and viola music
  RT Oboe and viola with string orchestra
  —Scores *(M1105)*
Concertos (Oboe and violin) *(M1040-1041)*
  BT Oboe and violin music
  RT Oboe and violin with orchestra
Concertos (Oboe and violin), Arranged
      (M1040-1041)
Concertos (Oboe and violin with chamber
      orchestra) *(M1040-1041)*
  BT Chamber-orchestra music
      Oboe and violin music
  RT Oboe and violin with chamber
      orchestra
  —Scores *(M1040)*
Concertos (Oboe and violin with string
      orchestra) *(M1105-6)*
  BT Oboe and violin music
  RT Oboe and violin with string orchestra
  —Solos with piano *(M1141)*
      BT Trios (Piano, oboe, violin), Arranged
Concertos (Oboe and violin with string
      orchestra), Arranged *(M1105-6)*
Concertos (Oboe and violoncello) *(M1040-1041)*
  RT Oboe and violoncello with orchestra
Concertos (Oboe), Arranged *(M1022-3)*
  —Solo with piano *(M1023)*
      BT Oboe and piano music, Arranged
Concertos (Oboe d'amore) *(M1034.O26; M1035.O26)*
  RT Oboe d'amore with orchestra
  —Solo with piano *(M1035.O26)*
      BT Oboe d'amore and piano music,
      Arranged
Concertos (Oboe d'amore with string
      orchestra) *(M1105-6)*
  BT String-orchestra music
  RT Oboe d'amore with string orchestra

Concertos (Oboe d'amore with string
orchestra), Arranged *(M1105-6)*

Concertos (Oboe, violin, violoncello)
(M1040-1041)
  BT Trios (Oboe, violin, violoncello)
  RT Oboe, violin, violoncello with orchestra

Concertos (Oboe, violin, violoncello with
string orchestra) *(M1105-6)*
  BT Trios (Oboe, violin, violoncello)
  RT Oboe, violin, violoncello with string
     orchestra

Concertos (Oboe with band) *(M1205-6)*
  RT Oboe with band
  —Scores *(M1205)*

Concertos (Oboe with chamber orchestra)
(M1022-3)
  BT Chamber-orchestra music
  RT Oboe with chamber orchestra
  —Solo with piano *(M1023)*
     BT Oboe and piano music, Arranged

Concertos (Oboe with instrumental ensemble)
  RT Oboe with instrumental ensemble

Concertos (Oboe with string ensemble)
(M960-962)
  RT Oboe with string ensemble

Concertos (Oboe with string orchestra)
(M1105-6)
  BT String-orchestra music
  RT Oboe with string orchestra
  —Solo with piano *(M1106)*
     BT Oboe and piano music, Arranged

Concertos (Oboe with string orchestra),
Arranged *(M1105-6)*
  —Scores *(M1105)*

Concertos (Oboes (2)) *(M1022-1023)*
  RT Oboes (2) with orchestra

Concertos (Oboes (2), trumpet with string
orchestra) *(M1140-1141)*
  BT Wind trios (Oboes (2), trumpet)
  RT Oboes (2), trumpet with string
     orchestra

Concertos (Oboes (2) with string orchestra)
(M1105-6)
  BT Oboe music (Oboes (2))
  RT Oboes (2) with string orchestra
  —Solos with piano *(M1123)*
     BT Trios (Piano, oboes (2)), Arranged

Concertos (Oboes (3) with string orchestra)
(M1122-1123)
  BT Woodwind trios (Oboes (3))
  RT Oboes (3) with string orchestra

Concertos (Oboes (4) with string orchestra)
(M1122-3)
  BT Woodwind quartets (Oboes (4))
  RT Oboes (4) with string orchestra

Concertos (Oboi d'amore (2) with string
orchestra) *(M1134.O26;*
M1135.O26)
  RT Oboi d'amore (2) with string orchestra

Concertos (Ondes Martenot) *(M1039.4.O5)*
  BT Ondes Martenot music
  RT Ondes Martenot with orchestra
  —Scores *(M1039.4.O5)*

Concertos (Ondes Martenot with string
orchestra) *(M1105-6)*
  BT Ondes Martenot music
  RT Ondes Martenot with string orchestra
  —Solo with piano *(M1106)*
     BT Ondes Martenot and piano music,
       Arranged

Concertos (Orchestra) *(M1042)*
  Note under Concertos

Concertos (Organ) *(M1105-6)*
  RT Organ with orchestra
  —Parts *(M1005)*
  —Parts (solo) *(M1005)*
  —Solo with piano *(M1006)*
     BT Piano and organ music, Arranged

Concertos (Organ, harp, timpani with string
orchestra) *(M1140-1141)*
  BT Trios (Organ, harp, timpani)
  RT Organ, harp, timpani with string
     orchestra

Concertos (Organ, piano, guitars (3),
percussion) *(M1040-1041)*
  BT Sextets (Organ, piano, guitars (3),
     percussion)
  RT Organ, piano, guitars (3), percussion
     with orchestra

Concertos (Organ with band) *(M1205)*
  BT Band music
  RT Organ with band

Concertos (Organ with brass ensemble)
  RT Organ with brass ensemble

Concertos (Organ with chamber orchestra)
(M1005-6)
  RT Organ with chamber orchestra

Concertos (Organ with instrumental ensemble)
  RT Organ with instrumental ensemble

Concertos (Organ with percussion ensemble)
  RT Organ with percussion ensemble

Concertos (Organ with string orchestra)
(M1105-6)
  RT Organ with string orchestra
  —Solo with piano *(M1106)*
     BT Piano and organ music, Arranged

Concertos (Organ with string orchestra),
Arranged *(M1105-6)*

Concertos (Organ with wind ensemble)
  RT Organ with wind ensemble

Concertos (Organs (3)) *(M1005-6)*
  BT Organ music (Organs (3))
  RT Organs (3) with orchestra

Concertos (Oud with string orchestra) *(M1137.4.O9)*
  RT Oud with string orchestra

Concertos (Panpipes) *(M1034.P; M1035.P)*
  RT Panpipes with orchestra

Concertos (Percussion) *(M1038-9)*
  RT Percussion with orchestra
  —Solo with piano *(M1039)*
     BT Percussion and piano music,
       Arranged
  Note under Percussion music

Concertos (Percussion and celesta with string
orchestra) *(M1140)*
  RT Percussion and celesta with string orchestra

Concertos (Percussion and organ with string orchestra) *(M1105-6)*
  RT Percussion and organ with string orchestra

Concertos (Percussion and piano) *(M1040-1041)*
  RT Percussion and piano with orchestra

Concertos (Percussion and piano with chamber orchestra) *(M1040-1041)*
  RT Percussion and piano with chamber orchestra

Concertos (Percussion and piano with instrumental ensemble)
  RT Percussion and piano with instrumental ensemble

Concertos (Percussion and piano with string orchestra) *(M1105-6)*
  BT Percussion and piano music
  RT Percussion and piano with string orchestra

Concertos (Percussion and timpani with string orchestra)
  USE Concertos (Percussion with string orchestra)

Concertos (Percussion with band) *(M1205-6)*
  RT Percussion with band
  —Scores *(M1205)*

Concertos (Percussion with chamber orchestra) *(M1038-9)*
  RT Percussion with chamber orchestra
  —Solos with piano *(M1039)*
    BT Percussion and piano music, Arranged

Concertos (Percussion with instrumental ensemble)
  RT Percussion with instrumental ensemble

Concertos (Percussion with jazz ensemble) *(M985)*
  RT Percussion with jazz ensemble

Concertos (Percussion with percussion ensemble)
  RT Percussion with percussion ensemble

Concertos (Percussion with string orchestra) *(M1105-M1106)*
  UF Concertos (Percussion and timpani with string orchestra)
  BT String-orchestra music
  RT Percussion with string orchestra

Concertos (P'i p'a) *(M1037.4.P5)*
  RT P'i p'a with orchestra

Concertos (Piano) *(M1010-1011)*
  RT Piano with orchestra
  NT Concertos (Harpsichord)
  Note under Concertos
  —2-piano scores *(M1011)*
    BT Piano music (Pianos (2)), Arranged
  — —Excerpts
    USE Concertos (Piano)—Excerpts— 2-piano scores
  —Cadenzas *(M1004.7; M1010.5)*
    Note under Concertos—Cadenzas
  —Excerpts
  — —2-piano scores *(M1011)*
    UF Concertos (Piano)—2-piano scores —Excerpts
    BT Piano music (Pianos (2)), Arranged

Concertos (Piano) *(M1010-1011)*
  (Continued)
  —Excerpts, Arranged
  —Parts (solo) *(M1010)*

Concertos (Piano, 1 hand) *(M1010-1011)*
  BT Piano music (1 hand)
  RT Piano (1 hand) with orchestra
  —2-piano scores *(M1011)*
    BT Piano music (Pianos (2)), Arranged

Concertos (Piano, 1 hand, with chamber orchestra) *(M1010-1011)*
  RT Piano (1 hand) with chamber orchestra

Concertos (Piano, 4 hands) *(M1010-1011)*
  BT Piano music (4 hands)
  RT Piano (4 hands) with orchestra
  —2-piano scores *(M1011)*
    BT Piano music (Pianos (2), 6 hands), Arranged

Concertos (Piano, 4 hands, with instrumental ensemble)
  RT Piano (4 hands) with instrumental ensemble

Concertos (Piano and synthesizer) *(M1040-M1041)*
  BT Piano and synthesizer with orchestra

Concertos (Piano), Arranged *(M1010-1011)*

Concertos (Piano, clarinet, percussion, violoncello) *(M1040-1041)*
  BT Quartets (Piano, clarinet, percussion, violoncello)
  RT Piano, clarinet, percussion, violoncello with orchestra

Concertos (Piano, clarinet, trombone, percussion) *(M1040-1041)*
  BT Quartets (Piano, clarinet, trombone, percussion)
  RT Piano, clarinet, trombone, percussion with orchestra

Concertos (Piano, clarinet, violin, violoncello) *(M1040-1041)*
  BT Quartets (Piano, clarinet, violin, violoncello)
  RT Piano, clarinet, violin, violoncello with orchestra

Concertos (Piano, clarinet, violin, violoncello with string orchestra) *(M1140-1141)*
  BT Quartets (Piano, clarinet, violin, violoncello)
  RT Piano, clarinet, violin, violoncello with string orchestra

Concertos (Piano, flute, horn with string orchestra) *(M1140-1141)*
  BT Trios (Piano, flute, horn)
  RT Piano, flute, horn with string orchestra

Concertos (Piano, flute, viola with string orchestra) *(M1105-6)*
  BT Trios (Piano, flute, viola)
  RT Piano, flute, viola with string orchestra
  —Scores *(M1105)*

Concertos (Piano, flute, violin with instrumental ensemble)
  BT Trios (Piano, flute, violin)
  RT Piano, flute, violin with instrumental ensemble

**Concertos (Piano, flute, violin with
    string orchestra)** *(M1105-6)*
  BT Trios (Piano, flute, violin)
  RT Piano, flute, violin with string orchestra
**Concertos (Piano, horn, glockenspiel,
    xylophone)** *(M1040-1041)*
  BT Quartets (Piano, horn, glockenspiel,
      xylophone)
  RT Piano, horn, glockenspiel, xylophone
      with orchestra
Concertos (Piano, horn, violin) *(M1040-1041)*
  BT Trios (Piano, horn, violin)
  RT Piano, horn, violin with orchestra
**Concertos (Piano, oboe, trumpet, violin,
    double bass with string orchestra)**
    (M1105-6)
  BT Quintets (Piano, oboe, trumpet, violin,
      double bass)
  RT Piano, oboe, trumpet, violin, double
      bass with string orchestra
  —Scores
Concertos (Piano quartet with string orchestra)
    (M1140-1141)
  BT Piano quartets
  RT Piano quartet with string orchestra
**Concertos (Piano quintet with string
    orchestra)** *(M1140-1141)*
  BT Piano quintets
  RT Piano quintet with string orchestra
**Concertos (Piano, saxophones (4), harp,
    percussion with string orchestra)**
    (M1140-M1141)
  BT Piano, saxophones (4), harp, percussion
      with string orchestra
      Septets (Piano, saxophones (4), harp,
      percussion)
Concertos (Piano trio) *(M1040-1041)*
  BT Piano trios
  RT Piano trio with orchestra
  —Scores *(M1040)*
  —Solos with piano *(M1041)*
      BT Quartets (Pianos (2), violin,
        violoncello), Arranged
Concertos (Piano trio with string orchestra)
    (M1105-6)
  BT Piano trios
  RT Piano trio with string orchestra
  —Scores *(M1105)*
**Concertos (Piano, trumpet, vibraphone, double
    bass)** *(M1040-1041)*
  BT Orchestral music
      Quartets (Piano, trumpet, vibraphone,
      double bass)
  RT Piano, trumpet, vibraphone, double bass
      with orchestra
  —Scores *(M1040)*
Concertos (Piano, trumpet, viola) *(M1040-1041)*
  BT Trios (Piano, trumpet, viola)
  RT Piano, trumpet, viola with orchestra
**Concertos (Piano, trumpets (3) with string
    orchestra)** *(M1105-6)*
  BT Quartets (Piano, trumpets (3))
      String-orchestra music
  RT Piano, trumpets (3) with string orchestra

**Concertos (Piano, violins (2) with string
    orchestra)** *(M1105-6)*
  BT String-orchestra music
      Trios (Piano, violins (2))
  RT Piano, violins (2) with string orchestra
Concertos (Piano with band) *(M1205)*
  BT Band music
  RT Piano with band
  —2-piano scores *(M1206)*
      BT Piano music (Pianos (2)), Arranged
Concertos (Piano with band), Arranged
    (M1257)
Concertos (Piano with brass ensemble)
    (M917)
  RT Piano with brass ensemble
Concertos (Piano with chamber orchestra)
    (M1010-1011)
  BT Chamber-orchestra music
  RT Piano with chamber orchestra
  —2-piano scores *(M1011)*
      BT Piano music (Pianos (2)), Arranged
Concertos (Piano with clarinet choir)
    (M1205-1206)
  RT Piano with clarinet choir
Concertos (Piano with dance orchestra)
    (M1353)
  RT Piano with dance orchestra
  —Scores *(M1353)*
Concertos (Piano with instrumental ensemble)
  RT Piano with instrumental ensemble
Concertos (Piano with percussion ensemble)
  RT Piano with percussion ensemble
Concertos (Piano with salon orchestra)
    (M1353)
  BT Salon-orchestra music
  RT Piano with salon orchestra
Concertos (Piano with string ensemble)
    (M910-912)
  RT Piano with string ensemble
  —2-piano scores *(M215)*
      BT Piano music (Pianos (2)), Arranged
Concertos (Piano with string orchestra)
    (M1105-6)
  BT String-orchestra music
  RT Piano with string orchestra
  —2-piano scores *(M1106)*
      BT Piano music (Pianos (2)), Arranged
**Concertos (Piano with string orchestra),
    Arranged** *(M1105-6)*
  —2-piano scores *(M1106)*
Concertos (Piano with wind ensemble)
  RT Piano with wind ensemble
Concertos (Piano with woodwind ensemble)
  RT Piano with woodwind ensemble
Concertos (Pianola) *(M1039.4.P5)*
  RT Pianola with orchestra
Concertos (Pianos (2)) *(M1010-1011)*
  BT Piano music (Pianos (2))
  RT Pianos (2) with orchestra
  —3-piano scores *(M1011)*
      BT Piano ensembles, Arranged
Concertos (Pianos (2)), Arranged
    (M1010-1011)

Concertos (Pianos (2), guitars (3), percussion)
   (M1040-1041)
  BT Sextets (Pianos (2), guitars (3), percussion)
  RT Pianos (2), guitars (3), percussion with
      orchestra
Concertos (Pianos (2), percussion)
   (M1040-1041)
  BT Pianos (2) with percussion ensemble
      Sextets (Pianos (2), percussion)
  RT Pianos (2), percussion with orchestra
Concertos (Pianos (2), percussion with string orchestra) *(M1140-1141)*
  BT Quartets (Pianos (2), percussion)
  RT Pianos (2), percussion with string orchestra
Concertos (Pianos (2) with band) *(M1205-6)*
  BT Piano music (Pianos (2))
  RT Pianos (2) with band
Concertos (Pianos (2) with brass band)
   (M1205; M1257)
  RT Pianos (2) with brass band
Concertos (Pianos (2) with chamber orchestra) *(M1010-M1011)*
  BT Piano music (Pianos (2))
  RT Pianos (2) with chamber orchestra
  —3-piano scores *(M1011)*
      BT Piano ensembles, Arranged
Concertos (Pianos (2) with dance orchestra)
   (M1353)
  RT Pianos (2) with dance orchestra
Concertos (Pianos (2) with instrumental ensemble)
  RT Pianos (2) with instrumental ensemble
Concertos (Pianos (2) with percussion ensemble)
  RT Pianos (2) with percussion ensemble
Concertos (Pianos (2) with string orchestra)
   (M1105-6)
  BT Piano music (Pianos (2))
  RT Pianos (2) with string orchestra
Concertos (Pianos (3)) *(M1010-1011)*
  BT Piano ensembles
  RT Pianos (3) with orchestra
Concertos (Pianos (3) with string orchestra)
  BT Piano ensembles
  RT Pianos (3) with string orchestra
  —Parts
Concertos (Piccolo) *(M1020-1021)*
  RT Piccolo with orchestra
  —Solo with piano *(M1021)*
      BT Piccolo and piano music, Arranged
Concertos (Piccolo with instrumental ensemble)
  BT Piccolo music
  RT Piccolo with instrumental ensemble
Concertos (Piccolo with string orchestra)
   (M1105-6)
  RT Piccolo with string orchestra
  —Solo with piano *(M1121)*
      BT Piccolo and piano music, Arranged
Concertos (Piccolo with string orchestra), Arranged *(M1105-6)*
  —Solo with piano *(M1106)*
      BT Piccolo and piano music, Arranged

Concertos (Piccolos (2)) *(M1020-1021)*
  BT Piccolo music (Piccolos (2))
  RT Piccolos (2) with orchestra
Concertos (Recorder) *(M1020-1021)*
  BT Concertos (Flute)
  RT Recorder with orchestra
Concertos (Recorder and trumpet with string orchestra) *(M1105-6)*
  BT Recorder and trumpet music
  RT Recorder and trumpet with string
      orchestra
Concertos (Recorder and viola da gamba with string orchestra) *(M1105-6)*
  BT Recorder and viola da gamba music
  RT Recorder and viola da gamba with
      string orchestra
  —Solos with piano *(M1141)*
      BT Trios (Piano, recorder, viola da
         gamba), Arranged
Concertos (Recorder and violin with string orchestra) *(M1105-6)*
  BT Recorder and violin music
  RT Recorder and violin with string
      orchestra
  —Solos with piano *(M1141)*
      BT Trios (Piano, recorder, violin),
         Arranged
Concertos (Recorder), Arranged
   (M1020-1021)
Concertos (Recorder with chamber orchestra)
   (M1020-1021)
  RT Recorder with chamber orchestra
Concertos (Recorder with instrumental ensemble)
  RT Recorder with instrumental ensemble
Concertos (Recorder with string ensemble)
  RT Recorder with string ensemble
Concertos (Recorder with string orchestra)
   (M1105-6)
  RT Recorder with string orchestra
  —Solo with piano *(M1121)*
      BT Recorder and piano music, Arranged
Concertos (Recorder with string orchestra), Arranged *(M1105-6)*
Concertos (Recorders (2)) *(M1020-1021)*
  BT Recorder music (Recorders (2))
  RT Recorders (2) with orchestra
  —Scores *(M1020)*
  —Solos with piano *(M1021)*
      BT Trios (Piano, recorders (2)), Arranged
Concertos (Recorders (2) with instrumental ensemble)
  RT Recorders (2) with instrumental
      ensemble
Concertos (Recorders (2) with plectral ensemble) *(M1360)*
  RT Recorders (2) with plectral ensemble
Concertos (Recorders (2) with string orchestra) *(M1105-6)*
  BT Recorder music (Recorders (2))
  RT Recorders (2) with string orchestra
  —Solos with piano *(M1121)*
      BT Trios (Piano, recorders (2)), Arranged

Concertos (Recorders (3) with string orchestra) *(M1120-1121)*
  BT Woodwind trios (Recorders (3))
  RT Recorders (3) with string orchestra
  —Solos with piano *(M1121)*
    BT Quartets (Piano, recorders (3)),
      Arranged
Concertos (Recorders (4) with string orchestra) *(M1134.R4; M1135.R5)*
  BT Woodwind quartets (Recorders (4))
  RT Recorders (4) with string orchestra
Concertos (Recorders (6) with string orchestra) *(M1105-6)*
  BT Woodwind sextets (Recorders (6))
  RT Recorders (6) with string orchestra
Concertos (Rhythm band) *(M1040-1041)*
  BT Rhythm bands and orchestras
  RT Rhythm band with orchestra
Concertos (Saxophone) *(M1034-5)*
  RT Saxophone with orchestra
  —Excerpts
  —Solo with piano *(M1035)*
    UF Concertos (Saxophone)—Solo
      with piano—Excerpts
    BT Saxophone and piano music,
      Arranged
  —Solo with piano *(M1035)*
    BT Saxophone and piano music,
      Arranged
  —Excerpts
    USE Concertos (Saxophone)—
      Excerpts—Solo with piano
Concertos (Saxophone and piano) *(M1040-1041)*
  BT Saxophone and piano music
  RT Saxophone and piano with orchestra
  —Scores *(M1040)*
Concertos (Saxophone and trumpet with band) *(M1205-M1206; M1257)*
  RT Saxophone and trumpet with band
Concertos (Saxophone and trumpet with string orchestra) *(M1140-1141)*
  BT Saxophone and trumpet music
  RT Saxophone and trumpet with string
    orchestra
Concertos (Saxophone and violin) *(M1040-1041)*
  RT Saxophone and violin with orchestra
Concertos (Saxophone with band) *(M1205-6)*
  RT Saxophone with band
  —Solo with piano *(M1206)*
    BT Saxophone and piano music, Arranged
Concertos (Saxophone with chamber orchestra) *(M1034-5)*
  BT Chamber-orchestra music
  RT Saxophone with chamber orchestra
  —Solo with piano *(M1035.S4)*
    BT Saxophone and piano music,
      Arranged
Concertos (Saxophone with dance orchestra) *(M1353)*
  RT Saxophone with dance orchestra
  —Scores *(M1353)*

Concertos (Saxophone with instrumental ensemble)
  RT Saxophone with instrumental ensemble
Concertos (Saxophone with percussion ensemble)
  RT Saxophone with percussion ensemble
Concertos (Saxophone with string ensemble)
  RT Saxophone with string ensemble
Concertos (Saxophone with string orchestra) *(M1105-6)*
  BT String-orchestra music
  RT Saxophone with string orchestra
  —Solo with piano *(M1106)*
    BT Saxophone and piano music,
      Arranged
Concertos (Saxophone with wind ensemble)
  RT Saxophone with wind ensemble
Concertos (Saxophones (4)) *(M1034.S4; M1035.S4)*
  BT Woodwind quartets (Saxophones (4))
  RT Saxophones (4) with orchestra
  —Solos with pianos (2) *(M1035.S4)*
    BT Sextets (Pianos (2), saxophones (4)),
      Arranged
Concertos (Saxophones (4) with band) *(M1205-M1206)*
  BT Saxophones (4) with band
    Woodwind quartets (Saxophones (4))
Concertos (Saxophones (4) with chamber orchestra) *(M1034.S4; M1035.S4)*
  BT Woodwind quartets (Saxophones (4))
  RT Saxophones (4) with chamber orchestra
Concertos (Saxophones (4) with string orchestra) *(M1134.S4; M1135.S4)*
  BT Woodwind quartets (Saxophones (4))
  RT Saxophones (4) with string orchestra
  —Scores *(M1105)*
Concertos (Shakuhachi) *(M1034.S5; M1035.S5)*
  RT Shakuhachi with orchestra
Concertos (Shakuhachi and biwa) *(M1040-1041)*
  BT Shakuhachi and biwa music
  RT Shakuhachi and biwa with orchestra
Concertos (Shakuhachi with string orchestra) *(M1134.S5; M1135.S5)*
  RT Shakuhachi with string orchestra
Concertos (Sheng) *(M1039.4.S5)*
  RT Sheng with orchestra
Concertos (Sitar) *(M1037.4.S58)*
  BT Sitar music
  RT Sitar with orchestra
Concertos (Sitar and tabla with instrumental ensemble)
  RT Sitar and tabla with instrumental
    ensemble
Concertos (String orchestra) *(M1142)*
  BT String-orchestra music
Concertos (String quartet) *(M1040-1041)*
  BT String quartets
  RT String quartet with orchestra
  —Solos with piano *(M1041)*
    BT Piano quintets, Arranged

Concertos (String quartet), Arranged
(M1040-1041)
—Solos with piano *(M1041)*
BT Piano quintets, Arranged
Concertos (String quartet with band)
(M1205-6)
BT String quartets
RT String quartet with band
—Scores*(M1205)*
**Concertos (String quartet with chamber
orchestra)** *(M1040-1041)*
BT String quartets
RT String quartet with chamber orchestra
—Scores*(M1040)*
**Concertos (String quartet with instrumental
ensemble)**
RT String quartet with instrumental
ensemble
Concertos (String quartet with jazz ensemble)
RT String quartet with jazz ensemble
**Concertos (String quartet with string
orchestra)** *(M1105-6)*
BT String quartets
RT String quartet with string orchestra
Concertos (String trio) *(M1040-1041)*
BT String trios
RT String trio with orchestra
Concertos (String trio with string orchestra)
(M1105-6)
BT String trios
RT String trio with string orchestra
Concertos (Tar) *(M1037.4.T3)*
BT Tar music
—Solo with piano *(M1037.4.T3)*
BT Tar and piano music, Arranged
Concertos (Tárogató with chamber orchestra)
(M1034.T3; M1035.T3)
RT Tárogató with chamber orchestra
—Solo with piano *(M1035.T3)*
BT Tárogató and piano music, Arranged
Concertos (Ti tzŭ) *(M1034.T6)*
RT Ti tzŭ with orchestra
Concertos (Ti tzŭ with chamber orchestra)
(M1034.T6)
RT Ti tzŭ with chamber orchestra
Concertos (Timpani) *(M1038-1039)*
RT Timpani with orchestra
—Solo with piano *(M1039)*
BT Timpani and piano music, Arranged
**Concertos (Timpani and piano with string
orchestra)** *(M1140-1141)*
RT Timpani and piano with string orchestra
Concertos (Timpani with band)
(M1205-M1206; M1257)
RT Timpani with band
Concertos (Timpani with brass ensemble)
RT Timpani with brass ensemble
Concertos (Timpani with string ensemble)
RT Timpani with string ensemble
Concertos (Trautonium) *(M1039.4T)*
BT Trautonium music
RT Trautonium with orchestra

Concertos (Trombone) *(M1032-3)*
RT Trombone with orchestra
—Solo with harpsichord and piano *(M1033)*
BT Trios (Harpsichord, piano,
trombone), Arranged
—Solo with piano *(M1033)*
BT Trombone and piano music,
Arranged
**Concertos (Trombone and timpani with string
orchestra)** *(M1140-1141)*
RT Trombone and timpani with string
orchestra
Concertos (Trombone and trumpet)
RT Trombone and trumpet with orchestra
—Solos with piano *(M1041)*
BT Trios (Piano, trombone, trumpet),
Arranged
Concertos (Trombone and trumpet with band)
(M1205-6)
BT Trombone and trumpet music
RT Trombone and trumpet with band
**Concertos (Trombone and trumpet with brass
band)** *(M1205; M1257)*
RT Trombone and trumpet with brass band
**Concertos (Trombone and trumpet with string
orchestra)** *(M1105-6)*
BT Trombone and trumpet music
RT Trombone and trumpet with string
orchestra
—Solo with piano *(M1106)*
BT Trios (Piano, trombone, trumpet),
Arranged
Concertos (Trombone with band) *(M1205)*
BT Band music
RT Trombone with band
—Scores and parts *(M1205)*
—Solo with piano *(M1206)*
BT Trombone and piano music,
Arranged
Concertos (Trombone with brass band)
(M1205-1206)
RT Trombone with brass band
—Solo with piano *(M1206)*
BT Trombone and piano music,
Arranged
Concertos (Trombone with chamber orchestra)
(M1032-3)
RT Trombone with chamber orchestra
—Solo with piano *(M1033)*
BT Trombone and piano music,
Arranged
**Concertos (Trombone with instrumental
ensemble)**
RT Trombone with instrumental ensemble
Concertos (Trombone with string ensemble)
RT Trombone with string ensemble
Concertos (Trombone with string orchestra)
(M1105-6)
RT Trombone with string orchestra
—Scores *(M1105)*
—Solo with piano *(M1106)*
BT Trombone and piano music, Arranged

Concertos (Trombones (2) with string
orchestra) *(M1132-1133)*
RT Trombones (2) with string orchestra
Concertos (Trombones (3), trumpets (3) with
band) *(M1205-6)*
BT Brass sextets (Trombones (3), trumpets
(3))
RT Trombones (3), trumpets (3) with band
Concertos (Trombones (3) with band)
(M1205-6)
BT Brass trios (Trombones (3))
RT Trombones (3) with band
Concertos (Trombones (4) with band)
(M1205-1206)
BT Brass quartets (Trombones (4))
RT Trombones (4) with band
Concertos (Trumpet) *(M1030-1031)*
RT Concertos (Cornet)
Trumpet with orchestra
—Solo with piano *(M1031)*
BT Trumpet and piano music, Arranged
Concertos (Trumpet and chimes with string
orchestra) *(M1140-1141)*
RT Trumpet and chimes with string
orchestra
Concertos (Trumpet and piano)
(M1040-1041)
BT Trumpet and piano music
RT Trumpet and piano with orchestra
Concertos (Trumpet and piano with chamber
orchestra) *(M1040-1041)*
RT Trumpet and piano with chamber orchestra
Concertos (Trumpet and piano with string
orchestra) *(M1105-6)*
BT String-orchestra music
Trumpet and piano music
RT Trumpet and piano with string
orchestra
—Solos with piano *(M1106)*
BT Trios (Pianos (2), trumpet),
Arranged
Concertos (Trumpet and timpani)
(M1040-M1041)
BT Trumpet and timpani with orchestra
Concertos (Trumpet and tuba with brass
ensemble)
RT Trumpet and tuba with brass ensemble
Concertos (Trumpet and tuba with
instrumental ensemble)
RT Trumpet and tuba with instrumental
ensemble
Concertos (Trumpet and violin with string
orchestra) *(M1105-6)*
BT Trumpet and violin music
RT Trumpet and violin with string orchestra
Concertos (Trumpet and violin with string
orchestra), Arranged *(M1105-6)*
Concertos (Trumpet), Arranged *(M1030-1031)*
Concertos (Trumpet, harp, chimes with string
orchestra) *(M1105-6)*
BT Trios (Trumpet, harp, chimes)
RT Trumpet, harp, chimes with string orchestra

Concertos (Trumpet with band) *(M1205)*
RT Trumpet with band
—Solo with piano *(M1206)*
BT Trumpet and piano music, Arranged
Note under Concertos
Concertos (Trumpet with band), Arranged
(M1257)
Concertos (Trumpet with brass band)
(M1205; M1257)
RT Trumpet with brass band
Concertos (Trumpet with chamber orchestra)
(M1030-1031)
RT Trumpet with chamber orchestra
—Scores *(M1030)*
—Solo with piano *(M1031)*
BT Trumpet and piano music, Arranged
Concertos (Trumpet with dance orchestra)
(M1353)
RT Trumpet with dance orchestra
Concertos (Trumpet with instrumental
ensemble)
RT Trumpet with instrumental ensemble
Concertos (Trumpet with percussion ensemble)
RT Trumpet with percussion ensemble
Concertos (Trumpet with string ensemble)
RT Trumpet with string ensemble
—Solo with piano *(M260-261)*
BT Trumpet and piano music, Arranged
Concertos (Trumpet with string orchestra)
(M1105-6)
BT String-orchestra music
RT Trumpet with string orchestra
—Solo with piano *(M1106)*
BT Trumpet and piano music, Arranged
Concertos (Trumpet with string orchestra),
Arranged *(M1105-6)*
Concertos (Trumpet with wind ensemble)
RT Trumpet with wind ensemble
Concertos (Trumpets (2)) *(M1030-1031)*
RT Trumpets (2) with orchestra
Concertos (Trumpets (2) with band)
(M1205-1206; M1257)
RT Trumpets (2) with band
Concertos (Trumpets (2) with instrumental
ensemble)
RT Trumpets (2) with instrumental ensemble
Concertos (Trumpets (2) with string
orchestra) *(M1105-6)*
BT Trumpet music (Trumpets (2))
RT Trumpets (2) with string orchestra
—Solos with piano *(M1131)*
BT Trios (Piano, trumpets (2)),
Arranged
Concertos (Trumpets (2) with string
orchestra), Arranged *(M1105-6)*
Concertos (Trumpets (3)) *(M1030-1031)*
BT Brass trios (Trumpets (3))
RT Trumpets (3) with orchestra
Concertos (Trumpets (3) with band)
(M1205-M1206; M1257)
BT Brass trios (Trumpets (3))
RT Trumpets (3) with band

Concertos (Trumpets (3) with string orchestra) *(M1130-1131)*
 BT Brass trios (Trumpets (3))
 RT Trumpets (3) with string orchestra
Concertos (Trumpets (4) with string orchestra) *(M1130-1131)*
 BT Brass quartets (Trumpets (4))
 RT Trumpets (4) with string orchestra
Concertos (Trumpets (5), percussion with string orchestra) *(M1140-1141)*
 BT Octets (Trumpets (5), percussion)
  Sextets (Trumpets (5), percussion)
 RT Trumpets (5), percussion with string orchestra
Concertos (Trumpets (8) with string orchestra) *(M1130-1131)*
 BT Brass octets (Trumpets (8))
 RT Trumpets (8) with string orchestra
Concertos (Tuba) *(M1034-5)*
 RT Tuba with orchestra
 —Solo with piano *(M1035)*
  BT Tuba and piano music, Arranged
Concertos (Tuba with band) *(M1205)*
 RT Tuba with band
 —Solo with piano *(M1206)*
  BT Tuba and piano music, Arranged
Concertos (Tuba with brass band) *(M1205-M1206; M1257)*
 RT Tuba with brass band
 —Solo with piano *(M1206; M1257)*
  BT Tuba with piano music, Arranged
Concertos (Tuba with brass ensemble)
 RT Tuba with brass ensemble
Concertos (Tuba with instrumental ensemble)
 RT Tuba with instrumental ensemble
Concertos (Tuba with percussion ensemble)
 RT Tuba with percussion ensemble
Concertos (Tuba with string ensemble)
 RT Tuba with string ensemble
Concertos (Tuba with string orchestra) *(M1105-6)*
 RT Tuba with string orchestra
 —Solo with piano *(M1106)*
  BT Tuba and piano music, Arranged
Concertos (Tuba with wind ensemble)
 RT Tuba with wind ensemble
Concertos (Vibraphone) *(M1039.4.X9)*
 RT Vibraphone with orchestra
 —Scores and parts *(M1039.4.X9)*
Concertos (Vibraphone with percussion ensemble)
 RT Vibraphone with percussion ensemble
Concertos (Viol with instrumental ensemble)
 RT Viol with instrumental ensemble
Concertos (Viola) *(M1014-1015)*
 RT Viola with orchestra
 —Solo with piano *(M1015)*
  BT Viola and piano music, Arranged
Concertos (Viola and double bass) *(M1040-1041)*
 BT Viola and double-bass music
 RT Viola and double bass with orchestra

Concertos (Viola and harp with string orchestra) *(M1140-1141)*
 BT Viola and harp music
 RT Viola and harp with string orchestra
Concertos (Viola and harpsichord with string orchestra) *(M1105-6)*
 BT Viola and harpsichord music
 RT Viola and harpsichord with string orchestra
Concertos (Viola and harpsichord with string orchestra), Arranged *(M1105-6)*
Concertos (Viola and organ with string orchestra) *(M1105-6)*
 BT Viola and organ music
 RT Viola and organ with string orchestra
Concertos (Viola and organ with string orchestra), Arranged *(M1105-6)*
Concertos (Viola and piano) *(M1040-1041)*
 BT Viola and piano music
 RT Viola and piano with orchestra
 —Scores *(M1040)*
 —Solos with piano *(M1041)*
  BT Trios (Pianos (2), viola), Arranged
Concertos (Viola and piano with band) *(M1205-6)*
 BT Viola and piano music
 RT Viola and piano with band
 —Scores *(M1205)*
Concertos (Viola and piano with string orchestra) *(M1105-6)*
 BT Viola and piano music
 RT Viola and piano with string orchestra
Concertos (Viola and violoncello) *(M1040-1041)*
 RT Viola and violoncello with orchestra
Concertos (Viola and violoncello with string orchestra) *(M1140-1141)*
 RT Viola and violoncello with string orchestra
Concertos (Viola), Arranged *(M1014-1015)*
 —Solo with piano *(M1015)*
  BT Viola and piano music, Arranged
Concertos (Viola da gamba) *(M1019)*
 RT Viola da gamba with orchestra
Concertos (Viola da gamba with string orchestra) *(M1105-6)*
 RT Viola da gamba with string orchestra
 —Solo with piano *(M1119)*
  BT Viola da gamba and piano music, Arranged
Concertos (Viola d'amore) *(M1019)*
 RT Viola d'amore with orchestra
 —Solo with piano *(M1019.V56)*
  BT Viola d'amore and piano music, Arranged
Concertos (Viola d'amore and guitar with string orchestra) *(M1140-1141)*
 BT Viola d'amore and guitar music
 RT Viola d'amore and guitar with string orchestra
Concertos (Viola d'amore and lute with string orchestra) *(M1105-6)*
 BT Viola d'amore and lute music
 RT Viola d'amore and lute with string orchestra

Concertos (Viola d'amore with chamber orchestra) *(M1019)*
   RT Viola d'amore with chamber orchestra
Concertos (Viola d'amore with string orchestra) *(M1105-6)*
   RT Viola d'amore with string orchestra
   —Solo with piano
       BT Viola d'amore and piano music, Arranged
Concertos (Viola pomposa with string orchestra) *(M1119)*
   RT Viola pomposa with string orchestra
Concertos (Viola with band) *(M1205-6)*
   BT Viola with band
Concertos (Viola with chamber orchestra) *(M1014-1015)*
   RT Viola with chamber orchestra
   —Solo with piano *(M1015)*
       BT Viola and piano music, Arranged
Concertos (Viola with instrumental ensemble)
   RT Viola with instrumental ensemble
Concertos (Viola with string ensemble)
   RT Viola with string ensemble
Concertos (Viola with string orchestra) *(M1105-6)*
   RT Viola with string orchestra
   —Solo with piano *(M1115)*
       BT Viola and piano music, Arranged
Concertos (Viola with string orchestra), Arranged *(M1105-6)*
   —Solo with piano *(M1106)*
       BT Viola and piano music, Arranged
Concertos (Viola with wind ensemble)
   RT Viola with wind ensemble
Concertos (Violas (2) with string orchestra) *(M1114-1115)*
   BT Viola music (Violas (2))
   RT Violas (2) with string orchestra
   —Solos with piano *(M1115)*
       BT Trios (Piano, violas (2)), Arranged
Concertos (Violas (4)) *(M1014-1015)*
   BT String quartets (Violas (4))
   RT Violas (4) with orchestra
Concertos (Violin) *(M1012-1013)*
   RT Violin with orchestra
   —Analysis, appreciation
   —Cadenzas *(M1004.7; M1012.5)*
   —Excerpts
   ——Solo with piano *(M1013)*
       BT Violin and piano music, Arranged
   —Excerpts, Arranged
   —Solo with piano *(M1013)*
       BT Violin and piano music, Arranged
   Example under reference from Solo with piano
Concertos (Violin and double bass) *(M1040-1041)*
   RT Violin and double bass with orchestra
   —Solos with piano *(M1041)*
       BT Trios (Piano, violin, double bass), Arranged
Concertos (Violin and double bass with instrumental ensemble)
   RT Violin and double bass with instrumental ensemble

Concertos (Violin and double bass with string orchestra) *(M1140-1141)*
   BT Violin and double-bass music
   RT Violin and double bass with orchestra
Concertos (Violin and harp) *(M1040-1041)*
   BT Violin and harp music
   RT Violin and harp with orchestra
Concertos (Violin and harpsichord) *(M1040-1041)*
   BT Concertos (Violin and piano)
       Violin and harpsichord music
   RT Violin and harpsichord with orchestra
Concertos (Violin and harpsichord with string orchestra) *(M1105-6)*
   BT Violin and harpsichord music
   RT Violin and harpsichord with string orchestra
   —Scores *(M1105)*
Concertos (Violin and organ with string orchestra) *(M1105-6)*
   BT Violin and organ music
   RT Violin and organ with string orchestra
   —Scores *(M1105)*
Concertos (Violin and piano) *(M1040-1041)*
   BT Violin and piano music
   RT Violin and piano with orchestra
   NT Concertos (Violin and harpsichord)
   —Solos with piano *(M1041)*
       BT Trios (Pianos (2), violin), Arranged
Concertos (Violin and piano with chamber orchestra) *(M1040-1041)*
   BT Violin and piano music
   RT Violin and piano with chamber orchestra
   —Scores *(M1040)*
   —Solos with piano *(M1041)*
       BT Trios (Pianos (2), violin), Arranged
Concertos (Violin and piano with string ensemble)
   RT Violin and piano with string ensemble
Concertos (Violin and piano with string orchestra) *(M1105-6)*
   BT Violin and piano music
   RT Violin and piano with string orchestra
   —Solos with piano *(M1106)*
       BT Trios (Pianos (2), violin), Arranged
Concertos (Violin and piano with wind ensemble)
   BT Violin and piano with wind ensemble
Concertos (Violin and viola) *(M1040-1041)*
   BT Violin and viola music
   RT Violin and viola with orchestra
   —Solos with piano *(M1041)*
       BT Trios (Piano, violin, viola), Arranged
Concertos (Violin and viola with chamber orchestra) *(M1040-1041)*
   BT Violin and viola music
   RT Violin and viola with chamber orchestra
   —Solos with piano *(M1041)*
       BT Trios (Piano, violin, viola), Arranged

Concertos (Violin and viola with instrumental ensemble)
  RT Violin and viola with instrumental ensemble
Concertos (Violin and viola with string orchestra) *(M1105-6)*
  BT String-orchestra music
     Violin and viola music
  RT Violin and viola with string orchestra
Concertos (Violin and violoncello) *(M1040-1041)*
  BT Violin and violoncello music
  RT Violin and violoncello with orchestra
  —Excerpts
  — —Solos with piano *(M1041)*
     BT Piano trios, Arranged
  —Solos with piano *(M1041)*
     BT Piano trios, Arranged
  Example under reference from Solos with piano
Concertos (Violin and violoncello with chamber orchestra) *(M1040-1041)*
  BT Violin and violoncello music
  RT Violin and violoncello with chamber orchestra
  —Solos with piano *(M1041)*
     BT Piano trios, Arranged
Concertos (Violin and violoncello with instrumental ensemble)
  RT Violin and violoncello with instrumental ensemble
Concertos (Violin and violoncello with string orchestra) *(M1105-6)*
  BT Violin and violoncello music
  RT Violin and violoncello with string orchestra
Concertos (Violin), Arranged *(M1012-1013)*
  —Solo with piano *(M1013)*
     BT Violin and piano music, Arranged
Concertos (Violin, viola, violoncello, double bass with string orchestra) *(M1140-1141)*
  BT String quartets (Violin, viola, violoncello, double bass)
  RT Violin, viola, violoncello, double bass with string orchestra
Concertos (Violin, violoncellos (2) with string orchestra) *(M1140-1141)*
  BT String trios (Violin, violoncellos (2))
  RT Violin, violoncellos (2) with string orchestra
Concertos (Violin with band) *(M1205-6)*
  RT Violin with band
Concertos (Violin with chamber orchestra) *(M1012-1013)*
  BT Chamber-orchestra music
  RT Violin with chamber orchestra
  —Solo with piano *(M1013)*
     BT Violin and piano music, Arranged
Concertos (Violin with instrumental ensemble)
  RT Violin with instrumental ensemble
Concertos (Violin with percussion ensemble)
  RT Violin with percussion ensemble
  Note under Percussion ensembles

Concertos (Violin with string ensemble)
  RT Violin with string ensemble
Concertos (Violin with string orchestra) *(M1105-6)*
  BT String-orchestra music
  RT Violin with string orchestra
  —Solo with piano *(M1106)*
     BT Violin and piano music, Arranged
Concertos (Violin with string orchestra), Arranged *(M1105-6)*
  —Solo with piano *(M1106)*
     BT Violin and piano music, Arranged
Concertos (Violin with wind ensemble)
  RT Violin with wind ensemble
Concertos (Violins (2)) *(M1012-1013)*
  BT Violin music (Violins (2))
  RT Violins (2) with orchestra
  —Solos with piano *(M1013)*
     BT Trios (Piano, violins (2)), Arranged
Concertos (Violins (2) and viola with chamber orchestra) *(M1040-1041)*
  RT Violins (2), viola with chamber orchestra
Concertos (Violins (2), viola) *(M1040-1041)*
  BT String trios (Violins (2), viola)
  RT Violins (2), viola with orchestra
Concertos (Violins (2), violas (2), violoncello with string orchestra) *(M1140-1141)*
  BT String quintets (Violins (2), violas (2), violoncello)
  RT Violins (2), violas (2), violoncello with string orchestra
Concertos (Violins (2), violas (2) with string orchestra) *(M1140-1141)*
  BT String quartets (Violins (2), violas (2))
  RT Violins (2), violas (2) with string orchestra
Concertos (Violins (2), violoncello with string orchestra) *(M1140-1141)*
  BT String trios (Violins (2), violoncello)
  RT Violins (2), violoncello with string orchestra
Concertos (Violins (2), violoncellos (2) with string orchestra) *(M1140-1141)*
  BT String quartets (Violins (2), violoncellos (2))
  RT Violins (2), violoncellos (2) with string orchestra
Concertos (Violins (2) with string ensemble)
  RT Violins (2) with string ensemble
Concertos (Violins (2) with string orchestra) *(M1105-6)*
  BT String-orchestra music
     Violin music (Violins (2))
  RT Violins (2) with string orchestra
  —Solos with piano *(M1113)*
     BT Trios (Piano, violins (2)), Arranged
Concertos (Violins (2) with string orchestra), Arranged
  —Solos with piano *(M1106)*
     BT Trios (Piano, violins (2)), Arranged
Concertos (Violins (3)) *(M1012-1013)*
  BT String trios (Violins (3))
  RT Violins (3) with orchestra
  —Scores *(M1012)*
  —Solos with piano *(M1013)*
     BT Quartets (Piano, violins (3)), Arranged

Concertos (Violins (3), viola, violoncello)
   (M1040-M1041)
  BT Violins (3), viola, violoncello with
      orchestra
Concertos (Violins (3), viola, violoncello with
    string orchestra) *(M1105-6)*
  BT String quintets (Violins (3), viola,
      violoncello)
  RT Violins (3), viola, violoncello with
      string orchestra
  —Scores *(M1105)*
Concertos (Violins (3) with string orchestra)
   (M1105-6)
  BT String-orchestra music
      String trios (Violins (3))
  RT Violins (3) with string orchestra
Concertos (Violins (3) with string orchestra),
    Arranged *(M1105-6)*
  —Scores and parts *(M1105)*
  —Solos with piano *(M1106)*
      BT Quartets (Piano, violins (3)),
         Arranged
Concertos (Violins (4) with string orchestra)
   (M1105-6)
  BT String quartets (Violins (4))
  RT Violins (4) with string orchestra
  —Solos with piano *(M1106)*
      BT Quintets (Piano, violins (4)),
         Arranged
Concertos (Violins (5)) *(M1012-1013)*
  BT String quintets (Violins (5))
  RT Violins (5) with orchestra
Concertos (Violoncello) *(M1016-1017)*
  RT Violoncello with orchestra
  —Analysis, appreciation
  —Excerpts
  — —Solo with piano *(M1017)*
      UF Concertos (Violoncello)—Solo
         with piano—Excerpts
      BT Violoncello and piano music,
         Arranged
  —Solo with piano *(M1017)*
      BT Violoncello and piano music,
         Arranged
  — —Excerpts
      USE Concertos (Violoncello)—
            Excerpts—Solo with piano
Concertos (Violoncello and double bass)
   (M1040-1041)
  RT Violoncello and double bass with
      orchestra
Concertos (Violoncello and harp)
   (M1040-1041)
  RT Violoncello and harp with orchestra
Concertos (Violoncello and harp with string
    orchestra) *(M1105-6)*
  BT Violoncello and harp music
  RT Violoncello and harp with string
      orchestra
Concertos (Violoncello and piano)
   (M1040-1041)
  RT Violoncello and piano with orchestra

Concertos (Violoncello), Arranged *(M1016-1017)*
  —Solo with piano *(M1017)*
      BT Violoncello and piano music,
         Arranged
Concertos (Violoncello piccolo with string
    orchestra) *(M1105-6)*
  BT Violoncello piccolo music
  RT Violoncello piccolo with string
      orchestra
Concertos (Violoncello with band)
   (M1205-6)
  RT Violoncello with band
  —Scores *(M1205)*
Concertos (Violoncello with brass band)
   (M1205; M1257)
  RT Violoncello with brass band
Concertos (Violoncello with chamber
    orchestra) *(M1016-1017)*
  RT Violoncello with chamber orchestra
  —Solo with piano *(M1017)*
      BT Violoncello and piano music,
         Arranged
Concertos (Violoncello with instrumental
    ensemble)
  RT Violoncello with instrumental ensemble
  —Solo with piano
      BT Violoncello and piano music,
         Arranged
Concertos (Violoncello with string ensemble)
  RT Violoncello with string ensemble
Concertos (Violoncello with string orchestra)
   (M1105-6)
  BT String-orchestra music
  RT Violoncello with string orchestra
  —Solo with piano *(M1106)*
      BT Violoncello and piano music,
         Arranged
Concertos (Violoncello with string orchestra),
    Arranged *(M1105-6)*
  —Solo with piano *(M1106)*
      BT Violoncello and piano music,
         Arranged
Concertos (Violoncello with wind ensemble)
  RT Violoncello with wind ensemble
Concertos (Violoncellos (2)) *(M1016-1017)*
  BT Violoncello music (Violoncellos (2))
  RT Violoncellos (2) with orchestra
  NT Violoncellos (2) with chamber orchestra
Concertos (Violoncellos (2) with chamber
    orchestra) *(M1016-1017)*
  RT Violoncellos (2) with chamber orchestra
Concertos (Violoncellos (2) with instrumental
    ensemble)
  RT Violoncellos (2) with instrumental
      ensemble
Concertos (Violoncellos (2) with string
    orchestra) *(M1105-6)*
  BT String-orchestra music
      Violoncello music (Violoncellos (2))
  RT Violoncellos (2) with string orchestra
  —Solos with piano *(M1117)*
      BT Trios (Piano, violoncellos (2)), Arranged

Concertos (Violoncellos (3)) *(M1016-1017)*
    BT   String trios (Violoncellos (3))
    RT   Violoncellos (3) with orchestra
Concertos (Wind instrument with instrumental ensemble)
    RT   Wind instrument with instrumental ensemble
Concertos (Xylophone) *(M1038-9)*
    RT   Xylophone with orchestra
    —Solo with piano *(M1039)*
        BT   Xylophone and piano music, Arranged
Concertos (Yang ch'in) *(M1039.4.Y35)*
    RT   Yang ch'in with orchestra
Concertos (Zither) *(M1037.4.Z6)*
    BT   Zither with orchestra
Concerts [May Subd Geog]
    BT   Amusements
        Music
    RT   Music—Performance
        Music festivals
    —Agents
      USE Concert agents
    —Program building
      UF   Program building (Music)
    —Programs *(ML25.7; ML40-ML44)*
      UF   Programs, Concert
      NT   Operas—Programs
    Example under Performing arts
Concord Summer Jazz Festival *(ML38)*
    BT   Jazz festivals—California
Concrete music
        Here are entered works in which the sounds produced were originally recorded on magnetic tape from natural sounds and subsequently rearranged or altered. The heading is used as a second heading when the tape is used with a specifically named medium or performance, *e.g.* 1. Quintets (Clarinet, flute, harp, viola, violoncello) 2. Concrete music.
    UF   Music, Concrete
        Musique concrète
        Tape-recorder music
    BT   Music
    RT   Electronic music
    NT   Monologues with music (Concrete music)
        Suites (Concrete music)
        Symphonies (Concrete music)
        Variations (Concrete music)
Conducting *(History, ML457; Instruction, MT85)*
        Here are entered works on orchestral conducting or a combination of orchestral and choral conducting. Works restricted to choral conducting are entered under the heading Conducting, Choral.
    BT   Music—Instruction and study
    RT   Bands (Music)
        Conductors (Music)
        Music—Performance

Conducting *(History, ML457; Instruction, MT85)*
    (Continued)
    RT   Orchestra
        Rehearsals (Music)
    NT   Conducting, Choral
Conducting, Choral *(History, ML457; Instruction, MT85)*
    UF   Choral conducting
    BT   Choral music
        Church music
        Conducting
    RT   Choirs (Music)
        Choral music
        Conductors (Music)
    Note under Conducting
Conductors (Music) [May Subd Geog]
    UF   Bandmasters
        Music—Biography
        Music conductors
    BT   Musicians
        Orchestra
    RT   Conducting
        Conducting, Choral
Conductus
    BT   Part-songs
        Part-songs, Sacred
Confitebimur tibi (Music)
    USE Psalms (Music)—75th Psalm
Confitebor tibi Domine in toto corde meo, in consilio (Music)
    USE Psalms (Music)—111th Psalm
Confitebor tibi Domine in toto corde meo, narrabo (Music)
    USE Psalms (Music)—9th Psalm
Confitebor tibi Domine in toto corde meo, quoniam audisti (Music)
    USE Psalms (Music)—138th Psalm
Confitemini Domino quoniam bonus, quoniam in aeternum (Music)
    USE Psalms (Music)—136th Psalm
Confitemini Domino quoniam bonus, quoniam in saeculum misericordia eius, Dicant qui redempti (Music)
Confitemini Domino quoniam bonus, quoniam in saeculum misericordia eius, Dicat nunc Israel
    USE Psalms (Music)—118th Psalm
Confitemini Domino quoniam bonus, quoniam in saeculum misericordia eius, Quis loquetur (Music)
    USE Psalms (Music)—106th Psalm
Conga (Drum)
    BT   Drum
        Musical instruments—Cuba
Congadas [May Subd Geog]
    BT   Folk-songs, Portuguese—Brazil
Conn organ music
    USE Electronic organ music (Conn registration)
Connsonata organ music
    USE Electronic organ music (Conn registration)
Conserva me, Domine (Music)
    USE Psalms (Music)—16th Psalm

Conservatories of music [May Subd Geog]
  (ML3795;MT1-MT5)
  UF Music—Conservatories
      Music conservatories
      Music schools
  BT Music
      Music—Instruction and study
      Schools
  NT Maîtrises
Contemporary Christian music [May Subd Geog]
  ML3187.5 (History and criticism)
  UF CCM
      Christian contemporary music
      Christian music, Contemporary
      Christian popular music
      Evangelical popular music
      Jesus music
      Popular music, Christian
  BT Gospel music
      Popular music
      Sacred songs
  NT Christian rock music
Contemporary music radio stations
  USE Popular music radio stations
Continuo
  USE Continuo *used as part of the
          specification of medium in headings,
          e.g.* Trio-Sonatas (Violins (2),
          continuo)
      Thorough bass
Continuo and bagpipe music
  USE Bagpipe and continuo music
Continuo and bassoon music
  USE Bassoon and continuo music
Continuo and cornett music
  USE Cornett and continuo music
Continuo and double-bass music
  USE Double-bass and continuo music
Continuo and dulcimer music
  USE Dulcimer and continuo music
Continuo and flageolet music
  USE Flageolet and continuo music
Continuo and flute music
  USE Flute and continuo music
Continuo and guitar music
  USE Guitar and continuo music
Continuo and hurdy-gurdy music
  USE Hurdy-gurdy and continuo music
Continuo and lyra-viol music
  USE Lyra-viol and continuo music
Continuo and mandolin music
  USE Mandolin and continuo music
Continuo and oboe d'amore music
  USE Oboe d'amore and continuo music
Continuo and oboe music
  USE Oboe and continuo music
Continuo and recorder music
  USE Recorder and continuo music
Continuo and saxophone music
  USE Saxophone and continuo music
Continuo and tenor violin music
  USE Tenor violin and continuo music

Continuo and trombone music
  USE Trombone and continuo music
Continuo and trumpet music
  USE Trumpet and continuo music
Continuo and unspecified instrument music
  USE Duets (Unspecified instrument and
          continuo)
Continuo and viol music
  USE Viol and continuo music
Continuo and viola da gamba music
  USE Viola da gamba and continuo music
Continuo and viola d'amore music
  USE Viola d'amore and continuo music
Continuo and viola music
  USE Viola and continuo music
Continuo and violin music
  USE Violin and continuo music
Continuo and violoncello music
  USE Violoncello and continuo music
Contra dances
  USE Country-dances
Contrabass players
  USE Double-bassists
Contrabassists
  USE Double-bassists
Contrabassoon (*History and construction,
      ML950-ML953; Instruction, MT 412*)
  UF Double bassoon
  BT Bassoon
Contrabassoon and piano music (*M253-254*)
  UF Piano and contrabassoon music
Contrabassoon and piano music, Arranged
      (*M253-254*)
  NT Contrabassoon with string
          ensemble—Solo with piano
Contrabassoon and piccolo music
      (*M288-289*)
  UF Piccolo and contrabassoon music
Contrabassoon music (*M75-79*)
  SA Concertos, Minuets, Sonatas, Suites,
          *and similar headings with specification
          of instruments which include specifications
          for contrabassoon; also* Trios [Quartets,
          etc.], Wind trios [quartets, etc.], *and*
          Woodwind trios [quartets, etc.] *followed
          by specifications which include
          contrabassoon; also* Wind ensembles,
          Woodwind ensembles, *and headings
          beginning with the words Contrabassoon or
          Contrabassoons.*
Contrabassoon with string ensemble
  RT Concertos (Contrabassoon with string
          ensemble)
  —Solo with piano (*M253-254*)
      BT Contrabassoon and piano music,
              Arranged
Contradance
  USE Country-dance
Contradances
  USE Country-dances
Contratenors
  USE Countertenors

Coplas [May Subd Geog] *(PQ6209.C6)*
> Here are entered collections of coplas.
> Works dealing with the copla as a liter-
> ary form are entered under the heading
> Copla.
> BT Folk-songs, Spanish

Coppélia (Ballet)
> BT Ballets

Copyright [May Subd Geog]
> —Adaptations [May Subd Geog]
>> UF Arrangement (Music)—Copyright
>> Copyright—Musical arrangements
> —Artistic performance [May Subd Geog] *(Z650)*
>> Here are entered works treating of the
>> intellectual property of actors,
>> musicians and other performing art-
>> tists in their performance. Works on
>> the protection of authors and com-
>> posers against unauthorized per-
>> formance of their works are entered
>> under the heading Copyright—Per-
>> forming rights.
>> BT Copyright—Music
> —Moving-picture music [May Subd Geog]
>> UF Moving-picture music—Copyright
>> BF Copyright—Music
> —Music [May Subd Geog] *(Z653)*
>> UF Music—Copyright
>> NT Copyright—Artistic performance
>> Copyright—Broadcasting rights
>> Copyright—Moving-picture music
>> Copyright—Operas
>> Musicians—Legal status, laws, etc.
> —Musical arrangements
>> USE Copyright—Adaptations
> —Operas [May Subd Geog]
>> UF Operas—Copyright
>> BT Copyright—Music
>> RT Copyright—Performing rights

Cornemuse
> USE Bagpipe

Cornet *(History and construction,
ML960-ML961)*
> UF Cornopean
> BT Brass instruments
> RT Trumpet
> —Orchestra studies *(MT446)*
>> BT Cornet—Studies and exercises
> —Studies and exercises *(MT445)*
>> NT Cornet—Orchestra studies

Cornet à bouquin
> USE Cornett

Cornet and baritone music
> USE Baritone and cornet music

Cornet and euphonium music *(M288-289)*
> UF Euphonium and cornet music

Cornet and euphonium with brass band
(M1205-1206; 1257)
> RT Concertos (Cornet and euphonium with
> brass band)

Cornet and organ music *(M182-6)*
> UF Organ and cornet music

Cornet and piano music *(M260-261)*
> UF Piano and cornet music
> NT Sonatas (Cornet and piano)
> Suites (Cornet and piano)

Cornet and piano music, Arranged
(M260-261)
> NT Concertos (Cornet with string
> orchestra)—Solo with piano
> Cornet with band—Solo with piano
> Cornet with brass band—Solo with piano

Cornet and piano music (Jazz) *(M260-261)*

Cornet and trumpet music *(M288-9)*
> UF Trumpet and cornet music
> NT Concertos (Cornet and trumpet)
> Cornet and trumpet with orchestra

Cornet and trumpet with orchestra
(M1040-1041)
> BT Cornet and trumpet music
> RT Concertos (Cornet and trumpet)

Cornet and trumpet with orchestra, Arranged
(M1040-1041)

Cornet music *(M85-89)*
> SA Concertos, Minuets, Sonatas, Suites,
> *and similar headings with
> specification of instruments;* Brass
> trios [quartets, etc.], Trios [Quartets,
> etc.], *and* Wind trios [quartets, etc.]
> *followed by specifications which
> include the cornet; also* Brass
> ensembles, Wind ensembles, *and
> headings that begin with the words
> cornet or cornets.*
> NT Concertos (Cornet)
> Cornet with orchestra

Cornet music, Arranged (Jazz)
> USE Cornet music (Jazz)

Cornet music (Cornets (2)) *(M288-9)*
Cornet music (Cornets (3))
> USE Brass trios (Cornets (3))
Cornet music (Cornets (4))
> USE Brass quartets (Cornets (4))

Cornet music (Jazz) *(M85-89)*
> UF Cornet music, Arranged (Jazz)

Cornet with band *(M1205)*
> RT Concertos (Cornet with band)
> NT Variations (Cornet with band)
> —Solo with piano *(M1205)*
>> BT Cornet and piano music, Arranged

Cornet with brass band *(M1205-M1206;
M1257)*
> RT Concertos (Cornet with brass band)
> —Solo with piano *(M1206)*
>> BT Cornet and piano music, Arranged

Cornet with instrumental ensemble
> RT Concertos (Cornet with instrumental
> ensemble)

Cornet with orchestra *(M1030-1031)*
> BT Cornet music
> Orchestral music
> RT Concertos (Cornet)

Cornet with orchestra, Arranged
(M1030-1031)

Cornet with string orchestra *(M1130-1131)*
   RT Concertos (Cornet with string orchestra)
Corneta
   USE Cornett
Cornets (4) with band *(M1205-6)*
   UF Four cornets with band
   BT Brass quartets (Cornets (4))
   RT Concertos (Cornets (4) with band)
Cornets (4) with band, Arranged *(M1257)*
   —Scores and parts *(M1257)*
Cornett *(ML990.C)*
   UF Cornet à bouquin
         Corneta
         Cornetto
         Zink
   BT Brass instruments
Cornett and continuo music
   UF Continuo and cornett music
   NT Sonatas (Cornett and continuo)
Cornett music *(M110.C)*
   NT Quartets (Cornett, trombone, violin, continuo)
Cornetto
   USE Cornett
Cornish folk-songs
   USE Folk-songs, Cornish
Cornopean
   USE Cornet
Coronation music
   UF Coronations—Music
   BT Music
Coronations [May Subd Geog]
   —Music
      USE Coronation music
Corpus Christi festival music
   BT Church music
         Sacred vocal music
Corridos *(Collections, PQ7260; History, PQ7180)*
   BT Folk-songs, Spanish—Mexico
Cortege of eagles (Ballet)
   BT Ballets
Cosaques
   UF Kozaki
   BT Dance music
Costume [May Subd Geog]
   UF Opera—Costume
Cotillions
   BT Dance music
Counterpoint *(History, ML446; Instruction, MT55)*
   BT Composition (Music)
         Music
         Music—Instruction and study
         Music—Theory
   NT Canon (Music)
         Descants
         Fugue
         Organum
         Schenkerian analysis
Countertenors
   UF Contratenors
         Counter tenors
   BT Singers

Country and western music
   USE Country music
Country-dances
   UF Contra dances
         Contradances
   BT Dance music
   NT Monferrinas
Country music [May Subd Geog]
      ML3523-ML3524 (History and criticism)
   UF Country and western music
         Hillbilly music
         Western and country music
   BT Folk music—United States
         Popular music
   SA Subdivisions *Methods (Country)* and *Studies and exercises (Country)* under names of musical instruments
   NT Bluegrass music
         Fiddle tunes
         Guitar—Methods (Country)
         Honky-tonk music
         Western swing (Music)
   —To 1931
   —1931-1940
   —1941-1950
   —1951-1960
   —1961-1970
   —1971-1980
   —1981-
   —United States
      USE Country music
Country music groups [May Subd Geog]
   BT Musical groups
Country musicians [May Subd Geog]
   UF Hillbilly musicians
   BT Musicians
   NT Bluegrass musicians
         Gospel musicians
Courantes
   BT Dance music
Cowboys [May Subd Geog]
   —Songs and music
Cradle songs
   USE Lullabies
Credo (Music) *(M2079.L3; M2099.L3)*
   UF Nicene Creed (Music)
Creole folk-songs
   USE Folk-songs, Creole
Cries [May Subd Geog] *(GT3450)*
   UF Street songs
   BT Street music and musicians
Criticism [May Subd Geog]
      Here are entered works on the principles of criticism in general and of literary criticism in particular. Criticism in a special field is entered under the appropriate heading, *e.g.* Art criticism; English literature—History and criticism; English poetry—History and criticism; Literature—History and criticism; Music—History and criticism.

Criticism [May Subd Geog]
   (Continued)
   SA *subdivision* History and criticism *under*
          literary, music, and film form headings, e.g.
          English literature—History and criticism;
          Chamber music—History and criticism;
          Erotic films—History and criticism; *also*
          subdivision Criticism and interpretation
          under names of persons active in the fine
          arts, music, and performing arts; and
          subdivision Criticism, interpretation, etc.
          under names of sacred books or their parts,
          e.g. Bible—Criticism, interpretation, etc.
   NT Music—History and criticism
Critics
   NT Music critics
Croatian folk-songs
   USE Folk-songs, Croatian
Cromorne
   USE Crumhorn
Crooning
   BT Singing
Crumhorn *(ML990.C8)*
   UF Cromorne
          Krummhorn
   BT Oboe
          Woodwind instruments
   —Methods *(MT520)*
Crumhorn music *(M110.C78)*
   NT Woodwind quartets (Crumhorns (4))
Csakan
   USE Czakan
Cuatro puertorriqueño *(ML1015-1018)*
   BT Musical instruments—Puerto Rico
   —Methods *(MT648)*
Cum invocarem (Music)
   USE Psalms (Music)—4th Psalm
Cuna lullabies
   USE Lullabies, Cuna
Curses in opera
   BT Blessing and cursing
          Opera
Curtall
   USE Bassoon
Customizing of guitars
   USE Guitar—Customizing
Cycles, Song
   USE Song cycles
Cymbal music *(M146)*
   NT Octets (Piano, clarinet, cymbals (2),
          violins (2), viola, violoncello)
Cymbalom
   USE Cimbalom
Cymbals *(ML1040)*
Czakan
   UF Csakan
   BT Flute
          Recorder (Musical instrument)
Czakan and piano music *(M240-242)*
   UF Piano and czakan music
Czardas
   UF Csárdás
   BT Dance music

Czech carols
   USE Carols, Czech
Czech folk-songs
   USE Folk-songs, Czech
Czech hymns
   USE Hymns, Czech
Czech songs
   USE Songs, Czech
Dakota folk-songs
   USE Folk-songs, Dakota
Dance band music
   USE Big band music
          Dance-orchestra music
Dance bands
   USE Big bands
          Dance orchestras
Dance music [May Subd Geog]
      Here are entered collections of miscel-
        laneous dance music. Music for in-
        dividual dances is entered under dance
        form, *e.g.:* Polkas, Waltzes.
      If the work is for a specific medium, a
        second heading is assigned, *e.g.* 1.
        Dance music. 2. Piano music.
      For an individual dance which is assigned
        a heading that is not qualified by
        medium, a second heading is assigned
        if the work is for a specific medium,
        e.g. 1. Mazurkas. 2. Piano music.
      For works consisting of dance music of an
        individual ethnic group, additional
        subject entry is made under the heading
        [ethnic group]—[place]—Music.
   BT Dancing
          Instrumental music
          Music
   NT Allemandes
          Ballet dance music
          Belly dance music
          Boleros
          Bourrées
          Cancans
          Cha-chas
          Clog-dance music
          Cosaques
          Cotillions
          Country-dances
          Courantes
          Czardas
          Dance-orchestra music
          Disco music
          Estampies
          Fandangos
          Folias (Music)
          Folk dance music
          Fox trots
          Frevos
          Furiants
          Galliards
          Galops
          Gavottes
          Hornpipes
          Jigs

Dance music [May Subd Geog]
   (Continued)
     NT Jotas
         Kolos
         Krakowiaks
         Ländler
         Mazurkas
         Merengues
         Minuets
         Morris-dances
         Pasillos
         Pasodobles
         Passamezzos
         Passepieds
         Pavans
         Polka-mazurkas
         Polkas
         Polonaises
         Quadrilles
         Redowas
         Reels (Music)
         Rigaudons
         Rumbas
         Salsa
         Saltarellos
         Sambas
         Sarabands
         Sardanas
         Schottisches
         Sicilianas
         Tangos
         Tarantellas
         Waltzes
   —History and criticism *(ML3400-3451)*
       NT Instrumentation and orchestration
            (Dance orchestra)
          Jazz music
   —Africa, West
       NT Gahu
   —Italy
       NT Monferrinas
   —Panama
       NT Tamboritos
   —Scotland
       NT Strathspeys
   —Spain
       NT Flamenco music
   —United States
       NT Rapping (Music)
Dance orchestra
   USE Dance orchestras
Dance-orchestra music *(M1350)*
   UF Dance band music
   BT Band music
        Dance music
        Instrumental music
        Orchestral music
   RT Jazz ensembles
   SA Concertos ([Solo instrument(s)] with
         dance orchestra); [Solo
         instrument(s)] with dance orchestra;
         Variations, Waltzes, *and similar*
         headings with specification of

Dance-orchestra music *(M1350)*
   (Continued)
   SA *instruments which include the*
         specification Dance orchestra
   NT Big band music
        Concertos (Dance orchestra)
        Overtures (Dance orchestra)
        Suites (Dance orchestra)
        Trumpet with dance orchestra
        Variations (Dance orchestra)
        Waltzes (Dance orchestra)
Dance orchestras [May Subd Geog]
   UF Dance bands
        Dance orchestra
   BT Bands (Music)
        Music
        Musical groups
        Orchestra
   NT Big bands
        Instrumentation and orchestration
          (Dance orchestra)
        Rock groups
Danish ballads
   USE Ballads, Danish
Danish folk-songs
   USE Folk-songs, Danish
Danish songs
   USE Songs, Danish
Ḍaph
       ML1038.D (History)
   UF Daf
        Daff
        Duff
   BT Frame drums
   BT Musical instruments—India
Ḍaph and piano music
   UF Piano and ḍaph music
Ḍaph music
   SA *Concertos; Minuets; Sonatas; Suites;* and
         similar headings with specification of
         instruments; *Trios [Quartets, etc.]* followed
         by specifications which include daph; also
         Percussion ensembles; Percussion music
         and headings that begin with the word Daph
De profundis (Music)
   USE Psalms (Music)—130th Psalm
Death in music
   BT Funeral music
        Music
        Program music
        Symbolism in music
Death songs
   BT Songs
Declamation, Musical
   USE Monologues with music
        Musical accentuation
Demung gantung
   USE Gender (Musical instrument)
DESC7 (Computer program)
   BT Computer programs
        MIDIM (Computer system)
        Music—Computer programs
   RT MIDIM7 (Computer program)

Deus, Deus meus respice in me (Music)
    USE Psalms (Music)—22d Psalm
Deus, auribus (Music)
    USE Psalms (Music)—44th Psalm
Deus, in adjutorium (Music)
    USE Psalms (Music)—70th Psalm
Deus in nomine tuo (Music)
    USE Psalms (Music)—54th Psalm
Deus misereatur (Music)
    USE Psalms (Music)—67th Psalm
Deus noster refugium (Music)
    USE Psalms (Music)—46th Psalm
Deus, quis similis (Music)
    USE Psalms (Music)—83d Psalm
Devotional exercises *(BV4800-BV4870; By*
        denomination, BX)
    NT Church music
        Hymns
        Hymns—Devotional use
Dictation, Musical
    USE Musical dictation
Diction
    RT Elocution
    NT Singing—Diction
Dies irae (Music)
    BT Sacred vocal music
        Sequences (Music)
Dilexi, quoniam (Music)
    USE Psalms (Music)—116th Psalm
Diligam te Domine (Music)
    USE Psalms (Music)—18th Psalm
Diminution (Music)
    USE Embellishment (Music)
Dingal Hindu hymns
    USE Hindu hymns, Dingal
Dinka folk-songs
    USE Folk-songs, Dinka
Direct radiator loudspeakers [May Subd Geog]
        TK5983
    UF Hornless loudspeakers
        Loudspeakers, Direct radiator
    BT Loudspeakers
Directors, Opera
    USE Opera producers and directors
Dirges
    BT Funeral hymns
        Laments
Dirty songs
    USE Bawdy songs
Disc jockeys [May Subd Geog]
    BT Radio and music
Disco music [May Subd Geog]
        ML3526 (History and criticism)
    UF Music, Disco
    BT Dance music
        Popular music
Disco musicians [May Subd Geog]
    BT Musicians
Discotheques [May Subd Geog]
    BT Music-halls (Variety-theaters, cabarets, etc.)
Dixi, Custodiam (Music)
    USE Psalms (Music)—39th Psalm

Dixieland music *(M1366)*
    UF Music, Dixieland
    BT Jazz ensembles
        Jazz music
Dixit Dominus (Music)
    USE Psalms (Music)—110th Psalm
Dixit injustus (Music)
    USE Psalms (Music)—36th Psalm
Dobro *(ML1015-1018)*
    BT Guitar
    —Methods *(MT599.D6)*
Dobro music *(M125-129)*
    BT Guitar music
Dobro with instrumental ensemble
    RT Concertos (Dobro with instrumental
        ensemble)
Dogri folk-songs
    USE Folk-songs, Dogri
Dolçaina
    USE Dulzaina
Dolzaina
    USE Dulzaina
Dombäck
    USE Tunbūk
Dombak
    USE Tunbūk
Dombra
    USE Domra
Domine, Dominus noster (Music)
    USE Psalms (Music)—8th Psalm
Domine, exaudi orationem meam, auribus
        percipe (Music)
    USE Psalms (Music)—143d Psalm
Domine, exaudi orationem meam, et clamor
        meus (Music)
    USE Psalms (Music)—102d Psalm
Domine, ne in furore tuo arguas me, neque in
        ira tua corripias me, miserere mei
        Domine (Music)
    USE Psalms (Music)—6th Psalm
Domine, non est (Music)
    USE Psalms (Music)—131st Psalm
Domine, quam multi sunt (Music)
    USE Psalms (Music)—3d Psalm
Domine, quis habitavit (Music)
    USE Psalms (Music)—15th Psalm
Domine, refugium (Music)
    USE Psalms (Music)—90th Psalm
Domini est terra (Music)
    USE Psalms (Music)—24th Psalm
Dominus illuminatio (Music)
    USE Psalms (Music)—27th Psalm
Dominus regit me (Music)
    USE Psalms (Music)—23d Psalm
Dominus regnavit, decorem indutus est (Music)
    USE Psalms (Music)—93d Psalm
Dominus regnavit, exultet terra (Music)
    USE Psalms (Music)—97th Psalm
Domra *(ML1015-1018)*
    UF Dombra
    BT Balalaika
        Lute

Domra *(ML1015-1018)*
  (Continued)
  —Methods
  — —Self-instruction *(MT643)*
  —Studies and exercises *(MT643.3)*
    BT Domra music
Domra and piano music *(M282-3)*
  UF Piano and domra music
  NT Sonatas (Domra and piano)
Domra and piano music, Arranged *(M282-3)*
  NT Concertos (Domra)—Solo with piano
    Concertos (Domra with chamber orchestra)
    —Solo with piano
Domra music *(M142.D6)*
  BT Balalaika music
    Lute music
  NT Concertos (Domra)
    Concertos (Domra with chamber orchestra)
    Domra—Studies and exercises
    Domra with chamber orchestra
    Domra with orchestra
Domra with chamber orchestra *(M1037.4.D64)*
  BT Domra music
  RT Concertos (Domra with chamber orchestra)
Domra with orchestra *(M1037.4.D64)*
  BT Domra music
  RT Concertos (Domra)
Don Chisciotte (Ballet)
  USE Don Quixote (Ballet)
Don Kikhot (Ballet)
  USE Don Quixote (Ballet)
Don Quixote (Ballet)
  UF Don Chisciotte (Ballet)
    Don Kikhot (Ballet)
  BT Ballets
Double bass *(ML920-925)*
  UF Bass viol
  —Orchestra studies *(MT331)*
    BT Double bass—Studies and exercises
  —Studies and exercises *(MT330)*
    NT Double bass—Orchestra studies
Double-bass and bassoon music
  USE Bassoon and double-bass music
Double-bass and clarinet music
  USE Clarinet and double-bass music
Double-bass and continuo music
  UF Continuo and double-bass music
  NT Sonatas (Double bass and continuo)
Double-bass and flute music
  USE Flute and double-bass music
Double-bass and guitar music *(M237-8)*
  UF Guitar and double-bass music
  NT Suites (Double bass and guitar)
Double-bass and harpsichord music *(M237-238)*
  UF Harpsichord and double-bass music
  NT Sonatas (Double bass and harpsichord)
Double-bass and oboe music
  USE Oboe and double-bass music

Double-bass and organ music *(M182-186)*
  UF Organ and double-bass music
Double-bass and percussion music
  USE Percussion and double-bass music
Double-bass and piano music *(M237-8)*
  UF Piano and double-bass music
  NT Minuets (Double bass and piano)
    Sonatas (Double bass and piano)
    Suites (Double bass and piano)
    Variations (Double bass and piano)
    Waltzes (Double bass and piano)
Double-bass and piano music, Arranged *(M237-8)*
  NT Concertos (Double bass)—Solo with piano
    Concertos (Double bass), Arranged—Solo with piano
    Concertos (Double bass with band)—Solo with piano
    Concertos (Double bass with string orchestra)—Solo with piano
    Double bass with orchestra—Solo with piano
    Double bass with string orchestra—Solo with piano
    Suites (Double bass with orchestra)—Solo with piano
    Variations (Double bass with string orchestra)—Solo with piano
Double-bass and piano music (Jazz)
Double-bass and saxophone music
  USE Saxophone and double-bass music
Double-bass and trombone music
  USE Trombone and double-bass music
Double-bass and trumpet music
  USE Trumpet and double-bass music
Double-bass and viola d'amore music
  USE Viola d'amore and double-bass music
Double-bass and viola music
  USE Viola and double-bass music
Double-bass and violin music
  USE Violin and double-bass music
Double-bass and violoncello music
  USE Violoncello and double-bass music
Double-bass and violone music
  USE Violone and double-bass music
Double bass makers [May Subd Geog]
  BT Stringed instrument makers
Double-bass music *(M55-58)*
  SA Concertos, Minuets, Sonatas, Suites, *and similar headings with specification of instruments;* String trios [quartets, etc.] *and* Trios [Quartets, etc.] *followed by specifications which include the double bass; also* String ensembles *and headings that begin with the words double bass or double basses*
  NT Suites (Double bass)
    Variations (Double bass)
Double-bass music (Double basses (2)) *(M286-7)*
  NT Sonatas (Double basses (2))

Double-bass music (Double basses (3))
    USE   String trios (Double basses (3))
Double-bass music (Double basses (4))
    USE   String quartets (Double basses (4))
Double-bass music (Double basses (5))
    USE   String quintets (Double basses (5))
Double-bass music (Double basses (8))
    USE   String octets (Double basses (8))
Double-bass players
    USE   Double-bassists
Double-bass viol
    USE   Violone
Double bass with band *(M1205-6)*
    RT   Concertos (Double bass with band)
    —Scores *(M1205)*
Double bass with chamber orchestra
        (M1018)
    RT   Concertos (Double bass with chamber
            orchestra)
Double bass with instrumental ensemble
    RT   Concertos (Double bass with
            instrumental ensemble)
Double bass with orchestra *(M1018)*
    RT   Concertos (Double bass)
    NT   Monologues with music (Double
            bass with orchestra)
            Suites (Double bass with orchestra)
    —Solo with piano *(M1018)*
        BT   Double-bass and piano music,
                Arranged
Double bass with string ensemble
Double bass with string orchestra *(M1105-6)*
    RT   Concertos (Double bass with string
            orchestra)
    NT   Variations (Double bass with string
            orchestra)
    —Solo with piano *(M1118)*
        BT   Double-bass and piano music,
                Arranged
Double basses (2) with orchestra *(M1018)*
    RT   Concertos (Double basses (2))
Double-bassists [May Subd Geog]
    UF   Bass players
            Bassists
            Contrabass players
            Contrabassists
            Double-bass players
    BT   Musicians
Double bassoon
    USE   Contrabassoon
Double quartets
    USE   String octets (Violins (4), violas (2),
            violoncellos (2))
Doxology *(BV194.D)*
    NT   Old Hundredth (Tune)
Dramatic music
        M1500-M1527.8 (Music compositions)
        ML1699-ML2100 (History)
        ML3857-ML3862 (Aesthetics)
    UF   Music, Dramatic
            Music, Theatrical
            Theatrical music

Dramatic music
        M1500-M1527.8 (Music compositions)
        ML1699-ML2100 (History)
        ML3857-ML3862 (Aesthetics)
    (Continued)
    BT   Music
    NT   Ballets
            Masques with music
            Music, Incidental
            Music in theaters
            Musical revue, comedy, etc.
            Musical revues, comedies, etc.
            Opera
            Operas
Dramaturgy
    USE   Subdivision Dramaturgy under
                names of composers, e.g. Wagner,
                Richard, 1813-1883—Dramaturgy
            Drama—Technique
            Opera—Dramaturgy
Drill (not military) *(GV1797)*
    NT   Baton twirling
            Drum majoring
            Marching bands
Drinking songs *(PN6237)*
    BT   Songs
    RT   Students' songs
Drone bass
    USE   Bourdon
Drum *(ML1035; Primitive, GN467.D8)*
    UF   Bass drum
            Side drum
            Snare drum
    BT   Percussion instruments
    NT   Bodhran
            Bronze drum
            Conga (Drum)
            Frame drums
            Hourglass drum
            Mridanga
            Pung (Drum)
            Stone drum
            Tambou
            Tambourin
            Timpani
            Tupan
    —Studies and exercises (Rock) *(MT662.3)*
        BT   Rock music
Drum and bagpipe music
    USE   Bagpipe and drum music
Drum and bugle-calls
    USE   Military calls
Drum and bugle corps
    USE   Bugle and drum corps
Drum and bugle music
    USE   Bugle and drum music
Drum and fife music
    USE   Fife and drum music
Drum and guitar music
    USE   Guitar and drum music
Drum and trumpet music
    USE   Trumpet and drum music

Drum corps
  USE Bugle and drum corps
Drum majorettes *(GV1797)*
  UF Majorettes
Drum majoring *(MT733.5)*
  BT Drill (not military)
  RT Baton twirling
Drum majors [May Subd Geog] *(MT733.5)*
  BT Bands (Music)
Drum music
  USE Percussion ensembles
        Percussion music
        Snare drum music
Drum players
  USE Drummers (Musicians)
Drummers (Musicians) [May Subd Geog]
  UF Drum players
  BT Musicians
Duda *(ML980)*
  UF Polish bagpipe
  BT Bagpipe
Duda music *(M145)*
Duets *(M177-M298.5)*
        Here are entered collections of composi-
        tions for various combinations of two
        instruments. Compositions for two un-
        specified instruments, or for one speci-
        fied and one unspecified instrument
        are entered under Duets followed by
        instrumental specification. Composi-
        tions for two specified instruments are
        entered under Bassoon and piano mu-
        sic, Violin music (Violins (2)), and
        similar headings. Compositions for
        two voices are entered under Sacred
        duets and Vocal duets.
  UF Duos
  SA Piano music (4 hands) *and similar*
        headings under other keyboard
        instruments
  NT Jazz duets
        Percussion ensembles
Duets (Unspecified instrument and cithern)
        (M298.5)
  UF Cithern and unspecified instrument
        music
Duets (Unspecified instrument and continuo)
  UF Continuo and unspecified instrument
        music
  NT Sonatas (Unspecified instrument and
        continuo)
        Suites (Unspecified instrument and
        continuo)
Duets (Unspecified instrument and flute)
  UF Flute and unspecified instrument music
Duets (Unspecified instrument and guitar)
  UF Guitar and unspecified instrument
        music
        Note under Chamber music
Duets (Unspecified instrument and organ)
        (M298.5)
  UF Organ and unspecified instrument music

Duets (Unspecified instrument and organ)
        (M298.5)
        (Continued)
  NT Chaconnes (Unspecified instrument and
        organ)
        Sonatas (Unspecified instrument and organ)
Duets (Unspecified instrument and piano)
        (M298.5-M298.6)
  UF Piano and unspecified instrument music
  NT Chaconnes (Unspecified instrument and
        piano)
        Variations (Unspecified instrument and
        piano)
        Note under Chamber music
Duets (Unspecified instruments (2))
        (M298.5)
  NT Sonatas (Unspecified instruments (2))
        Suites (Unspecified instruments (2))
        Note under Chamber music
Dulcian *(History, ML990.C; Instruction, MT553.C)*
  UF Curtal
        Dolcian
        Dolcino
        Dolzoni
        Dulzian
  BT Bassoon
Dulcian music
        M110.D
  SA *Concertos, Minuets, Sonatas, Suites,* and
        similar headings with specification of
        instruments; *Trios [Quartets, etc.], Wind*
        trios [quartets, etc.], and *Woodwind trios*
        [quartets,etc.] followed by specifications
        which include the dulcian; also *Wind*
        ensembles, Woodwind ensembles, and
        headings that begin with the words
        Dulcian or Dulcians
Dulcimer *(ML1015-1018)*
  UF Cembalo
        Epinette
        Hackbrett
        Hammered dulcimer
        Salterio tedesco
  NT Appalachian dulcimer
        Cimbalom
        Gusli
        Kantele (Musical instrument)
        Kokle
        Santūr
        Yang ch'in
Dulcimer and continuo music
  UF Continuo and dulcimer music
  NT Sonatas (Dulcimer and continuo)
Dulcimer and guitar music *(M292-3)*
  UF Guitar and dulcimer music
Dulcimer and harp music *(M292-293)*
  UF Harp and dulcimer music
  NT Sonatas (Dulcimer and harp)
Dulcimer and piano music
        (Collections, M284.D85; Separate
        works, M285.D85
  UF Piano and dulcimer

Dulcimer music *(M142.D8)*

Dulcimer with string orchestra
- RT Concertos (Dulcimer with string orchestra)

Dulzaina *(ML990.D8)*
- UF Dolçaina
- Dolzaina
- BT Musical instruments—Spain
- Woodwind instruments

Dulzian
- USE Dulcian

Dumy
- BT Folk-songs

Duos
- USE Duets

Dutch folk-songs
- USE Folk-songs, Dutch

Dutch hymns
- USE Hymns, Dutch

Dutch songs
- USE Songs, Dutch

Dynamics (Music)
- USE Music—Interpretation (Phrasing, dynamics, etc.)

Dzongkha songs
- USE Songs, Dzongkha

Ear training *(MT35)*
- BT Music—Instruction and study
- RT Musical dictation

Early Christian hymns
- USE Hymns, Early Christian

Easter [May Subd Geog]
—Hymns
- USE Easter hymns
—Songs and music
- USE Easter music

Easter carols
- USE Carols

Easter hymns
- UF Easter—Hymns
- BT Easter music
- Hymns

Easter music
- UF Easter—Songs and music
- BT Church music
- Holidays—Songs and music
- Music
- Sacred vocal music
- NT Carols
- Easter hymns

Eastman School Festival of American Music
(ML38.R67E2)
- UF Eastman School of Music, Rochester, N.Y. Festival of American Music
- Festival of American Music, Rochester, N.Y.
- BT Music festivals—New York (State)

Eastman School of Music, Rochester, N.Y. Festival of American Music
- USE Eastman School Festival of American Music

Ecce nunc (Music)
- USE Psalms (Music)—134th Psalm

Ecce, quam bonum (Music)
- USE Psalms (Music)—133d Psalm

Education [May Subd Geog]
- NT Music in education

Education, Musical
- USE Music—Instruction and study

Electric guitar
ML1015
- UF Guitar, Electric
- BT Guitar
- Musical instruments, Electronic
- NT Bass guitar

Electric musical instruments
- USE Musical instruments, Electronic

Electronic equipment for guitars
- USE Guitar—Electronic equipment

Electronic harpsichord *(ML697)*
- UF Harpsichord, Electronic
- BT Musical instruments, Electronic

Electronic harpsichord music *(M20-32)*
- NT Quartets (Electronic harpsichord, castanets, percussion, violoncello)

Electronic keyboard (Synthesizer)
ML1092
- UF Keyboard, Electronic (Synthesizer)
- BT Synthesizer (Musical instrument)

Electronic music
Here are entered works in which the sounds produced were originally recorded on magnetic tape from electronic instruments, or from a combination of electronic instruments and other sources, and subsequently rearranged or altered, or performed live. The heading is used as a medium of performance after the names of specific forms, *e.g.* 1. Suites (Electronic music) It is used as a second heading when a tape recording is used with specifically named conventional instruments, *e.g.* 1. Quintets (Clarinet, flute, harp, viola, violoncello) 2. Electronic music.
- UF Electrophonic music
- Music, Electronic
- Tape-recorder music
- BT Music
- Technology and the arts
- RT Concrete music
- NT Canons, fugues, etc. (Electronic music)
- Choruses, Sacred (Mixed voices) with electronic music
- Choruses, Secular (Men's voices) with electronic music
- Choruses, Secular (Mixed voices) with electronic music
- Choruses, Secular (Women's voices) with electronic music
- Computer music
- Monologues with music (Electronic music)
- Overtures (Electronic music)
- Sacred songs (High voice) with electronic music

Electronic music
(*Continued*)
  NT Sacred songs (Medium voice) with
        electronic music
      Songs (High voice) with electronic music
      Songs (Medium voice) with electronic
        music
      Suites (Electronic music)
      Symphonies (Electronic music)
      Synthesizer music
      Vocal quartets with electronic music
Electronic musical instruments
  USE Musical instruments, Electronic
Electronic organ *(ML597)*
  UF Organ, Electronic
  BT Musical instruments, Electronic
      Organ
  NT Allen organ
      Baldwin organ
      Hammond organ
      Kimball organ
      Minshall-Estey organ
      Silvertone organ
      Welte-Lichtton-Orgel
      Wurlitzer organ
  —Construction *(ML597)*
  --Registration *(MT192)*
        Example under Organ—Registration
Electronic organ and flute music
  USE Flute and electronic organ music
Electronic organ music *(M14.8; M14.85)*
  SA Concertos, Sonatas, Suites, Waltzes,
        and similar headings with
        specification of instruments; also
        Trios [Quartets, etc.] *followed by*
        specifications which include the
        electronic organ; and headings
        beginning with the words Electronic
        organ or Electronic organs
Electronic organ music (Conn registration)
        (M14.8; M14.85)
  UF Conn organ music
      Connsonata organ music
Electronic organ music (Hammond
        registration) *(M14.8; M14.85)*
  UF Hammond organ music
Electronic organ music (Organs (2))
        (M180-181)
Electronic organ music (Organs (4))
        (M180-181)
Electronic organ music (Silvertone
        registration *(M14.8; M14.85)*
  UF Silvertone organ music
Electronic organ music (Thomas registration)
        (M14.8; M14.85)
  UF Thomas organ music
Electronic organ with orchestra
        (M1005-M1006)
  NT Concertos (Electronic organ)
Electronic percussion instruments
        ML1092
  UF Drum machine
      Electronic drum

Electronic percussion instruments
        ML1092
(*Continued*)
  UF Percussion instruments, Electronic
      Rhythm machine
  BT Percussion instruments
      Synthesizer (Musical instruments)
Electronic piano *(ML697)*
  UF Fender-Rhodes (Musical instrument)
      Piano, Electronic
      Rhodes (Musical instrument)
  BT Musical instruments, Electronic
Electronic piano music
Electronium *(ML1092)*
  UF Elektronium
Electronium music *(M175.E4)*
  NT Quartets (Electronium, piano,
        percussion, viola)
Electrophonic music
  USE Electronic music
Electrophonic musical instruments
  USE Musical instruments, Electronic
Electrostatic loudspeakers
  UF Capacitor loudspeakers
  BT Direct radiator loudspeakers
Elektronium
  USE Electronium
Embellishment (Music) *(MT80)*
  UF Diminution (Music)
      Ornaments (Music)
  BT Music—Instruction and study
      Musical notation
  RT Variation (Music)
  NT Embellishment (Vocal music)
      Music—Performance
Embellishment (Vocal music) *(MT80)*
  UF Coloratura
      Fioriture
  BT Embellishment (Music)
      Music—Instruction and study
      Vocal music—History and criticism
  NT Music—Performance
Emblems, National [May Subd Geog]
  NT National songs
EMI Abbey Road Studios (London, England)
  USE Abbey Road Studios (London, England)
EMI Recording Studios (London, England)
  USE Abbey Road Studios (London, England)
EMI Studios (London, England)
  USE Abbey Road Studios (London, England)
Emperor's new clothes (Ballet)
  BT Ballets
Endowments [May Subd Geog]
  NT Music—Endowments
English carols
  USE Carols, English
English folk-songs
  USE Folk-songs, English
English guitar *(ML1015-1018)*
  UF Cetra
  BT Cithern
      Guitar
English guitar music *(M142.E5)*

English Hindu hymns
   USE Hindu hymns, English
English horn *(ML940-941)*
   BT Woodwind instruments
   RT Oboe
   —Orchestra studies *(MT376)*
      BT English horn—Studies and exercises
   —Studies and exercises *(MT376)*
      NT English horn—Orchestra studies
English-horn and bassoon music
   USE Bassoon and English-horn music
English-horn and clarinet music
   USE Clarinet and English-horn music
English horn and flute music *(M288-9)*
   UF Flute and English-horn music
   BT Flute music
   NT Concertos (English horn and flute with string orchestra)
English horn and flute with string orchestra *(M1105-6)*
   BT English horn and flute music
        String-orchestra music
   RT Concertos (English horn and flute with string orchestra)
English horn and guitar music *(M296-7)*
   UF Guitar and English horn music
English horn and harp music *(M296-7)*
   UF Harp and English horn music
   NT Concertos (English horn and harp with string orchestra)
        English horn and harp with string orchestra
English horn and harp with string orchestra *(M1105-6)*
   BT English horn and harp music
   RT Concertos (English horn and harp with string orchestra)
   —Scores and parts *(M1105)*
English horn and harpsichord music *(M246.2)*
   UF Harpsichord and English horn music
English horn and oboe music *(M288-9)*
   UF Oboe and English horn music
   NT Concertos (English horn and oboe with string orchestra)
        English horn and oboe with string orchestra
English horn and oboe with string orchestra *(M1105-6)*
   BT English horn and oboe music
   RT Concertos (English horn and oboe with string orchestra)
   —Scores *(M1105)*
English horn and organ music *(M182-4))*
   UF Organ and English-horn music
   NT Suites (English horn and organ)
English horn and piano music *(M246.2)*
   UF Piano and English-horn music
   NT Sonatas (English horn and piano)
English horn and piano music, Arranged *(M246.2)*
   NT Concertos (English horn with chamber orchestra)—Solo with piano

English horn and piano music, Arranged *(M246.2)*
   (Continued)
   NT Concertos (English horn with string orchestra)—Solo with piano
        English horn with string orchestra—Solo with piano
English horn and trombone music *(M288-289)*
   UF Trombone and English horn music
English horn and trumpet music *(M288-9)*
   UF Trumpet and English horn music
   NT Concertos (English horn and trumpet with string orchestra)
        English horn and trumpet with string orchestra
English horn and trumpet with string orchestra *(M1105-6)*
   BT English horn and trumpet music
   RT Concertos (English horn and trumpet with string orchestra)
   —Solos with piano *(M1106)*
      BT Trios (Piano, English horn, trumpet), Arranged
English horn and violin music *(M290-M291)*
   UF Violin and English horn music
English horn and violoncello music *(M290-291)*
   UF Violoncello and English horn music
English horn and violoncello with orchestra *(M1040-1041)*
   RT Concertos (English horn and violoncello)
English horn, flute, viola, violoncello with string orchestra *(M1140-1141)*
   BT Quartets (English horn, flute, viola, violoncello)
   RT Concertos (English horn, flute, viola, violoncello with string orchestra)
English-horn music *(M110.E5)*
   SA Concertos, Minuets, Sonatas, Suites, *and similar headings with specification of instruments;* Trios [Quartets, etc.], Wind trios [quartets, etc.], *and* Woodwind trios [quartets, etc.] *followed by specifications which include the English horn; also* Wind ensembles, Woodwind ensembles, *and headings that begin with the words English horn or English horns*
   NT Bassoon and English-horn music
English-horn music (English horns (2)) *(M288-9)*
   NT Concertos (English horns (2)) with string orchestra
        English horns (2) with string orchestra
English-horn music (English horns (2)) with string orchestra
   NT Concertos (English horns (2))
English horn with chamber orchestra *(M1034-5)*
   RT Concertos (English horn with chamber orchestra)

English horn with orchestra *(M1034.E5;*
  M1035.E5)
  RT Concertos (English horn)
  —Scores and parts *(M1034.E)*
English horn with string orchestra
  (M1105-6)
  RT Concertos (English horn with string
    orchestra)
  —Solo with piano
    BT English horn and piano music,
      Arranged
English horns (2) with string orchestra
  (M1134.E5; M1135.E5)
  BT English-horn music (English horns (2))
  RT Concertos (English horns (2)) with
    string orchestra
English hymns
  USE Hymns, English
English language [May Subd Geog]
  —Conversation and phrase books (for
    musicians, musicologists, etc.)
    BT Music—Terminology
English literature [May Subd Geog]
  —Musical settings
    Example under reference from Musical
      settings; Settings, Musical
English lullabies
  USE Lullabies, English
English madrigals (Music)
  USE Madrigals (Music), English
English part-songs
  USE Part-songs, English
English songs
  USE Songs, English
Enharmonic organ
  USE Organ
Enka [May Subd Geog]
  BT Popular music—Japan
Enkyoku *(Collections, PL761; History,*
    PL731)
  UF Eikyoku
  BT Songs, Japanese
Ensemble playing *(MT728)*
  BT Chamber music—History and criticism
Ensemble singing
  BT Singing
  RT Vocal ensembles
  NT Barbershop singing
Ensembles, Chamber music
  USE Chamber music groups
Ensembles, Musical
  USE Musical groups
Ensembles (Music)
  USE Viol ensembles, *and similar headings*
    for ensembles of like instruments
    Instrumental ensembles
    Jazz ensembles
    Percussion ensembles
    Sacred vocal ensembles
    String ensembles
    Vocal ensembles
    Wind ensembles

Entr'acte music *(M1510-1518; History, ML2000)*
  UF Act-tune
  BT Music, Incidental
    Overture
  NT Tonadilla
Eolian harp
  USE Aeolian harp
Epiphany
  —Songs and music
    USE Epiphany music
Epiphany hymns
  BT Hymns
Epiphany music
  UF Epiphany—Songs and music
  BT Church music
    Music
    Sacred vocal music
Epithalamia *(English, PR1195.E6)*
  UF Wedding songs
Erh hu *(ML927.E)*
  BT Hu ch'in
    Musical instruments—China
    Stringed instruments, Bowed
  RT Nan hu
Erh hu and yang ch'in music
  UF Yang ch'in and erh hu music
Erh hu music *(M59.E7)*
  NT Trios (Piano, san hsien, erh hu)
Eripe me, Domine (Music)
  USE Psalms (Music)—140th Psalm
Erotic songs [May Subd Geog]
  UF Sex—Songs and music
    Songs, Erotic
  BT Erotic poetry
    Erotica
    Music and erotica
    Songs
  RT Bawdy songs
Eructavit cor meum (Music)
  USE Psalms (Music)—45th Psalm
Erzlaute
  USE Archlute
Eskimo folk-songs
  USE Folk-songs, Eskimo
Eskimo music
  USE Eskimos—Music
Eskimos [May Subd Geog]
  —Music
    UF Eskimo music
    NT Folk-songs, Eskimo
Estampies
  UF Istanpittas
    Stampitas
  BT Dance music
Estonian ballads
  USE Ballads, Estonian
Estonian folk-songs
  USE Folk-songs, Estonian
Ethics [May Subd Geog]
  NT Music and morals
Ethiopian folk-songs
  USE Folk-songs, Ethiopian

Ethnic performing arts [May Subd Geog]
    UF Minority performing arts
         Performing arts, Ethnic
    BT Performing arts
Ethnomusicological collections
    USE *subdivision* Ethnomusicological
         collections *under names of persons,*
         families, and corporate bodies
Ethnomusicologists [May Subd Geog]
    BT Ethnologists
         Folklorists
         Musicologists
    RT Ethnomusicology
Ethnomusicology [May Subd Geog]
        (ML3797.7-3799)
    BT Ethnology
         Musicology
    RT Ethnomusicologists
    NT Sound recordings in ethnomusicology
Eunuch flute
    USE Kazoo
Euphonium *(ML965-8)*
    BT Brass instruments
    RT Baritone (Musical instrument)
         Trombone
Euphonium (Chladni's)
    USE Clavicylinder
Euphonium and cornet music
    USE Cornet and euphonium music
Euphonium and marimba music *(M298)*
    UF Marimba and euphonium music
Euphonium and percussion music *(M298)*
    UF Percussion and euphonium music
Euphonium and piano music *(M270.B37;*
        M271.B37)
    UF Piano and euphonium music
    NT Suites (Euphonium and piano)
         Variations (Euphonium and piano)
Euphonium and tuba music *(M288-289)*
    UF Tuba and euphonium music
Euphonium, horns (4) with band
        (M1205-1206)
    BT Brass quintets (Euphonium, horns (4))
    RT Concertos (Euphonium, horns (4) with
         band)
Euphonium music *(M90-94)*
    SA Concertos, Minuets, Sonatas, Suites *and*
        similar headings with specification of
        instruments; Brass trios [quartets,
        etc.], Trios [Quartets, etc.], *and*
        Wind trios [quartets, etc.], *followed*
        by specifications which include the
        euphonium; also Brass ensembles,
        Wind ensembles, *and headings that*
        begin with the words euphonium or
        euphoniums
Euphonium with band *(M1205-M1206; M1257)*
    RT Concertos (Euphonium with band)
Euphonium with wind ensemble
    RT Concertos (Euphonium with wind
         ensemble)
Euphoniums (2) with band *(M1205-M1206; M1257)*
    RT Concertos (Euphoniums (2) with band)

Eurythmy *(BP596.R5)*
    BT Rhythm
Evening-service music
    BT Sacred vocal music
    RT Vespers (Music)
    NT Magnificat (Music)
         Synagogue music—Evening services
Exaltabo te, Deus (Music)
    USE Psalms (Music)—145th Psalm
Exaltabo te, Domine (Music)
    USE Psalms (Music)—30th Psalm
Exaudi, Deus orationem meam (Music)
    USE Psalms (Music)—55th Psalm
Exsultets (Liturgy)
    USE Exultets (Liturgy)
Exsurgat Deus (Music)
    USE Psalms (Music)—68th Psalm
Extemporization (Music)
    USE Improvisation (Music)
Exultate Deo (Music)
    USE Psalms (Music)—81st Psalm
Exultate, justi (Music)
    USE Psalms (Music)—33d Psalm
Fados *(M1781-2)*
    BT Folk-songs, Portuguese
Fake books (Music)
    USE Fakebooks (Music)
Fakebooks (Music)
    UF Fake books (Music)
    BT Jazz music
         Popular music
Fandangos
    BT Dance music
Fanfares *(M1270)*
    BT Band music
         Brass band music
         Military music
    RT Military calls
         Trumpet-calls
    NT Bugle-calls
Fang songs
    USE Songs, Fang
Faroese folk-songs
    USE Folk-songs, Faroese
Faroese songs
    USE Songs, Faroese
Faulx bourdon
    USE Fauxbourdon
Fauxbourdon
    UF Faulx bourdon
    BT Bourdon
Feadóg stáin
    USE Penny whistle
Feature films
    NT Musical revues, comedies, etc.
Feminism and music [May Subd Geog] *(ML82)*
    BT Feminism and the arts
         Music
Festival of American Music, Rochester, N.Y.
    USE Eastman School Festival of American
         Music
Fiddle
    USE Violin

Fiddle playing
  USE Fiddling
Fiddle tunes [May Subd Geog]
  BT Country music
      Violin music
  NT Fiddling
Fiddlers [May Subd Geog]
  BT Violinists
Fiddling *(Instruction and study, MT279)*
  UF Fiddle playing
  BT Fiddle tunes
      Folk music
      Violin
Fife *(History, ML935)*
  BT Flute
      Woodwind instruments
Fife and drum bands
  USE Fife and drum corps
Fife and drum corps [May Subd Geog]
  UF Drum and fife corps
      Fife and drum bands
  BT Bands (Music)
Fife and drum music *(M1270)*
  UF Drum and fife music
  BT Fife music
      Percussion music
Fife music *(M60-62)*
  NT Fife and drum music
Fife music (Fifes (2)) *(M288-9)*
Film music
  USE Moving-picture music
Fingering (Piano playing)
  USE Piano—Instruction and study—
        Fingering
      Piano—Studies and exercises—
        Fingering
Finnish folk-songs
  USE Folk-songs, Finnish
Finnish hymns
  USE Hymns, Finnish
Finnish songs
  USE Songs, Finnish
Finno-Ugric folk-songs
  USE Folk-songs, Finno-Ugric
Fioriture
  USE Embellishment (Vocal music)
Firebird (Ballet) *(GV1790.F)*
  BT Ballets
First performances of musical works
  USE Music—First performances
Flageolet *(ML935-6)*
  BT Flute
      Woodwind instruments
  RT Recorder (Musical instrument)
  NT Galoubet
      Melody flute
      Penny whistle
Flageolet and continuo music
  UF Continuo and flageolet music
  NT Sonatas (Flageolet and continuo)
Flageolet and piano music *(M240-242)*
  UF Piano and flageolet music

Flageolet and violin music *(M290)*
  UF Violin and flageolet music
Flageolet and violin music, Arranged *(M290)*
Flageolet music *(M60-62)*
  BT Flute music
      Recorder music
Flageolet music, Arranged *(M63-64)*
Flageolet music (Flageolets (2)) *(M288-9)*
Flageolet music (Flageolets (2)), Arranged
      (M288-9)
Flageolet tunes
  USE Harmonics (Music)
Flamenco music
  UF Cante flamenco
      Cante hondo
  BT Dance music—Spain
      Folk dance music—Spain
      Folk music—Spain
      Folk-songs, Spanish
      Gypsies—Music
Flicorno
  USE Fluegelhorn
Flue pipes (Organ pipes)
  UF Flues (Organ pipes)
  BT Organ-pipes
Fluegelhorn *(ML975-7)*
  UF Flicorno
      Flugelhorn
  BT Brass instruments
  NT Alto horn
  —Studies and exercises (Jazz) *(MT493.3)*
Fluegelhorn and organ music
  UF Organ and fluegelhorn music
  NT Chorale preludes (Fluegelhorn and
        organ)
Fluegelhorn and piano music *(M270.F;*
      M271.F)
  UF Piano and fluegelhorn music
Fluegelhorn and piano music, Arranged
      (M270.F; M271.F)
  NT Fluegelhorn with string orchestra—Solo
        with piano
Fluegelhorn music *(M110.F53)*
  NT Brass quartets (Baritone, fluegelhorn,
        horn, trumpet)
Fluegelhorn with band [May Subd Geog]
      (M1205-M1206)
Fluegelhorn with string orchestra
      (M1134.F7; M1135.F7)
  RT Concertos (Fluegelhorn with string
       orchestra)
  —Solo with piano *(M1135.F7)*
    BT Fluegelhorn and piano music,
        Arranged
Flues (Organ pipes)
  USE Flue pipes (Organ pipes)
Flugelhorn
  USE Fluegelhorn
Flute *(History, ML935-ML937)*
  UF Alto flute
      Boehm flute
  BT Woodwind instruments

Flute *(History, ML935-ML937)*
   (Continued)
     NT Bānsurī
         Czakan
         Fife
         Flageolet
         Galoubet
         Hsiao
         Hsüan (Musical instrument)
         Huang chung (Musical instrument)
         Nāy
         Piccolo
         Recorder (Musical instrument)
         Ryūteki
         Shakuhachi
         Shinobue
         Taegūm
         Tanso
         Ti tzū
         Tibia (Musical instrument)
   —Construction *(ML936)*
   —Fingering charts *(MT348)*
   —Orchestra studies *(MT346)*
     BT Flute—Studies and exercises
   —Studies and exercises *(MT345)*
     NT Flute—Orchestra studies
   Example under reference from Melody
      instruments
Flute and accordion music *(M298)*
   UF Accordion and flute music
Flute and banjo music *(M296-297)*
   UF Banjo and flute music
Flute and bassoon music
   USE Bassoon and flute music
Flute and celesta music *(M298)*
   UF Celesta and flute music
Flute and chime music *(M298)*
   UF Chime and flute music
Flute and cimbalom music *(M298)*
   UF Cimbalom and flute music
Flute and clarinet music
   USE Clarinet and flute music
Flute and continuo music
   UF Continuo and flute music
   NT Marches (Flute and continuo)
        Minuets (Flute and continuo)
        Rondos (Flute and continuo)
        Sonatas (Flute and continuo)
        Suites (Flute and continuo)
        Variations (Flute and continuo)
Flute and double-bass music *(M290-291)*
   UF Double-bass and flute music
Flute and electronic organ music *(M182-186)*
   UF Electronic organ and flute music
   BT Flute and organ music
Flute and English-horn music
   USE English horn and flute music
Flute and guitar music *(M296-7)*
   UF Guitar and flute music
   NT Potpourris (Flute and guitar)
        Sonatas (Flute and guitar)
        Suites (Flute and guitar)
        Variations (Flute and guitar)

Flute and guitar music, Arranged *(M296-7)*
Flute and guitar with orchestra *(M1040-1041)*
   RT Concertos (Flute and guitar)
Flute and guitar with string orchestra
      (M1140-1141)
   RT Concertos (Flute and guitar with string
       orchestra)
Flute and harp music *(M296-7)*
   UF Harp and flute music
   NT Concertos (Flute and harp)
        Concertos (Flute and harp with string
         orchestra)
        Flute and harp with orchestra
        Flute and harp with string orchestra
        Rondos (Flute and harp)
        Sonatas (Flute and harp)
        Suites (Flute and harp)
        Variations (Flute and harp)
Flute and harp music, Arranged *(M296-7)*
Flute and harp with orchestra *(M1040-1041)*
   BT Flute and harp music
   RT Concertos (Flute and harp)
Flute and harp with string ensemble
   RT Concertos (Flute and harp with string
       ensemble)
Flute and harp with string orchestra *(M1105-6)*
   UF Harp and flute with string orchestra
   BT Flute and harp music
   RT Concertos (Flute and harp with string
       orchestra)
Flute and harpsichord music *(M240-242)*
   UF Harpsichord and flute music
   NT Concertos (Flute and harpsichord with
       string orchestra)
        Flute and harpsichord with string
         orchestra
        Minuets (Flute and harpsichord)
        Sonatas (Flute and harpsichord)
        Suites (Flute and harpsichord)
        Variations (Flute and harpsichord)
Flute and harpsichord with string ensemble
   NT Concertos (Flute and harpsichord
       with string ensemble)
Flute and harpsichord with string orchestra
      (M1105-6)
   BT Flute and harpsichord music
   RT Concertos (Flute and harpsichord with
       string orchestra)
   NT Suites (Flute and harpsichord with
       string orchestra)
   —Scores *(M1105)*
Flute and horn music *(M288-9)*
   UF Horn and flute music
   NT Concertos (Flute and horn with string
       orchestra)
        Flute and horn with string orchestra
Flute and horn with string orchestra *(M1105-6)*
   BT Flute and horn music
       String-orchestra music
   RT Concertos (Flute and horn with string
       orchestra)
   NT Variations (Flute and horn with string
       orchestra)

Flute and hurdy-gurdy music *(M298)*
UF   Hurdy-gurdy and flute music
Flute and keyboard instrument music
    (M240-M242)
UF   Keyboard instrument and flute music
Flute and koto music *(M296-7)*
UF   Koto and flute music
Flute and lute music *(M296-297)*
UF   Lute and flute music
NT   Sonatas (Flute and lute)
Flute and marimba music *(M298)*
UF   Marimba and flute music
NT   Suites (Flute and marimba)
Flute and oboe d'amore with string orchestra
    (M1140-1141)
RT   Concertos (Flute and oboe d'amore
     with string orchestra)
Flute and oboe music *(M288-9)*
UF   Oboe and flute music
NT   Concertos (Flute and oboe)
    Concertos (Flute and oboe with
     chamber orchestra)
    Concertos (Flute and oboe with string
     orchestra)
    Flute and oboe with chamber orchestra
    Flute and oboe with orchestra
    Flute and oboe with string orchestra
    Suites (Flute and oboe)
Flute and oboe with chamber orchestra
    (M1040-1041)
BT   Flute and oboe music
RT   Concertos (Flute and oboe with
     chamber orchestra)
Flute and oboe with orchestra *(M1040-1041)*
BT   Flute and oboe music
RT   Concertos (Flute and oboe)
—Solos with piano *(M1041)*
    BT   Trios (Piano, flute, oboe), Arranged
Flute and oboe with string orchestra
    (M1105-6)
BT   Flute and oboe music
RT   Concertos (Flute and oboe with string
     orchestra)
NT   Variations (Flute and oboe with string
     orchestra)
—Scores *(M1105)*
—Solos with piano *(M1141)*
    BT   Trios (Piano, flute, oboe), Arranged
Flute and oboe with string orchestra,
    Arranged *(M1105-6)*
Flute and organ music *(M182-186)*
UF   Organ and flute music
NT   Choral preludes (Flute and organ)
    Flute and electronic organ music
    Sonatas (Flute and organ)
    Suites (Flute and organ)
    Variations (Flute and organ)
Flute and percussion music *(M298)*
UF   Percussion and flute music
NT   Concertos (Flute and percussion with
     string orchestra)
    Flute and percussion with string
     orchestra

Flute and percussion music *(M298)*
    (Continued)
NT   Sonatas (Flute and percussion)
    Suites (Flute and percussion)
Flute and percussion with string orchestra
    (M1105-6)
BT   Flute and percussion music
RT   Concertos (Flute and percussion with
     string orchestra)
Flute and piano music *(M240-242)*
UF   Piano and flute music
NT   Canons, fugues, etc. (Flute and piano)
    Concertos (Flute and piano with string
     orchestra)
    Flute and piano with string orchestra
    Marches (Flute and piano)
    Passacaglias (Flute and piano)
    Polkas (Flute and piano)
    Recorder and harpsichord music
    Rondos (Flute and piano)
    Sonatas (Flute and piano)
    Suites (Flute and piano)
    Variations (Flute and piano)
    Waltzes (Flute and piano)
Flute and piano music, Arranged *(M243-4)*
NT   Ballets arranged for flute and piano
    Concertos (Flute)—Solo with piano
    Concertos (Flute with chamber
     orchestra)—Solo with piano
    Concertos (Flute with string orchestra)
     —Solo with piano
    Concertos (Flute with string orchestra),
     Arranged—Solo with piano
    Flute with chamber orchestra—Solo
     with piano
    Flute with orchestra—Solo with piano
    Flute with string ensemble—Solo with
     piano
    Flute with string orchestra—Solo with
     piano
    Rondos (Flute with orchestra)—Solo
     with piano
    Suites (Flute with orchestra)—Solo with
     piano
    Suites (Flute with string orchestra)—
     Solo with piano
    Suites (Flute with string orchestra),
     Arranged—Solo with piano
    Variations (Flute with orchestra)—Solo
     with piano
Flute and piano with orchestra
    (M1040-1041)
RT   Concertos (Flute and piano)
Flute and piano with string ensemble
NT   Concertos (Flute and piano with
     string ensemble)
Flute and piano with string orchestra
    (M1105-6)
BT   Flute and piano music
RT   Concertos (Flute and piano with string
     orchestra)
—Scores *(M1105)*

Flute and piccolo music *(M288-289)*
UF   Piccolo and flute music
Flute and piccolo with flute ensemble
Flute and recorder music *(M288-9)*
UF   Recorder and flute music
NT   Concertos (Flute and recorder with
string orchestra)
Flute and recorder with string orchestra
Sonatas (Flute and recorder)
Flute and recorder with string orchestra
(M1105-6)
BT   Flute and recorder music
RT   Concertos (Flute and recorder with
string orchestra)
Flute and saxophone music *(M288-289)*
UF   Saxophone and flute music
Flute and tabla music *(M298)*
UF   Tabla and flute music
Flute and trombone music *(M288-9)*
UF   Trombone and flute music
NT   Concertos (Flute and trombone with
chamber orchestra)
Flute and trombone with chamber orchestra
(M1040-1041)
BT   Flute and trombone music
RT   Concertos (Flute and trombone with
chamber orchestra)
NT   Suites (Flute and trombone with
chamber orchestra)
Flute and trumpet music *(M288-9)*
UF   Trumpet and flute music
NT   Concertos (Flute and trumpet with
string orchestra)
Flute and trumpet with string orchestra
Flute and trumpet with string orchestra
(M1105-6)
BT   Flute and trumpet music
RT   Concertos (Flute and trumpet with
string orchestra)
NT   Canons, fugues, etc. (Flute and trumpet
with string orchestra)
Flute and unspecified instrument music
USE   Duets (Unspecified instrument and flute)
Flute and vibraphone music *(M298)*
UF   Vibraphone and flute music
Flute and viola d'amore music *(M290-291)*
UF   Viola d'amore and flute music
NT   Concertos (Flute and viola d'amore
with string orchestra)
Flute and viola d'amore with string
orchestra
Flute and viola d'amore with string orchestra
(M1105-6)
BT   Flute and viola d'amore music
String-orchestra music
RT   Concertos (Flute and viola d'amore
with string orchestra)
Flute and viola music *(M290-291)*
UF   Viola and flute music
NT   Sonatas (Flute and viola)
Flute and viola with instrumental ensemble
RT   Concertos (Flute and viola with
instrumental ensemble)

Flute and viola with string ensemble
RT   Concertos (Flute and viola with string
ensemble)
Flute and violin music *(M290-291)*
UF   Violin and flute music
NT   Canons, fugues, etc. (Flute and violin)
Concertos (Flute and violin)
Concertos (Flute and violin with string
orchestra)
Flute and violin with orchestra
Flute and violin with string orchestra
Sonatas (Flute and violin)
Suites (Flute and violin)
Variations (Flute and violin)
Flute and violin with orchestra
(M1040-1041)
BT   Flute and violin music
RT   Concertos (Flute and violin)
—Solos with piano *(M1041)*
BT   Trios (Piano, flute, violin), Arranged
Flute and violin with string orchestra
(M1105-6)
BT   Flute and violin music
String-orchestra music
RT   Concertos (Flute and violin with string
orchestra)
NT   Suites (Flute and violin with string
orchestra)
Flute and violoncello music *(M290-291)*
UF   Violoncello and flute music
NT   Canons, fugues, etc. (Flute and
violoncello)
Concertos (Flute and violoncello with
string orchestra)
Flute and violoncello with string
orchestra
Minuets (Flute and violoncello)
Sonatas (Flute and violoncello)
Suites (Flute and violoncello)
Flute and violoncello with string orchestra
(M1105-6)
BT   Flute and violoncello music
RT   Concertos (Flute and violoncello with
string orchestra)
BT   Concertos (Flute and violoncello with
string orchestra)
—Scores *(M1105)*
Flute clock
USE   Musical clock
Flûte enchantée (Ballet)
USE   Magic flute (Ballet)
Flute ensembles *(M955-956; M957.2;*
M958-959)
Here are entered compositions for ten or
more flutes and collections of compo-
sitions for a varying number of flutes.
When used in conjunction with specific
solo instrument(s), the designation Flute
ensemble may stand for any number of
flutes.
SA   Concertos ([Solo instrument(s)] with flute
ensemble); Suites, Variations, Waltzes,
and similar headings with specifications

Flute ensembles *(M955-956; M957.2;*
      M958-959)
  (Continued)
  SA *of instruments which include the specifica-*
        tion Flute ensemble
  Note under Woodwind ensembles
Flute, horn, harp with string orchestra
      (M1105-6)
  BT String-orchestra music
      Trios (Flute, horn, harp)
  RT Concertos (Flute, horn, harp with string
      orchestra)
Flute makers
  BT Woodwind instrument makers
Flute music *(M60-64)*
  SA Concertos, Minuets, Sonatas, Suites,
      and similar headings with
      specification of instruments; Trios
      [Quartets, etc.], Wind trios [quartets,
      etc.], *and* Woodwind trios [quartets,
      etc.] *followed by specifications which*
      include the flute; also Wind
      ensembles, Woodwind ensembles,
      and headings that begin with the
      words flute or flutes
  NT English horn and flute music
      Flageolet music
      Marches (Flute)
      Passacaglias (Flute)
      Potpourris (Flute)
      Recorded accompaniments (Flute)
      Rondos (Flute)
      Sonatas (Flute)
      Suites (Flute)
      Variations (Flute)
  —Interpretation (Phrasing, dynamics, etc.)
      (MT140; MT145)
Flute music, Arranged *(M63-64)*
  NT Operas arranged for flute
Flute music (Flutes (2)) *(M288-9)*
  NT Canons, fugues, etc. (Flutes (2))
      Concertos (Flutes (2))
      Concertos (Flutes (2) with chamber
        orchestra)
      Concertos (Flutes (2) with string
        orchestra)
      Flutes (2) with chamber orchestra
      Flutes (2) with orchestra
      Flutes (2) with string orchestra
      Marches (Flutes (2))
      Minuets (Flutes (2))
      Sonatas (Flutes (2))
      Suites (Flutes (2))
      Variations (Flutes (2))
  Note under Chamber music
Flute music (Flutes (2)), Arranged *(M288-9)*
  NT Overtures arranged for flutes (2)
Flute music (Flutes (3))
  USE Woodwind trios (Flutes (3))
Flute music (Flutes (4))
  USE Woodwind quartets (Flutes (4))
Flute music (Flutes (5))
  USE Woodwind quintets (Flutes (5))

Flute music (Flutes (6))
  USE Woodwind sextets (Flutes (6))
Flute music (Flutes (7))
  USE Woodwind septets (Flutes (7))
Flute music (Flutes (8))
  USE Woodwind octets (Flutes (8))
Flute music (Flutes (9))
  USE Woodwind nonets (Flutes (9))
Flute music (Jazz) *(M60-64)*
Flute, oboe d'amore, viola d'amore with string
      orchestra *(M1105-6)*
  BT Trios (Flute, oboe d'amore, viola
      d'amore)
  RT Concertos (Flute, oboe d'amore, viola
      d'amore with string orchestra)
Flute, oboe d'amore, violin with string
      orchestra *(M1140-1141)*
  BT Trios (Flute, oboe d'amore, violin)
  RT Concertos (Flute, oboe d'amore, violin with
string orchestra)
Flute, oboe, trumpet with string orchestra
      (M1105-6)
  BT String orchestra music
      Wind trios (Flute, oboe, trumpet)
  RT Concertos (Flute, oboe, trumpet with string
orchestra)
Flute, oboe, violin, violoncello with orchestra
      (M1040-1041)
  BT Quartets (Flute, oboe, violin,
      violoncello)
  RT Concertos (Flute, oboe, violin,
      violoncello)
Flute, oboe, violin with string orchestra
      (M1140-1141)
  BT Trios (Flute, oboe, violin)
  RT Concertos (Flute, oboe, violin with
      string orchestra)
Flute-players [May Subd Geog] *(ML937)*
  UF Flutists
      Music—Biography
  BT Musicians
Flute-playing clock
  USE Musical clock
Flute, saxophone, harp with string orchestra
      (M1105-6)
  BT Trios (Flute, saxophone, harp)
  RT Concertos (Flute, saxophone, harp with
      string orchestra)
Flute, timpani, violin with string orchestra
      (M1140-1141)
  BT Trios (Flute, timpani, violin)
  RT Concertos (Flute, timpani, violin with
      string orchestra)
Flute, viola, violoncello with string orchestra
      (M1105-6)
  BT Trios (Flute, viola, violoncello)
  RT Concertos (Flute, viola, violoncello with
      string orchestra)
Flute with accordion ensemble
  BT Accordion ensembles
  RT Concertos (Flute with accordion
      ensemble)

Flute with band *(M1205-6)*
RT Concertos (Flute with band)
NT Suites (Flute with band)
Flute with band, Arranged *(M1257)*
—Scores and parts *(M1257)*
Flute with brass ensemble
RT Concertos (Flute with brass ensemble)
Flute with chamber orchestra *(M1020-1021)*
RT Concertos (Flute with chamber
      orchestra)
NT Rondos (Flute with chamber orchestra)
      Suites (Flute with chamber orchestra)
      Variations (Flute with chamber
      orchestra)
—Solo with piano *(M1021)*
      BT Flute and piano music, Arranged
Flute with chamber orchestra, Arranged
      (M1020-1021)
Flute with flute ensemble
RT Concertos (Flute with flute ensemble)
Flute with instrumental ensemble
RT Concertos (Flute with instrumental
      ensemble)
NT Rondos (Flute with instrumental
      ensemble)
      Variations (Flute with instrumental
      ensemble)
Flute with jazz ensemble *(M1366)*
RT Concertos (Flute with jazz ensemble)
Flute with orchestra *(M1020-1021)*
BT Orchestral music
RT Concertos (Flute)
NT Polonaises (Flute with orchestra)
      Recorder with orchestra
      Rondos (Flute with orchestra)
      Suites (Flute with orchestra)
      Symphonies (Flute with orchestra)
      Variations (Flute with orchestra)
—Solo with piano *(M1021)*
      BT Flute and piano music, Arranged
Flute with orchestra, Arranged
      (M1020-1021)
—Scores *(M1020)*
Flute with percussion ensemble
RT Concertos (Flute with percussion
      ensemble)
NT Suites (Flute with percussion ensemble)
Flute with string ensemble
RT Concertos (Flute with string ensemble)
—Solo with piano
      BT Flute and piano music, Arranged
Flute with string orchestra *(M1105-6)*
RT Concertos (Flute with string orchestra)
NT Canons, fugues, etc. (Flute with string
      orchestra)
      Rondos (Flute with string orchestra)
      Suites (Flute with string orchestra)
      Variations (Flute with string orchestra)
—Solo with piano *(M1106)*
      BT Flute and piano music, Arranged
Flute with string orchestra, Arranged
      (M1105-6)

Flute with wind ensemble
RT Concertos (Flute with wind ensemble)
Flute with woodwind ensemble
RT Concertos (Flute with woodwind
      ensemble)
Flutes (2), glockenspiel with string orchestra
      (M1105-6)
UF Two flutes and glockenspiel with string
      orchestra
BT String-orchestra music
      Trios (Flutes (2), glockenspiel)
RT Concertos (Flutes (2), glockenspiel with
      string orchestra)
Flutes (2), marimba with string orchestra
      (M1105-6)
UF Two flutes, marimba with string
      orchestra
BT String-orchestra music
      Trios (Flutes (2), marimba)
RT Concertos (Flutes (2), marimba with
      string orchestra)
—Scores *(M1105)*
**Flutes (2), viola, violoncello with string
      orchestra** *(M1140-1141)*
BT Quartets (Flutes (2), viola, violoncello)
RT Concertos (Flutes (2), viola, violoncello .
      with string orchestra)
**Flutes (2), violin, violoncello with string
      orchestra** *(M1140-1141)*
BT Quartets (Flutes (2), violin, violoncello)
RT Concertos (Flutes (2), violin,
      violoncello with string orchestra)
Flutes (2), violin with string orchestra
      (M1140-1141)
BT Trios (Flutes (2), violin)
RT Concertos (Flutes (2), violin with string
      orchestra)
**Flutes (2), violoncello with string
      orchestra** *(M1140-1141)*
BT Trios (Flutes (2), violoncello)
RT Concertos (Flutes (2), violoncello with
      string orchestra)
Flutes (2) with chamber orchestra
      (M1020-1021)
UF Two flutes with chamber orchestra
BT Chamber-orchestra music
      Flute music (Flutes (2))
RT Concertos (Flutes (2) with chamber
      orchestra)
Flutes (2) with flute ensemble
RT Concertos (Flutes (2) with flute ensemble)
Flutes (2) with orchestra *(M1020-1021)*
UF Two flutes with orchestra
BT Flute music (Flutes (2))
RT Concertos (Flutes (2))
—Solos with piano *(M1021)*
      BT Trios (Piano, flutes (2)), Arranged
Flutes (2) with string ensemble
Flutes (2) with string orchestra *(M1105-6)*
UF Two flutes with string orchestra
BT Flute music (Flutes (2))
RT Concertos (Flutes (2) with string orchestra)

Flutes (2) with string orchestra *(M1105-6)*
(*Continued*)
  NT Canons, fugues, etc. (Flutes (2) with
        string orchestra)
      Suites (Flutes (2) with string orchestra)
Flutes (3) and harp with orchestra
      (M1040-1041)
  BT Quartets (Flutes (3), harp)
  RT Concertos (Flutes (3) and harp)
Flutes (3) with band *(M1205-1206)*
  BT Woodwind trios (Flutes (3))
  RT Concertos (Flutes (3) with band)
  —Scores and parts *(M1205)*
Flutes (3) with string orchestra
      (M1120-1121)
  BT Woodwind trios (Flutes (3))
  RT Concertos (Flutes (3) with string
        orchestra)
  NT Suites (Flutes (3) with string orchestra)
Flutes (4) with band *(M1205-6)*
  BT Woodwind quartets (Flutes (4))
  RT Concertos (Flutes (4) with band)
Flutes (4) with band, Arranged *(M1257)*
  —Scores and parts *(M1257)*
Flutes (4) with chamber orchestra
      (M1020-1021)
  BT Woodwind quartets (Flutes (4))
  RT Concertos (Flutes (4) with chamber
        orchestra)
Flutes (4) with orchestra *(M1020-1021)*
Flutists
  USE Flute-players
Folias (Music)
      This heading is used without specification
      of medium. For works for a specific
      medium, a second heading is assigned,
      e.g. 1. Folias (Music) 2. Guitar mu-
      sic.
  UF Follias (Music)
  BT Dance music
      Songs
      Variations
Folk dance music [May Subd Geog] *(M1627)*
      Here are entered collections of miscel-
      laneous folk dance music. Music for
      individual dances is entered under
      dance form, *e.g.* Square dance music.
      If the collection also contains dance in-
      struction, two headings are used, *e.g.*
      1. Folk dancing. 2. Folk dance music.
      If the collection is for a medium other
      than piano, additional heading is used
      for the medium, *e.g.* 1. Folk dance mu-
      sic. 2. Orchestral music, Arranged.
      For works consisting of Folk dance music
      of an individual ethnic group, an addi-
      tional subject entry is made under the
      heading [ethnic group]—[place]—Music.
  UF National dances
  BT Dance music
      Folk music
      Music

Folk dance music [May Subd Geog] *(M1627)*
(*Continued*)
  —Poland
    NT Krakowiaks
  —Spain
    NT Flamenco music
  Note under Folk dancing
Folk dancing [May Subd Geog]
  BT National music
  RT Folk music
Folk dancing, Embu [May Subd Geog]
  UF Embu folk dancing
Folk music [May Subd Geog]
      For works consisting of folk music of an
      individual ethnic group, an additional
      subject entry is made under the heading
      [ethnic group]—[place]—Music.
  BT Folklore
      Music
      National music
  RT Folk dancing
  NT Fiddling
      Folk dance music
      Folk-songs
  —Mexico
    NT Mariachi
  —Spain
    NT Flamenco music
  —Thailand
    NT Pīphāt music
  —United States
    NT Blues (Music)
        Country music
        Folk-rock music
Folk music groups [May Subd Geog]
  BT Musical groups
Folk-rock music [May Subd Geog]
  UF Ecology rock music
      Folkrock music
      Soft rock music
  BT Folk music—United States
      Rock music—United States
Folk singers [May Subd Geog]
  UF Folksingers
  BT Singers
  —Japan
    NT Goze
Folk-songs [May Subd Geog] *(Folk poetry,*
      PN1341-PN1345; Music, M1627;
      Music literature, ML3545)
      Here are entered collections of folk-songs
      in various unrelated languages. Works
      in a single language or group of lan-
      guages are entered under this heading
      with language qualifier, *e.g.* Folk-
      songs, English; Folk-songs, Slavic. For
      works consisting of folk-songs of an
      individual ethnic group, additional sub-
      ject entries are made under the heading
      [ethnic group]—Music and under the
      heading Folk music—[place] or Music—
      [place].

Folk-songs [May Subd Geog] (*Folk poetry,*
　　PN1341-PN1345; Music, M1627;
　　Music literature, ML3545)
　　(*Continued*)
　　BT　Folk music
　　　　Music
　　　　National music
　　　　Songs
　　　　Vocal music
　　RT　Ballads
　　　　National songs
　　NT　Carols
　　　　Dumy
　　　　Folk poetry
　　　　Lays
　　　　Play-party
　　　　Rice—Planting—Songs and music
　　　　Work-songs
　　—Accompaniment (*MT68*)
　　　　BT　Musical accompaniment
　　—Criticism, Textual
　　—Instrumental settings
　　Example under reference from Instru-
　　　　mental settings
Folk-songs, Abkhaz [May Subd Geog]
　　(*M1766-1767*)
　　UF　Abkhaz folk-songs
Folk-songs, Acoli [May Subd Geog]
　　UF　Acoli folk-songs
Folk-songs, Adyghe [May Subd Geog]
　　(*M1766-1767*)
　　UF　Adyghe folk-songs
Folk-songs, Adzhar [May Subd Geog] (*M1766.A3;*
　　M1767.A3)
　　UF　Adzhar folk-songs
Folk-songs, Agri [May Subd Geog]
　　UF　Agri folk-songs
Folk-songs, Ainu [May Subd Geog]
　　UF　Ainu folk-songs
Folk-songs, Aka (Central African Republic)
　　[May Subd Geog]
　　UF　Aka folk-songs (Central African
　　　　Republic)
Folk-songs, Akan [May Subd Geog]
　　UF　Akan folk-songs
Folk-songs, Albanian [May Subd Geog]
　　UF　Albanian folk-songs
Folk-songs, Ambo (Zambia) [May Subd Geog]
　　UF　Ambo (Zambia) folk-songs
Folk-songs, Antandroy [May Subd Geog]
　　UF　Antandroy folk-songs
Folk-songs, Arabic [May Subd Geog]
　　UF　Arabic folk-songs
Folk-songs, Armenian [May Subd Geog]
　　UF　Armenian folk-songs
Folk-songs, Aromanian [May Subd Geog]
　　UF　Aromanian folk-songs
Folk-songs, Australian (Aboriginal) [May Subd
Geog]
　　UF　Australian (Aboriginal) folk-songs
Folk-songs, Awadhi [May Subd Geog]
　　UF　Awadhi folk-songs

Folk-songs, Bamileke [May Subd Geog]
　　UF　Bamileke folk-songs
Folk-songs, Banjarese [May Subd Geog]
　　UF　Banjarese folk-songs
Folk-songs, Bantu [May Subd Geog]
　　UF　Bantu folk-songs
Folk-songs, Basque [May Subd Geog]
　　UF　Basque folk-songs
Folk-songs, Bassari [May Subd Geog]
　　UF　Bassari folk-songs
Folk-songs, Béarnais [May Subd Geog]
　　UF　Béarnais folk-songs
Folk-songs, Bella Coola [May Subd Geog]
　　UF　Bella Coola folk-songs
Folk-songs, Bengali [May Subd Geog]
　　UF　Bengali folk-songs
Folk-songs, Bhili [May Subd Geog]
　　UF　Bhili folk-songs
Folk-songs, Bhojpuri [May Subd Geog]
　　UF　Bhojpuri folk-songs
Folk-songs, Bohemian
　　USE　Folk-songs, Czech
Folk-songs, Bosavi [May Subd Geog]
　　UF　Bosavi folk-songs
Folk-songs, Breton [May Subd Geog]
　　UF　Breton folk-songs
Folk-songs, Buin [May Subd Geog]
　　UF　Buin folk-songs
Folk-songs, Bulgarian [May Subd Geog]
　　UF　Bulgarian folk-songs
　　BT　Folk-songs, Slavic
Folk-songs, Bundeli [May Subd Geog]
　　UF　Bundeli folk-songs
Folk-songs, Burgundian [May Subd Geog]
　　UF　Burgundian folk-songs
Folk-songs, Burmese [May Subd Geog]
　　UF　Burmese folk-songs
Folk-songs, Byelorussian [May Subd Geog]
　　UF　Byelorussian folk-songs
Folk-songs, Cajun French [May Subd Geog]
　　UF　Cajun French folk-songs
Folk-songs, Catalan [May Subd Geog]
　　UF　Catalan folk-songs
　　NT　Goigs
Folk-songs, Chakma [May Subd Geog]
　　UF　Chakma folk-songs
Folk-songs, Chechen [May Subd Geog]
　　(*M1766-1767*)
　　UF　Chechen folk-songs
Folk-songs, Chhattisgarhi [May Subd Geog]
　　UF　Chhattisgarhi folk-songs
Folk-songs, Chinese [May Subd Geog]
　　UF　Chinese folk-songs
Folk-songs, Chuvash [May Subd Geog]
　　(*M1766-1767*)
　　UF　Chuvash folk-songs
Folk-songs, Cornish [May Subd Geog]
　　UF　Cornish folk-songs
Folk-songs, Creole [May Subd Geog]
　　UF　Creole folk-songs
Folk-songs, Croatian [May Subd Geog]
　　UF　Croatian folk-songs
　　BT　Folk-songs, Slavic

Folk-songs, Czech [May Subd Geog]
UF Czech folk-songs
Folk-songs, Bohemian
BT Folk-songs, Slavic
Folk-songs, Dakota [May Subd Geog]
UF Dakota folk-songs
Folk-songs, Danish [May Subd Geog]
UF Danish folk-songs
BT Folk-songs, Scandinavian
Folk-songs, Dargwa [May Subd Geog]
UF Dargwa folk-songs
Folk-songs, Dimasa [May Subd Geog]
UF Dimasa folk-songs
Folk-songs, Dinka [May Subd Geog]
UF Dinka folk-songs
Folk-songs, Dogri [May Subd Geog]
UF Dogri folk-songs
Folk-songs, Dutch [May Subd Geog]
UF Dutch folk-songs
Folk-songs, Embu [May Subd Geog]
UF Embu folk-songs
Folk-songs, English [May Subd Geog]
UF English folk-songs
—United States
NT Spirituals (Songs)
Note under Folk-songs
Folk-songs, Eskimo [May Subd Geog]
UF Eskimo folk-songs
BT Eskimos—Music
Folk-songs, Estonian [May Subd Geog]
UF Estonian folk-songs
Folk-songs, Ethiopian [May Subd Geog]
UF Ethiopian folk-songs
Folk-songs, Faroese [May Subd Geog]
UF Faroese folk-songs
BT Folk-songs, Scandinavian
Folk-songs, Finnish [May Subd Geog]
UF Finnish folk-songs
Folk-songs, Finno-Ugric [May Subd Geog]
UF Finno-Ugric folk-songs
Folk-songs, French [May Subd Geog]
UF French folk-songs
Folk-songs, Friesian [May Subd Geog]
UF Friesian folk-songs
Folk-songs, Friulian [May Subd Geog]
UF Friulian folk-songs
Folk-songs, Fulah [May Subd Geog]
UF Fulah folk-songs
Folk-songs, Gã [May Subd Geog]
UF Gã folk-songs
Folk-songs, Gaelic [May Subd Geog]
UF Gaelic folk-songs
Folk-songs, Ganda [May Subd Geog]
UF Ganda folk-songs
Folk-songs, Garhwali [May Subd Geog]
UF Garhwali folk-songs
Folk-songs, Garo [May Subd Geog]
UF Garo folk-songs
Folk-songs, Gascon [May Subd Geog]
UF Gascon folk-songs
Folk-songs, Gayo [May Subd Geog]
UF Gayo folk-songs

Folk-songs, Gbaya [May Subd Geog]
UF Gbaya folk-songs
Folk-songs, German [May Subd Geog]
UF German folk-songs
NT Folk-songs, Low German
—Switzerland
NT Yodels
Folk-songs, Gondi [May Subd Geog]
UF Gondi folk-songs
Folk-songs, Greek [May Subd Geog]
UF Greek folk-songs
Folk-songs, Greek (Modern) [May Subd Geog]
UF Greek folk-songs, Modern
Modern Greek folk-songs
Folk-songs, Guarani [May Subd Geog]
UF Guarani folk-songs
Folk-songs, Gujarati [May Subd Geog]
UF Gujarati folk-songs
Folk-songs, Gujuri [May Subd Geog]
UF Gujuri folk-songs
Folk-songs, Hebrew [May Subd Geog]
UF Hebrew folk-songs
Folk-songs, Himachali [May Subd Geog]
UF Himachali folk-songs
Folk-songs, Hindi [May Subd Geog]
UF Hindi folk-songs
Folk-songs, Hungarian [May Subd Geog]
UF Hungarian folk-songs
Folk-songs, Iatmul [May Subd Geog]
UF Iatmul folk-songs
Folk-songs, Icelandic [May Subd Geog]
UF Icelandic folk-songs
BT Folk-songs, Scandinavian
Folk-songs, Indic [May Subd Geog]
UF Indic folk-songs
Folk-songs, Ingush [May Subd Geog]
(M1766-1767)
UF Ingush folk-songs
Folk-songs, Irish [May Subd Geog]
UF Irish folk-songs
Folk-songs, Italian [May Subd Geog]
UF Italian folk-songs
Folk-songs, Japanese [May Subd Geog]
UF Japanese folk-songs
Saibara
Folk-songs, Javanese [May Subd Geog]
UF Javanese folk-songs
Folk-songs, Kalmyk [May Subd Geog]
UF Kalmyk folk-songs
Folk-songs, Kamba [May Subd Geog]
UF Kamba folk-songs
Folk-songs, Kangri [May Subd Geog]
UF Kangri folk-songs
Folk-songs, Kannada [May Subd Geog]
UF Kannada folk-songs
Folk-songs, Karamojong [May Subd Geog]
UF Karamojong folk-songs
Folk-songs, Karelian [May Subd Geog]
UF Karelian folk-songs
Folk-songs, Karo-Batak [May Subd Geog]
UF Karo-Batak folk-songs
Folk-songs, Kashubian [May Subd Geog]
UF Kashubian folk-songs

Folk-songs, Kazakh [May Subd Geog]
    UF   Kazakh folk-songs
Folk-songs, Kemak [May Subd Geog]
    UF   Kemak folk-songs
Folk-songs, Khakass [May Subd Geog]
    UF   Khakass folk-songs
Folk-songs, Khanty [May Subd Geog]
    UF   Khanty folk-songs
Folk-songs, Kikuyu [May Subd Geog]
    UF   Kikuyu folk-songs
Folk-songs, Kimbundu [May Subd Geog]
    UF   Kimbundu folk-songs
Folk-songs, Konkani [May Subd Geog]
    UF   Konkani folk-songs
Folk-songs, Korean [May Subd Geog]
    UF   Korean folk-songs
Folk-songs, Kpelle [May Subd Geog]
    UF   Kpelle folk-songs
Folk-songs, Kuanua [May Subd Geog]
    UF   Kuanua folk-songs
Folk-songs, Kului [May Subd Geog]
    UF   Kului folk-songs
Folk-songs, Kurdish [May Subd Geog]
    UF   Kurdish folk-songs
Folk-songs, Kurukh [May Subd Geog]
    UF   Kurukh folk-songs
Folk-songs, Ladakhi [May Subd Geog]
    UF   Ladakhi folk-songs
Folk-songs, Ladino [May Subd Geog]
    UF   Ladino folk-songs
Folk-songs, Langue d'oc [May Subd Geog]
    UF   Langue d'oc folk-songs
Folk-songs, Lao [May Subd Geog]
    UF   Lao folk-songs
Folk-songs, Latvian [May Subd Geog]
    UF   Latvian folk-songs
Folk-songs, Lepcha [May Subd Geog]
    UF   Lepcha folk-songs
Folk-songs, Lithuanian [May Subd Geog]
    UF   Lithuanian folk-songs
Folk-songs, Livonian [May Subd Geog]
    UF   Livonian folk-songs
Folk-songs, Lobi [May Subd Geog]
    UF   Lobi folk-songs
Folk-songs, Low German [May Subd Geog]
    UF   Low German folk-songs
    BT   Folk-songs, German
Folk-songs, Lunda [May Subd Geog]
    UF   Lunda folk-songs
Folk-songs, Lushai [May Subd Geog]
    UF   Lushai folk-songs
Folk-songs, Macedonian [May Subd Geog]
        (M1724-1725)
    UF   Macedonian folk-songs
Folk-songs, Maithili [May Subd Geog]
    UF   Maithili folk-songs
Folk-songs, Malagasy [May Subd Geog]
    UF   Malagasy folk-songs
Folk-songs, Malay [May Subd Geog]
    UF   Malay folk-songs
Folk-songs, Malayalam [May Subd Geog]
    UF   Malayalam folk-songs

Folk-songs, Mandailing [May Subd Geog]
    UF   Mandailing folk-songs
Folk-songs, Mandingo [May Subd Geog]
    UF   Mandingo folk-songs
Folk-songs, Mansi [May Subd Geog]
    UF   Mansi folk-songs
Folk-songs, Manx [May Subd Geog]
    UF   Manx folk-songs
Folk-songs, Maori [May Subd Geog]
    UF   Maori folk-songs
Folk-songs, Marathi [May Subd Geog]
    UF   Marathi folk-songs
Folk-songs, Mari [May Subd Geog]
    UF   Mari folk-songs
Folk-songs, Marwari [May Subd Geog]
    UF   Marwari folk-songs
Folk-songs, Moldavian [May Subd Geog]
    UF   Moldavian folk-songs
Folk-songs, Mongolian [May Subd Geog]
    UF   Mongolian folk-songs
Folk-songs, Mundari [May Subd Geog]
    UF   Mundari folk-songs
Folk-songs, Ngbaka ma'bo [May Subd Geog]
    UF   Ngbaka ma'bo folk-songs
Folk-songs, Nimadi [May Subd Geog]
    UF   Nimadi folk-songs
Folk-songs, Norwegian [May Subd Geog]
    UF   Norwegian folk-songs
    BT   Folk-songs, Scandinavian
Folk-songs, Nuer [May Subd Geog]
    UF   Nuer folk-songs
Folk-songs, Old French [May Subd Geog]
    UF   Old French folk-songs
Folk-songs, Oriya [May Subd Geog]
    UF   Oriya folk-songs
Folk-songs, Paite [May Subd Geog]
    UF   Paite folk-songs
Folk-songs, Panjabi [May Subd Geog]
    UF   Panjabi folk-songs
Folk-songs, Papuan [May Subd Geog]
    UF   Papuan folk-songs
Folk-songs, Pennsylvanian German
        [May Subd Geog]
    UF   Pennsylvanian German folk-songs
Folk-songs, Polish [May Subd Geog]
    UF   Polish folk-songs
    BT   Folk-songs, Slavic
Folk-songs, Portuguese [May Subd Geog]
    UF   Portuguese folk-songs
    NT   Fados
    —Brazil
        NT   Congadas
Folk-songs, Provençal [May Subd Geog]
    UF   Provençal folk-songs
Folk-songs, Punu [May Subd Geog]
    UF   Punu folk-songs
Folk-songs, Quechua [May Subd Geog]
    UF   Quechua folk-songs
Folk-songs, Raeto-Romance [May Subd Geog]
    UF   Raeto-Romance folk-songs
Folk-songs, Rajasthani [May Subd Geog]
    UF   Rajasthani folk-songs

Folk-songs, Romanian [May Subd Geog]
    UF Romanian folk-songs
Folk-songs, Romany [May Subd Geog]
    UF Romany folk-songs
Folk-songs, Ruanda [May Subd Geog]
    UF Ruanda folk-songs
Folk-songs, Rundi [May Subd Geog]
    UF Rundi folk-songs
Folk-songs, Russian [May Subd Geog]
    UF Russian folk-songs
    BT Folk-songs, Slavic
    NT Byliny
        Chastushki
Folk-songs, Salampasu [May Subd Geog]
    UF Salampasu folk-songs
Folk-songs, Sambalpuri [May Subd Geog]
    UF Sambalpuri folk-songs
Folk-songs, Samoan [May Subd Geog]
    UF Samoan folk-songs
Folk-songs, Santali [May Subd Geog]
    UF Santali folk-songs
Folk-songs, Sardinian [May Subd Geog]
    UF Sardinian folk-songs
Folk-songs, Scandinavian [May Subd Geog]
    UF Scandinavian folk-songs
    NT Folk-songs, Danish
        Folk-songs, Faroese
        Folk-songs, Icelandic
        Folk-songs, Norwegian
        Folk-songs, Swedish
Folk-songs, Serbo-Croatian [May Subd Geog]
    UF Serbo-Croatian folk-songs
Folk-songs, Simelungun [May Subd Geog]
    UF Simelungun folk-songs
Folk-songs, Sinhalese [May Subd Geog]
    UF Sinhalese folk-songs
Folk-songs, Slavic [May Subd Geog]
    UF Slavic folk-songs
    NT Folk-songs, Bulgarian
        Folk-songs, Croatian
        Folk-songs, Czech
        Folk-songs, Polish
        Folk-songs, Russian
        Folk-songs, Slovak
        Folk-songs, Slovenian
        Folk-songs, Sorbian
        Folk-songs, Ukrainian
    Note under Folk-songs
Folk-songs, Slovak [May Subd Geog]
    UF Slovak folk-songs
    BT Folk-songs, Slavic
Folk-songs, Slovenian [May Subd Geog]
    UF Slovenian folk-songs
    BT Folk-songs, Slavic
Folk-songs, Somali [May Subd Geog]
    UF Somali folk-songs
Folk-songs, Sorbian [May Subd Geog]
    UF Sorbian folk-songs
    BT Folk-songs, Slavic
Folk-songs, Southern Slavic [May Subd Geog]
    UF Southern Slavic folk-songs

Folk-songs, Spanish [May Subd Geog]
    UF Spanish folk-songs
    NT Coplas
        Flamenco music
  —Mexico
    NT Corridos
  —Peru
    NT Mulizas
Folk-songs, Sranan [May Subd Geog]
    UF Sranan folk-songs
Folk-songs, Sundanese [May Subd Geog]
    UF Sundanese folk-songs
Folk-songs, Swedish [May Subd Geog]
    UF Swedish folk-songs
    BT Folk-songs, Scandinavian
Folk-songs, Tahitian [May Subd Geog]
    UF Tahitian folk-songs
Folk-songs, Tamazight [May Subd Geog]
    UF Tamazight folk-songs
Folk-songs, Tamil [May Subd Geog]
    UF Tamil folk-songs
Folk-songs, Tatar [May Subd Geog]
    UF Tatar folk-songs
Folk-songs, Teda [May Subd Geog]
    UF Teda folk-songs
Folk-songs, Teke [May Subd Geog]
    UF Teke folk-songs
Folk-songs, Telugu [May Subd Geog]
    UF Telugu folk-songs
Folk-songs, Tewa [May Subd Geog]
    UF Tewa folk-songs
Folk-songs, Thai [May Subd Geog]
    UF Thai folk-songs
Folk-songs, Tibetan [May Subd Geog]
    UF Tibetan folk-songs
Folk-songs, Tlingit [May Subd Geog]
    UF Tlingit folk-songs
Folk-songs, Tsogo [May Subd Geog]
    UF Tsogo folk-songs
Folk-songs, Tsonga [May Subd Geog]
    UF Tsonga folk-songs
Folk-songs, Tswana [May Subd Geog]
    UF Tswana folk-songs
Folk-songs, Turkish [May Subd Geog]
    UF Turkish folk-songs
Folk-songs, Tuvinian [May Subd Geog]
    UF Tuvinian folk-songs
Folk-songs, Ukrainian [May Subd Geog]
    UF Ukrainian folk-songs
    BT Folk-songs, Slavic
    NT Kolomyîky
Folk-songs, Urdu [May Subd Geog]
    UF Urdu folk-songs
Folk-songs, Uzbek [May Subd Geog]
    UF Uzbek folk-songs
Folk-songs, Vietnamese [May Subd Geog]
    UF Vietnamese folk-songs
Folk-songs, Walloon [May Subd Geog]
    UF Walloon folk-songs
Folk-songs, Welsh [May Subd Geog]
    UF Welsh folk-songs

Folk-songs, Yiddish [May Subd Geog]
    UF   Yiddish folk-songs
Folk-songs, Yoruba [May Subd Geog]
    UF   Yoruba folk-songs
Folk-songs, Zande [May Subd Geog]
    UF   Zande folk-songs
Folk-songs, Zarma [May Subd Geog]
    UF   Zarma folk-songs
Folksingers
    USE Folk singers
Follias (Music)
    USE Folias (Music)
Form, Musical
    USE Musical form
Four clarinets with string orchestra
    USE Clarinets (4) with string orchestra
Four cornets with band
    USE Cornets (4) with band
Four flutes with band
    USE Flutes (4) with band
Four harpsichords with orchestra
    USE Harpsichords (4) with orchestra
Four harpsichords with string orchestra
    USE Harpsichords (4) with string orchestra
Four horns with band
    USE Horns (4) with band
Four horns with orchestra
    USE Horns (4) with orchestra
Four saxophones with chamber orchestra
    USE Saxophones (4) with chamber orchestra
Four saxophones with string orchestra
    USE Saxophones (4) with string orchestra
Four trumpets with string orchestra
    USE Trumpets (4) with string orchestra
Four violins with string orchestra
    USE Violins (4) with string orchestra
Fourth of July
    —Songs and music *(M1629.3.F6)*
        Example under Holidays—Songs and
            music
Fox trots
    BT   Dance music
Frame drums
    BT   Drum
    NT   Ḍaph
Fraternity songs *(M1960)*
    UF   Sorority songs
    BT   Students' songs—United States
    SA   *subdivision* Songs and music *under*
           names of fraternities, e.g. Phi Kappa
           Psi—Songs and music
French ballads
    USE Ballads, French
French folk-songs
    USE Folk-songs, French
French Hindu hymns
    USE Hindu hymns, French
French horn
    USE Horn (Musical instrument)
French lullabies
    USE Lullabies, French
French part-songs
    USE Part-songs, French

French songs
    USE Songs, French
Frevos
    BT   Dance music
Friesian folk-songs
    USE Folk-songs, Friesian
Fuging tunes
    USE Hymns, English
Fugue *(ML448; MT59)*
        Here are entered works on the fugue as a
           musical form. Scores are entered under
           the heading Canons, fugues, etc.
    UF   Ricercare
    BT   Counterpoint
    RT   Canon (Music)
    Example under Musical form
Fugues
    USE Canons, fugues, etc.
Fuguing tunes
    USE Hymns, English
Fulah folk-songs
    USE Folk-songs, Fulah
Funeral hymns
    BT   Funeral music
          Hymns
    NT   Dirges
Funeral music
    BT   Church music
          Music
          Sacred vocal music
    RT   Memorial music
    NT   Death in music
          Funeral hymns
          Requiems
Furiants
    BT   Dance music
Gã folk-songs
    USE Folk-songs, Gã
Gaelic folk-songs
    USE Folk-songs, Gaelic
Gaelic songs
    USE Songs, Gaelic
Gagaku
    BT   Music—Japan
    RT   Bugaku
          Tōgaku
Gagliarde
    USE Galliards
Gahu
    BT   Dance music—Africa, West
          Percussion ensembles
Gaillardes
    USE Galliards
Gaita *(ML980)*
    UF   Spanish bagpipe
    BT   Bagpipe
Galin-Paris-Chevé method (Music) *(MT20)*
    BT   Music—Instruction and study
          Musical notation
          Sight-reading (Music)
          Sight-singing
          Singing—Methods

Gallegan ballads
USE Ballads, Gallegan
Galliards
UF Gagliarde
Gaillardes
BT Dance music
Galops
BT Dance music
Galoubet *(ML935-7)*
UF Txistu
BT Flageolet
Flute
Recorder (Musical instrument)
Woodwind instruments
Galoubet and tambourin music *(M298)*
UF Tambourin and galoubet music
Galoubet music *(M110.G)*
Galoubet music (Galoubets (2)) *(M288-9)*
Gamelan *(ML1251)*
UF Gamelang
BT Orchestra
Percussion instruments
NT Khjai Mendung (Gamelan)
Gamelan music
Gamelang
USE Gamelan
Games with music *(M1993)*
UF Action songs
BT Children's songs
Play-party
RT Singing games
NT Musical card games
Garhwali folk-songs
USE Folk-songs, Garhwali
Gascon folk-songs
USE Folk-songs, Gascon
Gathering of Traditional Indiana Fiddlers and
Other Folks
USE Battle Ground Fiddlers' Gathering,
Battle Ground, Ind.
Gavottes
BT Dance music
Gayo folk-songs
USE Folk-songs, Gayo
Gazoo
USE Kazoo
Gender (Musical instrument)
UF Demung gantung
Kliningan
Slentem gantung
BT Musical instruments—Indonesia
Percussion instruments
Georgian hymns
USE Hymns, Georgian
German ballads
USE Ballads, German
German folk-songs
USE Folk-songs, German
German lullabies
USE Lullabies, German
German part-songs
USE Part-songs, German

German songs
USE Songs, German
Germanic ballads
USE Ballads, Germanic
Gifted children
NT Children as musicians
Giselle (Ballet) *(GV1790.G5)*
BT Ballets
Glass harmonica *(ML1055)*
UF Glasses, Musical
Harmonica, Glass
Musical glasses
Glass-harmonica and lute music *(M298)*
UF Lute and glass-harmonica music
Glass-harmonica and piano music *(M284.G6;*
M285.G6)
UF Piano and glass-harmonica music
Glass-harmonica music *(M165)*
SA Concertos, Minuets, Sonatas, Suites,
and similar headings with
specification of instruments; Trios
[Quartets, etc.] *followed by*
specifications which include the glass
harmonica; also headings that begin
with the words glass harmonica or
glass harmonicas
Glees, catches, rounds, etc.
UF Catches
Rounds
BT Song-books
Vocal music
RT Canons, fugues, etc. (Vocal)
Glockenspiel *(History, ML1040)*
UF Bell-lyra
Orchestral bells
BT Percussion instruments
Glockenspiel and celesta music *(M284.G65;*
M285.G65)
UF Celesta and glockenspiel music
Glockenspiel and harpsichord music
(M284.G65; M285.G65)
UF Harpsichord and glockenspiel music
Glockenspiel music *(M147)*
SA Concertos, Minuets, Sonatas, Suites,
and similar headings with
specification of instruments; Trios
[Quartets, etc.] *followed by*
specifications which include the
glockenspiel; also Percussion
ensembles, Percussion music, *and*
headings that begin with the words
glockenspiel or glockenspiels
NT Glockenspiel with string orchestra
Quartets (Piano, flute, harp,
glockenspiel)
Quintets (Pianos (4), glockenspiel)
Quintets (Trombone, glockenspiel,
percussion)
Trios (Piano, clarinet, glockenspiel)
Glockenspiel with string orchestra *(M1105-6)*
BT Glockenspiel music
RT Concertos (Glockenspiel with string orchestra)

Gloria in excelsis Deo (Music)
 BT Masses
Gluck-Piccinni controversy *(ML1727.35)*
 BT Opera
 RT Guerre des Bouffons
Goigs *(ML3086)*
 BT Folk-songs, Catalan
   Hymns, Spanish
Gondi folk-songs
 USE Folk-songs, Gondi
Gong
 USE Tamtam
Good Friday music *(Part-songs, M2078.G5,*
   M2088.G5, M2098.G5; Catholic
   liturgical music, M2149.4.G7)
 BT Holy-Week music
   Lenten music
 RT Passion-music
Gospel music [May Subd Geog]
   M2198-M2199 (Music)
   ML3186.8-ML3187 (History and criticism)
 UF Music, Gospel
 BT Afro-Americans—Music
   Popular music
   Sacred songs
 NT Revivals—Hymns
Gospel musicians [May Subd Geog] *(ML385-403)*
 BT Country musicians
   Musicians
Goura (Musical instrument)
 BT Musical instruments—Africa
Goze [May Subd Geog]
 BT Blind musicians—Japan
   Folk singers—Japan
   Minstrels—Japan
   Women musicians—Japan
Graceland Mansion (Memphis, Tenn.)
 BT Dwellings—Tennessee
Graduals (Liturgical books) *(Roman Catholic,*
   primarily non-musical, BX2043; Roman
   Catholic, primarily musical, M2148-
   M2148.5)
 BT Liturgies
Graduals (Music) *(M2079.L416)*
 BT Propers (Music)
Greek drama
 —Incidental music
   BT Music, Greek and Roman
     Music, Incidental
     Opera
Greek folk-songs
 USE Folk-songs, Greek
Greek folk-songs, Modern
 USE Folk-songs, Greek (Modern)
Greek hymns
 USE Hymns, Greek
   Hymns, Greek (Classical)
Greek music
 USE Music, Greek and Roman
Greek songs, Modern
 USE Songs, Greek (Modern)
Gregorian chant
 USE Chants (Plain, Gregorian, etc.)

Grimilds hœvn (Ballad) *(PT8050.G)*
 BT Ballads, Danish
Ground bass *(ML448)*
 UF Basso ostinato
   Ostinato
 BT Composition (Music)
   Variation (Music)
Groupies [May Subd Geog]
 BT Rock music—Fans
Groups, Chamber music
 USE Chamber music groups
Groups, Rock
 USE Rock groups
Guarani folk-songs
 USE Folk-songs, Guarani
Guarani songs
 USE Songs, Guarani
Gŭdulka *(ML927.G)*
Guerre des Bouffons *(ML1727.33)*
 UF Bouffons, Guerre des
 BT Opera
 RT Gluck-Piccinni controversy
Gueux
 —Songs and music *(PT5484)*
   BT Songs, Dutch
Guitar *(ML1015-ML1018)*
 UF Spanish guitar
 RT Vihuela
 NT Balalaika
   Bandurria
   Charango
   Cithern
   Dobro
   Electric guitar
   English guitar
   Harp-lute guitar
   Hawaiian guitar
   Lyre-guitar
   Ukulele
   Yüeh ch'in
 —Construction
   NT Guitar—Customizing
 —Customizing
   UF Customizing of guitars
   BT Guitar—Construction
 —Electronic equipment
   UF Electronic equipment for guitars
   BT Electronic apparatus and appliances
 —Group instruction
   USE Guitar—Methods—Group
     instruction
 —Instruction and study *(MT580)*
   NT Guitar music—Teaching pieces
 —Methods *(MT582)*
 — —Group instruction *(MT582)*
   UF Guitar—Group instruction
 — —Self-instruction *(MT588)*
   UF Guitar—Self-instruction
 —Methods (Bluegrass) *(General, MT582;*
   Self-instructors, MT588)
 —Methods (Blues) *(MT582)*
   BT Blues (Music)

Guitar *(ML1015-ML1018)*
　(Continued)
　—Methods (Country) *(General, MT582;*
　　　Self-instructors, MT588)
　　BT Country music
　—Methods (Ragtime) *(MT582)*
　　BT Ragtime music
　—Self-instruction
　　USE Guitar—Methods—
　　　Self-instruction
　—Tuning *(History, ML3809; Instruction,*
　　MT165)
　Example under Stringed instruments
Guitar, Electric
　USE Electric guitar
Guitar, Harp-lute
　USE Harp-lute guitar
Guitar, Hawaiian
　USE Hawaiian guitar
Guitar, Steel
　USE Hawaiian guitar
Guitar and accordion music
　USE Accordion and guitar music
Guitar and Appalachian dulcimer music
　USE Appalachian dulcimer and guitar music
Guitar and banjo music
　USE Banjo and guitar music
Guitar and bassoon music
　USE Bassoon and guitar music
Guitar and clarinet music
　USE Clarinet and guitar music
Guitar and concertina music
　USE Concertina and guitar music
Guitar and continuo music
　UF Continuo and guitar music
　NT Sonatas (Guitar and continuo)
Guitar and double-bass music
　USE Double-bass and guitar music
Guitar and drum music *(M298)*
　UF Drum and guitar music
Guitar and dulcimer music
　USE Dulcimer and guitar music
Guitar and English horn music
　USE English horn and guitar music
Guitar and flute music
　USE Flute and guitar music
Guitar and harp music *(M292-293)*
　UF Harp and guitar music
Guitar and harp with chamber orchestra
　　(M1040-1041)
　RT Concertos (Guitar and harp with
　　chamber orchestra)
Guitar and harpsichord music *(M276-7)*
　UF Harpsichord and guitar music
　NT Concertos (Guitar and harpsichord with
　　string orchestra)
　　Guitar and harpsichord with string
　　　orchestra
　　Sonatas (Guitar and harpsichord)
　　Suites (Guitar and harpsichord)
Guitar and harpsichord music, Arranged
　　(M276-7)

Guitar and harpsichord with string orchestra
　　(M1140-1141)
　BT Guitar and harpsichord music
　RT Concertos (Guitar and harpsichord with
　　string orchestra)
Guitar and horn music
　USE Horn and guitar music
Guitar and mandolin music
　UF Mandolin and guitar music
Guitar and oboe d'amore music
　USE Oboe d'amore and guitar music
Guitar and oboe music
　USE Oboe and guitar music
Guitar and organ music *(M182-186)*
　UF Organ and guitar music
Guitar and penny whistle music
　USE Penny whistle and guitar music
Guitar and percussion music
　USE Percussion and guitar music
Guitar and percussion music, Arranged
　　(M298)
Guitar and piano music *(M276-7)*
　UF Piano and guitar music
　NT Concertos (Guitar and piano with string
　　orchestra)
　　Guitar and piano with string orchestra
　　Marches (Guitar and piano)
　　Polonaises (Guitar and piano)
　　Potpourris (Guitar and piano)
　　Rondos (Guitar and piano)
　　Sonatas (Guitar and piano)
　　Suites (Guitar and piano)
　　Variations (Guitar and piano)
　　Waltzes (Guitar and piano)
Guitar and piano music, Arranged *(M276-7)*
　NT Concertos (Guitar)—Solo with piano
　　Concertos (Guitar), Arranged—Solo
　　　with piano
　　Concertos (Guitar with chamber
　　　orchestra)—Solo with piano
　　Concertos (Guitar with string
　　　orchestra)—Solo with piano
　　Guitar with orchestra—Solo with piano
　　Overtures arranged for guitar and piano
　　Suites (Guitar with chamber orchestra)
　　　—Solo with piano
　　Suites (Guitar with orchestra)—Solo
　　　with piano
Guitar and piano with jazz ensemble
　RT Concertos (Guitar and piano with jazz
　　ensemble)
Guitar and piano with string orchestra
　　(M1140-1141)
　BT Guitar and piano music
　RT Concertos (Guitar and piano with string
　　orchestra)
Guitar and piccolo music
　USE Piccolo and guitar music
Guitar and recorder music
　USE Recorder and guitar music
Guitar and saxophone music
　USE Saxophone and guitar music

Guitar and trumpet music
    USE Trumpet and guitar music
Guitar and unspecified instrument music
    USE Duets (Unspecified instrument and
         guitar)
Guitar and viola d'amore music
    USE Viola d'amore and guitar music
Guitar and viola music
    USE Viola and guitar music
Guitar and violin music
    USE Violin and guitar music
Guitar and violoncello music
    USE Violoncello and guitar music
Guitar band
    USE Plectral ensembles
Guitar music *(M125-129)*
    SA Concertos, Minuets, Sonatas, Suites,
        *and similar headings with
        specification of instruments;* Trios
        [Quartets, etc.] *followed by
        specifications which include the
        guitar; also* Plectral ensembles *and
        headings that begin with the words
        guitar or guitars*
    NT Canons, fugues, etc. (Guitar)
        Dobro music
        Hawaiian-guitar music
        Minuets (Guitar)
        Overtures (Guitar)
        Passacaglias (Guitar)
        Potpourris (Guitar)
        Recorded accompaniments (Guitar)
        Rondos (Guitar)
        Sonatas (Guitar)
        Suites (Guitar)
        Tablature (Musical notation)
        Variations (Guitar)
        Waltzes (Guitar)
    —Teaching pieces *(MT585)*
        BT Guitar—Instruction and study
Guitar music (Guitars (2)) *(M292-3)*
    NT Concertos (Guitars (2))
        Concertos (Guitars (2) with chamber
            orchestra)
        Guitars (2) with chamber orchestra
        Guitars (2) with orchestra
        Passacaglias (Guitars (2))
        Rondos (Guitars (2))
        Sonatas (Guitars (2))
        Suites (Guitars (2))
        Variations (Guitars (2))
        Waltzes (Guitars (2))
Guitar music (Guitars (2)), Arranged
        (M292-3)
    NT Overtures arranged for guitars (2)
Guitar music (Guitars (3))
    USE Trios (Guitars (3))
Guitar music (Guitars (4))
    USE Quartets (Guitars (4))
Guitar music (Guitars (5))
    USE Quintets (Guitars (5))
Guitar music (Jazz) *(M125-129)*
    NT Guitar with jazz ensemble

Guitar music (Ragtime) *(M125-129)*
    BT Ragtime music
Guitar violoncello
    USE Arpeggione
Guitar with chamber orchestra *(M1037.4.G8)*
    BT Chamber-orchestra music
    RT Concertos (Guitar with chamber
            orchestra)
    NT Suites (Guitar with chamber orchestra)
Guitar with instrumental ensemble
    RT Concertos (Guitar with instrumental
            ensemble)
Guitar with jazz ensemble *(M1366)*
    BT Guitar music (Jazz)
Guitar with orchestra *(M1037.4.G8)*
    BT Orchestral music
    RT Concertos (Guitar)
    NT Suites (Guitar with orchestra)
        Variations (Guitar with orchestra)
    —Solo with piano *(M1037.4.G8)*
        BT Guitar and piano music, Arranged
Guitar with orchestra, Arranged
        (M1037.4.G8)
Guitar with plectral ensemble
    NT Concertos (Guitar with plectral ensemble)
Guitar with string ensemble
    RT Concertos (Guitar with string
            ensemble)
Guitar with string orchestra *(M1105-6)*
    RT Concertos (Guitar with string
            orchestra)
    NT Variations (Guitar with string
            orchestra)
Guitar with string orchestra, Arranged
        (M1105-6)
Guitare d'amour
    USE Arpeggione
Guitarists [May Subd Geog] *(Biography: collective,
        ML399; individual, ML419)*
Guitars (2) with chamber orchestra
        (M1037.4.G8)
    UF Two guitars with chamber orchestra
    BT Guitar music (Guitars (2))
    RT Concertos (Guitars (2) with chamber
            orchestra)
Guitars (2) with jazz ensemble *(M1366)*
    RT Concertos (Guitars (2) with jazz
            ensemble)
Guitars (2) with orchestra *(M1037.4.G8)*
    BT Guitar music (Guitars (2))
    RT Concertos (Guitars (2))
Guitars (3) with chamber orchestra
        (M1037.4.G8)
    BT Trios (Guitars (3))
    RT Concertos (Guitars (3) with chamber
            orchestra)
Guitars (4) with orchestra *(M1037.4.G8)*
    BT Orchestral music
        Quartets (Guitars (4))
    RT Concertos (Guitars (4))
Gujarati folk-songs
    USE Folk-songs, Gujarati

Gujarati songs
  USE Songs, Gujarati
Gujuri folk-songs
  USE Folk-songs, Gujuri
Gujuri songs
  USE Songs, Gujuri
Gumlā *(Instruction, MT725.G8)*
  BT Musical instruments—Nepal
     Percussion instruments
Gusli *(Russian, ML1015.G8)*
  BT Dulcimer
  NT Kanklės
     Kantele (Musical instrument)
Gusli music (Guslis (2)) *(M292-293)*
Guslis (2) with chamber orchestra
     (M1037.4.G85)
  RT Concertos (Guslis (2) with chamber
     orchestra)
Gypsies [May Subd Geog]
  —Music
     NT Flamenco music
Gypsy musicians
  USE Musicians, Gypsy
Hackbrett
  USE Dulcimer
Haegŭm *(ML927.H)*
  BT Musical instruments—Korea
     Stringed instruments, Bowed
Haegŭm music *(M59.H3)*
Halur
  USE Bānsurī
Hammered dulcimer
  USE Dulcimer
Hammered stringed instruments
  USE Stringed instruments
Hammond organ *(ML597)*
  UF Hammond electric organ
  BT Electronic organ
     Organ
  —Registration *(MT192)*
     Example under Organ—Registration
Hammond organ music
  USE Electronic organ music (Hammond
     registration)
Hand bell ringing
  USE Handbell ringing
Hand-organ
  USE Barrel organ
Handbell and organ music *(M183-4)*
  UF Organ and handbell music
Handbell and organ music, Arranged
     (M185-6)
Handbell music *(M147)*
  BT Handbell ringing
Handbell ringing *(MT710)*
  UF Bell ringing
     Hand bell ringing
  BT Bells
     Carillons
  NT Handbell music
Handbells [May Subd Geog]
  BT Bells

Handicapped children [May Subd Geog]
  —Education [May Subd Geog]
  — —Music
     BT Music—Instruction and study—
        Juvenile
Hardanger fiddle *(ML760)*
  UF Hardangerfele
     Hardingfele
  BT Violin
Hardanger-fiddle music *(M59)*
Hardanger fiddle with string orchestra
     (M1119.H37)
  RT Concertos (Hardanger fiddle with string
        orchestra)
Hardangerfele
  USE Hardanger fiddle
Hardingfele
  USE Hardanger fiddle
Harmonic analysis (Music) *(MT50)*
  UF Music—Harmonic analysis
  BT Harmony
     Music—Theory
     Musical analysis
  NT Schenkerian analysis
Harmonic dictation
  USE Musical dictation
Harmonica *(ML1088)*
  UF Mouth harmonica
     Mouth organ
  BT Mouth organs
Harmonica, Glass
  USE Glass harmonica
Harmonica and harp music
     (M296-M297)
  UF Harp and harmonica music
Harmonica and harpsichord music
     (M284.M6; M285.M6)
  UF Harpsichord and harmonica music
  NT Sonatas (Harmonica and harpsichord)
Harmonica and piano music *(M284.M6;
     M285.M6)*
  UF Piano and harmonica music
  NT Sonatas (Harmonica and piano)
     Suites (Harmonica and piano)
Harmonica and piano music, Arranged
     (M284.M6; M285.M6)
  NT Concertos (Harmonica)—Solo with
     piano
Harmonica band
  USE Harmonica ensembles
Harmonica ensembles
     Here are entered works for three or more
        harmonicas and collections of compo-
        sitions for a varying number of har-
        monicas.
  UF Harmonica band
  NT Waltzes (Harmonica ensemble)
Harmonica music *(M175.M8)*
  SA Concertos, Sonatas, Suites, Waltzes,
     *and similar headings with
     specification of instruments;* Trios
     [Quintets, etc.] *followed by*

Harmonica music *(M175.M8)*
  (Continued)
  SA   *specifications which include the*
        harmonica; also headings that begin
        with the words Harmonica or
        Harmonicas
Harmonica players [May Subd Geog]
  BT   Musicians
Harmonica with chamber orchestra
        (M1039.4.M6)
  RT   Concertos (Harmonica with chamber
        orchestra)
Harmonica with orchestra *(M1039.4.M6)*
  RT   Concertos (Harmonica)
  NT   Suites (Harmonica with orchestra)
Harmonica with string orchestra
        (M1139.4.M6)
  RT   Concertos (Harmonica with string
        orchestra)
  NT   Suites (Harmonica with string
        orchestra)
Harmonics (Music)
  UF   Flageolet tones
        Overtones (Music)
        Partials (Music)
  BT   Music—Acoustics and physics
  NT   Bass guitar—Instruction and study—
        Harmonics
Harmonium
  USE Reed-organ
Harmonium, Bichromatic
  USE Bichromatic harmonium
Harmonometer (Mechanical musical
        instrument)
Harmony *(Acoustics, ML3815; Aesthetics,*
        ML3852; History, ML444;
        Instruction, MT50; Psychology,
        ML3836)
  BT   Composition (Music)
        Music
        Music—Instruction and study
        Music—Theory
  RT   Thorough bass
        Tonality
  SA   *subdivision* Harmony *under names of*
        composers, e.g. Wagner, Richard,
        1813-1883—Harmony
  NT   Bourdon
        Cadence (Music)
        Chromatic alteration (Music)
        Harmonic analysis (Music)
        Melody
        Modulation (Music)
        Musical intervals and scales
        Organ-point
        Solmization
        Suspension (Music)
        Symmetrical inversion (Music)
        Twelve-tone system
  —Mechanical aids *(MT50)*
        UF   Chromophone

Harmony, Keyboard *(MT224)*
  UF   Keyboard harmony
  BT   Improvisation (Music)
        Piano—Instruction and study
Harmony (Aesthetics) *(BH301.H3)*
  BT   Music
        Music—Philosophy and aesthetics
Harp *(History and construction, ML1005-ML1006)*
  UF   Celtic harp
        Irish harp
  NT   Aeolian harp
        Clavi-harp
        Harp-lute guitar
        Harp zither
        Kantele (Musical instrument)
        Kokle
  —Construction *(ML1006)*
  —Instruction and study *(MT540-548)*
        NT   Harp music—Teaching pieces
  —Orchestra studies *(MT546)*
        BT   Harp—Studies and exercises
  —Studies and exercises
        NT   Harp—Orchestra studies
  Example under Stringed instruments
Harp and alpenhorn music
  USE Alpenhorn and harp music
Harp and clarinet music
  USE Clarinet and harp music
Harp and clarinet with string orchestra
  USE Clarinet and harp with string orchestra
Harp and dulcimer music
  USE Dulcimer and harp music
Harp and English horn music
  USE English horn and harp music
Harp and flute music
  USE Flute and harp music
Harp and flute with string orchestra
  USE Flute and harp with string orchestra
Harp and guitar music
  USE Guitar and harp music
Harp and harmonica music
  USE Harmonica and harp music
Harp and harpsichord music *(M272-273)*
  UF   Harpsichord and harp music
  NT   Sonatas (Harp and harpsichord)
Harp and horn music
  USE Horn and harp music
Harp and lute music *(M292-3)*
  UF   Lute and harp music
  NT   Concertos (Harp and lute)
        Harp and lute with orchestra
Harp and lute with orchestra *(M1040-1041)*
  BT   Harp and lute music
  RT   Concertos (Harp and lute)
Harp and oboe music
  USE Oboe and harp music
Harp and organ music *(M182-4)*
  UF   Organ and harp music
  NT   Harp and organ with string orchestra
Harp and organ with string orchestra *(M1105-6)*
  BT   Harp and organ music
  RT   Concertos (Harp and organ with string orchestra)

Harp and percussion music
USE Percussion and harp music
Harp and piano music *(M272-3)*
UF Piano and harp music
NT Concertos (Harp and piano)
Harp and piano with orchestra
Sonatas (Harp and piano)
Variations (Harp and piano)
Harp and piano music, Arranged *(M272-3)*
NT Chaconnes (Harp with string orchestra)
—Solo with piano
Concertos (Harp)—Solo with piano
Concertos (Harp with string orchestra)
—Solo with piano
Concertos (Harp with string orchestra),
Arranged—Solo with piano
Harp with band—Solo with piano
Harp with orchestra—Solo with piano
Harp with string orchestra—Solo with
piano
Harp and piano with orchestra
(M1040-1041)
BT Harp and piano music
RT Concertos (Harp and piano)
Harp and recorder music
USE Recorder and harp music
Harp and saxophone music
USE Saxophone and harp music
Harp and trumpet music
USE Trumpet and harp music
Harp and vibraphone music *(M298)*
UF Vibraphone and harp music
Harp and viola music
USE Viola and harp music
Harp and violin music
USE Violin and harp music
Harp and violoncello music
USE Violoncello and harp music
Harp ensembles *(M965-M969)*
Here are entered compositions for ten or
more harps and collections of compo-
sitions for a varying number of harps.
BT Plectral ensembles
Harp-lute
USE Kora (Musical instrument)
Harp-lute guitar *(ML1015-1018)*
UF Guitar, Harp-lute
BT Guitar
Harp
Lute
Harp-lute guitar and piano music *(M282-3)*
UF Piano and harp-lute guitar music
Harp-lute guitar music *(M142.H2)*
NT Suites (Harp-lute guitar)
Harp music *(M115-119)*
SA Concertos, Minuets, Sonatas, Suites,
*and similar headings with
specification of instruments;* Trios
[Quartets, etc.] *followed by
specifications which include the
harp; also* Plectral ensembles *and
headings that begin with the words
harp or harps.*

Harp music *(M115-119)*
(Continued)
NT Chaconnes (Harp)
Marches (Harp)
Potpourris (Harp)
Sonatas (Harp)
Suites (Harp)
Variations (Harp)
Waltzes (Harp)
—Bibliography *(ML128.H3)*
— —Graded lists *(ML132.H3)*
UF Harp music—Graded lists
—Graded lists
USE Harp music—Bibliography—
Graded lists
—Teaching pieces *(MT545)*
BT Harp—Instruction and study
Harp music (Harps (2)) *(M292-3)*
NT Concertos (Harps (2))
Concertos (Harps (2) with string
orchestra)
Harps (2) with orchestra
Harps (2) with string orchestra
Sonatas (Harps (2))
Suites (Harps (2))
Harp music (Harps (2)), Arranged *(M292-3)*
Harp music (Harps (3))
USE Trios (Harps (3))
Harp music (Harps (4))
USE Quartets (Harps (4))
Harp music (Harps (5))
USE Quintets (Harps (5))
Harp music (Jazz)
M115-M119
Harp, violin, violoncello with orchestra
(M1040-1041)
BT Trios (Harp, violin, violoncello)
RT Concertos (Harp, violin, violoncello)
—Scores *(M1040)*
Harp with band *(M1205-1206)*
RT Concertos (Harp with band)
—Solo with piano *(M1206)*
BT Harp and piano music, Arranged
Harp with brass ensemble
RT Concertos (Harp with brass ensemble)
NT Variations (Harp with brass ensemble)
Harp with chamber orchestra *(M1036-7)*
RT Concertos (Harp with chamber orchestra)
NT Suites (Harp with chamber orchestra)
Variations (Harp with chamber orchestra)
Harp with chamber orchestra, Arranged
(M1036-7)
—Scores *(M1036)*
Harp with instrumental ensemble
RT Concertos (Harp with instrumental
ensemble)
Harp with orchestra *(M1036-7)*
RT Concertos (Harp)
NT Suites (Harp with orchestra)
Symphonies (Harp with orchestra)
Variations (Harp with orchestra)
—Solo with piano *(M1037)*
BT Harp and piano music, Arranged

Harp with string orchestra *(M1105-6)*
 RT Concertos (Harp with string orchestra)
 NT Chaconnes (Harp with string orchestra)
 —Solo with piano *(M1106)*
   BT Harp and piano music, Arranged
Harp with string orchestra, Arranged
   (M1105-6)
 —Scores
Harp zither
   (History, ML1015.H; Instruction,
   MT634.H37)
 UF MacArthur harp
 BT Harp
   Zither
Harpists [May Subd Geog] *(Biography: collective,*
   ML399; individual, ML419)
Harps (2), percussion with string orchestra
   (M1140-1141)
 BT Sextets (Harps (2), percussion)
 RT Concertos (Harps (2), percussion with
   string orchestra)
Harps (2) with chamber orchestra
   (M1036-1037)
 RT Concertos (Harps (2) with chamber
   orchestra)
Harps (2) with orchestra *(M1036-7)*
 BT Harp music (Harps (2))
 RT Concertos (Harps (2))
Harps (2) with string ensemble
 RT Concertos (Harps (2) with string
   ensemble)
Harps (2) with string orchestra *(M1105-6)*
 BT Harp music (Harps (2))
 RT Concertos (Harps (2) with string
   orchestra)
 NT Suites (Harps (2) with string orchestra)
Harps (4) with string orchestra *(M1136-1137)*
 BT Quartets (Harps (4))
 RT Concertos (Harps (4) with string
   orchestra)
 NT Suites (Harps (4) with string orchestra)
Harpsichord *(History and construction,*
   ML650-ML697)
 UF Cembalo
   Clavecin
   Clavicembalo
   Spinet
   Virginal
 RT Piano
 NT Claviorganum
   Keyboards
 Example under Musical instruments
Harpsichord, Electronic
 USE Electronic harpsichord
Harpsichord and bassoon music
 USE Bassoon and harpsichord music
Harpsichord and celesta music
 USE Celesta and harpsichord music
Harpsichord and clarinet music
 USE Clarinet and harpsichord music
Harpsichord and double-bass music
 USE Double-bass and harpsichord music

Harpsichord and English horn music
 USE English horn and harpsichord music
Harpsichord and flute music
 USE Flute and harpsichord music
Harpsichord and glockenspiel music
 USE Glockenspiel and harpsichord music
Harpsichord and guitar music
 USE Guitar and harpsichord music
Harpsichord and harmonica music
 USE Harmonica and harpsichord music
Harpsichord and harp music
 USE Harp and harpsichord music
Harpsichord and lute music
 USE Lute and harpsichord music
Harpsichord and mandolin music
 USE Mandolin and harpsichord music
Harpsichord and oboe d'amore music
 USE Oboe d'amore and harpsichord music
Harpsichord and oboe music
 USE Oboe and harpsichord music
Harpsichord and organ music *(M182-4)*
 UF Organ and harpsichord music
 NT Passacaglias (Harpsichord and organ)
   Sonatas (Harpsichord and organ)
Harpsichord and organ music, Arranged
   (M185-6)
Harpsichord and organ with chamber
   orchestra *(M1040-1041)*
 RT Concertos (Harpsichord and organ with
   chamber orchestra)
Harpsichord and percussion music
 USE Percussion and harpsichord music
Harpsichord and piano music *(M214)*
 UF Piano and harpsichord music
 NT Concertos (Harpsichord and piano)
   Concertos (Harpsichord and piano with
   dance orchestra)
   Harpsichord and piano with dance orchestra
   Harpsichord and piano with orchestra
   Harpsichord and piano with wind ensemble
Harpsichord and piano music, Arranged
 NT Concertos (Harpsichord)—Solo with
   piano
   Concertos (Harpsichord with chamber
   orchestra)—Solo with piano
   Concertos (Harpsichord with
   instrumental ensemble)—Solo with
   piano
   Concertos (Harpsichord with string
   orchestra)—Solo with piano
   Variations (Harpsichord with string
   orchestra)—2-piano scores
Harpsichord and piano with dance orchestra
   (M1353)
 BT Harpsichord and piano music
 RT Concertos (Harpsichord and piano with
   dance orchestra)
Harpsichord and piano with orchestra
   (M1010-1011)
 BT Harpsichord and piano music
 RT Concertos (Harpsichord and piano)

Harpsichord and piano with wind ensemble
    (M915-917)
    BT Harpsichord and piano music
    RT Concertos (Harpsichord and piano with
        wind ensemble)
    NT Wind ensembles
Harpsichord and piccolo music
    USE Piccolo and harpsichord music
Harpsichord and recorder music
    USE Recorder and harpsichord music
Harpsichord and trumpet music
    USE Trumpet and harpsichord music
Harpsichord and viola da gamba music
    USE Viola da gamba and harpsichord music
Harpsichord and viola d'amore music
    USE Viola d'amore and harpsichord music
Harpsichord and viola music
    USE Viola and harpsichord music
Harpsichord and viola pomposa music
    USE Viola pomposa and harpsichord music
Harpsichord and violin music
    USE Violin and harpsichord music
Harpsichord and violoncello music
    USE Violoncello and harpsichord music
Harpsichord and violone music
    USE Violone and harpsichord music
Harpsichord duets
    USE Harpsichord music (4 hands)
        Harpsichord music (Harpsichords (2))
Harpsichord, flute, harp with string orchestra
    (M1105-6)
    BT Trios (Harpsichord, flute, harp)
    RT Concertos (Harpsichord, flute, harp
        with string orchestra)
    NT Suites (Harpsichord, flute, harp with
        string orchestra)
Harpsichord, flute, oboe with string orchestra
    (M1105-6)
    BT Trios (Harpsichord, flute, oboe)
    RT Concertos (Harpsichord, flute, oboe
        with string orchestra)
    NT Suites (Harpsichord, flute, oboe with
        string orchestra)
    BT Concertos (Harpsichord, flute, oboe
        with string orchestra)
    —Scores *(M1105-6)*
Harpsichord, flute, violin with string orchestra
    (M1105-6)
    BT String-orchestra music
        Trios (Harpsichord, flute, violin)
    RT Concertos (Harpsichord, flute, violin
        with string orchestra)
Harpsichord, flutes (2) with string orchestra
    (M1105-6)
    UF Two flutes, harpsichord with string orchestra
    BT String-orchestra music
        Trios (Harpsichord, flutes (2))
    RT Concertos (Harpsichord, flutes (2) with
        string orchestra)
**Harpsichord, guitars (2), harp, double bass
    with orchestra** *(M1040-1041)*
    BT Quintets (Harpsichord, guitars (2),
        harp, double bass)

**Harpsichord, guitars (2), harp, double bass
    with orchestra** *(M1040-1041)*
    (Continued)
    RT Concertos (Harpsichord, guitars (2),
        harp, double bass)
Harpsichord makers [May Subd Geog]
    BT Musical instrument makers
Harpsichord music *(M20-39)*
    UF Virginal music
    BT Keyboard instrument music
        Piano music
    SA Concertos, Minuets, Sonatas, Suites,
        *and similar headings with
        specification of instruments;* Trios
        [Quartets, etc.] *followed by
        specifications which include the
        harpsichord; also headings that begin
        with the words harpsichord or
        harpsichords*
    NT Canons, fugues, etc. (Harpsichord)
        Chaconnes (Harpsichord)
        Chorale preludes (Harpsichord)
        Claviorganum music
        Minuets (Harpsichord)
        Polonaises (Harpsichord)
        Rondos (Harpsichord)
        Sonatas (Harpsichord)
        Suites (Harpsichord)
        Thorough bass—Realizations
        Variations (Harpsichord)
    —Instructive editions *(MT245-7)*
        BT Piano music—Instructive
            editions
Harpsichord music, Arranged
    NT Chaconnes (Harpsichord), Arranged
        Overtures arranged for harpsichord
Harpsichord music, Arranged (Jazz)
    USE Harpsichord music (Jazz)
Harpsichord music (4 hands) *(M200-M204;
        M207-M212)*
    UF Harpsichord duets
Harpsichord music (Harpsichords (2))
    (M214-215)
    UF Harpsichord duets
    NT Canons, fugues, etc. (Harpsichords (2))
        Concertos (Harpsichords (2))
        Concertos (Harpsichords (2) with string
            orchestra)
        Harpsichords (2) with orchestra
        Harpsichords (2) with string orchestra
        Sonatas (Harpsichords (2))
        Suites (Harpsichords (2))
**Harpsichord music (Harpsichords (2)),
        Arranged** *(M215)*
    NT Concertos (Harpsichord)—
            2-harpsichord scores
Harpsichord music (Harpsichords (3))
    (M216)
    UF Harpsichord trios (Harpsichords (3))
    NT Concertos (Harpsichords (3) with string
            orchestra)
        Harpsichords (3) with string orchestra

Harpsichord music (Harpsichords (4))
    (M216)
    UF Harpsichord quartets (Harpsichords (4))
    NT Concertos (Harpsichords (4))
         Concertos (Harpsichords (4) with string
           orchestra)
         Harpsichords (4) with orchestra
         Harpsichords (4) with string orchestra
         Variations (Harpsichords (4))
Harpsichord music (Jazz) *(M20-32)*
    UF Harpsichord music, Arranged (Jazz)
Harpsichord, piano, harp with string orchestra
    (M1140-1141)
    BT Trios (Harpsichord, piano, harp)
    RT Concertos (Harpsichord, piano, harp
         with string orchestra)
Harpsichord, piano, violin with orchestra
    (M1040-1041)
    BT Trios (Harpsichord, piano, violin)
    RT Concertos (Harpsichord, piano, violin)
Harpsichord players
    USE Harpsichordists
Harpsichord quartets (Harpsichords (4))
    USE Harpsichord music (Harpsichords (4))
Harpsichord realizations of thorough bass
    USE Thorough bass—Realizations
Harpsichord trios (Harpsichords (3))
    USE Harpsichord music (Harpsichords (3))
Harpsichord, violin, violoncello with string
    orchestra *(M1140-1141)*
    BT Trios (Harpsichord, violin, violoncello)
    RT Concertos (Harpsichord, violin,
         violoncello with string orchestra)
Harpsichord, violins (2), violoncello with
    orchestra *(M1040-M1041)*
    BT Quartets (Harpsichord, violins (2),
         violoncello)
    NT Concertos (Harpsichord, violins (2),
         violoncello)
Harpsichord with chamber orchestra
    (M1010-1011)
    RT Concertos (Harpsichord with chamber
         orchestra)
Harpsichord with instrumental ensemble
    BT Concertos (Harpsichord with chamber
         orchestra)
    NT Concertos (Harpsichord with chamber
         orchestra)
Harpsichord with orchestra *(M1010-1011)*
    BT Orchestral music
    RT Concertos (Harpsichord)
Harpsichord with percussion ensemble
Harpsichord with string ensemble
    (M910-912)
    BT String ensembles
    RT Concertos (Harpsichord with string
         ensemble)
Harpsichord with string orchestra *(M1105-6)*
    RT Concertos (Harpsichord with string
         orchestra)
    NT Variations (Harpsichord with string
         orchestra)
    —Scores *(M1105)*

Harpsichordists [May Subd Geog]
    UF Harpsichord players
    BT Musicians
Harpsichords (2) with orchestra
    (M1010-1011)
    UF Two harpsichords with orchestra
    BT Harpsichord music (Harpsichords (2))
    RT Concertos (Harpsichords (2))
Harpsichords (2) with string orchestra
    (M1105-6)
    UF Two harpsichords with string orchestra
    BT Harpsichord music (Harpsichords (2))
    RT Concertos (Harpsichords (2) with string
         orchestra)
Harpsichords (3) with string orchestra
    (M1105-6)
    UF Three harpsichords with string
         orchestra
    BT Harpsichord music (Harpsichords (3))
    RT Concertos (Harpsichords (3) with string
         orchestra)
Harpsichords (4) with orchestra
    (M1010-1011)
    UF Four harpsichords with orchestra
    BT Harpsichord music (Harpsichords (4))
    RT Concertos (Harpsichords (4))
Harpsichords (4) with string orchestra
    (M1105-6)
    UF Four harpsichords with string orchestra
    BT Harpsichord music (Harpsichords (4))
    RT Concertos (Harpsichords (4) with string
         orchestra)
Hawaiian guitar *(ML1015)*
    UF Guitar, Hawaiian
         Guitar, Steel
         Steel guitar
    BT Guitar
    —Instruction and study *(MT590)*
         NT Hawaiian-guitar music—Teaching
            pieces
Hawaiian-guitar band
    USE Plectral ensembles
Hawaiian-guitar music *(M142.H3)*
    BT Guitar music
    NT Plectral ensembles
    —Teaching pieces *(MT590.5)*
         BT Hawaiian guitar—Instruction and
            study
Heavy metal (Music) [May Subd Geog]
    BT Rock music
Hebrew folk-songs
    USE Folk-songs, Hebrew
Hebrew hymns
    USE Hymns, Hebrew
Hebrew music
    USE Jews—Music
Heckelphone *(ML990.H4)*
    BT Oboe
Heckelphone music *(M110.H4)*
    NT Quintets (Harpsichord, English horn,
         heckelphone, oboe, oboe d'amore)
         Quintets (Piano, English horn,
         heckelphone, oboe, oboe d'amore)

Heckelphone music *(M110.H4)*
  (Continued)
    NT Woodwind quartets (English horn,
        heckelphone, oboe, oboe d'amore)
      Woodwind trios (English horn,
        heckelphone, oboe)
Helicon bass
  USE Tuba
Hiang te
  USE So na
Hichiriki *(ML990.H5)*
  BT Musical instruments—Japan
      Oboe
Hichiriki music *(M110.H)*
  NT Quintets (Piano, hichiriki, harp, violin,
      violoncello)
Hillbilly music
  USE Country music
Hillbilly musicians
  USE Country musicians
Himachali folk-songs
  USE Folk-songs, Himachali
Hindi lullabies
  USE Lullabies, Hindi
Hindu hymns *(BL1226.3)*
  UF Hinduism—Hymns
      Hymns, Hindu
  BT Chants (Hindu)
  SA *subdivision* Hymns *under names of*
      individual Hindu sects, e.g.
      Vaishnavism—Hymns
  NT Sivaism—Hymns
Hindu hymns, Bengali [Marathi, etc.]
Hindu hymns, Dingal [May Subd Geog]
    (BL1226.3)
  UF Dingal Hindu hymns
Hindu hymns, English [May Subd Geog]
  UF English Hindu hymns
Hindu hymns, French [May Subd Geog]
  UF French Hindu hymns
Hindu hymns, Kannada [May Subd Geog]
  UF Kannada Hindu hymns
Hindu hymns, Marathi [May Subd Geog]
  UF Marathi Hindu hymns
Hindu hymns, Sanskrit [May Subd Geog]
  UF Sanskrit Hindu hymns
Hindu hymns, Telugu [May Subd Geog]
  UF Telugu Hindu hymns
Hindustani music
  USE Music, Hindustani
Hispanic Americans [May Subd Geog]
  —Music
      NT Alabados
Hmar hymns
  USE Hymns, Hmar
Hobo songs *(M1977.H6; M1978.H6)*
  UF Tramps—Songs and music
Holy Saturday music *(Catholic liturgical*
    music, M2149.4.H8)
  BT Holy-Week music
Holy-Week music
  BT Church music
      Lenten music

Holy-Week music
  (Continued)
  BT Sacred vocal music
  NT Good Friday music
      Holy Saturday music
      Maundy Thursday music
      Palm Sunday music
      Tenebrae service music
Hommel
  USE Noordsche balk
Honky-tonk music [May Subd Geog] *(ML3528)*
  BT Country music
Horn (Musical instrument) *(ML955-8)*
  UF French horn
  BT Brass instruments
  RT Tuba
  NT Alpenhorn
      Alto horn
      Lur
      Post horn
      Russian horn
      Shophar
  —Orchestra studies *(MT426)*
    BT Horn (Musical instrument)—Studies
      and exercises
  —Studies and exercises *(MT425)*
    NT Horn (Musical instrument)—
      Orchestra studies
Horn and bassoon music
  USE Bassoon and horn music
Horn and cimbalom music *(M298)*
  UF Cimbalom and horn music
Horn and clarinet music
  USE Clarinet and horn music
Horn and flute music
  USE Flute and horn music
Horn and guitar music *(M296-7)*
  UF Guitar and horn music
Horn and guitar music, Arranged *(M296-7)*
Horn and harp music *(M296-297)*
  UF Harp and horn music
Horn and harp with orchestra *(M1040-1041)*
  RT Concertos (Horn and harp)
Horn and oboe music *(M288-9)*
  UF Oboe and horn music
Horn and organ music *(M182-4)*
  UF Organ and horn music
  NT Chorale preludes (Horn and organ)
      Suites (Horn and organ)
      Variations (Horn and organ)
Horn and percussion music *(M298)*
  UF Percussion and horn music
Horn and piano music *(M255-7)*
  UF Piano and horn music
  NT Marches (Horn and piano)
      Rondos (Horn and piano)
      Sonatas (Horn and piano)
      Suites (Horn and piano)
      Variations (Horn and piano)
      Waltzes (Horn and piano)
Horn and piano music, Arranged *(M258-9)*
  NT Concertos (Horn)—Solo with piano

Horn and piano music, Arranged *(M258-9)*
(Continued)
  NT Concertos (Horn with string ensemble)
        —Solo with piano
      Concertos (Horn with string orchestra)
        —Solo with piano
      Horn with band—Solo with piano
      Horn with orchestra—Solo with piano
      Horn with string ensemble—Solo with
        piano
      Horn with string orchestra—Solo with
        piano
      Rondos (Horn with orchestra)—Solo
        with piano
      Variations (Horn with orchestra)—Solo
        with piano
Horn and trombone music
      (M288-M289)
  UF Trombone and horn music
Horn and trombone with orchestra
      (M1040-1041)
  RT Concertos (Horn and trombone)
Horn and trumpet music
      (M288-M289)
  UF Trumpet and horn music
Horn and violin music *(M290-291)*
  UF Violin and horn music
Horn and violoncello music *(M290-291)*
  UF Violoncello and horn music
Horn ensembles *(M955-956; M957.4;*
        M958-959)
      Here are entered compositions for ten or
        more horns and collections of compo-
        sitions for a varying number of horns.
      When used in conjunction with specific
        solo instrument(s), the designation Horn
        ensemble may stand for any number of
        horns.
  SA Concertos ([Solo instrument(s)] with horn
        ensemble); [Solo instrument(s)] with horn
        ensemble; Suites, Variations, Waltzes, *and*
        similar headings with specification of
        instruments which include the specification
        of Horn ensemble
      Note under Brass ensembles
Horn music *(M80-84)*
  SA Concertos, Minuets, Sonatas, Suites,
        and similar headings with
        specification of instruments; Brass
        trios [quartets, etc.], Trios [Quartets,
        etc.], *and* Wind trios [quartets, etc.]
        followed by specifications which
        include the horn; also Brass
        ensembles, Wind ensembles, *and*
        headings that begin with the words
        horn or horns
  NT Hunting music
      Recorded accompaniments (Horn)
      Sonatas (Horn)
Horn music (Horns (2)) *(M288-9)*
  NT Canons, fugues, etc. (Horns (2))
      Concertos (Horns (2))

Horn music (Horns (2)) *(M288-9)*
(Continued)
  NT Concertos (Horns (2) with string
        orchestra)
      Horns (2) with orchestra
      Horns (2) with string orchestra
      Sonatas (Horns (2))
Horn music (Horns (3))
  USE Brass trios (Horns (3))
Horn music (Horns (4))
  USE Brass quartets (Horns (4))
Horn music (Horns (5))
  USE Brass quintets (Horns (5))
Horn music (Horns (6))
  USE Brass sextets (Horns (6))
Horn music (Horns (7))
  USE Brass septets (Horns (7))
Horn music (Horns (8))
  USE Brass octets (Horns (8))
Horn players *(ML399; ML419)*
Horn, trombone, trumpets (2), tuba with
        instrumental ensemble
  BT Brass quintets (Horn, trombone,
        trumpets (2), tuba)
  RT Concertos (Horn, trombone, trumpets
        (2), tuba with instrumental
        ensemble)
  NT Variations (Horn, trombone, trumpets
        (2), tuba with instrumental
        ensemble)
Horn, trombone, trumpets (2), tuba with
        orchestra *(M1040-1041)*
  BT Brass quintets (Horn, trombone,
        trumpets (2), tuba)
  RT Concertos (Horn, trombone, trumpets
        (2), tuba)
Horn, trombone, trumpets (2), tuba with
        string orchestra *(M1140-1141)*
  BT Brass quintets (Horn, trombone,
        trumpets (2), tuba)
  RT Concertos (Horn, trombone, trumpets
        (2), tuba with string orchestra)
Horn, trombones (2), trumpets (2) with
        chamber orchestra *(M1040-1041)*
  BT Brass quintets (Horn, trombones (2),
        trumpets (2))
  RT Concertos (Horn, trombones (2),
        trumpets (2) with chamber orchestra)
Horn, trombones (2), trumpets (2) with
        orchestra *(M1040-1041)*
  BT Brass quintets (Horn, trombones (2),
        trumpets (2))
  RT Concertos (Horn, trombones (2),
        trumpets (2))
Horn, trombones (2), trumpets (2) with string
        orchestra *(M1140-1141)*
  BT Brass quintets (Horn, trombones (2),
        trumpets (2))
  RT Concertos (Horn, trombones (2),
        trumpets (2) with string orchestra)
Horn with band *(M1205)*
  BT Band music

Horn with band *(M1205)*
  (Continued)
  RT Concertos (Horn with band)
  —Solo with piano *(M1206)*
      BT Horn and piano music, Arranged
Horn with band, Arranged *(M1257)*
  —Scores *(M1257)*
Horn with chamber orchestra *(M1028-9)*
  RT Concertos (Horn with chamber
      orchestra)
Horn with horn ensemble
  RT Concertos (Horn with horn ensemble)
Horn with instrumental ensemble
  RT Concertos (Horn with instrumental
      ensemble)
Horn with orchestra *(M1028-9)*
  BT Orchestral music
  RT Concertos (Horn)
  NT Rondos (Horn with orchestra)
      Variations (Horn with orchestra)
  —Solo with piano *(M1029)*
      BT Horn and piano music, Arranged
Horn with orchestra, Arranged *(M1028-9)*
Horn with percussion ensemble
  RT Concertos (Horn with percussion
      ensemble)
Horn with string ensemble
  RT Concertos (Horn with string ensemble)
  —Solo with piano
      BT Horn and piano music, Arranged
Horn with string orchestra *(M1105-6)*
  RT Concertos (Horn with string orchestra)
  NT Suites (Horn with string orchestra)
  —Solo with piano *(M1129)*
      BT Horn and piano music, Arranged
Horn with string orchestra, Arranged *(M1105-6)*
  —Scores *(M1105)*
Hornpipes
  BT Dance music
Horns (2), oboes (2) with string orchestra
      (M1140-1141)
  BT Wind quartets (Horns (2), oboes (2))
  RT Concertos (Horns (2), oboes (2) with
      string orchestra)
Horns (2), trombones (2), trumpets (2), tuba
      with orchestra *(M1040-1041)*
  BT Brass septets (Horns (2), trombones (2),
      trumpets (2), tuba)
  RT Concertos (Horns (2), trombones (2),
      trumpets (2), tuba)
Horns (2) with orchestra *(M1028-9)*
  UF Two horns with orchestra
  BT Horn music (Horns (2))
  RT Concertos (Horns (2))
Horns (2) with string orchestra *(M1105-6)*
  UF Two horns with string orchestra
  BT Horn music (Horns (2))
  RT Concertos (Horns (2) with string
      orchestra)
Horns (3) with band *(M1205-6)*
  BT Brass trios (Horns (3))
  RT Concertos (Horns (3) with band)

Horns (3) with orchestra *(M1028-9)*
  BT Brass trios (Horns (3))
  RT Concertos (Horns (3))
Horns (3) with string orchestra
      (M1128-1129)
  BT Brass trios (Horns (3))
  RT Concertos (Horns (3) with string
      orchestra)
Horns (4) with band *(M1205-6)*
  UF Four horns with band
  BT Brass quartets (Horns (4))
  NT Concertos (Horns (4) with band)
Horns (4) with orchestra *(M1028-9)*
  UF Four horns with orchestra
  BT Brass quartets (Horns (4))
  RT Concertos (Horns (4))
  —Scores *(M1028)*
Hourglass drum
  BT Drum
      Percussion instruments
  NT Changgo
      Kotsuzumi
Hsiao *(ML980)*
  BT Flute
Hsiao music *(M110.H7)*
Hsüan (Musical instrument)
  BT Flute
      Musical instruments—China
      Wind instruments
Hu ch'in *(ML927.H)*
  UF Ching hu
  BT Musical instruments—China
      Stringed instruments, Bowed
  NT Erh hu
      Nan hu
      Pan hu
Hu ch'in music *(M175.H8)*
Hu ch'in with instrumental ensemble
  RT Concertos (Hu ch'in with instrumental
      ensemble)
Hu ch'in with orchestra *(M1039.4.H83)*
  RT Concertos (Hu ch'in)
Huang chung (Musical instrument) *(ML990)*
  BT Flute
      Musical instruments—China
Hummel
  USE Noordsche balk
Humorous songs
  UF Comic songs
      Songs, Humorous
  BT Songs
      Wit and humor, Musical
  NT Bawdy songs
      Nonsense songs
Hungarian ballads
  USE Ballads, Hungarian
Hungarian folk-songs
  USE Folk-songs, Hungarian
Hungarian hymns
  USE Hymns, Hungarian
Hungarian madrigals (Music)
  USE Madrigals (Music), Hungarian

Hunting music
  BT Horn music
      Instrumental music
      Music
  RT Trumpet-calls
  NT Bugle-calls
      Hunting songs
Hunting songs [May Subd Geog] *(M1977.H8;*
      English poetry, PR1195.H9; History,
      ML3780)
  BT Hunting music
      Songs
Hurdy-gurdies (2) with instrumental ensemble
  RT Concertos (Hurdy-gurdies (2) with
      instrumental ensemble)
Hurdy-gurdies (2) with orchestra
      (M1039.4.H87)
  UF Two hurdy-gurdies with orchestra
  BT Hurdy-gurdy music (Hurdy-gurdies (2))
  RT Concertos (Hurdy-gurdies (2))
Hurdy-gurdy *(ML1086)*
      Not to be confused with the barrel and
      piano organs used chiefly by street
      musicians.
  UF Vielle
  BT Musical instruments
Hurdy-gurdy and bagpipe music
  USE Bagpipe and hurdy-gurdy music
Hurdy-gurdy and continuo music
  UF Continuo and hurdy-gurdy music
  NT Suites (Hurdy-gurdy and continuo)
Hurdy-gurdy and flute music
  USE Flute and hurdy-gurdy music
Hurdy-gurdy and percussion music
      M298
  UF Percussion and hurdy-gurdy music
Hurdy-gurdy and viol music *(M990)*
  UF Viol and hurdy-gurdy music
Hurdy-gurdy and violin music
  UF Violin and hurdy-gurdy music
Hurdy-gurdy music *(M175.H9)*
  SA Concertos, Minuets, Sonatas, Suites, *and*
      similar headings with specification of
      instruments; Trios [Quartets, etc.]
      followed by specifications which include
      the hurdy-gurdy; also Instrumental
      ensembles *and headings that begin with the*
      words Hurdy-gurdy or Hurdy-gurdies
Hurdy-gurdy music (Hurdy-gurdies (2))
      (M298)
  NT Concertos (Hurdy-gurdies (2))
      Hurdy-gurdies (2) with orchestra
      Suites (Hurdy-gurdies (2))
Hurdy-gurdy with chamber orchestra
      (M1039.4.H87)
  NT Concertos (Hurdy-gurdy with chamber
      orchestra)
Hurdy-gurdy with instrumental ensemble
  RT Concertos (Hurdy-gurdy with
      instrumental ensemble)
Hurdy-gurdy with orchestra *(M1039.4.H87)*
  RT Concertos (Hurdy-gurdy)

Husor
  USE Bānsurī
Hydraulic organ *(ML553)*
  UF Hydraulus
      Water organ
  BT Organ
  NT Barrel organ, Hydraulic
Hydraulus
  USE Hydraulic organ
Hymn festivals *(BV341)*
  BT Hymns
      Music festivals
Hymn playing
  USE Hymns—Accompaniment
Hymn tunes
      Here, with appropriate subdivisions, are
      entered works about hymn tunes. Col-
      lections of hymn tunes (without ac-
      companying text) are entered under
      the heading Tune-books.
  BT Hymns
  RT Tune-books
  NT Chorale
      Old Hundredth (Tune)
  Note under Tune-books
Hymn writers [May Subd Geog] *(BV325)*
  UF Hymnists
  BT Hymns—History and criticism
      Poets
  NT Women hymn writers
Hymnists
  USE Hymn writers
Hymnology
  USE Hymns
Hymns [May Subd Geog]
      (BV301-BV525; Hymns with music,
      M2115-M2145)
      Here are entered general collections of
      hymns as well as hymns of a particular
      Christian denomination, with qualifi-
      cation, when appropriate, by language,
      e.g. Hymns, English. Duplicate entry
      is made for the latter under the name
      of the denomination with subdivision
      Hymns, *e.g.* Baptists—Hymns.
  UF Christian hymns
      Hymnology
  BT Church music
      Devotional exercises
      Sacred songs
      Sacred vocal music
  RT Canticles
      Christian poetry
      Psalmody
  SA *names of individual hymns, e.g.* Gloria
      in excelsis Deo
  NT Advent hymns
      Bible—Use in hymns
      Carols
      Christmas—Poetry
      Easter hymns
      Epiphany hymns
      Funeral hymns

Hymns [May Subd Geog]
  (BV301-BV525; Hymns with music,
   M2115-M2145)
 (Continued)
 NT Hymn festivals
   Hymn tunes
   Lenten hymns
   Revivals—Hymns
   Seamen—Hymns
   Sequences (Music)
   Soldiers—Hymns
   Sunday-schools—Hymns
   Te Deum laudamus (Music)
   Tune-books
 —Accompaniment *(MT240)*
  UF Hymn playing
  BT Musical accompaniment
  RT Chants (Plain, Gregorian, etc.)—
     Accompaniment
 —Concordances
  USE Hymns—Indexes
 —Devotional use
  BT Devotional exercises
 —History and criticism *(BV310-340;*
   Music, ML3086, ML3186)
  NT Hymn writers
 —Homiletical use *(BV4235.H94)*
  UF Hymn sermons
  BT Preaching
 —Indexes
  UF Hymns—Concordances
 —Metrics and rhythmics *(BV335)*
 —Orchestrations
 —Versification
  USE Hymns—Metrics and rhythmics
Hymns, African
 UF Hymns, Black—Africa
Hymns, Afrikaans, [Danish, English, etc.]
Hymns, American
 USE Hymns, English
Hymns, Arikara [Choctaw, Cree, etc.]
 UF Indians of North America—Hymns
Hymns, Black [May Subd Geog]
 UF Black hymns
 —Africa
  USE Hymns, African
Hymns, Bohemian
 USE Hymns, Czech
Hymns, Buddhist
 USE Buddhist hymns
Hymns, Byzantine
 USE Hymns, Greek
Hymns, Cheyenne
 UF Cheyenne hymns
Hymns, Chinese [May Subd Geog]
 UF Chinese hymns
Hymns, Czech
 UF Czech hymns
   Hymns, Bohemian
Hymns, Danish
 RT Hymns, Norwegian
Hymns, Dutch [May Subd Geog]
 UF Dutch hymns

Hymns, Early Christian *(BV320)*
 UF Early Christian hymns
Hymns, Egyptian [May Subd Geog]
 PJ1585
 UF Egyptian hymns
Hymns, English [May Subd Geog]
 UF American hymns
   English hymns
   Fuging tunes
   Fuguing tunes
   Hymns, American
 —United States
  NT Spirituals (Songs)
 Note under Hymns
Hymns, Finnish [May Subd Geog]
 UF Finnish hymns
Hymns, French [May Subd Geog]
 UF French hymns
Hymns, Georgian [May Subd Geog]
 UF Georgian hymns
Hymns, German [May Subd Geog]
 UF German hymns
 NT Chorale
   Chorale prelude
   Chorales
   Hymns, Low German
Hymns, Greek
  Here are entered Christian hymns in the
   Greek language, whether ancient, By-
   zantine or modern. Pre-Christian clas-
   sical hymns are entered under the
   heading Hymns, Greek (Classical).
 UF Greek hymns
   Hymns, Byzantine
Hymns, Greek (Classical)
  Here are entered pre-Christian classical
   hymns. Christian hymns in ancient,
   Byzantine or modern Greek are entered
   under Hymns, Greek.
 UF Greek hymns
 Note under Hymns, Greek
Hymns, Guaymi [May Subd Geog]
 UF Guaymi hymns
Hymns, Hawaiian [May Subd Geog]
 UF Hawaiian hymns
Hymns, Hebrew [May Subd Geog]
 UF Hebrew hymns
   Hymns, Jewish
 BT Jewish hymns
 RT Hymns, Yiddish
 NT Piyutim
Hymns, Hindu
 USE Hindu hymns
Hymns, Hmar *(BV510.H)*
 UF Hmar hymns
Hymns, Hungarian [May Subd Geog]
 UF Hungarian hymns
Hymns, Irish [May Subd Geog]
 UF Irish hymns
Hymns, Islamic
 USE Islamic hymns
Hymns, Jaina
 USE Jaina hymns

Hymns, Jewish
  USE Hymns, Hebrew
        Hymns, Yiddish
        Jewish hymns
Hymns, Korean [May Subd Geog]
  UF Korean hymns
Hymns, Latin [May Subd Geog]
  UF Latin hymns
Hymns, Low German
  UF Low German hymns
  BT Hymns, German
Hymns, Luo *(BV510.L)*
  UF Luo hymns
Hymns, Lushai [May Subd Geog]
  UF Lushai hymns
Hymns, Lwo (Sudan) [May Subd Geog]
  UF Lwo hymns (Sudan)
Hymns, Mahican
  UF Mahican hymns
Hymns, Malay [May Subd Geog] *(BV510.M)*
  UF Malay hymns
Hymns, Muslim
  USE Islamic hymns
Hymns, Norwegian
  UF Norwegian hymns
  RT Hymns, Danish
Hymns, Paite [May Subd Geog] *(M2143)*
  UF Paite hymns
Hymns, Ramadan
  USE Ramadan hymns
Hymns, Revival
  USE Revivals—Hymns
Hymns, Romanian [May Subd Geog]
  UF Romanian hymns
Hymns, Scandinavian [May Subd Geog]
  UF Scandinavian hymns
Hymns, Serbo-Croatian [May Subd Geog]
  UF Serbo-Croatian hymns
Hymns, Sikh
  USE Sikh hymns
Hymns, Sindhi [May Subd Geog]
  UF Sindhi hymns
Hymns, Sivaite
  USE Sivaism—Hymns
Hymns, Spanish [May Subd Geog]
  UF Spanish hymns
  NT Alabados
        Goigs
Hymns, Sumerian [May Subd Geog]
  UF Sumerian hymns
Hymns, Swedish [May Subd Geog]
Hymns, Tamil [May Subd Geog]
  UF Tamil hymns
Hymns, Tswana [May Subd Geog]
  UF Tswana hymns
Hymns, Ukrainian [May Subd Geog]
  UF Ukrainian hymns
Hymns, Vietnamese [May Subd Geog]
  UF Vietnamese hymns
Hymns, Welsh [May Subd Geog]
  UF Welsh hymns
Hymns, Xhosa [May Subd Geog]
  UF Xhosa hymns

Hymns, Yiddish
  UF Hymns, Jewish
        Yiddish hymns
  BT Jewish hymns
  RT Hymns, Hebrew
Hymns to Apollo
  BT Music, Greek and Roman
Hyon kum
  USE Hyŏn'gŭm
Hyŏn'gŭm *(ML1015.H)*
  UF Hyon kum
  BT Musical instruments—Korea
        Zither
Hyŏn'gŭm music *(M142.H9)*
Icelandic folk-songs
  USE Folk-songs, Icelandic
Ichigenkin *(ML1015-1018)*
  BT Koto
        Musical instruments—Japan
Ichigenkin music *(M142.I3)*
Ida Rosen Prize
  BT Music librarianship—Awards
Imitation (in music) *(ML430)*
  UF Music, Imitation in
  BT Composition (Music)
Impresarios [May Subd Geog] *(ML429)*
  BT Opera
  RT Concert agents
Impressionism (Music) *(ML197)*
  UF Music, Impressionism in
  BT Music
        Music—Philosophy and aesthetics
        Style, Musical
Improvisation (Music) *(MT68)*
  UF Extemporization (Music)
  BT Music
        Music—Performance
  NT Chance composition
        Harmony, Keyboard
        Rapping (Music)
In convertendo (Music)
  USE Psalms (Music)—126th Psalm
In exitu Israel (Music)
  USE Psalms (Music)—114th Psalm
In nomine (Music)
In te, Domine, speravi, non confundar in
        aeternum, in justitia tua libera me,
        Inclina (Music)
  USE Psalms (Music)—31st Psalm
Inca music
  USE Incas—Music
Incas
  —Music *(ML3575)*
      UF Inca music
           Music, Inca
Incidental music
  USE Music, Incidental
Inclina Domine (Music)
  USE Psalms (Music)—86th Psalm
Incunabula
  —Music *(ML112)*
      UF Music—Incunabula
Indian music (American Indian)
  USE Indians—Music

Indians
  —Music *(E59.M9; ML3547)*
      UF Indian music (American Indian)
          Music—Indians
          Musical instruments—Indians
Indians of Central America
  —Music *(ML3572)*
Indians of Mexico
  —Music *(F1219.3.M; ML3570)*
Indians of North America
  —Hymns
      USE Hymns, Arikara, [Choctaw, Cree,
           etc.]
  —Music *(E98.M9; ML3557)*
          The music or works about music of
          a particular tribe are entered under
          Indians of North America—[local
          subdivision]—Music, and under the
          name of the tribe with the subdivision
          Music.
  —Arizona
  — —Music
      NT Chicken scratch music
  —[local subdivision]
  — —Music
  Note under Indians of North America—Music
Indic folk-songs
  USE Folk-songs, Indic
Indonesian songs
  USE Songs, Indonesian
Industry and music
  USE Music in industry
Information theory in aesthetics
  NT Information theory in music
Information theory in music
  BT Information theory in aesthetics
      Music
Ingush folk-songs
  USE Folk-songs, Ingush
Ingush songs
  USE Songs, Ingush
Instruction
  USE *subdivision* Instruction and study *under*
       Music *and under names of musical
       instruments*
Instrumental ensembles *(M900-M949;
      M960-M985)*
          Here are entered compositions for ten or
          more solo instruments belonging to
          various families.
          Compositions for ten or more like solo
          instruments are entered under Re-
          corder ensembles, Viol ensembles, and
          similar headings.
          Compositions for ten or more different
          solo instruments of the same family are
          entered as follows: bowed stringed
          instruments under String ensembles;
          wind instruments under Wind ensembles;
          brass instruments under Brass ensembles;
          woodwind instruments under Woodwind
          ensembles; plectral instruments under
          Plectral ensembles; and percussion

Instrumental ensembles *(M900-M949;
      M960-M985)*
  (Continued)
          instruments under Percussion ensembles.
          The qualifier Instrumental ensemble
          stands for two or more different solo
          instruments when used in conjunction
          with specific solo instrument(s) or voi-
          ce(s), in headings for choruses, and in
          other headings as specified, *e.g.* Mono-
          logues with music.
  UF Brass choir music
      Ensembles (Music)
  BT Organ with instrumental ensemble
  SA Concertos ([Solo instrument(s)] with
      instrumental ensemble); [Solo
      instrument(s)] with instrumental
      ensemble; Suites, Variations,
      Waltzes, *and similar headings with
      specification of instruments which
      include the specification
      Instrumental ensemble*
  NT Canons, fugues, etc. (Instrumental
      ensemble)
      Chorale preludes (Instrumental
      ensemble)
      Overtures (Instrumental ensemble)
      Polkas (Instrumental ensemble)
      Polonaises (Instrumental ensemble)
      Suites (Instrumental ensemble)
      Suites (Pianos (2) with instrumental
      ensemble)
      Symphonies (Instrumental ensemble)
      Variations (Instrumental ensemble)
      Violin and piano with instrumental
      ensemble
      Vocal ensembles with instrumental
      ensemble
Instrumental ensembles, Arranged
Instrumental masses
  USE Organ masses
Instrumental music [May Subd Geog] *(M5-1459)*
  UF Music, Instrumental
  BT Music
  SA Piano music, Violoncello and
      harpsichord music, *and similar
      headings*
  NT Accordion ensembles
      Band music
      Chamber music
      Chamber-orchestra music
      Concertina ensembles
      Dance music
      Dance-orchestra music
      Hunting music
      Jazz nonets
      Jazz quartets
      Jazz quintets
      Jazz septets
      Jazz sextets
      Jazz trios
      Military music
      Orchestral music

Instrumental music [May Subd Geog] *(M5-1459)*
    (Continued)
    NT Percussion music
          Piano music
          Plectral ensembles
          Popular instrumental music
          Salon-orchestra music
          Solo instrument music
          String instrument music
          String-orchestra music
          Violoncello and harpsichord music
    —Bibliography
    — —Graded lists *(ML132.I5)*
        UF Instrumental music—Graded lists
    —Graded lists
        USE Instrumental music—Bibliography
               —Graded lists
    —History and criticism *(ML460-547)*
        RT Musical instruments
        SA *various forms of instrumental music,*
            e.g. Sonata, Symphony
        NT Bands (Music)
            Orchestra
    —Instruction and study *(MT170)*
        BT Music—Instruction and study
        SA *subdivision* Instruction and study
            under names of musical
            instruments, e.g. Piano—
            Instruction and study
Instrumental settings
    USE *subdivision* Instrumental settings *under*
          headings for vocal music, e.g. Folk-
          songs—Instrumental settings;
          Operas—Instrumental settings;
          Spirituals (Songs)—Instrumental
          settings
Instrumentalisten
    USE Stadtpfeifer
Instrumentation and orchestration *(History,*
        ML455; Instruction, MT70)
    UF Orchestration
    BT Chamber orchestra
          Composition (Music)
          Music
          Music—Instruction and study
          Music—Theory
          Orchestra
    RT Arrangement (Music)
          Musical instruments
Instrumentation and orchestration (Band)
        (ML455; MT73)
    BT Bands (Music)
          Military music—History and criticism
          Wind instruments
    NT Instrumentation and orchestration
          (Brass band)
**Instrumentation and orchestration (Brass
        band)** *(History and criticism,*
        ML455; Instruction and study,
        MT73)
    BT Brass bands
          Brass instruments
          Instrumentation and orchestration (Band)

**Instrumentation and orchestration (Dance
        orchestra)** *(MT86)*
    BT Dance music—History and criticism
          Dance orchestras
          Jazz music
Instruments, Musical
    USE Musical instruments
Intellectual life
    Here are entered general works on learning
        and scholarship, literature, the arts, etc.
        Works on literature, art, music, motion
        pictures, etc. produced for a mass audience
        are entered under Popular culture.
International Festival of Jazz
    BT Jazz festivals—Belgium
Interpretation, Musical
    USE Music—Interpretation (Phrasing,
          dynamics, etc.)
Intervals (Music)
    USE Musical intervals and scales
Intonarium
    USE Tonarius
Introits (Music)
    BT Propers (Music)
          Psalms (Music)
Inversion, Symmetrical
    USE Symmetrical inversion (Music)
Irish ballads
    USE Ballads, Irish
Irish folk-songs
    USE Folk-songs, Irish
Irish harp
    USE Harp
Irish songs
    USE Songs, Irish
Isadora (Ballet)
    BT Ballets
Islam [May Subd Geog]
    —Hymns
        USE Islamic hymns
Islam and music
    USE Music—Religious aspects—Islam
Islamic hymns *(BP183.5)*
    UF Hymns, Islamic
          Hymns, Muslim
          Islam—Hymns
          Muslim hymns
    NT Ramadan hymns
Istanpittas
    USE Estampies
Italian folk-songs
    USE Folk-songs, Italian
Italian lullabies
    USE Lullabies, Italian
Italian songs
    USE Songs, Italian
Jacobite ballads and songs
    USE Jacobites—Poetry
Jaina hymns *(BL1377.3)*
    UF Hymns, Jaina
          Jainism—Hymns
Jaina hymns, Gujarati [May Subd Geog] *(BL1377.3)*
    UF Gujarati Jaina hymns

Japanese ballads
    USE Ballads, Japanese
Japanese Buddhist hymns
    USE Buddhist hymns, Japanese
Japanese folk-songs
    USE Folk-songs, Japanese
Japanese lullabies
    USE Lullabies, Japanese
Japanese songs
    USE Songs, Japanese
Javanese folk-songs
    USE Folk-songs, Javanese
Jaw bone, Musical *(ML1040)*
    UF Musical jaw bone
    BT Percussion instruments
Jaw harp
    USE Jew's harp
Jaw's-harp
    USE Jew's harp
Jazz audiences [May Subd Geog]
        ML3505.8-ML3509
    BT Music audiences
Jazz band music
    USE Big band music
Jazz bands
    USE Big bands
Jazz dance
    BT Dancing
Jazz duets *(M1366)*
    BT Duets
Jazz ensemble with chamber orchestra
        (M1040-1041)
    BT Jazz ensembles
    RT Concertos (Jazz ensemble with chamber
          orchestra)
    NT Monologues with music (Jazz ensemble
          with chamber orchestra)
    —Scores *(M1040)*
Jazz ensemble with orchestra *(M1040-1041)*
    BT Jazz ensembles
    RT Concertos (Jazz ensemble)
    NT Suites (Jazz ensemble with orchestra)
Jazz ensemble with string orchestra
        (M1140-1141)
    BT Jazz ensembles
    RT Concertos (Jazz ensemble with string
          orchestra)
Jazz ensembles *(M900-949; M960-985)*
        Here are entered single jazz compositions
          for ten or more solo instruments, also
          collections of jazz compositions for
          any number or combination of solo
          instruments.
        When used in conjunction with specific
          solo instrument(s), the qualifier jazz
          ensemble may stand for any number or
          combination of solo instruments.
    UF Ensembles (Music)
    RT Dance-orchestra music
    SA Concertos (Solo instrument(s)) with
          jazz ensemble; [Solo instrument(s)]
          with jazz ensemble

Jazz ensembles *(M900-949; M960-985)*
    (Continued)
    NT Big band music
          Choruses, Sacred (Mixed voices) with
            jazz ensemble
          Concertos (Jazz ensemble)
          Concertos (Jazz ensemble with chamber
            orchestra)
          Concertos (Jazz ensemble with string
            orchestra)
          Dixieland music
          Jazz ensemble with chamber orchestra
          Jazz ensemble with orchestra
          Jazz ensemble with string orchestra
          Jazz vocals
          Percussion with jazz ensemble
          Saxophone with jazz ensemble
          Suites (Jazz ensemble)
          Vocalises (High voice) with jazz
            ensemble
Jazz festivals [May Subd Geog]
    BT Music festivals
    —Belgium
        NT International Festival of Jazz
    —California
        NT Concord Summer Jazz Festival
Jazz music [May Subd Geog] *(ML3561)*
    UF Be bop music
          Bebop music
          Swing music
    BT Afro-Americans—Music
          Dance music—History and criticism
          Music
    SA Jazz quintets, Jazz septets, *and similar*
          headings; and various headings for
          instrumental music followed by the
          qualifying adjective (Jazz), *e.g.* Piano
          music (Jazz); *also subdivisions*
          Methods (Jazz) *and* Studies and
          exercises (Jazz) *under names of*
          instruments or groups of instruments,
          e.g. Saxophone—Studies and
          exercises (Jazz); Wind instruments—
          Methods (Jazz)
    NT Big band music
          Big bands
          Blues (Songs, etc.)
          Dixieland music
          Fakebooks (Music)
          Gospel music
          Instrumentation and orchestration
            (Dance orchestra)
          Jazz quintets
          Jazz septets
          Jazz vocals
          Ragtime music
          Western swing (Music)
    —Interpretation (Phrasing, dynamics, etc.)
        (MT75)
Jazz musicians [May Subd Geog]
    BT Musicians
    NT Women jazz musicians

Jazz nonets
    BT Instrumental music
Jazz octet with orchestra *(M1040-1041)*
    RT Concertos (Jazz octet)
         Jazz octets
Jazz octets
    RT Concertos (Jazz octet)
         Jazz octet with orchestra
Jazz quartet with chamber orchestra
         (M1040-1041)
    BT Chamber-orchestra music
         Jazz quartets
Jazz quartet with orchestra *(M1040-1041)*
    BT Jazz quartets
    RT Concertos (Jazz quartet)
Jazz quartets
    BT Instrumental music
         Quartets (Piano, percussion,
           vibraphone, double bass)
    NT Concertos (Jazz quartet)
         Jazz quartet with chamber orchestra
         Jazz quartet with orchestra
         Suites (Jazz quartet)
Jazz quintet with band *(M1205-1206)*
    RT Concertos (Jazz quintet with band)
    NT Suites (Jazz quintet with band)
Jazz quintet with orchestra *(M1040-1041)*
    BT Jazz quintets
    RT Concertos (Jazz quintet)
Jazz quintet with string orchestra
         (M1140-1141)
    BT Jazz quintets
    RT Concertos (Jazz quintet with string
         orchestra)
Jazz quintets
    BT Instrumental music
         Jazz music
    NT Concertos (Jazz quintet)
         Concertos (Jazz quintet with string
           orchestra)
         Jazz quintet with orchestra
         Jazz quintet with string orchestra
         Monologues with music (Jazz quintet)
Jazz septets
    BT Instrumental music
         Jazz music
Jazz sextet with band
    M1205-M1206
    NT Suites (Jazz sextet with band)
Jazz sextet with orchestra *(M1040-M1041)*
Jazz sextets
    BT Instrumental music
Jazz songs
    USE Jazz vocals
Jazz trio with chamber orchestra *(M1040-1041)*
    RT Concertos (Jazz trio with chamber
         orchestra)
    NT Suites (Jazz trio with chamber
         orchestra)
Jazz trio with orchestra *(M1040-1041)*
    BT Jazz trios
    RT Concertos (Jazz trio)

Jazz trios
    BT Instrumental music
    NT Concertos (Jazz trio)
         Jazz trio with orchestra
         Suites (Jazz trio)
Jazz vocals
         Here are entered songs performed in jazz
           style by a vocalist, vocal ensemble, or
           chorus, generally accompanied by a
           solo instrument, jazz ensemble, or big
           band.
    UF Jazz songs
         Scat singing
         Songs, Jazz
         Vocals, Jazz
    BT Big band music
         Jazz ensembles
         Jazz music
         Popular music
         Songs
Jesus Christ
    —Crucifixion
    — —Songs and music
         USE Passion-music
    —Passion
    — —Music
         USE Passion-music
    — —Songs and music
         USE Passion-music
    —Seven last words
    — —Songs and music
         USE Passion-music
Jewish composers
    USE Composers, Jewish
Jewish hymns
    UF Hymns, Jewish
         Jews—Hymns
    BT Synagogue music
    NT Hymns, Hebrew
         Hymns, Yiddish
         Piyutim
Jewish liturgical music
    USE Synagogue music
Jewish music
    USE Jews—Music
Jewish musicians
    USE Musicians, Jews
Jews. Liturgy and ritual.
    USE Judaism—Liturgy
Jews [May Subd Geog]
    —Hymns
         USE Jewish hymns
    —Music
         UF Hebrew music
            Jewish music
            Music, Hebrew
            Music, Jewish
         NT Klezmer music
            Music in synagogues
            Music in the Bible
            Synagogue music

Jew's harp
ML1087
UF Jaw harp
Jaw's-harp
Trump
BT Musical instruments
Jew's harp music *(M175.J4)*
SA Concertos, Minuets, Sonatas, Suites, *and similar headings with specification of instruments;* Trios [Quartets, etc.] *followed by specifications which include the Jew's harp; also* Percussion ensembles *and headings that begin with the words Jew's harp or Jew's harps*

Jigs
UF Gigues
BT Dance music
Jodel
USE Yodel and yodeling
Jody calls
UF Cadence calls
Cadences (Soldiers' songs)
Calls, Cadence
Calls, Jody
Chants, Jody
Jody chants
BT War-songs
Jody chants
USE Jody calls
Jongleurs
USE Minstrels
Troubadours
Trouvères
Jōruri
BT Monologues with music (Shamisen)
NT Katōbushi
Joseph Legende (Ballet)
USE Legend of Joseph (Ballet)
Josephlegende (Ballet)
USE Legend of Joseph (Ballet)
Jotas
BT Dance music
Jubilate Deo omnis terra, Servite Domino (Music)
USE Psalms (Music)—100th Psalm
Jubilate Deo omnis terra, psalmum dicite (Music)
USE Psalms (Music)—66th Psalm
Jubilee singers *(ML400)*
Judaism—Liturgy
Judica me, Deus (Music)
USE Psalms (Music)—43d Psalm
Juke boxes
USE Jukeboxes
Jukeboxes
UF Juke boxes
BT Musical instruments (Mechanical)
Juvenile music
USE Music—Juvenile
Juvenile opera
USE Opera—Juvenile
Kabardian songs
USE Songs, Kabardian

Kabuki music
UF Kabuki plays—Incidental music
BT Music—Japan
Kabuki plays
—Incidental music
USE Kabuki music
Kaen *(M1089.K)*
UF Khen
BT Mouth organs
Musical instruments—Laos
Musical instruments—Thailand
Kagok
BT Sijo
Songs, Korean
Kalinga ballads
USE Ballads, Kalinga
Kalmyk folk-songs
USE Folk-songs, Kalmyk
Kamba folk-songs
USE Folk-songs, Kamba
Kanklės *(Lithuanian, ML509)*
BT Gusli
Kantele (Musical instrument)
Musical instruments—Lithuania
Kannada ballads
USE Ballads, Kannada
Kannada folk-songs
USE Folk-songs, Kannada
Kannada Hindu hymns
USE Hindu hymns, Kannada
Kantele (Musical instrument) *(Finnish, ML509)*
BT Dulcimer
Gusli
Harp
NT Kanklės
Kantele music *(M142.K)*
Kanze school [May Subd Geog]
(Performance, PN2924.5.N6)
BT Nō
Karamojong folk-songs
USE Folk-songs, Karamojong
Karelian folk-songs
USE Folk-songs, Karelian
Karnatic music
USE Music, Karnatic
Karo-Batak folk-songs
USE Folk-songs, Karo-Batak
Kashubian folk-songs
USE Folk-songs, Kashubian
Katarimono
BT Monologues with music
Music—Japan
NT Sekkyō jōruri
Katōbushi
BT Jōruri
Monologues with music (Shamisen)
Kayagŭm
USE Kayakeum
Kayakeum *(ML1015.K39; ML1018.K39)*
UF Kayagŭm
Kayakko
BT Musical instruments—Korea
Zither

Kayakeum music *(M142.K39)*
Kayakeum players [May Subd Geog]
    BT Musicians—Korea
Kayakko
    USE Kayakeum
Kazakh folk-songs
    USE Folk-songs, Kazakh
Kazoo *(Instruction, MT533.K36)*
    UF Bazoo
        Eunuch flute
        Gazoo
        Tommy talker
        Zarah
    BT Mirliton
Kechruk
    USE Angklung
Kei
    BT Musical instruments—Japan
        Percussion instruments
Kemak folk-songs
    USE Folk-songs, Kemak
Kemanak *(ML1040.K4)*
    BT Percussion instruments
Kettledrum
    USE Timpani
Keyboard, Electronic (Synthesizer)
    USE Electronic keyboard (Synthesizer)
Keyboard harmony
    USE Harmony, Keyboard
Keyboard instrument and flute music
    USE Flute and keyboard instrument music
Keyboard instrument and oboe music
    USE Oboe and keyboard instrument music
Keyboard instrument and recorder music
    USE Recorder and keyboard instrument music
Keyboard instrument and violin music
    USE Violin and keyboard instrument music
Keyboard instrument music
    UF Keyboard music
    SA Concertos, Minuets, Sonatas, Suites,
        and similar headings with specification
        of instruments; Trios [Quartets, etc.] *fol-*
        lowed by specifications which include
        keyboard instrument(s); also headings that
        begin with the words Keyboard instrument
        or Keyboard instruments
    NT Clavichord music
        Harpsichord music
        Organ music
        Piano music
Keyboard instrument music (Keyboard
    instruments (2))
Keyboard instruments *(ML549)*
    NT Celesta
        Clavi-harp
        Organ
        Piano
    —Tuning
Keyboard music
    USE Keyboard instrument music
Keyboards *(ML549-697)*
    BT Harpsichord
        Organ

Keyboards *(ML549-697)*
    (Continued)
    BT Piano
        Reed-organ
Keyed fiddle *(ML760)*
    UF Key fiddle
        Nyckelgiga
        Nyckelharpa
        Schlüsselfidel
        Schlüsselfiedel
    BT Musical instruments—Sweden
        Stringed instruments, Bowed
Keyed fiddle music *(M59)*
    SA Concertos, Minuets, Sonatas, Suites,
        and similar headings with specifi-
        cation of instruments; String trios
        [quartets, etc.] *and* Trios [Quartets,
        etc.] *followed by specifications*
        which include the keyed fiddle; also
        headings that begin with the words
        Keyed fiddle or Keyed fiddles
Keyed fiddle music (Keyed fiddles (2))
    (M286-287)
Keyed fiddle with orchestra *(M1019.K)*
    NT Concertos (Keyed fiddle)
Keyed harp
    USE Clavi-harp
Keys (Music theory)
    USE Tonality
Keys (Musical instruments)
    USE *subdivision* Keys *under names of*
        individual instruments, e.g. Piano—
        Keys
Khakass folk-songs
    USE Folk-songs, Khakass
Khanty folk-songs
    USE Folk-songs, Khanty
Khayāl
    USE Khyāl (Musical form)
Khen
    USE Kaen
Khil-khuur
    USE Morin khuur
Khjai Mendung (Gamelan)
    UF Venerable Dark Cloud
    BT Gamelan
Khyāl (Musical form)
    UF Khayāl
    BT Music, Hindustani
        Vocal music—India
Kikuyu folk-songs
    USE Folk-songs, Kikuyu
Kimball organ *(ML597)*
    BT Electronic organ
        Organ
Kindergarten [May Subd Geog]
    —Music *(M1990; Instruction and study,*
        MT920-MT925)
        UF Music—Kindergarten
        BT Children's songs
            Music
            Music—Instruction and study
        NT Nursery schools—Music

Kit (Musical instrument)
  USE Pochette
Kithara
  USE Cithara
Klezmer music [May Subd Geog]
  BT Jews—Music
      Popular music
Kliningan
  USE Gender (Musical instrument)
Ko tsuzumi
  USE Kotsuzumi
Kobsa
  USE Kobza
Kobza *(ML1015.K6)*
  UF Kobsa
  BT Lute
      Musical instruments—Ukraine
Kobza music *(M142.K55)*
Kobzari [May Subd Geog]
  BT Musicians
Kokle *(ML1015.K64)*
  BT Dulcimer
      Harp
      Musical instruments—Latvia
Kolintang *(ML1040)*
  BT Musical instruments—Indonesia
      Percussion instruments
Kolomyiky
  BT Folk-songs, Ukrainian
Kolos
  BT Dance music
Komunko *(ML1015-1018)*
  UF Kum
  BT Musical instruments—Korea
      Zither
Komunko music *(M42.K58)*
Konkani folk-songs
  USE Folk-songs, Konkani
Kora (Musical instrument) *(ML1015-1018)*
  UF Harp-lute
  BT Musical instruments—Africa
Kora music *(M142.K595)*
Koran
  —Musical declamation
    USE Koran—Recitation
  —Recitation *(BP131.6)*
      UF Koran—Musical declamation
      BT Music, Islamic
      NT Hafiz
Korean ballads
  USE Ballads, Korean
Korean Buddhist hymns
  USE Buddhist hymns, Korean
Korean folk-songs
  USE Folk-songs, Korean
Korean hymns
  USE Hymns, Korean
Korean songs
  USE Songs, Korean
Koto *(ML1015-1018)*
  BT Musical instruments—Japan
      Zither
  NT Ichigenkin

Koto and clarinet music
  USE Clarinet and koto music
Koto and flute music
  USE Flute and koto music
Koto and shakuhachi music
  USE Shakuhachi and koto music
Koto music *(M142.K6)*
  NT Concertos (Koto)
      Koto with orchestra
      Quartets (Shakuhachi, kotos (2), shamisen)
      Quartets (Shakuhachi, kotos (3))
      Sextets (Shakuhachi, biwa, kotos (2),
        shamisen, percussion)
      Sextets (Shakuhachi, guitar, kotos (2),
        percussion, double bass)
      Sonatas (Koto)
      Suites (Kotos (6))
Koto with orchestra *(M1037.4.K68)*
  BT Koto music
  RT Concertos (Koto)
Kotsuzumi *(ML1038.K7)*
  UF Ko tsuzumi
  BT Hourglass drum
      Musical instruments—Japan
Kouta *(History, PL732.K6; Collections, PL762.K6)*
  BT Ballads, Japanese
      Songs, Japanese
Kōwaka *(PN2924.5.K6)*
  BT Theater—Japan
Kpelle folk-songs
  USE Folk-songs, Kpelle
Krakowiaks
  BT Dance music
      Folk dance music—Poland
Kului folk-songs
  USE Folk-songs, Kului
Kum
  USE Komunko
Kumiuta
  BT Songs, Japanese
      Songs with koto
      Songs with shamisen
Kunstpfeifer
  USE Stadtpfeifer
Kurukh folk-songs
  USE Folk-songs, Kurukh
Kurukh songs
  USE Songs, Oraon
Kyrie eleison (Music)
  BT Masses
La pa
  USE So na
Labels [May Subd Geog] *(Commercial art,*
      NC1002.L3; Shipment of goods,
      HF5773.L3)
  NT Violin—Labels
Labor and laboring classes [May Subd Geog]
      (HD4801-8942)
  —Songs and music *(Collections,*
        M1977.L3; History and criticism,
        ML3780; Political songs,
        M1664-M1665.L3; Single songs,
        M1978.L3)

Labor and laboring classes [May Subd Geog]
    (HD4801-8942)
    —Songs and music
    (Continued)
        RT   Work-songs
        SA   Lumbermen—Songs and music;
                Miners—Songs and music; *and*
                similar headings
        NT   Lumbermen—Songs and music
             Miners—Songs and music
Ladakhi folk-songs
    USE   Folk-songs, Ladakhi
Ladino ballads
    USE   Ballads, Ladino
Laetatus sum (Music)
    USE   Psalms (Music)—122d Psalm
Lakota songs
    USE   Songs, Lakota
Lamentations
    USE   Laments
Lamentations of Jeremiah (Music)
    BT   Laments
         Tenebrae service music
Laments [May Subd Geog]
    UF   Complancha
         Lamentations
    NT   Dirges
         Lamentations of Jeremiah (Music)
Ländler
    BT   Dance music
         Waltzes
    NT   Schuhplattler
Langleik
    USE   Noordsche balk
Language and languages *(P1-P410)*
    —Rhythm
        BT   Rhythm
Language and music
    USE   Music and language
Lao folk-songs
    USE   Folk-songs, Lao
Latin hymns
    USE   Hymns, Latin
Latvian folk-songs
    USE   Folk-songs, Latvian
Latvian Song Festival *(ML36)*
    UF   Vispārjiē latviesu dziešmu svētki
    BT   Music festivals—Canada
         Music festivals—United States
Latvian songs
    USE   Songs, Latvian
Lauda, anima mea (Music)
    USE   Psalms (Music)—146th Psalm
Lauda Jerusalem Dominum (Music)
    USE   Psalms (Music)—147th Psalm
Laudate Dominum de caelis (Music)
    USE   Psalms (Music)—148th Psalm
Laudate Dominum in sanctis eius (Music)
    USE   Psalms (Music)—150th Psalm
Laudate Dominum omnes gentes (Music)
    USE   Psalms (Music)—117th Psalm
Laudate Dominum quoniam bonus (Music)
    USE   Psalms (Music)—147th Psalm

Laudate nomen Domini (Music)
    USE   Psalms (Music)—135th Psalm
Laudate, pueri, Dominum (Music)
    USE   Psalms (Music)—113th Psalm
Lauds (Music)
    BT   Morning-service music
Lays *(PN1351-1525; French, PQ1317,*
            PQ1323.L3; Medieval, PN691)
    BT   Folk-songs
Left-hand piano music
    USE   Piano music (1 hand)
Legend of Joseph (Ballet)
    UF   Joseph Legende (Ballet)
         Josephlegende (Ballet)
    BT   Ballets
Leitmotiv *(MT90; Wagner, MT100.W2)*
    BT   Music
         Opera
         Program music
Lent [May Subd Geog] *(BV85-95)*
    —Hymns
        USE   Lenten hymns
    —Songs and music
        USE   Lenten music
Lenten hymns
    UF   Lent—Hymns
    BT   Hymns
    RT   Lenten music
Lenten music *(M2088.L5; M2098.L5)*
    UF   Lent—Songs and music
    BT   Church music
         Sacred vocal music
    RT   Lenten hymns
    NT   Good Friday music
         Holy-Week music
         Passion-music
Lepcha folk-songs
    USE   Folk-songs, Lepcha
Levavi oculos (Music)
    USE   Psalms (Music)—121st Psalm
Libraries, Music
    USE   Music libraries
Librettists [May Subd Geog] *(ML2110)*
    UF   Opera—Librettists
    BT   Libretto
         Musicians
Libretto
        Here are entered works on the history
            and criticism of the libretto and on li-
            bretto-writing. *Cf.* note under Librettos.
    NT   Librettists
Librettos *(ML48-49)*
        Here are entered collections of miscel-
            laneous librettos. Collections of libret-
            tos limited to a specific form are en-
            tered under that form, *e.g.* Operas—
            Librettos; Oratorios—Librettos. *Cf.*
            note under Libretto.
Ligature (Music)
    USE   Musical notation
          Neumes
Likembe
    USE   Mbira

Lincoln, Abraham, 1809-1865 *(E457)*
—Music
RT Lincoln, Abraham, 1809-1865—
Songs and music
—Musical settings
—Songs and music
RT Lincoln, Abraham, 1809-1865—
Music
Lingala songs
USE Songs, Lingala
Literature *(PN45)*
NT Music and literature
Literature and music
USE Music and literature
Lithuanian ballads
USE Ballads, Lithuanian
Lithuanian folk-songs
USE Folk-songs, Lithuanian
Liturgical drama
BT Opera
Liturgies *(BV170-BV199; Particular*
denominations, BX)
NT Hymns
Liuto attiorbato
USE Archlute
Lord's prayer (Music)
Loudspeakers [May Subd Geog]
TK5983
UF Loud-speakers
Speakers (Loudspeakers)
BT Electroacoustic transducers
Sound—Equipment and supplies
NT Direct radiator loudspeakers
Love songs [May Subd Geog]
BT Songs
Low German folk-songs
USE Folk-songs, Low German
Low German hymns
USE Hymns, Low German
Low German songs
USE Songs, Low German
Lullabies
UF Cradle songs
Slumber songs
BT Children's songs
Nursery rhymes
Songs
Lullabies, American [May Subd Geog]
UF American lullabies
Lullabies, Brazilian [May Subd Geog]
UF Brazilian lullabies
Lullabies, Cuna [May Subd Geog]
UF Cuna lullabies
Lullabies, English [May Subd Geog]
UF English lullabies
Lullabies, French [May Subd Geog]
UF French lullabies
Lullabies, German [May Subd Geog]
UF German lullabies
Lullabies, Hindi [May Subd Geog]
UF Hindi lullabies
Lullabies, Italian [May Subd Geog]
UF Italian lullabies

Lullabies, Japanese [May Subd Geog]
UF Japanese lullabies
Lullabies, Malay [May Subd Geog]
UF Malay lullabies
Lullabies, Mongo [May Subd Geog]
UF Mongo lullabies
Lullabies, Norwegian [May Subd Geog]
UF Norwegian lullabies
Lullabies, Panjabi [May Subd Geog]
UF Panjabi lullabies
Lullabies, Provençal [May Subd Geog]
UF Provençal lullabies
Lullabies, Puerto Rican [May Subd Geog]
UF Puerto Rican lullabies
Lullabies, Russian [May Subd Geog]
UF Russian lullabies
Lullabies, Salvadorian [May Subd Geog]
UF Salvadorian lullabies
Lullabies, Spanish [May Subd Geog]
UF Spanish lullabies
Lullabies, Tamil [May Subd Geog]
UF Tamil lullabies
Lullabies, Thai [May Subd Geog]
UF Thai lullabies
Lullabies, Urdu [May Subd Geog]
UF Urdu lullabies
Lumbermen [May Subd Geog] *(TS805-TS806;*
Labor, HD8039.L9)
—Songs and music *(M1977.L8;*
M1978.L8)
BT Labor and laboring classes—Songs
and music
Lunda folk-songs
USE Folk-songs, Lunda
Lur *(ML990.L8)*
BT Brass instruments
Horn (Musical instrument)
RT Alpenhorn
Lur music *(M175.L87)*
Lushai hymns
USE Hymns, Lushai
Lushai songs
USE Songs, Lushai
Lute *(ML1010-1013)*
UF Colascione
RT Vihuela
NT Archlute
Bağlama
Bandura
Bandurria
Biwa
Bouzouki
Domra
Harp-lute guitar
Kobza
Mandola
Oud
P'i p'a
San hsien
Sarod
Tambura
Tar (Musical instrument)
Theorbo

Lute and cithern music
USE Cithern and lute music
Lute and flute music
USE Flute and lute music
Lute and glass-harmonica music
USE Glass-harmonica and lute music
Lute and harp music
USE Harp and lute music
Lute and harpsichord music *(M282.L88;*
M283.L88)
UF Harpsichord and lute music
BT Lute and piano music
NT Sonatas (Lute and harpsichord)
Lute and organ music *(M182-186)*
UF Organ and lute music
Lute and piano music *(M282.L88;*
M283.L88)
UF Piano and lute music
NT Lute and harpsichord music
Lute and recorder music
USE Recorder and lute music
Lute and viol music
USE Viol and lute music
Lute and viola da gamba music
USE Viola da gamba and lute music
Lute and viola d'amore music
USE Viola d'amore and lute music
Lute and viola d'amore with string orchestra
(M1140-1141)
RT Concertos (Lute and viola d'amore with
string orchestra)
Lute and violin music
USE Violin and lute music
Lute music *(M140-141)*
SA Concertos, Minuets, Sonatas, Suites,
and similar headings with
specification of instruments; Trios
[Quartets, etc.] *followed by*
specifications which include the lute;
also Plectral ensembles *and headings*
that begin with the words lute or
lutes
NT Canons, fugues, etc. (Lute)
Domra music
Mandola music
Oud music
Sarod music
Sonatas (Lute)
Suites (Lute)
Tablature (Musical notation)
Lute music (Lutes (2)) *(M292-3)*
NT Suites (Lutes (2))
Lute players
USE Lutenists
Lute with string orchestra *(M1105-6)*
RT Concertos (Lute with string orchestra)
Lutenists *(Biography: collective, ML399;*
individual, ML419)
UF Lute players
Lutes (2) with string orchestra
(M1137.4.L88)
RT Concertos (Lutes (2) with string
orchestra)

Lutheran Church [May Subd Geog]
(BX8001-BX8080)
—Hymns *(BV410; Vocal music, M2126)*
NT Chorale
Chorales
Lwo hymns (Sudan)
USE Hymns, Lwo (Sudan)
Lyra viol *(ML760)*
UF Lyro-viol
Viola bastarda
BT Viola da gamba
Lyra-viol and continuo music
UF Continuo and lyra-viol music
Lyra-viol music *(M142.L)*
NT Suites (Lute, violin, lyra viol)
Suites (Theorbo, violin, lyra viol)
Suites (Violin, lyra viol, continuo)
Lyra-viol music (Lyra-viols (2)) *(M990)*
Lyra-viol music (Lyra-viols (3))
USE String trios (Lyra-viols (3))
Lyre *(ML162-9)*
NT Lyre-guitar
Lyre-guitar *(ML1015-1018)*
UF Apollo lyre
BT Cithara
Guitar
Lyre
Lyre-guitar music *(M135-7)*
NT Trios (Flute, lyre-guitar, violin)
Lyre-guitar music (Lyre-guitars (2))
(M292-3)
Lyric drama
USE Opera
Lyricists [May Subd Geog]
UF Songwriters
BT Poets
Lyro-viol
USE Lyra viol
Ma t'ou ch'in
USE Morin khuur
Macedonian folk-songs
USE Folk-songs, Macedonian
Madrigal *(PN1493; German literature,*
PT581.M3)
Here are entered works on the madrigal
as a literary or musical form. Collec-
tions of madrigals in literature are en-
tered under Madrigals. Musical works
composed in the form of the madrigal
are entered under Madrigals (Music).
BT Choral music
Part-songs
Notes under Madrigals; Madrigals (Music)
Madrigal comedies
Here are entered musical works com-
posed in the form of the madrigal
comedy. A second heading for
medium is assigned if a specific
medium of performance is given in the
work.
UF Comedies, Madrigal
BT Madrigals (Music), Italian

Madrigals *(English literature, PR1195.M2)*
> Here are entered collections of madrigals
> in literature. Musical works composed
> in the form of the madrigal are entered
> under Madrigals (Music). Works on
> the madrigal as a literary or musical
> form are entered under Madrigal.

> BT Songs
> Vocal music

Notes under Madrigal; Madrigals (Music)

Madrigals (Music)
> Here are entered musical works com-
> posed in the form of the madrigal. The
> heading is qualified by language when
> the text is in one language only.
> A second heading for medium is assigned
> if a specific medium of performance is
> given in the work.
> Works on the madrigal as a literary or
> musical form are entered under Madri-
> gal. Collections of madrigals in litera-
> ture are entered under Madrigals.

> BT Part-songs
> Vocal duets
> Vocal ensembles
> Vocal nonets
> Vocal octets
> Vocal quartets
> Vocal quintets
> Vocal septets
> Vocal sextets
> Vocal trios

Notes under Madrigal; Madrigals; Part-songs

Madrigals (Music), English
> UF English madrigals (Music)

Madrigals (Music), English [Spanish, etc.]

Madrigals (Music), Hungarian
> UF Hungarian madrigals (Music)

Madrigals (Music), Italian
> UF Italian madrigals (Music)
> NT Madrigal comedies

Note under Madrigals (Music)

Madrigals (Music), Portuguese
> UF Portuguese madrigals (Music)

Magic and music
> USE Music and magic

Magic flute (Ballet)
> UF Flûte enchantée (Ballet)
> Volshebnaia fleia (Ballet)
> Zauberflöte (Ballet)
> BT Ballets

Magnificat (Music) *(M2079)*
> BT Evening-service music

Mahican hymns
> USE Hymns, Mahican

Maîtrises *(ML3027)*
> BT Chapels (Music)
> Choirs (Music)
> Church music—Catholic Church
> Church music—France
> Conservatories of music
> Music—Instruction and study—France

Malagasy folk-songs
> USE Folk-songs, Malagasy

Malagasy songs
> USE Songs, Malagasy

Malay hymns
> USE Hymns, Malay

Malayalam folk-songs
> USE Folk-songs, Malayalam

Manambu songs
> USE Songs, Manambu

Mandola
> UF Mandora
> Mandore
> BT Lute

Mandola and Jew's harp with string orchestra *(M1140-M1141)*
> NT Concertos (Mandola and Jew's harp
> with string orchestra)

Mandola music *(M142.M25)*
> BT Lute music
> SA Concertos, Minuets, Sonatas, Suites,
> *and similar headings with specification*
> *of instruments;* Trios [Quartets, etc.]
> *followed by specifications which include*
> *the Mandola; also* Plectral ensembles
> *and headings that begin with the words*
> *Mandola or Mandolas*

Mandolin
> ML1015.M2 (History)
> MT600-MT608 (Instruction)
> UF Bandolim
> NT Bağlama
> —Methods (Bluegrass) *(General, MT602;*
> *Self-instructors, MT608)*

Mandolin and continuo music
> UF Continuo and mandolin music
> NT Sonatas (Mandolin and continuo)

Mandolin and guitar music
> USE Guitar and mandolin music

Mandolin and harpsichord music *(M278-9)*
> UF Harpsichord and mandolin music
> BT Mandolin and piano music
> NT Sonatas (Mandolin and harpsichord)

Mandolin and piano music *(M278-9)*
> UF Piano and mandolin music
> NT Mandolin and harpsichord music
> Sonatas (Mandolin and piano)
> Suites (Mandolin and piano)

Mandolin and piano music, Arranged *(M278-9)*
> NT Concertos (Mandolin)—Solo with piano
> Concertos (Mandolin with string
> orchestra)—Solo with piano

Mandolin and viola music
> USE Viola and mandolin music

Mandolin bands
> USE Mandolin orchestras

Mandolin music *(M130-134)*
> SA Concertos, Minuets, Sonatas, Suites,
> *and similar headings with*
> *specification of instruments;* Trios
> [Quartets, etc.] *followed by*
> *specifications which include the*

Mandolin music *(M130-134)*
   (Continued)
   SA   *mandolin; also* Plectral ensembles
         and headings that begin with the
         words mandolin or mandolins
Mandolin music (Jazz) *(M130-134)*
Mandolin music (Mandolins (2)) *(M292-3)*
   NT   Concertos (Mandolins (2) with string
         orchestra)
         Mandolins (2) with string orchestra
Mandolin orchestra music
   USE Plectral ensembles
Mandolin orchestras [May Subd Geog]
   UF   Mandolin bands
   BT   Bands (Music)
         Orchestra
Mandolin players
   USE Mandolinists
Mandolin with chamber orchestra
         (M1037.4.M3)
   NT   Suites (Mandolin with chamber
         orchestra)
Mandolin with orchestra *(M1037.4.M3)*
   RT   Concertos (Mandolin)
Mandolin with string orchestra *(M1105-6)*
   RT   Concertos (Mandolin with string
         orchestra)
Mandolinists *(Biography: collective, ML399;*
         individual, ML419)
   UF   Mandolin players
Mandolins (2) with string orchestra
         (M1105-6)
   BT   Mandolin music (Mandolins (2))
   RT   Concertos (Mandolins (2) with string
         orchestra)
Mandora
   USE Mandola
Mandore
   USE Mandola
Manipuri songs
   USE Songs, Manipuri
Mannerism (Music) [May Subd Geog]
   BT   Music
Mansi folk-songs
   USE Folk-songs, Mansi
Manualo *(ML1055.M26)*
   BT   Musical instruments (Mechanical)
         Player-piano
Manuscripts [May Subd Geog] *(Z105-Z115;*
         Z6601-Z6625)
   NT   Music—Manuscripts
   —Exhibitions
         NT   Music—Manuscripts—Exhibitions
Manuscripts, Musical
   USE *subdivision* Manuscripts *under names of*
         composers, e.g. Wagner, Richard,
         1813-1883—Manuscripts
         Music—Manuscripts
Manx ballads
   USE Ballads, Manx
Manx folk-songs
   USE Folk-songs, Manx

Maori folk-songs
   USE Folk-songs, Maori
Maori songs
   USE Songs, Maori
Maraca
   BT   Percussion instruments
Maraca music *(M175.M)*
   NT   Quintets (Electronic organs (4),
         maracas)
Marathi folk-songs
   USE Folk-songs, Marathi
Marathi Hindu hymns
   USE Hindu hymns, Marathi
Marathi songs
   USE Songs, Marathi
March (Music)
   BT   Military music—History and criticism
Marches
         Here are entered collections of march
         music for various mediums. Individual
         marches and collections of marches for
         a specific medium are entered under
         the heading followed by specification
         of medium.
   UF   Quick-steps
Marches (Accordion) *(M175.A4)*
   BT   Accordion music
Marches (Band) *(M1247; M1260)*
   BT   Band music
Marches (Chamber orchestra) *(M1046;*
         M1060)
   BT   Chamber-orchestra music
Marches (Clarinet and piano) *(M248-252)*
   BT   Clarinet and piano music
Marches (Flute) *(M60-64)*
   BT   Flute music
Marches (Flute and continuo)
   BT   Flute and continuo music
Marches (Flute and piano) *(M240-244)*
   BT   Flute and piano music
Marches (Flutes (2)) *(M288-9)*
   BT   Flute music (Flutes (2))
Marches (Flutes (2), percussion) *(M385)*
Marches (Guitar and piano) *(M276-7)*
   BT   Guitar and piano music
Marches (Harp) *(M115-119)*
   BT   Harp music
Marches (Horn and piano) *(M255-259)*
   BT   Horn and piano music
Marches (Instrumental ensemble) *(M985)*
Marches (Oboe and continuo)
   BT   Oboe and continuo music
Marches (Orchestra) *(M1046; M1060)*
   BT   Orchestral music
Marches (Organ) *(M6-M7; M11-13)*
   BT   Organ music
Marches (Percussion, trombones (2), trumpets
         (3), tuba) *(M785)*
Marches (Piano) *(M28)*
   BT   Piano music
Marches (Piano, 4 hands) *(M200-M201;*
         M204)
   BT   Piano music (4 hands)

Marches (Piano (4 hands) and reed-organ)
    (M191-5)
  BT Piano music (4 hands) and reed-organ music
**Marches (Piano, bassoon, clarinet, flute, oboe,
    trumpet, violin, viola, violoncello)**
    (M920-924)
  BT Nonets (Piano, bassoon, clarinet, flute,
      oboe, trumpet, violin, viola,
      violoncello)
Marches (Pianos (2)) *(M214-215)*
  BT Piano music (Pianos (2))
Marches (Piccolo and piano) *(M240-244)*
  BT Piccolo and piano music
Marches (Salon orchestra) *(M1350)*
  BT Salon-orchestra music
Marches (Saxophone and piano) *(M268-9)*
  BT Saxophone and piano music
Marches (String orchestra) *(M1145; M1160)*
  BT String-orchestra music
Marches (Trombone and piano) *(M262-3)*
  BT Trombone and piano music
Marches (Trumpet) *(M85-89)*
  BT Trumpet music
Marches (Trumpet and organ) *(M182-186)*
  BT Trumpet and organ music
Marches (Trumpet and piano) *(M260-261)*
  BT Trumpet and piano music
Marches (Tuba with instrumental ensemble)
  BT Tuba with instrumental ensemble
Marches (Tubas (2))
    (M288-M289)
  BT Tuba music (Tubas (2))
Marches (Ukulele and piano) *(M282-3)*
  BT Ukulele and piano music
Marches (Violin and continuo)
  BT Violin and continuo music
Marches (Violin and harpsichord)
    (M217-218; M221-3)
  BT Violin and harpsichord music
Marches (Violin and piano)
    (M217-M218; M221-M223)
  BT Violin and piano music
Marches (Violins (3)) *(M349-353)*
  BT String trios (Violins (3))
Marches (Voice with piano)
  BT Songs with piano
Marches (Wind ensemble) *(M955-7)*
  BT Wind ensembles
Marching bands *(MT733.4)*
  BT Bands (Music)
      Drill (not military)
Mariachi *(ML3485)*
  BT Bands (Music)
      Folk music—Mexico
Marimba *(ML1040)*
  UF Marimbaphone
  BT Percussion instruments
  RT Vibraphone
      Xylophone
Marimba and clarinet music
  USE Clarinet and marimba music
Marimba and euphonium music
  USE Euphonium and marimba music

Marimba and flute music
  USE Flute and marimba music
Marimba and organ music *(M182-186)*
  UF Organ and marimba music
Marimba and piano music *(M284-5)*
  UF Piano and marimba music
  NT Suites (Marimba and piano)
Marimba and piano music, Arranged
    (M284-5)
  NT Concertos (Marimba)—Solo with piano
      Marimba with orchestra, Arranged—
        Solo with piano
      Suites (Marimba with orchestra)—Solo
        with piano
Marimba and piano with string orchestra
    (M1140-1141)
  RT Concertos (Marimba and piano with
      string orchestra)
Marimba and saxophone music
  USE Saxophone and marimba music
Marimba and trumpet music
  USE Trumpet and marimba music
Marimba music *(M175.X6)*
  SA Concertos, Minuets, Sonatas, Suites,
      *and similar headings with
      specification of instruments;* Trios
      [Quartets, etc.] *followed by
      specifications which include the
      marimba; also* Percussion ensembles,
      Percussion music, *and headings that
      begin with the words marimba or
      marimbas*
  NT Trios (Flute, guitar, marimba)
      Trios (Flute, marimba, vibraphone)
Marimba with band *(M1205-M1206; M1257)*
  RT Concertos (Marimba with band)
Marimba with orchestra *(M1038-9)*
  BT Orchestral music
  RT Concertos (Marimba)
  NT Suites (Marimba with orchestra)
Marimba with orchestra, Arranged
    (M1038-9)
  —Solo with piano *(M1039)*
    BT Marimba and piano music, Arranged
Marimba with string orchestra
    (M1138-1139)
  RT Concertos (Marimba with string
      orchestra)
Marimbaphone
  USE Marimba
Marine trumpet
  USE Sea-trumpet
Martenot (Musical instrument)
  USE Ondes Martenot
Martenot's ondes musicales
  USE Ondes Martenot
Marwari folk-songs
  USE Folk-songs, Marwari
Marwari songs
  USE Songs, Marwari
Mary, Blessed Virgin, Saint *(BT595-680)*
  —Songs and music
    BT Church music

Mary, Blessed Virgin, Saint *(BT595-680)*
—Songs and music
(Continued)
    BT Sacred vocal music
    NT Ave Maria (Music)
        Ave Maris Stella (Music)
        Ave Regina coelorum (Music)
        Regina caeli laetare (Music)
        Salve Regina (Music)
        Stabat Mater dolorosa (Music)
Masques with music *(M1520-M1526)*
  BT Dramatic music
      Masques
—Excerpts, Arranged
—Vocal scores with piano *(M1523)*
Mass (Music) *(ML3088)*
  BT Church music
      Church music—Catholic Church
      Lord's Supper (Liturgy)
  NT Organ mass
Mass media and music *(ML3849)*
  UF Music and mass media
  BT Mass media and the arts
Mass media and the arts [May Subd Geog]
  NT Mass media and music
Masses *(M2010-M2014.5)*
    Here are entered Masses for mixed
      voices and collections of Masses
      for various groups of voices (men's,
      mixed, women's, etc.).
  BT Sacred vocal music
  RT Communion-service music
  NT Agnus Dei (Music)
      Gloria in excelsis Deo (Music)
      Kyrie eleison (Music)
      Propers (Music)
      Requiems
—Juvenile *(M2190)*
  UF Children's masses
—Piano scores *(M33)*
  BT Piano music, Arranged
Example under reference from Arias
Masses, Instrumental
  USE Organ masses
Masses, Organ
  USE Organ masses
Masses, Private
  USE Private masses
Masses, Unaccompanied *(M2011)*
Masses (Children's voices)
Masses (Equal voices)
Masses (Men's voices)
Masses (Unison)
Masses (Women's voices)
Matthäus-Passion (Ballet)
  USE Saint Matthew Passion (Ballet)
Matthäuspassion (Ballet)
  USE Saint Matthew Passion (Ballet)
Maundy Thursday music *(M2048.M35; M2058.M35)*
  BT Holy-Week music
Mazurkas
  BT Dance music
  RT Redowas

Mbira *(ML1015-1018)*
  UF Likembe
  BT Musical instruments—Africa
      Sanza
Mbira music *(ML142.M)*
Measured music *(ML174)*
    The term is here restricted to medieval
      music in mensural notation.
  UF Music, Measured
  BT Music—500-1400
      Musical meter and rhythm
      Musical notation
Mechanical organs *(History, ML1058)*
  UF Automatic organs
  BT Musical instruments (Mechanical)
      Organ
  NT Band organ
      Barrel organ
      Calliope
      Musical clock
Medea (Ballet) *(GV1790.M)*
  BT Ballets
Medieval music
  USE *subdivisions* 500-1400 *and* 15th century
      under music headings
      Music—500-1400
      Music—15th century
Meistersinger *(Literature, PT245; Music, ML183)*
  BT Bards and bardism
      Minstrels
  RT Minnesingers
Mellophone
  USE Alto horn
Melodeon (Button-key accordion) *(Instruction, MT681)*
  BT Button-key accordions
Melodeon (Reed organ)
  USE Reed-organ
Melodic analysis
  UF Analysis, Melodic
      Music—Melodic analysis
  BT Melody
      Musical analysis
Melodic dictation
  USE Musical dictation
Melodica *(ML980)*
  UF Scaletta
Melodrama *(Literature, PN1910-PN1919; Music: aesthetics, ML3861; History, ML2050)*
  BT Music
      Opera
      Operetta
Melody *(Aesthetics, ML3851; History, ML440; Instruction, MT47; Psychology, ML3834)*
  BT Composition (Music)
      Harmony
      Music
      Music—Theory
  NT Melodic analysis
      Raga

Melody flute
  BT Flageolet
     Penny whistle
Melody instrument music
  USE Unspecified instrument *used as part of*
     the specification of medium in
     headings, e.g. Sextets (Unspecified
     instruments (6)); Suites (Piano,
     unspecified instruments (2)); *also,*
     Duets, *with instrumental*
     specification
     Brass instrument music
     Solo instrument music
     String instrument music
     Wind instrument music
     Woodwind instrument music
Melody instruments
  USE *headings for melody instruments, e.g.*
     Flute; Recorder (Musical
     instrument); Violin
Memento Domine David (Music)
  USE Psalms (Music)—132d Psalm
Memorial music
  BT Church music
     Music
     Sacred vocal music
  RT Funeral music
Memory *(Psychology, BF370-BF385;*
     Psychology, Educational, LB1063)
  NT Music—Memorizing
Mendzan
  USE Menzan
Menzan *(ML1040)*
  UF Mendzan
  RT Xylophone
Merchant seamen's songs
  USE Sea songs
Merengue (Dance)
  UF Meringue (Dance)
Merengues
  BT Dance music
Merry-go-round music
  USE Calliope music
Meter
  USE Musical meter and rhythm
Metrometer
  USE Metronome
Metronome *(ML1080)*
  UF Chronometer (Music)
     Metrometer
  BT Tempo (Music)
Microtones
     Here is entered material on musical
        intervals smaller than the semitone.
  UF Quarter-tones
     Third-tones
  BT Microtonic music
     Music—Acoustics and physics
     Tonality
  RT Musical intervals and scales
  NT Bichromatic harmonium

Microtonic music
     This heading is used (1) for discussion of
        music employing microtones, and (2)
        as additional heading for compositions
        employing microtones. Thus a sonata
        composed for a quarter-tone piano is
        entered under two headings: 1. Sona-
        tas (Piano) 2. Microtonic music.
  UF Music, Microtonic
     Music, Quarter-tone
     Quarter-tone music
  BT Music
  NT Microtones
Middle English songs
  USE Songs, Middle English
Middle High German songs
  USE Songs, German (Middle High German)
MIDI (Standard)
  UF Musical Instrument Digital Interface
  BT Analog-to-digital converters—Standards
MIDIM (Computer system)
  BT Music—Data processing
  NT MIDIM7 (Computer program)
MIDIM7 (Computer program)
  BT MIDIM (Computer system)
     Music—Computer programs
Midsummer night's dream (Ballet)
  BT Ballets
Military calls *(M1270; UH40-UH45)*
  UF Calls, Military
     Drum and bugle-calls
  BT Military music
  RT Bugle-calls
     Fanfares
     Trumpet-calls
Military music [May Subd Geog] *(M1270)*
  UF Armies—Music
     Music, Military
  BT Instrumental music
     Music
  RT Band music
  SA *subdivision* Songs and music *under*
     individual wars and names of
     individual military services, e.g.
     World War, 1939-1945—Songs and
     music; United States. Army—Songs
     and music
  NT Bugle-calls
     Fanfares
     Military calls
     Pipe band music
     Trumpet-calls
     War-songs
  —Handbooks, manuals, etc.
     UF Military music—Manuals, text-books,
        etc.
  —History and criticism *(ML1300-1354)*
     RT Music and war
        Music in the army
     NT Bands (Music)
        Instrumentation and orchestration
           (Band)
        March (Music)

Military music [May Subd Geog] *(M1270)*
> *(Continued)*
> —Text-books
>> UF   Military music—Manuals, textbooks,
>>> etc.

Miners [May Subd Geog] *(Labor, HD8039.M6-*
> *HD8039.M7)*
> —Songs and music *(American literature,*
>> *PS595.M5; Music, M1977.M5;*
>> *Musical history, ML3780)*
> BT   Labor and laboring classes—Songs
>> and music

Minimal music [May Subd Geog]
> UF   Meditative music
>> Music, Minimal
>> Repetitive music
>> Systematic music
> BT   Music

Minnesingers *(German literature: collections,*
> *PT1419-PT1426; History, PT217;*
> *Manners and customs, GT3650)*
> BT   Bards and bardism
>> Minstrels
> RT   Meistersinger
>> Troubadours
>> Trouvères

Minshall-Estey organ *(ML597)*
> BT   Electronic organ
> —Methods *(MT192)*

Minstrel shows
> UF   Afro-American minstrel shows
>> Blackfaced minstrel shows
>> Negro minstrel shows
> BT   Afro-Americans in the performing arts
>> Musical revues, comedies, etc.
>> Vaudeville—United States
> RT   Blackface entertainers

Minstrels [May Subd Geog] *(Manners and customs,*
> *GT3650; Musical history,*
> *ML182-183 (Medieval), ML2870*
> *(Modern))*
> UF   Jongleurs
> RT   Bards and bardism
> NT   Charans
>> Meistersinger
>> Minnesingers
>> Troubadours
>> Trouvères
> —Japan
>> NT   Goze

Minuet *(Dancing, GV1796.M5; Musica form:*
> *history, ML3465; Instruction, MT64)*
> RT   Scherzo

Minuets
>> Here are entered collections of minuet
>> music for various mediums. Individual
>> minuets and collections of minuets for
>> a specific medium are entered under
>> the heading followed by specification
>> of medium.
> BT   Dance music

Minuets (Accordion ensemble) *(M1362)*
> BT   Accordion ensembles

Minuets (Band) *(M1249; M1266)*
> BT   Band music

Minuets (Bassoon, flute, guitar) *(M375-9)*
> BT   Trios (Bassoon, flute, guitar)

Minuets (Bassoons (2), clarinets (2), horns
> **(2), oboes (2))** *(M855-9)*

Minuets (Clarinet and piano) *(M248-252)*
> BT   Clarinet and piano music

Minuets (Double bass and piano)
> *(M237-238)*
> BT   Double-bass and piano music

Minuets (Flute and continuo)
> BT   Flute and continuo music

Minuets (Flute and harpsichord) *(M240-244)*
> BT   Flute and harpsichord music

Minuets (Flute and violoncello) *(M290-291)*
> BT   Flute and violoncello music

Minuets (Flutes (2)) *(M288-289)*
> BT   Flute music (Flutes (2))

Minuets (Guitar) *(M125-9)*
> BT   Guitar music

Minuets (Harpsichord) *(M32)*
> BT   Harpsichord music
>> Minuets (Piano)

Minuets (Oboe and continuo)
> BT   Oboe and continuo music

Minuets (Orchestra) *(M1049; M1060)*
> BT   Orchestral music

Minuets (Organ) *(M6-M7; M11-M13)*
> BT   Organ music

Minuets (Piano) *(M32)*
> BT   Piano music
> NT   Minuets (Harpsichord)

Minuets (Piano, 4 hands) *(M204; M211)*
> BT   Piano music (4 hands)

Minuets (Piano trio) *(M310-314)*
> BT   Piano trios

Minuets (Pianos (2)) *(M214-215)*
> BT   Piano music (Pianos (2))

Minuets (Recorder) *(M60-64)*
> BT   Recorder music

Minuets (Recorder and piano) *(M240-244)*
> BT   Recorder and piano music

Minuets (Recorders (2)) *(M288-289)*
> BT   Recorder music (Recorders (2))

Minuets (Recorders (2) with plectral
> **ensemble)** *(M1360)*
> BT   Recorders (2) with plectral ensemble

Minuets (String orchestra) *(M1145; M1160)*
> BT   String-orchestra music

Minuets (String quartet) *(M450-454)*
> BT   String quartets

Minuets (String trio) *(M349-353)*
> BT   String trios

Minuets (Violin and continuo)
> BT   Violin and continuo music

Minuets (Violin and piano) *(M217-M218;*
> *M221-M223)*
> BT   Violin and piano music

Minuets (Violins (2), viola) *(M349-353)*
> BT   String trios (Violins (2), viola)

Minuets (Violins (2), violoncello) *(M349-353)*
> BT   String trios (Violins (2), violoncello)

Minuets (Violins (3)) *(M349-353)*
  BT String trios (Violins (3))
Minuets (Violoncello and piano) *(M229-M230;*
  M233-M236)
  BT Violoncello and piano music
Mirliton
  BT Wind instruments
  NT Kazoo
Miserere mei, Deus, miserere mei (Music)
  USE Psalms (Music)—57th Psalm
Miserere mei, Deus, secundum magnum
    misericordiam (Music)
  USE Psalms (Music)—51st Psalm
Misericordias Domine (Music)
  USE Psalms (Music)—89th Psalm
Missions [May Subd Geog] *(BV2000-BV3705)*
  —Hymns *(BV465.M5)*
  —Music
Mixture stops
  UF Compound stops
    Mixtures (Organ stops)
    Stops, Mixture
  BT Organ stops
Mixtures (Organ stops)
  USE Mixture stops
Mnemonics *(Psychology, BF380-BF385)*
  NT Music—Memorizing
Mock trumpet
  USE Chalumeau (Single-reed musical
      instrument)
Modern Greek songs
  USE Songs, Greek (Modern)
Modes, Musical
  USE Musical intervals and scales
Modulation (Music) *(Music, MT52)*
  BT Harmony
    Music—Instruction and study
    Music—Theory
    Musical accompaniment
Mongolian ballads
  USE Ballads, Mongolian
Mongolian folk-songs
  USE Folk-songs, Mongolian
Mongolian songs
  USE Songs, Mongolian
Monochord *(ML3809)*
  BT Music—Acoustics and physics
    Musical temperament
Monologues with music *(M1625-6)*
      Here, followed by specification of accom-
        panying medium, are entered secular
        musical works in which spoken lan-
        guage is an integral part. The specifica-
        tion (Instrumental ensemble) stands
        for two or more different solo instru-
        ments; (Voice) for a solo voice of high,
        low, or medium range; and (Chorus)
        for men's, mixed, women's, or chil-
        dren's voices in two or more parts. Sa-
        cred works are entered under Sacred
        monologues with music.
      Headings are printed below only if spe-
        cific cross references are needed.

Monologues with music *(M1625-6)*
    (Continued)
  UF Declamation, Musical
    Musical declamation
    Narration with music
    Recitations with music
    Speaking with music
  BT Music
  NT Katarimono
    Rapping (Music)
    Sacred monologues with music
    Sekkyō jōruri
  Note under Monologues; Sacred monologues
    with music
Monologues with music, Sacred
  USE Sacred monologues with music
Monologues with music (Chorus with band)
  BT Choruses with band
Monologues with music (Chorus with chamber
      orchestra)
  BT Choruses with chamber orchestra
  —Vocal scores with piano
Monologues with music (Chorus with
      electronic music) *(M1625)*
  BT Choruses with electronic music
Monologues with music (Chorus with
      instrumental ensemble)
  BT Choruses with instrumental ensemble
Monologues with music (Chorus with
      orchestra)
  BT Choruses with orchestra
  —Scores
Monologues with music (Chorus with piano)
      (M1626)
  BT Choruses with piano
Monologues with music (Chorus with piano,
      4 hands)
  BT Choruses with piano, 4 hands
Monologues with music (Concrete music)
      (M1625)
  BT Concrete music
Monologues with music (Double bass with
      orchestra) *(M1625)*
  BT Double bass with orchestra
Monologues with music (Electronic music)
      (M1625)
  BT Electronic music
Monologues with music (Jazz ensemble with
      chamber orchestra) *(M1625-6)*
  BT Jazz ensemble with chamber orchestra
  —Scores *(M1625)*
Monologues with music (Jazz quintet) *(M1625)*
  BT Jazz quintets
Monologues with music (Orchestra) *(M1625)*
  BT Orchestral music
Monologues with music (Piano) *(M1626)*
  BT Piano music
Monologues with music (Piano, 4 hands) *(M1626)*
  BT Piano music (4 hands)
Monologues with music (Pianos (2) with
      chamber orchestra) *(M1625)*
  BT Piano music (Pianos (2))
    Pianos (2) with chamber orchestra

Monologues with music (Plectral ensemble)
    (M1625)
  BT Plectral ensembles
Monologues with music (Shamisen)
  BT Shamisen music
  NT Jōruri
       Katōbushi
       Naniwabushi
       Shinnai
Monologues with music (Violin with orchestra)
    M1625
  BT Violin with orchestra
Monologues with music (Vocal duet with instrumental ensemble)
    (M1625-1626)
  BT Vocal duets with instrumental ensemble
Monologues with music (Vocal octet with chamber orchestra) *(M1625-6)*
Monologues with music (Vocal quartet with instrumental ensemble)
    (M1625-1626)
  BT Vocal quartets with instrumental ensemble
Monologues with music (Vocal trio with orchestra) *(M1625-6)*
  BT Vocal trios with orchestra
Monologues with music (Voice with instrumental ensemble) *(M1625)*
Morals and music
  USE Music and morals
Moravian ballads and songs [May Subd Geog]
Morin khuur *(ML927.M67)*
  UF Khil-khuur
       Ma t'ou ch'in
  BT Musical instruments—Asia, Central
       Stringed instruments, Bowed
Morning-service music
  BT Sacred vocal music
  NT Lauds (Music)
Morris-dances
  BT Dance music
Motet
    Here are entered works on the motet as a musical form. Musical works composed in the form are entered under Motets.
  BT Choral music
       Church music
       Church music—Catholic Church
       Part-songs
       Part-songs, Sacred
  Example under Musical form
  Note under Motets
Motets
    Here are entered musical works composed in the form of the motet. Works on the motet as a musical form are entered under Motet.
    A second heading for medium is assigned if a specific medium of performance is given in the work.
  BT Part-songs
       Part-songs, Sacred

Motets
  (Continued)
  BT Sacred duets
       Sacred nonets
       Sacred octets
       Sacred quartets
       Sacred quintets
       Sacred septets
       Sacred sextets
       Sacred trios
  NT Anthems
  Notes under Motet; Part-songs; Part-songs, Sacred
Motives, themes
  USE subdivisions Themes, motives under literary or art forms or under names of persons other than literary authors and Themes, motives, Literary under music compositions for general discussions of the themes, etc., occurring or possible in the form or in the person's creative work.
Mount Pilot Festival *(ML37)*
  BT Music festivals—North Carolina
Mountain dulcimer
  USE Appalachian dulcimer
Mouth harmonica
  USE Harmonica
Mouth organ
  USE Harmonica
Mouth organs *(ML1088)*
  BT Musical instruments
  NT Harmonica
       Kaen
       Sheng (Musical instrument)
       Shō
Mouthpieces (Music)
  USE Brass instruments—Mouthpieces
Moving-picture music [May Subd Geog] *(ML2075)*
  UF Film music
       Moving-pictures—Musical accompaniment
  BT Moving-pictures, Musical
       Music
       Musical accompaniment
  RT Silent film music
  —Copyright
    USE Copyright—Moving-picture music
  —Excerpts
  ——Vocal scores with accordion *(M1507-8)*
  ——Vocal scores with piano *(M1507-8)*
    UF Moving-picture music—Vocal scores with piano—Excerpts
  —Piano scores *(M1527)*
    BT Piano music, Arranged
  —Scores *(M1527)*
    UF Moving-pictures—Musical scores
       Moving-pictures, Musical—Scores
  —Vocal scores with piano *(M1507-8)*
  ——Excerpts
    USE Moving-picture music—Excerpts—Vocal scores with piano
Moving picture music, Arranged

Moving-pictures [May Subd Geog] *(PN1992-PN1999)*
  —Musical accompaniment
    USE Moving-picture music
  —Musical scores
    USE Moving-picture music—Scores
Moving-pictures, Musical [May Subd Geog]
    (PN1995.9.M86)
  UF Musical moving-pictures
    Musicals (Motion pictures)
    Operatic moving-pictures
  NT Moving-picture music
    Operas—Film and video adaptations
    Rock films
  —History and criticism
  —Scores
    USE Moving-picture music—Scores
Moving-pictures and music
  UF Music and moving-pictures
  BT Moving-pictures and the arts
Moving-pictures and the arts [May Subd Geog]
    (PN1995.25)
  NT Moving-pictures and music
Mozartiana (Ballet)
  BT Ballets
Mṛdangam
  USE Mṛidanga
Mṛidanga *(ML1035)*
  UF Mṛdangam
  BT Drum
Mṛidanga and vina music
  USE Vina and mṛidanga music
Mṛidanga and violin music
  USE Violin and mṛidanga music
Mṛidanga music *(M146)*
  BT Percussion music
Mulisas
  USE Mulizas
Mulizas
  UF Mulisas
  BT Folk-songs, Spanish—Peru
Mundari folk-songs
  USE Folk-songs, Mundari
Musette
  USE Bagpipe
Museums [May Subd Geog] *(AM)*
  NT Music museums
Museums, Music
  USE Music museums
Music [May Subd Geog]
    For works consisting of music of an in-
      dividual ethnic group, additional sub-
      ject entry is made under the heading
      [ethnic group]—[place]—Music.
  UF Classical music
    Music, Classical
  SA *subdivision* Songs and music *under*
    individual subjects, classes of
    persons, names of individuals,
    institutions, societies, etc., e.g.
    Aeronautics—Songs and music;
    subdivision Music *under individual*
    ethnic groups, e.g. Afro-Americans—
    Music; Navajo Indians—Music; *and*

Music [May Subd Geog]
(Continued)
  SA *headings beginning with the words*
    Music *or* Musical
  NT Advent music
    Arrangement (Music)
    Ascension Day music
    Bands (Music)
    Big band music
    Big bands
    Blind, Music for the
    Carillons
    Chamber music
    Chance compositions
    Chimes
    Choral music
    Christmas music
    Church music
    Composition (Music)
    Computer music
    Concerts
    Concrete music
    Conservatories of music
    Coronation music
    Counterpoint
    Dance music
    Dance orchestras
    Death in music
    Dramatic music
    Easter music
    Electronic music
    Epiphany music
    Feminism and music
    Folk dance music
    Folk music
    Folk-songs
    Funeral music
    Harmony
    Harmony (Aesthetics)
    Hunting music
    Impressionism (Music)
    Improvisation (Music)
    Information theory in music
    Instrumental music
    Instrumentation and orchestration
    Jazz music
    Kindergarten—Music
    Leitmotiv
    Mannerism (Music)
    Melodrama
    Melody
    Memorial music
    Microtonic music
    Military music
    Minimal music
    Monologues with music
    Moving-picture music
    National music
    National socialism and music
    National songs
    New Age music
    Paleography, Musical
    Pantomimes with music

Music [May Subd Geog]
   (*Continued*)
    NT Passion-music
        Pastoral music (Secular)
        Patriotic music
        Peru in music
        Popular music
        Program music
        Radio music
        Realism in music
        Romanticism in music
        Sacred monologues with music
        School music
        Singing
        Solmization
        Songs
        Sound
        Street music and musicians
        Symbolism in music
        Symphony orchestras
        Television music
        Titles of musical compositions
        Tragedy in music
        Transposition (Music)
        Vibrato
        Virtuosity in music
        Vocal music
        Voice
        Wedding music
   —To 500
      UF Ancient music
          Music, Ancient
      SA *subdivision* To 500 *under music*
          headings
      NT Music, Greek and Roman
          Music in the Bible
   — —Theory
      USE Music—Theory—To 500
   —500-1400
      UF Medieval music
          Music, Medieval
      SA *subdivision* 500-1400 *under music*
          headings
      NT Chants (Plain, Gregorian, etc.)
          Measured music
          Organum
          Tonus peregrinus
   — —Theory
      USE Music—Theory—500-1400
   —15th century
      UF Medieval music
          Music, Medieval
          Music, Renaissance
          Renaissance music
      SA *subdivision* 15th century *under*
          music headings
   — —Theory
      USE Music—Theory—15th century
   —16th century
      UF Music, Renaissance
          Renaissance music
      SA *subdivision* 16th century *under*
          music headings

Music [May Subd Geog]
   (*Continued*)
   —16th century
   — —Theory
      USE Music—Theory—16th century
   —17th century
      UF Baroque music
          Music, Baroque
          Music, Renaissance
          Renaissance music
      SA *subdivision* 17th century *under*
          music headings
   — —Theory
      USE Music—Theory—17th century
   —18th century
      UF Baroque music
          Classical period music
          Music, Baroque
          Music, Classical period
      SA *subdivision* 18th century *under*
          music headings
   — —Theory
      USE Music—Theory—18th century
   —19th century
      UF Classical period music
          Music, Classical period
          Music, Romantic period
          Romantic period music
      SA *subdivision* 19th century *under*
          music headings
   — —Theory
      USE Music—Theory—19th century
   —20th century
      SA *subdivision* 20th century *under*
          music headings
      NT Neoclassicism (Music)
   — —Theory
      USE Music—Theory—20th century

GENERAL SUBDIVISIONS

   —Acoustics and physics (*ML3805-3817*)
      UF Acoustics
      BT Music—Theory
      RT Sound
      NT Harmonics (Music)
          Microtones
          Monochord
          Musical intervals and scales
          Musical temperament
          Tone color (Music)
   —Aesthetics
      USE Music—Philosophy and aesthetics
   —Almanacs, yearbooks, etc. (*ML13-21*)
      UF Music—Yearbooks
      RT Music—Chronology
      NT Music calendars
   —Analysis, appreciation
      USE Music appreciation
          Musical analysis
   —Analytical guides
      USE Music appreciation
          Musical analysis

Music [May Subd Geog]
(Continued)
—Anecdotes, facetiae, satire, etc. *(ML65)*
 UF Anecdotes, Musical
   Musicians—Anecdotes, facetiae,
    satire, etc.
—Appreciation
 USE Music appreciation
—Bibliography *(ML111-158)*
 NT International inventory of musical
   sources
   Music—First performances
— —Catalogs, Microfilm
— —Catalogs, Publishers' [May Subd Geog]
   (ML145)
 NT Music printing—Plate numbers
— —Graded lists
 UF Music—Graded lists
—Bio-bibliography *(Dictionaries,*
   ML105-ML107; History and criticism,
   ML385-ML429)
 UF Composers—Dictionaries
   Music—Biography
   Musicians—Dictionaries
 BT Musicians
  Example under Biography
—Biography
 USE Flute-players, Organists, Pianists,
   and similar headings
   Composers
   Conductors (Music)
   Flute-players
   Music—Bio-bibliography
   Music teachers
   Musicians
   Organists
   Pianists
   Singers
—Cataloging
 USE Cataloging of music
—Chinese influences
 BT China—Civilization
—Chronology *(ML161)*
 BT Music—History and criticism
 RT Music—Almanacs, yearbooks, etc.
 NT Music printing—Plate numbers
—Classification
 USE Classification—Music
—Competitions *(ML76)*
 BT Music—Examinations, questions, etc.
   Music festivals
—Composition
 USE Composition (Music)
—Computer programs
 NT DESC7 (Computer program)
   MIDIM7 (Computer program)
   Music Major (Computer program)
   PR1XM (Computer program)
—Conservatories
 USE Conservatories of music
—Copyright
 USE Copyright—Music

Music [May Subd Geog]
(Continued)
—Data processing
 NT MIDIM (Computer system)
—Dictionaries *(ML100-110)*
 SA *subdivision* Dictionaries *under*
   various headings, e.g. Chamber
   music—Dictionaries; Opera—
   Dictionaries
 NT Music—Terminology
—Dictionaries, Juvenile
—Discography *(ML156)*
—Dynamics, phrasing
 USE Music—Interpretation (Phrasing,
   dynamics, etc.)
—Economic aspects [May Subd Geog]
—Editing *(ML63)*
 BT Musicology
—Elementary theory
 USE Music—Theory, Elementary
—Endowments
—Examinations, questions, etc. *(MT9)*
 NT Music—Competitions
   Musical ability—Testing
—Exhibitions *(Catalogs, ML141;*
   Instruments, ML462)
 BT Music museums
 NT Music—Manuscripts—Exhibitions
   Musical instruments—Catalogs and
    collections
   Musical instruments—Exhibitions
—First performances [May Subd Geog]
 UF First performances of musical works
   Music—Premiere performances
   Premiere performances of musical works
 BT Music—Bibliography
 SA *subdivision* First performances *under*
   headings for music compositions,
   e.g. Operas—First performances
—Graded lists
 USE Music—Bibliography—Graded
   lists
—Handbooks, manuals, etc.
 UF Music—Manuals, text-books, etc.
—Harmonic analysis
 USE Harmonic analysis (Music)
—Historiography *(ML)*
 UF Music—History and criticism—
   Methods
   Music—History and criticism—
   Theory, etc.
 RT Musicology
 NT Musical criticism
—History and criticism *(ML159-3795)*
 SA *headings of the type* Music—[period
   subdivision]—History and
   criticism; Songs—[period
   subdivision]—History and
   criticism
 NT Music—Chronology
   Music—Performance—History
   Music, Origin of
  Note under Criticism

Music [May Subd Geog]
  —History and criticism *(ML159-3795)*
  (Continued)
  — —Methods
    USE Music—Historiography
      Musical criticism
  — —Outlines, syllabi, etc.
    UF Music—Outlines, syllabi, etc.
  — —Theory, etc.
    USE Music—Historiography
      Musical criticism
  —Iconography
    USE Music in art
  —Incunabula
    USE Incunabula—Music
  —Indians
    USE Indians—Music
  —Instruction and study [May Subd Geog] *(MT)*
    UF Education, Musical
      Music—Study and teaching
      Music education
      Musical education
      Musical instruction
    SA *subdivision* Instruction and study
      under names of musical
      instruments, e.g. Piano—
      Instruction and study
    NT Chromatic alteration (Music)
      Composition (Music)
      Conducting
      Conservatories of music
      Counterpoint
      Ear training
      Embellishment (Music)
      Embellishment (Vocal music)
      Galin-Paris-Chevé method (Music)
      Harmony
      Instrumental music—Instruction and
        study
      Instrumentation and orchestration
      Kindergarten—Music
      Modulation (Music)
      Music—Interpretation (Phrasing,
        dynamics, etc.)
      Music—Manuals, text-books, etc.
      Music—Memorizing
      Music—Teacher training
      Music appreciation
      Music in universities and colleges
      Music teachers
      Musical accompaniment
      Musical form
      Sight-reading (Music)
      Singing—Instruction and study
      Tempo (Music)
      Thorough bass
      Transposition (Music)
      Virtuosity in music
    Example under Teaching; *and under*
    reference from Instruction
  — —Juvenile
    BT Music—Juvenile literature
    NT Handicapped children—Education
      —Music

Music [May Subd Geog]
  (Continued)

GEOGRAPHIC SUBDIVISIONS

  — —France
    NT Maîtrises
  —Interpretation (Phrasing, dynamics, etc.)
    UF Dynamics (Music)
      Interpretation, Musical
      Music—Dynamics, phrasing
      Music—Phrasing, dynamics
      Musical interpretation
      Phrasing (Music)
    BT Music—Instruction and study
      Music—Performance
  —Inventions and patents
    USE Musical inventions and patents
  —Juvenile
    UF Children's music
      Juvenile music
      Music, Children's
      Music, Juvenile
      subdivision Juvenile *under headings*
      for music compositions for works
      to be performed by children, e.g.
      Operas—Juvenile
    NT Children's songs
  —Juvenile literature *(ML3930)*
    NT Music—Instruction and study—
      Juvenile
      Musical instruments—Juvenile
      literature
  —Kindergarten
    USE Kindergarten—Music
  —Manuscripts [May Subd Geog] *(ML93-98)*
    UF Manuscripts, Musical
    BT Manuscripts
    RT Paleography, Musical
    SA *subdivision* Manuscripts *under*
      names of composers, e.g. Wagner,
      Richard, 1813-1883—Manuscripts
  — —Exhibitions
    BT Manuscripts—Exhibitions
      Music—Exhibitions
  —Melodic analysis
    USE Melodic analysis
  —Memorizing *(MT82)*
    BT Memory
      Mnemonics
      Music—Instruction and study
  Example under Memory
  —Modes
    USE Musical intervals and scales
  —Museums
    USE Music museums
  —Notation
    USE Musical notation
  —Nursery schools
    USE Nursery schools—Music
  —Outlines, syllabi, etc.
    USE Music—History and criticism—
      Outlines, syllabi, etc.

Music [May Subd Geog]
   (Continued)
   —Performance *(ML457)*
      UF Musical performance
      BT Embellishment (Music)
          Embellishment (Vocal music)
      RT Concerts
          Conducting
      NT Improvisation (Music)
          Music—Interpretation (Phrasing,
              dynamics, etc.)
          Notes inégales
          Piano—Performance
          Rehearsals (Music)
          Singing
          Tonguing (Wind instrument playing)
          Violin—Performance
          Virtuosity in music
   — —History
      BT Music—History and criticism
   —Philosophy and aesthetics
      (ML3800-3920)
      UF Music—Aesthetics
      BT Aesthetics
          Music—Theory
      NT Classicism in music
          Harmony (Aesthetics)
          Impressionism (Music)
          Music and architecture
          Realism in music
          Romanticism in music
          Style, Musical
          Symbolism in music
   —Phrasing, dynamics
      USE Music—Interpretation (Phrasing,
            dynamics, etc.)
   —Physiological aspects *(ML3820-3822)*
      UF Physiological aspects of music
      BT Senses and sensation
      NT Amusia
          Music—Physiological effect
          Music, Influence of
          Music therapy
          Vocal registers
          Voice
   —Physiological effect *(ML3920)*
   UF Music, Effect of
      Music, Physical effect of
      Music, Physiological effect of
   BT Music—Physiological aspects
      Music, Influence of
   NT Music therapy
      Plants, Effect of music on
   —Plagiarism
      USE Plagiarism in music
   —Poetry
      UF Musicians—Poetry
      BT Music and literature
      NT Music—Quotations, maxims, etc.
   Example under Poetry
   —Premiere performances
      USE Music—First performances

Music [May Subd Geog]
   (Continued)
   —Proofreading
      USE Proofreading—Music
   —Psychology *(ML3830-3838)*
      NT Amusia
          Music and color
          Music therapy
          Musical ability—Testing
          Symbolism in music
   —Publishing [May Subd Geog] *(ML112-ML112.5)*
      UF Music publishing
      BT Publishers and publishing
      NT Popular music—Writing and publishing
   Example under Publishers and publishing
   —Quotations, maxims, etc. *(ML66)*
      BT Music—Poetry
          Music and literature
   Example under Aphorisms and apothegms;
      Maxims; Proverbs; Quotations
   —Reading
      USE Score reading and playing
          Sight-reading (Music)
   —Religious aspects
      UF Religion and music
   — —Baptists [Catholic Church, etc.]
   — —Buddhism
      UF Buddhism and music
      NT Music, Buddhist
   — —Buddhism [Christianity, etc.]
   — —Christianity
      NT Church music
          Music in churches
   — —Islam
      UF Islam and music
      NT Music, Islamic
   — —Judaism
      NT Music in synagogues
          Synagogue music
   —Rudiments
      USE Music—Theory, Elementary
   —Sketches
      USE Musical sketches
   —Societies, etc. *(ML25-28)*
      UF Clubs, Musical
          Music clubs
          Music societies
          Musical clubs
          Musical societies
      NT Choral societies
          Church music—Societies, etc.
   —Study and teaching
      USE Music—Instruction and study
   —Sunday-schools
      USE Sunday-schools—Hymns
   —Teacher training [May Subd Geog]
      UF Music teachers, Training of
      BT Music—Instruction and study
   —Terminology *(ML108)*
      BT Music—Dictionaries
      NT English language—Conversation and
          phrase books (for musicians,
          musicologists, etc.)

Music [May Subd Geog]
  (Continued)
  —Text-books
      Here are entered works discussing music
      textbooks. Individual music textbooks are
      entered under the specific subject, e.g.
      Music—Theory.
    UF Music—Manuals, text-books, etc.
    BT Music—Instruction and study
  —Thematic catalogs
    UF Thematic catalogs (Music)
    SA *subdivision* Thematic catalogs *under*
        names of individual composers
        and under special musical forms,
        e.g. Symphonies—Thematic
        catalogs
  —Theory
    UF Music theory
        Theory of music
    NT Chants (Plain, Gregorian, etc.)—
        Instruction and study
        Chromatic alteration (Music)
        Composition (Music)
        Counterpoint
        Harmonic analysis (Music)
        Harmony
        Instrumentation and orchestration
        Melody
        Modulation (Music)
        Music—Acoustics and physics
        Music—Philosophy and aesthetics
        Musical analysis
        Musical form
        Musical intervals and scales
        Musical meter and rhythm
        Musical temperament
        Schenkerian analysis
        Thorough bass
        Transposition (Music)
        Twelve-tone system
  — —To 500
    UF Music—To 500—Theory
  — —500-1400
    UF Music—500-1400—Theory
  — —15th century
    UF Music—15th century—Theory
  — —16th century
    UF Music—16th century—Theory
  — —17th century
    UF Music—17th century—Theory
  — —18th century
    UF Music—18th century—Theory
  — —19th century
    UF Music—19th century—Theory
  — —20th century
    UF Music—20th century—Theory
  Note under Music—Text-books

GENERAL SUBDIVISIONS

  — —Computer-assisted instruction
    NT Music Major (Computer program)

Music [May Subd Geog]
  (Continued)
  —Theory, Elementary *(MT7)*
    UF Music—Elementary theory
        Music—Rudiments
  —Therapeutic use
    USE Music therapy
  — —Yearbooks
    USE Music—Almanacs, yearbooks, etc.

GEOGRAPHIC SUBDIVISIONS

  —Egypt
    NT Sistrum
  —Flanders
    BT Music—France
  —France
    NT Music—Flanders
  —India
    NT Music, Hindustani
        Music, Karnatic
        Raga
        Vedas—Recitation
  —Japan
    NT Gagaku
        Kabuki music
        Katarimono
        Nō music
        Shigin
  —Latin America
  —Scotland
    NT Bagpipe
        Pibroch
        Pibrochs
  —United States
    NT Music Week
  —Wales
    NT Pennillion singing
Music, Aleatory
  USE Chance composition
        Chance compositions
Music, Ancient
  USE *subdivision* To 500 *under music*
        headings
        Music—To 500
Music, Baroque
  USE *subdivisions* 17th century *and* 18th
        century *under music headings*
        Music—17th century
        Music—18th century
Music, Buddhist [May Subd Geog]
  UF Buddhist music
      Buddhists—Music
  BT Music—Religious aspects—Buddhism
  NT Chants (Buddhist)
Music, Byzantine
  UF Byzantine music
  BT Music, Greek and Roman
Music, Chance
  USE Chance composition
        Chance compositions
Music, Children's
  USE Music—Juvenile

Music, Chiming clock
　USE　Chiming clock music
Music, Choral
　USE　Choral music
Music, Classical
　USE　Music
Music, Classical period
　USE　*subdivisions* 18th century *and* 19th
　　　　century *under music headings*
　　　　Music—18th century
　　　　Music—19th century
Music, Community
　USE　Community music
Music, Computer
　USE　Computer music
Music, Concrete
　USE　Concrete music
Music, Disco
　USE　Disco music
Music, Dixieland
　USE　Dixieland music
Music, Dramatic
　USE　Dramatic music
Music, Effect of
　USE　Music—Physiological effect
　　　　Music, Influence of
　　　　Music and morals
　　　　Music therapy
Music, Electronic
　USE　Electronic music
Music, Gospel
　USE　Gospel music
Music, Greek (Ancient)
　USE　Music, Greek and Roman
Music, Greek and Roman
　UF　Greek music
　　　　Music, Greek (Ancient)
　　　　Music, Roman
　　　　Roman music
　BT　Music—To 500
　NT　Greek drama—Incidental music
　　　　Hymns to Apollo
　　　　Music, Byzantine
Music, Hebrew
　USE　Jews—Music
Music, Hindustani *(M1808-9)*
　　　　Here is entered vocal or instrumental
　　　　　music of the Hindustani system, native
　　　　　to northern India, as differentiated from
　　　　　the Karnatic system, native to southern
　　　　　India.
　UF　Hindustani music
　BT　Music—India
　NT　Khyāl (Musical form)
Music, Imitation in
　USE　Imitation (in music)
Music, Impressionism in
　USE　Impressionism (Music)
Music, Inca
　USE　Incas—Music
Music, Incidental *(Aesthetics, ML3860;*
　　　　History, ML2000)
　UF　Incidental music

Music, Incidental *(Aesthetics, ML3860;*
　　　　History, ML2000)
　(Continued)
　BT　Dramatic music
　　　　Music in theaters
　NT　Entr'acte music
　　　　Greek drama—Incidental music
　　　　Overture
　　　　Pageants
　　　　Radio plays with music
　—Excerpts
　— —Vocal scores with piano *(M1518)*
　　　　UF　Music, Incidental—Vocal scores
　　　　　　with piano—Excerpts
　—Excerpts, Arranged
　—Piano scores *(M1513)*
　—Vocal scores with piano *(M1513)*
　— —Excerpts
　　　　USE　Music, Incidental—Excerpts—
　　　　　　Vocal scores with piano
Music, Influence of *(ML3920)*
　UF　Music, Effect of
　BT　Music—Physiological aspects
　NT　Music—Physiological effect
　　　　Music and morals
　　　　Music in the army
　　　　Music therapy
Music, Instrumental
　USE　Instrumental music
Music, Islamic [May Subd Geog]
　UF　Music, Muslim
　　　　Muslim music
　　　　Muslims—Music
　BT　Music—Religious aspects—Islam
Music, Jewish
　USE　Jews—Music
Music, Juvenile
　USE　Music—Juvenile
Music, Karnatic [May Subd Geog] *(M1808-1809)*
　　　　Here is entered vocal or instrumental
　　　　　music of the Karnatic system, native
　　　　　to southern India, as differentiated from
　　　　　the Hindustani system, native to northern
　　　　　India.
　UF　Carnatic music
　　　　Karnatic music
　BT　Music—India
　—Theory
Music, Magical use of
　USE　Music and magic
Music, Measured
　USE　Measured music
Music, Medieval
　USE　*subdivisions* 500-1400 *and* 15th century
　　　　under music headings
　　　　Music—500-1400
　　　　Music—15th century
Music, Microtonic
　USE　Microtonic music
Music, Military
　USE　Military music
Music, Minimal
　USE　Minimal music

Music, Muslim
  USE Music, Islamic
Music, National
  USE National music
Music, Origin of *(ML3800)*
  BT Music—History and criticism
Music, Passover
  USE Passover music
Music, Pastoral
  USE Pastoral music
Music, Patriotic
  USE Patriotic music
Music, Physical effect of
  USE Music—Physiological effect
        Music therapy
Music, Physiological effect of
  USE Music—Physiological effect
Music, Plagiarism in
  USE Plagiarism in music
Music, Popular
  USE Popular music
Music, Popular (Songs, etc.)
  USE Popular music
  —Japan
      NT Enka
Music, Printing of
  USE Music printing
Music, Quarter-tone
  USE Microtonic music
Music, Religious
  USE Church music
        Synagogue music
Music, Renaissance
  USE *subdivisions* 15th century, 16th century,
        and 17th century *under music headings*
        Music—15th century
        Music—16th century
        Music—17th century
Music, Rhythm and blues
  USE Rhythm and blues music
Music, Roman
  USE Music, Greek and Roman
Music, Romantic period
  USE *subdivision* 19th century *under music*
        headings
        Music—19th century
Music, Sacred
  USE Church music
        Synagogue music
Music, Soul
  USE Soul music
Music, Sufi [May Subd Geog]
  UF Sufi music
Music, Theatrical
  USE Dramatic music
Music, Turkmen [May Subd Geog]
  UF Turkmen music
Music, Vocal
  USE Vocal music
Music analysis
  USE Musical analysis

Music and architecture *(ML3849)*
  UF Architecture and music
  BT Aesthetics
        Music—Philosophy and aesthetics
        Musical form
Music and art
  USE Art and music
Music and color *(ML3840)*
  UF Color and music
        Color-music
        Music of colors
  BT Music—Psychology
        Wave-motion, Theory of
Music and communism
  USE Communism and music
Music and erotica
  BT Erotica
  NT Erotic songs
Music and industry
  USE Music in industry
Music and language *(ML3849)*
  UF Language and music
  BT Language and languages
  RT Music and literature
        Musical accentuation
Music and literature *(ML80; ML3849)*
  UF Literature and music
        Music and poetry
        Poetry and music
  BT Literature
  RT Music and language
        Musicians in literature
  NT Music—Poetry
        Music—Quotations, maxims, etc.
        Musical fiction
        Musicians as authors
Music and magic
  UF Magic and music
        Music, Magical use of
Music and mass media
  USE Mass media and music
Music and morals *(ML3920)*
  UF Morals and music
        Music, Effect of
  BT Music, Influence of
Music and moving-pictures
  USE Moving-pictures and music
Music and mythology *(ML80; ML3849)*
  UF Mythology and music
Music and poetry
  USE Music and literature
Music and race
  UF Race and music
  BT Nationalism in music
Music and radio
  USE Radio and music
Music and romanticism
  USE Romanticism in music
Music and society
  UF Society and music
        Sociology and music
  NT Music and morals
        Music and state

Music and state [May Subd Geog] *(ML3795)*
    UF State and music
    BT Music and society
    NT Musicians—Legal status, laws, etc.
Music and television
    USE Television and music
Music and war
    UF War and music
    RT Military music—History and criticism
        Music in the army
    SA *subdivisions* Music and the war, Music
        and the revolution, *etc. and* Songs
        and music *under individual wars, e.g.*
        World War, 1939-1945—Music and
        the war; World War, 1939-1945—
        Songs and music
Music and youth [May Subd Geog]
    UF Youth and music
    BT Youth
Music appreciation
    UF Analytical guides (Music)
        Appreciation of music
        Music—Analysis, appreciation
        Music—Analytical guides
        Music—Appreciation
        Musical appreciation
    BT Music—Instruction and study
    RT Musical analysis
    SA *subdivision* Analysis, appreciation *under*
        headings for music compositions
    —Music collections *(MT6.5)*
Music archaeology [May Subd Geog]
    UF Archaeology, Music
        Archeomusicology
        Archeo-musicology
    BT Archaeology
        Musicology
Music as recreation
    BT Community music
        Music in the home
    NT Musical recreations
Music audiences [May Subd Geog]
    BT Performing arts—Audiences
    NT Jazz audiences
Music box *(ML1066)*
    UF Musical box
    BT Musical instruments (Mechanical)
Music box books
    USE Musical books
Music box music *(M174.M85)*
Music calendars *(ML13-21)*
    BT Music—Almanacs, yearbooks, etc.
Music chapels
    USE Chapels (Music)
Music clubs
    USE Music—Societies, etc.
Music conductors
    USE Conductors (Music)
Music conservatories
    USE Conservatories of music
Music critics [May Subd Geog]
    BT Musical criticism

Music education
    USE Music—Instruction and study
Music festivals [May Subd Geog] *(ML35-38)*
    UF Musical festivals
    BT Art festivals
        Festivals
        Performing arts festivals
    RT Concerts
    NT Hymn festivals
        Jazz festivals
        Music—Competitions
        Music Week
        Saint Cecilia's Day
    —Canada
        NT Latvian Song Festival
    —Germany (West)
        NT Ostdeutsche Musiktage
    —Indiana
        NT Battle Ground Fiddlers' Gathering,
            Battle Ground, Ind.
    —New York (State)
        NT Eastman School Festival of
            American Music
    —North Carolina
        NT Mount Pilot Festival
    —United States
        NT Latvian Song Festival
Music for meditation
    UF Meditation music
Music for playgrounds
    USE Playground music
Music for silent films
    USE Silent film music
Music for the blind
    USE Blind, Music for the
Music for the visually handicapped
    BT Visually handicapped
    NT Blind, Music for the
Music-halls [May Subd Geog] *(Architecture,*
    NA6820-6840)
    UF Concert halls
    RT Theaters
    —Scotland
        NT Saint Cecilia's Hall (Edinburgh, Lothian)
    —Switzerland
        NT Casino (Bern, Switzerland)
Music-halls (Variety-theaters, cabarets, etc.)
    [May Subd Geog] *(PN1960-1969)*
    UF Cabarets
        Night clubs
        Nightclubs
        Variety shows (Theater)
        Variety-theaters
    RT Vaudeville
    NT Discotheques
        Strip-tease
    —Law and legislation [May Subd Geog]

    GEOGRAPHIC SUBDIVISIONS

    —England
        NT Penny theaters
    —Japan
        NT Yose

Music in advertising
  NT Singing commercials
Music in armies
  USE Music in the army
Music in art *(ML85; N8226)*
      Here are entered works dealing with the
        representation of musical subjects in art.
  UF Music—Iconography
      Musical iconography
  BT Art
  RT Art and music
  NT Musical instruments in art
      Rāgamālā painting
Music in book-plates [May Subd Geog]
      (Z994.5.M87)
Music in Christian education
  BT Church music
      Music in religious education
Music in churches *(ML3001)*
      Here are entered discussions as to the
        desirability, etc. of having music in the
        church.
  BT Music—Religious aspects—Christianity
  RT Church music
      Psalmody
  NT Music in synagogues
Music in education
Music in industry
  UF Industry and music
      Music and industry
Music in monasteries [May Subd Geog]
  BT Church music
      Monasteries
Music in physical education *(ML3923)*
  UF Physical education and music
  BT Physical education and training
Music in prisons *(ML3920)*
  UF Prisons, Music in
  BT Prisons
Music in religious education
  BT Religious education
  NT Music in Christian education
Music in synagogues *(M3195)*
  BT Jews—Music
      Music—Religious aspects—Judaism
      Music in churches
Music in the army *(Military science, UH40-UH45)*
  UF Armies—Music
      Music in armies
  BT Community music
      Music, Influence of
  RT Military music—History and criticism
      Music and war
      War-songs
Music in the Bible *(ML166)*
      Here are entered works on music and
        musical instruments in the Bible.
  UF Bible—Music
      Bible—Musical instruments
      Bible. O.T. Psalms—Music
      Musical instruments in the Bible
  BT Jews—Music
      Music—To 500

Music in the home *(ML67)*
  BT Chamber music—History and criticism
  NT Music as recreation
Music in theaters
      Here are entered works on music as an
        adjunct to theatrical productions.
  BT Dramatic music
      Theater
  NT Music, Incidental
Music in universities and colleges [May Subd Geog]
      (ML63; Instruction, MT18)
  BT Music—Instruction and study
      Universities and colleges
  RT Students' songs
  SA *subdivision* Songs and music *under*
      names of universities and colleges,
      e.g. Harvard University—Songs and
      music
Music librarianship *(ML111)*
  NT Cataloging of music
      Classification—Music
      Subject headings—Music
Music libraries [May Subd Geog] *(Catalogs,*
      ML136-ML139; Forming of libraries,
      ML111)
  UF Libraries, Music
  BT Libraries, Special
  NT Sound recording libraries
  —Shelving
      USE Shelving (for music)
  Example under Libraries, Special
Music Major (Computer program)
  BT Computer programs
      Music—Computer programs
      Music—Theory—Computer-assisted
        instruction
Music museums [May Subd Geog] *(Instruments,*
      ML462; Libraries, exhibitions,
      ML136-ML141)
  UF Museums, Music
      Music—Museums
  BT Museums
  NT Music—Exhibitions
      Musical instruments—Catalogs and collections
      Theater—Museums and collections
Music of colors
  USE Music and color
Music of the spheres
Music plate numbers
  USE Music printing—Plate numbers
Music printing [May Subd Geog]
      (ML112-ML112.5)
  UF Music, Printing of
      Type and type-founding—Music-type
  BT Printing
  NT Music title-pages
  —Law and legislation [May Subd Geog]
  —Plate numbers
      UF Music plate numbers
          Plate numbers, Music
      BT Music—Bibliography—Catalogs,
            Publishers'
          Music—Chronology

Music publishers [May Subd Geog]
    BT Publishers and publishing
Music publishing
    USE Music—Publishing
Music reading
    USE Score reading and playing
         Sight-reading (Music)
Music-recorders *(ML1090)*
    UF Melograph
         Pianograph
    BT Musical instruments (Mechanical)
         Piano
Music Room from Norfolk House (Interior
        decoration)
    USE Brettingham, Matthew, 1699-1769.
         Norfolk House Music Room
Music rooms and equipment
    UF Rooms, Music
Music schools
    USE Conservatories of music
Music societies
    USE Music—Societies, etc.
Music supervision in schools
    USE School music supervision
Music teachers [May Subd Geog] *(ML3795)*
    UF Music—Biography
    BT Music—Instruction and study
         Musicians
         Teachers
Music teachers, Training of
    USE Music—Teacher training
Music theory
    USE Music—Theory
Music therapy [May Subd Geog] *(ML3919-ML3920)*
    UF Music—Therapeutic use
         Music, Effect of
         Music, Physical effect of
         Musical therapy
    BT Music—Physiological aspects
         Music—Physiological effect
         Music—Psychology
         Music, Influence of
         Occupational therapy
         Recreational therapy
         Therapeutics, Physiological
    NT Musical instruments for the handicapped
         Tarantella
Music therapy for the aged [May Subd Geog]
    ML3919-ML3920)
    UF Geriatric music therapy
    BT Music therapy
Music title-pages [May Subd Geog]
    UF Sheet-music covers
    BT Music printing
         Title-page
Music trade [May Subd Geog]
    ML3790
    NT Musical instruments—Catalogs, Manufacturers'
    —Credit guides
Music video direction
    USE Music videos—Production and direction
Music video production
    USE Music videos—Production and direction

Music videos [May Subd Geog] *(PN1992.8.M87)*
    UF Videos, Music
    BT Television programs
         Video recordings
    RT Television music
    NT Rock videos
  —Direction
    USE Music videos—Production and direction
  —Production and direction
    UF Music video direction
         Music video production
         Music videos—Direction
Music Week *(ML200.5)*
    UF National Music Week
    BT Music—United States
         Music festivals
    RT Community music
Musica ficta
    USE Chromatic alteration (Music)
Música norteña
    USE Popular music—Mexico
         Popular music—Texas
Musical ability
    UF Ability, Musical
         Musical talent
  —Testing
    BT Music—Examinations, questions, etc.
         Music—Psychology
Musical accentuation
    UF Accentuation (Music)
         Declamation, Musical
         Musical declamation
    RT Music and language
         Singing—Diction
Musical accompaniment *(Instruction, MT68;*
    Organ, MT190; Piano, MT239)
    UF Accompaniment, Musical
    BT Composition (Music)
         Music—Instruction and study
         Piano—Instruction and study
    NT Chants (Plain, Gregorian, etc.)—
         Accompaniment
         Folk-songs—Accompaniment
         Hymns—Accompaniment
         Modulation (Music)
         Moving-picture music
         Songs—Accompaniment
         Thorough bass
         Transposition (Music)
Musical analysis
    UF Analysis, Musical
         Analytical guides (Music)
         Music—Analysis, appreciation
         Music—Analytical guides
         Music analysis
    BT Music—Theory
    RT Music appreciation
    SA *subdivision* Analysis, appreciation *under*
        headings for music compositions
    NT Harmonic analysis (Music)
         Melodic analysis
         Schenkerian analysis
  —Music collections *(MT6.5)*

Musical appreciation
  USE Music appreciation
Musical books [May Subd Geog]
  UF Melody books
      Music box books
  BT Books
Musical box
  USE Music box
Musical card games *(M1985)*
  BT Games with music
      Musical recreations
Musical clock *(History, ML1067)*
      Here are entered works about clocks
          equipped with mechanical organs.
          Works about clocks equipped with
          carillons or other chiming mechanisms
          are entered under the heading
          Chiming clocks.
  UF Clock, Musical
      Flötenuhr
      Flötenwerk
      Flute clock
      Flute-playing clock
      Laufwerk
      Spieluhr
  BT Mechanical organs
  Note under Chiming clocks
Musical clock music *(M174.M)*
Musical clubs
  USE Music—Societies, etc.
Musical comedies
  USE Musical revues, comedies, etc.
Musical comedy
  USE Musical revue, comedy, etc.
Musical composition
  USE Composition (Music)
Musical compositions, Titles of
  USE Titles of musical compositions
Musical criticism [May Subd Geog] *(ML3880-3916)*
  UF Music—History and criticism—
          Methods
      Music—History and criticism—Theory,
          etc.
  BT Music—Historiography
      Musicology
  NT Music critics
      Newspapers—Sections, columns, etc.—
          Reviews
Musical declamation
  USE Monologues with music
      Musical accentuation
      Singing—Diction
Musical dictation *(MT35)*
  UF Dictation, Musical
      Harmonic dictation
      Melodic dictation
  RT Ear training
Musical education
  USE Music—Instruction and study
Musical ensembles
  USE Musical groups

Musical extravaganza
  USE Musical revue, comedy, etc.
Musical farce
  USE Musical revue, comedy, etc.
Musical festivals
  USE Music festivals
Musical fiction
  UF Musical novels
  BT Music and literature
  NT Musicians in literature
      Wagner, Richard, 1813-1883, in fiction,
          drama, poetry, etc.
Musical form *(History, ML448; Instruction,*
          MT58-MT64)
  UF Form, Musical
  BT Composition (Music)
      Music—Instruction and study
      Music—Theory
  SA *names of particular musical forms, e.g.*
          Fugue; Motet; Opera; Sonata
  NT Cadence (Music)
      Coda (Music)
      Music and architecture
      Parody (Music)
      Scherzo
Musical glasses
  USE Glass harmonica
Musical groups [May Subd Geog]
  UF Ensembles, Musical
      Groups, Musical
      Musical ensembles
  NT Bands (Music)
      Brass bands
      Chamber music groups
      Chamber orchestra
      Choirs (Music)
      Choral societies
      Country music groups
      Dance orchestras
      Folk music groups
      Rock groups
      Symphony orchestras
Musical iconography
  USE Music in art
Musical instruction
  USE Music—Instruction and study
Musical instrument collections
  USE Musical instruments—
          Catalogs and collections
Musical Instrument Digital Interface
  USE MIDI (Standard)
Musical instrument makers [May Subd Geog]
  UF Musical instruments—Makers
  BT Musicians
  NT Clavichord makers
      Harpsichord makers
      Organ-builders
      Piano makers
      Stringed instrument makers
      Wind instrument makers

Musical instruments [May Subd Geog] *(Collections, descriptive catalogs, exhibitions, ML462; History, ML460-ML1055; Industry, HD9999.M8; Instruction, MT170-MT805)*

For works about musical instruments of an individual ethnic group, additional subject entry is made under the heading [ethnic group]—[place]—Music.

UF Instruments, Musical
    Organology (Music)
RT Instrumental music—History and criticism
    Instrumentation and orchestration
SA *groups of instruments, e.g.* Percussion instruments; Stringed instruments; Stringed instruments, Bowed; Wind instruments; *also names of the individual musical instruments, e.g.* Accordion, Harpsichord, Organ, Piano
NT Hurdy-gurdy
    Mouth organs
    Musical instruments, Electronic
    Orchestra
    Tuning
—Catalogs and collections [May Subd Geog] *(ML461-462)*
    UF Musical instrument collections
        Musical instruments—Collections
    BT Music—Exhibitions
        Music museums
    SA *subdivision* Musical instrument collections *under names of persons, families, and corporate bodies*
—Catalogs, Manufacturers' *(ML155)*
    BT Music trade
—Collections
    USE Musical instruments—Catalogs and collections
—Construction
—Dictionaries *(ML102)*
    SA *subdivision* Dictionaries *under names of instruments, e.g.* Piano—Dictionaries
—Exhibitions *(ML462)*
    BT Music—Exhibitions
—Indians
    USE Indians—Music
—Juvenile literature *(ML3930)*
    BT Music—Juvenile literature
    NT Rhythm bands and orchestras
—Makers
    USE Musical instrument makers
—Studies and exercises
—Studies and exercises (Jazz)
—Tariff
    USE Tariff on stringed instruments
         Tariff on wind instruments

GEOGRAPHIC SUBDIVISIONS

—Africa
    NT Goura (Musical instrument)
        Kora (Musical instrument)
        Mbira
        Sanza

Musical instruments [May Subd Geog] *(Collections, descriptive catalogs, exhibitions, ML462; History, ML460-ML1055; Industry, HD9999.M8; Instruction, MT170-MT805)*

Geographic Subdivisions
(Continued)
—Africa, French-speaking West
    NT Balo
—Andes Region
    NT Charango
—Asia, Central
    NT Morin khuur
—Brazil
    NT Berimbau
—China
    NT Cheng (Musical instrument)
        Ch'in (Musical instrument)
        Erh hu
        Hsüan (Musical instrument)
        Hu ch'in
        Huang chung (Musical instrument)
        Nan hu
        Pan hu
        Sheng (Musical instrument)
        So na
        Yang ch'in
        Yüeh ch'in
—Cuba
    NT Conga (Drum)
—Greece
    NT Bouzouki
—India
    NT Bānsurī
        Ḍaph
        Sarod
        Shehnai
        Sitar
        Tabla
—Indonesia
    NT Angklung
        Gender (Musical instrument)
        Kolintang
—Iran
    RT Santūr
        Tunbūk
—Ireland
    NT Bodhran
—Japan
    NT Biwa
        Hichiriki
        Ichigenkin
        Kei
        Koto
        Kotsuzumi
        Ryūteki
        Shakuhachi
        Shamisen
        Shinobue
        Shō
—Kenya
    NT Zumari

Musical instruments [May Subd Geog] *(Collections,
        descriptive catalogs, exhibitions, ML62;
        History, ML460-ML1055; Industry,
        HD9999.M8; Instruction, MT170-MT805)*
Geographic Subdivisions
(Continued)
—Korea
    NT   Changgo
         Haegŭm
         Hyŏn'gŭm
         Kayakeum
         Komunko
         P'illyul
         Taegŭm
         Tanso
—Laos
    NT   Kaen
—Latvia
    NT   Kokle
—Lithuania
    NT   Kanklės
—Nepal
    NT   Gumlā
—Pakistan
    NT   Bānsurī
—Puerto Rico
    NT   Cuatro puertorriqueño
—Russian S.F.S.R.
    NT   Russian horn
—Soviet Union
    NT   Bayan
—Spain
    NT   Alboka
         Dulzaina
—Sweden
    NT   Keyed fiddle
         Tambi
—Thailand
    NT   Kaen
—Turkey
    NT   Saz
—Ukraine
    NT   Kobza
—Yugoslavia
    NT   Tambura
Musical instruments, Ancient [May Subd Geog]
        (ML162-169)
UF   Ancient musical instruments
NT   Psaltery
—Greece
    NT   Aulos
         Cithara
—Rome
    NT   Tibia (Musical instrument)
Musical instruments, Electronic *(ML1092)*
UF   Electric musical instruments
     Electronic musical instruments
     Electrophonic musical instruments
BT   Musical instruments (Mechanical)
NT   Clavioline
     Electric guitar
     Electronic harpsichord
     Electronic organ

Musical instruments, Electronic *(ML1092)*
    (Continued)
         Electronic piano
         Ondes Martenot
         Synthesizer (Musical instrument)
         Trautonium
Musical instruments (Mechanical) *(History,
        ML1050-ML1055; Instruction, MT700)*
    NT   Aeolian-vocalion
         Jukeboxes
         Manualo
         Mechanical organs
         Music box
         Music-recorders
         Musical instruments, Electronic
         Organina
         Pianola
         Player-organ
         Player-piano
         Pyrophone
         Violano-virtuoso
Musical instruments for the handicapped
    BT   Music therapy
Musical instruments in art
    BT   Music in art
Musical instruments in the Bible
    USE   Music in the Bible
Musical instruments industry [May Subd Geog]
        (HD9999.M8)
Musical interpretation
    USE   Music—Interpretation (Phrasing,
          dynamics, etc.)
Musical intervals and scales *(ML3809)*
    UF   Intervals (Music)
         Modes, Musical
         Music—Modes
         Musical modes
         Scales (Music)
    BT   Harmony
         Music—Acoustics and physics
         Music—Theory
    RT   Microtones
    NT   Raga
         Tonality
         Tonus peregrinus
         Twelve-tone system
Musical inventions and patents
    UF   Music—Inventions and patents
Musical jaw bone
    USE   Jaw bone, Musical
Musical landmarks [May Subd Geog] *(ML198-370)*
Musical medleys
    USE   Potpourris
Musical meter and rhythm *(Aesthetics,
        ML3850; History of composition,
        ML437; Instruction in composition,
        MT42; Physics: acoustics, ML3813;
        Piano, MT233; Psychology, ML3832)*
    UF   Meter
    BT   Music—Theory
         Rhythm
    NT   Chants (Plain, Gregorian, etc.)—
         Instruction and study

Musical meter and rhythm *(Aesthetics,*
ML3850; History of composition,
ML437; Instruction in composition,
MT42; Physics: acoustics, ML3813;
Piano, MT233; Psychology, ML3832)
(Continued)
- NT Measured music
  Musical notation
  Neumes
  Syncopation
  Tempo (Music)
—Studies and exercises *(MT42)*

Musical modes
  USE Musical intervals and scales

Musical moving-pictures
  USE Moving-pictures, Musical

Musical notation *(History, ML431;*
Instruction, MT35; Reform, ML432)
- UF Ligature (Music)
  Music—Notation
  Notation, Musical
- BT Musical meter and rhythm
- NT Braille music-notation
  Embellishment (Music)
  Galin-Paris-Chevé method (Music)
  Measured music
  Musical shorthand
  Neumes
  Notes inégales
  Paleography, Musical
  Solmization
  Tablature (Musical notation)
  Tone-word system
  Tonic sol-fa

Musical novels
  USE Musical fiction

Musical paleography
  USE Paleography, Musical

Musical parodies
  USE Wit and humor, Musical

Musical parody
  USE Parody (Music)

Musical performance
  USE Music—Performance

Musical pitch *(Acoustics, ML3807-ML3809;*
Psychology, ML3830)
- UF Pitch, Musical
- BT Tuning
- NT Organ-pipes

Musical play
  USE Musical revue, comedy, etc.

Musical radio programs
  USE Radio programs, Musical

Musical realism
  USE Realism in music

Musical recreations
- UF Recreations, Musical
- BT Amusements
  Music as recreation
- NT Musical card games

Musical research
  USE Musicology

Musical revue, comedy, etc. [May Subd Geog]
Here are entered works on musical revue,
  comedy, etc. Musical works composed
  for musical revues, comedies, etc. are
  entered under Musical revues, comedies,
  etc.
- UF Musical comedy
  Musical extravaganza
  Musical farce
  Musical play
- BT Dramatic music
  Zarzuela
- NT Pantomime (Christmas entertainment)
—Authorship
  USE Musical revue, comedy, etc.—
    Writing and publishing
—Direction
  USE Musical revue, comedy, etc.—
    Production and direction
—Production and direction *(MT955)*
  UF Musical revue, comedy, etc.—
    Direction
—Writing and publishing
  UF Musical revue, comedy, etc.—
    Authorship
  BT Composition (Music)
Note under Musical revues, comedies, etc.

Musical revues, comedies, etc. *(M1500-M1508)*
Here are entered musical works composed
  for musical revues, comedies, etc. Works
  on musical revue, comedy, etc., are entered
  under Musical revue, comedy, etc.
- UF Musical comedies
  Operettas
- BT Dramatic music
- NT College operas, revues, etc.
  Minstrel shows
  Tonadillas
—Stage guides
  (MT955)
—Stories, plots, etc.
  BT Plots (Drama, novel, etc.)
Note under Musical revue, comedy, etc.

Musical saw *(ML1055)*
- UF Saw, Musical

Musical saw music *(M175 .M9)*
- NT Septets (Piano, guitar, clavioline,
  musical saw, percussion, vibraphone,
  xylophone)

Musical settings
  USE *subdivision* Musical settings *under*
    headings for authors, e.g. Shakespeare,
    William, 1564-1616—Musical settings;
    also under headings for literature, poetry,
    drama,etc., e.g. English literature—
    Musical settings *for musical scores or*
    sound recordings in which the writings or
    words of an author or authors have been
    set to music

Musical shorthand *(MT35)*
- BT Musical notation
  Shorthand

Musical sketches

  Here are entered tentative drafts or preliminary studies, in manuscript, facsimile or transcription, for musical works.

  UF Composers' sketches

    Music—Sketches

    Sketches, Musical

Musical societies

  USE Music—Societies, etc.

Musical style

  USE Style, Musical

Musical talent

  USE Musical ability

Musical temperament *(ML3809)*

  UF Temperament, Musical

  BT Music—Acoustics and physics

    Music—Theory

    Tuning

  NT Monochord

Musical therapy

  USE Music therapy

Musical time

  USE Tempo (Music)

Musical variation

  USE Variation (Music)

Musical wit and humor

  USE Wit and humor, Musical

Musicians [May Subd Geog] *(ML385-403)*

  UF Music—Biography

  SA Flute-players, Pianists, Singers, *and similar headings*

  NT Aged musicians

    Bagpipers

    Bandsmen

    Biwa players

    Blues musicians

    Calypso musicians

    Children as musicians

    Church musicians

    Composers

    Conductors (Music)

    Country musicians

    Disco musicians

    Double-bassists

    Drummers (Musicians)

    Flute-players

    Gospel musicians

    Harmonica players

    Harpsichordists

    Jazz musicians

    Kobzari

    Librettists

    Music—Bio-bibliography

    Music critics

    Music teachers

    Musical instrument makers

    Musicologists

    Oboe players

    Physically handicapped musicians

    Physicians as musicians

    Pianists

Musicians [May Subd Geog] *(ML385-403)*

 (Continued)

  NT Reggae musicians

    Rock musicians

    Singers

    Sitar players

    Soul musicians

    Stadtpfeifer

    Street music and musicians

    Trade-unions—Musicians

    Trumpet players

    Viol players

    Violinists

    Violists

    Violoncellists

    Women musicians

 —Anecdotes, facetiae, satire, etc.

  USE Music—Anecdotes, facetiae, satire, etc.

 —Autographs *(ML93-98)*

  Example under Signatures (Writing)

 —Dictionaries

  USE Music—Bio-bibliography

 —Legal status, laws, etc. [May Subd Geog] *(ML63)*

  BT Copyright—Music

    Music and state

 —Pensions [May Subd Geog]

  UF Musicians—Salaries, pensions, etc.

 —Poetry

  USE Music—Poetry

 —Salaries, etc. [May Subd Geog] *(ML3795)*

  UF Musicians—Salaries, pensions, etc.

 —France

 ——Portraits

    NT Titon du Tillet, Évrard, 1677-1762. Parnasse françois

 —Great Britain

  NT Waits

 —Japan

  NT Biwa players

    Shakuhachi players

 —Korea

  NT Kayakeum players

Musicians, Afro-American

  USE Afro-American musicians

Musicians, Basque

  UF Basque musicians

Musicians, Black [May Subd Geog]

  UF Black musicians

Musicians, Blind

  USE Blind musicians

Musicians, Celtic

  UF Celtic musicians

Musicians, Gipsy

  USE Musicians, Gypsy

Musicians, Gypsy

  UF Gipsy musicians

    Gypsy musicians

    Musicians, Gipsy

Musicians, Jewish

  UF Jewish musicians

  NT Cantors, Jewish

Musicians, Physically handicapped
    USE Physically handicapped musicians
Musicians, Street
    USE Street music and musicians
Musicians, Town
    USE Stadtpfeifer
        Waits
Musicians, Women
    USE Women musicians
Musicians as authors
    BT Music and literature
Musicians in literature
    BT Musical fiction
    RT Music and literature
Musicians' wives [May Subd Geog]
    BT Wives
    NT Rock musicians' wives
Musico-callisthenics *(Callisthenics, GV463,*
      GV464; Music, M1993)
Musicologists [May Subd Geog]
    BT Musicians
        Scholars
    RT Musicology
    NT Ethnomusicologists
Musicology [May Subd Geog] *(ML)*
    UF Musical research
        Research, Musical
    RT Music—Historiography
        Musicologists
    NT Ethnomusicology
        Music—Editing
        Music archaeology
        Musical criticism
        Paleography, Musical
    —Almanacs, yearbooks, etc.
        UF Musicology—Yearbooks
    —Yearbooks
        USE Musicology—Almanacs,
            yearbooks, etc.
Musique concrète
    USE Concrete music
Muslim hymns
    USE Islamic hymns
Muslim music
    USE Music, Islamic
Muslims [May Subd Geog] *(DS38)*
    —Music
        USE Music, Islamic
Mythology and music
    USE Music and mythology
Nagauta
    BT Ballads, Japanese
        Songs, Japanese
Nan hu *(ML927.N)*
    BT Hu ch'in
        Musical instruments—China
        Stringed instruments, Bowed
    RT Erh hu
Nan hu music *(M59.N)*
Naniwabushi
    BT Monologues with music (Shamisen)
        Sekkyō jōruri

Narration with music
    USE *subdivision* Readings with music *under*
        subjects, e.g. American poetry—20th
        century—Readings with music;
        Monologues with music
        Sacred monologues with music
National music [May Subd Geog] *(M1627-1844)*
    UF Music, National
    BT Music
    RT Patriotic music
    SA *subdivision* Songs and music *under*
        armies and navies, e.g. United States.
        Army—Songs and music; United
        States. Navy—Songs and music
    NT Folk dancing
        Folk music
        Folk-songs
        National songs
    —History and criticism *(ML3545)*
        RT Nationalism in music
National Music Week
    USE Music Week
National socialism and music
    UF Nazi music
    BT Music
National songs [May Subd Geog]
    UF Anthems, National
        National anthems
        Patriotic songs
        Songs, National
        Songs, Patriotic
    BT Emblems, National
        Music
        National music
        Patriotic music
        Songs
    RT Folk-songs
    NT Political ballads and songs
        War-songs
    —United States
        NT State songs
Nationalism and music
    USE Nationalism in music
Nationalism in music
    UF Nationalism and music
    RT National music—History and criticism
    NT Music and race
Natural trumpet
    USE Trumpet
Nature in music
    USE Program music
Nāy *(ML990.N)*
    UF Ney
        Quṣaba
    BT Flute
Nāy and zarb music
    UF Zarb and nāy music
Nazi music
    USE National socialism and music
Ndebele songs (Zimbabwe)
    USE Songs, Ndebele (Zimbabwe)
Negro minstrel shows
    USE Minstrel shows

Negro spirituals
    USE   Spirituals (Songs)
Nepali songs
    USE   Songs, Nepali
Neumes *(ML174)*
    UF   Ligature (Music)
    BT   Chants (Plain, Gregorian, etc.)—
           Instruction and study
        Musical meter and rhythm
        Musical notation
    RT   Paleography, Musical
New Age music
       ML3529
    BT   Music
New wave music [May Subd Geog]
    BT   Rock music
    RT   Punk rock music
New Year [May Subd Geog] *(GT4905)*
    —Songs and music
       USE   New Year music
New Year music
    UF   New Year—Songs and music
    NT   Synagogue music—Rosh ha-Shanah
           services
Newari songs
    USE   Songs, Newari
Ngbaka ma'bo folk-songs
    USE   Folk-songs, Ngbaka ma'bo
Nicene Creed (Music)
    USE   Credo (Music)
Night clubs
    USE   Music-halls (Variety-theaters, cabarets,
           etc.)
Nightclubs
    USE   Music-halls (Variety-theaters, cabarets,
           etc.)
Nisi Dominus (Music)
    USE   Psalms (Music)—127th Psalm
Nō music
    BT   Music—Japan
    NT   Utai
Noardske balke
    USE   Noordsche balk
Noli aemulari (Music)
    USE   Psalms (Music)—37th Psalm
Non nobis, Domine (Music)
    USE   Psalms (Music)—115th Psalm
Nonets *(M900-986)*
       Here are entered collections of composi-
          tions for nine instruments belonging to
          various families and in various combi-
          nations; and compositions for nine
          specific instruments belonging to vari-
          ous families, followed by specification
          of instruments (including the specifi-
          cation Unspecified instrument(s)).
       Compositions for nine bowed stringed in-
          struments are entered under String no-
          nets; for nine wind instruments under
          Wind nonets; for nine brass instru-
          ments under Brass nonets; and for nine
          woodwind instruments under Woodwind

Nonets *(M900-986)*
   (Continued)
       nonets, with or without specification of
         instruments in each case.
       Compositions for nine plectral instru-
         ments are entered under Plectral en-
         sembles, except those for guitars and
         /or harps, which are entered under
         Nonets followed by specification of in-
         struments.
       Compositions for nine percussionists are
         entered under Percussion ensembles.
       Compositions for nine solo voices are en-
         tered under Sacred nonets or Vocal
         nonets.
       Headings with specification of instru-
         ments are printed below only if spe-
         cific cross references are needed.
    SA   Suites, Variations, Waltzes, *and similar*
        headings with specification of
        instruments
Nonets, Brass
    USE   Brass nonets
Nonets, Sacred
    USE   Sacred nonets
Nonets, Secular
    USE   Vocal nonets
Nonets, String
    USE   String nonets
Nonets, Vocal
    USE   Vocal nonets
Nonets, Wind
    USE   Wind nonets
Nonets, Woodwind
    USE   Woodwind nonets
Nonets (Bassoon, clarinet, flute, horn, oboe,
        violin, viola, violoncello, double
        bass) *(M960-962)*
    NT   Suites (Bassoon, clarinet, flute, horn,
         oboe, violin, viola, violoncello,
         double bass)
    Note under Nonets
Nonets (Bassoon, clarinet, flute, horn, oboe,
        violins (2), viola, violoncello)
        (M960-962)
Nonets (Bassoon, clarinet, flute, horn, violins
        (2), viola, violoncello, double bass)
        (M960-962)
    NT   Variations (Bassoon, clarinet, flute,
         horn, violins (2), viola, violoncello,
         double bass)
Nonets (Bassoon, clarinet, flute, oboe,
        trumpet, violin, viola, violoncello,
        double bass) *(M960-962)*
    NT   Suites (Bassoon, clarinet, flute, oboe,
         trumpet, violin, viola, violoncello,
         double bass)
Nonets (Bassoon, clarinet, flute, oboe, violins
        (2), viola, violoncello, double bass)
        (M960-962)
    NT   Suites (Bassoon, clarinet, flute, oboe,
         violins (2), viola, violoncello, double
         bass)

Nonets (Bassoon, clarinet, oboe, percussion, violins (2), viola, violoncello, double bass) *(M985)*
  NT Suites (Bassoon, clarinet, oboe, percussion, violins (2), viola, violoncello, double bass)
Nonets (Bassoon, clarinets (3), flute, trombone, trumpets (2), percussion) *(M985)*
Nonets (Bassoon, flute, horn, piccolo, trombone, trumpet, viola, violoncello, double bass) *(M960-962)*
Nonets (Clarinet, flute, guitar, percussion, violin, viola, violoncello) *(M985)*
Nonets (Clarinet, flute, trumpet, mandolin, xylophone, violins (2), viola, violoncello) *(M985)*
Nonets (Clarinets (2), horns (2), hurdy-gurdies (2), violas (2), violoncello) *(M985)*
Nonets (Clarinets (2), horns (2), violins (2), violas (2), violoncello) *(M960-962)*
  NT Suites (Clarinets (2), horns (2), violins (2), violas (2), violoncello)
Nonets (Clarinets (3), cornet, trombone, trumpet, violin, viola, violoncello) *(M960-962)*
  NT Suites (Clarinets (3), cornet, trombone, trumpet, violin, viola, violoncello)
Nonets (Flute, horns (2), oboe, violins (2), violas (2), violoncello) *(M960-962)*
Nonets (Flute, horns (2), oboe, violins (2), violas (2), violoncello), Arranged *(M963-4)*
Nonets (Harpsichord, bassoon, clarinets (2), horns (2), oboes (2), percussion) *(M935)*
  NT Suites (Harpsichord, bassoon, clarinets (2), horns (2), oboes (2), percussion)
Nonets (Harpsichord, violins (4), violas (3), violoncello) *(M910-912)*
  BT Nonets (Piano, violins (4), violas (3), violoncello)
Nonets (Harpsichord, violins (4), violas (3), violoncello), Arranged *(M913-914)*
Nonets (Horns (2), oboes (2), violins (2), violas (2), violoncello) *(M960-962)*
  NT Suites (Horns (2), oboes (2), violins (2), violas (2), violoncello)
Nonets (Percussion, violins (2), viola, violoncello) *(M985)*
  NT Suites (Percussion, violins (2), viola, violoncello)
Nonets (Piano, bassoon, clarinet, flute, horn, oboe, trombone, trumpet, tuba) *(M915-917)*
Nonets (Piano, bassoon, clarinet, flute, horn, trombone, trumpet, violin, violoncello) *(M920-922)*
Nonets (Piano, bassoon, clarinet, flute, oboe, trumpet, violin, viola, violoncello) *(M920-922)*
  NT Marches (Piano, bassoon, clarinet, flute, oboe, trumpet, violin, viola, violoncello)

Nonets (Piano, bassoon, clarinet, flute, oboe, violins (2), viola, violoncello) *(M920-922)*
Nonets (Piano, bassoon, clarinet, flutes (2), horn, oboe, trombone, trumpet) *(M915-917)*
Nonets (Piano, bassoon, clarinets (2), English horn, flute, horn, oboe, trumpet) *(M915-917)*
  NT Suites (Piano, bassoon, clarinets (2), English horn, flute, horn, oboe, trumpet)
Nonets (Piano, bassoon, clarinets (2), English horn, oboe, piccolo, violin, violoncello) *(M920-922)*
Nonets (Piano, bassoon, clarinets (2), trumpet, violins (2), violoncello, double bass) *(M920-922)*
Nonets (Piano, bassoons (2), flute, horn, oboe, violin, violoncello, double bass) *(M920-922)*
  NT Variations (Piano, bassoons (2), flute, horn, oboe, violin, violoncello, double bass)
Nonets (Piano, clarinet, English horn, flute, trombones (2), percussion, violin) *(M947)*
Nonets (Piano, clarinet, flute, horn, oboe, trombone, trumpet, violin, viola) *(M920-922)*
Nonets (Piano, clarinets (2), flute, percussion, violins (2), viola, violoncello) *(M985)*
Nonets (Piano, flute, percussion, violin, viola, violoncello) *(M985)*
Nonets (Piano, horn, trombone, tuba, percussion, viola, violoncello, double bass) *(M945-7)*
Nonets (Piano, horn, trombone, tuba, percussion, violin, violoncello, double bass) *(M945-7)*
Nonets (Piano, violins (4), violas (3), violoncello) *(M910-912)*
  NT Nonets (Harpsichord, violins (4), violas (3), violoncello)
Nonets (Pianos (2), bassoon, flutes (4), trombone, percussion) *(M985)*
Nonets (Pianos (2), flutes (3), trumpet, violoncellos (3)) *(M920-922)*
Nonets (Saxophone, guitar, percussion, violins (2), viola, violoncello, double basses (2)) *(M985)*
Nonsense songs
  BT Humorous songs
Noordsche balk *(ML760)*
  UF Hommel
      Hummel
      Langleik
      Noardske balke
      Scheitholt
  BT Zither
Norteno music
  USE Popular music—Mexico
       Popular music—Texas

Norwegian ballads
    USE Ballads, Norwegian
Norwegian folk-songs
    USE Folk-songs, Norwegian
Norwegian hymns
    USE Hymns, Norwegian
Norwegian lullabies
    USE Lullabies, Norwegian
Notation, Musical
    USE Musical notation
Notched rattle *(GN477.R)*
    UF Bone rattle
        Rattle, Notched
    BT Percussion instruments
Notes inégales
    BT Music—Performance
        Musical notation
Nunc dimittis (Music)
    BT Canticles
Nun's fiddle
    USE Sea-trumpet
Nursery rhymes *(PN6110.C4; PZ8.3)*
    BT Children's songs
    NT Lullabies
Nursery schools [May Subd Geog] *(LB1140)*
    —Music
        UF Music—Nursery schools
        BT Children's songs
            Kindergarten—Music
Nutcracker (Ballet)
    BT Ballets
Oboe *(History and construction, ML940-ML943)*
    BT Woodwind instruments
    RT English horn
    NT Crumhorn
        Heckelphone
        Hichiriki
        Pommer
        Shawm
        Shehnai
        So na
    —Orchestra studies *(MT366)*
        BT Oboe—Studies and exercises
    —Reeds
        Example under Reeds (Music)
    —Studies and exercises *(MT365)*
        NT Oboe—Orchestra studies
Oboe, Pastoral
    USE Pipe (Musical instrument)
Oboe and bassoon music
    USE Bassoon and oboe music
Oboe and clarinet music
    USE Clarinet and oboe music
Oboe and claves music [May Subd Geog] *(M298)*
    UF Claves and oboe music
Oboe and continuo music
    UF Continuo and oboe music
    NT Marches (Oboe and continuo)
        Minuets (Oboe and continuo)
        Sonatas (Oboe and continuo)
        Suites (Oboe and continuo)
        Variations (Oboe and continuo)

Oboe and double-bass music *(M290-291)*
    UF Double-bass and oboe music
Oboe and English horn music
    USE English horn and oboe music
Oboe and flute music
    USE Flute and oboe music
Oboe and guitar music *(M296-7)*
    UF Guitar and oboe music
    NT Sonatas (Oboe and guitar)
        Variations (Oboe and guitar)
Oboe and harp music *(M296-7)*
    UF Harp and oboe music
    NT Concertos (Oboe and harp)
        Concertos (Oboe and harp with string
          orchestra)
        Oboe and harp with orchestra
        Oboe and harp with string orchestra
        Sonatas (Oboe and harp)
Oboe and harp with chamber orchestra
        (M1040-1041)
    RT Concertos (Oboe and harp with
          chamber orchestra)
Oboe and harp with orchestra *(M1040-1041)*
    BT Oboe and harp music
    RT Concertos (Oboe and harp)
Oboe and harp with string orchestra *(M1105-6)*
    BT Oboe and harp music
    RT Concertos (Oboe and harp with string
          orchestra)
    —Scores and parts *(M1105)*
Oboe and harpsichord music *(M245-6)*
    UF Harpsichord and oboe music
    NT Concertos (Oboe and harpsichord with
          string orchestra)
        Oboe and harpsichord with string
          orchestra
        Sonatas (Oboe and harpsichord)
        Suites (Oboe and harpsichord)
        Variations (Oboe and harpsichord)
    Note under Chamber music
Oboe and harpsichord with string orchestra
        (M1105-6)
    BT Oboe and harpsichord music
    RT Concertos (Oboe and harpsichord
          with string orchestra)
Oboe and horn music
    USE Horn and oboe music
Oboe and keyboard instrument music
        (M245-M246)
    UF Keyboard instrument and oboe music
Oboe and organ music *(M182-4)*
    UF Organ and oboe music
    NT Chorale preludes (Oboe and organ)
        Sonatas (Oboe and organ)
        Suites (Oboe and organ)
        Variations (Oboe and organ)
Oboe and percussion music *(M298)*
    UF Percussion and oboe music
Oboe and percussion with string orchestra
        (M1140-1141)
    RT Concertos (Oboe and percussion with
          string orchestra)

Oboe and piano music *(M245-6)*
  UF Piano and oboe music
  NT Rondos (Oboe and piano)
      Sonatas (Oboe and piano)
      Suites (Oboe and piano)
      Variations (Oboe and piano)
Oboe and piano music, Arranged *(M247)*
  NT Concertos (Oboe)—Solo with piano
      Concertos (Oboe), Arranged—Solo with
        piano
      Concertos (Oboe with chamber
        orchestra)—Solo with piano
      Concertos (Oboe with string orchestra)
        —Solo with piano
      Oboe with band—Solo with piano
      Oboe with chamber orchestra—Solo
        with piano
      Oboe with orchestra—Solo with piano
      Oboe with string orchestra—Solo with
        piano
      Suites (Oboe with chamber orchestra)—
        Solo with piano
      Suites (Oboe with string orchestra)—
        Solo with piano
      Variations (Oboe with band)—Solo with
        piano
Oboe and piano with string ensemble
  NT Concertos (Oboe and piano with
        string ensemble)
Oboe and piccolo music *(M288-289)*
  UF Piccolo and oboe music
Oboe and recorder music *(M288-9)*
  UF Recorder and oboe music
  NT Concertos (Oboe and recorder with
        string orchestra)
      Oboe and recorder with string orchestra
Oboe and recorder with string orchestra
        (M1105-6)
  BT Oboe and recorder music
  RT Concertos (Oboe and recorder with
        string orchestra)
Oboe and theorbo music *(M296-297)*
  UF Theorbo and oboe music
  NT Suites (Oboe and theorbo)
Oboe and trombone music *(M288-289)*
  UF Trombone and oboe music
Oboe and trumpet music *(M288-9)*
  UF Trumpet and oboe music
  NT Concertos (Oboe and trumpet with
        string orchestra)
      Oboe and trumpet with string orchestra
Oboe and trumpet with string orchestra
        (M1105-6)
  BT Oboe and trumpet music
  RT Concertos (Oboe and trumpet with
        string orchestra)
Oboe and viola music *(M290-291)*
  UF Viola and oboe music
  NT Concertos (Oboe and viola with string
        orchestra)
      Oboe and viola with string orchestra

Oboe and viola with string orchestra
        (M1105-6)
  BT Oboe and viola music
  RT Concertos (Oboe and viola with string
        orchestra)
Oboe and violin music *(M290-291)*
  UF Violin and oboe music
  NT Concertos (Oboe and violin)
      Concertos (Oboe and violin with
        chamber orchestra)
      Concertos (Oboe and violin with string
        orchestra)
      Oboe and violin with chamber
        orchestra
      Oboe and violin with orchestra
      Oboe and violin with string orchestra
Oboe and violin with chamber orchestra
        (M1040-1041)
  BT Chamber-orchestra music
      Oboe and violin music
  RT Concertos (Oboe and violin with
        chamber orchestra)
Oboe and violin with orchestra
        (M1040-1041)
  BT Oboe and violin music
      Orchestral music
  RT Concertos (Oboe and violin)
Oboe and violin with string orchestra
        (M1105-6)
  BT Oboe and violin music
  RT Concertos (Oboe and violin with string
        orchestra)
Oboe and violoncello music *(M290-291)*
  NT Oboe and violoncello with string
        orchestra
      Suites (Oboe and violoncello)
      Variations (Oboe and violoncello)
Oboe and violoncello with orchestra
        (M1040-1041)
  RT Concertos (Oboe and violoncello)
Oboe and violoncello with string orchestra
        (M1140-1141)
  BT Oboe and violoncello music
  NT Suites (Oboe and violoncello with
        string orchestra)
Oboe d'amore and continuo music
  UF Continuo and oboe d'amore music
  NT Suites (Oboe d'amore and continuo)
Oboe d'amore and guitar music
        (M296-297)
  UF Guitar and oboe d'amore music
Oboe d'amore and harpsichord music
        (M270.026; M271.026)
  UF Harpsichord and oboe d'amore music
Oboe d'amore and piano music *(M270.026;*
        M271.026)
  UF Piano and oboe d'amore music
Oboe d'amore and piano music, Arranged
        (M270.026; M271.026)
  NT Concertos (Oboe d'amore)—Solo with
        piano

Oboe d'amore music *(M65-69)*
  SA Concertos, Minuets, Sonatas, Suites,
      *and similar headings with
      specification of instruments;* Trios
      [Quartets, etc.], Wind trios [quartets,
      etc.], *and* Woodwind trios [quartets,
      etc.] *followed by specifications which
      include the oboe d'amore; also* Wind
      ensembles, Woodwind ensembles,
      *and headings that begin with the
      words Oboe d'amore or Oboi
      d'amore*
  NT Trios (Flute, oboe d'amore, percussion)
      Trios (Harpsichord, flute, oboe d'amore)
Oboe d'amore with orchestra *(M1034.O26;
      M1035.O26)*
  RT Concertos (Oboe d'amore)
Oboe d'amore with string orchestra *(M1105-6)*
  RT Concertos (Oboe d'amore with string
      orchestra)
  —Scores *(M1105)*
Oboe music *(M65-69)*
  SA Concertos, Minuets, Sonatas, Suites,
      *and similar headings with
      specification of instruments;* Trios
      [Quartets, etc.], Wind trios [quartets,
      etc.], *and* Woodwind trios [quartets,
      etc.] *followed by specifications which
      include the oboe; also* Wind
      ensembles, Woodwind ensembles,
      *and headings that begin with the
      words oboe or oboes*
  NT Recorded accompaniments (Oboe)
      Sonatas (Oboe)
      Suites (Oboe)
Oboe music (Oboes (2)) *(M288-9)*
  NT Concertos (Oboes (2) with string
      orchestra)
      Oboes (2) with string orchestra
      Sonatas (Oboes (2))
      Suites (Oboes (2))
Oboe music (Oboes (3))
  USE Woodwind trios (Oboes (3))
Oboe music (Oboes (4))
  USE Woodwind quartets (Oboes (4))
Oboe players [May Subd Geog]
  UF Oboists
  BT Musicians
Oboe, violin, violoncello with orchestra
      (M1040-1041)
  BT Trios (Oboe, violin, violoncello)
  RT Concertos (Oboe, violin, violoncello)
Oboe, violin, violoncello with string orchestra
      (M1105-6)
  BT Trios (Oboe, violin, violoncello)
  RT Concertos (Oboe, violin, violoncello
      with string orchestra)
Oboe with band *(M1205-6)*
  BT Band music
  RT Concertos (Oboe with band)
  NT Variations (Oboe with band)
  —Solo with piano *(M1206)*
      BT Oboe and piano music, Arranged

Oboe with chamber orchestra *(M1022-3)*
  BT Chamber-orchestra music
  RT Concertos (Oboe with chamber
      orchestra)
  NT Suites (Oboe with chamber orchestra)
      Variations (Oboe with chamber
      orchestra)
  —Solo with piano *(M1023)*
      BT Oboe and piano music, Arranged
Oboe with instrumental ensemble
  RT Concertos (Oboe with instrumental
      ensemble)
Oboe with orchestra *(M1022-3)*
  RT Concertos (Oboe)
  NT Variations (Oboe with orchestra)
  —Solo with piano *(M1023)*
      BT Oboe and piano music, Arranged
Oboe with orchestra, Arranged
      (M1022-3)
Oboe with string ensemble *(M960-962)*
  RT Concertos (Oboe with string ensemble)
Oboe with string orchestra *(M1105-6)*
  RT Concertos (Oboe with string orchestra)
  NT Canons, fugues, etc. (Oboe with string
      orchestra)
      Passacaglias (Oboe with string
      orchestra)
      Suites (Oboe with string orchestra)
      Variations (Oboe with string orchestra)
  BT Concertos (Oboe with string orchestra)
  —Solo with piano *(M1106)*
      BT Oboe and piano music, Arranged
Oboe with string orchestra, Arranged
      (M1105-6)
  —Scores and parts *(M1105-6)*
Oboes (2), trumpet with string orchestra
      (M1140-1141)
  BT Wind trios (Oboes (2), trumpet)
  RT Concertos (Oboes (2), trumpet with
      string orchestra)
Oboes (2) with orchestra *(M1022-1023)*
  RT Concertos (Oboes (2))
Oboes (2) with string orchestra *(M1105-6)*
  BT Oboe music (Oboes (2))
  RT Concertos (Oboes (2) with string
      orchestra)
Oboes (3) with string orchestra
      (M1122-1123)
  BT Woodwind trios (Oboes (3))
  RT Concertos (Oboes (3) with string
      orchestra)
  NT Suites (Oboes (3) with string orchestra)
Oboes (4) with string orchestra *(M1122-3)*
  BT Woodwind quartets (Oboes (4))
  RT Concertos (Oboes (4) with string
      orchestra)
Oboi d'amore (2) with string orchestra
      (M1134.O26; M1135.O26)
  RT Concertos (Oboi d'amore (2) with
      string orchestra)
Oboists
  USE Oboe players

Ocarina *(ML990.O3)*
   BT   Woodwind instruments
   —Methods *(MT526)*
   — —Self-instruction *(MT526)*
         UF   Ocarina—Self-instruction
   —Self-instruction
         USE   Ocarina—Methods—
               Self-instruction
Ocarina and piano music *(M270-271)*
   UF   Piano and ocarina music
Ocarina music *(M110.O3)*
Occupational therapy [May Subd Geog]
         (Psychotherapy, RC487;
         Rehabilitation, RM735-735.7)
   NT   Music therapy
Octets *(M800-886)*
         Here are entered collections of composi-
         tions for eight instruments belonging
         to various families and in various com-
         binations; and compositions for eight
         specific instruments belonging to vari-
         ous families, followed by specification
         of instruments (including the specifi-
         cation Unspecified instruments)).
         Compositions for eight bowed stringed
         instruments are entered under String
         octets; for eight wind instruments un-
         der Wind octets; for eight brass instru-
         ments under Brass octets; and for eight
         woodwind instruments under Wood-
         wind octets, with or without specifica-
         tion of instruments in each case.
         Compositions for eight plectral instru-
         ments are entered under Plectral en-
         sembles, except those for guitars and-
         /or harps, which are entered under
         Octets followed by specification of in-
         struments.
         Compositions for eight percussionists are
         entered under Percussion ensembles.
         Compositions for eight solo voices are en-
         tered under Sacred octets or Vocal oc-
         tets.
         Headings with specification of instru-
         ments are printed below only if spe-
         cific cross references are needed.
   SA   Suites, Variations, Waltzes, *and similar*
         headings with specification of
         instruments
Octets, Brass
   USE   Brass octets
Octets, Sacred
   USE   Sacred octets
Octets, Secular
   USE   Vocal octets
Octets, String
   USE   String octets
Octets, Vocal
   USE   Vocal octets
Octets, Wind
   USE   Wind octets
Octets, Woodwind
   USE   Woodwind octets

Octets (Bassoon, clarinet, flute, horn, harp,
   violin, viola, double bass)
         (M880-882)
Octets (Bassoon, clarinet, flute, horn, oboe,
   trombone, trumpet, double bass)
         (M860-862)
Octets (Bassoon, clarinet, flute, horn, trumpet,
   violin, violoncello, double bass)
         (M860-862)
Octets (Bassoon, clarinet, flute, horn, trumpet,
   violin, violoncello, double bass),
   Arranged *(M863-4)*
Octets (Bassoon, clarinet, flute, horn, violin,
   viola, violoncello, double bass)
         (M860-862)
   NT   Suites (Bassoon, clarinet, flute, horn,
         violin, viola, violoncello, double
         bass)
Octets (Bassoon, clarinet, flute, horn, violins
   (2), viola, violoncello) *(M860-862)*
   NT   Variations (Bassoon, clarinet, flute,
         horn, violins (2), viola, violoncello)
Octets (Bassoon, clarinet, flute, horns (2),
   oboe, percussion) *(M885)*
Octets (Bassoon, clarinet, flute, horns (2),
   violin, viola, violoncello)
         (M860-862)
Octets (Bassoon, clarinet, flute, oboe, violin,
   viola, violoncello, double bass)
         (M860-862)
Octets (Bassoon, clarinet, flute, oboe, violins
   (2), viola, violoncello) *(M860-862)*
   NT   Bassoon, clarinet, flute, oboe, violins
         (2), viola, violoncello with string
         orchestra
         Concertos (Bassoon, clarinet, flute,
         oboe, violins (2), viola, violoncello
         with string orchestra)
         Suites (Bassoon, clarinet, flute, oboe,
         violins (2), viola, violoncello)
Octets (Bassoon, clarinet, horn, oboe, violin,
   viola, violoncello, double bass)
         (M860-862)
Octets (Bassoon, clarinet, horn, oboe, violins
   (2), viola, violoncello) *(M860-862)*
Octets (Bassoon, clarinet, horn, violin, violas
   (2), violoncello, double bass)
         (M860-862)
Octets (Bassoon, clarinet, horn, violins (2),
   viola, violoncello, double bass)
         (M860-862)
Octets (Bassoon, clarinets (2), flute, horn,
   oboe, violin, double bass)
         (M860-862)
Octets (Clarinet, flute, horn, trumpet,
   percussion, vibraphone, violin,
   violoncello) *(M885)*
   NT   Suites (Clarinet, flute, horn, trumpet,
         percussion, vibraphone, violin,
         violoncello)
Octets (Clarinet, flute, oboe, percussion,
   violin, viola, violoncello) *(M885)*

Octets (Clarinet, flute, saxophone, percussion,
    vibraphone, violin, voice) *(M885)*
Octets (Clarinet, horns (2), violin, violas (2),
    violoncello, double bass)
    (M860-862)
Octets (Clarinets (2), flute, drums, percussion,
    viola, violoncello, double bass)
    (M885)
    NT   Suites (Clarinets (2), flute, drums,
         percussion, viola, violoncello, double
         bass)
Octets (Clarinets (2), harp, violins (2), viola,
    violoncello, double bass)
    (M880-882)
Octets (Clarinets (2), horns (2), violins (2),
    viola, double bass) *(M860-862)*
    NT   Suites (Clarinets (2), horns (2), violins
         (2), viola, double bass)
Octets (Clarinets (2), horns (4), harp, double
    bass) *(M880-882)*
Octets (Clarinets (2), horns (4), harp, double
    bass), Arranged *(M883-4)*
Octets (Flute, horns (2), oboes (2), violins (2),
    violoncello) *(M860-862)*
Octets (Flute, horns (2), violins (2), viola,
    violoncello, double bass)
    (M860-862)
    NT   Suites (Flute, horns (2), violins (2),
         viola, violoncello, double bass)
Octets (Flutes (2), trumpets (5), percussion)
    (M885)
    NT   Suites (Flutes (2), trumpets (5),
         percussion)
Octets (Harpsichord, bassoon, clarinet, flute,
    horn, oboe, viola, violoncello)
    (M820-822)
Octets (Harpsichord, guitar, violins (6))
    (M830-832)
Octets (Harpsichord, recorders (7))
    (M815-817)
    BT   Octets (Piano, flutes (7))
Octets (Horns (2), oboes (2), violins (2),
    viola, violoncello) *(M860-862)*
    NT   Suites (Horns (2), oboes (2), violins (2),
         viola, violoncello)
Octets (Horns (2), trombones (2), trumpets
    (2), tuba, percussion) *(M885)*
Octets (Horns (2), trombones (2), trumpets
    (2), tuba, percussion), Arranged
    (M885)
Octets (Organ, trombones (3), trumpets (3),
    percussion) *(M885)*
Octets (Percussion, violins (2), viola,
    violoncello) *(M885)*
Octets (Piano, bassoon, clarinet, flute,
    trumpet, percussion, violin,
    violoncello) *(M845-7)*
Octets (Piano, clarinet, cymbals (2), violins
    (2), viola, violoncello) *(M845-849)*
    BT   Cymbal music
Octets (Piano, clarinet, flute, guitar, mandolin,
    accordion, percussion, double bass)
    (M832)

Octets (Piano, clarinet, flute, violins (2), viola,
    violoncello, double bass)
    (M820-822)
Octets (Piano, clarinets (2), flute, trombone,
    trumpets (2), percussion)
    (M845-7)
Octets (Piano, flute, horn, oboe, violin, viola,
    violoncello, double bass)
    (M820-822)
Octets (Piano, flute, violins (2), violas (2),
    violoncellos (2)) *(M820-822)*
Octets (Piano, flutes (7)) *(M815-817)*
    NT   Octets (Harpsichord, recorders (7))
Octets (Piano, horn, violins (2), violas (2),
    violoncello, double bass)
    (M820-822)
Octets (Piano, horns (2), trombone, trumpets
    (2), percussion) *(M845-7)*
Octets (Piano, percussion, vibraphone, violins
    (2), viola, violoncello, double bass)
    (M845-7)
Octets (Piano, recorders (3), violins (2), viola,
    violoncello) *(M820-822)*
    NT   Variations (Piano, recorders (3), violins
         (2), viola, violoncello)
Octets (Piano, recorders (6), guitar) *(M835)*
Octets (Piano, trombones (2), trumpets (3),
    percussion, double bass) *(M845-7)*
Octets (Piano, trombones (3), trumpets (4))
    (M815-817)
Octets (Piano, trombones (3), trumpets (4)),
    Arranged *(M818-819)*
Octets (Pianos (2), bassoon, clarinets (2),
    English horn, horn, trombone)
    (M815-817)
Octets (Pianos (2), chimes (2), violins (2),
    violoncellos (2)) *(M845-7)*
Octets (Pianos (2), percussion, violoncellos
    (4)) *(M835)*
Octets (Recorder, percussion, double bass)
    NT   Variations (Recorder, percussion,
         double bass)
Octets (Trombones (3), trumpets (3),
    percussion) *(M885)*
Octets (Trumpets (4), percussion) *(M885)*
    NT   Suites (Trumpets (4), percussion)
         Note under Percussion music
Octets (Trumpets (5), percussion) *(M885)*
    NT   Concertos (Trumpets (5), percussion
         with string orchestra)
         Trumpets (5), percussion with string
         orchestra
Offertories (Music)
    BT   Propers (Music)
         Sacred vocal music
Old Hundredth (Tune) *(ML3186)*
    BT   Doxology
         Hymn tunes
Old Norse ballads
    USE   Ballads, Old Norse
Omnes gentes, plaudite (Music)
    USE   Psalms (Music)—47th Psalm

Ondes Martenot *(ML1092)*
  UF Martenot (Musical instrument)
       Martenot's ondes musicales
       Ondes musicales
       Ondium Martenot
  BT Musical instruments, Electronic
Ondes Martenot and percussion music *(M298)*
  UF Percussion and ondes Martenot music
Ondes Martenot and piano music *(M284.O5;*
       M285.O5)
  UF Piano and ondes Martenot music
  NT Sonatas (Ondes Martenot and piano)
       Suites (Ondes Martenot and piano)
Ondes Martenot and piano music, Arranged
       (M284.O5; M285.O5)
  NT Concertos (Ondes Martenot with string
       orchestra)—Solo with piano
Ondes Martenot music *(M175.O5)*
  NT Concertos (Ondes Martenot)
       Concertos (Ondes Martenot with string
       orchestra)
       Ondes Martenot with orchestra
       Ondes Martenot with string orchestra
       Quartets (Ondes Martenot (2), guitar,
       percussion)
       Quartets (Ondes Martenot (4))
       Sextets (Ondes Martenot (6))
       Trios (Ondes Martenot (2), percussion)
       Trios (Piano, ondes Martenot,
       percussion)
Ondes Martenot music (Ondes Martenot (2))
       (M298)
Ondes Martenot music (Ondes Martenot (3))
  USE Trios (Ondes Martenot (3))
Ondes Martenot music (Ondes Martenot (6))
  USE Sextets (Ondes Martenot (6))
Ondes Martenot with orchestra *(M1039.4.O5)*
  BT Ondes Martenot music
  RT Concertos (Ondes Martenot)
Ondes Martenot with string orchestra *(M1105-6)*
  BT Ondes Martenot music
  RT Concertos (Ondes Martenot with string
       orchestra)
Ondes musicales
  USE Ondes Martenot
Ondium Martenot
  USE Ondes Martenot
Opera [May Subd Geog] *(Aesthetics, ML3858;*
       History and criticism, ML1700-ML2110)
       Here are entered works about opera.
         Musical works composed in this form
         are entered under the heading Operas.
  UF Comic opera
       Lyric drama
       Opera—History and criticism
       Opera, Comic
       Operas—History and criticism
  BT Drama
       Dramatic music
  NT Acting in opera
       Ballad opera
       Ballet

Opera [May Subd Geog] *(Aesthetics, ML3858;*
       History and criticism, ML1700-ML2110)
  (Continued)
  NT Curses in opera
       Gluck-Piccinni controversy
       Greek drama—Incidental music
       Guerre des Bouffons
       Impresarios
       Leitmotiv
       Liturgical drama
       Melodrama
       Operetta
       Overture
       Turks in opera
       Women in opera
  Example under Musical form; Performing arts;
       Vocal music—History and criticism
  Note under Operas
  —Biography
     NT Opera producers and directors
  —Costume
     USE Costume
  —Dictionaries *(ML102)*
     NT Operas—Stories, plots, etc.
     Example under Music—Dictionaries
  —Direction
     USE Opera—Production and direction
  —Dramaturgy *(ML3858)*
     Here are entered discussions of the
       technique of writing operas.
     UF Dramaturgy
     RT Operas—Stage guides
     SA *subdivision* Dramaturgy *under names*
          of composers, e.g. Wagner, Richard,
          1813-1883—Dramaturgy
  —History and criticism
     USE Opera
  —Juvenile
     UF Children's opera
          Juvenile opera
          Opera, Children's
          Opera, Juvenile
          School opera
  —Librettists
     USE Librettists
  —Librettos
     USE Opera—Librettos
  —Production and direction *(MT955)*
     UF Opera—Direction
          Opera direction
          Opera production
     NT Opera producers and directors
  —Stories, plots, etc.
     USE Operas—Stories, plots, etc.

       GEOGRAPHIC SUBDIVISIONS

  —China
     NT Operas, Chinese—History and
          criticism
  —Korea
     NT Ch'anggŭk
          P'ansori

Opera, Children's
USE Opera—Juvenile
Opera, Comic
USE Opera
Operetta
Zarzuela
Opera companies [May Subd Geog]
UF Companies, Opera
Opera direction
USE Opera—Production and direction
Opera directors and producers
USE Opera producers and directors
Opera-glasses *(Manners and customs,*
GT2370)
Opera-houses
USE Theaters
Opera producers and directors [May Subd Geog]
UF Directors, Opera
Opera directors and producers
Producers, Opera
BT Opera—Biography
Opera—Production and direction
Opera production
USE Opera—Production and direction
Operas *(M1500-M1508)*
Here are entered musical works com-
posed in this form. Works about opera
are entered under the heading Opera.
UF Operettas
Puppet operas
Singspiels
BT Dramatic music
NT Ballad operas
College operas, revues, etc.
Operatic scenes
Radio operas
Revolutionary operas
Television operas
Tonadillas
Zarzuelas
Example under reference from Arias
Note under Opera
—To 500
—500-1400
—15th century
—16th century
—17th century
—18th century
—19th century
—20th century

GENERAL SUBDIVISIONS

—Analysis, appreciation *(MT95; MT100)*
—Bibliography
— —Graded lists
—Cadenzas
Example under reference from Cadenzas
—Chorus scores with piano
—Chorus scores without accompaniment
(M1502)
—Copyright
USE Copyright—Operas

Operas *(M1500-M1508)*
(Continued)
—Discography *(ML156.4.O46)*
— —Methodology *(ML110-112)*
—Excerpts *(M1505-8)*
NT Overtures
Suites (Orchestra)
— —Parts *(M1505-6)*
UF Operas—Scores—Excerpts
— —Scores *(M1505-6)*
UF Operas—Scores—Excerpts
— —Vocal scores with guitar *(M1508)*
UF Operas—Vocal scores with guitar
—Excerpts
— —Vocal scores with piano *(M1507-8)*
UF Operas—Vocal scores with piano
—Excerpts
—Excerpts, Arranged
—Film and video adaptations
BT Film adaptations
Moving-pictures, Musical
—First performances [May Subd Geog]
Example under Music—First performances
—History and criticism
USE Opera—History and criticism
—Instructive editions
—Instrumental settings
Example under reference from Instru-
mental settings
—Interpretation (Phrasing, dynamics, etc.)
—Juvenile *(M1995)*
Example under Music—Juvenile
—Librettos *(ML48)*
UF Operas—Librettos
NT Operas—Scenarios
Operas—Stories, plots, etc.
Note under Librettos
—Parts *(M1500)*
— —Excerpts
USE Operas—Excerpts—Parts
—Parts (solo)
—Piano scores *(M33)*
BT Piano music, Arranged
—Piano scores (4 hands) *(M208)*
—Programs *(ML40)*
BT Concerts—Programs
—Scenarios *(ML48-50.2)*
BT Operas—Librettos
Example under reference from Scenarios
—Scores *(M1500)*
— —Excerpts
USE Operas—Excerpts—Scores
—Scores and parts *(M1500)*
—Scores and parts (solo)
—Simplified editions
—Stage guides *(MT955)*
BT Theaters—Stage-setting and scenery
RT Opera—Dramaturgy
Example under reference from Stage
guides
—Stories, plots, etc. *(MT95; MT100)*
UF Opera—Stories, plots, etc.

Operas *(M1500-M1508)*
—Stories, plots, etc. *(MT95; MT100)*
(Continued)
    UF   Operetta—Stories, plots, etc.
            Stories of operas
        BT   Opera—Dictionaries
              Operas—Librettos
              Plots (Drama, novel, etc.)
        SA   *subdivision* Stories of operas *under*
             names of individual composers, e.g.
             Wagner, Richard, 1813-1883—Stories
             of operas
—Teaching pieces
—Themes, motives, Literary
—Vocal scores with accordion
—Vocal scores with continuo
—Vocal scores with guitar *(M1503)*
— —Excerpts
      USE Operas—Excerpts—Vocal
            scores with guitar
—Vocal scores with harpsichord *(M1503)*
—Vocal scores with keyboard instrument
    (M1503)
—Vocal scores with organ
—Vocal scores with piano *(M1503)*
— —Excerpts
      USE Operas—Excerpts—Vocal
            scores with piano
—Vocal scores with piano (4 hands)
    (M1503)
—Vocal scores with piano and organ
—Vocal scores with pianos (2) *(M1503)*
—Vocal scores without accompaniment
    (M1502)
Operas, Chinese [May Subd Geog]
    M1805.3-1805.4
    Here are entered Chinese musical
        dramas, including Peking operas, and,
        with local subdivision, regional operas
        written and performed in the style of a
        particular locality.
    UF   Chinese operas
          Ching chü
          Jingju
          Operas, Peking
          Peking operas
          P'ing chü (Chinese operas)
    BT   Chinese drama
    —History and criticism
        BT   Opera—China
    —Production and direction *(MT955)*
Operas, Peking
    USE Operas, Chinese
Operas arranged for flute *(M64)*
    BT   Flute music, Arranged
Operas arranged for flute, violin, viola, and
    violoncello) *(M463-4)*
    BT   Quartets (Flute, violin, viola,
          violoncello), Arranged
Operas arranged for string quartets
    (M453-4)
    BT   String quartets, Arranged

Operas arranged for violin and piano
    (M222-3)
    BT   Violin and piano music, Arranged
Operatic moving-pictures
    USE Moving-pictures, Musical
Operatic scenes *(M1509)*
    BT   Operas
    RT   College operas, revues, etc.
Operetta [May Subd Geog] *(ML1900)*
    UF   Comic opera
          Musical farce
          Opera, Comic
    BT   Opera
    NT   Melodrama
          Singspiel
          Zarzuela
    —Stories, plots, etc.
        USE Operas—Stories, plots, etc.
Operettas
    USE Musical revues, comedies, etc.
          Operas
          Tonadillas
          Zarzuelas
Ophicleide *(ML990.O)*
    BT   Brass instruments
          Serpent (Musical instrument)
          Tuba
Oraon songs
    USE Songs, Oraon
Oratorio [May Subd Geog] *(Aesthetics, ML3867;*
    History and criticism,
    ML3201-ML3251)
    BT   Church music
    NT   Cantata
          Passion-music—History and criticism
Oratorios *(M2000-M2007)*
    BT   Sacred vocal music
    NT   Pantomimes with music, Sacred
    Example under reference from Arias
    —Analytical guides *(MT110-115)*
    —Excerpts, Arranged
    —Juvenile *(M2190)*
        UF   Children's oratorios
    —Librettos
    Note under Librettos
Oratorios arranged for string quartets
    (M453-4)
    BT   String quartets, Arranged
Oratorios arranged for string quintets
    (M553-4)
    BT   String quintets, Arranged
Orchestra *(ML1200-1251)*
    BT   Chamber music—History and criticism
          Instrumental music—History and
          criticism
          Musical instruments
    RT   Bands (Music)
          Conducting
    SA   *subdivision* Orchestras and bands *under*
          names of individual universities and
          colleges, e.g. Harvard University—
          Orchestras and bands

Orchestra *(ML1200-1251)*
  (Continued)
    NT Chamber orchestra
        Chapels (Music)
        Conductors (Music)
        Dance orchestras
        Gamelan
        Instrumentation and orchestration
        Mandolin orchestras
        Orchestral music
        Pīphāt
        Rhythm bands and orchestras
        Symphony orchestras
Orchestra music
  USE Orchestral music
Orchestral bells
  USE Glockenspiel
Orchestral music *(M1000-1049)*
    UF Orchestra music
    BT Instrumental music
        Orchestra
    SA [Solo instrument(s)] with orchestra
    NT Accordion with orchestra
        Band music
        Bassoon, clarinet, flute, horn, oboe with
          orchestra
        Bassoon, clarinet, flute, oboe, harp with
          orchestra
        Canons, fugues, etc. (Orchestra)
        Chamber-orchestra music
        Chorale preludes (Orchestra)
        Concertos
        Concertos (Bassoon, clarinet, English
          horn, flute)
        Concertos (Clarinets (2))
        Concertos (Jazz octet)
        Concertos (Jazz quartet)
        Concertos (Piano, trumpet, vibraphone,
          double bass)
        Cornet with orchestra
        Dance-orchestra music
        Flute with orchestra
        Guitar with orchestra
        Guitars (4) with orchestra
        Harpsichord with orchestra
        Horn with orchestra
        Marches (Orchestra)
        Marimba with orchestra
        Minuets (Orchestra)
        Monologues with music (Orchestra)
        Oboe and violin with orchestra
        Overtures
        Passacaglias (Orchestra)
        Piano (4 hands) with orchestra
        Pianos (3) with orchestra
        Polkas (Orchestra)
        Polonaises (Orchestra)
        Potpourris (Orchestra)
        Recorder with orchestra
        Rondos (Orchestra)
        Sacred monologues with music
          (Orchestra)

Orchestral music *(M1000-1049)*
  (Continued)
    NT Salon-orchestra music
        String-orchestra music
        String quartet with orchestra
        Suites (Orchestra)
        Symphonic poems
        Symphonies
        Trautonium with orchestra
        Trombone with orchestra
        Trumpet and piano with orchestra
        Variations (Orchestra)
        Viola da gamba with orchestra
        Viola d'amore with orchestra
        Violin and harpsichord with orchestra
        Violin and piano with orchestra
        Violin and viola with orchestra
        Violins (2) with orchestra
        Vocal ensembles with orchestra
        Waltzes (Orchestra)
  Note under Wit and humor, Musical
  —Analysis, appreciation *(MT125; MT130)*
  —Parts *(M1045)*
  —Scores *(M1045)*
  —Scores and parts *(M1045)*
Orchestral music, Arranged *(M1060-1075)*
        Subdivided in the same manner as the
          heading Orchestral music.
  Note under Folk dance music
Orchestration
  USE Instrumentation and orchestration
Orga-sonic organ
  USE Baldwin organ
Organ *(History and criticism, ML550-649)*
    UF Enharmonic organ
        Pipe-organ
    BT Keyboard instruments
    RT Organs
    NT Archiphone
        Claviorganum
        Electronic organ
        Hammond organ
        Hydraulic organ
        Keyboards
        Kimball organ
        Mechanical organs
        Player-organ
        Reed-organ
        Welte-Lichtton-Orgel
        Wurlitzer organ
  Example under Musical instruments
  —Construction *(ML550-597)*
      NT Organ-pipes
          Organ stops
  —History
      BT Church music
  —Instruction and study *(MT180)*
      NT Chants (Plain, Gregorian, etc.)—
          Accompaniment
          Organ music—Teaching pieces
  —Methods *(MT182)*
  —Methods (Jazz) *(MT182)*

Organ *(History and criticism, ML550-649)*
   (Continued)
     —Registration *(MT189)*
       UF Registration (Organ)
       BT Organ—Studies and exercises
       SA *subdivision* Registration *under*
           individual types of organ, e.g.
           Electronic organ—Registration;
           Hammond organ—Registration
       NT Organ stops
   —Studies and exercises *(MT185-191)*
       BT Organ music
       NT Organ—Registration
Organ, Electronic
   USE Electronic organ
Organ and alpenhorn music
   USE Alpenhorn and organ music
Organ and bass trombone music
   USE Bass trombone and organ music
Organ and bassoon music
   USE Bassoon and organ music
Organ and bugle music
   USE Bugle and organ music
Organ and clarinet music
   USE Clarinet and organ music
Organ and cornet music
   USE Cornet and organ music
Organ and double-bass music
   USE Double-bass and organ music
Organ and English-horn music
   USE English horn and organ music
Organ and fluegelhorn music
   USE Fluegelhorn and organ music
Organ and flute music
   USE Flute and organ music
Organ and guitar music
   USE Guitar and organ music
Organ and handbell music
   USE Handbell and organ music
Organ and harp music
   USE Harp and organ music
Organ and harpsichord music
   USE Harpsichord and organ music
Organ and horn music
   USE Horn and organ music
Organ and lute music
   USE Lute and organ music
Organ and marimba music
   USE Marimba and organ music
Organ and oboe music
   USE Oboe and organ music
Organ and percussion music
   USE Percussion and organ music
Organ and piano music
   USE Piano and organ music
Organ and recorder music
   USE Recorder and organ music
Organ and saxophone music
   USE Saxophone and organ music
Organ and timpani music
   USE Timpani and organ music
Organ and trombone music
   USE Trombone and organ music

Organ and trumpet music
   USE Trumpet and organ music
Organ and unspecified instrument music
   USE Duets (Unspecified instrument and
       organ)
Organ and viola da gamba music
   USE Viola da gamba and organ music
Organ and viola d'amore music
   USE Viola d'amore and organ music
Organ and viola music
   USE Viola and organ music
Organ and violin music
   USE Violin and organ music
Organ and violoncello music
   USE Violoncello and organ music
Organ-builders [May Subd Geog]
   BT Musical instrument makers
Organ grinders [May Subd Geog]
   UF Barrel organ players
       Barrel organists
   BT Street music and musicians
Organ, harp, timpani with string orchestra
      (M1140-1141)
   BT Trios (Organ, harp, timpani)
   RT Concertos (Organ, harp, timpani with
       string orchestra)
Organ mass *(ML647)*
   BT Mass (Music)
Organ masses *(M14.3)*
   UF Instrumental masses
       Masses, Instrumental
       Masses, Organ
Organ music *(M6-14)*
   BT Church music
       Keyboard instrument music
   SA Concertos, Minuets, Sonatas, Suites,
       and similar headings with
       specification of instruments; Trios
       [Quartets, etc.] *followed by*
       specifications which include the
       organ; also headings that begin with
       the words organ or organs
   NT Calliope music
       Canons, fugues, etc. (Organ)
       Chaconnes (Organ)
       Chorale preludes
       Claviorganum music
       Marches (Organ)
       Minuets (Organ)
       Organ—Studies and exercises
       Overtures (Organ)
       Passacaglias (Organ)
       Player-organ music
       Reed-organ music
       Rondos (Organ)
       Sonatas (Organ)
       Suites (Organ)
       Symphonic poems (Organ)
       Symphonies (Organ)
       Tablature (Musical notation)
       Thorough bass—Realizations
       Variations (Organ)

Organ music *(M6-14)*
   (Continued)
   —Bibliography
   — —Graded lists *(ML132.O)*
       UF Organ music—Graded lists
   —Graded lists
     USE Organ music—Bibliography—
         Graded lists
   —History and criticism
   —Instructive editions *(MT195-7)*
   —Teaching pieces *(MT193)*
      BT Organ—Instruction and study
Organ music, Arranged *(M12-13)*
   NT Concerti grossi arranged for organ
      Overtures arranged for organ
      Symphonies arranged for organ
Organ music (4 hands) *(M180-181)*
   NT Canons, fugues, etc. (Organ, 4 hands)
      Sonatas (Organ, 4 hands)
      Suites (Organ, 4 hands)
      Variations (Organ, 4 hands)
Organ music (Jazz)
   NT Organ music (Ragtime)
Organ music (Organs (2)) *(M180-181)*
   NT Canons, fugues, etc.(Organs (2))
      Sonatas (Organs (2))
Organ music (Organs (3)) *(M180-181)*
   NT Concertos (Organs (3))
Organ music (Ragtime) *(M6-13.5)*
   BT Organ music (Jazz)
      Ragtime music
Organ, piano, guitars (3), percussion with
      orchestra *(M1040-1041)*
   BT Sextets (Organ, piano, guitars (3),
        percussion)
   RT Concertos (Organ, piano, guitars (3),
        percussion)
Organ-pipes *(ML595)*
   BT Musical pitch
      Organ—Construction
   RT Organ stops
   NT Flue pipes (Organ pipes)
      Reed pipes (Organ pipes)
Organ-player
   USE Player-organ
Organ-point *(MT59)*
   UF Pedal point
   BT Harmony
   RT Bourdon
Organ realizations of thorough bass
   USE Thorough bass—Realizations
Organ stops
   UF Stops, Organ
   BT Organ—Construction
      Organ—Registration
   RT Organ-pipes
   NT Mixture stops
      Rohrflöte
Organ with band *(M1205)*
   RT Concertos (Organ with band)
   —Solo with piano *(M1206)*
      BT Piano and organ music, Arranged

Organ with brass ensemble
   RT Concertos (Organ with brass ensemble)
Organ with chamber orchestra *(M1105-6)*
   RT Concertos (Organ with chamber orchestra)
Organ with instrumental ensemble
   RT Concertos (Organ with instrumental
        ensemble)
      Instrumental ensembles
   NT Instrumental ensembles
      Suites (Organ with instrumental
        ensemble)
Organ with orchestra *(M1005-6)*
   RT Concertos (Organ)
   NT Symphonies (Organ with orchestra)
   —Solo with piano *(M1006)*
      BT Piano and organ music, Arranged
Organ with percussion ensemble
   RT Concertos (Organ with percussion
        ensemble)
Organ with string orchestra *(M1105-6)*
   RT Concertos (Organ with string orchestra)
   NT Passacaglias (Organ with string orchestra)
      Suites (Organ with string orchestra)
      Symphonies (Organ with string orchestra)
      Variations (Organ with string orchestra)
Organ with string orchestra, Arranged *(M1105-6)*
   —Score and parts *(M1105)*
Organ with wind ensemble
   RT Concertos (Organ with wind ensemble)
Organa
      Here are entered musical works composedin
        the form of organum. Works on organum
        as a musical form are entered under the
        heading Organum.
   BT Part-songs, Sacred
Organina *(MT35)*
   BT Musical instruments (Mechanical)
Organists [May Subd Geog] *(Biography: collective,*
      ML396; individual, ML416)
   UF Music—Biography
   BT Church musicians
Organology (Music)
   USE Musical instruments
Organs [May Subd Geog]
   RT Organ
   SA *subdivisions* Organ *or* Organs *under*
       names of churches, cathedrals, etc.
   —France
      NT Saint-Sernin de Toulouse (Church)—
        Organ
Organs (3) with orchestra *(M1005-6)*
   RT Concertos (Organs (3))
Organum *(Musical history, ML174)*
      Here are entered works on organum as a
        musical form. Musical works composed in
        the form are entered under the heading
        Organa.
   BT Counterpoint
      Music—500-1400
   Note under Organa
Oriya folk-songs
   USE Folk-songs, Oriya

Ornaments (Music)
   USE Embellishment (Music)
Ossetic songs
   USE Songs, Ossetic
Ostdeutsche Musiktage *(ML37.G3S36)*
   BT Music festivals—Germany (West)
Oud *(ML1015.O9)*
   UF 'Ud
   BT Lute
Oud music *(M142.O9)*
   BT Lute music
   NT Suites (Oud, violins (2), viola,
           violoncello)
Oud with string orchestra *(M1137.4.O9)*
   RT Concertos (Oud with string orchestra)
   NT Suites (Oud with string orchestra)
Overtones (Music)
   USE Harmonics (Music)
Overture *(History and criticism, ML1261)*
   BT Music, Incidental
         Opera
   NT Entr'acte music
Overtures *(M1004)*
         Here are entered overtures for orchestra.
           Overtures for other media are entered
           under this heading followed by specifi-
           cation of medium, e.g. *Overtures*
           (Chamber orchestra)
   BT Ballets—Excerpts
         Operas—Excerpts
         Orchestral music
   RT Symphonic poems
Overtures, Arranged *(M1060)*
Overtures (Band) *(M1204)*
   BT Band music
Overtures (Band), Arranged *(M1255)*
Overtures (Chamber orchestra) *(M1004)*
   BT Chamber-orchestra music
   Note under Overtures
Overtures (Clarinet and piano) *(M248-252)*
   BT Clarinet and piano music
Overtures (Dance orchestra) *(M1356)*
   BT Dance-orchestra music
   —Scores *(M1356)*
Overtures (Electronic music) *(M1473)*
   BT Electronic music
Overtures (Guitar) *(M125-7)*
   BT Guitar music
Overtures (Instrumental ensemble) *(M985)*
   BT Instrumental ensembles
Overtures (Organ) *(M6-M7; M11)*
   BT Organ music
Overtures (Organ), Arranged
   USE Overtures arranged for organ
Overtures (Piano) *(M25)*
   BT Piano music
Overtures (Piano, 4 hands) *(M200-M201;*
         M204)
   BT Piano music (4 hands)
Overtures (Piano, 4 hands), Arranged
   USE Overtures arranged for piano (4 hands)
Overtures (Piano), Arranged
   USE Overtures arranged for piano

Overtures (Pianos (2)) *(M214-215)*
   BT Piano music (Pianos (2))
Overtures (Recorders (5)) *(M555-M556;*
         M557.2)
   BT Woodwind quintets (Recorders (5))
Overtures (Salon orchestra) *(M1350)*
   BT Salon-orchestra music
Overtures (String orchestra) *(M1104)*
   BT String-orchestra music
Overtures (String orchestra), Arranged
         (M1106)
   —Scores and parts
Overtures (Trumpet with string orchestra)
         (M1130-M1131)
   BT Trumpet with string orchestra)
Overtures (Violin with orchestra)
         (M1012-1013)
   BT Violin with orchestra
Overtures (Violin with string orchestra)
         (M1112-1113)
   BT Violin with string orchestra
Overtures (Wind ensemble) *(M955-7)*
   BT Wind ensembles
Overtures arranged for accordion *(M175.A4)*
   BT Accordion music
Overtures arranged for bassoons (3),
         clarinets (2), horns (2), oboes (2)
         (M958-M959)
   BT Wind nonets (Bassoons (3), clarinets (2),
          horns (2), oboes (2)), Arranged
Overtures arranged for flute, guitar, viola
         (M383-4)
   BT Trios (Flute, guitar, viola), Arranged
Overtures arranged for flute, guitar, violin
         (M383-4)
   BT Trios (Flute, guitar, violin), Arranged
Overtures arranged for flute, violin, viola,
         violoncello) *(M463-4)*
   BT Quartets (Flute, violin, viola,
          violoncello), Arranged
Overtures arranged for flutes (2) *(M288-9)*
   BT Flute music (Flutes (2)), Arranged
Overtures arranged for flutes (4) *(M458-459)*
   BT Woodwind quartets (Flutes (4)), Arranged
Overtures arranged for guitar and piano
         (M276-7)
   BT Guitar and piano music, Arranged
Overtures arranged for guitar, violin, viola
         (M373-4)
   BT Trios (Guitar, violin, viola), Arranged
Overtures arranged for guitars (2) *(M292-3)*
   BT Guitar music (Guitars (2)), Arranged
Overtures arranged for harpsichord *(M35)*
   BT Harpsichord music, Arranged
         Overtures arranged for piano
Overtures arranged for organ *(M12-13)*
   UF Overtures (Organ), Arranged
   BT Organ music, Arranged
Overtures arranged for piano *(M35)*
   UF Overtures (Piano), Arranged
   BT Piano music, Arranged
   NT Overtures arranged for harpsichord
   —Excerpts *(M35)*

Overtures arranged for piano (4 hands)
(*M209*)
 UF   Overtures (Piano, 4 hands), Arranged
 BT   Piano music (4 hands), Arranged
Overtures arranged for piano (6 hands)
(*M213*)
 BT   Piano music (6 hands), Arranged
Overtures arranged for piano (Pianos (2), 8
hands) (*M216*)
 BT   Piano music (Pianos (2), 8 hands),
       Arranged
Overtures arranged for piano, flute, guitar
(*M338-9*)
 BT   Trios (Piano, flute, guitar), Arranged
Overtures arranged for piano trios
(*M313-314*)
 BT   Piano trios, Arranged
Overtures arranged for string quartets
(*M453-4*)
 BT   String quartets, Arranged
Overtures arranged for violin and piano
(*M222-3*)
 BT   Violin and piano music, Arranged
Overtures arranged for violins (2), violoncello
(*M352-3*)
 BT   String trios (Violins (2), violoncello),
       Arranged
P.R.1 X.M. (Computer program)
 USE   PR1XM (Computer program)
Pageants [May Subd Geog] (*PN3202-PN3299;*
       Manners and customs,
       GT3980-4099)
 BT   Music, Incidental
       Pantomimes with music
 —Vocal scores with organ (*M1523*)
 —Vocal scores with piano (*M1523*)
Paite folk-songs
 USE   Folk-songs, Paite
Paite hymns
 USE   Hymns, Paite
Paleography, Musical (*ML174*)
 UF   Musical paleography
 BT   Music
       Musical notation
       Musicology
 RT   Music—Manuscripts
       Neumes
Palm Sunday music (*M2048.P4; M2058.P4*)
 BT   Holy-Week music
Pan hu (*ML927*)
 BT   Hu ch'in
       Musical instruments—China
       Stringed instruments, Bowed
Pan-pipes
 USE   Panpipes
Pandean pipes
 USE   Panpipes
Pandora music (*M142.P*)
 SA   Concertos, Minuets, Sonatas, Suites,
       and similar headings with
       specification of instruments; also
       Trios [Quartets, etc.] *followed by*

Pandora music (*M142.P*)
 (*Continued*)
 SA   *specifications which include the*
       pandora; also Plectral ensembles; *and*
       headings beginning with the words
       Pandora or Pandoras
Pandore
 USE   Pandora (Musical instrument)
Pandur
 USE   Tambura
Panjabi folk-songs
 USE   Folk-songs, Panjabi
Panjabi lullabies
 USE   Lullabies, Panjabi
Panpipes
       ML990.P3 (History, construction)
       MT533.P3 (Instruction)
 UF   Antara
       Nai
       Pan-pipes
       Pandean pipes
       Pan's pipes
       Sico
       Siku
       Syrinx (Musical instrument)
       Zampoña
 BT   Pipe (Musical instrument)
       Woodwind instruments
Panpipes music (*M110.P*)
Panpipes with orchestra (*M1034.P;*
       M1035.P)
 RT   Concertos (Panpipes)
Pan's pipes
 USE   Panpipes
P'ansori
 BT   Ballads, Korean
       Opera—Korea
Panto
 USE   Pantomime (Christmas entertainment)
Pantomime [May Subd Geog] (*Drama,*
       PN1985-PN1988; Music, ML3460)
       Here are entered works on plays or
       entertainments in which the performers
       express themselves by mute gestures,
       often to the accompaniment of music.
       Collections of pantomimes are entered
       under Pantomimes.
 RT   Ballet
 NT   Pantomime (Christmas entertainment)
 Note under Pantomimes
Pantomime (Christmas entertainment)
       [May Subd Geog]
       Here are entered works on those tradi-
       tional British Christmas entertain-
       ments based on certain nursery or
       popular tales dramatized in a manner
       deriving from the European commedia
       dell'arte and harlequinade with a free
       admixture of music-hall comedy rou-
       tines, song, dance, melodrama, opulent
       tableaux, and audience participation.
 UF   Christmas pantomime

Pantomime (Christmas entertainment)
    [May Subd Geog]
  (Continued)
  UF Panto
  BT Musical revue, comedy, etc.
      Pantomime
      Vaudeville
Pantomimes *(PN6120.P3-PN6120.P4)*
      Here are entered collections of pantomimes.
      Works on plays or entertainments in which
      the performers express themselves by mute
      gestures, often to the accompaniment of
      music, are entered under Pantomime.
  —*Note under* Pantomime
  —Copyright
Pantomimes with music *(M1520-1526)*
  BT Cantatas, Secular
      Music
  RT Ballets
  NT Pageants
  —Piano scores *(M33)*
  —Vocal scores with piano *(M1523)*
Pantomimes with music, Juvenile *(M1995)*
Pantomimes with music, Sacred
      (M1520-1526)
  BT Cantatas, Sacred
      Oratorios
  —Vocal scores with piano *(M1523)*
Pantomimes with music arranged for piano
      (Pianos (2)) *(M1523)*
  BT Piano music (Pianos (2)), Arranged
Papuan folk-songs
  USE Folk-songs, Papuan
Paratum cor meum
  USE Psalms (Music)—108th Psalm
Parlor organ
  USE Reed-organ
Parodies (Music)
  USE Wit and humor, Musical
Parody (Music)
  UF Musical parody
  BT Musical form
      Vocal music—History and criticism
  SA *subdivision* Parodies, imitations, etc. *under*
      names of individual composers
Part-songs *(M1578-1607)*
      The term Part-songs is here defined as a
      type of vocal chamber music which
      may be performed by solo voices or a
      choral ensemble, with or without dou-
      bling or even with replacement by in-
      struments; it applies to early music
      through the beginning of the seven-
      teenth century and other works com-
      posed in a similar manner.
      Here are entered collections of secular
      part-songs and separately published
      secular part-songs with texts in more
      than one language. Part-songs with
      texts in one language are entered un-
      der Part-songs, English [French, Ger-
      man, etc.]

Part-songs *(M1578-1607)*
  (Continued)
      Part-songs composed in a form are en-
      tered under the name of the form, *e.g.*
      Chansons, Polyphonic; Madrigals
      (Music); etc.
  UF Part-songs, Secular
      Secular part-songs
  BT Choral music
      Songs
      Vocal duets
      Vocal ensembles
      Vocal music
      Vocal nonets
      Vocal octets
      Vocal quartets
      Vocal quintets
      Vocal septets
      Vocal sextets
      Vocal trios
  RT Choruses, Secular
  NT Canons, fugues, etc. (Vocal)
      Clausulae (Part-songs)
      Conductus
      Madrigal
      Madrigals (Music)
      Motet
      Motets
      Rondos (Vocal)
  Notes under Madrigals (Music); Motets
Part-songs, Anglo-Norman
  UF Anglo-Norman part-songs
Part-songs, English
  UF English part-songs
  NT Anthems
Part-songs, English, [French, German, etc.]
  Notes under Part-songs; Part-songs, Sacred
Part-songs, French
  UF French part-songs
Part-songs, German
  UF German part-songs
Part-songs, Italian
  NT Ballate
      Villanelle (Part-songs)
Part-songs, Latin
  UF Latin part-songs
  NT Part-songs, Sacred
Part-songs, Middle English [May Subd Geog]
  UF Middle English part-songs
Part-songs, Old French [May Subd Geog]
  UF Old French part-songs
Part-songs, Sacred *(M2081-2099)*
      Here are entered collections of sacred
      part-songs and separately published
      sacred part-songs.
      Sacred part-songs with texts in a language
      other than Latin are assigned a second
      heading, *e.g.:* Part-songs, English,
      [French, German, etc.]
      Sacred part-songs composed in a form are
      entered under the name of the form,
      e.g.: Anthems, Motets, etc.

Part-songs, Sacred *(M2081-2099)*
    (Continued)
    UF Sacred part-songs
    BT Choral music
         Choruses, Sacred
         Church music
         Part-songs, Latin
         Sacred duets
         Sacred nonets
         Sacred octets
         Sacred quartets
         Sacred quintets
         Sacred septets
         Sacred sextets
         Sacred trios
         Sacred vocal music
    NT Anthem
         Anthems
         Clausulae (Part-songs)
         Conductus
         Motet
         Motets
         Organa
    Notes under Motets
Part-songs, Secular
    USE Part-songs
Part-songs, Spanish
    Note under Villancicos (Music)
Partita
    USE Suite (Music)
         Variation (Music)
Pasillos
    BT Dance music
Paso dobles
    USE Pasodobles
Pasodobles
    UF Paso dobles
    BT Dance music
Passacaglia
Passacaglias
        Here are entered collections of pass-
          acaglia music for various mediums. In-
          dividual passacaglias and collections of
          passacaglias for a specific medium are
          entered under the heading followed by
          specification of medium.
    UF Passacailles
Passacaglias (Band) *(M1245)*
    BT Band music
    —Scores and parts *(M1245)*
Passacaglias (Band), Arranged *(M1258)*
    —Scores and parts *(M1258)*
Passacaglias (Bassoon and piano) *(M253-4)*
    BT Bassoon and piano music
Passacaglias (Clarinet, horn, violin, viola,
      violoncello) *(M560-562)*
Passacaglias (Flute) *(M60-62)*
    BT Flute music
Passacaglias (Flute and piano) *(M240-242)*
    BT Flute and piano music
    NT Passacaglias (Recorder and
         harpsichord)

Passacaglias (Guitar) *(M125-9)*
    BT Guitar music
Passacaglias (Guitars (2)) *(M292-3)*
    BT Guitar music (Guitars (2))
Passacaglias (Guitars (2)), Arranged
    (M292-3)
Passacaglias (Harpsichord and organ)
    (M182-186)
    BT Harpsichord and organ music
Passacaglias (Oboe with string orchestra)
    (M1122-1123)
    BT Oboe with string orchestra
Passacaglias (Orchestra) *(M1045)*
    BT Orchestral music
    —Scores
Passacaglias (Orchestra), Arranged *(M1060)*
Passacaglias (Organ) *(M6-M7; M11)*
    BT Organ music
Passacaglias (Organ with string orchestra)
    (M1105-6)
    BT Organ with string orchestra
    —Solo with piano *(M1106)*
        BT Piano and organ music, Arranged
Passacaglias (Piano) *(M25)*
    BT Piano music
Passacaglias (Piano), Arranged *(M32.8-38.5)*
Passacaglias (Piano quintet) *(M510-512)*
    BT Piano quintets
Passacaglias (Piano quintet), Arranged
    (M513-514)
Passacaglias (Piano with orchestra)
    (M1010-1011)
    BT Piano with orchestra
    —2-piano scores *(M1011)*
        BT Piano music (Pianos (2)), Arranged
Passacaglias (Pianos (2)) *(M214)*
    BT Piano music (Pianos (2))
Passacaglias (Recorder and harpsichord)
    (M240-242)
    BT Passacaglias (Flute and piano)
        Recorder and harpsichord music
Passacaglias (String orchestra) *(M1145)*
    BT String-orchestra music
Passacaglias (String orchestra), Arranged
    (M1160)
    —Scores
Passacaglias (Viola) *(M45-47)*
    BT Viola music
Passacaglias (Viola), Arranged *(M48-49)*
Passacaglias (Violin) *(M40-42)*
    BT Violin music
Passacaglias (Violin and viola) *(M286-7)*
    BT Violin and viola music
Passacaglias (Violoncello and piano)
    (M229-M230; M233)
    BT Violoncello and piano music
Passacaglias (Violoncellos (2)) *(M286-7)*
    BT Violoncello music (Violoncellos (2))
Passacaglias (Violoncellos (2)), Arranged
    (M286-7)
Passacailles
    USE Passacaglias

Passamezzos
UF Pass'e mezzi
BT Dance music
RT Pavans

Pass'e mezzi
USE Passamezzos

Passepieds
BT Dance music

Passion-music
UF Jesus Christ—Crucifixion—Songs and
music
Jesus Christ—Passion—Music
Jesus Christ—Passion—Songs and
music
Jesus Christ—Seven last words—Songs
and music
BT Lenten music
Music
Passion-plays
Sacred vocal music
RT Good Friday music
NT Stabat Mater dolorosa (Music)
Stations of the Cross—Songs and music
—History and criticism
BT Church music
Oratorio

Passover music
UF Music, Passover
Seder music
BT Synagogue music

Pastoral music (Sacred)
USE Church music
Sacred vocal music

Pastoral music (Secular) [May Subd Geog]
UF Music, Pastoral
Pastorale (Music)
BT Music
NT Shepherds' songs

Pastoral oboe
USE Pipe (Musical instrument)

Pastorale (Music)
USE Pastoral music (Secular)

Patriotic music [May Subd Geog]
UF Music, Patriotic
Patriotic songs
Songs, Patriotic
BT Music
RT National music
NT National songs

Patriotic songs
USE National songs
Patriotic music

Pavan *(GV1796.P3)*
Here are entered works on the pavan.
Music for the dance is entered under
the heading Pavans followed by
specification of medium.

Pavans
BT Dance music
RT Passamezzos
Note under Pavan

Pedal point
USE Organ-point

Pedaling (Piano playing)
USE Piano—Instruction and study—Pedaling
Piano—Studies and exercises—Pedaling

Pedalling (Piano playing)
USE Piano—Instruction and study—Pedaling
Piano—Studies and exercises—Pedaling

Peking operas
USE Operas, Chinese

Penitential Psalms (Music)
UF Psalms (Music), Penitential
BT Psalms (Music)
NT Psalms (Music)—6th Psalm
Psalms (Music)—32d Psalm
Psalms (Music)—51st Psalm
Psalms (Music)—102d Psalm
Psalms (Music)—130th Psalm
Psalms (Music)—143d Psalm

Pennillion singing *(ML3653)*
BT Music—Wales

Pennsylvania German folk-songs
USE Folk-songs, Pennsylvania German

Pennsylvania German songs
USE Songs, Pennsylvania German

Penny theaters [May Subd Geog]
BT Music-halls (Variety theaters, cabarets,
etc.)—England

Penny whistle *(ML990.P45)*
UF Feadóg stáin
Tin whistle
Whistle
BT Flageolet
Pipe (Musical instrument)
NT Melody flute

Penny whistle and guitar music *(M296-297)*
UF Guitar and penny whistle music

Penny whistle music *(M110.P)*

Pentecost festival music

Percussion and accordion music
USE Accordion and percussion music

Percussion and banjo music *(M298)*
UF Banjo and percussion music

Percussion and bass clarinet music
USE Bass clarinet and percussion music

Percussion and bassoon music
USE Bassoon and percussion music

Percussion and celesta music *(M298)*
UF Celesta and percussion music
NT Percussion and celesta with string
orchestra

Percussion and celesta with string orchestra
(M1105-6)
BT Percussion and celesta music
RT Concertos (Percussion and celesta with
string orchestra)

Percussion and clarinet music
USE Clarinet and percussion music

Percussion and double-bass music *(M298)*
UF Double-bass and percussion music

Percussion and euphonium music
USE Euphonium and percussion music

Percussion and flute music
USE Flute and percussion music

Percussion and guitar music *(M298)*
 UF Guitar and percussion music
Percussion and harp music *(M298)*
 UF Harp and percussion music
Percussion and harpsichord music *(M284.P4;*
    M285.P4)
 UF Harpsichord and percussion music
Percussion and horn music
 USE Horn and percussion music
Percussion and hurdy-gurdy music
 USE Hurdy-gurdy and percussion music
Percussion and oboe music
 USE Oboe and percussion music
Percussion and ondes Martenot music
 USE Ondes Martenot and percussion music
Percussion and organ music *(M182-6)*
 UF Organ and percussion music
 NT Percussion and organ with string orchestra
Percussion and organ with string orchestra
    (M1105-6)
 BT Percussion and organ music
 RT Concertos (Percussion and organ with
    string orchestra)
 —Scores and parts *(M1105)*
Percussion and piano music *(M284-5)*
 UF Piano and percussion music
 NT Concertos (Percussion and piano with
    string orchestra)
    Percussion and piano with instrumental
    ensemble
    Percussion and piano with string orchestra
    Suites (Percussion and piano)
    Trios (Piano (4 hands), percussion)
    Variations (Percussion and piano)
    Waltzes (Percussion and piano)
Percussion and piano music, Arranged *(M284-5)*
 NT Concertos (Percussion)—Solo with
    piano
    Concertos (Percussion with chamber
    orchestra)—Solos with piano
    Percussion with chamber orchestra—
    Solo with piano
    Percussion with orchestra—Solo with
    piano
Percussion and piano with chamber orchestra
    (M1040-1041)
 RT Concertos (Percussion and piano with
    chamber orchestra)
Percussion and piano with instrumental
    ensemble
 BT Percussion and piano music
 RT Concertos (Percussion and piano with
    instrumental ensemble)
 NT Variations (Percussion and piano with
    instrumental ensemble)
Percussion and piano with orchestra *(M1040-1041)*
 RT Concertos (Percussion and piano)
Percussion and piano with string orchestra
    (M1105-6)
 BT Percussion and piano music
    String-orchestra music
 RT Concertos (Percussion and piano with
    string orchestra)

Percussion and piccolo music
 USE Piccolo and percussion music
Percussion and recorder music
 USE Recorder and percussion music
Percussion and sarrusophone music
 USE Sarrusophone and percussion music
Percussion and saxophone music
 USE Saxophone and percussion music
Percussion and timpani with string orchestra   .
 USE Timpani and percussion with string
    orchestra
Percussion and trombone music
 USE Trombone and percussion music
Percussion and trumpet music
 USE Trumpet and percussion music
Percussion and tuba music
 USE Tuba and percussion music
Percussion and viola music *(M298)*
 UF Viola and percussion music
 NT Sonatas (Percussion and viola)
    Variations (Percussion and viola)
Percussion and violin music *(M298)*
 UF Violin and percussion music
 NT Sonatas (Percussion and violin)
Percussion and violoncello music *(M298)*
 UF Violoncello and percussion music
 NT Sonatas (Percussion and violoncello)
Percussion bands
 USE Percussion ensembles
    Rhythm bands and orchestras
    Steel band (Musical ensemble)
Percussion ensembles
    Here are entered compositions for two or
    more percussionists, each playing one
    or many percussion instruments. Com-
    positions for one percussionist playing
    two or more different percussion in-
    struments are entered under Percus-
    sion music. The designation Percus-
    sion ensemble is also used in conjunc-
    tion with a specified solo in-
    strument(s), *e.g.* Concertos (Violin
    with percussion ensemble); Piano,
    flute, zither with percussion ensemble;
    Violin with percussion ensemble. *Cf.*
    note under Percussion music for form
    of other headings which include per-
    cussion instruments.
 UF Drum music
    Ensembles (Music)
    Percussion bands
 BT Duets
    Percussion music
 SA Concertos, *followed by specifications of*
    instruments which include percussion
    instruments or the word percussion;
    and Percussion with band [orchestra,
    string orchestra, etc.]
 NT Gahu
    Steel band music
    Notes under Instrumental ensembles; Percus-
    sion music

Percussion instruments *(History and*
     criticism, ML1030-1040)
  UF Instruments, Percussion
  NT Bones (Musical instrument)
       Bongo
       Celesta
       Claves
       Drum
       Electronic percussion instruments
       Gamelan
       Gender (Musical instrument)
       Glockenspiel
       Guṃlā
       Hourglass drum
       Jaw bone, Musical
       Jew's harp
       Kei
       Kemanak
       Kolintang
       Maraca
       Marimba
       Notched rattle
       Pīphāt
       Rhythm bands and orchestras
       Sistrum
       Tabla
       Tambourine
       Timpani
       Vibraphone
       Xylophone
  Example under Musical instruments
  —Methods *(MT655)*
Percussion instruments, Electronic
  USE Electronic percussion instruments
Percussion music *(M146)*
       Here are entered compositions for one
       percussionist playing two or more dif-
       ferent percussion instruments. Com-
       positions for one percussion instru-
       ment are entered under specific per-
       cussion instruments, *e.g.* Timpani mu-
       sic; Xylophone music. Compositions
       for two or more percussionists are en-
       tered under Percussion ensembles.
       The word percussion may stand for any
       number of percussionists when used in
       other headings, *e.g.* Choruses, Secular
       (Mixed voices) with percussion; Con-
       certos (Percussion); Octets (Trumpets
       (4), Percussion); Percussion with or-
       chestra; Songs with percussion. *Cf.*
       note under Percussion ensembles for
       form of headings for specified solo in-
       strument(s) with two or more percus-
       sionists.
  UF Drum music
  BT Instrumental music
  SA Concertos, Minuets, Sonatas, Suites,
      and similar headings with
      specification of instruments; Trios
      [Quartets, etc.] *followed by*
      specifications which include

Percussion music *(M146)*
  (Continued)
  SA *percussion instruments or the word*
      percussion; also headings that begin
      with the word percussion
  NT Bagpipe and drum music
       Bugle and drum music
       Fife and drum music
       Mridanga music
       Percussion ensembles
       Pipe band music
       Pīphāt music
       Recorded accompaniments (Drum)
       Symphonies (Percussion)
  Notes under Nonets; Octets; Quartets; Quin-
     tets; Septets; Sextets; Trios
Percussion with band *(M1205-6)*
  RT Concertos (Percussion with band)
Percussion with chamber orchestra *(M1038-9)*
  BT Chamber-orchestra music
  RT Concertos (Percussion with chamber
      orchestra)
  —Solo with piano *(M1039)*
      BT Percussion and piano music,
         Arranged
Percussion with instrumental ensemble
  RT Concertos (Percussion with
      instrumental ensemble)
Percussion with jazz ensemble *(M985)*
  BT Jazz ensembles
  RT Concertos (Percussion with jazz
      ensemble)
Percussion with orchestra *(M1038-9)*
  RT Concertos (Percussion)
  NT Suites (Percussion with orchestra)
       Variations (Percussion with orchestra)
  Note under Percussion music
  —Solo with piano *(M1039)*
      BT Percussion and piano music,
         Arranged
  —Solo with pianos (2) *(M1039)*
      BT Trios (Pianos (2), percussion),
         Arranged
Percussion with percussion ensemble
  RT Concertos (Percussion with percussion
      ensemble)
Percussion with string orchestra *(M1105-M1106)*
  UF Percussion and timpani with string
      orchestra
  RT Concertos (Percussion with string orchestra)
Performances
  USE *subdivision* Performances *under names*
      of individual composers, performing
      artists, etc.
Performing arts [May Subd Geog]
  SA *subdivision* Performances *under names*
      of individual composers, performing
      artists, etc.; and other art forms per-
      formed on stage or screen, e.g. Ballet,
      Concerts, Opera, *etc.*
  —Festivals
     USE Performing arts festivals

Performing arts festivals [May Subd Geog]
 UF Performing arts—Festivals
 NT Music festivals
Peru in music
 BT Music
Petroushka (Ballet) *(GV1790)*
 UF Petrouchka (Ballet)
   Petrushka (Ballet)
 BT Ballets
Philharmonie (Berlin, Germany)
 UF Philharmonie Concert Hall (Berlin,
   Germany)
 BT Music-halls—Germany (West)
Phonotapes—Catalogs
 SA *subdivision* Phonotape catalogs *under*
   topical headings, names of individual
   persons, and names of individual
   corporate bodies for lists or catalogs
   of sound recordings or phonotapes,
   e.g. Radio journalism—Phonotape catalogs
Phrasing (Music)
 USE Music—Interpretation (Phrasing,
   dynamics, etc.)
Physical education and music
 USE Music in physical education
Physical education and training [May Subd Geog]
   (GV201-GV555)
 NT Music in physical education
Physically handicapped musicians
   [May Subd Geog]
 UF Musicians, Physically handicapped
 BT Musicians
   Physically handicapped
 NT Blind musicians
Physicians as musicians *(R707.3)*
 BT Musicians
Physiological aspects of music
 USE Music—Physiological aspects
P'i P'a *(ML1015-1018)*
 UF Chinese lute
   Pipa
 BT Lute
P'i P'a music *(M142.P6)*
P'i P'a with orchestra *(M1037.4.P5)*
 RT Concertos (P'i P'a)
Pianists [May Subd Geog] *(Biography: collective,*
   ML397; individual, ML417)
 UF Music—Biography
 BT Musicians
Piano *(ML650-749)*
 UF Fortepiano
   Pianoforte
   Tangentenflügel
 BT Keyboard instruments
 RT Harpsichord
 NT Archicembalo
   Clavichord
   Keyboards
   Music-recorders
   Pianola
   Player-piano
   Sambuca lincea
 Example under Musical instruments

Piano *(ML650-749)*
 (Continued)
 —Catalogs and collections [May Subd Geog]
 —Catalogs, Manufacturers'
 —Chord diagrams *(MT248)*
  BT Piano—Instruction and study
    Piano—Methods—Self-instruction
  Example under Tablature (Musical nota-
   tion)
 —Construction *(ML652-697)*
  NT Piano makers
    Piano numbers
 —Customizing
  UF Customizing of pianos
  BT Piano—Construction
 —Dictionaries *(ML102)*
  Example under Musical instruments—
   Dictionaries
 —Group instruction
  USE Piano—Methods—Group
    instruction
 —History *(ML650-697)*
 —Identification
 —Instruction and study [May Subd Geog]
   (MT220-MT255; Juvenile,
   MT745-MT758)
  NT Chiroplast
    Harmony, Keyboard
    Musical accompaniment
    Piano—Chord diagrams
    Piano—Practicing
    Piano music—Teaching pieces
    Technicon
  Example under Instrumental music—In-
   struction and study; Music—Instruction
   and study
 — —Fingering
  UF Fingering (Piano playing)
 — —Juvenile *(MT745-758)*
 — —Pedaling *(MT227)*
  UF Pedaling (Piano playing)
    Pedalling (Piano playing)
 —Keys
  Example under reference from Keys
   (Musical instruments)
 —Maintenance and repair *(ML652)*
 —Methods *(MT222)*
 — —Group instruction
  UF Piano—Group instruction
 — —Juvenile *(MT746)*
 — —Self-instruction *(MT248)*
  UF Piano—Self-instruction
  NT Piano—Chord diagrams
 —Methods (Bluegrass)
  BT Bluegrass music
 —Methods (Blues)
 —Methods (Boogie woogie) *(MT239)*
 —Methods (Country) *(MT239)*
 —Methods (Jazz) *(MT239)*
 —Methods (Ragtime) *(MT239)*
  BT Ragtime music
 —Methods (Rock) *(MT239)*

Piano *(ML650-749)*
  (Continued)
  —Orchestra studies *(MT240)*
    BT Piano—Studies and exercises
  —Performance *(ML700-742)*
    UF Piano playing
    BT Music—Performance
        Piano music—Interpretation
          (Phrasing, dynamics, etc.)
  —Practicing *(MT220)*
    UF Piano practicing
    BT Piano—Instruction and study
  —Self-instruction
    USE Piano—Methods—Self-instruction
  —Strings
    Example under reference from Strings
      (Musical instrument parts)
  —Studies and exercises *(MT225-240)*
    BT Piano music
    NT Piano—Orchestra studies
  — —Fingering
    UF Fingering (Piano playing)
  — —Juvenile *(MT755)*
  — —Pedaling *(MT227)*
    UF Pedaling (Piano playing)
        Pedalling (Piano playing)
  —Studies and exercises (Bluegrass)
    BT Bluegrass music
  —Studies and exercises (Blues) *(MT239)*
    BT Piano music (Blues)
  —Studies and exercises (Jazz) *(MT239)*
  —Studies and exercises (Rock) *(MT239)*
    BT Rock music
  —Tuning
    BT Piano technicians
    Example under Tuning
Piano, Electronic
  USE Electronic piano
Piano (1 hand) with chamber orchestra
    (M1010-1011)
  RT Concertos (Piano, 1 hand, with
      chamber orchestra)
  NT Suites (Piano, 1 hand, with chamber
      orchestra)
Piano (1 hand) with orchestra *(M1010-1011)*
  BT Piano music (1 hand)
  RT Concertos (Piano, 1 hand)
  NT Variations (Piano, 1 hand, with
      orchestra)
  —2-piano scores *(M1011)*
    BT Piano music (Pianos (2)), Arranged
Piano (4 hands) and reed-organ music
    (M191-3)
  UF Reed-organ and piano music (4 hands)
  NT Marches (Piano (4 hands) and reed-organ)
Piano (4 hands) with instrumental ensemble
  RT Concertos (Piano, 4 hands, with
      instrumental ensemble)
Piano (4 hands) with orchestra *(M1010-1011)*
  BT Orchestral music
      Piano music (4 hands)
  RT Concertos (Piano, 4 hands)

Piano accordion
  USE Accordion
Piano and accordion music
  USE Accordion and piano music
Piano and alto horn music
  USE Alto horn and piano music
Piano and arpeggione music
  USE Arpeggione and piano music
Piano and balalaika music
  USE Balalaika and piano music
Piano and bandonion music
  USE Bandonion and piano music
Piano and baritone music
  USE Baritone and piano music
Piano and bass clarinet music
  USE Bass clarinet and piano music
Piano and bass trombone music
  USE Bass trombone and piano music
Piano and basset-horn music
  USE Basset-horn and piano music
Piano and bassoon music
  USE Bassoon and piano music
Piano and chime music
  USE Chime and piano music
Piano and cimbalom music
  USE Cimbalom and piano music
Piano and clarinet music
  USE Clarinet and piano music
Piano and contrabassoon music
  USE Contrabassoon and piano music
Piano and cornet music
  USE Cornet and piano music
Piano and czakan music
  USE Czakan and piano music
Piano and ḍaph music
  USE Ḍaph and piano music
Piano and domra music
  USE Domra and piano music
Piano and double-bass music
  USE Double-bass and piano music
Piano and dulcimer music
  USE Dulcimer and piano music
**Piano and electronic organ with jazz
    ensemble**
Piano and English horn music
  USE English horn and piano music
Piano and euphonium music
  USE Euphonium and piano music
Piano and flageolet music
  USE Flageolet and piano music
Piano and fluegelhorn music
  USE Fluegelhorn and piano music
Piano and flute music
  USE Flute and piano music
Piano and glass-harmonica music
  USE Glass-harmonica and piano music
Piano and guitar music
  USE Guitar and piano music
Piano and harmonica music
  USE Harmonica and piano music
Piano and harp-lute guitar music
  USE Harp-lute guitar and piano music

Piano and harp music
    USE Harp and piano music
Piano and harpsichord music
    USE Harpsichord and piano music
Piano and horn music
    USE Horn and piano music
Piano and lute music
    USE Lute and piano music
Piano and mandolin music
    USE Mandolin and piano music
Piano and marimba music
    USE Marimba and piano music
Piano and oboe d'amore music
    USE Oboe d'amore and piano music
Piano and oboe music
    USE Oboe and piano music
Piano and ocarina music
    USE Ocarina and piano music
Piano and ondes Martenot music
    USE Ondes Martenot and piano music
Piano and organ music *(M182-4)*
    UF Organ and piano music
    NT Chorale preludes (Piano and organ)
        Suites (Piano and organ)
        Variations (Piano and organ)
Piano and organ music, Arranged *(M186)*
    NT Concertos (Organ)—Solo with piano
        Concertos (Organ with string orchestra)
            —Solo with piano
        Organ with band—Solo with piano
        Organ with orchestra—Solo with piano
        Passacaglias (Organ with string
            orchestra)—Solo with piano
        Symphonies (Organ with orchestra)—
            Solo with piano
        Symphonies arranged for organ and
            piano
Piano and percussion music
  USE Percussion and piano music
Piano and piccolo music
  USE Piccolo and piano music
Piano and recorder music
  USE Recorder and piano music
Piano and reed-organ music, Arranged
        (M194-5)
Piano and saxhorn music
  USE Saxhorn and piano music
Piano and saxophone music
  USE Saxophone and piano music
Piano and shakuhachi music
  USE Shakuhachi and piano music
Piano and shinobue music
  USE Shinobue and piano music
Piano and synthesizer music *(M284.E4;*
        M285.E4)
    UF Synthesizer and piano music
Piano and synthesizer with orchestra
        (M1040-M1041)
    NT Concertos (Piano and synthesizer)
Piano and tárogató music
    USE Tárogató and piano music
Piano and timpani music
    USE Timpani and piano music

Piano and trombone music
    USE Trombone and piano music
Piano and trumpet music
    USE Trumpet and piano music
Piano and tuba music
    USE Tuba and piano music
Piano and ukulele music
    USE Ukulele and piano music
Piano and unspecified instrument music
    USE Duets (Unspecified instrument and piano)
Piano and vibraphone music
    USE Vibraphone and piano music
Piano and viola da gamba music
    USE Viola da gamba and piano music
Piano and viola d'amore music
    USE Viola d'amore and piano music
Piano and viola music
    USE Viola and piano music
Piano and violin music
    USE Violin and piano music
Piano and violoncello music
    USE Violoncello and piano music
Piano and wind instrument music
    USE Wind instrument and piano music
Piano and xylophone music
    USE Xylophone and piano music
Piano, clarinet, percussion, violoncello with
        orchestra *(M1040-1041)*
    BT Quartets (Piano, clarinet, percussion,
            violoncello)
    RT Concertos (Piano, clarinet, percussion,
            violoncello)
Piano, clarinet, trombone, percussion with
        orchestra *(M1040-1041)*
    BT Quartets (Piano, clarinet, trombone,
            percussion)
    RT Concertos (Piano, clarinet, trombone,
            percussion)
Piano, clarinet, violin, violoncello with
        orchestra *(M1040-1041)*
    BT Quartets (Piano, clarinet, violin,
            violoncello)
    RT Concertos (Piano, clarinet, violin,
            violoncello)
Piano, clarinet, violin, violoncello with
        string orchestra *(M1140-1141)*
    BT Quartets (Piano, clarinet, violin,
            violoncello)
    RT Concertos (Piano, clarinet, violin,
            violoncello with string orchestra)
Piano duets
    USE Piano music (4 hands)
        Piano music (Pianos (2))
Piano ensembles *(M216)*
        Here are entered compositions for 3 or
            more pianos.
    UF Piano music (Pianos (3))
        Piano music (Pianos (4))
    NT Concertos (Pianos (3))
        Concertos (Pianos (3) with string orchestra)
        Pianos (3) with string orchestra
        Suites (Piano ensemble)
    Note under Chamber music

Piano ensembles, Arranged *(M216)*
>   NT   Concertos (Pianos (2))—3-piano scores
>   Concertos (Pianos (2) with chamber
>   orchestra)—3-piano scores

Piano, flute, horn with string orchestra
>   *(M1140-1141)*
>   BT   Trios (Piano, flute, horn)
>   RT   Concertos (Piano, flute, horn with
>   string orchestra)

Piano, flute, viola with string orchestra
>   *(M1105-6)*
>   BT   Trios (Piano, flute, viola)
>   RT   Concertos (Piano, flute, viola with
>   string orchestra)

Piano, flute, violin with instrumental ensemble
>   BT   Trios (Piano, flute, violin)
>   RT   Concertos (Piano, flute, violin with
>   instrumental ensemble)

Piano, flute, violin with string orchestra
>   *(M1105-6)*
>   BT   Trios (Piano, flute, violin)
>   RT   Concertos (Piano, flute, violin with
>   string orchestra)

Piano, horn, glockenspiel, xylophone with
>   **orchestra** *(M1040-1041)*
>   BT   Quartets (Piano, horn, glockenspiel,
>   xylophone)
>   RT   Concertos (Piano, horn, glockenspiel,
>   xylophone)

Piano, horn, violin with orchestra
>   *(M1040-1041)*
>   BT   Trios (Piano, horn, violin)
>   RT   Concertos (Piano, horn, violin)

Piano makers [May Subd Geog]
>   BT   Musical instrument makers

Piano music *(M20-39)*
>   UF   Piano music (2 hands)
>   BT   Instrumental music
>   Keyboard instrument music
>   SA   Concertos, Trios [Quartets, etc.]
>   *followed by specifications which*
>   *include the piano; also headings that*
>   *begin with the words piano or pianos*
>   NT   Basset-horn and piano music
>   Canons, fugues, etc. (Piano)
>   Chaconnes (Piano)
>   Chorale preludes (Piano)
>   Clavichord music
>   Harpsichord music
>   Marches (Piano)
>   Minuets (Piano)
>   Monologues with music (Piano)
>   Overtures (Piano)
>   Passacaglias (Piano)
>   Piano—Studies and exercises
>   Piano quartets
>   Piano quintets
>   Piano trios
>   Player-piano music
>   Polkas (Piano)
>   Polonaises (Piano)
>   Potpourris (Piano)
>   Prepared piano music

Piano music *(M20-39)*
>   *(Continued)*
>   NT   Recorded accompaniments (Piano)
>   Rondos (Piano)
>   Sacred monologues with music (Piano)
>   Sonatas (Piano)
>   Suites (Piano)
>   Thorough bass—Realizations
>   Variations (Piano)
>   Waltzes (Piano)
>   *Note under* Chance compositions
>   —Analysis, appreciation *(MT140; MT145)*
>   —Bibliography *(ML128.P3)*
>   — —Graded lists *(ML132.P)*
>   UF   Piano music—Graded lists
>   —Graded lists
>   USE   Piano music—Bibliography—
>   Graded lists
>   —History and criticism *(ML700-749)*
>   —Instructive editions *(MT245-7)*
>   NT   Harpsichord music—Instructive
>   editions
>   —Interpretation (Phrasing, dynamics, etc.)
>   *(ML700; MT235)*
>   NT   Piano—Performance
>   —Simplified editions *(M38.3)*
>   —Teaching pieces *(MT243)*
>   BT   Piano—Instruction and study
>   NT   Piano music (Boogie woogie)—
>   Teaching pieces

Piano music, Arranged *(M32.8-38.5)*
>   NT   Concerti grossi arranged for piano
>   Masses—Piano scores
>   Moving-picture music—Piano scores
>   Operas—Piano scores
>   Overtures arranged for piano
>   Symphonic poems arranged for piano
>   Symphonies arranged for piano

Piano music, Arranged (Jazz)
>   USE   Piano music (Jazz)

Piano music (1 hand) *(M26; M26.2)*
>   UF   Left-hand piano music
>   Right-hand piano music
>   NT   Canons, fugues, etc. (Piano, 1 hand)
>   Concertos (Piano, 1 hand)
>   Piano (1 hand) with orchestra
>   Sonatas (Piano, 1 hand)
>   Suites (Piano, 1 hand)
>   Waltzes (Piano, 1 hand)

Piano music (1 hand), Arranged *(M26;*
>   *M26.2)*

Piano music (2 hands)
>   USE   Piano music

Piano music (3 hands) *(M205)*
>   NT   Sonatas (Piano, 3 hands)
>   Variations (Piano, 3 hands)

Piano music (4 hands) *(M200-M201; M204)*
>   UF   Piano duets
>   NT   Canons, fugues, etc. (Piano, 4 hands)
>   Clavichord music (4 hands)
>   Concertos (Piano, 4 hands)
>   Marches (Piano, 4 hands)
>   Minuets (Piano, 4 hands)

Piano music (4 hands) *(M200-M201; M204)*
(Continued)
   NT Monologues with music (Piano, 4 hands)
      Overtures (Piano, 4 hands)
      Piano (4 hands) with orchestra
      Polkas (Piano, 4 hands)
      Polonaises (Piano, 4 hands)
      Potpourris (Piano, 4 hands)
      Quartets (Piano (4 hands), violin, violoncello)
      Quintets (Piano (4 hands), horn, trombone, guitar)
      Rondos (Piano, 4 hands)
      Sonatas (Piano, 4 hands)
      Suites (Piano, 4 hands)
      Suites (Piano (4 hands), cymbals, drum, tambourine, triangle)
      Variations (Piano, 4 hands)
      Waltzes (Piano, 4 hands)
Piano music (4 hands), Arranged *(M207-211)*
   NT Ballets—Piano scores (4 hands)
      Concerti grossi arranged for piano (4 hands)
      Overtures arranged for piano (4 hands)
      Requiems arranged for piano (4 hands)
      Symphonic poems arranged for piano (4 hands)
      Symphonies arranged for piano (4 hands)
Piano music (5 hands) *(M213)*
   Note under Piano trios
Piano music (6 hands) *(M213)*
   NT Canons, fugues, etc. (Piano, 6 hands)
   Note under Piano trios
Piano music (6 hands), Arranged *(M213)*
   NT Overtures arranged for piano (6 hands)
Piano music (8 hands) *(M213)*
Piano music (Blues) *(M20-M32)*
   BT Blues (Music)
   NT Piano—Studies and exercises (Blues)
Piano music (Boogie woogie) *(M20-32)*
   UF Boogie-woogie music
   BT Piano music (Jazz)
  —Teaching pieces *(MT239)*
      BT Piano music—Teaching pieces
Piano music (Jazz) *(M20-32)*
   UF Piano music, Arranged (Jazz)
   NT Piano music (Boogie woogie)
      Piano music (Ragtime)
      Piano with jazz ensemble
   Example under Jazz music
Piano music (Pianos (2)) *(M214)*
   UF Piano duets
   NT Canons, fugues, etc. (Pianos (2))
      Chorale preludes (Pianos (2))
      Concertos (Pianos (2))
      Concertos (Pianos (2) with band)
      Concertos (Pianos (2) with chamber orchestra)
      Concertos (Pianos (2) with string orchestra)
      Marches (Pianos (2))
      Minuets (Pianos (2))

Piano music (Pianos (2)) *(M214)*
(Continued)
   NT Monologues with music (Pianos (2) with chamber orchestra)
      Overtures (Pianos (2))
      Passacaglias (Pianos (2))
      Pianos (2) with band
      Pianos (2) with chamber orchestra
      Pianos (2) with instrumental ensemble
      Pianos (2) with orchestra
      Pianos (2) with string ensemble
      Pianos (2) with string orchestra
      Polkas (Pianos (2))
      Polonaises (Pianos (2))
      Potpourris (Pianos (2))
      Quartets (Pianos (2), flute, viola)
      Quartets (Pianos (2), percussion)
      Quartets (Pianos (2), trombone, percussion)
      Quartets (Pianos (2), violin, violoncello)
      Quintets (Pianos (2), percussion, double bass)
      Rondos (Pianos (2))
      Sonatas (Pianos (2))
      Suites (Pianos (2))
      Suites (Pianos (2) with chamber orchestra)
      Suites (Pianos (2) with instrumental ensemble)
      Variations (Pianos (2))
      Waltzes (Pianos (2))
Piano music (Pianos (2), 5 hands) *(M216)*
Piano music (Pianos (2), 6 hands) *(M216)*
Piano music (Pianos (2), 6 hands), Arranged *(M216)*
   NT Concertos (Piano, 4 hands)—2-piano scores
Piano music (Pianos (2), 8 hands) *(M216)*
   NT Rondos (Pianos (2), 8 hands)
      Variations (Pianos (2), 8 hands)
Piano music (Pianos (2), 8 hands), Arranged *(M216)*
   NT Overtures arranged for piano (Pianos (2), 8 hands)
      Symphonic poems arranged for piano (Pianos (2), 8 hands)
      Symphonies arranged for piano (Pianos (2), 8 hands)
Piano music (Pianos (2)), Arranged *(M215)*
   NT Ballets—2-piano scores
      Concerti grossi arranged for piano (Pianos (2))
      Concertos (Harpsichord)—2-piano scores
      Concertos (Harpsichord with string orchestra)—2-piano scores
      Concertos (Piano)—2-piano scores
      Concertos (Piano)—Excerpts—2-piano scores
      Concertos (Piano, 1 hand)—2-piano scores
      Concertos (Piano with band)—2-piano scores
      Concertos (Piano with chamber orchestra)—2-piano scores
      Concertos (Piano with string ensemble)—2-piano scores

Piano music (Pianos (2)), Arranged *(M215)*
(Continued)
  NT Concertos (Piano with string orchestra)
        —2-piano scores
      Pantomimes with music arranged for
        piano (Pianos (2))
      Passacaglias (Piano with orchestra)—
        2-piano scores
      Piano (1 hand) with orchestra—2-piano
        scores
      Piano with band—2-piano scores
      Piano with chamber orchestra—2-piano
        scores
      Piano with orchestra—2-piano scores
      Piano with orchestra, Arranged—
        2-piano scores
      Piano with string orchestra—2-piano
        scores
      Rondos (Piano with orchestra)—2-piano
        scores
      Suites (Piano with chamber orchestra)
        —2-piano scores
      Suites (Piano with orchestra)—2-piano
        scores
      Symphonic poems arranged for piano
        (Pianos (2))
      Symphonies arranged for piano (Pianos
        (2))
      Symphonies arranged for piano (Pianos
        (2))—Excerpts
      Variations (Piano, 1 hand, with
        orchestra)—2-piano scores
      Variations (Piano with chamber
        orchestra), Arranged—2-piano scores
      Variations (Piano with orchestra)—
        2-piano scores
      Variations (Piano with string orchestra)
        —2-piano scores
      Waltzes (Piano with orchestra)—
        2-piano scores
Piano music (Pianos (3))
  USE Piano ensembles
Piano music (Pianos (4))
  USE Piano ensembles
Piano music (Ragtime) *(M20-32)*
  BT Piano music (Jazz)
      Ragtime music
Piano music (Solovox registration) *(M25.2; M38.2)*
  BT Solovox
Piano numbers *(ML652)*
  BT Piano—Construction
**Piano, oboe, trumpet, violin, double bass with
    string orchestra** *(M1105-6)*
  BT Quintets (Piano, oboe, trumpet, violin,
        double bass)
  RT Concertos (Piano, oboe, trumpet, violin,
        double bass with string orchestra)
Piano-player
  USE Player-piano
Piano playing
  USE Piano—Performance
Piano practicing
  USE Piano—Practicing

Piano quartet *(ML1165)*
      Here are entered works dealing with the
        piano quartet as a musical form.
Piano quartet with string orchestra
    (M1140-1141)
  BT Piano quartets
  RT Concertos (Piano quartet with string
        orchestra)
Piano quartets *(M410-412)*
      Here, with appropriate subdivisions, are
        entered compositions for piano, violin,
        viola and violoncello.
      Compositions for piano and three other
        solo instruments are entered under the
        heading Quartets followed by specifi-
        cation of instruments, *e.g.* Quartets
        (Piano, violins (2), violoncello)
  UF Quartets, Piano
      Quartets (Piano, violin, viola,
        violoncello)
  BT Piano music
      Viola music
      Violin music
      Violoncello music
  NT Canons, fugues, etc. (Piano quartet)
      Concertos (Piano quartet with string
        orchestra)
      Piano quartet with string orchestra
      Quartets (Harpsichord, violin, viola,
        violoncello)
      Suites (Piano quartet)
      Variations (Piano quartet)
  Notes under Quartets; Sonatas
  —Parts
  —Scores
  —Scores and parts
Piano quartets, Arranged *(M413-414)*
  NT Suites (String trio with orchestra)—
        Solos with piano
Piano quintet with string orchestra
    (M1140-1141)
  BT Piano quintets
  RT Concertos (Piano quintet with string
        orchestra)
Piano quintets *(M510-512)*
      Here, with appropriate subdivisions, are
        entered compositions for piano, violins
        (2), viola and violoncello.
      Compositions for piano and four other
        solo instruments are entered under the
        heading Quintets followed by specifi-
        cation of instruments, *e.g.* Quintets
        (Piano, oboe, violin, viola, violoncello)
  UF Quintets, Piano
      Quintets (Piano, violins (2), viola,
        violoncello)
  BT Piano music
      Viola music
      Violin music
      Violoncello music
  NT Concertos (Piano quintet with string
        orchestra)
      Passacaglias (Piano quintet)

Piano quintets *(M510-512)*
> *(Continued)*
> NT Piano quintet with string orchestra
> Quintets (Harpsichord, violins (2), viola, viola da gamba)
> Quintets (Harpsichord, violins (2), viola, violoncello)
> Quintets (Piano (1 hand), violins (2), viola, violoncello)
> Rondos (Piano quintet)
> Suites (Piano quintet)
> Suites (Piano, violins (2), viola, violoncello)
> Variations (Piano quintet)
> *Note under* Quintets
> —Parts
> —Scores
> —Scores and parts

Piano quintets, Arranged *(M513-514)*
> NT Concertos (String quartet)—Solos with piano
> Concertos (String quartet), Arranged—Solos with piano

Piano realizations of thorough bass
> USE Thorough bass—Realizations

Piano, saxophone, percussion, double bass with orchestra *(M1040-1041)*
> BT Quartets (Piano, saxophone, percussion, double bass)
> NT Variations (Piano, saxophone, percussion, double bass with orchestra)

Piano, saxophones (4), harp, percussion with string orchestra) *(M1140-M1141)*
> BT Septets (Piano, saxophones (4), harp, percussion)
> NT Concertos (Piano, saxophones (4), harp, percussion with string orchestra)

Piano technicians
> NT Piano—Tuning

Piano trio with orchestra *(M1040-1041)*
> BT Piano trios
> RT Concertos (Piano trio)
> —Solos with piano *(M1041)*
> > BT Quartets (Pianos (2), violin, violoncello), Arranged

Piano trio with string orchestra *(M1105-6)*
> BT Piano trios
> RT Concertos (Piano trio with string orchestra)

Piano trios *(M310-312)*
> Here, with appropriate subdivisions, are entered compositions for piano, violin and violoncello.
> Compositions for piano and two other solo instruments are entered under the heading Trios, followed by specification of instruments, *e.g.* Trios (Piano, clarinet, violoncello); Trios (Piano, violins (2))
> Compositions for three pianos are entered under the heading Piano music (Pianos (3))

Piano trios *(M310-312)*
> *(Continued)*
> Compositions for three players at one piano are entered under the headings Piano music (5 hands) or Piano music (6 hands)
> UF Trios, Piano
> Trios (Piano, violin, violoncello)
> BT Piano music
> Violin music
> Violoncello music
> NT Concertos (Piano trio)
> Concertos (Piano trio with string orchestra)
> Minuets (Piano trio)
> Piano trio with orchestra
> Piano trio with string orchestra
> Potpourris (Piano trio)
> Suites (Piano trio)
> Trios (Harpsichord, violin, viola da gamba)
> Trios (Harpsichord, violin, violoncello)
> Variations (Piano trio)
> *Notes under* Chamber music; Sonatas; Trios
> —Parts
> — —Collections
> —Scores
> —Scores and parts

Piano trios, Arranged *(M313-314)*
> NT Concertos (Violin and violoncello)—Excerpts—Solos with piano
> Concertos (Violin and violoncello)—Solos with piano
> Concertos (Violin and violoncello with chamber orchestra)—Solos with piano
> Overtures arranged for piano trios
> Symphonies arranged for piano trios
> Violin and violoncello with orchestra—Solos with piano

Piano, trumpet, vibraphone, double bass with orchestra *(M1040-1041)*
> BT Quartets (Piano, trumpet, vibraphone, double bass)
> RT Concertos (Piano, trumpet, vibraphone, double bass)

Piano, trumpet, viola with orchestra *(M1040-1041)*
> BT Trios (Piano, trumpet, viola)
> RT Concertos (Piano, trumpet, viola)
> —Scores *(M1041)*

Piano, trumpets (2) with string orchestra *(M1140-1141)*
> BT Trios (Piano, trumpets (2))

Piano, trumpets (3) with string orchestra *(M1105-6)*
> BT Quartets (Piano, trumpets (3))
> String-orchestra music
> RT Concertos (Piano, trumpets (3) with string orchestra)
> —Scores *(M1105)*

Piano, violins (2) with string orchestra *(M1105-6)*
  UF Two violins, piano with string orchestra
  BT String-orchestra music
      Trios (Piano, violins (2))
  RT Concertos (Piano, violins (2) with
      string orchestra)
  —Scores *(M1105)*

Piano with band *(M1205)*
  RT Concertos (Piano with band)
  NT Potpourris (Piano with band)
      Variations (Piano with band)
  —2-piano scores *(M1206)*
      BT Piano music (Pianos (2)), Arranged
  —Scores *(M1205)*

Piano with band, Arranged *(M1257)*
  —Scores (reduced) and parts *(M1257)*

Piano with brass ensemble *(M917)*
  RT Concertos (Piano with brass ensemble)

Piano with chamber orchestra *(M1010-1011)*
  RT Concertos (Piano with chamber
      orchestra)
  NT Suites (Piano with chamber orchestra)
      Variations (Piano with chamber
      orchestra)
  —2-piano scores *(M1011)*
      BT Piano music (Pianos (2)), Arranged
  —Scores *(M1010)*

Piano with chamber orchestra, Arranged
    (M1010-1011)

Piano with clarinet choir *(M1205-1206)*
  RT Concertos (Piano with clarinet choir)
  NT Variations (Piano with clarinet choir)

Piano with dance orchestra *(M1353)*
  RT Concertos (Piano with dance orchestra)

Piano with instrumental ensemble
  RT Concertos (Piano with instrumental
      ensemble)
  NT Suites (Piano with instrumental
      ensemble)

Piano with jazz ensemble
  BT Piano music (Jazz)

Piano with orchestra *(M1010-1011)*
  RT Concertos (Piano)
  NT Canons, fugues, etc. (Piano with
      orchestra)
      Passacaglias (Piano with orchestra)
      Polonaises (Piano with orchestra)
      Rondos (Piano with orchestra)
      Suites (Piano with orchestra)
      Symphonies (Piano with orchestra)
      Variations (Piano with orchestra)
      Waltzes (Piano with orchestra)
  —2-piano scores *(M1011)*
      BT Piano music (Pianos (2)), Arranged
  —Excerpts, Arranged
  —Scores *(M1010)*
  —Scores and parts *(M1010)*

Piano with orchestra, Arranged
  —2-piano scores *(M1011)*
      BT Piano music (Pianos (2)), Arranged

Piano with percussion ensemble
  RT Concertos (Piano with percussion ensemble)

Piano with salon orchestra *(M1353)*
  BT Salon-orchestra music
      String-orchestra music
  RT Concertos (Piano with salon orchestra)
  —Parts

Piano with string ensemble *(M910-912)*
  RT Concertos (Piano with string ensemble)

Piano with string orchestra *(M1105-6)*
  RT Concertos (Piano with string orchestra)
  NT Suites (Piano with string orchestra)
      Variations (Piano with string orchestra)
  —2-piano scores *(M1106)*
      BT Piano music (Pianos (2)), Arranged

Piano with string orchestra, Arranged
  —Scores and parts *(M1160)*

Piano with wind ensemble
  RT Concertos (Piano with wind ensemble)

Piano with woodwind ensemble
  RT Concertos (Piano with woodwind
      ensemble)

Pianoforte
  USE Piano

Pianograph
  USE Music-recorders

Pianola *(History, ML1055; Instruction and*
    study, MT150, MT700)
  BT Musical instruments (Mechanical)
      Piano
  RT Player-piano

Pianola with orchestra *(M1039.4.P5)*
  RT Concertos (Pianola)

**Pianos (2), guitars (3), percussion with
orchestra** *(M1040-1041)*
  BT Sextets (Pianos (2), guitars (3),
      percussion)
  RT Concertos (Pianos (2), guitars (3),
      percussion)

Pianos (2), percussion with orchestra
    (M1040)
  BT Pianos (2) with percussion
      Sextets (Pianos (2), percussion)
  RT Concertos (Pianos (2), percussion)
  —Scores *(M1040)*

Pianos (2), percussion with string orchestra
    (M1140-1141)
  BT Quartets (Pianos (2), percussion)
  RT Concertos (Pianos (2), percussion with
      string orchestra)

Pianos (2) with band *(M1205-6)*
  BT Piano music (Pianos (2))
  RT Concertos (Pianos (2) with band)

Pianos (2) with brass band *(M1205; M1257)*
  RT Concertos (Pianos (2) with brass band)

Pianos (2) with chamber orchestra
    (M1010-1011)
  BT Piano music (Pianos (2))
  RT Concertos (Pianos (2) with chamber
      orchestra)
  NT Monologues with music (Pianos (2)
      with chamber orchestra)
      Suites (Pianos (2) with chamber
      orchestra)

Pianos (2) with dance orchestra *(M1353)*
   RT Concertos (Pianos (2) with dance
       orchestra)
   NT Variations (Pianos (2) with dance
       orchestra)

Pianos (2) with instrumental ensemble
   UF Two pianos with instrumental ensemble
   BT Piano music (Pianos (2))
   RT Concertos (Pianos (2) with instrumental
       ensemble)
   NT Suites (Pianos (2) with instrumental
       ensemble)

Pianos (2) with orchestra *(M1010-1011)*
   UF Two pianos with orchestra
   BT Piano music (Pianos (2))
   RT Concertos (Pianos (2))
   NT Suites (Pianos (2) with orchestra)
       Variations (Pianos (2) with orchestra)
   —2-piano scores *(M1011)*
   —Parts *(M1010)*
   —Scores *(M1010)*

Pianos (2) with percussion
   NT Pianos (2), percussion with orchestra

Pianos (2) with percussion ensemble
   RT Concertos (Pianos (2) with percussion
       ensemble)
   NT Concertos (Pianos (2), percussion)
       Suites (Pianos (2) with percussion
       ensemble)

Pianos (2) with string ensemble *(M910-914)*
   BT Piano music (Pianos (2))

Pianos (2) with string orchestra *(M1105-6)*
   BT Piano music (Pianos (2))
   RT Concertos (Pianos (2) with string
       orchestra)
   NT Suites (Pianos (2) with string orchestra)

Pianos (3) with orchestra *(M1010-1011)*
   UF Three pianos with orchestra
   BT Orchestral music
   RT Concertos (Pianos (3))
   NT Suites (Pianos (3) with orchestra)

Pianos (3) with string orchestra
   UF Three pianos with string orchestra
   BT Piano ensembles
   RT Concertos (Pianos (3) with string orchestra)

Pibroch *(ML980)*
       Here are entered works about pibroch.
        Musical works composed in this form
        are entered under the heading Pibrochs.
   UF Piobaireachd
   BT Bagpipe music
       Music—Scotland
       Variations (Bagpipe)
   Note under Pibrochs

Pibrochs *(M145)*
       Here are entered musical works composed in
        this form. Works about pibroch are entered
        under the heading Pibroch.
   UF Piobaireachd
   BT Bagpipe music
       Music—Scotland
       Variations (Bagpipe)
   Note under Pibroch

Piccolo *(ML935-7)*
   BT Flute

Piccolo and bassoon music
   USE Bassoon and piccolo music

Piccolo and berimbau music *(M296-297)*
   UF Berimbau and piccolo music

Piccolo and clarinet music
   USE Clarinet and piccolo music

Piccolo and contrabassoon music
   USE Contrabassoon and piccolo music

Piccolo and flute music
   USE Flute and piccolo music

Piccolo and guitar music *(M296-297)*
   UF Guitar and piccolo music

Piccolo and harpsichord music *(M240-244)*
   UF Harpsichord and piccolo music

Piccolo and oboe music
   USE Oboe and piccolo music

Piccolo and percussion music *(M298)*
   UF Percussion and piccolo music

Piccolo and piano music *(M240-242)*
   UF Piano and piccolo music
   NT Marches (Piccolo and piano)
       Rondos (Piccolo and piano)

Piccolo and piano music, Arranged *(M243-4)*
   NT Concertos (Piccolo)—Solo with piano
       Concertos (Piccolo with string
        orchestra)—Solo with piano
       Concertos (Piccolo with string
        orchestra), Arranged—Solo with piano

Piccolo music *(M110.P5)*
   SA Concertos, Minuets, Sonatas, Suites,
       and similar headings with
       specification of instruments; Trios
       [Quartets, etc.], Wind trios [quartets,
       etc.] *and* Woodwind trios [quartets, etc.]
       followed by specifications which
       include the piccolo; also Wind
       ensembles, Woodwind ensembles *and*
       headings that begin with the words
       piccolo or piccolos
   NT Concertos (Piccolo with instrumental
       ensemble)
       Piccolo with instrumental ensemble

Piccolo music (Piccolos (2)) *(M288-9)*
   NT Concertos (Piccolos (2))
       Piccolos (2) with orchestra

Piccolo with instrumental ensemble
   BT Piccolo music
   RT Concertos (Piccolo with instrumental
       ensemble)

Piccolo with orchestra *(M1020-1021)*
   RT Concertos (Piccolo)

Piccolo with string orchestra *(M1105-6)*
   RT Concertos (Piccolo with string orchestra)

Piccolos (2) with orchestra *(M1020-1021)*
   BT Piccolo music (Piccolos (2))
   RT Concertos (Piccolos (2))
   —Scores *(M1020)*

P'illyul *(ML990.P)*
   UF P'iri
   BT Musical instruments—Korea
       Woodwind instruments

P'illyul music *(M110.P54)*

Piobaireachd
USE Pibroch
Pibrochs

Pipa
USE P'i p'a

Pipe, Shepherd's
USE Pipe (Musical instrument)

Pipe (Musical instrument)
UF Bamboo pipe
Oboe, Pastoral
Pastoral oboe
Pipe, Shepherd's
Pipes (Musical instruments)
Quena
Shepherd's pipe
Symphonet
BT Woodwind instruments
NT Alboka
Panpipes
Penny whistle

Pipe band music
UF Bagpipe band music
BT Bagpipe and drum music
Bagpipe music
Band music
Military music
Percussion music

Pipe bands [May Subd Geog]
UF Bagpipe bands
Pipes and drums
BT Bands (Music)

Pipe music *(M60-64)*
RT Bagpipe music
NT Quartets (Pipes (3), guitar)
Suites (Pipes (4))
Variations (Pipes (4))
Woodwind quartets (Pipes (4))

Pipe-organ
USE Organ

Pipers, Town
USE Stadtpfeifer

Pipers (Bagpipes)
USE Bagpipers

Pipes (Musical instruments)
USE Pipe (Musical instrument)

Pipes and drums
USE Pipe bands

Pīphāt *(ML1251)*
BT Orchestra
Percussion instruments

Pīphāt music *(M985)*
BT Folk-music—Thailand
Percussion music

Pitch, Musical
USE Musical pitch

Pitch-pipe
USE Pitchpipe

Pitchpipe *(ML990.P)*
UF Pitch-pipe

Piyutim *(BM670.P5)*
UF Piyyutim

Piyutim *(BM670.P5)*
(Continued)
BT Hymns, Hebrew
Jewish hymns

Piyyutim
USE Piyutim

Plagiarism in music *(ML63)*
UF Music—Plagiarism
Music, Plagiarism in

Plain chant
USE Chants (Plain, Gregorian, etc.)

Plain song
USE Chants (Plain, Gregorian, etc.)

Plants, Effect of music on
BT Music—Physiological effect

Plate numbers, Music
USE Music printing—Plate numbers

Play-party *(GV1771)*
UF Swinging plays
BT Dancing
Folk dancing
Folk-songs
Games
RT Singing games
NT Games with music

Player-organ *(ML1050-ML1055; Analytical guides, MT150; Instruction, MT700)*
UF Aeolian pipe-organ
Organ-player
BT Musical instruments (Mechanical)
Organ

Player-organ music
BT Organ music

Player-organ rolls

Player-piano *(ML1050-ML1055; Analytical guides, MT150; Instruction, MT700)*
UF Piano-player
BT Musical instruments (Mechanical)
Piano
RT Pianola
NT Manualo

Player-piano music *(M20-M32)*
Here are entered recordings made from player-pianos and scores of works intended for performance on player pianos. The perforated rolls intended for use on player pianos and textual works about such rolls are entered under Player-piano rolls.
BT Piano music
Note under Player-piano rolls

Player-piano rolls *(M174)*
Here are entered the perforated rolls intended for use on player pianos and textual works about such rolls. Recordings made from player-pianos and scores of works intended for performance on player pianos are entered under Player-piano music.
Note under Player-piano music

Playground music
UF Music for playgrounds
Playgrounds—Music
BT Community music

Playgrounds [May Subd Geog] *(GV421-GV433)*
　—Music
　　USE Playground music
Plectral ensembles *(M1360)*
　　　Here are entered compositions for 3 or
　　　more solo plectral instruments and col-
　　　lections of compositions for any num-
　　　ber of solo plectral instruments, with
　　　the following exception; compositions
　　　for 3 or more guitars and/or harps are
　　　entered under Trios, [Quartets, etc.]
　　　followed by specification of instru-
　　　ments.
　UF Banjo band
　　　Guitar band
　　　Hawaiian-guitar band
　　　Mandolin orchestra music
　　　Ukulele band
　BT Banjo music
　　　Hawaiian-guitar music
　　　Instrumental music
　　　Ukulele music
　　　Zither music
　NT Accordion with plectral ensemble
　　　Concertos (Accordion with plectral
　　　　ensemble)
　　　Harp ensembles
　　　Monologues with music (Plectral
　　　　ensemble)
　　　Recorders (2) with plectral ensemble
　　　Suites (Plectral ensemble)
　　　Symphonies (Plectral ensemble)
　Notes under Instrumental ensembles; Nonets;
　　　Octets; Quartets; Quintets; Septets;
　　　Sextets; Trios
Plectral ensembles, Arranged
Plectral instruments
　USE Stringed instruments
Plots (Drama, novel, etc.) *(Drama, PN1683;*
　　　Fiction, PN3378)
　NT Musical revues, comedies, etc.—Stories,
　　　　plots, etc.
　　　Operas—Stories, plots, etc.
Plucked dulcimer
　USE Appalachian dulcimer
Pochette *(ML760)*
　UF Kit (Musical instrument)
　　　Pocket fiddle
　　　Taschengeige
　BT Violin
Pocket fiddle
　USE Pochette
Poetry and music
　USE Music and literature
Polish carols
　USE Carols, Polish
Polish folk-songs
　USE Folk-songs, Polish
Political ballads and songs [May Subd Geog]
　UF Political songs
　BT Ballads
　　　National songs
　　　Songs

Political ballads and songs [May Subd Geog]
　(Continued)
　NT Protest songs
　　　Revolutionary ballads and songs
Political songs
　USE Political ballads and songs
Polka-mazurkas
　BT Dance music
Polkas
　　　Here are entered collections of polka music
　　　　for various mediums. Individual polkas and
　　　　collections of polkas for a specific medium
　　　　are entered under the heading followed by
　　　　specification of medium.
　BT Dance music
　NT Schottisches
　Note under Dance music
Polkas (Accordion) *(M175.A4)*
　BT Accordion music
Polkas (Band) *(M1248; M1264)*
　BT Band music
　—Parts
　—Scores
Polkas (Chamber orchestra) *(M1048)*
　BT Chamber-orchestra music
　—Scores *(M1048)*
Polkas (Chorus with orchestra)
　BT Choruses with orchestra
Polkas (Flute and piano) *(M240-244)*
　BT Flute and piano music
Polkas (Instrumental ensemble)
　BT Instrumental ensembles
Polkas (Orchestra) *(M1048; M1060)*
　BT Orchestral music
Polkas (Piano) *(M31)*
　BT Piano music
Polkas (Piano, 4 hands)
　BT Piano music (4 hands)
Polkas (Piano, flutes (2)) *(M315-317)*
　BT Trios (Piano, flutes (2))
Polkas (Pianos (2)) *(M214-215)*
　BT Piano music (Pianos (2))
Polkas (String orchestra) *(M1145; M1160)*
　BT String-orchestra music
Polkas (String quartet) *(M450-454)*
　BT String quartets
Polkas (Trumpet and piano) *(M260-261)*
　BT Trumpet and piano music
Polkas (Violin and piano) *(M217-M218;*
　　　M221-M223)
　BT Violin and piano music
Polkas (Voice with piano)
　BT Songs with piano
Polkas (Zither) *(M135-9)*
　BT Zither music
Polonaises
　　　Here are entered collections of polonaise
　　　　music for various mediums. Individual
　　　　polonaises and collections of polonaises
　　　　for a specific medium are entered under
　　　　the heading followed by specification of
　　　　medium.
　BT Dance music

Polonaises (Accordion ensemble) *(M1362)*
　BT　Accordion ensembles
Polonaises (Band) *(M1249; M1266)*
　BT　Band music
　—Scores and parts *(M1249; M1266)*
Polonaises (Bassoon and piano) *(M253-254)*
　BT　Bassoon and piano music
Polonaises (Bassoon, clarinet, flute)
　　　(M355-9)
Polonaises (Chamber orchestra) *(M1049;*
　　　M1060)
　BT　Chamber-orchestra music
Polonaises (Flute with orchestra)
　　　(M1020-1021)
　BT　Flute with orchestra
　—Parts *(M1020)*
Polonaises (Guitar and piano) *(M276-7)*
　BT　Guitar and piano music
Polonaises (Guitar, violins (2), viola,
　　　violoncello) *(M570-572)*
　BT　Quintets (Guitar, violins (2), viola,
　　　violoncello)
Polonaises (Harpsichord) *(M32)*
　BT　Harpsichord music
Polonaises (Instrumental ensemble)
　　　(M900-985)
　BT　Instrumental ensembles
Polonaises (Orchestra) *(M1049; M1060)*
　BT　Orchestral music
Polonaises (Piano) *(M32)*
　BT　Piano music
Polonaises (Piano, 4 hands)
　BT　Piano music (4 hands)
Polonaises (Piano with orchestra)
　　　(M1010-1011)
　BT　Piano with orchestra
Polonaises (Pianos (2)) *(M214-215)*
　BT　Piano music (Pianos (2))
Polonaises (Violin and harpsichord)
　　　(M217-218)
　BT　Violin and harpsichord music
Polonaises (Violin and piano) *(M217-M218;*
　　　M221-M223)
　BT　Violin and piano music
Polonaises (Violin and violoncello) *(M286-7)*
　BT　Violin and violoncello music
Polonaises (Violin with chamber orchestra)
　　　(M1012-1013)
　BT　Violin with chamber orchestra
Polonaises (Violin with orchestra)
　　　(M1012-1013)
　BT　Violin with orchestra
Polonaises (Violin with string orchestra)
　　　(M1112-1113)
　BT　Violin with string orchestra
Polonaises (Violoncello and piano) *(M230;*
　　　M233)
　BT　Violoncello and piano music
Polytonality
　　　ML3811 (Acoustics and physics)
　　　MT46 (Instruction)
　BT　Tonality

Pommer *(ML990.P6)*
　BT　Bassoon
　　　Oboe
　　　Shawm
　　　Woodwind instruments
Pop music stations
　USE　Popular music radio stations
Popular culture
　　　Here are entered works on literature,
　　　　art, music, motion pictures, etc.
　　　　produced for a mass audience. General
　　　　works on learning and scholarship,
　　　　literature, the arts, etc. are entered
　　　　under Intellectual life.
　Note under Intellectual life
Popular instrumental music [May Subd Geog]
　　　ML3649-ML3541 (History and criticism)
　UF　Popular music, Instrumental
　　　Popular songs (Instrumental settings)
　　　Songs, Popular (Instrumental settings)
　BT　Instrumental music
　　　Popular music
　—To 1901
　—1901-1910
　—1911-1920
　—1921-1930
　—1931-1940
　—1941-1950
　—1951-1960
　—1961-1970
　—1971-1980
　—1981-
Popular music [May Subd Geog]
　　　M1627-M1844 (Music)
　　　ML3469-ML3541 (History and criticism)
　　　Here are entered popular vocal music and
　　　　collections containing both popular
　　　　instrumental and vocal music.
　UF　Music, Popular
　　　Music, Popular (Songs, etc.)
　　　Popular songs
　　　Popular vocal music
　　　Songs, Popular
　　　Vocal music, Popular
　BT　Music
　NT　Blues (Music)
　　　Calypso (Music)
　　　Contemporary Christian music
　　　Country music
　　　Disco music
　　　Fakebooks (Music)
　　　Gospel music
　　　Jazz vocals
　　　Klezmer music
　　　Popular instrumental music
　　　Reggae music
　　　Rhythm and blues music
　　　Rock music
　　　Salsa
　　　Soul music
　　　Steel band music

Popular music [May Subd Geog]
      M1627-M1844 (Music)
      ML3469-ML3541 (History and criticism)
  (Continued)
  —To 1901
  —1901-1910
  —1911-1920
  —1921-1930
  —1931-1940
  —1941-1950
  —1951-1960
  —1961-1970
  —1971-1980
  —1981-
  —Homiletical use
      UF Homiletical use of popular music
      BT Preaching
  —Religious aspects
      ML3470-ML3505
  — —Baptists, [Catholic church, etc.]
  — —Buddhism [Christianity, etc.]
  —Writing and publishing
      MT67
      UF Songwriting
      BT Authorship
          Composition (Music)
          Music—Publishing
  —Arizona
      NT Chicken scratch music
  —Jamaica
  —Japan
      M1813.18-M1813.2 (Music)
      ML3501 (History and criticism)
  —Louisiana
      NT Zydeco music
  —Mexico
      M1683.18-M1683.2 (Music)
      ML3485 (History and criticism)
      UF Música norteña
          Norteno music
  —Texas
      UF Música norteña
          Norteno music
  —Trinidad
  —United States
      M1630.18-M1630.2 (Music)
      ML3476.8-ML3481 (History and criticism)
      NT Rapping (Music)
Popular music, Christian
  USE Contemporary Christian music
Popular music, Instrumental
  USE Popular instrumental music
Popular music radio stations [May Subd Geog]
      (PN1991.67.P67)
  UF Contemporary music radio stations
      Pop music stations
  BT Radio and music
Popular music record industry
  USE Sound recording industry
Popular songs
  USE Popular music
Popular songs (Instrumental settings)
  USE Popular instrumental music

Popular vocal music
  USE Popular music
Portuguese folk-songs
  USE Folk-songs, Portuguese
Portuguese madrigals (Music)
  USE Madrigals (Music), Portuguese
Portuguese school song-books
  USE School song-books, Portuguese
Portuguese songs
  USE Songs, Portuguese
Positions (Violin playing)
  USE Violin—Instruction and study—
      Positions
Post horn *(ML990.P67)*
  BT Horn (Musical instrument)
Post horn music *(M110.P)*
Potpourris
      Here are entered collections of potpourri
      music for various mediums. Individual
      potpourris and collections of potpour-
      ris for a specific medium are entered
      under the heading followed by specifi-
      cation of medium.
  UF Medleys, Musical
      Musical medleys
Potpourris (Band) *(M1268)*
  BT Band music
Potpourris (Bassoon and piano)
      M248-M252
  BT Bassoon and piano music
Potpourris (Clarinet and piano)
      M248-M252
  BT Clarinet and piano music
Potpourris (Concertina and guitar) *(M298)*
  BT Concertina and guitar music
Potpourris (Flute) *(M60-64)*
  BT Flute music
Potpourris (Flute and guitar) *(M296-7)*
  BT Flute and guitar music
Potpourris (Flute, guitar, viola) *(M380-384)*
  BT Trios (Flute, guitar, viola)
Potpourris (Flute, guitar, violin) *(M380-384)*
  BT Trios (Flute, guitar, violin)
Potpourris (Guitar) *(M125-9)*
  BT Guitar music
Potpourris (Guitar and piano) *(M276-7)*
  BT Guitar and piano music
Potpourris (Harp) *(M115-119)*
  BT Harp music
Potpourris (Orchestra) *(M1075)*
  BT Orchestral music
Potpourris (Piano) *(M39)*
  BT Piano music
Potpourris (Piano, 4 hands) *(M212)*
  BT Piano music (4 hands)
Potpourris (Piano, bassoon, clarinet, guitar, violin) *(M540-544)*
  BT Quintets (Piano, bassoon, clarinet, guitar, violin)
Potpourris (Piano trio) *(M313-314)*
  BT Piano trios
Potpourris (Piano with band) *(M1268)*
  BT Piano with band

Potpourris (Pianos (2)) *(M214-215)*
  BT Piano music (Pianos (2))
Potpourris (Salon orchestra) *(M1350)*
  BT Salon-orchestra music
Potpourris (String orchestra) *(M1160)*
  BT String-orchestra music
Potpourris (Viola with string orchestra)
  BT Viola with string orchestra
Potpourris (Violin and guitar) *(M294-295)*
  BT Violin and guitar music
Potpourris (Violin and piano) *(M221)*
  BT Violin and piano music
Potpourris (Violin and violoncello with
         orchestra) *(M1040-1041)*
  BT Violin and violoncello with orchestra
Potpourris (Violin with orchestra)
         (M1012-1013)
  BT Violin with orchestra
  —Solo with piano
      BT Violin and piano music, Arranged
Potpourris (Violins (2)) *(M286-287)*
  BT Violin music (Violins (2))
Potpourris (Violoncello and guitar) *(M294-M295)*
  BT Violoncello and guitar music
Potpourris (Violoncello and piano) *(M235-6)*
  BT Violoncello and piano music
Potpourris (Violoncello with orchestra)
         (M1016-1017)
  BT Violoncello with orchestra
  —Solo with piano *(M1017)*
      BT Violoncello and piano music,
          Arranged
PR1XM (Computer program)
  UF P.R.1 X.M. (Computer program)
  BT Computer programs
      Music—Computer programs
Preaching [May Subd Geog] *(BV4200-4235)*
  NT Hymns—Homiletical use
      Popular music—Homiletical use
Preludes and fugues
  USE Canons, fugues, etc.
Premiere performances of musical works
  USE Music—First performances
Prepared piano music *(M20-38.5)*
          Here are entered piano works to be per-
              formed on a piano with its sound artifi-
              cially altered by various devices, *e.g.*
              metal clips or bolts attached to the
              strings; strips of paper, rubber, felt,
              etc., inserted across the strings; altered
              tuning of the unison strings; etc. The
              heading is given as a second heading if
              a prepared piano is part of an ensemble
              of 2 or more voices and/or instru-
              ments, or if the work is composed in a
              form, (i.e. a sonata, suite, etc.), *e.g.*
              1.Vocalises (Low voice) with piano.
              2.Prepared piano music; 1. Sonatas
              (Piano) 2. Prepared piano music.
  BT Piano music
Presbyterian Church [May Subd Geog]
         (BX8901-BX9225)
  —Hymns *(BV430-431)*

Printing [May Subd Geog] *(Z116-Z265)*
  NT Music printing
Prisoners as artists [May Subd Geog] *(NX164.P7)*
  BT Artists
  NT Prisoners' songs
      Prisoners' writings
Prisoners' songs *(M1977.C55; M1978.C55)*
  BT Prisoners as artists
      Songs
  RT Prisons—Songs and music
Prisons [May Subd Geog] *(HV8301-9920)*
  NT Music in prisons
  —Songs and music
      RT Prisoners' songs
Prisons, Music in
  USE Music in prisons
Producers, Opera
  USE Opera producers and directors
Program building (Music)
  USE Concerts—Program building
Program music *(Aesthetics, ML3855;*
         History, ML3300-3354)
  UF Nature in music
  BT Music
  RT Symbolism in music
  NT Death in music
      Leitmotiv
      Tragedy in music
Proofreading *(Z254)*
  —Music *(MT35)*
      UF Music—Proofreading
Propers (Music) *(M2148.2)*
  UF Propers of the Mass (Music)
  BT Masses
  NT Graduals (Music)
      Introits (Music)
      Offertories (Music)
Propers of the Mass (Music)
  USE Propers (Music)
Protest songs [May Subd Geog] *(M1977.P75;*
         M1978.P75)
  BT Political ballads and songs
      Songs
      Topical songs
  RT Radicalism—Songs and music
Provençal folk-songs
  USE Folk-songs, Provençal
Provençal lullabies
  USE Lullabies, Provençal
Provençal songs
  USE Songs, Provençal
Psalmody *(BV290)*
          Here are entered works on the singing of
              Psalms in public worship
  RT Church music
      Hymns
      Music in churches
Psalms (Music)
          Individual psalms by number.
  UF Bible. O.T. Psalms—Music
  BT Sacred vocal music
  NT Introits (Music)
      Penitential Psalms (Music)

Psalms (Music)
(Continued)

GENERAL SUBDIVISIONS

—1st Psalm
　　UF　Beatus vir, qui non abiit (Music)
—2d Psalm
　　UF　Quare fremuerent gentes (Music)
—3d Psalm
　　UF　Domine, quam multi sunt (Music)
—4th Psalm
　　UF　Cum invocarem (Music)
—6th Psalm
　　UF　Domine, ne in furore tuo arguas me,
　　　　neque in ira tua corripias me,
　　　　miserere mei Domine (Music)
　　BT　Penitential Psalms (Music)
—8th Psalm
　　UF　Domine, Dominus noster (Music)
—9th Psalm
　　UF　Confitebor tibi Domine in toto corde
　　　　meo, narrabo (Music)
—12th Psalm
　　UF　Salvum me fac Domine (Music)
—13th Psalm
　　UF　Usquequo, Domine (Music)
—15th Psalm
　　UF　Domine, quis habitavit (Music)
—16th Psalm
　　UF　Conserva me, Domine (Music)
—18th Psalm
　　UF　Diligam te Domine (Music)
—19th Psalm *(M2079.2.L19;*
　　　　M2099.2.L19)
　　UF　Coeli enarrant (Music)
—22d Psalm
　　UF　Deus, Deus meus respice in me
　　　　(Music)
—23d Psalm
　　UF　Dominus regit me (Music)
—24th Psalm
　　UF　Domini est terra (Music)
—27th Psalm
　　UF　Dominus illuminatio (Music)
—28th Psalm
　　UF　Ad te, Domine, clamabo (Music)
—30th Psalm
　　UF　Exaltabo te, Domine (Music)
—31st Psalm
　　UF　In te, Domine, speravi, non
　　　　confundar in aeternum, in justitia
　　　　tua libera me, Inclina (Music)
—32d Psalm
　　UF　Beati quorum (Music)
　　BT　Penitential Psalms (Music)
—33d Psalm
　　UF　Exultate, justi (Music)
—34th Psalm
　　UF　Benedicam Dominum (Music)
—36th Psalm
　　UF　Dixit injustus (Music)

Psalms (Music)
GENERAL SUBDIVISIONS
(Continued)
—37th Psalm
　　UF　Noli aemulari (Music)
—39th Psalm
　　UF　Dixi, Custodiam (Music)
—41st Psalm
　　UF　Beatus qui intelligit (Music)
—42d Psalm
　　UF　Quemadmodum (Music)
—43d Psalm
　　UF　Judica me, Deus (Music)
—44th Psalm
　　UF　Deus, auribus (Music)
—45th Psalm
　　UF　Eructavit cor meum (Music)
—46th Psalm
　　UF　Deus noster refugium (Music)
—47th Psalm
　　UF　Omnes gentes, plaudite (Music)
—51st Psalm
　　UF　Miserere mei, Deus, secundum
　　　　magnum misericordiam (Music)
　　BT　Penitential Psalms (Music)
—54th Psalm
　　UF　Deus in nomine tuo (Music)
—55th Psalm
　　UF　Exaudi, Deus orationem meam
　　　　(Music)
—57th Psalm
　　UF　Miserere mei, Deus, miserere mei
　　　　(Music)
—66th Psalm
　　UF　Jubilate Deo omnis terra, psalmum
　　　　dicite (Music)
—67th Psalm
　　UF　Deus misereatur (Music)
—68th Psalm
　　UF　Exsurgat Deus (Music)
—69th Psalm
　　UF　Salvum me fac Deus (Music)
—70th Psalm
　　UF　Deus, in adjutorium (Music)
—74th Psalm
　　UF　Ut quid, Deus (Music)
—75th Psalm
　　UF　Confitebimur tibi (Music)
—78th Psalm
　　UF　Attendite, popule (Music)
—80th Psalm
　　UF　Qui regis Israel (Music)
—81st Psalm
　　UF　Exultate Deo (Music)
—83d Psalm
　　UF　Deus, quis similis (Music)
—84th Psalm
　　UF　Quam dilecta (Music)
—85th Psalm
　　UF　Benedixisti, Domine (Music)
—86th Psalm
　　UF　Inclina Domine (Music)

Psalms (Music)
GENERAL SUBDIVISIONS
(Continued)

—89th Psalm
    UF Misericordias Domine (Music)
—90th Psalm
    UF Domine, refugium (Music)
—91st Psalm
    UF Qui habitat (Music)
—93d Psalm
    UF Dominus regnavit, decorem indutus
        est (Music)
—95th Psalm
    UF Venite, exultemus Domino
        (Music)
—96th Psalm
    UF Cantate Domino canticum novum,
        cantate Domino (Music)
—97th Psalm
    UF Dominus regnavit, exultet terra
—98th Psalm
    UF Cantate Domino canticum novum,
        quia mirabilia fecit (Music)
—100th Psalm
    UF Jubilate Deo omnis terra, Servite
        Domino (Music)
—102d Psalm
    UF Domine, exaudi orationem meam, et
        clamor meus (Music)
    BT Penitential Psalms (Music)
—103d Psalm
    UF Benedic, anima mea Domino et
        omnia (Music)
—104th Psalm
    UF Benedic, anima mea Domino,
        Domine Deus (Music)
—106th Psalm
    UF Confitemini Domino quoniam bonus,
        quoniam in saeculum misericordia
        eius, Quis loquetur (Music)
—107th Psalm
—108th Psalm
    UF Paratum cor meum
—110th Psalm
    UF Dixit Dominus (Music)
—111th Psalm
    UF Confitebor tibi Domine in toto corde
        meo, in consilio (Music)
—112th Psalm
    UF Beatus vir, qui timet Dominum
        (Music)
—113th Psalm
    UF Laudate, pueri, Dominum
        (Music)
—114th Psalm
    UF In exitu Israel (Music)
—115th Psalm
    UF Non nobis, Domine (Music)
—116th Psalm
    UF Dilexi, quoniam (Music)
—117th Psalm
    UF Laudate Dominum omnes gentes
        (Music)

Psalms (Music)
GENERAL SUBDIVISIONS
(Continued)

—118th Psalm
    UF Confitemini Domino quoniam bonus,
        quoniam in saeculum misericordia
        eius, Dicat nunc Israel
—119th Psalm
    UF Beati immaculati (Music)
—120th Psalm
    UF Ad Dominum (Music)
—121st Psalm
    UF Levavi oculos (Music)
—122d Psalm
    UF Laetatus sum (Music)
—126th Psalm
    UF In convertendo (Music)
—127th Psalm
    UF Nisi Dominus (Music)
—128th Psalm
    UF Beati omnes (Music)
—129th Psalm
    UF Saepe expugnauerunt me (Music)
—130th Psalm
    UF De profundis (Music)
    BT Penitential Psalms (Music)
—131st Psalm
    UF Domine, non est (Music)
—132d Psalm
    UF Memento Domine David (Music)
—133d Psalm
    UF Ecce, quam bonum (Music)
—134th Psalm
    UF Ecce nunc (Music)
—135th Psalm
    UF Laudate nomen Domini (Music)
—136th Psalm
    UF Confitemini Domino quoniam bonus,
        quoniam in aeternum (Music)
—137th Psalm
    UF Super flumina (Music)
—138th Psalm
    UF Confitebor tibi Domine in toto corde
        meo, quoniam audisti (Music)
—140th Psalm
    UF Eripe me, Domine (Music)
—142d Psalm
    UF Voce mea ad Dominum clamavi,
        voce mea ad Dominum
        deprecatus sum (Music)
—143d Psalm
    UF Domine, exaudi orationem meam,
        auribus percipe (Music)
    BT Penitential Psalms (Music)
—144th Psalm
    UF Benedictus Dominus (Music)
—145th Psalm
    UF Exaltabo te, Deus (Music)
—146th Psalm
    UF Lauda, anima mea (Music)
—147th Psalm
    UF Lauda Jerusalem Dominum (Music)
        Laudate Dominum quoniam bonus (Music)

Psalms (Music)
 GENERAL SUBDIVISIONS
 (Continued)
  —148th Psalm
   UF Laudate Dominum de caelis (Music)
  —149th Psalm
   UF Cantate Domino canticum novum,
    laus eius (Music)
  —150th Psalm
   UF Laudate Dominum in sanctis eius
    (Music)
Psalms (Music), Penitential
 USE Penitential Psalms (Music)
Psaltery
  ML1015.P8
 UF Ala
 BT Musical instruments, Ancient
  Stringed instruments
Public-school music
 USE School music
Publishers and publishing [May Subd Geog]
  Z278-Z550
 RT Music—Publishing
  Music publishers
 SA subdivision *Publishing* under types of
  published material, under headings for
  literature on particular topics, and under
  names of individual corporate bodies, e.g.
  Music—Publishing; English imprints—
  Publishing; Business literature—Publishing;
  Catholic church—Publishing; and sub-
  division *Publication and distribution* under
  individual sacred works, e.g. *Bible—*
  Publication and distribution
Puerto Rican lullabies
 USE Lullabies, Puerto Rican
Pung (Drum) *(ML1035)*
 BT Drum
Punk culture *(Indirect)*
 RT Punk rock music
Punk rock groups
 USE Rock groups
Punk rock music *(Indirect) (ML3534)*
 RT New wave music
 BT New wave music
  Punk culture
  Rock music
Punk rock musicians
 USE Rock musicians
Puppet operas
 USE Operas
Quadrilles
 BT Dance music
Quam dilecta (Music)
 USE Psalms (Music)—84th Psalm
Quare fremuerent gentes (Music)
 USE Psalms (Music)—2d Psalm
Quarter-tone music
 USE Microtonic music
Quarter-tones
 USE Microtones
Quartet, String
 USE String quartet

Quartets *(M400-486)*
  Here are entered collections of compositions for four instruments belonging to
  various families and in various combinations; and compositions for four specific instruments belonging to various
  families, followed by specification of
  instruments (including the specification: Unspecified instrument(s))
  Compositions for four bowed stringed instruments are entered under String
  quartets; for four wind instruments under Wind quartets; for four brass instruments under Brass quartets; and
  for four woodwind instruments under
  Woodwind quartets, with or without
  specification of instruments in each
  case.
  Compositions for piano, violin, viola and
  violoncello are entered under Piano
  quartets.
  Compositions for four plectral instruments are entered under Plectral ensembles, except those for guitars and-
  /or harps, which are entered under
  Quartets followed by specification of
  instruments.
  Compositions for four percussionists are
  entered under Percussion ensembles.
  Compositions for four solo voices are en-
  tered under Sacred quartets or Vocal
  quartets.
  Headings with specification of instru-
  ments are printed below only if spe-
  cific cross references are needed.
 RT Suites, Variations, Waltzes, *and similar*
  headings with specification of
  instruments
 Notes under Chamber music; Sonatas
Quartets, Arranged
Quartets, Barbershop
 USE Barbershop quartets
Quartets, Brass
 USE Brass quartets
Quartets, Piano
 USE Piano quartets
Quartets, Sacred
 USE Sacred quartets
Quartets, Secular
 USE Vocal quartets
Quartets, String
 USE String quartets
Quartets, Vocal
 USE Vocal quartets
Quartets, Wind
 USE Wind quartets
Quartets, Woodwind
 USE Woodwind quartets
Quartets (Bassoon, clarinet, oboe, guitar) *(M475-7)*
Quartets (Bassoon, clarinet, oboe, viola) *(M460-462)*
Quartets (Bassoon, clarinet, trombone, violin)
  (M460-462)
 RT Suites (Bassoon, clarinet, trombone, violin)

Quartets (Bassoon, flute, oboe, double bass)
    (M460-462)
Quartets (Bassoon, flute, violin, violoncello)
    (M460-462)
  RT Bassoon, flute, violin, violoncello with
       orchestra
**Quartets (Bassoon, horn, trumpet, double
    bass)** *(M460-462)*
  NT Bassoon, horn, trumpet, double bass
       with orchestra
       Concertos (Bassoon, horn, trumpet,
         double bass)
Quartets (Bassoon, horn, violin, viola) *(M460-462)*
Quartets (Bassoon, oboe, viola, violoncello)
    (M460-462)
Quartets (Bassoon, oboe, violin, viola) *(M460-462)*
  NT Bassoon, oboe, violin, viola with
       orchestra
       Concertos (Bassoon, oboe, violin, viola)
Quartets (Bassoon, oboe, violin, violoncello)
    (M460-462)
  NT Bassoon, oboe, violin, violoncello with
       chamber orchestra
       Bassoon, oboe, violin, violoncello with
         orchestra
       Concertos (Bassoon, oboe, violin,
         violoncello)
       Concertos (Bassoon, oboe, violin,
         violoncello with chamber orchestra)
Quartets (Bassoon, violin, viola, violoncello)
    (M460-462)
Quartets (Cimbalom, violin, viola, double bass)
    (M470-472)
  BT Cimbalom music
**Quartets (Cimbalom, violin, viola, double
    bass), Arranged** *(M473-4)*
Quartets (Clarinet, flute, harp, violin)
    (M480-482)
Quartets (Clarinet, flute, oboe, violoncello)
    (M460-462)
Quartets (Clarinet, flute, trombone, viola)
    (M460-462)
Quartets (Clarinet, flute, trumpet, violoncello)
    (M460-462)
  NT Suites (Clarinet, flute, trumpet, violoncello)
Quartets (Clarinet, flute, violin, violoncello)
    (M460-462)
  NT Clarinet, flute, violin, violoncello with
       chamber orchestra
       Concertos (Clarinet, flute, violin,
         violoncello with chamber orchestra)
       Variations (Clarinet, flute, violin, violoncello)
Quartets (Clarinet, guitar, violin, viola) *(M480-482)*
Quartets (Clarinet, guitars (2), violin) *(M480-482)*
Quartets (Clarinet, harp, celesta, violin) *(M485)*
  NT Clarinet, harp, celesta, violin with string
       orchestra
       Concertos (Clarinet, harp, celesta,
         violin with string orchestra)
**Quartets (Clarinet, harp, vibraphone, double
    bass)** *(M485)*
Quartets (Clarinet, harp, violin, viola) *(M480-482)*

Quartets (Clarinet, harp, violin, violoncello)
    (M480-484)
  NT Clarinet, harp, violin, violoncello with
       string orchestra
       Concertos (Clarinet, harp, violin,
         violoncello with string orchestra)
Quartets (Clarinet, oboe, harp, viola)
    (M480-482)
**Quartets (Clarinet, percussion, violin, double
    bass)** *(M485)*
Quartets (Clarinet, violin, viola, violoncello)
    (M460-462)
Quartets (Clarinet, violins (2), violoncello)
    (M460-462)
Quartets (Cornets (3), drum) *(M485)*
Quartets (Cornett, trombone, violin, continuo)
  BT Cornett music
**Quartets (Electronic harpsichord, castanets,
    percussion, violoncello)** *(M445-7)*
  BT Castanet music
      Electronic harpsichord music
**Quartets (Electronium, piano, percussion,
    viola)** *(M485)*
  BT Electronium music
**Quartets (English horn, flute, viola,
    violoncello)** *(M460-464)*
  NT Concertos (English horn, flute, viola,
       violoncello with string orchestra)
       English horn, flute, viola, violoncello
         with string orchestra
**Quartets (English horn, violin, violoncello,
    double bass)** *(M460-462)*
**Quartets (Flute, glass harmonica, viola,
    violoncello)** *(M485)*
Quartets (Flute, guitar, percussion, viola)
    (M485)
Quartets (Flute, guitar, viola, violoncello)
    (M480-482)
**Quartets (Flute, guitar, viola, violoncello),
    Arranged** *(M483-4)*
Quartets (Flute, guitar, violin, viola)
    (M480-482)
  NT Suites (Flute, guitar, violin, viola)
Quartets (Flute, guitars (3)) *(M475-7)*
Quartets (Flute, harp, tamtam, violoncello)
    (M485)
Quartets (Flute, harp, vibraphone, violoncello)
    (M485)
  NT Suites (Flute, harp, vibraphone, violoncello)
Quartets (Flute, harp, violin, viola) *(M481-2)*
Quartets (Flute, oboe, synthesizer, violin)
    (M485)
  BT Synthesizer music
Quartets (Flute, oboe, viola, violoncello)
    (M460-462)
**Quartets (Flute, oboe, viola, violoncello),
    Arranged** *(M463-4)*
Quartets (Flute, oboe, violin, violoncello)
    (M460-462)
  NT Concertos (Flute, oboe, violin,
       violoncello)
       Flute, oboe, violin, violoncello with
         orchestra

Quartets (Flute, saxophone, violin, violoncello)
(M460-462)
Quartets (Flute, shakuhachi, biwa, harp)
(M475-479)
   BT Biwa music
       Shakuhachi music
Quartets (Flute, violas (2), violoncello)
(M460-462)
Quartets (Flute, violin, viola, violoncello)
(M460-462)
   NT Suites (Flute, violin, viola, violoncello)
Quartets (Flute, violin, viola, violoncello),
   Arranged
   NT Operas arranged for flute, violin, viola,
       and violoncello
       Overtures arranged for flute, violin,
       viola, violoncello
Quartets (Flute, violins (2), viola)
(M460-462)
   NT Rondos (Flute, violins (2), viola)
       Suites (Flute, violins (2), viola)
Quartets (Flute, violins (2), violoncello)
(M460-462)
   NT Variations (Flute, violins (2),
       violoncello)
       Waltzes (Flute, violins (2), violoncello)
Quartets (Flutes (2), viola, violoncello)
(M460-462)
   NT Concertos (Flutes (2), viola, violoncello
       with string orchestra)
       Flutes (2), viola, violoncello with string
       orchestra
Quartets (Flutes (2), violin, viola) (M460-462)
Quartets (Flutes (2), violin, violoncello)
(M460-462)
   NT Concertos (Flutes (2), violin,
       violoncello with string orchestra)
       Flutes (2), violin, violoncello with
       string orchestra
Quartets (Flutes (3), harp) (M475-479)
   NT Concertos (Flutes (3) and harp)
       Flutes (3) and harp with orchestra
Quartets (Guitar, violin, viola, violoncello)
(M470-472)
Quartets (Guitar, violin, viola, violoncello),
   Arranged (M473-4)
Quartets (Guitar, violins (2), violoncello)
(M470-472)
Quartets (Guitars (4)) (M465-7)
   UF Guitar music (Guitars (4))
   NT Concertos (Guitars (4))
       Guitars (4) with orchestra
       Suites (Guitars (4))
Quartets (Guitars (4)), Arranged (M468-9)
Quartets (Harp, violin, viola, violoncello)
(M470-472)
Quartets (Harp, violins (2), violoncello)
(M470-472)
Quartets (Harps (4)) (M465-7)
   UF Harp music (Harps (4))
   NT Concertos (Harps (4) with string orchestra)
       Harps (4) with string orchestra
       Suites (Harps (4) with string orchestra)

Quartets (Harpsichord, bassoon, oboes (2))
(M415-417)
Quartets (Harpsichord, bassoon, clarinet,
   oboe) (M415-417)
   BT Quartets (Piano, bassoon, clarinet,
       oboe)
   NT Suites (Harpsichord, bassoon, clarinet,
       oboe)
Quartets (Harpsichord, bassoon, cornet,
   recorder) (M415-417)
   BT Quartets (Piano, bassoon, cornet,
       recorder)
Quartets (Harpsichord, bassoon, flute, viola da
   gamba) (M420-422)
   BT Quartets (Piano, bassoon, flute,
       violoncello)
Quartets (Harpsichord, bassoon, flute, violin)
(M420-422)
   BT Quartets (Piano, bassoon, flute, violin)
Quartets (Harpsichord, bassoon, oboe,
   recorder) (M415-417)
   BT Quartets (Piano, bassoon, flute, oboe)
Quartets (Harpsichord, bassoon, oboe,
   trumpet) (M415-417)
   NT Suites (Harpsichord, bassoon, oboe,
       trumpet)
Quartets (Harpsichord, bassoon, oboe, violin)
(M420-422)
   BT Quartets (Piano, bassoon, oboe, violin)
Quartets (Harpsichord, bassoon, oboe, violin),
   Arranged (M423-4)
Quartets (Harpsichord, bassoon, oboe,
   violoncello) (M420-422)
   BT Quartets (Piano, bassoon, oboe,
       violoncello)
Quartets (Harpsichord, flute, oboe, double
   bass) (M421-2)
   BT Quartets (Piano, flute, oboe, double
       bass)
Quartets (Harpsichord, flute, oboe, viola)
(M420-422)
Quartets (Harpsichord, flute, oboe, violin)
(M420-422)
   BT Quartets (Piano, flute, oboe, violin)
Quartets (Harpsichord, flute, oboe,
   violoncello) (M420-422)
   BT Quartets (Piano, flute, oboe, violoncello)
Quartets (Harpsichord, flute, recorders (2))
(M415-417)
   BT Quartets (Piano, flute, recorders (2))
Quartets (Harpsichord, flute, violin, viola)
(M420-422)
   BT Quartets (Piano, flute, violin, viola)
   NT Suites (Harpsichord, flute, violin, viola)
Quartets (Harpsichord, flute, violin, viola da
   gamba) (M420-422)
   BT Quartets (Piano, flute, violin, viola da
       gamba)
Quartets (Harpsichord, flute, violin,
   violoncello) (M420-422)
   BT Quartets (Piano, flute, violin, violoncello)
   NT Suites (Harpsichord, flute, violin,
       violoncello)

Quartets (Harpsichord, flute, violins (2))
(M420-422)
　BT　Quartets (Piano, flute, violins (2))
Quartets (Harpsichord, flutes (2), recorder)
(M415-417)
　BT　Quartets (Piano, flutes (2), recorder)
Quartets (Harpsichord, flutes (2), violoncello)
(M420-422)
　BT　Quartets (Piano, flutes (2), violoncello)
Quartets (Harpsichord, horn, oboe, violin)
(M420-422)
　BT　Quartets (Piano, horn, oboe, violin)
Quartets (Harpsichord, horns (2), violin)
(M420-422)
　BT　Quartets (Piano, horns (2), violin)
Quartets (Harpsichord, oboe, percussion, violoncello) *(M445-7)*
　BT　Quartets (Piano, oboe, percussion, violoncello)
　NT　Suites (Harpsichord, oboe, percussion, violoncello)
Quartets (Harpsichord, oboe, recorder, violin)
(M420-422)
　BT　Quartets (Piano, flute, oboe, violin)
Quartets (Harpsichord, oboe, viola, violoncello) *(M420-422)*
　BT　Quartets (Piano, oboe, viola, violoncello)
Quartets (Harpsichord, oboe, violin, viola)
(M420-422)
　BT　Quartets (Piano, oboe, violin, viola)
Quartets (Harpsichord, oboes (2), recorder)
(M415-417)
　BT　Quartets (Piano, oboes (2), recorder)
Quartets (Harpsichord, oboes (2), trumpet)
(M415-417)
　BT　Quartets (Piano, oboes (2), trumpet)
Quartets (Harpsichord, oboes (2), violoncello)
(M420-422)
　BT　Quartets (Piano, oboes (2), violoncello)
Quartets (Harpsichord, recorder, violin, violoncello) *(M420-422)*
　BT　Quartets (Piano, recorder, violin, violoncello)
Quartets (Harpsichord, recorder, violins (2))
(M420-422)
　BT　Quartets (Piano, flute, violins (2))
Quartets (Harpsichord, recorders (3))
(M415-417)
　BT　Quartets (Piano, flutes (3))
　NT　Chaconnes (Harpsichord, recorders (3))
　　　Suites (Harpsichord, recorders (3))
Quartets (Harpsichord, trumpet, violins (2))
(M420-422)
　RT　Quartets (Piano, trumpet, violins (2))
Quartets (Harpsichord, viole da gamba (3))
(M412.4)
Quartets (Harpsichord, violin, viola, violoncello) *(M410-412)*
　BT　Piano quartets
Quartets (Harpsichord, violin, violas (2))
(M410-411; M412.4)
　BT　Quartets (Piano, violin, violas (2))

Quartets (Harpsichord, violins (2), viola)
(M410-411; M412.4)
　BT　Quartets (Piano, violins (2), viola)
　NT　Suites (Harpsichord, violins (2), viola)
Quartets (Harpsichord, violins (2), viola da gamba) *(M410-411; M412.4)*
　BT　Quartets (Piano, violins (2), violoncello)
　NT　Suites (Harpsichord, violins (2), viola da gamba)
Quartets (Harpsichord, violins (2), violoncello) *(M410-M411; M412.4)*
　BT　Quartets (Piano, violins (2), violoncello)
　NT　Concertos (Harpsichord, violins (2), violoncello)
　　　Harpsichord, violins (2), violoncello with orchestra
　　　Suites (Harpsichord, violins (2), violoncello)
　　　Trio-sonatas
Quartets (Harpsichord, violins (2), violone)
(M412.4)
Quartets (Harpsichord, violins (3))
(M410-M411; M412.2)
　BT　Quartets (Piano, violins (3))
　NT　Canons, fugues, etc. (Harpsichord, violins (3))
Quartets (Harpsichord, wind instruments (3))
(M415-417)
　BT　Quartets (Piano, wind instruments (3))
Quartets (Horn, violin, viola, violoncello)
(M460-462)
Quartets (Horns (2), viola, violoncello)
(M460-462)
Quartets (Lute, mandolin, violin, viola)
(M470-472)
Quartets (Oboe, viola, violoncellos (2))
(M460-462)
　NT　Suites (Oboe, viola, violoncellos (2))
Quartets (Oboe, violin, viola, violoncello)
(M460-462)
　NT　Variations (Oboe, violin, viola, violoncello)
Quartets (Ondes Martenot (2), guitar, percussion) *(M485)*
　BT　Ondes Martenot music
Quartets (Ondes Martenot (4)) *(M485)*
　BT　Ondes Martenot music
Quartets (Organ, cornets (3)) *(M400-402)*
Quartets (Organ, cornets (3)), Arranged
(M403-4)
Quartets (Organ, flute, percussion, violoncello) *(M400-402)*
Quartets (Organ, flutes (2), violoncello)
(M400-402)
Quartets (Organ, horn, trombone, trumpet)
(M400-402)
Quartets (Organ, oboes (2), recorder)
(M400-402)
Quartets (Organ, oboes (2), violoncello)
(M400-402)
Quartets (Organ, violin, viola, violoncellos)
(M400-402)
Quartets (Organ, violins (2), viola) *(M400-402)*

Quartets (Organ, violins (2), viola da gamba)
(M400-402)
- BT Quartets (Organ, violins (2), violoncello)
- NT Canons, fugues, etc. (Organ, violins (2), viola da gamba)
      Suites (Organ, violins (2), viola da gamba)

Quartets (Organ, violins (2), violoncello)
(M400-402)
- NT Quartets (Organ, violins (2), viola da gamba)
      Suites (Organ, violins (2), violoncello)

Quartets (Organ, violins (3)) *(M400-402)*

Quartets (Organ, viols (3)) *(M990)*
- BT String trios (Viols (3))
- NT Canons, fugues, etc. (Organ, viols (3))

Quartets (Piano (4 hands), violin, violoncello)
- BT Piano music (4 hands)
- NT Waltzes (Piano (4 hands), violin, violoncello)

Quartets (Piano, bassoon, clarinet, flute)
(M415-417)

Quartets (Piano, bassoon, clarinet, oboe)
(M415-417)
- NT Quartets (Harpsichord, bassoon, clarinet, oboe)
      Suites (Piano, bassoon, clarinet, oboe)

Quartets (Piano, bassoon, clarinet, oboe), Arranged *(M418-419)*
- NT Suites (Bassoon, clarinet, oboe with string orchestra), Arranged—Solos with piano

Quartets (Piano, bassoon, clarinet, viola)
(M420-422)

Quartets (Piano, bassoon, cornet, recorder)
(M415-417)
- NT Quartets (Harpsichord, bassoon, cornet, recorder)

Quartets (Piano, bassoon, flute, oboe)
(M415-417)
- NT Quartets (Harpsichord, bassoon, oboe, recorder)

Quartets (Piano, bassoon, flute, violin)
(M420-422)
- NT Quartets (Harpsichord, bassoon, flute, violin)

Quartets (Piano, bassoon, flute, violoncello)
(M420-422)
- NT Quartets (Harpsichord, bassoon, flute, viola da gamba)

Quartets (Piano, bassoon, oboe, violin)
(M420-422)
- NT Quartets (Harpsichord, bassoon, oboe, violin)

Quartets (Piano, bassoon, oboe, violoncello)
(M420-422)
- NT Quartets (Harpsichord, bassoon, oboe, violoncello)

Quartets (Piano, chimes, violin, violoncello)
(M445-7)

Quartets (Piano, clarinet, flute, oboe)
(M415-417)

Quartets (Piano, clarinet, flute, oboe), Arranged *(M418-419)*

Quartets (Piano, clarinet, flute, violin)
(M420-422)

Quartets (Piano, clarinet, flute, violoncello)
(M420-422)

Quartets (Piano, clarinet, flutes (2)) *(M415-417)*

Quartets (Piano, clarinet, oboe, trombone)
(M415-417)

Quartets (Piano, clarinet, percussion, violoncello) *(M445-7)*
- NT Concertos (Piano, clarinet, percussion, violoncello)
      Piano, clarinet, percussion, violoncello with orchestra

Quartets (Piano, clarinet, trombone, percussion) *(M445-449)*
- NT Concertos (Piano, clarinet, trombone, percussion)
      Piano, clarinet, trombone, percussion with orchestra

Quartets (Piano, clarinet, trombone, trumpet)
(M415-417)

Quartets (Piano, clarinet, trombone, trumpet), Arranged *(M418-419)*
- NT Concertos (Clarinet, trombone, trumpet with string orchestra)—Solos with piano

Quartets (Piano, clarinet, trumpet, percussion)
(M445-7)
- NT Suites (Piano, clarinet, trumpet, percussion)

Quartets (Piano, clarinet, violin, violoncello)
(M420-422)
- NT Concertos (Piano, clarinet, violin, violoncello)
      Concertos (Piano, clarinet, violin, violoncello with string orchestra)
      Piano, clarinet, violin, violoncello with orchestra
      Piano, clarinet, violin, violoncello with string orchestra
      Suites (Piano, clarinet, violin, violoncello)

Quartets (Piano, clarinets (3)) *(M415-417)*

Quartets (Piano, cornets (3)) *(M415-417)*
- NT Variations (Piano, cornets (3))
      Waltzes (Piano, cornets (3))

Quartets (Piano, cornets (3)), Arranged
(M418-419)

Quartets (Piano, English horn, flute, viola)
(M420-424)

Quartets (Piano, flute, guitar, violin)
(M440-442)

Quartets (Piano, flute, harp, glockenspiel)
(M445-7)
- BT Glockenspiel music

Quartets (Piano, flute, harp, vibraphone)
(M445-7)

Quartets (Piano, flute, oboe, double bass)
(M421-2)
- NT Quartets (Harpsichord, flute, oboe, double bass)

Quartets (Piano, flute, oboe, harp) *(M435-7)*
Quartets (Piano, flute, oboe, percussion)
    (M445-7)
Quartets (Piano, flute, oboe, violin)
    (M420-422)
  NT Quartets (Harpsichord, flute, oboe,
       violin)
       Quartets (Harpsichord, flute, recorder,
       violin)
Quartets (Piano, flute, oboe, violoncello)
    (M420-422)
  NT Quartets (Harpsichord, flute, oboe,
       violoncello)
Quartets (Piano, flute, percussion, violoncello)
Quartets (Piano, flute, recorders (2))
    (M415-417)
  NT Quartets (Harpsichord, flute, recorders
       (2))
Quartets (Piano, flute, viola, violoncello)
    (M420-422)
Quartets (Piano, flute, violin, viola)
    (M420-422)
  NT Quartets (Harpsichord, flute, violin,
       viola)
Quartets (Piano, flute, violin, viola da gamba)
    (M420-422)
  NT Quartets (Harpsichord, flute, violin,
       viola da gamba)
       Suites (Piano, flute, violin,
       viola da gamba)
Quartets (Piano, flute, violin, violoncello)
    (M420-422)
  NT Quartets (Harpsichord, flute, violin,
       violoncello)
       Suites (Piano, flute, violin, violoncello)
       Variations (Piano, flute, violin,
       violoncello)
Quartets (Piano, flute, violin, violoncello),
    Arranged *(M423-4)*
  NT Symphonies arranged for piano, flute,
       violin, violoncello
Quartets (Piano, flute, violins (2))
    (M420-422)
  NT Quartets (Harpsichord, flute, violins
       (2))
       Quartets (Harpsichord, recorder, violins
       (2))
Quartets (Piano, flutes (2), recorder)
    (M415-417)
  NT Quartets (Harpsichord, flutes (2),
       recorder)
Quartets (Piano, flutes (2), violoncello)
    (M420-422)
  NT Quartets (Harpsichord, flutes (2),
       violoncello)
Quartets (Piano, flutes (3)) *(M415-417)*
  NT Quartets (Harpsichord, recorders (3))
Quartets (Piano, flutes (3)), Arranged
    (M418-419)
  NT Suites (Flutes (3) with string orchestra)
       —Solos with piano
Quartets (Piano, guitar, drums (2), double
    bass) *(M445-7)*

Quartets (Piano, guitar, mandolins (2))
    (M425-7)
Quartets (Piano, guitar, mandolins (2)),
    Arranged *(M428-9)*
Quartets (Piano, horn, glockenspiel,
    xylophone) *(M445-449)*
  NT Concertos (Piano, horn, glockenspiel,
       xylophone)
       Piano, horn, glockenspiel, xylophone
       with orchestra
Quartets (Piano, horn, oboe, violin)
    (M420-422)
  NT Quartets (Harpsichord, horn, oboe,
       violin)
Quartets (Piano, horn, trombone, double bass)
    (M420-422)
Quartets (Piano, horns (2), violin)
    (M420-422)
  NT Quartets (Harpsichord, horns (2),
       violin)
Quartets (Piano, oboe, percussion, violoncello)
    (M445-7)
  NT Quartets (Harpsichord, oboe,
       percussion, violoncello)
Quartets (Piano, oboe, viola, violoncello)
    (M420-422)
  NT Quartets (Harpsichord, oboe, viola,
       violoncello)
Quartets (Piano, oboe, violin, viola)
    (M420-422)
  NT Quartets (Harpsichord, oboe, violin,
       viola)
Quartets (Piano, oboe, violin, violoncello)
    (M420-422)
  NT Suites (Piano, oboe, violin, violoncello)
Quartets (Piano, oboe, violin, violoncello),
    Arranged *(M423-4)*
Quartets (Piano, oboes (2), recorder)
    (M415-417)
  NT Quartets (Harpsichord, oboes (2),
       recorder)
Quartets (Piano, oboes (2), trumpet)
    (M415-417)
  NT Quartets (Harpsichord, oboes (2),
       trumpet)
Quartets (Piano, oboes (2), violoncello)
    (M420-422)
  NT Quartets (Harpsichord, oboes (2),
       violoncello)
Quartets (Piano, percussion, vibraphone,
    double bass) *(M485)*
  NT Jazz quartets
Quartets (Piano, recorder, violin, violoncello)
    (M420-422)
  NT Quartets (Harpsichord, recorder, violin,
       violoncello)
Quartets (Piano, recorders (3)) *(M415-417)*
Quartets (Piano, recorders (3)), Arranged
    (M418-419)
  NT Concertos (Recorders (3) with string
       orchestra)—Solos with piano
Quartets (Piano, recorders (3)), Juvenile
    (M1413-1417)

Quartets (Piano, reed-organ, flute, xylophone)
(M405-409)
  BT Reed-organ music
Quartets (Piano, saxophone, percussion, double bass) *(M445-7)*
  NT Piano, saxophone, percussion, double bass with orchestra
Quartets (Piano, saxophone, trumpet, percussion) *(M485)*
Quartets (Piano, saxophones (2), vibraphone) *(M445-7)*
Quartets (Piano, trombone, trumpets (2)) *(M415-417)*
Quartets (Piano, trombones (3)) *(M415-417)*
Quartets (Piano, trombones (3)), Arranged *(M418-419)*
  NT Trombones (3) with band—Solos with piano
Quartets (Piano, trumpet, vibraphone, double bass) *(M445-7)*
  NT Concertos (Piano, trumpet, vibraphone, double bass)
       Piano, trumpet, vibraphone, double bass with orchestra
Quartets (Piano, trumpet, violins (2)) *(M420-422)*
  RT Quartets (Harpsichord, trumpet, violins (2))
Quartets (Piano, trumpets (3)) *(M415-417)*
  NT Concertos (Piano, trumpets (3) with string orchestra)
       Piano, trumpets (3) with string orchestra
Quartets (Piano, trumpets (3)), Arranged *(M418-419)*
  NT Trumpets (3) with band—Solos with piano
Quartets (Piano, viole da gamba (3)) *(M412.4)*
Quartets (Piano, violin, viola, violoncello)
  USE Piano quartets
Quartets (Piano, violin, violas (2)) *(M410-M411; M412.4)*
  NT Quartets (Harpsichord, violin, violas (2))
Quartets (Piano, violin, violoncello, double bass) *(M410-M411; M412.4)*
Quartets (Piano, violins (2), double bass) *(M410-M411; M412.4)*
Quartets (Piano, violins (2), viola) *(M412.4)*
  NT Quartets (Harpsichord, violins (2), viola)
Quartets (Piano, violins (2), violoncello) *(M410-M411; M412.4)*
  NT Quartets (Harpsichord, violins (2), viola da gamba)
       Quartets (Harpsichord, violins (2), violoncello)
       Suites (Harpsichord, violins (2), viola da gamba)
       Suites (Piano, violins (2), violoncello)
       Waltzes (Piano, violins (2), violoncello)
  Notes under Piano quartets; Quartets

Quartets (Piano, violins (2), violoncello), Arranged *(M413-414)*
Quartets (Piano, violins (3)) *(M410-M411; M412.2)*
  NT Canons, fugues, etc. (Piano, violins (3))
       Quartets (Harpsichord, violins (3))
       Suites (Piano, violins (3))
Quartets (Piano, violins (3)), Arranged *(M413-414)*
  NT Concertos (Violins (3))—Solos with piano
       Concertos (Violins (3) with string orchestra), Arranged—Solos with piano
       Violins (3) with orchestra—Solos with piano
Quartets (Piano, violoncellos (3)), Arranged *(M413-414)*
  NT Violoncellos (3) with orchestra—Solos with piano
Quartets (Piano, wind instruments (3)) *(M415-417)*
  NT Quartets (Harpsichord, wind instruments (3))
Quartets (Piano, wind instruments (3)), Arranged *(M418-419)*
Quartets (Pianos (2), flute, viola) *(M445-7)*
  BT Piano music (Pianos (2))
Quartets (Pianos (2), percussion) *(M445-7)*
  BT Piano music (Pianos (2))
  NT Concertos (Pianos (2), percussion with string orchestra)
       Pianos (2), percussion with string orchestra
Quartets (Pianos (2), trombone, percussion) *(M445-7)*
  BT Piano music (Pianos (2))
Quartets (Pianos (2), violin, violoncello) *(M445-7)*
  BT Piano music (Pianos (2))
Quartets (Pianos (2), violin, violoncello), Arranged *(M448-9)*
  NT Concertos (Piano trio)—Solos with piano
       Piano trio with orchestra—Solos with piano
Quartets (Pianos (2), violins (2)) *(M445-7)*
Quartets (Pipes (3), guitar) *(M475-479)*
  BT Pipe music
Quartets (Recorders (3), violin) *(M460-462)*
  NT Suites (Recorders (3), violin)
Quartets (Reed-organ, violins (2), violoncello) *(M405-7)*
  BT Reed-organ music
Quartets (Shakuhachi, kotos (2), shamisen)
  BT Koto music
       Shakuhachi music
       Shamisen music
Quartets (Shakuhachi, kotos (3))
  BT Koto music
       Shakuhachi music
Quartets (Shakuhachi, kotos (3)), Arranged
Quartets (Zithers (2), violin, viola) *(M470-472)*

Quechua folk-songs
  USE Folk-songs, Quechua
Quemadmodum (Music)
  USE Psalms (Music)—42d Psalm
Quena
  USE Pipe (Musical instrument)
Qui habitat (Music)
  USE Psalms (Music)—91st Psalm
Qui regis Israel (Music)
  USE Psalms (Music)—80th Psalm
Quick-steps
  USE Marches
Quintets *(M500-586)*

> Here are entered collections of compositions for five instruments belonging to various families and in various combinations; and compositions for five specific instruments belonging to various families, followed by specification of instruments (including the specification: Unspecified instrument(s))
>
> Compositions for five bowed stringed instruments are entered under String quintets; for five wind instruments under Wind quintets; for five brass instruments under Brass quintets; and for five woodwind instruments under Woodwind quintets, with or without specification of instruments in each case.
>
> Compositions for piano, violins (2), viola and violoncello are entered under Piano quintets.
>
> Compositions for five plectral instruments are entered under Plectral ensembles, except those for guitars and /or harps, which are entered under Quintets followed by specification of instruments.
>
> Compositions for five percussionists are entered under Percussion ensembles.
>
> Compositions for five solo voices are entered under Sacred quintets or Vocal quintets.
>
> Headings with specification of instruments are printed below only if specific cross references are needed.

  SA Suites, Variations, Waltzes, *and similar headings with specification of instruments*
Quintets, Brass
  USE Brass quintets
Quintets, Piano
  USE Piano quintets
Quintets, Sacred
  USE Sacred quintets
Quintets, Secular
  USE Vocal quintets
Quintets, String
  USE String quintets
Quintets, Vocal
  USE Vocal quintets
Quintets, Wind
  USE Wind quintets

Quintets, Woodwind
  USE Woodwind quintets
Quintets (Accordion, violins (2), viola, violoncello) *(M585)*
Quintets (Accordions (4), double bass) *(M585)*
Quintets (Accordions (4), double bass), Arranged *(M585)*
Quintets (Basset horn, clarinet, violin, viola, violoncello) *(M560-564)*
Quintets (Basset horn, clarinets (3), vibraphone) *(M585)*
Quintets (Bassoon, clarinet, flute, horn, violoncello) *(M560-562)*
  NT Bassoon, clarinet, flute, horn, violoncello with string orchestra
    Concertos (Bassoon, clarinet, flute, horn, violoncello with string orchestra)
Quintets (Bassoon, clarinet, flute, oboe, harp) *(M575-7)*
  NT Bassoon, clarinet, flute, oboe, harp with orchestra
    Concertos (Bassoon, clarinet, flute, oboe, harp)
Quintets (Bassoon, clarinet, flute, oboe, violoncello) *(M560-562)*
Quintets (Bassoon, clarinet, horn, violin, viola) *(M560-562)*
Quintets (Bassoon, clarinet, horn, violoncello, double bass) *(M560-562)*
Quintets (Bassoon, clarinet, oboe, violin, double bass) *(M560-562)*
Quintets (Bassoon, clarinet, oboe, violin, violoncello) *(M560-562)*
Quintets (Bassoon, clarinet, oboe, violin, violoncello), Arranged *(M563-4)*
Quintets (Bassoon, clarinet, violin, viola, violoncello) *(M560-562)*
  NT Suites (Bassoon, clarinet, violin, viola, violoncello)
Quintets (Bassoon, flute, horn, violin, viola) *(M560-562)*
  NT Suites (Bassoon, flute, horn, violin, viola)
Quintets (Bassoon, flute, trombone, trumpet, viola) *(M560-562)*
Quintets (Bassoon, oboe, violin, viola, double bass) *(M560-562)*
  NT Suites (Bassoon, oboe, violin, viola, double bass)
Quintets (Bassoon, violin, violas (2), violoncello) *(M560-562)*
Quintets (Bassoon, violins (2), viola, violoncello) *(M560-562)*
Quintets (Bassoons (2), oboes (2), percussion) *(M585)*
Quintets (Bassoons (2), oboes (2), percussion), Arranged *(M585)*
Quintets (Ch'in, violin, viola, violoncello, double bass) *(M570-574)*
  BT Ch'in music
Quintets (Cimbalom, violins (2), viola, violoncello) *(M570-574)*
  BT Cimbalom music

Quintets (Clarinet, flute, harp, viola, violoncello) *(M580-582)*
Notes under Concrete music; Electronic music

Quintets (Clarinet, flute, harp, violin, violoncello) *(M580-582)*
  NT Suites (Clarinet, flute, harp, violin, violoncello)

Quintets (Clarinet, flute, oboe, harp, percussion) *(M585)*
  NT Clarinet, flute, oboe, harp, percussion with orchestra
      Concertos (Clarinet, flute, oboe, harp, percussion)

Quintets (Clarinet, flute, violin, viola, violoncello) *(M560-562)*

Quintets (Clarinet, harp, vibraphone, violin, violoncello) *(M585)*

Quintets (Clarinet, horn, trombone, trumpet, viola) *(M560-562)*

Quintets (Clarinet, oboe, harp, violin, violoncello) *(M580-582)*

Quintets (Clarinet, oboe, violin, viola, double bass) *(M560-562)*

Quintets (Clarinet, oboe, violin, viola, violoncello) *(M560-562)*

Quintets (Clarinet, violas (2), violoncellos (2)) *(M560-562)*

Quintets (Clarinet, violin, viola, violoncello, double bass) *(M560-562)*

Quintets (Clarinet, violins (2), viola, violoncello) *(M560-562)*
  NT Canons, fugues, etc. (Clarinet, violins (2), viola, violoncello)
      Suites (Clarinet, violins (2), viola, violoncello)
      Variations (Clarinet, violins (2), viola, violoncello)

Quintets (Clarinets (2), flute, viola, violoncello) *(M560-562)*

Quintets (Clarinets (2), violin, viola, violoncello) *(M560-564)*
  NT Suites (Clarinets (2), violin, viola, violoncello)

Quintets (Electronic organs (4), maracas) *(M585)*
  BT Maraca music

Quintets (Flute, guitar, violin, viola, violoncello) *(M580-582)*

Quintets (Flute, harp, percussion, viola, violoncello) *(M585)*

Quintets (Flute, harp, violin, viola, violoncello) *(M580-582)*
  NT Suites (Flute, harp, violin, viola, violoncello)

Quintets (Flute, horn, marimba, violin, violoncello) *(M585)*

Quintets (Flute, oboe, glass harmonica, viola, violoncello) *(M585)*

Quintets (Flute, oboe, harp, viola, violoncello) *(M580-582)*

Quintets (Flute, oboe, harp, viola, violoncello), Arranged *(M583-4)*

Quintets (Flute, oboe, violin, viola, violoncello) *(M560-562)*
  NT Suites (Flute, oboe, violin, viola, violoncello)

Quintets (Flute, trumpet, percussion, viola) *(M585)*
  NT Suites (Flute, trumpet, percussion, viola)

Quintets (Flute, violin, violas (2), violoncello) *(M560-562)*

Quintets (Flute, violin, violas (2), violoncello), Arranged *(M563-4)*

Quintets (Flute, violins (2), viola, violoncello) *(M560-562)*
  NT Variations (Flute, violins (2), viola, violoncello)
  Note under Quintets

Quintets (Flute, violins (2), viola, violoncello), Arranged *(M563-4)*
  NT Symphonies arranged for flute, violins (2), viola, violoncello

Quintets (Flutes (2), guitar, viola, violoncello) *(M580-582)*

Quintets (Flutes (2), violins (2), violoncello) *(M560-562)*

Quintets (Flutes (3), percussion) *(M585)*

Quintets (Guitar, violins (2), viola, violoncello) *(M570-572)*
  NT Polonaises (Guitar, violins (2), viola, violoncello)

Quintets (Guitar, violins (2), viola, violoncello), Arranged

Quintets (Guitars (5)) *(M565-7)*
  UF Guitar music (Guitars (5))
  NT Suites (Guitars (5))

Quintets (Harp, violins (2), viola, violoncello) *(M570-572)*

Quintets (Harps (5)) *(M565-569)*
  UF Harp music (Harps (5))

Quintets (Harpsichord, bassoon, clarinet, flute, horn) *(M515-517)*
  BT Quintets (Piano, bassoon, clarinet, flute, horn)

Quintets (Harpsichord, bassoon, clarinet, flute, horn), Arranged *(M518-519)*

Quintets (Harpsichord, bassoon, English horn, oboes (2)) *(M515-517)*
  BT Quintets (Piano, bassoon, English horn, oboes (2))
  NT Suites (Harpsichord, bassoon, English horn, oboes (2))

Quintets (Harpsichord, bassoon, flute, horn, oboe) *(M515-517)*
  BT Quintets (Piano, bassoon, flute, horn, oboe)

Quintets (Harpsichord, bassoon, flute, oboe, viola) *(M520-522)*
  BT Quintets (Piano, bassoon, flute, oboe, viola)

Quintets (Harpsichord, bassoon, flute, oboe, viola), Arranged *(M523-4)*

Quintets (Harpsichord, bassoon, flute, oboe, violin) *(M520-522)*
  BT Quintets (Piano, bassoon, flute, oboe, violin)

Quintets (Harpsichord, bassoon, flute, oboe, violin), Arranged *(M523-4)*

Quintets (Harpsichord, bassoon, oboe, recorder, violin) *(M520-522)*
    BT Quintets (Piano, bassoon, flute, oboe, violin)

Quintets (Harpsichord, English horn, heckelphone, oboe, oboe d'amore) *(M515-519)*
    BT Heckelphone music

Quintets (Harpsichord, flute, harp, viola, violoncello) *(M540-542)*
    BT Quintets (Piano, flute, harp, viola, violoncello)

Quintets (Harpsichord, flute, oboe, viola, violoncello) *(M520-522)*
    BT Quintets (Piano, flute, oboe, viola, violoncello)

Quintets (Harpsichord, flute, oboe, violin, viola) *(M520-522)*

Quintets (Harpsichord, flute, oboe, violin, violoncello) *(M520-522)*
    BT Quintets (Piano, flute, oboe, violin, violoncello)

Quintets (Harpsichord, flute, oboes (2), viola da gamba) *(M520-522)*
    BT Quintets (Piano, flute, oboes (2), violoncello)

Quintets (Harpsichord, flute, percussion, viola, double bass) *(M545-7)*
    NT Quintets (Piano, flute, percussion, viola, double bass)

Quintets (Harpsichord, flute, viole da gamba (2), violoncello) *(M990)*

Quintets (Harpsichord, flute, violin, viola, violoncello) *(M520-522)*
    BT Quintets (Piano, flute, violin, viola, violoncello)

Quintets (Harpsichord, flute, violin, viole da gamba (2)) *(M520-522)*
    BT Quintets (Piano, flute, violin, viole da gamba (2))
    NT Suites (Harpsichord, flute, violin, viole da gamba (2))

Quintets (Harpsichord, flute, violins (2), violoncello) *(M520-522)*
    BT Quintets (Piano, flute, violins (2), violoncello)

Quintets (Harpsichord, flute, viols (2), violoncello) *(M520-522)*
    BT Viol music (Viols (2))

Quintets (Harpsichord, flutes (2), recorders (2)) *(M515-517)*
    BT Quintets (Piano, flutes (2), recorders (2))

Quintets (Harpsichord, flutes (2), violins (2)) *(M520-522)*
    BT Quintets (Piano, flutes (2), violins (2))

Quintets (Harpsichord, guitars (2), harp, double bass) *(M530-534)*
    NT Concertos (Harpsichord, guitars (2), harp, double bass)
          Harpsichord, guitars (2), harp, double bass with orchestra

Quintets (Harpsichord, horns (2), violin, violoncello) *(M520-522)*
    BT Quintets (Piano, horns (2), violin, violoncello)
    NT Suites (Harpsichord, horns (2), violin, violoncello)

Quintets (Harpsichord, horns (2), violins (2)) *(M520-522)*
    BT Quintets (Piano, horns (2), violins (2))
    NT Suites (Harpsichord, horns (2), violins (2))

Quintets (Harpsichord, oboe, violin, viola da gamba, violoncello) *(M520-522)*

Quintets (Harpsichord, oboes (2), recorders (2)) *(M515-517)*
    BT Quintets (Piano, oboes (2), recorders (2))

Quintets (Harpsichord, recorder, violins (2), violoncello) *(M520-522)*
    BT Quintets (Piano, recorder, violins (2), violoncello)

Quintets (Harpsichord, recorders (2), violins (2)) *(M520-522)*
    BT Quintets (Piano, recorders (2), violins (2))

Quintets (Harpsichord, recorders (3), viola da gamba) *(M520-522)*
    BT Quintets (Piano, flutes (3), violoncello)

Quintets (Harpsichord, recorders (4)) *(M515-517)*
    BT Quintets (Piano, recorders (4))

Quintets (Harpsichord, trumpet, violin, viola, violoncello) *(M520-522)*
    BT Quintets (Piano, trumpet, violin, viola, violoncello)

Quintets (Harpsichord, trumpet, violins (2), viola) *(M520-522)*
    RT Quintets (Piano, trumpet, violins (2), viola)

Quintets (Harpsichord, violins (2), viola, viola da gamba) *(M510-512)*
    BT Piano quintets

Quintets (Harpsichord, violins (2), viola, violoncello) *(M510-512)*
    BT Piano quintets

Quintets (Harpsichord, violins (2), violas (2)) *(M510-512)*
    BT Quintets (Piano, violins (2), violas (2))
    NT Suites (Harpsichord, violins (2), violas (2))

Quintets (Harpsichord, violins (2), violoncellos (2)) *(M510-512)*
    BT Quintets (Piano, violins (2), violoncellos (2))

Quintets (Harpsichord, violins (2), viols (2)) *(M510-512)*
    BT Quintets (Piano, violins (2), viols (2))
          Viol music

Quintets (Harpsichord, violins (3), viola da gamba) *(M510-512)*
    BT Quintets (Piano, violins (3), violoncello)
    NT Canons, fugues, etc. (Harpsichord, violins (3), viola da gamba)

Quintets (Harpsichord, violins (3), violoncello) *(M510-512)*
BT   Quintets (Piano, violins (3), violoncello)

Quintets (Harpsichord, violins (4)) *(M510-512)*
BT   Quintets (Piano, violins (4))

Quintets (Harpsichord, viols (2), viola d'amore, viola da gamba) *(M990)*
BT   Viol music

Quintets (Horn, oboe, violas (2), violoncello) *(M560-562)*

Quintets (Horn, violin, violas (2), violoncello) *(M560-562)*

Quintets (Horn, violins (2), viola, violoncello) *(M560-562)*

Quintets (Horn, violins (2), viola, violoncello), Arranged *(M563-4)*

Quintets (Horns (2), violin, viola, violoncello) *(M560-562)*
NT   Suites (Horns (2), violin, viola, violoncello)

Quintets (Horns (2), violins (2), violoncello) *(M560-562)*

Quintets (Kettledrums, violins (2), viola, violoncello) *(M585)*

Quintets (Oboe, guitar, percussion, viola, double bass) *(M585)*

Quintets (Oboe, violins (2), viola, violoncello) *(M560-562)*
NT   Suites (Oboe, violins (2), viola, violoncello)

Quintets (Organ, baritone, cornets (2), trombone) *(M500-502)*
NT   Canons, fugues, etc. (Organ, baritone, cornets (2), trombone)

Quintets (Organ, baritone, cornets (2), trombone), Arranged *(M503-4)*

Quintets (Organ, trombones (2), trumpets (2)) *(M500-502)*

Quintets (Organ, trombones (2), trumpets (2)), Arranged *(M503-4)*

Quintets (Organ, violin, viols (3)) *(M500-502)*
BT   Viol music

Quintets (Organ, violins (2), viola, violoncello) *(M500-502)*

Quintets (Organ, violins (2), viols (2)) *(M500-502)*
BT   Viol music

Quintets (Percussion, violins (2), viola, violoncello) *(M585)*

Quintets (Piano (1 hand), violins (2), viola, violoncello) *(M510-514)*
BT   Piano quintets

Quintets (Piano (4 hands), horn, trombone, guitar) *(M535-7)*
BT   Piano music (4 hands)

Quintets (Piano, bassoon, clarinet, English horn, flute) *(M515-517)*

Quintets (Piano, bassoon, clarinet, English horn, flute), Arranged *(M518-519)*
NT   Concertos (Bassoon, clarinet, English horn, flute)—Solos with piano

Quintets (Piano, bassoon, clarinet, flute, horn) *(M515-517)*
NT   Quintets (Harpsichord, bassoon, clarinet, flute, horn)

Quintets (Piano, bassoon, clarinet, flute, oboe) *(M515-517)*
NT   Suites (Piano, bassoon, clarinet, flute, oboe)

Quintets (Piano, bassoon, clarinet, flute, oboe), Arranged *(M518-M519)*
NT   Concertos (Piano, bassoon, clarinet, flute, oboe)

Quintets (Piano, bassoon, clarinet, guitar, violin)
NT   Potpourris (Piano, bassoon, clarinet, guitar, violin)

Quintets (Piano, bassoon, clarinet, horn, oboe) *(M515-517)*

Quintets (Piano, bassoon, clarinet, horn, oboe), Arranged *(M518-519)*
NT   Concertos (Bassoon, clarinet, horn, oboe)—Solos with piano

Quintets (Piano, bassoon, English horn, oboes (2)) *(M515-517)*
NT   Quintets (Harpsichord, bassoon, English horn, oboes (2))
Suites (Piano, bassoon, English horn, oboes (2))

Quintets (Piano, bassoon, flute, harp, violoncello) *(M540-542)*

Quintets (Piano, bassoon, flute, horn, oboe) *(M515-517)*
NT   Quintets (Harpsichord, bassoon, flute, horn, oboe)

Quintets (Piano, bassoon, flute, horn, oboe), Arranged *(M518-519)*
NT   Concertos (Bassoon, flute, horn, oboe)—Solos with piano

Quintets (Piano, bassoon, flute, oboe, saxophone) *(M515-517)*

Quintets (Piano, bassoon, flute, oboe, viola) *(M520-522)*
NT   Quintets (Harpsichord, bassoon, flute, oboe, viola)

Quintets (Piano, bassoon, flute, oboe, violin) *(M520-522)*
NT   Quintets (Harpsichord, bassoon, flute, oboe, violin)
Quintets (Harpsichord, bassoon, oboe, recorder, violin)

Quintets (Piano, bassoon, oboe, violin, violoncello), Arranged *(M523-4)*
NT   Bassoon, oboe, violin, violoncello with orchestra—Solos with piano

Quintets (Piano, bassoon, trumpets (2), harp) *(M535-7)*

Quintets (Piano, bassoons (2), clarinets (2)) *(M515-517)*

Quintets (Piano, clarinet, flute, horn, viola) *(M520-522)*

Quintets (Piano, clarinet, flute, viola, violoncello) *(M520-522)*

Quintets (Piano, clarinet, flute, violin, violoncello) *(M520-522)*

Quintets (Piano, clarinet, flute, violin, violoncello), Arranged *(M523-4)*
   NT Symphonies arranged for piano, clarinet, flute, violin, violoncello
Quintets (Piano, clarinet, horn, violin, violoncello) *(M520-522)*
Quintets (Piano, clarinet, violin, viola, violoncello) *(M520-522)*
Quintets (Piano, clarinet, violin, viola, violoncello), Arranged *(M523-4)*
Quintets (Piano, clarinet, violins (3)) *(M520-522)*
Quintets (Piano, clarinets (2), flute, oboe) *(M515-517)*
Quintets (Piano, clarinets (2), violin, violoncello) *(M520-522)*
Quintets (Piano, clarinets (4)) *(M515-517)*
Quintets (Piano, clarinets (4)), Arranged *(M518-519)*
   NT Clarinets (4) with orchestra—Solos with piano
Quintets (Piano, English horn, heckelphone, oboe, oboe d'amore) *(M515-519)*
   BT Heckelphone music
Quintets (Piano, English horn, violins (2), viola) *(M520-522)*
Quintets (Piano, flute, harp, viola, violoncello) *(M540-542)*
   NT Quintets (Harpsichord, flute, harp, viola, violoncello)
Quintets (Piano, flute, oboe, viola, violoncello) *(M520-522)*
   NT Quintets (Harpsichord, flute, oboe, viola, violoncello)
Quintets (Piano, flute, oboe, violin, viola) *(M520-522)*
Quintets (Piano, flute, oboe, violin, violoncello) *(M520-522)*
   NT Quintets (Harpsichord, flute, oboe, violin, violoncello)
Quintets (Piano, flute, oboes (2), violoncello) *(M520-522)*
   NT Quintets (Harpsichord, flute, oboes (2), viola da gamba)
Quintets (Piano, flute, percussion, viola, double bass) *(M545-7)*
   BT Quintets (Harpsichord, flute, percussion, viola, double bass)
Quintets (Piano, flute, percussion, violoncello) *(M545-7)*
   NT Variations (Piano, flute, percussion, violoncello)
Quintets (Piano, flute, trumpet, violin, violoncello) *(M520-522)*
Quintets (Piano, flute, violin, viola, violoncello) *(M520-522)*
   NT Quintets (Harpsichord, flute, violin, viola, violoncello)
       Suites (Piano, flute, violin, viola, violoncello)
Quintets (Piano, flute, violin, viola, violoncello), Arranged *(M523-4)*

Quintets (Piano, flute, violin, viole da gamba (2)) *(M520-522)*
   NT Quintets (Harpsichord, flute, violin, viole da gamba (2))
Quintets (Piano, flute, violins (2), violoncello) *(M520-522)*
   NT Quintets (Harpsichord, flute, violins (2), violoncello)
Quintets (Piano, flutes (2), recorders (2)) *(M515-517)*
   NT Quintets (Harpsichord, flutes (2), recorders (2))
Quintets (Piano, flutes (2), violins (2))
   NT Quintets (Harpsichord, flutes (2), violins (2))
Quintets (Piano, flutes (3), violoncello) *(M520-522)*
   NT Quintets (Harpsichord, recorders (3), viola da gamba)
Quintets (Piano, flutes (4)) *(M515-517)*
Quintets (Piano, hichiriki, harp, violin, violoncello) *(M540-544)*
   BT Hichiriki music
Quintets (Piano, horn, percussion, violin, violoncello) *(M545-7)*
Quintets (Piano, horns (2), violin, violoncello) *(M520-522)*
   NT Quintets (Harpsichord, horns (2), violin, violoncello)
Quintets (Piano, horns (2), violins (2)) *(M520-522)*
   NT Quintets (Harpsichord, horns (2), violins (2))
       Suites (Piano, horns (2), violins (2))
Quintets (Piano, horns (4)) *(M515-517)*
Quintets (Piano, horns (4)), Arranged *(M518-519)*
   NT Concertos (Horns (4))—Solos with piano
Quintets (Piano, oboe, trumpet, violin, double bass) *(M520-522)*
   NT Concertos (Piano, oboe, trumpet, violin, double bass with string orchestra)
       Piano, oboe, trumpet, violin, double bass with string orchestra
Quintets (Piano, oboe, violin, viola, violoncello) *(M520-522)*
   Note under Piano quintets
Quintets (Piano, oboes (2), recorders (2)) *(M515-517)*
   NT Quintets (Harpsichord, oboes (2), recorders (2))
Quintets (Piano, percussion, violoncellos (3)) *(M545-7)*
Quintets (Piano, piccolo, trombone, trumpet, percussion) *(M545-7)*
Quintets (Piano, recorder, violins (2), violoncello) *(M520-522)*
   NT Quintets (Harpsichord, recorder, violins (2), violoncello)
Quintets (Piano, recorders (2), violins (2)) *(M520-522)*
   NT Quintets (Harpsichord, recorders (2), violins (2))

Quintets (Piano, recorders (4)) *(M515-517)*
  NT   Quintets (Harpsichord, recorders (4))
Quintets (Piano, recorders (4)), Arranged
    (M518-519)
Quintets (Piano, shō, harp, violin, violoncello)
    (M540-544)
  BT   Shō music
Quintets (Piano, trombone, trumpet,
    xylophone, violin) *(M545-7)*
  BT   Xylophone music
Quintets (Piano, trumpet, violin, viola,
    violoncello) *(M520-522)*
  NT   Quintets (Harpsichord, trumpet, violin,
       viola, violoncello)
Quintets (Piano, trumpet, violins (2), viola)
    (M520-522)
  RT   Quintets (Harpsichord, trumpet, violins
       (2), viola)
Quintets (Piano, trumpets (4)) *(M515-517)*
Quintets (Piano, violin, viola, violoncello,
    double bass) *(M510-512)*
Quintets (Piano, violin, viola, violoncello,
    double bass), Arranged *(M513-514)*
Quintets (Piano, violin, violas (2), violoncello)
    (M512.4)
Quintets (Piano, violins (2), viola, violoncello)
  USE   Piano quintets
Quintets (Piano, violins (2), violas (2))
    (M510-512)
  NT   Quintets (Harpsichord, violins (2),
       violas (2))
Quintets (Piano, violins (2), violoncellos (2))
    (M510-512)
  NT   Quintets (Harpsichord, violins (2),
       violoncellos (2))
Quintets (Piano, violins (2), viols (2))
    (M510-512)
  BT   Viol music
  NT   Quintets (Harpsichord, violins (2), viols (2))
Quintets (Piano, violins (3), violoncello)
    (M510-512)
  NT   Canons, fugues, etc. (Piano, violins (3),
       violoncello)
       Quintets (Harpsichord, violins (3), viola
       da gamba)
       Quintets (Harpsichord, violins (3),
       violoncello)
Quintets (Piano, violins (4)) *(M510-512)*
  NT   Quintets (Harpsichord, violins (4))
Quintets (Piano, violins (4)), Arranged *(M513-514)*
  NT   Concertos (Violins (4) with string
       orchestra)—Solos with piano
Quintets (Piano, wind instruments (4)) *(M515-517)*
Quintets (Piano, wind instruments (4)),
    Arranged *(M518-519)*
Quintets (Pianos (2), percussion, double bass)
    (M585)
  BT   Piano music (Pianos (2))
Quintets (Pianos (4), glockenspiel) *(M585)*
  BT   Glockenspiel music
Quintets (Pianos (4), glockenspiel), Arranged
    (M585)

Quintets (Recorders (2), lute, violin, viola)
    (M580-584)
Quintets (Recorders (2), violins (2),
    violoncello) *(M560-562)*
Quintets (Sitar, percussion, unspecified
    instruments (3)) *(M586)*
  BT   Sitar music
Quintets (Trombone, glockenspiel, percussion)
    (M585)
  BT   Glockenspiel music
Quodlibet (Music)
  UF   Quotlibet (Music)
Quotlibet (Music)
  USE   Quodlibet (Music)
Quṣaba
  USE   Nāy
Race and music
  USE   Music and race
Racket (Musical instrument) *(History, ML990.R;*
    Instruction, MT533.R)
  UF   Cervelas
       Cervelat
       Cortaldi
       Cortalli
       Rackett
       Rankett
  BT   Woodwind instruments
Radicalism [May Subd Geog]
  —Songs and music
     RT   Protest songs
Radio and music [May Subd Geog] *(General, ML68;*
    Analytical guides, MT150)
  UF   Music and radio
  NT   Disc jockeys
       Popular music radio stations
Radio music
  BT   Music
Radio operas *(M1527.5)*
  BT   Operas
  —Vocal scores with piano *(M1527.5)*
Radio plays with music
  BT   Music, Incidental
Radio programs, Musical [May Subd Geog]
  UF   Musical radio programs
Raga
  UF   Ragini
  BT   Melody
       Music—India
       Musical intervals and scales
Rāgamālā painting [May Subd Geog]
  BT   Music in art
Ragini
  USE   Raga
Ragtime music *(M1366)*
  BT   Jazz music
  NT   Guitar—Methods (Ragtime)
       Guitar music (Ragtime)
       Organ music (Ragtime)
       Piano—Methods (Ragtime)
       Piano music (Ragtime)
Rajasthani folk-songs
  USE   Folk-songs, Rajasthani

Raluana folk-songs
USE Folk-songs, Raluana
Ramadan hymns *(BP183.5)*
UF Hymns, Ramadan
BT Islamic hymns
Rap (Music)
USE Rapping (Music)
Rap songs
USE Rapping (Music)
Rappin' (Music)
USE Rapping (Music)
Rapping (Music)
UF Rap (Music)
Rap songs
Rappin' (Music)
BT Dance music—United States
Improvisation (Music)
Monologues with music
Popular music—United States
Ratsmusikanten
USE Stadtpfeifer
Ratsmusizi
USE Stadtpfeifer
Rattle *(Primitive music, GN467.R)*
NT Clapper (Musical instrument)
Sistrum
Rattle, Notched
USE Notched rattle
Realism in music
UF Musical realism
BT Aesthetics
Music
Music—Philosophy and aesthetics
RT Romanticism in music
Recitations with music
USE *subdivision* Readings with music *under
subjects, e.g.* American poetry—20th
century—Readings with music;
Monologues—Readings with music
Monologues with music
Sacred monologues with music
Recorded accompaniments
Here are entered recordings to be used as
accompaniments for playing or sing-
ing. Recordings to be used with vari-
ous or unspecified instruments or
voices are entered under the heading
without specification of medium. Re-
cordings to be used with a specific in-
strument, voice, etc., are entered under the heading followed by specifica-
tion of medium, *e.g.* Recorded accom-
paniments (Flute); Recorded
accompaniments (Soprano)
Recorded accompaniments (Alto)
BT Songs (Low voice) with piano
Recorded accompaniments (Bassoon)
BT Bassoon music
Recorded accompaniments (Clarinet)
BT Clarinet music
Recorded accompaniments (Drum)
BT Percussion music

Recorded accompaniments (Flute)
BT Flute music
Note under Recorded accompaniments
Recorded accompaniments (Guitar)
BT Guitar music
Recorded accompaniments (Horn)
BT Horn music
Recorded accompaniments (Oboe)
BT Oboe music
Recorded accompaniments (Piano)
BT Piano music
Recorded accompaniments (Recorder)
BT Recorder music
Recorded accompaniments (Saxophone)
BT Saxophone music
Recorded accompaniments (Soprano)
BT Songs (High voice) with piano
Note under Recorded accompaniments
Recorded accompaniments (Trumpet)
BT Trumpet music
Recorded accompaniments (Viola)
BT Viola music
Recorded accompaniments (Violin)
BT Violin music
Recorded accompaniments (Violoncello)
BT Violoncello music
Recorded music industry
USE Sound recording industry
Recorder (Musical instrument) *(ML935-6)*
UF Block flute
Blockflute
Song flute
BT Flute
Woodwind instruments
RT Flageolet
NT Czakan
Galoubet
Tonette
Example under reference from Melody
instruments
Recorder (Physical instrument)
USE Recording instruments
Recorder and accordion music *(M298)*
UF Accordion and recorder music
Recorder and bassoon music
USE Bassoon and recorder music
Recorder and celesta music *(M298)*
UF Celesta and recorder music
NT Suites (Recorder and celesta)
Recorder and continuo music
UF Continuo and recorder music
NT Sonatas (Recorder and continuo)
Suites (Recorder and continuo)
Variations (Recorder and continuo)
Recorder and flute music
USE Flute and recorder music
Recorder and guitar music *(M296-7)*
UF Guitar and recorder music
NT Sonatas (Recorder and guitar)
Suites (Recorder and guitar)
Recorder and guitar music, Arranged
(M296-7)

Recorder and harp music *(M296-297)*
UF Harp and recorder music
Recorder and harpsichord music *(M240-242)*
UF Harpsichord and recorder music
BT Flute and piano music
NT Passacaglias (Recorder and
harpsichord)
Sonatas (Recorder and harpsichord)
Suites (Recorder and harpsichord)
Variations (Recorder and harpsichord)
Recorder and harpsichord music, Arranged
(M243-4)
Recorder and keyboard instrument music
(M270.R4-M271.R4)
UF Keyboard instrument and recorder music
Recorder and lute music *(M296-7)*
UF Lute and recorder music
NT Suites (Recorder and lute)
Recorder and lute music, Arranged *(M296-7)*
Recorder and oboe music
USE Oboe and recorder music
Recorder and organ music *(M182-4)*
UF Organ and recorder music
NT Sonatas (Recorder and organ)
Recorder and percussion music *(M298)*
UF Percussion and recorder music
Recorder and piano music *(M240-242)*
UF Piano and recorder music
NT Canons, fugues, etc. (Recorder and piano)
Minuets (Recorder and piano)
Sonatas (Recorder and piano)
Suites (Recorder and piano)
Variations (Recorder and piano)
Recorder and piano music, Arranged *(M243-4)*
NT Concertos (Recorder with string
orchestra)—Solo with piano
Suites (Recorder with string orchestra)
—Solo with piano
Recorder and tenor violin music *(M290-291)*
UF Tenor violin and recorder music
NT Suites (Recorder and tenor violin)
Recorder and trumpet music *(M288-9)*
UF Trumpet and recorder music
NT Concertos (Recorder and trumpet with
string orchestra)
Recorder and trumpet with string
orchestra
Recorder and trumpet with string orchestra
(M1105-6)
BT Recorder and trumpet music
RT Concertos (Recorder and trumpet with
string orchestra)
Recorder and viola da gamba music *(M290-291)*
UF Viola da gamba and recorder music
NT Concertos (Recorder and viola da
gamba with string orchestra)
Recorder and viola da gamba with
string orchestra
Recorder and viola da gamba with string
orchestra *(M1105-6)*
BT Recorder and viola da gamba music
RT Concertos (Recorder and viola da
gamba with string orchestra)

Recorder and viola music *(M290-291)*
UF Viola and recorder music
Recorder and violin music *(M290-291)*
UF Violin and recorder music
NT Concertos (Recorder and violin with
string orchestra)
Recorder and violin with string orchestra
Recorder and violin with string orchestra
(M1105-6)
BT Recorder and violin music
RT Concertos (Recorder and violin with
string orchestra)
Recorder and violoncello music *(M290-291)*
UF Violoncello and recorder music
Recorder ensembles *(M955-M956; M957.2;*
M958-M959)
Here are entered compositions for ten or
more recorders and collections of
compositions for a varying number of
recorders.
Notes under Instrumental ensembles; Wood-
wind ensembles
Recorder music *(M60-64)*
SA Concertos, Minuets, Sonatas, Suites,
and similar headings with
specification of instruments; Trios
[Quartets, etc.], Wind trios [quartets,
etc.], *and* Woodwind trios [quartets,
etc.] *followed by specifications which*
include the recorder; also Wind
ensembles, Woodwind ensembles,
and headings that begin with the
words recorder or recorders
NT Flageolet music
Minuets (Recorder)
Recorded accompaniments (Recorder)
Suites (Recorder)
Variations (Recorder)
Recorder music, Arranged *(M63-64)*
Recorder music (Recorders (2)) *(M288-9)*
NT Canons, fugues, etc. (Recorders (2))
Concertos (Recorders (2))
Concertos (Recorders (2) with string
orchestra)
Minuets (Recorders (2))
Recorders (2) with orchestra
Recorders (2) with plectral ensemble
Recorders (2) with string orchestra
Sonatas (Recorders (2))
Suites (Recorders (2))
Variations (Recorders (2))
Recorder music (Recorders (2)), Arranged
(M288-9)
Recorder music (Recorders (3))
USE Woodwind trios (Recorders (3))
Recorder music (Recorders (4))
USE Woodwind quartets (Recorders (4))
Recorder music (Recorders (5))
USE Woodwind quintets (Recorders (5))
Recorder music (Recorders (6))
USE Woodwind sextets (Recorders (6))
Recorder music (Recorders (7))
USE Woodwind septets (Recorders (7))

Recorder music (Recorders (8))
USE Woodwind octets (Recorders (8))
Recorder players *(Biography: collective,*
ML399; individual, ML417)
Recorder with chamber orchestra *(M1020-1021)*
RT Concertos (Recorder with chamber
orchestra)
Recorder with instrumental ensemble
RT Concertos (Recorder with instrumental
ensemble)
Recorder with orchestra *(M1020-1021)*
BT Flute with orchestra
Orchestral music
RT Concertos (Recorder)
Recorder with string ensemble
RT Concertos (Recorder with string ensemble)
Recorder with string orchestra *(M1105-6)*
BT String-orchestra music
RT Concertos (Recorder with string orchestra)
NT Suites (Recorder with string orchestra)
Recorders (2) with instrumental ensemble
RT Concertos (Recorders (2) with
instrumental ensemble)
Recorders (2) with orchestra *(M1020-1021)*
UF Two recorders with orchestra
BT Recorder music (Recorders (2))
RT Concertos (Recorders (2))
Recorders (2) with plectral ensemble *(M1360)*
BT Plectral ensembles
Recorder music (Recorders (2))
RT Concertos (Recorders (2) with plectral
ensemble)
NT Minuets (Recorders (2) with plectral
ensemble)
Recorders (2) with string ensemble
NT Suites (Recorders (2) with string
ensemble)
Recorders (2) with string orchestra *(M1105-6)*
UF Two recorders with string orchestra
BT Recorder music (Recorders (2))
RT Concertos (Recorders (2) with string
orchestra)
Recorders (3) with string orchestra *(M1120-1121)*
BT Woodwind trios (Recorders (3))
RT Concertos (Recorders (3) with string
orchestra)
Recorders (4) with string orchestra
(M1134.R4; M1135.R4)
BT Woodwind quartets (Recorders (4))
RT Concertos (Recorders (4) with string
orchestra)
Recorders (6) with string orchestra *(M1105-6)*
BT Woodwind sextets (Recorders (6))
RT Concertos (Recorders (6) with string
orchestra)
Recreational therapy *(General, RM736.7;*
Psychotherapy, RC489.R4)
NT Music therapy
Recreations, Musical
USE Musical recreations
Redowas
BT Dance music
RT Mazurkas

Reed-organ [May Subd Geog] *(ML597)*
UF Cabinet organ
Harmonium
Melodeon (Reed organ)
Parlor organ
Vocalion
BT Organ
NT Bichromatic harmonium
Keyboards
Sheng (Musical instrument)
Shō
—Methods *(MT202)*
— —Self-instruction *(MT208)*
UF Reed-organ—Self-instruction
—Self-instruction
USE Reed-organ—Methods—
Self-instruction
Reed-organ and piano music (4 hands)
USE Piano (4 hands) and reed-organ music
Reed-organ music *(M15-17)*
BT Organ music
NT Quartets (Piano, reed-organ, flute,
xylophone)
Quartets (Reed-organ, violins (2),
violoncello)
Sheng music
Trios (Reed-organ, harps (2))
Variations (Harpsichord, reed-organ,
celesta, vibraphone, violins (2), viola,
violoncello)
Reed-organ music, Arranged *(M18-19)*
Reed-organ music (4 hands) *(M190)*
NT Suites (Reed-organ, 4 hands)
Reed-organ music (Reed-organs (2)) *(M190)*
Reed-organ music (Reed-organs (2)), Arranged
(M190)
Reed pipes (Organ pipes)
UF Reeds (Organ pipes)
BT Organ-pipes
Reeds (Music)
USE *subdivision* Reeds *under specific*
instruments and types of
instruments, e.g. Oboe—Reeds;
Woodwind instruments—Reeds
Reeds (Organ pipes)
USE Reed pipes (Organ pipes)
Reels (Music)
BT Dance music
NT Strathspeys
Reggae music [May Subd Geog]
ML3532 (History and criticism)
BT Popular music
Reggae musicians [May Subd Geog]
BT Musicians
Regina Caeli laetare (Music)
UF Regina Coeli laetare (Music)
BT Antiphons (Music)
Mary, Blessed Virgin, Saint—Songs and
music
Registers, Vocal
USE Vocal registers
Registration (Organ)
USE Organ—Registration

Rehearsals (Music)
    BT   Music—Performance
    RT   Conducting
Religion and music
    USE Music—Religious aspects
Religious education [May Subd Geog]
    NT   Music in religious education
Religious music
    USE Church music
          Synagogue music
Renaissance music
    USE *subdivisions* 15th century, 16th century,
          and 17th century *under music headings*
          Music—15th century
          Music—16th century
          Music—17th century
Requiems *(M2010-M2014)*
    BT   Funeral music
          Masses
    —Excerpts
    — —Vocal scores *(M2011)*
         UF   Requiems—Vocal scores—Excerpts
    — —Vocal scores with piano *(M2014)*
         UF   Requiems—Vocal scores with
                piano—Excerpts
    —Scores *(M2010)*
    —Vocal scores *(M2011)*
    — —Excerpts
         USE Requiems—Excerpts—Vocal scores
    —Vocal scores with organ *(M2013)*
    —Vocal scores with piano *(M2013)*
    — —Excerpts
         USE Requiems—Excerpts—Vocal
              scores with piano
Requiems, Unaccompanied *(M2011)*
    UF   Unaccompanied requiems
Requiems (Equal voices)
    —Vocal scores with organ *(M2013)*
Requiems (Men's voices) *(M2010-2011; M2013)*
Requiems (Unison)
    —Vocal scores with organ *(M2013.5)*
Requiems (Women's voices)
    —Vocal scores with organ *(M2013)*
Requiems arranged for piano (4 hands) *(M208)*
    BT   Piano music (4 hands), Arranged
Research, Musical
    USE Musicology
Respiration *(QP121)*
    BT   Singing
          Voice
          Voice culture
Responses (Music)
    UF   Responsories
    BT   Sacred vocal music
Responsories
    USE Responses (Music)
Revivals [May Subd Geog] *(BV3750-3797)*
    —Hymns *(BV460)*
         UF   Camp-meeting hymns
               Hymns, Revival
               Revival hymns
         BT   Gospel music
               Hymns

Revolutionary ballads and songs [May Subd Geog]
    BT   Ballads
          Campaign songs
          Political ballads and songs
          Songs
          War-songs
Revolutionary ballads and songs, Russian
         [May Subd Geog]
    UF   Russian revolutionary ballads and songs
Revolutionary operas [May Subd Geog]
    BT   Operas
Rhythm *(Dancing, GV1595; Physical*
         training, GV463; Physiology, QP301,
         QP465; Psychology, BF475)
    BT   Aesthetics
    RT   Cycles
    NT   Eurythmy
          Musical meter and rhythm
Rhythm and blues music [May Subd Geog]
    ML3521 (History and criticism)
    UF   Music, Rhythm and blues
          Rhythm 'n' blues music
    BT   Afro-Americans—Music
          Popular music
    RT   Rock music
          Soul music
Rhythm band with orchestra *(M1040-1041)*
    RT   Concertos (Rhythm band)
Rhythm bands and orchestras
    UF   Percussion bands
          Toy orchestras
    BT   Bands (Music)
          Children as musicians
          Musical instruments—Juvenile literature
          Orchestra
          Percussion instruments
    NT   Concertos (Rhythm band)
          Suites (Rhythm band)
Rhythm 'n' blues music
    USE Rhythm and blues music
Rhythmic games
    USE Games with music
Ribald songs
    USE Bawdy songs
Rice [May Subd Geog] *(Botany, QK495.G74;*
         Culture, SB191.R5)
    —Planting *(Agriculture, SB191.5;*
         Folklore, GR8951; Customs,
         GT5899)
    — —Songs and music
         BT   Folk-songs
             Work-songs
Right-hand piano music
    USE Piano music (1 hand)
Rite of spring (Ballet)
    UF   Sacre du printemps (Ballet)
    BT   Ballets
Rock-a-billy music
    USE Rockabilly music
Rock and roll bands
    USE Rock groups
Rock and roll groups
    USE Rock groups

Rock and roll music
  USE Rock music
Rock bands
  USE Rock groups
Rock groups [May Subd Geog]
  UF Bands, Rock
      Groups, Rock
      Punk rock groups
      Rock and roll bands
      Rock and roll groups
      Rock bands
      Rock-n-roll bands
      Rock-n-roll groups
  BT Dance orchestras
      Musical groups
      Rock music
  RT Rock musicians
Rock music [May Subd Geog]
    ML3533.8-ML3534 (History and criticism)
  UF Rock and roll music
      Rock-n-roll music
  BT Afro-Americans—Music
      Popular music
  SA subdivisions *Methods (Rock)* and *Studies*
      and exercises (Rock) under names of
      musical instruments
  NT Christian rock music
      Drum—Studies and exercises (Rock)
      Heavy metal (Music)
      New wave music
      Piano—Studies and exercises (Rock)
      Punk rock music
      Rock groups
      Rockabilly music
  —To 1961
  —1961-1970
  —1971-1980
  —1981-
  —Fans
      BT Fans (Persons)
      NT Groupies
  —Religious aspects
  — —Baptists, [Catholic Church, etc.]
  — —Buddhism, [Christianity, etc.]
  —United States
      NT Folk-rock music
Rock music, Christian
  USE Christian rock music
Rock musicians [May Subd Geog]
  UF Punk rock musicians
  BT Musicians
  RT Rock groups
Rock musicians' wives [May Subd Geog]
  BT Musicians' wives
Rock-n-roll bands
  USE Rock groups
Rock-n-roll groups
  USE Rock groups
Rock-n-roll music
  USE Rock music
Rock videos [May Subd Geog] *(PN1992.8.M87)*
  UF Videos, Rock
  BT Music videos

Rockabilly music [May Subd Geog]
  UF Rock-a-billy music
  BT Country music
      Rock music
Rohrflöte
  UF Chimney flute
  BT Organ stops
Roman music
  USE Music, Greek and Roman
Romanian ballads
  USE Ballads, Romanian
Romanian folk-songs
  USE Folk-songs, Romanian
Romanian hymns
  USE Hymns, Romanian
Romanian songs
  USE Songs, Romanian
Romantic period music
  USE *subdivision* 19th century *under music*
      headings
      Music—19th century
Romanticism in music *(ML196)*
  UF Music and romanticism
  BT Music
      Music—Philosophy and aesthetics
      Style, Musical
  RT Realism in music
Romany folk-songs
  USE Folk-songs, Romany
Rondo *(History, ML1165; Instruction, MT62)*
Rondos
    Here are entered collections of rondo mu-
    sic for various mediums. Individual
    rondos and collections of rondos for a
    specific medium are entered under the
    heading followed by specification of
    medium.
Rondos (Accordion) *(M175.A4)*
  BT Accordion music
Rondos (Balalaika and piano)
    (Collections, M282.B3; Separate
    works, M283.B3)
  BT Balalaika and piano music
Rondos (Band) *(M1203)*
  BT Band music
  —Scores
Rondos (Baritone and piano) *(M262-3)*
  BT Baritone and piano music
Rondos (Bassoon and continuo)
  BT Bassoon and continuo music
Rondos (Bassoon and violin with instrumental
    ensemble)
  BT Bassoon and violin with instrumental
      ensemble
Rondos (Bassoon, clarinet, flute, oboe),
    Arranged *(M458-9)*
Rondos (Bassoon with orchestra)
    (M1026-1027)
  BT Bassoon with orchestra
  —Solo with piano *(M1027)*
      BT Bassoon and piano music, Arranged
Rondos (Clarinet and piano) *(M248-252)*
  BT Clarinet and piano music

Rondos (Clarinet with chamber orchestra)
(M1024-5)
  BT Clarinet with chamber orchestra
  —Scores *(M1024)*
Rondos (Flute) *(M60-62)*
  BT Flute music
Rondos (Flute and continuo)
  BT Flute and continuo music
Rondos (Flute and harp) *(M296-7)*
  BT Flute and harp music
Rondos (Flute and piano) *(M240-242)*
  BT Flute and piano music
Rondos (Flute, violins (2), viola) *(M460-462)*
  BT Quartets (Flute, violins (2), viola)
Rondos (Flute, violins (2), viola), Arranged
(M463-4)
Rondos (Flute with chamber orchestra)
(M1020-1021)
  BT Flute with chamber orchestra
Rondos (Flute with instrumental ensemble)
  BT Flute with instrumental ensemble
Rondos (Flute with orchestra) *(M1020-1021)*
  BT Flute with orchestra
  —Solo with piano *(M1021)*
      BT Flute and piano music, Arranged
Rondos (Flute with orchestra), Arranged
(M1020-1021)
Rondos (Flute with string orchestra)
(M1105-6)
  BT Flute with string orchestra
  —Scores *(M1105)*
Rondos (Guitar) *(M125-7)*
  BT Guitar music
Rondos (Guitar and piano) *(M276-7)*
  BT Guitar and piano music
Rondos (Guitars (2)) *(M292-3)*
  BT Guitar music (Guitars (2))
Rondos (Guitars (3)) *(M365-7)*
  BT Trios (Guitars (3))
Rondos (Harpsichord) *(M25)*
  BT Harpsichord music
      Rondos (Piano)
Rondos (Horn and piano) *(M255-7)*
  BT Horn and piano music
Rondos (Horn with orchestra) *(M1028-9)*
  BT Horn with orchestra
  —Solo with piano *(M1029)*
      BT Horn and piano music, Arranged
Rondos (Oboe and piano) *(M245-M246; M247)*
  BT Oboe and piano music
Rondos (Orchestra) *(M1045; M1060)*
  BT Orchestral music
Rondos (Orchestra), Arranged *(M1060)*
  —Scores *(M1060)*
Rondos (Organ) *(M7; M11)*
  BT Organ music
Rondos (Organ), Arranged *(M12-13)*
Rondos (Piano) *(M25)*
  BT Piano music
  NT Rondos (Harpsichord)
Rondos (Piano, 4 hands) *(M200-M201; M204)*
  BT Piano music (4 hands)
Rondos (Piano), Arranged

Rondos (Piano quintet) *(M510-512)*
  BT Piano quintets
Rondos (Piano with orchestra)
(M1010-1011)
  BT Piano with orchestra
  —2-piano scores *(M1011)*
      BT Piano music (Pianos (2)), Arranged
Rondos (Pianos (2)) *(M214-215)*
  BT Piano music (Pianos (2))
Rondos (Pianos (2), 8 hands) *(M216)*
  BT Piano music (Pianos (2), 8 hands)
Rondos (Pianos (2)), Arranged *(M215)*
Rondos (Pianos, 4 hands), Arranged
(M207-211)
Rondos (Piccolo and piano) *(M240-242)*
  BT Piccolo and piano music
Rondos (Saxophone and piano) *(M268-269)*
  BT Saxophone and piano music
Rondos (String orchestra) *(M1145)*
  BT String-orchestra music
  —Scores *(M1145)*
Rondos (String quartet) *(M450-452)*
  BT String quartets
Rondos (Trumpet and piano) *(M260-261)*
  BT Trumpet and piano music
Rondos (Trumpet with orchestra)
(M1030-1031)
  BT Trumpet with orchestra
Rondos (Viola and double bass) *(M286-287)*
  BT Viola and double-bass music
Rondos (Viola and piano) *(M224-6)*
  BT Viola and piano music
Rondos (Viola and piano), Arranged
(M227-8)
Rondos (Viola with orchestra) *(M1014-1015)*
  BT Viola with orchestra
  —Solo with piano *(M1015)*
      BT Viola and piano music, Arranged
Rondos (Violin and continuo)
  BT Violin and continuo music
Rondos (Violin and piano) *(M221)*
  BT Violin and piano music
Rondos (Violin with chamber orchestra)
(M1012-1013)
  BT Violin with chamber orchestra
  —Solo with piano *(M1013)*
      BT Violin and piano music, Arranged
Rondos (Violin with orchestra)
(M1012-1013)
  BT Violin with orchestra
  —Solo with piano *(M1013)*
      BT Violin and piano music, Arranged
Rondos (Violin with string ensemble)
  BT Violin with string ensemble
Rondos (Violin with string orchestra) *(M1105-6)*
  BT Violin with string orchestra
  —Solo with piano *(M1106)*
      BT Violin and piano music, Arranged
Rondos (Violoncello and double-bass) *(M286-287)*
  BT Violoncello and double-bass music
Rondos (Violoncello and piano) *(M229-M230;
M233)*
  BT Violoncello and piano music

Rondos (Violoncello with orchestra)
    (M1016-1017)
  BT Violoncello with orchestra
Rondos (Vocal)
  BT Choruses
        Part-songs
        Vocal music
Rooms, Music
  USE Music rooms and equipment
Rosh ha-Shanah *(BM695.N5)*
  —Music
  USE Synagogue music—Rosh
          ha-Shanah services
Ruanda folk-songs
  USE Folk-songs, Ruanda
Ruanda songs
  USE Songs, Ruanda
Rumbas
  BT Dance music
Russian ballads
  USE Ballads, Russian
Russian folk-songs
  USE Folk-songs, Russian
Russian horn *(ML990.R8)*
  BT Brass instruments
        Horn (Musical instrument)
        Musical instruments—Russian S.F.S.R.
Russian lullabies
  USE Lullabies, Russian
Russian revolutionary ballads and songs
  USE Revolutionary ballads and songs,
          Russian
Ryukyu ballads
  USE Ballads, Ryukyu
Ryukyu songs
  USE Songs, Ryukyu
Ryūteki *(ML990.R9)*
  BT Flute
        Musical instruments—Japan
Ryūteki and shō music *(M288-9)*
  UF Shō and ryūteki music
  NT Sonatas (Ryūteki and shō)
Sackbut *(ML990.S3)*
  BT Trombone
Sacre du printemps (Ballet)
  USE Rite of spring (Ballet)
Sacred cantatas
  USE Cantatas, Sacred
Sacred choruses
  USE Choruses, Sacred
Sacred duets
  BT Choruses, Sacred
        Sacred vocal music
  RT Vocal duets
  NT Anthems
        Motets
        Part-songs, Sacred
Sacred duets, Unaccompanied
Sacred duets with chamber orchestra
    (M2018-2019)
  —Scores *(M2018)*
Sacred duets with continuo

Sacred duets with guitar *(M2062.2; M2063.2)*
Sacred duets with harpsichord
  BT Sacred duets with piano
Sacred duets with instrumental ensemble
    (M2018-2019)
Sacred duets with orchestra *(M2018-2019)*
  —Vocal scores with piano
    BT Sacred duets with piano
Sacred duets with organ
Sacred duets with piano
  NT Sacred duets with harpsichord
        Sacred duets with orchestra—Vocal
          scores with piano
Sacred duets with string orchestra
    (M2018-2019)
Sacred monologues with music
        Here, followed by specification of accom-
        panying medium, are entered sacred
        musical works in which spoken lan-
        guage is an integral part. The specifica-
        tion (Instrumental ensemble) stands
        for two or more different solo instru-
        ments; (Voice) for solo voice of high,
        low, or medium range; and (Chorus)
        for men's, mixed, women's, or chil-
        dren's voices in two or more parts.
        Secular works are entered under
        Monologues with music.
        Headings are printed below only if spe-
        cific cross references are needed.
  UF Monologues with music, Sacred
        Narration with music
        Recitations with music
        Sacred recitations with music
        Speaking with music
  BT Monologues with music
        Music
  Note under Monologues with music
Sacred monologues with music (Chorus with
        instrumental ensemble)
    (M1625-1626)
  BT Choruses, Sacred, with instrumental
        ensemble
Sacred monologues with music (Chorus with
        orchestra) *(M1625-6)*
  BT Choruses, Sacred, with orchestra
  —Vocal scores with organ
    BT Choruses, Sacred, with organ
  —Vocal scores with piano *(M1626)*
    BT Choruses, Sacred, with piano
Sacred monologues with music (Orchestra)
    (M1625)
  BT Orchestral music
Sacred monologues with music (Piano)
    (M1626)
  BT Piano music
Sacred monologues with music (Voice with
        orchestra) *(M1625)*
  BT Sacred songs with orchestra
Sacred music
  USE Church music
        Synagogue music

Sacred nonets
- UF Nonets, Sacred
- BT Choruses, Sacred
  - Sacred vocal music
- RT Vocal nonets
- NT Anthems
  - Motets
  - Part-songs, Sacred
- *Note under* Nonets

Sacred octets
- UF Octets, Sacred
- BT Choruses, Sacred
  - Sacred vocal music
- RT Vocal octets
- NT Anthems
  - Motets
  - Part-songs, Sacred
- *Note under* Octets

Sacred octets with continuo

Sacred octets with instrumental ensemble
  (M2018-2019)

Sacred part-songs
- USE Part-songs, Sacred

Sacred quartets
- UF Quartets, Sacred
- BT Choruses, Sacred
  - Sacred vocal music
- RT Vocal quartets
- NT Anthems
  - Motets
  - Part-songs, Sacred
- *Note under* Quartets

Sacred quartets, Unaccompanied

Sacred quartets with band (M2018-2019)

Sacred quartets with guitar (M2061.4;
  M2062.4; M2063.4; M2064.4;
  M2072.4; M2073.4; M2074.4)

Sacred quartets with instrumental ensemble
  (M2018-2019)

Sacred quartets with organ (M2062.4;
  M2072.4)

Sacred quartets with piano (M2061.4;
  M2062.4; M2063.4; M2064.4;
  M2072.4; M2073.4; M2074.4)

Sacred quartets with string orchestra
  (M2018-2019)

**Sacred quartets with string orchestra and
  organ** (M2018-2019)

Sacred quintets
- UF Quintets, Sacred
- BT Choruses, Sacred
  - Sacred vocal music
- RT Vocal quintets
- NT Anthems
  - Motets
  - Part-songs, Sacred
- *Note under* Quintets

Sacred quintets with chamber orchestra
  (M2018-2019)
—Vocal scores with pianos (2) (M2019)
- BT Sacred quintets with pianos (2)

Sacred quintets with instrumental ensemble
  (M2018-2019)

Sacred quintets with piano (M2061.5;
  M2062.5; M2063.5; M2064.5;
  M2072.5; M2073.5; M2074.5)
Sacred quintets with pianos (2) (M2061.5;
  M2062.5; M2063.5; M2064.5;
  M2072.5; M2073.5; M2074.5)
- NT Sacred quintets with chamber orchestra
  - —Vocal scores with pianos (2)

Sacred recitations with music
- USE Sacred monologues with music

Sacred septets
- UF Septets, Sacred
- BT Choruses, Sacred
  - Sacred vocal music
- RT Vocal septets
- NT Anthems
  - Motets
  - Part-songs, Sacred
- *Note under* Septets

Sacred sextets
- UF Sextets, Sacred
- BT Choruses, Sacred
  - Sacred vocal music
- RT Vocal sextets
- NT Anthems
  - Motets
  - Part-songs, Sacred
- *Note under* Sextets

Sacred sextets with chamber orchestra
  (M2018-2019)
Sacred sextets with continuo
Sacred sextets with instrumental ensemble
  (M2018-2019)

Sacred songs
> Here are entered works for solo voice
> with sacred texts. Works with secular
> texts are entered under the heading
> Songs. This heading is also qualified as
> appropriate by voice range and specifi-
> cation of accompaniment, *e.g.* Sacred
> songs (High voice) with piano; Sacred
> songs with string orchestra; Sacred
> songs, Unaccompanied.
- UF Arias
  - Art songs
  - Songs, Sacred
- BT Sacred vocal music
  - Songs
- NT Bhajans
  - Contemporary Christian music
  - Gospel music
  - Hymns
  - Solo cantatas, Sacred
- *Note under* Songs

Sacred songs, Unaccompanied
- *Note under* Sacred songs

Sacred songs (High voice)

**Sacred songs (High voice) with chamber
  orchestra**
—Vocal scores with piano (M2014)

Sacred songs (High voice) with continuo
- NT Solo cantatas, Sacred (High voice)—
  - Vocal scores with continuo

Sacred songs (High voice) with electronic music *(M2103.3)*
> BT   Electronic music

Sacred songs (High voice) with harpsichord *(M2110-2114)*
> BT   Sacred songs (High voice) with piano

Sacred songs (High voice) with instrumental ensemble *(M2103.3)*

Sacred songs (High voice) with lute

Sacred songs (High voice) with orchestra
> —Vocal scores with piano
>> BT   Sacred songs (High voice) with piano

Sacred songs (High voice) with organ *(M2110-2114)*
> NT   Solo cantatas, Sacred (High voice)—Vocal scores with organ

Sacred songs (High voice) with piano *(M2110-2114)*
> NT   Sacred songs (High voice) with harpsichord
> Sacred songs (High voice) with orchestra—Vocal scores with piano
> *Note under* Sacred songs

Sacred songs (High voice) with reed-organ *(M2110-2113)*

Sacred songs (High voice) with string orchestra

Sacred songs (High voice) with viol *(M2103.3)*

Sacred songs (Low voice) with chamber orchestra
> —Vocal scores with piano
>> BT   Sacred songs (Low voice) with piano

Sacred songs (Low voice) with continuo
> NT   Solo cantatas, Sacred (Low voice)—Vocal scores with continuo

Sacred songs (Low voice) with harpsichord *(M2110-2114)*
> BT   Sacred songs (Low voice) with piano

Sacred songs (Low voice) with instrumental ensemble *(M2103.3)*

Sacred songs (Low voice) with orchestra
> —Vocal scores with piano
>> BT   Sacred songs (Low voice) with piano

Sacred songs (Low voice) with organ *(M2110-2114)*

Sacred songs (Low voice) with piano *(M2110-2114)*
> NT   Sacred songs (Low voice) with chamber orchestra—Vocal scores with piano
> Sacred songs (Low voice) with harpsichord
> Sacred songs (Low voice) with orchestra—Vocal scores with piano
> Sacred songs (Low voice) with string orchestra—Vocal scores with piano

Sacred songs (Low voice) with string orchestra
> —Vocal scores with piano
>> BT   Sacred songs (Low voice) with piano

Sacred songs (Low voice) with viola *(M2113.3)*

Sacred songs (Medium voice)

Sacred songs (Medium voice) with band *(M1205; M1257)*
> —Scores

Sacred songs (Medium voice) with chamber orchestra
> —Vocal scores with piano *(M2104)*
>> BT   Sacred songs (Medium voice) with piano
> —Vocal scores with pianos (2)

Sacred songs (Medium voice) with electronic music *(M2103.3)*
> BT   Electronic music

Sacred songs (Medium voice) with guitar *(M2110-2114)*

Sacred songs (Medium voice) with harpsichord *(M2110-2114)*
> BT   Sacred songs (Medium voice) with piano

Sacred songs (Medium voice) with instrumental ensemble *(M2103.3)*

Sacred songs (Medium voice) with orchestra

Sacred songs (Medium voice) with organ *(M2110-2114)*

Sacred songs (Medium voice) with piano *(M2110-2114)*
> NT   Sacred songs (Medium voice) with chamber orchestra—Vocal scores with piano
> Sacred songs (Medium voice) with harpsichord
> Sacred songs (Medium voice) with string orchestra—Vocal scores with piano

Sacred songs (Medium voice) with reed-organ *(M2110-2113)*

Sacred songs (Medium voice) with string orchestra *(M2103.3)*
> —Vocal scores with piano
>> BT   Sacred songs (Medium voice) with piano

Sacred songs with continuo
> NT   Solo cantatas, Sacred—Vocal scores with continuo

Sacred songs with guitar *(M2112-2113)*

Sacred songs with harpsichord
> BT   Sacred songs with piano

Sacred songs with instrumental ensemble *(M2103.3)*

Sacred songs with lute *(M2103.3)*

Sacred songs with orchestra
> NT   Sacred monologues with music (Voice with orchestra)

Sacred songs with organ *(M2110; M2112)*

Sacred songs with piano *(M2110; M2112)*
> NT   Sacred songs with harpsichord

Sacred songs with string orchestra *(M2103.3; M2104)*
> *Note under* Sacred songs

Sacred trios
> UF   Trios, Sacred
> BT   Choruses, Sacred
> Sacred vocal music
> RT   Vocal trios
> NT   Anthems
> Motets
> Part-songs, Sacred
> *Note under* Trios

Sacred trios, Unaccompanied

Sacred trios with chamber orchestra *(M2103.3)*
> —Vocal scores with piano *(M2104)*
>> BT   Sacred trios with piano

Sacred trios with harpsichord
   BT Sacred trios with piano
Sacred trios with instrumental ensemble
     (M2018-2019)
Sacred trios with orchestra *(M2018-2019)*
   —Vocal scores with piano *(M2019)*
     BT Sacred trios with piano
Sacred trios with organ
Sacred trios with piano
   NT Sacred trios with chamber orchestra—
       Vocal scores with piano
      Sacred trios with harpsichord
      Sacred trios with orchestra—Vocal
       scores with piano
Sacred trios with string orchestra
     (M2018-2019)
Sacred vocal ensembles *(M2018-2019.5)*
   UF Ensembles (Music)
   BT Vocal ensembles
Sacred vocal ensembles with instrumental
     ensemble *(M2018-2019)*
Sacred vocal music [May Subd Geog] *(M1999)*
     Here are entered collections of miscel-
     laneous sacred vocal compositions.
     Works on sacred music are entered un-
     der the headings Church music and
     Synagogue music—History and criti-
     cism.
   UF Pastoral music (Sacred)
      Vocal music, Sacred
   BT Vocal music
   NT Advent music
      All Saints' Day music
      Amens (Music)
      Antiphonaries (Music)
      Antiphons (Music)
      Ascension Day music
      Candlemas music
      Cantatas, Sacred
      Carols
      Chants
      Chants (Anglican)
      Chants (Buddhist)
      Chants (Hindu)
      Chants (Jewish)
      Chants (Plain, Gregorian, etc.)
      Chorales
      Christmas music
      Communion-service music
      Corpus Christi festival music
      Dies irae (Music)
      Easter music
      Epiphany music
      Evening-service music
      Funeral music
      Holy-Week music
      Hymns
      Lenten music
      Mary, Blessed Virgin, Saint—Songs and
       music
      Masses
      Memorial music
      Morning-service music

Sacred vocal music [May Subd Geog] *(M1999)*
   (Continued)
   NT Offertories (Music)
      Oratorios
      Part-songs, Sacred
      Passion-music
      Psalms (Music)
      Responses (Music)
      Sacred duets
      Sacred nonets
      Sacred octets
      Sacred quartets
      Sacred quintets
      Sacred septets
      Sacred sextets
      Sacred songs
      Sacred trios
      Song of Solomon (Music)
      Synagogue music
      Wedding music
   Note under Church music
   —Analysis, appreciation
Saepe expugnauerunt me (Music)
   USE Psalms (Music)—129th Psalm
Safety songs *(M1978.S15; M1997.S15)*
   BT Topical songs
Sailors' songs
   USE Sea songs
Saint Cecilia's Day *(Indirect)*
   UF St. Cecilia's Day
   BT Music festivals
Saint Cecilia's Hall (Edinburgh, Lothian)
   BT Music-halls—Scotland
Saint Matthew Passion (Ballet)
   UF Matthäus-Passion (Ballet)
      Matthäuspassion (Ballet)
   BT Ballets
Saint-Sernin de Toulouse (Church)
   —Organ *(ML594)*
     BT Organs—France
Salon-orchestra music *(M1350)*
   BT Instrumental music
      Orchestral music
   RT Chamber-orchestra music
   SA Suites, Variations, Waltzes, *and similar*
      headings with specification of
      instruments which include the
      specification Salon orchestra
   NT Concertos (Piano with salon orchestra)
      Marches (Salon orchestra)
      Overtures (Salon orchestra)
      Piano with salon orchestra
      Potpourris (Salon orchestra)
      Suites (Salon orchestra)
      Waltzes (Salon orchestra)
Salsa [May Subd Geog]
   BT Popular music
Saltarellos
   BT Dance music
Salterio tedesco
   USE Dulcimer
Salvadorian lullabies
   USE Lullabies, Salvadorian

Salve Regina (Music)
   BT Antiphons (Music)
         Mary, Blessed Virgin, Saint—Songs and
            music
Salvum me fac Deus (Music)
   USE Psalms (Music)—69th Psalm
Salvum me fac Domine (Music)
   USE Psalms (Music)—12th Psalm
Sambalpuri folk-songs
   USE Folk-songs, Sambalpuri
Sambas
   BT Dance music
Sambuca lincea *(ML697.A2)*
   BT Piano
Samisen
   USE Shamisen
Samoan folk-songs
   USE Folk-songs, Samoan
San hsien *(ML1015-1018)*
   BT Lute
San hsien music *(M142.S)*
   NT Trios (Piano, san hsien, erh hu)
Sānāyī
   USE Shehnai
Sanctus (Music) *(M2079)*
Sangen
   USE Shamisen
Sansa
   USE Sanza
Sanskrit Hindu hymns
   USE Hindu hymns, Sanskrit
Santali folk-songs
   USE Folk-songs, Santali
Santir
   USE Santūr
Santūr *(ML1015-1018)*
   UF Santir
   BT Dulcimer
         Musical instruments—Iran
Santūr and tabla music
   UF Tabla and santūr music
Santūr music *(M142.S3)*
Sanza *(ML1015-1018)*
   UF Sansa
         Zanza
   BT Musical instruments—Africa
   NT Mbira
Sarabands
   BT Dance music
Sarangi *(ML927.S4)*
Sarangi and tabla music
   UF Tabla and sarangi music
Sardanas
         This heading is used without specification
           of instruments. A second heading is
           assigned if the work is for a medium
           other than piano (2 hands).
   BT Dance music
Sardinian folk-songs
   USE Folk-songs, Sardinian
Sarod
   BT Lute
         Musical instruments—India

Sarod and sitar music
   UF Sitar and sarod music
Sarod and tabla music
   UF Tabla and sarod music
Sarod music
   BT Lute music
Sarrusophone
   BT Bassoon
         Brass instruments
Sarrusophone and percussion music *(M298)*
   UF Percussion and sarrusophone music
Satirical songs *(Indirect)*
   BT Songs
Saxophone *(ML975)*
   BT Woodwind instruments
   NT Tárogató
   —Methods (Jazz) *(MT502)*
   —Reeds
   —Studies and exercises (Jazz)
         Example under Jazz music
Saxophone and clarinet music
   USE Clarinet and saxophone music
Saxophone and continuo music
   UF Continuo and saxophone music
   NT Sonatas (Saxophone and continuo)
Saxophone and double-bass music
         (M290-291)
   UF Double-bass and saxophone music
Saxophone and flute music
   USE Flute and saxophone music
Saxophone and guitar music *(M296-7)*
   UF Guitar and saxophone music
   NT Saxophone and guitar with jazz
         ensemble
Saxophone and guitar with jazz ensemble
         (M1366)
   BT Saxophone and guitar music
Saxophone and harp music *(M296-297)*
   UF Harp and saxophone music
Saxophone and marimba music *(M298)*
   UF Marimba and saxophone music
Saxophone and organ music *(M182-186)*
   UF Organ and saxophone music
Saxophone and percussion music *(M298)*
   UF Percussion and saxophone music
Saxophone and piano music *(M268-9)*
   UF Piano and saxophone music
   NT Concertos (Saxophone and piano)
         Marches (Saxophone and piano)
         Rondos (Saxophone and piano)
         Saxophone and piano with orchestra
         Sonatas (Saxophone and piano)
         Suites (Saxophone and piano)
Saxophone and piano music, Arranged
         (M268-9)
   NT Concertos (Saxophone)—Excerpts—
         Solo with piano
         Concertos (Saxophone)—Solo with
         piano
         Concertos (Saxophone with band)—
         Solo with piano
         Concertos (Saxophone with chamber
         orchestra)—Solo with piano

Saxophone and piano music, Arranged *(M268-9)*
  (Continued)
  NT Concertos (Saxophone with string
        orchestra)—Solo with piano
      Saxophone with band—Solo with piano
      Saxophone with chamber orchestra—
        Solo with piano
      Saxophone with orchestra—Solo with
        piano
      Saxophone with orchestra, Arranged—
        Solo with piano
      Saxophone with string orchestra—Solo
        with piano
      Suites (Saxophone with orchestra)—
        Solo with piano
      Suites (Saxophone with string
        orchestra)—Solo with piano
Saxophone and piano music, Arranged (Jazz)
  USE Saxophone and piano music (Jazz)
Saxophone and piano music (Jazz) *(M268-9)*
  UF Saxophone and piano music, Arranged
        (Jazz)
Saxophone and piano with orchestra
        (M1040-1041)
  BT Saxophone and piano music
  RT Concertos (Saxophone and piano)
Saxophone and tambourine music *(M298)*
  UF Tambourine and saxophone music
Saxophone and trumpet music *(M288-9)*
  UF Trumpet and saxophone music
  NT Concertos (Saxophone and trumpet
        with string orchestra)
      Saxophone and trumpet with
        string orchestra
Saxophone and trumpet with band
        (M1205-M1206; M1257)
  RT Concertos (Saxophone and trumpet
        with band)
  NT Suites (Saxophone and trumpet with band)
Saxophone and trumpet with string orchestra
        (M1140-1141)
  BT Saxophone and trumpet music
  RT Concertos (Saxophone and trumpet
        with string orchestra)
Saxophone and tuba music *(M288-289)*
  UF Tuba and saxophone music
Saxophone and violin with orchestra *(M1040-1041)*
  RT Concertos (Saxophone and violin)
Saxophone and violoncello music *(M290-291)*
  UF Violoncello and saxophone music
Saxophone music *(M105-109)*
  SA Concertos, Minuets, Sonatas, Suites,
        and similar headings with
        specification of instruments; Trios
        [Quartets, etc.], Wind trios [quartets,
        etc.], *and* Woodwind trios [quartets,
        etc.] *followed by specifications which*
        include the saxophone; also Wind
        ensembles, Woodwind ensembles,
        and headings that begin with the
        words saxophone or saxophones
  NT Recorded accompaniments (Saxophone)
      Saxophone with instrumental ensemble

Saxophone music, Arranged *(M108-9)*
Saxophone music (Jazz) *(M105-7)*
  NT Saxophone with jazz ensemble
Saxophone music (Saxophones (2)) *(M288-9)*
Saxophone music (Saxophones (2)), Arranged
        (M288-9)
Saxophone music (Saxophones (3))
  USE Woodwind trios (Saxophones (3))
Saxophone music (Saxophones (4))
  USE Woodwind quartets (Saxophones (4))
Saxophone players
  USE Saxophonists
Saxophone with band *(M1205-6)*
  RT Concertos (Saxophone with band)
  —Solo with piano *(M1206)*
      BT Saxophone and piano music,
            Arranged
Saxophone with chamber orchestra
        (M1034-5)
  RT Concertos (Saxophone with chamber
        orchestra)
  —Solo with piano *(M1035)*
      BT Saxophone and piano music,
            Arranged
Saxophone with chamber orchestra, Arranged
        (M1034-5)
  —Scores and parts *(M1034)*
Saxophone with dance orchestra *(M1353)*
  RT Concertos (Saxophone with dance
        orchestra)
Saxophone with instrumental ensemble
  BT Saxophone music
  RT Concertos (Saxophone with
        instrumental ensemble)
Saxophone with jazz ensemble *(M1366)*
  BT Jazz ensembles
      Saxophone music (Jazz)
Saxophone with orchestra *(M1034-5)*
  RT Concertos (Saxophone)
  NT Suites (Saxophone with orchestra)
      Symphonies (Saxophone with orchestra)
  —Solo with piano *(M1035)*
      BT Saxophone and piano music,
            Arranged
Saxophone with orchestra, Arranged
        (M1034-5)
  —Solo with piano *(M1035.S4)*
      BT Saxophone and piano music,
            Arranged
Saxophone with percussion ensemble
  RT Concertos (Saxophone with percussion
        ensemble)
Saxophone with string ensemble
  RT Concertos (Saxophone with string
        ensemble)
Saxophone with string orchestra *(M1105-6)*
  BT String orchestra music
  RT Concertos (Saxophone with string
        orchestra)
  NT Suites (Saxophone with string
        orchestra)
  —Solo with piano *(M1106)*
      BT Saxophone and piano music, Arranged

Saxophone with wind ensemble
- RT Concertos (Saxophone with wind ensemble)
- NT Suites (Saxophone with wind ensemble)

Saxophones (4) with band
(M1205-M1206)
- BT Woodwind quartets (Saxophones (4))
- NT Concertos (Saxophones (4) with band)

Saxophones (4) with chamber orchestra
(M1034.S4; M1035.S4)
- BT Woodwind quartets (Saxophones (4))
- RT Concertos (Saxophones (4) with chamber orchestra)
- NT Suites (Saxophones (4) with chamber orchestra)

Saxophones (4) with orchestra *(M1034.S4; M1035.S4)*
- BT Woodwind quartets (Saxophones (4))
- RT Concertos (Saxophones (4))
- NT Symphonies (Saxophones (4) with orchestra)

Saxophones (4) with string orchestra
(M1134.S4; M1135.S4)
- BT Woodwind quartets (Saxophones (4))
- RT Concertos (Saxophones (4) with string orchestra)

Saxophonists [May Subd Geog] *(Biography: collective, ML399; individual, ML419)*
- UF Saxophone players

Saz *(ML1015-1018)*
- BT Musical instruments—Turkey

Saz music *(M142.S)*

Scales (Music)
- USE Musical intervals and scales

Scaletta
- USE Melodica

Scandinavian folk-songs
- USE Folk-songs, Scandinavian

Scat singing
- USE Jazz vocals

Schalmei
- USE Shawm

Scheitholt
- USE Noordsche balk

Schenker analysis
- USE Schenkerian analysis

Schenker family
- USE Schenk family

Schenker system
- USE Schenkerian analysis

Schenkerian analysis
- UF Schenker analysis
  Schenker system
  Schenkerian theory
- BT Counterpoint
  Harmonic analysis (Music)
  Music—Theory
  Musical analysis

Schenkerian theory
- USE Schenkerian analysis

Scherzo
- BT Musical form
- RT Minuet

School music [May Subd Geog]
- UF Public-school music
- BT Music
- —Public relations
  - USE Public relations—School music

School music supervision
- UF Music supervision in schools
  School music supervisors
- BT School supervision

School music supervisors
- USE School music supervision

School opera
- USE Opera—Juvenile

School song-books *(M1994)*
- Here are entered song-books for use in American and English schools.
- BT Song-books
  Songs—United States
  Songs, English
- NT Children's songs
  Choral singing—Juvenile

School song-books, Afrikaner *(M1990-1994)*
- UF Afrikaner school song-books

School song-books, Catholic *(M1994)*

School song-books, French, [German, etc.]

School song-books, Hebrew
- USE School song-books, Jewish

School song-books, Jewish
- UF School song-books, Hebrew
  School song-books, Yiddish

School song-books, Lutheran *(M1994)*

School song-books, Portuguese
- UF Portuguese school song-books

School song-books, Yiddish
- USE School song-books, Jewish

School supervision [May Subd Geog] *(LB2801-LB2822)*
- NT School music supervision

Schottisches
- UF Schottishes
- BT Dance music
  Polkas

Score reading and playing *(MT85)*
- UF Music—Reading
  Music reading
- RT Sight-reading (Music)
- NT Sight-singing

Sea songs [May Subd Geog] *(Collections, M1977.S2; History and criticism, ML3780; Poetry, PN6110.S4)*
- UF Boatmen's songs
  Chanteys
  Chantys
  Merchant seamen's songs
  Sailors' songs
  Seamen's songs
  Shanties
- BT Songs
- NT Seamen—Hymns

Sea-trumpet *(Medieval stringed instrument, ML760)*
- UF Marine trumpet
  Nun's fiddle
  Tromba marina

Seamen [May Subd Geog] *(Labor, HD8039.S4-*
HD8039.S42)
—Hymns *(BV463)*
Here are entered collections of hymns
for the use of seamen exclusively.
Hymns intended for the use of sol-
diers and seamen are entered under
the heading Soldiers—Hymns.
BT Hymns
Sea songs
Note under Soldiers—Hymns
Seamen's songs
USE Sea songs
Secular part-songs
USE Part-songs
Seder music
USE Passover music
Seises
UF Six (Dance)
BT Choirboys
Sekkyō jōruri [May Subd Geog] *(Collections,*
PL768.J6; History, PL738.J6)
BT Monologues with music
Senses and sensation *(Epistemology, BD214;*
Physiology, QP431-QP499; Psychology,
BF231-BF299)
NT Music—Physiological aspects
Septets *(M700-786)*
Here are entered collections of composi-
tions for seven instruments belonging
to various families and in various com-
binations; and compositions for seven
specific instruments belonging to various families, followed by specification
of instruments (including the specification: Unspecified instrument(s))
Compositions for seven bowed stringed
instruments are entered under String
septets; for seven wind instruments under Wind septets; for seven brass instruments under Brass septets; for
seven woodwind instruments under
Woodwind septets, with or without
specification of instruments in each
case.
Compositions for seven plectral instruments are entered under Plectral ensembles, except those for guitars and-
/or harps, which are entered under
Septets followed by specification of instruments.
Compositions for seven percussionists are
entered under Percussion ensembles.
Compositions for seven solo voices are
entered under Sacred septets or Vocal
septets.
Headings with specification of instruments are printed below only if specific cross references are needed.
SA Suites, Variations, Waltzes, *and similar*
headings with specification of
instruments

Septets, Brass
USE Brass septets
Septets, Sacred
USE Sacred septets
Septets, Secular
USE Vocal septets
Septets, String
USE String septets
Septets, Vocal
USE Vocal septets
Septets, Wind
USE Wind septets
Septets, Woodwind
USE Woodwind septets
Septets (Piano, flute, zither, percussion)
(M745-749)
BT Zither music
Septets (Piano, guitar, clavioline, musical saw,
percussion, vibraphone, xylophone)
(M785)
BT Clavioline music
Musical saw music
Septets (Piano, saxophones (4), harp, percussion)
(M745-M749)
NT Concertos (Piano, saxophones (4), harp,
percussion with string orchestra)
Piano, saxophones (4), harp, percussion
with string orchestra
Sequences (Music)
BT Hymns
RT Tropes (Music)
NT Dies irae (Music)
Stabat Mater dolorosa (Music)
Seraphic dialogue (Ballet)
BT Ballets
Serbo-Croatian ballads
USE Ballads, Serbo-Croatian
Serbo-Croatian folk-songs
USE Folk-songs, Serbo-Croatian
Serpent *(Musical instrument) (History,*
ML980)
BT Brass instruments
NT Ophicleide
Service books (Music)
UF Choir books
Church music—Choruses and choir
books
Church music—Service books
BT Choruses, Sacred
NT Antiphonaries (Music)
—Baptists [Catholic Church, etc.]
Setar
USE Sitar
Settings, Musical
USE *subdivision* Musical settings *under*
headings for authors, e.g.
Shakespeare, William, 1564-1616—
Musical settings; *also under headings*
for literature, poetry, drama, etc.,
e.g. English literature—Musical
settings

Sextets *(M600-686)*

Here are entered collections of compositions for six instruments belonging to various families and in various combinations; and compositions for six specific instruments belonging to various families, followed by specification of instruments (including the specification: Unspecified instrument(s))

Compositions for six bowed stringed instruments are entered under String sextets; for six wind instruments under Wind sextets; for six brass instruments under Brass sextets; and for six woodwind instruments under Woodwind sextets, with or without specification of instruments in each case.

Compositions for six plectral instruments are entered under Plectral ensembles, except those for guitars and/or harps, which are entered under Sextets followed by specification of instruments.

Compositions for six percussionists are entered under Percussion ensembles.

Compositions for six solo voices are entered under Sacred sextets or Vocal sextets.

Headings with specification of instruments are printed below only if specific cross references are needed.

- SA Suites, Variations, Waltzes, *and similar headings with specification of instruments*

Sextets, Brass
  USE Brass sextets
Sextets, Sacred
  USE Sacred sextets
Sextets, Secular
  USE Vocal sextets
Sextets, String
  USE String sextets
Sextets, Vocal
  USE Vocal sextets
Sextets, Wind
  USE Wind sextets
Sextets, Woodwind
  USE Woodwind sextets
Sextets (Bassoon, clarinet, oboe, violin, viola, violoncello) *(M660-664)*
  NT Bassoon, clarinet, oboe, violin, viola, violoncello with orchestra
     Concertos (Bassoon, clarinet, oboe, violin, viola, violoncello)
Sextets (Chimes, xylophone, violins (2), viola, violoncello) *(M685)*
  BT Chime music
  NT Chimes, xylophone, violins (2), viola, violoncello with string orchestra
     Concertos (Chimes, xylophone, violins (2), viola, violoncello with string orchestra)
Sextets (Clarinet, flute, violin, violoncello, double bass, percussion) *(M685)*

Sextets (Cornetts (2), violins (2), continuos (2))
Sextets (Harps (2), percussion) *(M685)*
  NT Concertos (Harps (2), percussion with string orchestra)
     Harps (2), percussion with string orchestra
Sextets (Ondes Martenot (6)) *(M685)*
  UF Ondes Martenot music (Ondes Martenot (6))
  BT Ondes Martenot music
Sextets (Organ, piano, guitars (3), percussion) *(M600-604)*
  NT Concertos (Organ, piano, guitars (3), percussion)
     Organ, piano, guitars (3), percussion with orchestra
Sextets (Percussion and violin) *(M685)*
Sextets (Piano (4 hands), bugle, clarinet, percussion, violin) *(M635)*
  BT Bugle music
Sextets (Piano, bassoon, clarinet, flute, horn, oboe) *(M615-619)*
Sextets (Piano, bassoon, clarinet, flute, horn, oboe), Arranged *(M618-619)*
  NT Concertos (Bassoon, clarinet, flute, horn, oboe with string orchestra)—Solos with piano
     Suites (Bassoon, clarinet, flute, horn, oboe with string orchestra)—Solos with piano
Sextets (Piano, horn, trombone, trumpets (2), tuba), Arranged *(M619)*
  NT Concertos (Horn, trombone, trumpets (2), tuba)—Solos with piano
Sextets (Pianos (2), guitars (3), percussion) *(M635)*
  NT Concertos (Pianos (2), guitars (3), percussion)
     Pianos (2), guitars (3), percussion with orchestra
Sextets (Pianos (2), percussion) *(M635)*
  NT Concertos (Pianos (2), percussion)
     Pianos (2), percussion with orchestra
Sextets (Pianos (2), saxophones (4)) *(M615-619)*
Sextets (Pianos (2), saxophones (4)), Arranged *(M618-619)*
  NT Concertos (Saxophones (4))—Solos with pianos (2)
Sextets (Shakuhachi, biwa, kotos (2), shamisen, percussion)
  BT Biwa music
     Koto music
     Shakuhachi music
     Shamisen music
Sextets (Shakuhachi, guitar, kotos (2), percussion, double bass) *(M685)*
  BT Koto music
     Shakuhachi music
Sextets (Trumpets (5), percussion) *(M685)*
  NT Concertos (Trumpets (5), percussion with string orchestra)
     Trumpets (5), percussion with string orchestra

Sextets (Unspecified instruments (6)) *(M686)*
   Example under reference from Melody instrument
     music; Unspecified instrument
Shakers [May Subd Geog] *(BX9751-BX9793)*
  —Hymns
Shakuhachi *(ML990.S5)*
  BT Flute
      Musical instruments—Japan
      Woodwind instruments
Shakuhachi and biwa music
  UF Biwa and shakuhachi music
  NT Concertos (Shakuhachi and biwa)
      Shakuhachi and biwa with orchestra
Shakuhachi and biwa with orchestra
     (M1040-1041)
  BT Shakuhachi and biwa music
  RT Concertos (Shakuhachi and biwa)
Shakuhachi and koto music
  UF Koto and shakuhachi music
Shakuhachi and piano music *(M270.S45;*
     M271.S45)
  UF Piano and shakuhachi music
Shakuhachi and shamisen music
  UF Shamisen and shakuhachi music
Shakuhachi music *(M110.S45)*
  NT Quartets (Flute, shakuhachi, biwa, harp)
      Quartets (Shakuhachi, kotos (2),
       shamisen)
      Quartets (Shakuhachi, kotos (3))
      Sextets (Shakuhachi, biwa, kotos (2),
       shamisen, percussion)
      Sextets (Shakuhachi, guitar, kotos (2),
       percussion, double bass)
Shakuhachi players [May Subd Geog]
  BT Musicians—Japan
Shakuhachi with orchestra *(M1034.S5;*
     M1035.S5)
  RT Concertos (Shakuhachi)
Shakuhachi with string orchestra
     (M1134.S5-M1135.S5)
  RT Concertos (Shakuhachi with string
      orchestra)
Shalm
  USE Shawm
Shamisen
  UF Samisen
      Sangen
  BT Musical instruments—Japan
Shamisen and shakuhachi music
  USE Shakuhachi and shamisen music
Shamisen music *(M142.S45)*
  NT Monologues with music (Shamisen)
      Quartets (Shakuhachi, kotos (2),
       shamisen)
      Sextets (Shakuhachi, biwa, kotos (2),
       shamisen, percussion)
Shamisen players [May Subd Geog]
  UF Shamisenists
Shamisenists
  USE Shamisen players
Shanties
  USE Sea songs

Shawm
  UF Chalumeau (Double-reed musical
      instrument)
      Schalmei
      Shalm
  BT Oboe
      Woodwind instruments
  NT Pommer
      So na
      Tárogató
      Zumari
Sheet-music covers
  USE Music title-pages
Shehnai
  UF Sānāyī
      Surnai
  BT Musical instruments—India
      Oboe
Shehnai and sitar music
  UF Sitar and shehnai music
Shehnai and tabla music
  UF Tabla and shehnai music
Shehnai and violin music
  UF Violin and shehnai music
  BT Shehnai music
      Violin music
Shehnai music
  NT Shehnai and violin music
Shelving (for music)
  UF Music libraries—Shelving
  BT Shelving (Furniture)
Shelving (Furniture) [May Subd Geog] *(NK2740)*
  NT Shelving (for music)
Sheng (Musical instrument) *(History,*
     ML1089.S5; Instruction, MT801.S5)
  BT Mouth organs
      Musical instruments—China
      Reed-organ
Sheng music *(M175.S5)*
  BT Reed-organ music
Sheng with orchestra *(M1039.4.S5)*
  RT Concertos (Sheng)
Shepherd's pipe
  USE Pipe (Musical instrument)
Shepherds' songs *(M1977-M1978.S48)*
  BT Pastoral music (Secular)
      Songs
Shigin
  BT Music—Japan
Shinnai
  UF Shinnaibushi
  BT Jōruri
      Monologues with music (Shamisen)
Shinnaibushi
  USE Shinnai
Shinobue *(History, ML990.S; Instruction,*
     MT358.S55)
  UF Shino
      Takebue
  BT Flute
      Musical instruments—Japan

Shinobue and piano music
(Collections, *M270.S47; Separate works,*
M271.S47)
UF Piano and shinobue music
Shō *(ML1050-1053)*
BT Mouth organs
Musical instruments—Japan
Reed-organ
Shō and ryūteki music
USE Ryūteki and shō music
Shō music *(M110.S)*
NT Quintets (Piano, shō, harp, violin, violoncello)
Shofar
USE Shophar
Shona songs
USE Songs, Shona
Shophar *(ML990.S)*
UF Shofar
BT Horn (Musical instrument)
Shophar-calls *(M110.S5)*
Shorthand *(Z53-Z100; English, Z54-Z57)*
NT Musical shorthand
Sicilianas
UF Sicilianos
Siciliennes
BT Dance music
Sicilianos
USE Sicilianas
Siciliennes
USE Sicilianas
Sight-reading (Music) *(MT236)*
UF Music—Reading
Music reading
BT Music—Instruction and study
RT Score reading and playing
NT Galin-Paris-Chevé method (Music)
Sight-singing
Sight-singing *(Instruction, MT870)*
UF Solfeggio
BT Score reading and playing
Sight-reading (Music)
Solmization
NT Galin-Paris-Chevé method (Music)
Tone-word system
Tonic sol-fa
Sijo [May Subd Geog]
BT Korean poetry
NT Kagok
Sikh hymns *(BL2018.32)*
UF Hymns, Sikh
Sikhism—Hymns
Sikh hymns, English, [etc.]
Sikhism [May Subd Geog] *(BL2017-2018.7)*
—Hymns
USE Sikh hymns
Silent film music *(M176)*
Here are entered musical works composed
or adapted to accompany silent films.
Works on the technique of composing,
adapting, or performing musical accompa
niments to silent films are entered under
Silent films—Musical accompaniment.

Silent film music *(M176)*
(*Continued*)
UF Music for silent films
BT Silent films—Musical accompaniment
RT Moving-picture music
Note under Silent films—Musical accompaniment
Silent films
—Musical accompaniment *(MT737)*
Here are entered works on the tech-
nique of composing, adapting, or
performing musical accompani-
ments to silent films. Musical works
composed or adapted to accompany
silent films are entered under Silent
film music.
Silvertone organ *(ML597)*
BT Electronic organ
—Methods
— —Self-instruction *(MT192)*
Silvertone organ music
USE Electronic organ music (Silvertone
registration)
Simelungun folk-songs
USE Folk-songs, Simelungun
Sindhi hymns
USE Hymns, Sindhi
Sindhi songs
USE Songs, Sindhi
Singers [May Subd Geog] *(Biography: collective,*
ML400; Individual, ML420)
UF Music—Biography
Vocalists
BT Musicians
NT Castrati
Choirboys
Countertenors
Folk singers
—Collective labor agreements
USE Collective labor agreements—
Singers
Singers, Afro-American
USE Afro-American singers
Singers, Jewish [May Subd Geog]
UF Jewish singers
Singers, Women
USE Women singers
Singers in literature
NT Shakespeare, William, 1564-1616—
Characters—Singers
Singing *(ML3877; MT820-MT821; MT853;*
MT855)
UF Vocal culture
BT Music
Music—Performance
RT Voice
Voice culture
NT Choral singing
Crooning
Ensemble singing
Respiration
Vocal registers
Yodel and yodeling

Singing *(ML3877; MT820-MT821; MT853; MT855)*
  (Continued)
  —Auditions
  —Breathing exercises
    BT Breathing exercises
  —Diction *(MT872)*
    UF Musical declamation
    BT Diction
    RT Musical accentuation
    NT Choral singing—Diction
  —Expression
    USE Singing—Interpretation (Phrasing,
        dynamics, etc.)
  —Instruction and study [May Subd Geog]
      (MT820-MT821; MT853; MT855;
      MT878)
    BT Music—Instruction and study
    NT Chants (Plain, Gregorian, etc.)—
        Instruction and study
  — —Juvenile *(MT898)*
  —Interpretation (Phrasing, dynamics, etc.)
    (MT892)
    UF Singing—Expression
  —Methods *(MT825-MT850; MT882)*
    NT Bel canto
        Galin-Paris-Chevé method (Music)
  — —Juvenile *(MT900)*
  — —Self-instruction *(MT893)*
  —Self-instruction
    USE Singing—Methods—
        Self-instruction
  —Studies and exercises *(MT870; MT885)*
    RT Vocalises
    NT Voice culture—Exercises
Singing, Barbershop
  USE Barbershop singing
Singing, Choral
  USE Choral singing
Singing, Community
  USE Community music
Singing commercials *(M1977.S5; M1978.S5)*
  UF Commercials, Singing
  BT Music in advertising
Singing games [May Subd Geog]
  RT Games with music
       Play-party
Singing registers
  USE Vocal registers
Singing societies
  USE Choral societies
Singspiel *(ML1950)*
  BT Operetta
  RT Ballad opera
Singspiels
  USE Operas
Sistrum *(ML1040)*
  BT Music—Egypt
       Percussion instruments
       Rattle
Sitar
  UF Citara
       Setar
  BT Musical instruments—India

Sitar and sarod music
  USE Sarod and sitar music
Sitar and shehnai music
  USE Shehnai and sitar music
Sitar and tabla music
  UF Tabla and sitar music
Sitar and tabla with instrumental ensemble
  RT Concertos (Sitar and tabla with
      instrumental ensemble)
Sitar and violin music
  USE Violin and sitar music
Sitar music *(M142.S5)*
  NT Concertos (Sitar)
       Quintets (Sitar, percussion, unspecified
         instruments (3))
       Sitar with orchestra
       Trios (Flute, sitar, tabla)
       Trios (Sitar, tabla, violin)
Sitar players [May Subd Geog]
  UF Sitarists
  BT Musicians
Sitar with orchestra *(M1037.4.S58)*
  BT Sitar music
  RT Concertos (Sitar)
Sitarists
  USE Sitar players
Sivaism *(BL1245.S5)*
  —Hymns *(BL1226.3)*
    UF Hymns, Sivaite
       Sivaite hymns
    BT Hindu hymns
Sivaite hymns
  USE Sivaism—Hymns
Siwa (Musical instrument) *(ML990.S6)*
  BT Trumpet
Six (Dance)
  USE Seises
Sketches, Musical
  USE Musical sketches
Slavic ballads and songs [May Subd Geog]
Slavic folk-songs
  USE Folk-songs, Slavic
Slavic songs
  USE Songs, Slavic
Slentem gantung
  USE Gender (Musical instrument)
Slovak folk-songs
  USE Folk-songs, Slovak
Slovenian folk-songs
  USE Folk-songs, Slovenian
Slumber songs
  USE Lullabies
Snare drum
    ML1038.S
  UF Side drum
  BT Drum
Snare drum music
    M146
  UF Drum music
  SA *Concertos; Minuets; Sonatas; Suites;*
      and similar headings with specification
      of instruments; *Trios [Quartets, etc.]*
      followed by specifications which include

Snare drum music
    M146
    (Continued)
    SA   snare drum; also *Percussion ensembles;*
            Percussion music, and headings that begin
            with the words Snare drum

So la
    USE So na

So na *(ML990.S)*
    UF Chi na
          Hiang te
          La pa
          So la
          Sona
          Suo na
          Ta ti
          Wa wa erh
          Wu li wa
    BT Musical instruments—China
          Oboe
          Shawm

So na music *(M110.S6)*

Society and music
    USE Music and society

Sociology and music
    USE Music and society

Sŏka *(PL731)*
    BT Songs, Japanese

Sol-fa system
    USE Tonic sol-fa

Soldiers
    —Hymns *(BV463)*
            Here are entered collections of hymns
               for the use of soldiers or soldiers
               and seamen. Hymns intended for
               the use of seamen only are entered
               under the heading Seamen—Hymns.
            BT Hymns
               War-songs
           Note under Seamen—Hymns

Solfeggio
    USE Sight-singing

Solmization *(MT44)*
    BT Harmony
          Music
          Musical notation
    NT Sight-singing

Solo cantatas
        Here are entered collections of sacred
          and secular solo cantatas for various
          ranges of voices (high, low, medium).
    UF Arias
    BT Cantatas
          Songs

Solo cantatas, Sacred
        Here are entered collections of sacred solo
          cantatas for various voice ranges (high,
          low, medium).
    BT Cantatas, Sacred
          Sacred songs
    Note under Solo cantatas, Secular
    —Vocal scores with continuo
            BT Sacred songs with continuo

Solo cantatas, Sacred (High voice)
        Here, with appropriate subdivisions, are
          entered collections and separates of
          sacred solo cantatas for high voice.
    Note under Solo cantatas, Secular (High voice)
    —Scores
    —Vocal scores with continuo
            BT Sacred songs (High voice) with
                continuo
    —Vocal scores with organ
            BT Sacred songs (High voice) with
                organ

Solo cantatas, Sacred (Low voice)
        Here, with appropriate subdivisions, are
          entered collections and separates of sa-
          cred solo cantatas for low voice.
    Note under Solo cantatas, Secular (Low voice)
    —Scores
    —Vocal scores with continuo
            BT Sacred songs (Low voice) with
                continuo

Solo cantatas, Sacred (Medium voice)
        Here, with appropriate subdivisions, are
          entered collections and separates of sa-
          cred solo cantatas for medium voice.
    Note under Solo cantatas, Secular (Medium
        voice)
    —Scores

Solo cantatas, Secular
        Cf. note under Solo cantatas, Sacred
    BT Cantatas, Secular
    —Vocal scores with continuo
            BT Songs with continuo

Solo cantatas, Secular (High voice)
        Cf. note under Solo cantatas, Sacred
         (High voice)
    —Vocal scores with continuo
            BT Songs (High voice) with continuo
    —Vocal scores with piano
            BT Songs (High voice) with piano

Solo cantatas, Secular (Low voice)
        Cf. note under Solo cantatas, Sacred
         (Low voice)
    —Vocal scores with continuo
            BT Songs (Low voice) with
                continuo

Solo cantatas, Secular (Medium voice)
        Cf. note under Solo cantatas, Sacred
         (Medium voice)
    —Vocal scores with continuo
            BT Songs (Medium voice) with continuo
    —Vocal scores with piano
            BT Songs (Medium voice) with piano

Solo instrument music *(M175.5)*
        Here are entered musical works for
          unspecified solo instrument.
    UF Melody instrument music
          Unspecified instrument music
    BT Instrumental music
    NT Brass instrument music
          String instrument music
          Wind instrument music
          Woodwind instrument music

Solo with piano
　　USE *subdivision* Solo with piano *after music headings in which the medium of performance is one solo instrument with accompanying ensemble, e.g.* Concertos (Violin)—Solo with piano; Violin with orchestra—Solo with piano.

Solor
　　USE Bānsurī

Solos with piano
　　USE *subdivision* Solos with piano *after music headings in which the medium of performance is two or more solo instruments with accompanying ensemble, e.g.* Concertos (Violin and violoncello)—Solos with piano; Violin and harp with orchestra—Solos with piano.

Solovox
　　NT Piano music (Solovox registration)

Somali folk-songs
　　USE Folk-songs, Somali

Sona
　　USE So na

Sonata *(Composition, MT62; History, ML1156)*
　　　Here are entered works dealing with the sonata as a musical form.
　　　Example under Instrumental music—History and criticism; Musical form

Sonatas
　　　Here are entered compositions of miscellaneous compositions for one or two solo instruments written in sonata form. Separate sonatas and collections of sonatas for a specific medium are entered under the heading followed by specification of medium.
　　　Compositions written in the sonata form for three or more solo instruments are entered under the headings for chamber music, *e.g.* Piano quartets; Piano trios; Quartets; String quartets; String trios; Trios; Wind trios.
　　UF Sonatinas
　　NT Trio-sonatas

Sonatas (Accordion) *(M175.A4)*
　　BT Accordion music

Sonatas (Alto horn and piano) *(M270-271)*
　　BT Alto horn and piano music

Sonatas (Arpeggione and piano) *(M239)*
　　BT Arpeggione and piano music

Sonatas (Balalaika and piano) *(M282-3)*
　　BT Balalaika and piano music

Sonatas (Band)
　　USE Symphonies (Band)

Sonatas (Baritone and piano) *(M262-3)*
　　BT Baritone and piano music

Sonatas (Bass clarinet and piano) *(M248-M252)*
　　BT Bass clarinet and piano music

Sonatas (Bass trombone and piano) *(M262-263)*
　　BT Bass trombone and piano music

Sonatas (Basset horn and piano) *(M270.B4; M271.B4)*
　　BT Basset-horn and piano music

Sonatas (Bassoon) *(M75-77)*
　　BT Bassoon music

Sonatas (Bassoon and clarinet) *(M288-9)*
　　BT Bassoon and clarinet music

Sonatas (Bassoon and continuo)
　　BT Bassoon and continuo music

Sonatas (Bassoon and flute) *(M288-9)*
　　BT Bassoon and flute music

Sonatas (Bassoon and guitar) *(M296-297)*
　　BT Bassoon and guitar music

Sonatas (Bassoon and harpsichord) *(M253-4)*
　　BT Bassoon and harpsichord music
　　　Sonatas (Bassoon and piano)

Sonatas (Bassoon and oboe) *(M288-9)*
　　BT Bassoon and oboe music

Sonatas (Bassoon and organ) *(M182-186)*
　　BT Bassoon and organ music

Sonatas (Bassoon and piano) *(M253-4)*
　　BT Bassoon and piano music
　　NT Sonatas (Bassoon and harpsichord)

Sonatas (Bassoon and piano), Arranged *(M253-4)*

Sonatas (Bassoon and viola) *(M290-291)*
　　BT Bassoon and viola music

Sonatas (Bassoon and violoncello) *(M290-291)*
　　BT Bassoon and violoncello music

Sonatas (Bassoons (2)) *(M288-9)*
　　BT Bassoon music (Bassoons (2))

Sonatas (Bassoons (2)), Arranged *(M288-9)*

Sonatas (Carillon) *(M172)*
　　BT Carillon music

Sonatas (Clarinet) *(M70-72)*
　　BT Clarinet music

Sonatas (Clarinet and continuo)
　　BT Clarinet and continuo music

Sonatas (Clarinet and flute) *(M288-9)*
　　BT Clarinet and flute music

Sonatas (Clarinet and harp) *(M296-M297)*
　　BT Clarinet and harp music

Sonatas (Clarinet and percussion) *(M298)*
　　BT Clarinet and percussion music

Sonatas (Clarinet and piano) *(M248-250)*
　　BT Clarinet and piano music

Sonatas (Clarinet and piano), Arranged *(M251-2)*

Sonatas (Clarinet and violoncello) *(M290-291)*
　　BT Clarinet and violoncello music

Sonatas (Clarinets (2)) *(M288-9)*
　　BT Clarinet music (Clarinets (2))

Sonatas (Clarinets (2)), Arranged *(M288-9)*

Sonatas (Clavichord) *(M23)*

Sonatas (Cornet and piano) *(M260-261)*
　　BT Cornet and piano music

Sonatas (Cornett and continuo)
　　BT Cornett and continuo music

Sonatas (Domra and piano) *(M282.D64; M283.D64)*
　　BT Domra and piano music

Sonatas (Double bass and continuo)
　　BT Double-bass and continuo music

Sonatas (Double bass and harpsichord) *(M237-238)*
　　BT Double-bass and harpsichord music

Sonatas (Double bass and piano) *(M237-8)*
   BT Double-bass and piano music
Sonatas (Double bass and piano), Arranged
      (M237-8)
Sonatas (Double basses (2)) *(M286-287)*
   BT Double-bass music (Double basses (2))
Sonatas (Dulcimer and continuo)
   BT Dulcimer and continuo music
Sonatas (Dulcimer and harp) *(M292-293)*
   BT Dulcimer and harp music
Sonatas (Electronic organ) *(M14.8; M14.85)*
Sonatas (English horn and piano) *(M246.2)*
   BT English horn and piano music
Sonatas (Flageolet and continuo)
   BT Flageolet and continuo music
Sonatas (Flute) *(M60-62)*
   BT Flute music
Sonatas (Flute and continuo)
   BT Flute and continuo music
Sonatas (Flute and guitar) *(M296-7)*
   BT Flute and guitar music
Sonatas (Flute and guitar), Arranged
      (M296-7)
Sonatas (Flute and harp) *(M296-7)*
   BT Flute and harp music
Sonatas (Flute and harpsichord) *(M241-2)*
   BT Flute and harpsichord music
       Sonatas (Flute and piano)
Sonatas (Flute and harpsichord), Arranged
      (M243-4)
Sonatas (Flute and lute) *(M296-297)*
   BT Flute and lute music
Sonatas (Flute and organ) *(M182-4)*
   BT Flute and organ music
Sonatas (Flute and organ), Arranged
      (M185-6)
Sonatas (Flute and percussion) *(M298)*
   BT Flute and percussion music
Sonatas (Flute and piano) *(M240-242)*
   BT Flute and piano music
   NT Sonatas (Flute and harpsichord)
       Sonatas (Recorder and harpsichord)
Sonatas (Flute and piano), Arranged
      (M243-4)
Sonatas (Flute and recorder) *(M288-289)*
   BT Flute and recorder music
Sonatas (Flute and viola) *(M290-291)*
   BT Flute and viola music
Sonatas (Flute and violin) *(M290-291)*
   BT Flute and violin music
Sonatas (Flute and violoncello) *(M290-291)*
   BT Flute and violoncello music
Sonatas (Flute), Arranged *(M63-4)*
Sonatas (Flutes (2)) *(M288-9)*
   BT Flute music (Flutes (2))
Sonatas (Guitar) *(M125-7)*
   BT Guitar music
Sonatas (Guitar and continuo)
   BT Guitar and continuo music
Sonatas (Guitar and harpsichord) *(M276-277)*
   BT Guitar and harpsichord music
Sonatas (Guitar and piano) *(M276-7)*
   BT Guitar and piano music

Sonatas (Guitar), Arranged *(M128-9)*
Sonatas (Guitars (2)) *(M292-3)*
   BT Guitar music (Guitars (2))
Sonatas (Guitars (2)), Arranged *(M292-3)*
Sonatas (Harmonica and harpsichord)
      (M284.M6; M285.M6)
   BT Harmonica and harpsichord music
Sonatas (Harmonica and piano) *(M284.M6;*
      M285.M6)
   BT Harmonica and piano music
Sonatas (Harp) *(M115-117)*
   BT Harp music
Sonatas (Harp and harpsichord) *(M272-273)*
   BT Harp and harpsichord music
Sonatas (Harp and piano) *(M272-3)*
   BT Harp and piano music
Sonatas (Harp), Arranged *(M118-119)*
Sonatas (Harps (2)) *(M292-3)*
   BT Harp music (Harps (2))
Sonatas (Harpsichord) *(M23)*
   BT Harpsichord music
       Sonatas (Piano)
Sonatas (Harpsichord and organ)
      (M182-186)
   BT Harpsichord and organ music
Sonatas (Harpsichord and viola)
   USE Sonatas (Viola and harpsichord)
Sonatas (Harpsichords (2)) *(M214)*
   BT Harpsichord music (Harpsichords (2))
Sonatas (Horn) *(M80-82)*
   BT Horn music
Sonatas (Horn and piano) *(M255-7)*
   BT Horn and piano music
Sonatas (Horn and piano), Arranged
Sonatas (Horns (2)) *(M288-9)*
   BT Horn music (Horns (2))
Sonatas (Horns (2)), Arranged *(M288-9)*
Sonatas (Koto) *(M142.K6)*
   BT Koto music
Sonatas (Lute) *(M140-141)*
   BT Lute music
Sonatas (Lute and harpsichord) *(M282.L88;*
      M283.L88)
   BT Lute and harpsichord music
Sonatas (Lute and harpsichord), Arranged
      (M282.L88; M283.L88)
Sonatas (Mandolin and continuo)
   BT Mandolin and continuo music
Sonatas (Mandolin and harpsichord)
   BT Mandolin and harpsichord music
Sonatas (Mandolin and piano) *(M278-9)*
   BT Mandolin and piano music
Sonatas (Oboe) *(M65-67)*
   BT Oboe music
Sonatas (Oboe and continuo)
   BT Oboe and continuo music
Sonatas (Oboe and guitar) *(M296-7)*
   BT Oboe and guitar music
Sonatas (Oboe and harp) *(M296-7)*
   BT Oboe and harp music
Sonatas (Oboe and harpsichord) *(M245-6)*
   BT Oboe and harpsichord music
       Sonatas (Oboe and piano)

Sonatas (Oboe and organ) *(M182-186)*
　　BT　Oboe and organ music
Sonatas (Oboe and piano) *(M245-6)*
　　BT　Oboe and piano music
　　NT　Sonatas (Oboe and harpsichord)
Sonatas (Oboe and piano), Arranged *(M247)*
Sonatas (Oboes (2)) *(M288-9)*
　　BT　Oboe music (Oboes (2))
Sonatas (Ondes Martenot and piano)
　　　　(M285.O5)
　　BT　Ondes Martenot and piano music
Sonatas (Organ) *(M8)*
　　BT　Organ music
　　RT　Symphonies (Organ)
Sonatas (Organ, 4 hands) *(M181)*
　　BT　Organ music (4 hands)
Sonatas (Organ), Arranged *(M12-13)*
Sonatas (Organs (2)) *(M181)*
　　BT　Organ music (Organs (2))
Sonatas (Percussion and viola) *(M298)*
　　BT　Percussion and viola music
Sonatas (Percussion and violin) *(M298)*
　　BT　Percussion and violin music
Sonatas (Percussion and violoncello) *(M298)*
　　BT　Percussion and violoncello music
Sonatas (Piano) *(M23)*
　　BT　Piano music
　　NT　Sonatas (Harpsichord)
　　Note under Microtonic music
Sonatas (Piano, 1 hand) *(Left hand, M26;*
　　　　Right hand, M26.2)
　　BT　Piano music (1 hand)
Sonatas (Piano, 3 hands) *(M205)*
　　BT　Piano music (3 hands)
Sonatas (Piano, 4 hands) *(M202)*
　　BT　Piano music (4 hands)
Sonatas (Piano, 4 hands), Arranged
　　　　(M207; M211)
Sonatas (Piano), Arranged
Sonatas (Pianos (2)) *(M214)*
　　BT　Piano music (Pianos (2))
Sonatas (Pianos (2)), Arranged *(M215)*
Sonatas (Recorder and continuo)
　　BT　Recorder and continuo music
Sonatas (Recorder and guitar) *(M296-7)*
　　BT　Recorder and guitar music
Sonatas (Recorder and guitar), Arranged
　　　　(M296-7)
Sonatas (Recorder and harpsichord)
　　　　(M240-242)
　　BT　Recorder and harpsichord music
　　　　Sonatas (Flute and piano)
Sonatas (Recorder and harpsichord), Arranged
　　　　(M243-4)
Sonatas (Recorder and organ) *(M182-4)*
　　BT　Recorder and organ music
Sonatas (Recorder and piano) *(M240-242)*
　　BT　Recorder and piano music
Sonatas (Recorder and piano), Arranged
　　　　(M243-4)
Sonatas (Recorders (2)) *(M288-9)*
　　BT　Recorder music (Recorders (2))
Sonatas (Recorders (2)), Arranged *(M288-9)*

Sonatas (Ryūteki and shō) *(M288-9)*
　　BT　Ryūteki and shō music
Sonatas (Saxhorn and piano) *(M266-7)*
　　BT　Saxhorn and piano music
Sonatas (Saxophone and continuo)
　　BT　Saxophone and continuo music
Sonatas (Saxophone and piano) *(M268-9)*
　　BT　Saxophone and piano music
Sonatas (Saxophone and piano), Arranged
　　　　(M268-9)
Sonatas (Tenor violin and continuo)
　　BT　Tenor violin and continuo music
Sonatas (Timpani and piano) *(M284.T5;*
　　　　M285.T5)
　　BT　Timpani and piano music
Sonatas (Trombone and organ) *(M182-186)*
　　BT　Trombone and organ music
Sonatas (Trombone and piano) *(M262-3)*
　　BT　Trombone and piano music
Sonatas (Trombone and piano), Arranged
　　　　(M262-3)
Sonatas (Trombones (2)) *(M288-289)*
　　BT　Trombone music (Trombones (2))
Sonatas (Trumpet and continuo)
　　BT　Trumpet and continuo music
Sonatas (Trumpet and harpsichord)
　　　　(M260-261)
　　BT　Sonatas (Trumpet and piano)
　　　　Trumpet and harpsichord music
Sonatas (Trumpet and harpsichord), Arranged
　　　　(M260-261)
Sonatas (Trumpet and organ) *(M182-4)*
　　BT　Trumpet and organ music
Sonatas (Trumpet and piano) *(M260-261)*
　　BT　Trumpet and piano music
　　NT　Sonatas (Trumpet and harpsichord)
Sonatas (Tuba and piano) *(M264-5)*
　　BT　Tuba and piano music
Sonatas (Unspecified instrument and
　　　　continuo)
　　BT　Duets (Unspecified instrument and
　　　　continuo)
Sonatas (Unspecified instrument and organ)
　　　　(M298.5)
　　BT　Duets (Unspecified instrument and
　　　　organ)
Sonatas (Unspecified instruments (2))
　　　　(M298.5)
　　BT　Duets (Unspecified instruments (2))
　　Note under Chamber music
Sonatas (Viola) *(M45-47)*
　　BT　Viola music
Sonatas (Viola and continuo)
　　BT　Viola and continuo music
Sonatas (Viola and double bass) *(M286-7)*
　　BT　Viola and double-bass music
Sonatas (Viola and double bass), Arranged
　　　　(M286-7)
Sonatas (Viola and guitar) *(M294-M295)*
　　BT　Viola and guitar music
Sonatas (Viola and harpsichord) *(M224-6)*
　　UF　Sonatas (Harpsichord and viola)
　　BT　Viola and harpsichord music

Sonatas (Viola and harpsichord), Arranged
 (M227-8)
Sonatas (Viola and organ)
 BT Viola and organ music
Sonatas (Viola and piano) *(M224-6)*
 BT Viola and piano music
Sonatas (Viola and piano), Arranged
 (M227-8)
 —Excerpts *(M227-8)*
Sonatas (Viola and viola d'amore)
 (M286-287)
 BT Viola and viola d'amore music
Sonatas (Viola and violoncello) *(M286-7)*
 BT Viola and violoncello music
Sonatas (Viola), Arranged *(M48-9)*
Sonatas (Viola da gamba and continuo)
 BT Viola da gamba and continuo music
Sonatas (Viola da gamba and harpsichord)
 (M239)
 BT Sonatas (Violoncello and piano)
  Viola da gamba and harpsichord music
Sonatas (Viola da gamba and harpsichord),
 Arranged *(M239)*
Sonatas (Viola da gamba and lute) *(M294-5)*
 BT Viola da gamba and lute music
Sonatas (Viola da gamba and organ) *(M184)*
 BT Viola da gamba and organ music
Sonatas (Viola d'amore and continuo)
 BT Viola d'amore and continuo music
Sonatas (Viola d'amore and double bass)
 (M286-7)
 BT Viola d'amore and double-bass music
Sonatas (Viola d'amore and guitar) *(M294-5)*
 BT Viola d'amore and guitar music
Sonatas (Viola d'amore and guitar), Arranged
 (M294-5)
Sonatas (Viola d'amore and harpsichord)
 (M239)
 BT Viola d'amore and harpsichord music
Sonatas (Viola d'amore and harpsichord),
 Arranged *(M239)*
Sonatas (Viola d'amore and piano) *(M239)*
 BT Viola d'amore and piano music
Sonatas (Viola d'amore and viola da gamba)
 BT Viola d'amore and viola da gamba music
Sonatas (Viola pomposa and harpsichord)
 (M239)
 BT Viola pomposa and harpsichord music
Sonatas (Violas (2)) *(M286-7)*
 BT Viola music (Violas (2))
Sonatas (Viole da gamba (2)) *(M286-7)*
 BT Viola da gamba music (Viole da gamba
  (2))
Sonatas (Violin) *(M42)*
 BT Violin music
Sonatas (Violin and continuo)
 BT Violin and continuo music
Sonatas (Violin and double bass) *(M286-7)*
 BT Violin and double-bass music
Sonatas (Violin and guitar) *(M294-5)*
 BT Violin and guitar music
Sonatas (Violin and guitar), Arranged
 (M294-5)

Sonatas (Violin and harp) *(M294-5)*
 BT Violin and harp music
Sonatas (Violin and harp), Arranged
 (M294-5)
Sonatas (Violin and harpsichord) *(M219)*
 BT Sonatas (Violin and piano)
  Violin and harpsichord music
Sonatas (Violin and harpsichord), Arranged
 (M222-3)
Sonatas (Violin and lute) *(M294-295)*
 BT Violin and lute music
Sonatas (Violin and organ) *(M182-4)*
 BT Violin and organ music
Sonatas (Violin and piano) *(M219)*
 BT Violin and piano music
 NT Sonatas (Violin and harpsichord)
Sonatas (Violin and piano), Arranged
 (M223)
Sonatas (Violin and viola) *(M286-7)*
 BT Violin and viola music
Sonatas (Violin and viola da gamba)
 (M286-7)
 BT Sonatas (Violin and violoncello)
  Violin and viola da gamba music
Sonatas (Violin and viola d'amore)
 (M286-287)
 BT Violin and viola d'amore music
Sonatas (Violin and violoncello) *(M286-7)*
 BT Violin and violoncello music
 NT Sonatas (Violin and viola da gamba)
Sonatas (Violin and violoncello), Arranged
 (M286-7)
Sonatas (Violins (2)) *(M286-7)*
 BT Violin music (Violins (2))
Sonatas (Violins (2)), Arranged
Sonatas (Violoncello) *(M50-52)*
 BT Violoncello music
Sonatas (Violoncello and continuo)
 BT Violoncello and continuo music
Sonatas (Violoncello and double bass)
 (M286-M287)
 BT Violoncello and double-bass music
Sonatas (Violoncello and harp) *(M294-295)*
 BT Violoncello and harp music
Sonatas (Violoncello and harpsichord)
 (M231)
 BT Sonatas (Violoncello and piano)
  Violoncello and harpsichord music
Sonatas (Violoncello and harpsichord),
 Arranged *(M235-6)*
Sonatas (Violoncello and organ) *(M182-4)*
 BT Violoncello and organ music
Sonatas (Violoncello and piano) *(M231)*
 BT Violoncello and piano music
 NT Sonatas (Viola da gamba and
  harpsichord)
  Sonatas (Violoncello and harpsichord)
Sonatas (Violoncello and piano), Arranged
 (M235-6)
Sonatas (Violoncellos (2)) *(M286-7)*
 BT Violoncello music (Violoncellos (2))
Sonatas (Violoncellos (2)), Arranged
 (M286-7)

Sonatas (Violone and harpsichord) *(M239)*
    BT Violone and harpsichord music
Sonatas (Xylophone) *(M175 X6)*
    BT Xylophone music
Sonatas (Zither) *(M135-7)*
    BT Zither music
Sonatinas
    USE Sonatas
Song bells
    USE Xylophone
Song-books *(M1977.C5)*
        Here are entered general collections of
          home and community songs, largely
          secular in content, arranged princi-
          pally for mixed voices and scored on
          two staves, as in their sacred counter-
          part, the hymnals.
    UF Community song-books
        Song-books, American
        Song-books, English
    BT Choruses
        Choruses, Secular
        Songs
    NT Glees, catches, rounds, etc.
        School song-books
Song-books, Afrikaner *(M1834)*
    UF Afrikaner song-books
Song-books, American
    USE Song-books
Song-books, Catholic
    UF Catholic song-books
Song-books, English
    USE Song-books
Song-books, French, [German, etc.]
Song-books, Sunday-school
    USE Sunday-school—Hymns
Song-books (Men's voices) *(M1977.C5)*
Song-books (Women's voices) *(M1977.C5)*
Song cycles *(M1621.4; M2113.4)*
    UF Cycles, Song
    BT Songs
Song flute
    USE Recorder (Musical instrument)
Song of Solomon (Music)
    UF Bible. O.T. Song of Solomon—Music
    BT Sacred vocal music
Songs [May Subd Geog]
        Here are entered works for solo voice
          with secular texts. Works for sacred
          texts are entered under the heading Sa-
          cred songs. For works consisting of art
          songs, this heading is qualified as ap-
          propriate by voice range and specifica-
          tion of accompaniment, *e.g.* Songs
          (High voice) with piano; Songs with
          orchestra; Songs, Unaccompanied. For
          works consisting of songs of ethnic or
          national character this heading is
          qualified by the name of the language
          or language group and subdivided by
          place, *e.g.* Songs, French; Songs, Eng-
          lish—United States; Songs, Slavic.

Songs [May Subd Geog]
    (Continued)
        For works consisting of songs of an
          individual ethnic group, additional subject
          entries are made under the headings [ethnic
          group]—[place]—Music and Music—
          [place]. For works consisting of songs of a
          national group, additional subject entry is
          made under the heading Music—[place].
    UF Arias
        Art songs
    BT Lyric poetry
        Music
        Poetry
        Vocal music
    SA *subdivision* Songs and music *under*
        subjects
    NT Ballads
        Bawdy songs
        Carnival songs
        Carols
        Children's songs
        Death songs
        Drinking songs
        Erotic songs
        Folias (Music)
        Folk-songs
        Humorous songs
        Hunting songs
        Jazz vocals
        Love songs
        Lullabies
        Madrigals
        National songs
        Part-songs
        Political ballads and songs
        Prisoners' songs
        Protest songs
        Revolutionary ballads and songs
        Sacred songs
        Satirical songs
        Sea songs
        Shepherds' songs
        Solo cantatas
        Song-books
        Song cycles
        Students' songs
        Topical songs
        Vocalises
        War-songs
        Work-songs
    Note under Sacred songs
    —Accompaniment *(MT68)*
        BT Musical accompaniment
    —History and criticism *(Aesthetics,*
        ML3875; History, ML2500-ML2862)
        NT Street music and musicians
    —Juvenile
        USE Children's songs
    —Texts
        UF Songsters (Books)

Songs [May Subd Geog]
  (Continued)
  GEOGRAPHIC SUBDIVISION
  —United States
    NT Campaign songs
        School song-books
        State songs
Songs, Abkhaz [May Subd Geog] *(M1766-1767)*
  UF Abkhaz songs
Songs, Adyghe *(M1766-1767)*
  UF Adyghe songs
Songs, Anglo-Saxon [May Subd Geog]
  UF Anglo-Saxon songs
Songs, Arabic [May Subd Geog]
  UF Arabic songs
Songs, Armenian [May Subd Geog]
  UF Armenian songs
Songs, Australian (Aboriginal)
  UF Australian songs
Songs, Azerbaijani *(M1766-1767)*
  UF Azerbaijani songs
Songs, Bajjika [May Subd Geog]
  UF Bajjika songs
Songs, Bantu
Songs, Bengali [May Subd Geog]
  UF Bengali songs
Songs, Braj [May Subd Geog]
  UF Braj songs
Songs, Breton [May Subd Geog]
  UF Breton songs
Songs, Burmese [May Subd Geog]
  UF Burmese songs
Songs, Cajun French [May Subd Geog]
  UF Cajun French songs
  BT Songs, French
Songs, Catalan [May Subd Geog]
  UF Catalan songs
Songs, Chechen [May Subd Geog] *(M1766-1767)*
  UF Chechen songs
Songs, Chinese [May Subd Geog]
  UF Chinese songs
Songs, Czech [May Subd Geog]
  UF Czech songs
Songs, Danish [May Subd Geog]
  UF Danish songs
Songs, Dutch [May Subd Geog]
  UF Dutch songs
  NT Gueux—Songs and music
Songs, Dzongkha [May Subd Geog]
  UF Dzongkha songs
Songs, English [May Subd Geog]
  UF English songs
  NT School song-books
  —United States
    NT Campaign songs
        State songs
  Note under Songs
Songs, English (Middle English,
    1100-1500)
  USE Songs, Middle English
Songs, Erotic
  USE Erotic songs

Songs, Fang [May Subd Geog]
  UF Fang songs
Songs, Faroese [May Subd Geog]
  UF Faroese songs
Songs, Finnish [May Subd Geog]
  UF Finnish songs
Songs, French [May Subd Geog]
  UF French songs
  NT Songs, Cajun French
  Note under Songs
Songs, Gaelic [May Subd Geog]
  UF Gaelic songs
Songs, Gallegan [May Subd Geog]
  UF Gallegan songs
Songs, German [May Subd Geog]
  UF German songs
  NT Songs, Low German
Songs, German (Middle High German)
  UF Middle High German songs
      Songs, Middle High German
Songs, Greek (Modern) [May Subd Geog]
  UF Greek songs, Modern
      Modern Greek songs
Songs, Guarani [May Subd Geog]
  UF Guarani songs
Songs, Gujarati [May Subd Geog]
  UF Gujarati songs
Songs, Gujuri [May Subd Geog]
  UF Gujuri songs
Songs, Hawaiian [May Subd Geog]
  UF Hawaiian songs
Songs, Hebrew [May Subd Geog]
  UF Hebrew songs
Songs, Humorous
  USE Humorous songs
Songs, Iatmul [May Subd Geog]
  UF Iatmul songs
Songs, Indic [May Subd Geog]
  UF Indic songs
Songs, Indonesian [May Subd Geog] *(M1824-1825)*
  UF Indonesian songs
Songs, Ingush [May Subd Geog] *(M1766-1767)*
  UF Ingush songs
Songs, Irish [May Subd Geog]
  UF Irish songs
Songs, Italian [May Subd Geog]
  UF Italian songs
Songs, Japanese [May Subd Geog]
  UF Japanese songs
  NT Enkyoku
      Kouta
      Kumiuta
      Nagauta
      Sōka
Songs, Jazz
  USE Jazz vocals
Songs, Kabardian [May Subd Geog] *(M1766.K26;*
    M1767.K26)
  UF Kabardian songs
Songs, Korean [May Subd Geog]
  UF Korean songs
  NT Kagok

Songs, Lakota [May Subd Geog]
    UF Lakota songs
Songs, Latin (Medieval and modern)
            [May Subd Geog]
    UF Latin songs, Medieval and modern
Songs, Latvian [May Subd Geog]
    UF Latvian songs
Songs, Lingala [May Subd Geog]
    UF Lingala songs
Songs, Low German [May Subd Geog]
            (M1734-1735)
    UF Low German songs
    BT Songs, German
Songs, Lushai [May Subd Geog]
    UF Lushai songs
Songs, Maithili [May Subd Geog]
    UF Maithili songs
Songs, Malagasy [May Subd Geog]
    UF Malagasy songs
Songs, Manambu [May Subd Geog]
    UF Manambu songs
Songs, Manipuri [May Subd Geog]
    UF Manipuri songs
Songs, Maori [May Subd Geog]
    UF Maori songs
Songs, Marathi [May Subd Geog]
    UF Marathi songs
Songs, Marwari [May Subd Geog]
    UF Marwari songs
Songs, Middle English [May Subd Geog]
    UF Middle English songs
            Songs, English (Middle English,
            1100-1500)
Songs, Middle High German
    USE Songs, German (Middle High German)
Songs, Mongolian [May Subd Geog]
    UF Mongolian songs
Songs, National
    USE National songs
Songs, Ndebele (Zimbabwe) [May Subd Geog]
    UF Ndebele songs (Zimbabwe)
Songs, Nepali [May Subd Geog]
    UF Nepali songs
Songs, Newari [May Subd Geog]
    UF Newari songs
Songs, Old French [May Subd Geog]
    UF Old French songs
Songs, Oraon [May Subd Geog]
    UF Kurukh songs
            Oraon songs
Songs, Oriya [May Subd Geog]
    UF Oriya songs
Songs, Ossetic [May Subd Geog] *(M1766-1767)*
    UF Ossetic songs
Songs, Patriotic
    USE National songs
            Patriotic music
Songs, Pennsylvania German [May Subd Geog]
    UF Pennsylvania German songs
Songs, Popular
    USE Popular music
Songs, Popular (Instrumental settings)
    USE Popular instrumental music

Songs, Portuguese [May Subd Geog]
    UF Portuguese songs
Songs, Provençal [May Subd Geog]
    UF Provençal songs
Songs, Romanian [May Subd Geog]
    UF Romanian songs
Songs, Ruanda [May Subd Geog]
    UF Ruanda songs
Songs, Ryukyu [May Subd Geog]
    UF Ryukyu songs
Songs, Sacred
    USE Sacred songs
Songs, Sambalpuri [May Subd Geog]
    UF Sambalpuri songs
Songs, Sanskrit [May Subd Geog]
    UF Sanskrit songs
Songs, Santali [May Subd Geog]
    UF Santali songs
Songs, Shona [May Subd Geog]
    UF Shona songs
Songs, Sindhi [May Subd Geog]
    UF Sindhi songs
Songs, Slavic [May Subd Geog]
    UF Slavic songs
    Note under Songs
Songs, Spanish [May Subd Geog]
    UF Spanish songs
Songs, Swedish [May Subd Geog]
    UF Swedish songs
Songs, Taensa [May Subd Geog]
    UF Taensa songs
Songs, Tamil [May Subd Geog] *(M1808-1809)*
    UF Tamil songs
Songs, Tatar [May Subd Geog] *(M1766-1767)*
    UF Tatar songs
Songs, Telugu [May Subd Geog]
    UF Telugu songs
Songs, Thai [May Subd Geog]
    UF Thai songs
Songs, Tibetan [May Subd Geog]
    UF Tibetan songs
Songs, Tivi [May Subd Geog]
    UF Tivi songs
Songs, Toda [May Subd Geog]
    UF Toda songs
Songs, Tsogo [May Subd Geog]
    UF Tsogo songs
Songs, Turkic [May Subd Geog]
    UF Turkic songs
Songs, Unaccompanied *(M1621.2)*
    Note under Songs
Songs, Uzbek *(M1766-1767)*
    UF Uzbek songs
Songs, Vietnamese [May Subd Geog]
    UF Vietnamese songs
Songs, Yakut [May Subd Geog] *(M1766.Y3;*
            M1767.Y3)
    UF Yakut songs
Songs, Yiddish [May Subd Geog]
    UF Yiddish songs
Songs (High voice)
Songs (High voice) with band *(M1613.3; M1614)*
    —Scores *(M1613.3)*

Songs (High voice) with chamber orchestra
—Vocal scores with piano
    BT Songs (High voice) with piano
Songs (High voice) with clarinet *(M1623.8;*
    M1624.7)
Songs (High voice) with continuo
    NT Solo cantatas, Secular (High voice)—
        Vocal scores with continuo
Songs (High voice) with electronic music
    (M1613.3)
    BT Electronic music
Songs (High voice) with flute *(M1623.8;*
    M1624.7)
Songs (High voice) with guitar *(M1623;*
    M1624)
Songs (High voice) with harp *(M1623.4;*
    M1624.4)
Songs (High voice) with harpsichord
    (M1619-1621)
    BT Songs (High voice) with piano
Songs (High voice) with instrumental
    ensemble *(M1613.3)*
Songs (High voice) with lute *(M1623.5)*
Songs (High voice) with mandolin *(M1623;*
    M1624)
Songs (High voice) with oboe *(M1623.8;*
    M1624.7)
Songs (High voice) with orchestra
—Vocal scores with piano
    BT Songs (High voice) with piano
Songs (High voice) with organ *(M1619-1621)*
Songs (High voice) with piano *(M1619-1621)*
    NT Recorded accompaniments (Soprano)
        Solo cantatas, Secular (High voice)—
          Vocal scores with piano
        Songs (High voice) with chamber
          orchestra—Vocal scores with piano
        Songs (High voice) with harpsichord
        Songs (High voice) with orchestra—
          Vocal scores with piano
        Songs (High voice) with string
          orchestra—Vocal scores with piano
    Note under Songs
Songs (High voice) with piano, 4 hands
    (M1619-1621)
Songs (High voice) with pianos (2)
    (M1619-1621)
Songs (High voice) with string orchestra
—Vocal scores with piano
    BT Songs (High voice) with piano
Songs (High voice) with viol *(M1623.8;*
    M1624.8)
Songs (High voice) with viola *(M1623.8;*
    M1624.8)
Songs (High voice) with violin *(M1623.8;*
    M1624.8)
Songs (High voice) with violoncello
    (M1623.8; M1624.8)
Songs (Low voice) with bandurria *(M1623;*
    M1624)
Songs (Low voice) with chamber orchestra
—Vocal scores with piano
    BT Songs (Low voice) with piano

Songs (Low voice) with clarinet *(M1623.8;*
    M1624.7)
Songs (Low voice) with continuo
    NT Solo cantatas, Secular (Low voice)—
        Vocal scores with continuo
Songs (Low voice) with guitar *(M1623; M1624)*
Songs (Low voice) with harpsichord
    (M1619-1621)
    BT Songs (Low voice) with piano
Songs (Low voice) with instrumental ensemble
    (M1613.3)
Songs (Low voice) with orchestra
—Vocal scores with piano
    BT Songs (Low voice) with piano
Songs (Low voice) with piano *(M1619-1621)*
    NT Recorded accompaniments (Alto)
        Songs (Low voice) with chamber
          orchestra—Vocal scores with piano
        Songs (Low voice) with harpsichord
        Songs (Low voice) with orchestra—
          Vocal scores with piano
        Songs (Low voice) with string orchestra
          —Vocal scores with piano
Songs (Low voice) with string orchestra
—Vocal scores with piano *(M1614)*
    BT Songs (Low voice) with piano
Songs (Medium voice)
Songs (Medium voice) with accordion
    (M1623.8; M1624.8)
Songs (Medium voice) with banjo *(M1623;*
    M1624)
Songs (Medium voice) with celesta
    (M1623.8; M1624.8)
Songs (Medium voice) with chamber orchestra
—Vocal scores with piano
    BT Songs (Medium voice) with piano
Songs (Medium voice) with continuo
    NT Solo cantatas, Secular (Medium voice)
        —Vocal scores with continuo
Songs (Medium voice) with electronic music
    (M1613.3)
    BT Electronic music
Songs (Medium voice) with flute *(M1623.8;*
    M1624.7)
Songs (Medium voice) with guitar *(M1623;*
    M1624)
Songs (Medium voice) with harp *(M1623.4;*
    M1624.4)
Songs (Medium voice) with harpsichord
    (M1619-1621)
    BT Songs (Medium voice) with piano
Songs (Medium voice) with instrumental
    ensemble *(M1613.3)*
Songs (Medium voice) with lute *(M1623.5;*
    M1624.5)
Songs (Medium voice) with oboe *(M1623.8;*
    M1624.7)
Songs (Medium voice) with orchestra
—Vocal scores with piano
    BT Songs (Medium voice) with piano
Songs (Medium voice) with piano *(M1619-1621)*
    NT Solo cantatas, Secular (Medium voice)
        —Vocal scores with piano

Songs (Medium voice) with piano *(M1619-1621)*
  (Continued)
    NT Songs (Medium voice) with chamber
        orchestra—Vocal scores with piano
        Songs (Medium voice) with harpsichord
        Songs (Medium voice) with orchestra
        —Vocal scores with piano
Songs (Medium voice) with violin *(M1623.8; M1624.8)*
Songs with accordion *(M1623.8; M1624.8)*
Songs with Appalachian dulcimer *(M1623; M1624)*
Songs with band
Songs with chamber orchestra
    NT Waltzes (Voice with chamber orchestra)
    —Scores and parts *(M1611; M1613)*
Songs with concertina *(M1623.8; M1624.8)*
Songs with continuo
    NT Solo cantatas, Secular—Vocal scores
        with continuo
Songs with dulcimer *(M1623; M1624)*
Songs with guitar *(M1623; M1624)*
Songs with harp-lute guitar *(M1623; M1624)*
Songs with harpsichord *(M1619-1621)*
    BT Songs with piano
Songs with instrumental ensemble *(M1613.3)*
Songs with kobza *(M1623; M1624)*
    BT Songs with lute
Songs with koto *(M1623; M1624)*
    NT Kumiuta
Songs with lute *(M1623.5; M1624.5)*
    NT Songs with kobza
        Songs with vihuela
Songs with mouth-organ
Songs with oboe *(M1623.8; M1624.7)*
Songs with orchestra *(M1611-M1613; M1614)*
    NT Waltzes (Voice with orchestra)
    Note under Songs
    —Scores *(M1611; M1613)*
    —Vocal scores with piano
        BT Songs with piano
Songs with percussion
    Note under Percussion music
Songs with piano *(M1619-1621)*
    NT Marches (Voice with piano)
        Polkas (Voice with piano)
        Songs with harpsichord
        Songs with orchestra—Vocal scores
        with piano
        Waltzes (Voice with piano)
Songs with pianos (2) *(M1619-1621)*
Songs with reed-organ *(M1619-1621)*
Songs with shamisen *(M1623; M1624)*
    NT Kumiuta
Songs with tar *(M1623-1624)*
Songs with ti tzŭ *(M1623.8; M1624.7)*
Songs with ukulele *(M1623; M1624)*
Songs with vihuela
    BT Songs with lute
Songs with viola da gamba *(M1623.8; M1624.8)*
    BT Songs with violoncello

Songs with violin *(M1623.8; M1624.8)*
Songs with violoncello *(M1623.8; M1624.8)*
    NT Songs with viola da gamba
Songsters (Books)
    USE Songs—Texts
Songwriters
    USE Composers
        Lyricists
Songwriting
    USE Popular music—Writing
        and publishing
Sorbian folk-songs
    USE Folk-songs, Sorbian
Sorority songs
    USE Fraternity songs
Soul music [May Subd Geog]
    ML3537 (History and criticism)
    UF Music, Soul
    BT Afro-Americans—Music
        Popular music
Soul musicians [May Subd Geog]
    BT Musicians
Sound *(QC220-246)*
    BT Music
    RT Music—Acoustics and physics
Sound recording industry [May Subd Geog]
    UF Popular music record industry
        Recorded music industry
Sound recording libraries [May Subd Geog]
    (ML111.5)
    BT Music libraries
Sound recordings [May Subd Geog]
    Here are entered comprehensive works on
        all types of media used for the recording
        of sound, including cylinders, analog discs,
        digital discs, films, tapes, and wires, as
        well as works on analog discs alone.
    —Catalogs *(Music, ML156-ML158)*
    —Dating *(ML1055)*
        UF Dating of sound recordings
    —Labels *(ML1055)*
        UF Labels, Record
            Record labels
        BT Labels
Southern Slavic folk-songs
    USE Folk-songs, Southern Slavic
Spain
    —History *(DP1-402)*
    — —Civil War, 1936-1939
    — — —Songs and music
Spanish ballads
    USE Ballads, Spanish
Spanish folk-songs
    USE Folk-songs, Spanish
Spanish guitar
    USE Guitar
Spanish hymns
    USE Hymns, Spanish
Spanish lullabies
    USE Lullabies, Spanish
Spanish songs
    USE Songs, Spanish

Speaking with music
    USE *subdivision* Readings with music *under*
             subjects, e.g. American poetry—20th
             century—Readings with music;
             Monologues—Readings with music
        Monologues with music
        Sacred monologues with music
Spirituals (Songs) [May Subd Geog] *(History and*
        criticism, ML3556; Music, M1670-M1671)
    UF Afro-American spirituals
        Negro spirituals
    BT Afro-Americans—Music
        Folk-songs, English—United States
        Hymns, English—United States
    —Instrumental settings
        Example under reference from Instrumental
        settings
Square dance music
    Note under Folk dance music
Sranan folk-songs
    USE Folk-songs, Sranan
St. Cecilia's Day
    USE Saint Cecilia's Day
Stabat Mater dolorosa (Music)
    BT Mary, Blessed Virgin, Saint—Songs
        and music
        Passion-music
        Sequences (Music)
Stadtmusikanten
    USE Stadtpfeifer
Stadtmusizi
    USE Stadtpfeifer
Stadtpfeifer [May Subd Geog]
    UF Instrumentalisten
        Kunstpfeifer
        Musicians, Town
        Pipers, Town
        Ratsmusikanten
        Ratsmusizi
        Stadtmusikanten
        Stadtmusizi
        Town musicians
        Town pipers
        Zinkenisten
    BT Musicians
    RT Waits
Stage band music
    USE Big band music
Stage bands
    USE Big bands
Stage guides
    USE subdivision Stage guides under headings
        for musical dramatic form, e.g. Operas—
        Stage guides
        Theaters—Stage-setting and scenery
State and music
    USE Music and state
State songs [May Subd Geog] *(M1657-8)*
        Here are entered collections of, and
        works on, state songs of the United
        States. State songs of individual states
        are entered under this heading subdivided
        by the name of the state.

State songs [May Subd Geog] *(M1657-8)*
    (Continued)
    BT National songs—United States
        Songs—United States
        Songs, English—United States
Stations of the Cross *(BX2040)*
    —Music
        USE Stations of the Cross—Songs and
          music
    —Songs and music
        UF Stations of the Cross—Music
        BT Passion-music
Steadfast tin soldier (Ballet)
    BT Ballets
Steel band (Musical ensemble) *(ML1351)*
    UF Percussion bands
    BT Bands (Music)
Steel band music [May Subd Geog]
    M1363
    BT Percussion ensembles
        Popular music
Stone drum
    BT Drum
Stops, Organ
    USE Organ stops
Strathspeys
    BT Dance music—Scotland
        Reels (Music)
Straw fiddle
    USE Xylophone
Street entertainers [May Subd Geog]
    NT Street music and musicians
Street music and musicians [May Subd Geog]
    UF Musicians, Street
        Street songs
    BT Music
        Musicians
        Songs—History and criticism
        Street entertainers
    NT Cries
        Organ grinders
Street songs
    USE Cries
        Street music and musicians
String ensembles *(M950-M954)*
        Here are entered compositions for ten or
        more different solo bowed stringed in-
        struments and collections of composi-
        tions for a varying number or combina-
        tion of different solo bowed stringed
        instruments. Compositions for ten or
        more like bowed stringed instruments
        and collections of compositions for a
        varying number of like bowed stringed
        instruments are entered under Viol en-
        sembles, Violoncello ensembles, and
        similar headings.
        When used in conjunction with specific
        solo instrument(s), the designation
        string ensemble may stand for any
        number and combination of solo
        stringed instruments.

String ensembles *(M950-M954)*
(Continued)

UF   Ensembles (Music)

SA   Concertos ([Solo instrument(s)] with
string ensemble); [Solo
instrument(s)] with string ensemble;
Suites, Variations, Waltzes, *and
similar headings with specification of
instruments which include the
specification String ensemble*

NT   Canons, fugues, etc. (String ensemble)
Harpsichord with string ensemble
Suites (String ensemble)
Waltzes (String ensemble)

Notes under Chamber music; Instrumental
ensembles

—Analytical guides *(MT140; MT145)*

String instrument music *(M59.5)*

Here are entered musical compositions
for an unspecified solo bowed string
instrument. Works for a specified instrument are entered under Violin music, Violoncello music, and similar
headings.

UF   Melody instrument music
Unspecified instrument music

BT   Instrumental music
Solo instrument music

String nonets *(M950-952)*

Here, followed by specification of instruments, are entered separate compositions and collections of compositions
for nine specific stringed instruments.
Collections of compositions for various
combinations of nine stringed instruments are entered under this heading
without specification.

UF   Nonets, String

SA   Suites, Variations, Waltzes, *and similar
headings with specification of
instruments*

Note under Nonets

**String nonets (Violins (3), violas (3),
violoncellos (3))** *(M950-952)*

String octets *(M850-852)*

Here, followed by specification of instruments, are entered separate compositions and collections of compositions
for eight specific stringed instruments.
Collections of compositions for various
combinations of eight stringed instruments are entered under this heading
without specification.

UF   Octets, String

SA   Suites, Variations, Waltzes, *and similar
headings with specification of
instruments*

Note under Octets

String octets (Double basses (8)) *(M850-854)*

UF   Double-bass music (Double basses (8))

**String octets (Violins (3), violas (2),
violoncellos (2), double bass)** *(M852)*

**String octets (Violins (4), violas (2),
violoncellos (2))** *(M850-852)*

UF   Double quartets

BT   String quartets

NT   Canons, fugues, etc. (Violins (4), violas
(2), violoncellos (2))

String octets (Violoncellos (8)) *(M850-852)*

UF   Violoncello music (Violoncellos (8))

String-orchestra music *(M1100-M1145)*

BT   Chamber orchestra music
Instrumental music
Orchestral music

SA   Concertos ([Solo instrument(s)] with
string orchestra; [Solo
instrument(s)] with string orchestra;
Suites, Variations, Waltzes, *and
similar headings with specification of
instruments which include the
specification String orchestra*

NT   Bassoon, clarinet, flute, horn,
violoncello with string orchestra
Bassoon, clarinet, flute, oboe, violins (2),
viola, violoncello with string
orchestra
Bassoon, clarinet, flute, oboe with string
orchestra
Bassoon, clarinet, flute with string
orchestra
Bassoon, clarinet, oboe with string
orchestra
Canons, fugues, etc. (String orchestra)
Chaconnes (String orchestra)
Chorale preludes (String orchestra)
Clarinet, flute, trumpet with string
orchestra
Clarinet, harp, violin, violoncello with
string orchestra
Concertos (Bassoon and clarinet with
string orchestra)
Concertos (Bassoon, clarinet, flute,
oboe, violins (2), viola, violoncello
with string orchestra)
Concertos (Clarinet and harp with
string orchestra)
Concertos (Clarinet, flute, trumpet with
string orchestra)
Concertos (Double bass with string
orchestra)
Concertos (Flute and harp with string
orchestra)
Concertos (Flute and horn with string
orchestra)
Concertos (Flute and oboe with string
orchestra)
Concertos (Flute and viola d'amore
with string orchestra)
Concertos (Flute and violin with string
orchestra)
Concertos (Flute, oboe, trumpet with
string orchestra)
Concertos (Flutes (2), glockenspiel with
string orchestra)

String-orchestra music *(M1100-M1145)*
  (Continued)
    NT Concertos (Flutes (2), marimba with
          string orchestra)
        Concertos (Harp with string orchestra)
        Concertos (Harpsichord, flutes (2) with
          string orchestra)
        Concertos (Horns (2) with string
          orchestra)
        Concertos (Mandolins (2) with string
          orchestra)
        Concertos (Oboe and harpsichord with
          string orchestra)
        Concertos (Oboe and trumpet with
          string orchestra)
        Concertos (Oboe d'amore with string
          orchestra)
        Concertos (Oboe with string orchestra)
        Concertos (Percussion with string
          orchestra)
        Concertos (Piano, trumpets (3) with
          string orchestra)
        Concertos (Piano, violins (2) with
          string orchestra)
        Concertos (Piano with string orchestra)
        Concertos (Saxophone with string
          orchestra)
        Concertos (String orchestra)
        Concertos (Trumpet and piano with
          string orchestra)
        Concertos (Trumpet with string
          orchestra)
        Concertos (Violin and viola with string
          orchestra)
        Concertos (Violin with string orchestra)
        Concertos (Violins (2) with string
          orchestra)
        Concertos (Violins (3) with string
          orchestra)
        Concertos (Violoncello with string
          orchestra)
        Concertos (Violoncellos (2) with string
          orchestra)
        English horn and flute with string
          orchestra
        Flute and horn with string orchestra
        Flute and viola d'amore with string
          orchestra
        Flute and violin with string orchestra
        Flute, horn, harp with string orchestra
        Flute, oboe, trumpet with string
          orchestra
        Flutes (2), glockenspiel with string
          orchestra
        Flutes (2), marimba with string
          orchestra
        Harpsichord, flute, violin with string
          orchestra
        Harpsichord, flutes (2) with string
          orchestra
        Marches (String orchestra)
        Minuets (String orchestra)

String-orchestra music *(M1100-M1145)*
  (Continued)
    NT Overtures (String orchestra)
        Passacaglias (String orchestra)
        Percussion and piano with string
          orchestra
        Piano, trumpets (3) with string
          orchestra
        Piano, violins (2) with string orchestra
        Piano with salon orchestra
        Potpourris (String orchestra)
        Recorder with string orchestra
        Rondos (String orchestra)
        Saxophone with string orchestra
        Suites (String orchestra)
        Symphonic poems (String orchestra)
        Symphonies (String orchestra)
        Trumpet and piano with string
          orchestra
        Trumpets (2) with string orchestra
        Variations (String orchestra)
        Viola d'amore with string orchestra
        Violin and viola with string orchestra
        Violins (2) with string orchestra
        Violins (3) with string orchestra
        Violoncello with string orchestra
        Violoncellos (2) with string orchestra
        Waltzes (String orchestra)
String-orchestra music, Arranged *(M1160)*
    NT Concerti grossi arranged for string
          orchestra
String printing
    UF Printing, String
    BT Prints—Technique
String quartet [May Subd Geog] *(History, ML1160;
          Instruction and study, MT728)*
    UF Quartet, String
    BT Chamber music—History and criticism
String quartet with band *(M1205-6)*
    BT String quartets
    RT Concertos (String quartet with band)
String quartet with chamber orchestra
          (M1040-1041)
    BT String quartets
    RT Concertos (String quartet with chamber
          orchestra)
String quartet with instrumental ensemble
    RT Concertos (String quartet with
          instrumental ensemble)
String quartet with jazz ensemble
    RT Concertos (String quartet with jazz
          ensemble)
    NT Suites (String quartet with jazz
          ensemble)
String quartet with orchestra *(M1040-1041)*
    BT Orchestral music
        String quartets
    RT Concertos (String quartet)
    NT Suites (String quartet with orchestra)
String quartet with string orchestra *(M1105-6)*
    BT String quartets
    RT Concertos (String quartet with string
          orchestra)

String quartet with string orchestra *(M1105-6)*
  (Continued)
  NT Suites (String quartet with string
        orchestra)
      Variations (String quartet with string
        orchestra)
String quartets *(M450-452)*
        Here, with appropriate subdivisions, are
          entered separate compositions and
          collections of compositions for violins
          (2), viola and violoncello.
        Separate compositions and collections for
          any other four specific stringed instru-
          ments are entered under this heading,
          followed by specification of instru-
          ments.
        Collections of compositions for various
          combinations of four stringed instru-
          ments are entered under this heading
          without subdivision or specification.
  UF Quartets, String
      String quartets (Violins (2), viola,
        violoncello)
  SA Suites, Variations, Waltzes, *and similar*
        headings with specification of
        instruments
  NT Canons, fugues, etc. (String quartet)
      Concertos (String quartet)
      Concertos (String quartet with band)
      Concertos (String quartet with chamber
        orchestra)
      Concertos (String quartet with string
        orchestra)
      Minuets (String quartet)
      Polkas (String quartet)
      Rondos (String quartet)
      String octets (Violins (4), violas (2),
        violoncellos (2))
      String quartet with band
      String quartet with chamber orchestra
      String quartet with orchestra
      String quartet with string orchestra
      Suites (String quartet)
      Variations (String quartet)
      Waltzes (String quartet)
  Notes under Chamber music; Quartets; Sonatas
  —Parts
  —Scores
  —Scores and parts
String quartets, Arranged *(M453-4)*
  NT Operas arranged for string quartets
      Oratorios arranged for string quartets
      Overtures arranged for string quartets
      Symphonies arranged for string quartets
String quartets (Double basses (4))
        (M450-M451; M452.4)
  UF Double-bass music (Double basses (4))
String quartets (Musical groups)
  USE Chamber music groups
String quartets (Violas (2), violoncellos (2))
        (M450-M451; M452.4)
  NT Canons, fugues, etc. (Violas (2),
        violoncellos (2))

String quartets (Violas (4)) *(M450-M451;*
        M452.4; M453-M454)
  UF Viola music (Violas (4))
  NT Concertos (Violas (4))
      Violas (4) with orchestra
**String quartets (Violin, viola, violoncello,
        double bass)** *(M450-M451; M452.4)*
  NT Concertos (Violin, viola, violoncello,
        double bass with string orchestra)
      Violin, viola, violoncello, double bass
        with string orchestra
String quartets (Violin, violas (2), violoncello)
        (M450-M451; M452.4)
**String quartets (Violins (2), viola d'amore,
        violoncello)** *(M450-M451; M452.4)*
String quartets (Violins (2), viola, violoncello)
  USE String quartets
String quartets (Violins (2), violas (2))
        (M450-M451; M452.4; M453-M454)
  NT Concertos (Violins (2), violas (2) with
        string orchestra)
      Violins (2), violas (2) with
        string orchestra
**String quartets (Violins (2), violoncello,
        double bass)** *(M450-M451; M452.4)*
String quartets (Violins (2), violoncellos (2))
        (M450-M451; M452.4; M453-M454)
  NT Concertos (Violins (2), violoncellos (2)
        with string orchestra)
      Violins (2), violoncellos (2) with string
        orchestra
String quartets (Violins (3), viola)
        (M450-M451; M452.4)
String quartets (Violins (3), violoncello)
        (M450-M451; M452.4)
  NT Suites (Violins (3), violoncello)
      Variations (Violins (3), violoncello)
String quartets (Violins (4)) *(M450-M451;*
        M452.2)
  UF Violin music (Violins (4))
  NT Concertos (Violins (4) with string
        orchestra)
      Suites (Violins (4))
      Violins (4) with string orchestra
String quartets (Violins (4)), Arranged
        (M453-4)
String quartets (Violoncellos (3), double bass)
        (M451; M452.4)
String quartets (Violoncellos (4))
        (M450-M451; M452.4)
  UF Violoncello music (Violoncellos (4))
  NT Canons, fugues, etc. (Violoncellos (4))
      Suites (Violoncellos (4))
      Variations (Violoncellos (4))
String quartets (Violoncellos (4)), Arranged
        (M453-4)
String quartets (Viols (4)) *(M990)*
  UF Viol music (Viols (4))
  NT Canons, fugues, etc. (Viols (4))
      Suites (Viols (4))
String quintets *(M550-552)*
        Here, followed by specification of
          instruments, are entered separate

String quintets *(M550-552)*
   (Continued)
        compositions and collections of
        compositions for five specific stringed
        instruments.
        Collections of compositions for various
        combinations of five stringed instru-
        ments are entered under this heading
        without specification.
  UF Quintets, String
  SA Suites, Variations, Waltzes, *and similar*
       headings with specification of
       instruments
  Notes under Chamber music; Quintets
String quintets, Arranged *(M553-4)*
  NT Oratorios arranged for string quintets
       Symphonies arranged for string quintets
String quintets (Double basses (5)) *(M550-M554)*
  UF Double-bass music (Double basses (5))
**String quintets (Violas (2), violoncellos (2),
    double bass)** *(M550-552)*
String quintets (Viole da gamba (5)) *(M550-552)*
  UF Viola da gamba music (Viole da gamba (5))
**String quintets (Violin, violas (2), violoncellos
    (2))** *(M550-552)*
**String quintets (Violin, violas (2), violoncellos
    (2)), Arranged** *(M553-4)*
**String quintets (Violins (2), viola, violoncello,
    double bass)** *(M550-552)*
  NT Canons, fugues, etc. (Violins (2), viola,
       violoncello, double bass)
       Suites (Violins (2), viola, violoncello,
       double bass)
       Waltzes (Violins (2), viola, violoncello,
       double bass)
**String quintets (Violins (2), viola, violoncello,
    double bass), Arranged** *(M553-4)*
**String quintets (Violins (2), viola, violoncellos
    (2))** *(M550-552)*
  NT Variations (Violins (2), viola,
       violoncellos (2))
**String quintets (Violins (2), violas (2),
    violoncello)** *(M550-552)*
  NT Canons, fugues, etc. (Violins (2), violas
       (2), violoncello)
       Concertos (Violins (2), violas (2),
       violoncello with string orchestra)
       Suites (Violins (2), violas (2),
       violoncello)
       Variations (Violins (2), violas (2),
       violoncello)
       Violins (2), violas (2), violoncello with
       string orchestra
**String quintets (Violins (2), violas (2),
    violoncello), Arranged** *(M553-4)*
String quintets (Violins (3), viola, double bass)
    (M550-552)
  NT Waltzes (Violins (3), viola, double bass)
String quintets (Violins (3), viola, violoncello)
    (M550-552)
  NT Canons, fugues, etc. (Violins (3), viola,
       violoncello)

String quintets (Violins (3), viola, violoncello)
    (M550-552)
  (Continued)
  NT Concertos (Violins (3), viola,
       violoncello with string orchestra)
       Variations (Violins (3), viola,
       violoncello)
       Violins (3), viola, violoncello with
       string orchestra
**String quintets (Violins (3), viola, violoncello),
    Arranged** *(M553-4)*
String quintets (Violins (4), violoncello)
    (M550-552)
String quintets (Violins (5)) *(M550-554)*
  UF Violin music (Violins (5))
  NT Concertos (Violins (5))
       Violins (5) with orchestra
String quintets (Viols (5)) *(M990)*
  UF Viol music (Viols (5))
  NT Canons, fugues, etc. (Viols (5))
       Suites (Viols (5))
String septets *(M750-752)*
        Here, followed by specification of instru-
        ments, are entered separate composi-
        tions and collections of compositions
        for seven specific stringed instruments.
        Collections of compositions for various
        combinations of seven stringed instru-
        ments are entered under this heading
        without specification.
  UF Septets, String
  SA Suites, Variations, Waltzes, *and similar*
       headings with specification of
       instruments
  Note under Septets
String septets (Violins (4), violoncellos (3))
    (M750-752)
String septets (Violoncellos (7)) *(M750-754)*
  UF Violoncello music (Violoncellos (7))
String septets (Viols (7)) *(M990)*
  UF Viol music (Viols (7))
  NT Canons, fugues, etc. (Viols (7))
String sextets *(M650-652)*
        Here, followed by specification of instru-
        ments, are entered separate composi-
        tions and collections of compositions
        for six specific stringed instruments.
        Collections of compositions for various
        combinations of six stringed instru-
        ments are entered under this heading
        without specification.
  UF Sextets, String
  SA Suites, Variations, Waltzes, *and similar*
       headings with specification of
       instruments
  Note under Sextets
**String sextets (Violins (2), viola, violoncellos
    (2), double bass)** *(M650-652)*
**String sextets (Violins (2), violas (2),
    violoncello, double bass)** *(M650-652)*
  NT Suites (Violins (2), violas (2),
       violoncello, double bass)

String sextets (Violins (2), violas (2), violoncellos (2)) *(M650-652)*
BT String trios
NT Suites (Violins (2), violas (2), violoncellos (2))
String sextets (Violins (2), violas (2), violoncellos (2)), Arranged *(M653-4)*
String sextets (Violins (3), viola, violoncellos (2)) *(M650-652)*
String sextets (Violins (3), violas (2), violoncello) *(M650-652)*
String sextets (Violins (4), violoncellos (2)) *(M650-652)*
String sextets (Violoncellos (6)) *(M650-654)*
UF Violoncello music (Violoncellos (6))
String sextets (Viols (6)) *(M990)*
NT Canons, fugues, etc. (Viols (6))
Suites (Viols (6))
String trio *(History, ML1165; Instruction and study, MT728)*
UF Trio, String
BT Chamber music—History and criticism
String trio with orchestra *(M1040-1041)*
BT String trios
RT Concertos (String trio)
NT Suites (String trio with orchestra)
—Scores *(M1040)*
String trio with string orchestra *(M1105-6)*
BT String trios
RT Concertos (String trio with string orchestra)
NT Canons, fugues, etc. (String trio with string orchestra)
Suites (String trio with string orchestra)
String trios *(M349-351)*
Here, with appropriate subdivisions, are entered separate compositions and collections of compositions for violin, viola and violoncello.
Separate compositions and collections for any other three specific stringed instruments are entered under this heading, followed by specification of instruments.
Collections of compositions for various combinations of three stringed instruments are entered under this heading without subdivision or specification.
UF String trios (Violin, viola, violoncello)
Trios, String
SA Suites, Variations, Waltzes, *and similar headings with specification of instruments*
NT Canons, fugues, etc. (String trio)
Concertos (String trio)
Concertos (String trio with string orchestra)
Minuets (String trio)
String sextets (Violins (2), violas (2), violoncellos (2))
String trio with orchestra
String trio with string orchestra

String trios *(M349-351)*
(Continued)
NT String trios (Violin, viola d'amore, viola da gamba)
String trios (Violin, viola d'amore, violoncello)
Suites (String trio)
Variations (String trio)
Notes under Chamber music; Sonatas; Trios
—Parts
—Scores
—Scores and parts
String trios, Arranged *(M352-3)*
String trios (Baryton, viola, violoncello) *(M349-351)*
BT Baryton music
NT Suites (Baryton, viola, violoncello)
String trios (Baryton, violin, violoncello) *(M349-351)*
BT Baryton music
String trios (Double basses (3)) *(M349-351)*
UF Double-bass music (Double basses (3))
String trios (Lyra-viols (3)) *(M990)*
UF Lyra-viol music (Lyra-viols (3))
String trios (Viol, viola d'amore, viola da gamba) *(M349-351)*
BT Viol music
String trios (Viola, violoncello, double bass) *(M349-351)*
String trios (Violas (3)) *(M349-M353)*
UF Viola music (Violas (3))
String trios (Violin, viola d'amore, viola da gamba) *(M349-351)*
BT String trios
String trios (Violin, viola d'amore, violoncello) *(M349-351)*
BT String trios
String trios (Violin, viola, double bass) *(M349-351)*
NT Suites (Violin, viola, double bass)
String trios (Violin, viola, viola da gamba) *(M349-351)*
NT Canons, fugues, etc. (Violin, viola, viola da gamba)
String trios (Violin, viola, violoncello)
USE String trios
String trios (Violin, violoncello, double bass) *(M349-351)*
NT Suites (Violin, violoncello, double bass)
String trios (Violin, violoncellos (2)) *(M349-353)*
NT Concertos (Violin, violoncellos (2) with string orchestra)
Violin, violoncellos (2) with string orchestra
String trios (Violins (2), viola) *(M349-351)*
NT Concertos (Violins (2), viola)
Minuets (Violins (2), viola)
Suites (Violins (2), viola)
Violins (2), viola with chamber orchestra
Violins (2), viola with orchestra
String trios (Violins (2), viola), Arranged *(M352-3)*

String trios (Violins (2), violoncello) *(M349-351)*
NT Concertos (Violins (2), violoncello with string orchestra)
　　Minuets (Violins (2), violoncello)
　　Suites (Violins (2), violoncello)
　　Variations (Violins (2), violoncello)
　　Violins (2), violoncello with string orchestra

String trios (Violins (2), violoncello), Arranged *(M352-3)*
NT Overtures arranged for violins (2), violoncello
　　Symphonies arranged for violins (2), violoncello

String trios (Violins (3)) *(M349-351)*
UF Violin music (Violins (3))
NT Canons, fugues, etc. (Violins (3))
　　Concertos (Violins (3))
　　Concertos (Violins (3) with string orchestra)
　　Marches (Violins (3))
　　Minuets (Violins (3))
　　Suites (Violins (3))
　　Violins (3) with orchestra
　　Violins (3) with string orchestra

String trios (Violins (3)), Arranged *(M352-3)*

String trios (Violoncellos (3)) *(M349-351)*
NT Concertos (Violoncellos (3))
　　Violoncellos (3) with orchestra

String trios (Viols (3)) *(M990)*
UF Viol music (Viols (3))
BT Viol music
NT Canons, fugues, etc. (Viols (3))
　　Quartets (Organ, viols (3))
　　Suites (Viols (3))

Stringed instrument makers [May Subd Geog]
BT Musical instrument makers
NT Banjo makers
　　Double bass makers
　　Violin makers

Stringed instruments *(ML750-ML925; ML1000-ML1018)*
　　Here is entered material on instruments employing strings, whether bowed, hammered, or plucked. Material restricted to bowed instruments is entered under Stringed instruments, Bowed.
UF Hammered stringed instruments
　　Plectral instruments
SA *names of stringed instruments, e.g.* Guitar, Harp
NT Bouzouki
　　Psaltery
　　Stringed instruments, Bowed
　　Tuning
Example under Musical instruments
—Construction *(ML755-1016)*
—Methods *(MT259)*
—Studies and exercises *(MT259)*
—Tariff
　　USE Tariff on stringed instruments

Stringed instruments, Bowed
UF Bowed instruments
　　Strings (Musical instruments)
BT Stringed instruments
SA *names of bowed instruments, e.g.* Viola, Violin
NT Erh hu
　　Haegŭm
　　Hu ch'in
　　Keyed fiddle
　　Morin khuur
　　Nan hu
　　Pan hu
　　Tuning
　　Vibrator (for bowed instruments)
Example under Musical instruments
Note under Stringed instruments
—Bow
　　UF Bow (Music)
　　　　Violin—Bow
　　　　Violoncello—Bow
—Construction *(ML755)*
—Methods *(MT259)*

Strings (Musical instrument parts)
USE *subdivision* Strings *under names of individual instruments, e.g.* Piano—Strings

Strings (Musical instruments)
USE Stringed instruments, Bowed

Strip-tease
BT Music-halls (Variety-theaters, cabarets, etc.)

Students' songs [May Subd Geog] *(Music, M1940-M1973; Poetry, PN6110.C7)*
　　Collections of the songs of a particular institution are entered here and also under the name of the institution, with subdivision Songs and music.
UF College songs
BT Songs
RT College verse
　　Drinking songs
　　Music in universities and colleges
—United States
　　NT Fraternity songs

Style, Musical
UF Musical style
BT Music—Philosophy and aesthetics
NT Classicism in music
　　Impressionism (Music)
　　Romanticism in music

Subject headings *(Z695)*
—Music
　　BT Music librarianship

Sue's Leg (Ballet)
BT Ballets

Sufi music
USE Music, Sufi

Suite (Music) *(Chamber music, ML1158; Orchestral music, ML1258)*
UF Partita

Suites

Here are entered collections of suite music for various mediums. Individual suites and collections of suites for a specific medium are entered under the heading followed by specification of medium.

Suites (Accordion) *(M175.A4)*
BT   Accordion music
Suites (Accordion with chamber orchestra)
(M1039.4.A3)
BT   Accordion with chamber orchestra
Suites (Accordion with orchestra)
(M1039.4.A3)
BT   Accordion with orchestra
—Scores *(M1039.4.A3)*
—Solo with piano *(M1039.4.A3)*
BT   Accordion and piano music, Arranged
Suites (Archiphone, violins (2)) *(M300-304)*
BT   Archiphone music
Suites (Bagpipe and continuo)
BT   Bagpipe and continuo music
Suites (Bagpipes (2))
BT   Bagpipe music (Bagpipes (2))
Suites (Balalaika and piano) *(M282-3)*
BT   Balalaika and piano music
Suites (Band) *(M1203)*
BT   Band music
Suites (Band), Arranged *(M1254)*
—Excerpts
—Scores
Suites (Baritone and cornet) *(M288-9)*
BT   Baritone and cornet music
Suites (Baryton, viola, violoncello)
(M349-351)
BT   String trios (Baryton, viola, violoncello)
Suites (Bassoon) *(M75-77)*
BT   Bassoon music
Suites (Bassoon and continuo)
BT   Bassoon and continuo music
Suites (Bassoon and English horn) *(M288-9)*
BT   Bassoon and English-horn music
Suites (Bassoon and flute) *(M288-9)*
BT   Bassoon and flute music
Suites (Bassoon and oboe) *(M288-9)*
BT   Bassoon and oboe music
Suites (Bassoon and organ) *(M182-186)*
BT   Bassoon and organ music
Suites (Bassoon and piano) *(M253-4)*
BT   Bassoon and piano music
Suites (Bassoon and tuba) *(M288-289)*
BT   Bassoon and tuba music
Suites (Bassoon and violin) *(M290-291)*
BT   Bassoon and violin music
Suites (Bassoon and violoncello) *(M290-291)*
BT   Bassoon and violoncello music
Suites (Bassoon, clarinet, English horn, flute, horn) *(M555-9)*
Suites (Bassoon, clarinet, flute, horn)
(M455-7)

Suites (Bassoon, clarinet, flute, horn, oboe, violin, viola, violoncello, double bass) *(M960-962)*
BT   Nonets (Bassoon, clarinet, flute, horn, oboe, violin, viola, violoncello, double bass)
Suites (Bassoon, clarinet, flute, horn, oboe with string orchestra) *(M1105-6)*
BT   Bassoon, clarinet, flute, horn, oboe with string orchestra
—Solos with piano *(M1106)*
BT   Sextets (Piano, bassoon, clarinet, flute, horn, oboe), Arranged
Suites (Bassoon, clarinet, flute, horn, violin, viola, violoncello, double bass)
(M860-862)
BT   Octets (Bassoon, clarinet, flute, horn, violin, viola, violoncello, double bass)
Suites (Bassoon, clarinet, flute, oboe, trumpet, violin, viola, violoncello, double bass) *(M960-962)*
BT   Nonets (Bassoon, clarinet, flute, oboe, trumpet, violin, viola, violoncello, double bass)
Suites (Bassoon, clarinet, flute, oboe, violins (2), viola, violoncello) *(M860-862)*
BT   Octets (Bassoon, clarinet, flute, oboe, violins (2), viola, violoncello)
Suites (Bassoon, clarinet, flute, oboe, violins (2), viola, violoncello, double bass)
(M960-962)
BT   Nonets (Bassoon, clarinet, flute, oboe, violins (2), viola, violoncello, double bass)
Suites (Bassoon, clarinet, oboe, percussion, violins (2), viola, violoncello, double bass) *(M985)*
BT   Nonets (Bassoon, clarinet, oboe, percussion, violins (2), viola, violoncello, double bass)
Suites (Bassoon, clarinet, oboe with string orchestra) *(M1105-6)*
BT   Bassoon, clarinet, oboe with string orchestra
—Scores *(M1105)*
Suites (Bassoon, clarinet, oboe with string orchestra), Arranged *(M1105-6)*
—Solos with piano *(M1106)*
BT   Quartets (Piano, bassoon, clarinet, oboe), Arranged
Suites (Bassoon, clarinet, trombone, violin)
(M460-M464)
BT   Quartets (Bassoon, clarinet, trombone, violin)
Suites (Bassoon, clarinet, violin, viola, violoncello) *(M560-562)*
BT   Quintets (Bassoon, clarinet, violin, viola, violoncello)
Suites (Bassoon, flute, horn, oboe, trumpet with string orchestra) *(M1140-1141)*
BT   Bassoon, flute, horn, oboe, trumpet with string orchestra

Suites (Bassoon, flute, horn, violin, viola)
    (M560-562)
   BT Quintets (Bassoon, flute, horn, violin,
       viola)
Suites (Bassoon, oboe, violin, viola, double
    bass) *(M560-562)*
   BT Quintets (Bassoon, oboe, violin, viola,
       double bass)
Suites (Bassoon with orchestra) *(M1026-7)*
   BT Bassoon with orchestra
  —Solo with piano *(M1027)*
      BT Bassoon and piano music, Arranged
Suites (Bassoon with string orchestra)
    (M1105-6)
   BT Bassoon with string orchestra
  —Solo with piano *(M1106)*
      BT Bassoon and piano music, Arranged
Suites (Bassoons (2)) *(M288-289)*
   BT Bassoon music (Bassoons (2))
Suites (Bassoons (2), clarinets (2), horns (2),
    oboes (2)) *(M855-7)*
Suites (Calliope, 4 hands) *(M298)*
   BT Calliope music (4 hands)
Suites (Carillon) *(M172)*
   BT Carillon music
Suites (Chamber orchestra) *(M1003)*
   BT Chamber-orchestra music
Suites (Chamber orchestra), Arranged
    (M1060)
Suites (Cimbalom) *(M142)*
   BT Cimbalom music
Suites (Clarinet) *(M70-72)*
   BT Clarinet music
Suites (Clarinet and flute) *(M288-9)*
   BT Clarinet and flute music
Suites (Clarinet and flute with chamber
    orchestra) *(M1040-1041)*
   BT Clarinet and flute with chamber
      orchestra
  —Scores *(M1040)*
Suites (Clarinet and flute with string
    orchestra) *(M1105-6)*
   BT Clarinet and flute with string
      orchestra
  —Scores *(M1105)*
Suites (Clarinet and oboe) *(M288-9)*
   BT Clarinet and oboe music
Suites (Clarinet and piano) *(M248-250)*
   BT Clarinet and piano music
Suites (Clarinet and piano), Arranged
    (M251-2)
Suites (Clarinet and tuba) *(M288-289)*
   BT Clarinet and tuba music
Suites (Clarinet and violin) *(M290-291)*
   BT Clarinet and violin music
Suites (Clarinet and violoncello) *(M290-291)*
   BT Clarinet and violoncello music
Suites (Clarinet), Arranged *(M73-74)*
Suites (Clarinet, English horn, flute, oboe with
    string orchestra) *(M1105-6)*
   BT Clarinet, English horn, flute, oboe with
      string orchestra
  —Scores *(M1105)*

Suites (Clarinet, flute, harp) *(M375-7)*
   BT Trios (Clarinet, flute, harp)
Suites (Clarinet, flute, harp, violin,
    violoncello) *(M580-582)*
   BT Quintets (Clarinet, flute, harp, violin,
      violoncello)
Suites (Clarinet, flute, horn, trumpet,
    percussion, vibraphone, violin,
    violoncello) *(M885)*
   BT Octets (Clarinet, flute, horn, trumpet,
      percussion, vibraphone, violin,
      violoncello)
Suites (Clarinet, flute, trombone) *(M355-7)*
Suites (Clarinet, flute, trumpet, violoncello)
    (M460-462)
   BT Quartets (Clarinet, flute, trumpet,
      violoncello)
Suites (Clarinet, flute, trumpet with string
    orchestra) *(M1105-6)*
   BT Clarinet, flute, trumpet with string
      orchestra
  —Scores *(M1105)*
Suites (Clarinet, oboe, viola) *(M360-362)*
   BT Trios (Clarinet, oboe, viola)
Suites (Clarinet, violin, violoncello) *(M360-362)*
   BT Trios (Clarinet, violin, violoncello)
Suites (Clarinet, violins (2), viola, violoncello)
    (M560-562)
   BT Quintets (Clarinet, violins (2), viola,
      violoncello)
Suites (Clarinet with orchestra) *(M1024-5)*
   BT Clarinet with orchestra
  —Solo with piano *(M1025)*
      BT Clarinet and piano music, Arranged
Suites (Clarinet with string orchestra)
    (M1105-6)
   BT Clarinet with string orchestra
  —Scores *(M1105)*
  —Solo with piano *(M1106)*
      BT Clarinet and piano music, Arranged
Suites (Clarinets (2)) *(M288-9)*
   BT Clarinet music (Clarinets (2))
Suites (Clarinets (2), flute, drums, percussion,
    viola, violoncello, double bass) *(M885)*
   BT Octets (Clarinets (2), flute, drums,
      percussion, viola, violoncello, double
      bass)
Suites (Clarinets (2), horns (2), violins (2),
    viola, double bass) *(M860-862)*
   BT Octets (Clarinets (2), horns (2), violins
      (2), viola, double bass)
Suites (Clarinets (2), horns (2), violins (2),
    violas (2), violoncello) *(M960-962)*
   BT Nonets (Clarinets (2), horns (2), violins
      (2), violas (2), violoncello)
Suites (Clarinets (2), violin, viola, violoncello)
    (M560-564)
   BT Quintets (Clarinets (2), violin, viola,
      violoncello)
Suites (Clarinets (2) with string orchestra)
    (M1124-5)
   BT Clarinets (2) with string orchestra

Suites (Clarinets (3), cornet, trombone, trumpet, violin, viola, violoncello) *(M960-962)*
   BT Nonets (Clarinets (3), cornet, trombone, trumpet, violin, viola, violoncello)

Suites (Clarinets (4) with string orchestra) *(M1124-1125)*
   RT Clarinets (4) with string orchestra

Suites (Clavichord) *(M24)*

Suites (Concrete music)
   BT Concrete music

Suites (Cornet and piano) *(M260-261)*
   BT Cornet and piano music

Suites (Dance orchestra) *(M1356)*
   BT Dance-orchestra music

Suites (Double bass) *(M55-57)*
   BT Double-bass music

Suites (Double bass and guitar) *(M237-8)*
   BT Double-bass and guitar music

Suites (Double bass and piano) *(M237-8)*
   BT Double-bass and piano music

Suites (Double bass), Arranged *(M58-59)*

Suites (Double bass with orchestra) *(M1018)*
   BT Double bass with orchestra
   —Solo with piano *(M1018)*
      BT Double-bass and piano music, Arranged

Suites (Electronic music) *(M1473)*
   BT Electronic music
   Note under Electronic music

Suites (English horn and organ) *(M182-186)*
   BT English horn and organ music

Suites (Euphonium and piano) *(M270.B37; M271.B37)*
   BT Euphonium and piano music

Suites (Flute) *(M60-62)*
   BT Flute music

Suites (Flute and continuo)
   BT Flute and continuo music

Suites (Flute and guitar) *(M296-7)*
   BT Flute and guitar music

Suites (Flute and harp) *(M296-7)*
   BT Flute and harp music

Suites (Flute and harpsichord) *(M240-242)*
   BT Flute and harpsichord music
      Suites (Flute and piano)

Suites (Flute and harpsichord with string orchestra) *(M1140-1141)*
   BT Flute and harpsichord with string orchestra

Suites (Flute and marimba) *(M298)*
   BT Flute and marimba music

Suites (Flute and oboe) *(M288-9)*
   BT Flute and oboe music

Suites (Flute and organ) *(M182-186)*
   BT Flute and organ music

Suites (Flute and percussion) *(M298)*
   BT Flute and percussion music

Suites (Flute and piano) *(M240-242)*
   BT Flute and piano music
   NT Suites (Flute and harpsichord)
      Suites (Recorder and harpsichord

Suites (Flute and piano), Arranged *(M243-4)*

Suites (Flute and trombone with chamber orchestra) *(M1040-1041)*
   BT Flute and trombone with chamber orchestra
   —Scores *(M1040)*

Suites (Flute and violin)
   BT Flute and violin music

Suites (Flute and violin with string orchestra) *(M1105-6)*
   BT Flute and violin with string orchestra
   —Solos with piano *(M1106)*
      BT Trios (Piano, flute, violin), Arranged

Suites (Flute and violoncello) *(M290-291)*
   BT Flute and violoncello music

Suites (Flute, guitar, viola) *(M380-382)*
   BT Trios (Flute, guitar, viola)

Suites (Flute, guitar, violin) *(M380-382)*
   BT Trios (Flute, guitar, violin)

Suites (Flute, guitar, violin, viola) *(M480-482)*
   BT Quartets (Flute, guitar, violin, viola)

Suites (Flute, guitar, violin, viola), Arranged *(M483-4)*

Suites (Flute, guitar, violoncello) *(M380-382)*
   BT Trios (Flute, guitar, violoncello)

Suites (Flute, harp, vibraphone, violoncello) *(M485)*
   BT Quartets (Flute, harp, vibraphone, violoncello)

Suites (Flute, harp, viola) *(M380-382)*
   BT Trios (Flute, harp, viola)

Suites (Flute, harp, violin, viola, violoncello) *(M580-582)*
   BT Quintets (Flute, harp, violin, viola, violoncello)

Suites (Flute, horns (2), violins (2), viola, violoncello, double bass) *(M860-862)*
   BT Octets (Flute, horns (2), violins (2), viola, violoncello, double bass)

Suites (Flute, lyre-guitar, violin) *(M380-382)*
   BT Trios (Flute, lyre-guitar, violin)

Suites (Flute, oboe, violin, viola, violoncello) *(M560-562)*
   BT Quintets (Flute, oboe, violin, viola, violoncello)

Suites (Flute, trumpet, percussion, viola) *(M585)*
   BT Quintets (Flute, trumpet, percussion, viola)

Suites (Flute, violin, viola, violoncello) *(M460-462)*
   BT Quartets (Flute, violin, viola, violoncello)

Suites (Flute, violin, viola, violoncello), Arranged *(M463-4)*

Suites (Flute, violin, violoncello) *(M360-364)*
   BT Trios (Flute, violin, violoncello)

Suites (Flute, violin, violoncello), Arranged *(M363-4)*

Suites (Flute, violins (2)) *(M360-362)*
   BT Trios (Flute, violins (2))

Suites (Flute, violins (2), viola) *(M460-462)*
    BT Quartets (Flute, violins (2), viola)
Suites (Flute with band) *(M1205-6)*
    BT Flute with band
Suites (Flute with band), Arranged *(M1257)*
    —Scores and parts *(M1257)*
Suites (Flute with chamber orchestra)
    (M1020-1021)
    BT Flute with chamber orchestra
Suites (Flute with orchestra) *(M1020-1021)*
    BT Flute with orchestra
    —Scores
    —Solo with piano *(M1021)*
        BT Flute and piano music, Arranged
Suites (Flute with percussion ensemble)
    BT Flute with percussion ensemble
Suites (Flute with string orchestra)
    (M1105-6)
    BT Flute with string orchestra
    —Solo with piano *(M1106)*
        BT Flute and piano music, Arranged
Suites (Flute with string orchestra), Arranged
    (M1105-6)
    —Solo with piano *(M1106)*
        BT Flute and piano music, Arranged
Suites (Flutes (2)) *(M288-9)*
    BT Flute music (Flutes (2))
Suites (Flutes (2), guitar) *(M375-7)*
    BT Trios (Flutes (2), guitar)
Suites (Flutes (2), trumpets (5), percussion)
    (M885)
    BT Octets (Flutes (2), trumpets (5),
        percussion)
Suites (Flutes (2) with string orchestra)
    (M1105-6)
    BT Flutes (2) with string orchestra
    —Scores *(M1105)*
Suites (Flutes (2) with string orchestra),
    Arranged *(M1105-6)*
    —Solo with piano *(M1106)*
        BT Trios (Piano, flutes (2)), Arranged
Suites (Flutes (3) with string orchestra)
    (M1105-6)
    BT Flutes (3) with string orchestra
    —Solos with piano *(M1106)*
        BT Quartets (Piano, flutes (3)),
        Arranged
Suites (Guitar) *(M125-7)*
    BT Guitar music
Suites (Guitar and harpsichord) *(M276-277)*
    BT Guitar and harpsichord music
Suites (Guitar and piano) *(M276-7)*
    BT Guitar and piano music
Suites (Guitar and piano), Arranged
    (M276-7)
Suites (Guitar), Arranged *(M128-9)*
Suites (Guitar, violin, viola) *(M370-372)*
    BT Trios (Guitar, violin, viola)
Suites (Guitar, violin, violoncello)
    (M370-372)
    BT Trios (Guitar, violin, violoncello)
Suites (Guitar, violin, violoncello), Arranged
    (M373-4)

Suites (Guitar with chamber orchestra)
    (M1037.4.G8)
    BT Guitar with chamber orchestra
    —Solo with piano *(M1037.4.G8)*
        BT Guitar and piano music, Arranged
Suites (Guitar with orchestra) *(M1037.4.G8)*
    BT Guitar with orchestra
    —Solo with piano *(M1037.4.G8)*
        BT Guitar and piano music, Arranged
Suites (Guitars (2)) *(M292-3)*
    BT Guitar music (Guitars (2))
Suites (Guitars (2)), Arranged *(M292-3)*
Suites (Guitars (4)) *(M465-7)*
    BT Quartets (Guitars (4))
Suites (Guitars (5)) *(M565-7)*
    BT Quintets (Guitars (5))
Suites (Harmonica and piano) *(M284.M6;*
    M285.M6)
    BT Harmonica and piano music
Suites (Harmonica with orchestra) *(M1039.4.M6)*
    BT Harmonica with orchestra
Suites (Harmonica with string orchestra)
    (M1139.4.M6)
    BT Harmonica with string orchestra
Suites (Harp) *(M115-117)*
    BT Harp music
Suites (Harp-lute guitar) *(M142.H2)*
    BT Harp-lute guitar music
Suites (Harp with chamber orchestra) *(M1036-7)*
    BT Harp with chamber orchestra
Suites (Harp with orchestra) *(M1036-7)*
    BT Harp with orchestra
Suites (Harps (2)) *(M292-3)*
    BT Harp music (Harps (2))
    —Excerpts *(M292-3)*
Suites (Harps (2) with string orchestra)
    (M1105-6)
    BT Harps (2) with string orchestra
    —Scores *(M1105)*
Suites (Harps (4) with string orchestra)
    (M1136-1137)
    BT Harps (4) with string orchestra
        Quartets (Harps (4))
Suites (Harpsichord) *(M24)*
    BT Harpsichord music
Suites (Harpsichord), Arranged *(M38)*
Suites (Harpsichord, bassoon, clarinet, oboe)
    (M415-417)
    BT Quartets (Harpsichord, bassoon,
        clarinet, oboe)
Suites (Harpsichord, bassoon, clarinet, oboe),
    Arranged *(M418-419)*
Suites (Harpsichord, bassoon, clarinets (2),
    horns (2), oboes (2), percussion)
    (M935)
    BT Nonets (Harpsichord, bassoon, clarinets
        (2), horns (2), oboes (2), percussion)
Suites (Harpsichord, bassoon, English horn,
    oboes (2)) *(M515-517)*
    BT Quintets (Harpsichord, bassoon, English
        horn, oboes (2))
        Suites (Piano, bassoon, English horn,
        oboes (2))

Suites (Harpsichord, bassoon, oboe, trumpet)
    (M415-417)
  BT Quartets (Harpsichord, bassoon, oboe,
        trumpet)
Suites (Harpsichord, flute, harp with string
      orchestra) *(M1105-6)*
  BT Harpsichord, flute, harp with string
        orchestra
    —Scores *(M1105)*
Suites (Harpsichord, flute, oboe with string
      orchestra)*(M1140-1141)*
  BT Harpsichord, flute, oboe with string
        orchestra
Suites (Harpsichord, flute, viola)
      (M320-322)
  BT Trios (Harpsichord, flute, viola)
Suites (Harpsichord, flute, viola), Arranged
      (M323-4)
Suites (Harpsichord, flute, viola da gamba)
      (M320-322)
  BT Trios (Harpsichord, flute, viola da
        gamba)
Suites (Harpsichord, flute, violin) *(M320-322)*
  BT Trios (Harpsichord, flute, violin)
Suites (Harpsichord, flute, violin, viola)
      (M420-422)
  BT Quartets (Harpsichord, flute, violin,
        viola)
Suites (Harpsichord, flute, violin, viola),
      Arranged *(M423-4)*
Suites (Harpsichord, flute, violin, viole da
      gamba (2)) *(M520-522)*
  BT Quintets (Harpsichord, flute, violin,
        viole da gamba (2))
Suites (Harpsichord, flute, violin, violoncello)
      (M420-422)
  BT Quartets (Harpsichord, flute, violin,
        violoncello)
      Suites (Piano, flute, violin,
        violoncello)
Suites (Harpsichord, flute, violoncello)
      (M320-322)
  BT Trios (Harpsichord, flute, violoncello)
Suites (Harpsichord, flutes (2)) *(M315-317)*
  BT Suites (Piano, flutes (2))
      Trios (Harpsichord, flutes (2))
Suites (Harpsichord, horns (2), violin,
      violoncello) *(M520-522)*
  BT Quintets (Harpsichord, horns (2),
        violin, violoncello)
Suites (Harpsichord, horns (2), violins (2))
      (M520-522)
  BT Quintets (Harpsichord, horns (2),
        violins (2))
Suites (Harpsichord, oboe, percussion,
      violoncello) *(M445-7)*
  BT Quartets (Harpsichord, oboe,
        percussion, violoncello)
    —Excerpts *(M445-7)*
Suites (Harpsichord, oboe, recorder)
      (M315-317)
  BT Trios (Harpsichord, oboe, recorder)

Suites (Harpsichord, recorders (2))
      (M315-317)
  BT Trios (Harpsichord, recorders (2))
Suites (Harpsichord, recorders (3))
      (M415-417)
  BT Quartets (Harpsichord, recorders (3))
Suites (Harpsichord, violas (2)) *(M310-M311;
      M312.4)*
  BT Trios (Harpsichord, violas (2))
Suites (Harpsichord, violas (2)), Arranged
      (M313-314)
Suites (Harpsichord, viole d'amore (2))
      (M310-M311; M312.4)
  BT Trios (Harpsichord, viole d'amore (2))
Suites (Harpsichord, viole d'amore (2)),
      Arranged *(M313-314)*
Suites (Harpsichord, violin, viola da gamba)
      (M310-312)
  BT Trios (Harpsichord, violin, viola da
        gamba)
Suites (Harpsichord, violin, violoncello)
      (M310-312)
  BT Trios (Harpsichord, violin, violoncello)
Suites (Harpsichord, violins (2)) *(M310-M311;
      M312.4)*
  BT Trios (Harpsichord, violins (2))
Suites (Harpsichord, violins (2), viola)
      (M410-M411; M412.4)
  BT Quartets (Harpsichord, violins (2),
        viola)
Suites (Harpsichord, violins (2), viola da
      gamba) *(M412.4)*
  BT Quartets (Harpsichord, violins (2), viola
        da gamba)
      Quartets (Piano, violins (2), violoncello)
Suites (Harpsichord, violins (2), violas (2))
      (M510-512)
  BT Quintets (Harpsichord, violins (2),
        violas (2))
Suites (Harpsichord, violins (2), violoncello)
      (M410-M411; M412.4)
  BT Quartets (Harpsichord, violins (2),
        violoncello)
Suites (Harpsichord, viols (2)) *(M310-M311;
      M312.4; M990)*
  BT Trios (Harpsichord, viols (2))
Suites (Harpsichords (2)) *(M214)*
  BT Harpsichord music (Harpsichords (2))
Suites (Harpsichords (2)), Arranged *(M215)*
Suites (Horn and organ) *(M182-186)*
  BT Horn and organ music
Suites (Horn and piano) *(M255-7)*
  BT Horn and piano music
Suites (Horn), Arranged *(M83-84)*
Suites (Horn, violin, violoncello) *(M360-362)*
  BT Trios (Horn, violin, violoncello)
Suites (Horn with string orchestra)
      (M1128-1129)
  BT Horn with string orchestra
Suites (Horns (2), baryton, violins (2), viola,
      violoncello, violone) *(M860-864)*
  BT Baryton music

Suites (Horns (2), oboes (2), violins (2), viola, violoncello) *(M860-862)*
  BT Octets (Horns (2), oboes (2), violins (2), viola, violoncello)
Suites (Horns (2), oboes (2), violins (2), violas (2), violoncello) *(M960-962)*
  BT Nonets (Horns (2), oboes (2), violins (2), violas (2), violoncello)
Suites (Horns (2), violin, viola, violoncello) *(M560-562)*
  BT Quintets (Horns (2), violin, viola, violoncello)
Suites (Hurdy-gurdies (2))
  BT Hurdy-gurdy music (Hurdy-gurdies (2))
Suites (Hurdy-gurdy and continuo)
  BT Hurdy-gurdy and continuo music
Suites (Instrumental ensemble) *(M900-985)*
  BT Instrumental ensembles
Suites (Instrumental ensemble), Arranged
Suites (Jazz ensemble)
  BT Jazz ensembles
Suites (Jazz ensemble with orchestra) *(M1040-1041)*
  BT Jazz ensemble with orchestra
Suites (Jazz quartet) *(M1366)*
  BT Jazz quartets
Suites (Jazz quintet with band) *(M1205-1206)*
  BT Jazz quintet with band
Suites (Jazz sextet with band)
  M1205-M1206
  BT Jazz sextet with band
Suites (Jazz trio)
  BT Jazz trios
Suites (Jazz trio with chamber orchestra) *(M1040-1041)*
  BT Jazz trio with chamber orchestra
Suites (Kotos (6)) *(M665-669)*
  BT Koto music
Suites (Lute) *(M140-141)*
  BT Lute music
Suites (Lute, violin, lyra viol) *(M990)*
  BT Lyra-viol music
Suites (Lutes (2)) *(M292-3)*
  BT Lute music (Lutes (2))
Suites (Lutes (2)), Arranged *(M292-3)*
Suites (Mandolin and piano) *(M278-9)*
  BT Mandolin and piano music
Suites (Mandolin with chamber orchestra) *(M1037.4.M3)*
  BT Mandolin with chamber orchestra
Suites (Marimba and piano) *(M284.X9; M285.X9)*
  BT Marimba and piano music
Suites (Marimba with orchestra) *(M1038-9)*
  BT Marimba with orchestra
  —Solo with piano *(M1039)*
    BT Marimba and piano music, Arranged
Suites (Oboe)
  BT Oboe music
Suites (Oboe and continuo)
  BT Oboe and continuo music

Suites (Oboe and harpsichord) *(M245-6)*
  BT Oboe and harpsichord music
Suites (Oboe and organ) *(M182-186)*
  BT Oboe and organ music
Suites (Oboe and piano) *(M245-6)*
  BT Oboe and piano music
Suites (Oboe and piano), Arranged *(M247)*
Suites (Oboe and theorbo) *(M296-297)*
  BT Oboe and theorbo music
Suites (Oboe and violoncello) *(M290-291)*
  BT Oboe and violoncello music
Suites (Oboe and violoncello with string orchestra) *(M1140-1141)*
  BT Oboe and violoncello with string orchestra
Suites (Oboe d'amore and continuo)
  BT Oboe d'amore and continuo music
Suites (Oboe, viola, violoncello) *(M360-362)*
  BT Trios (Oboe, viola, violoncello)
Suites (Oboe, viola, violoncellos (2)) *(M460-462)*
  BT Quartets (Oboe, viola, violoncellos (2))
Suites (Oboe, violin, viola) *(M360-362)*
  BT Trios (Oboe, violin, viola)
Suites (Oboe, violins (2), viola, violoncello) *(M560-562)*
  BT Quintets (Oboe, violins (2), viola, violoncello)
Suites (Oboe with chamber orchestra) *(M1022-3)*
  BT Oboe with chamber orchestra
  —Solo with piano *(M1023)*
    BT Oboe and piano music, Arranged
Suites (Oboe with string orchestra) *(M1105-6)*
  BT Oboe with string orchestra
  —Scores *(M1105)*
  —Solo with piano *(M1123)*
    BT Oboe and piano music, Arranged
Suites (Oboes (2)) *(M288-289)*
  BT Oboe music (Oboes (2))
Suites (Oboes (3) with string orchestra) *(M1122-1123)*
  BT Oboes (3) with string orchestra
Suites (Ondes Martenot and piano)
  BT Ondes Martenot and piano music
Suites (Orchestra) *(M1003)*
  BT Ballets—Excerpts
      Operas—Excerpts
      Orchestral music
  —Excerpts
  —|—Scores *(M1003)*
    UF Suites (Orchestral)—Scores—Excerpts
  —Scores
  —|—Excerpts
    USE Suites (Orchestra)—Excerpts—Scores
Suites (Orchestra), Arranged *(M1060)*
  —Excerpts
  —|—Scores
    UF Suites (Orchestra), Arranged—Scores—Excerpts

Suites (Orchestra), Arranged *(M1060)*
  (Continued)
  —Scores
  — —Excerpts
      USE Suites (Orchestra), Arranged—
          Excerpts—Scores
Suites (Organ) *(M9)*
  BT Organ music
Suites (Organ, 4 hands) *(M180-181)*
  BT Organ music (4 hands)
Suites (Organ), Arranged *(M12-13)*
Suites (Organ, violin, viola) *(M300-302)*
  BT Trios (Organ, violin, viola)
Suites (Organ, violin, viola da gamba)
      (M300-302)
  BT Trios (Organ, violin, viola da gamba)
Suites (Organ, violins (2), viola da gamba)
      (M400-402)
  BT Quartets (Organ, violins (2), viola da
      gamba)
Suites (Organ, violins (2), violoncello)
      (M400-402)
  BT Quartets (Organ, violins (2),
      violoncello)
Suites (Organ with instrumental ensemble)
  BT Organ with instrumental ensemble
Suites (Organ with string orchestra)
      (M1108-1109)
  BT Organ with string orchestra
Suites (Oud, violins (2), viola, violoncello)
      (M570-574)
  BT Oud music
Suites (Oud with string orchestra)
      (M1137.4.O9)
  BT Oud with string orchestra
Suites (Percussion) *(M146)*
Suites (Percussion and piano)
  BT Percussion and piano music
Suites (Percussion, violins (2), viola,
      violoncello) *(M985)*
  BT Nonets (Percussion, violins (2), viola,
      violoncello)
Suites (Percussion with orchestra)
      (M1038-9)
  BT Percussion with orchestra
  —Scores *(M1038)*
Suites (Piano) *(M24)*
  BT Piano music
Suites (Piano, 1 hand) *(Left hand, M26;
      Right hand, M26.2)*
  BT Piano music (1 hand)
Suites (Piano, 1 hand, with chamber
      orchestra) *(M1010-1011)*
  BT Piano (1 hand) with chamber orchestra
Suites (Piano, 4 hands) *(M203)*
  BT Piano music (4 hands)
Suites (Piano, 4 hands), Arranged *(M211)*
Suites (Piano (4 hands), cymbals, drum,
      tambourine, triangle) *(M585)*
  BT Piano music (4 hands)
Suites (Piano and organ) *(M182-4)*
  BT Piano and organ music

Suites (Piano and organ), Arranged *(M185-186)*
Suites (Piano), Arranged *(M24)*
Suites (Piano, bassoon, clarinet, flute, oboe)
      (M515-517)
  BT Quintets (Piano, bassoon, clarinet, flute,
      oboe)
Suites (Piano, bassoon, clarinet, oboe)
      (M415-417)
  BT Quartets (Piano, bassoon, clarinet,
      oboe)
Suites (Piano, bassoon, clarinets (2), English
      horn, flute, horn, oboe, trumpet)
      (M915-917)
  BT Nonets (Piano, bassoon, clarinets (2),
      English horn, flute, horn, oboe,
      trumpet)
Suites (Piano, bassoon, English horn, oboes
      (2)) *(M515-517)*
  BT Quintets (Piano, bassoon, English horn,
      oboes (2))
  NT Suites (Harpsichord, bassoon, English
      horn, oboes (2))
Suites (Piano, bassoon, oboe) *(M315-317)*
  BT Trios (Piano, bassoon, oboe)
Suites (Piano, clarinet, flute) *(M315-317)*
  BT Trios (Piano, clarinet, flute)
Suites (Piano, clarinet, horn) *(M315-317)*
  BT Trios (Piano, clarinet, horn)
Suites (Piano, clarinet, trumpet, percussion)
      (M455-7)
  BT Quartets (Piano, clarinet, trumpet,
      percussion)
Suites (Piano, clarinet, violin) *(M320-322)*
  BT Trios (Piano, clarinet, violin)
Suites (Piano, clarinet, violin), Arranged
      (M323-4)
Suites (Piano, clarinet, violin, violoncello)
      (M420-422)
  BT Quartets (Piano, clarinet, violin,
      violoncello)
Suites (Piano ensemble) *(M216)*
  BT Piano ensembles
Suites (Piano, flute, oboe) *(M315-317)*
  BT Trios (Piano, flute, oboe)
Suites (Piano, flute, violin) *(M320-322)*
  BT Trios (Piano, flute, violin)
Suites (Piano, flute, violin, viola da gamba)
      (M420-422)
  BT Quartets (Piano, flute, violin, viola da
      gamba)
Suites (Piano, flute, violin, viola, violoncello)
      (M522-4)
  BT Quintets (Piano, flute, violin, viola,
      violoncello)
Suites (Piano, flute, violin, viola, violoncello),
      Arranged *(M523-4)*
Suites (Piano, flute, violin, violoncello)
      (M420-422)
  BT Quartets (Piano, flute, violin,
      violoncello)
  NT Suites (Harpsichord, flute, violin,
      violoncello)

Suites (Piano, flutes (2)) *(M315-317)*
  BT Trios (Piano, flutes (2))
  NT Suites (Harpsichord, flutes (2))
Suites (Piano, horns (2), violins (2))
    (M520-522)
  BT Quintets (Piano, horns (2), violins (2))
Suites (Piano, oboe, violin, violoncello)
    (M420-422)
  BT Quartets (Piano, oboe, violin,
    violoncello)
Suites (Piano, percussion, violin) *(M340-342)*
  BT Trios (Piano, percussion, violin)
Suites (Piano quartet) *(M410-412)*
  BT Piano quartets
Suites (Piano quartet), Arranged *(M413-414)*
Suites (Piano quintet) *(M510-512)*
  BT Piano quintets
Suites (Piano trio) *(M310-312)*
  BT Piano trios
Suites (Piano, trombone, trumpet)
    (M315-317)
  BT Trios (Piano, trombone, trumpet)
Suites (Piano, unspecified instruments (2))
    (M386)
  Example under references from Melody instru-
    ment music; Unspecified instrument music
Suites (Piano, viole d'amore (2)) *(M310-M311;
    M312.4)*
  BT Trios (Piano, viole d'amore (2))
Suites (Piano, violins (2)) *(M310-M311;
    M312.4)*
  BT Trios (Piano, violins (2))
Suites (Piano, violins (2)), Arranged
    (M313-314)
Suites (Piano, violins (2), viola, violoncello)
    (M510-512)
  BT Piano quintets
Suites (Piano, violins (2), violoncello)
    (M412.4)
  BT Quartets (Piano, violins (2), violoncello)
Suites (Piano, violins (2), violoncello),
    Arranged *(M413-414)*
Suites (Piano, violins (3)) *(M412.2)*
  BT Quartets (Piano, violins (3))
Suites (Piano, violoncellos (2)) *(M310-M311;
    M312.4)*
  BT Trios (Piano, violoncellos (2))
Suites (Piano, violoncellos (2)), Arranged
    (M313-314)
Suites (Piano with chamber orchestra)
    (M1010-1011)
  BT Piano with chamber orchestra
  —2-piano scores *(M1011)*
    BT Piano music (Pianos (2)), Arranged
  —Scores *(M1010)*
Suites (Piano with instrumental ensemble)
  BT Piano with instrumental ensemble
Suites (Piano with orchestra) *(M1010-1011)*
  BT Piano with orchestra
  —2-piano scores *(M1011)*
    BT Piano music (Pianos (2)), Arranged

Suites (Piano with string orchestra)
    (M1105-6)
  BT Piano with string orchestra
Suites (Piano with string orchestra), Arranged
    (M1160)
  —Scores (reduced) and parts
Suites (Pianos (2)) *(M214)*
  BT Piano music (Pianos (2))
Suites (Pianos (2)), Arranged *(M215)*
Suites (Pianos (2) with chamber orchestra)
    (M1010-1011)
  BT Piano music (Pianos (2))
    Pianos (2) with chamber orchestra
Suites (Pianos (2) with instrumental
    ensemble)
  BT Instrumental ensembles
    Piano music (Pianos (2))
    Pianos (2) with instrumental ensemble
Suites (Pianos (2) with orchestra)
    (M1010-1011)
  BT Pianos (2) with orchestra
Suites (Pianos (2) with percussion ensemble)
  BT Pianos (2) with percussion ensemble
Suites (Pianos (2) with string orchestra)
    (M1105-6)
  BT Pianos (2) with string orchestra
  —Scores *(M1105)*
Suites (Pianos (3) with orchestra)
    (M1010-1011)
  BT Pianos (3) with orchestra
  —Scores *(M1010)*
Suites (Pipes (4)) *(M455-459)*
  BT Pipe music
Suites (Plectral ensemble) *(M1360)*
  BT Plectral ensembles
Suites (Recorder)
  BT Recorder music
Suites (Recorder and celesta) *(M298)*
  BT Recorder and celesta music
Suites (Recorder and continuo)
  BT Recorder and continuo music
Suites (Recorder and guitar) *(M296-7)*
  BT Recorder and guitar music
Suites (Recorder and guitar), Arranged
    (M296-7)
Suites (Recorder and harpsichord)
    (M240-242)
  BT Recorder and harpsichord music
    Suites (Flute and piano)
Suites (Recorder and lute) *(M296-M297)*
  BT Recorder and lute music
Suites (Recorder and piano) *(M240-242)*
  BT Recorder and piano music
Suites (Recorder and piano), Arranged
    (M243-4)
Suites (Recorder and tenor violin)
    (M290-291)
  BT Recorder and tenor violin music
Suites (Recorder, guitar, violoncello) *(M380-382)*
  BT Trios (Recorder, guitar, violoncello)
Suites (Recorder, violin, viola) *(M360-362)*
  BT Trios (Recorder, violin, viola)

Suites (Recorder with string orchestra)
    (M1105-6)
  BT Recorder with string orchestra
  —Solo with piano *(M1121)*
    BT Recorder and piano music, Arranged
Suites (Recorders (2)) *(M288-9)*
  BT Recorder music (Recorders (2))
Suites (Recorders (2)), Arranged *(M288-9)*
Suites (Recorders (2), continuo) *(M315-319)*
Suites (Recorders (2), guitar) *(M375-7)*
  BT Trios (Recorders (2), guitar)
Suites (Recorders (2) with string ensemble)
  BT Recorders (2) with string ensemble
Suites (Recorders (3), violin) *(M460-462)*
  BT Quartets (Recorders (3), violin)
Suites (Reed-organ, 4 hands) *(M190)*
  BT Reed-organ music (4 hands)
Suites (Rhythm band) *(M1420; MT810)*
  BT Rhythm bands and orchestras
Suites (Salon orchestra) *(M1350)*
  BT Salon-orchestra music
Suites (Saxophone and piano) *(M268-9)*
  BT Saxophone and piano music
Suites (Saxophone and trumpet with band)
    (M1205-M1206; M1257)
  BT Saxophone and trumpet with band
Suites (Saxophone with orchestra)
    (M1034-5)
  BT Saxophone with orchestra
  —Solo with piano *(M1035)*
    BT Saxophone and piano music,
      Arranged
Suites (Saxophone with string orchestra)
    (M1105-6)
  BT Saxophone with string orchestra
  —Solo with piano *(M1106)*
    BT Saxophone and piano music,
      Arranged
Suites (Saxophone with wind ensemble)
  BT Saxophone with wind ensemble
Suites (Saxophones (4) with chamber
    orchestra) *(M1034-5)*
  BT Saxophones (4) with chamber orchestra
Suites (String ensemble) *(M950-952)*
  BT String ensembles
Suites (String orchestra) *(M1103)*
  BT String-orchestra music
Suites (String orchestra), Arranged *(M1160)*
Suites (String quartet) *(M450-452)*
  BT String quartets
Suites (String quartet), Arranged *(M453-4)*
Suites (String quartet with jazz ensemble)
  BT String quartet with jazz ensemble
Suites (String quartet with orchestra)
    (M1040-1041)
  BT String quartet with orchestra
Suites (String quartet with string orchestra)
    (M1140-1141)
  BT String quartet with string orchestra
Suites (String trio) *(M349-351)*
  BT String trios
Suites (String trio), Arranged *(M352-3)*

Suites (String trio with orchestra) *(M1040)*
  BT String trio with orchestra
  —Solos with piano *(M1041)*
    BT Piano quartets, Arranged
Suites (String trio with string orchestra)
    (M1105-6)
  BT String trio with string orchestra
  —Scores *(M1105)*
Suites (Theorbo, violin, lyra viol) *(M990)*
  BT Lyra-viol music
    Theorbo music
Suites (Trombone and piano) *(M262-3)*
  BT Trombone and piano music
Suites (Trombone and timpani with string
    orchestra) *(M1140-1141)*
  BT Trombone and timpani with string
    orchestra
Suites (Trombone and trumpet with band)
    (M1205; M1257)
  BT Trombone and trumpet with band
  —Scores *(M1205)*
Suites (Trombone, viola, violoncello)
    (M360-362)
  BT Trios (Trombone, viola, violoncello)
Suites (Trumpet and continuo)
  BT Trumpet and continuo music
Suites (Trumpet and marimba) *(M298)*
  BT Trumpet and marimba music
Suites (Trumpet and organ) *(M182-186)*
  BT Trumpet and organ music
Suites (Trumpet and piano) *(M260-261)*
  BT Trumpet and piano music
Suites (Trumpet with orchestra) *(M1030-1031)*
  BT Trumpet with orchestra
  —Solo with piano *(M1031)*
    BT Trumpet and piano music, Arranged
Suites (Trumpet with string orchestra)
    (M1130-1)
  BT Trumpet with string orchestra
  —Solo with piano *(M1131)*
    BT Trumpet and piano music, Arranged
Suites (Trumpet with string orchestra),
    Arranged *(M1105-6)*
  —Scores *(M1105)*
Suites (Trumpets (2)) *(M288-289)*
  BT Trumpet music (Trumpets (2))
Suites (Trumpets (2) with string orchestra)
    (M1130-1131)
  BT Trumpets (2) with string orchestra
  —Solos with piano *(M1131)*
    BT Trios (Piano, trumpets (2)),
      Arranged
Suites (Trumpets (4), percussion)
  BT Octets (Trumpets (4), percussion)
Suites (Tuba) *(M95-98)*
  BT Tuba music
Suites (Tuba and piano) *(M264-5)*
  BT Tuba and piano music
Suites (Unspecified instrument and continuo)
  BT Duets (Unspecified instrument and
    continuo)
Suites (Unspecified instrument with band)
    (M1205-M1206; M1257)

Suites (Unspecified instruments (2))
    (M298.5)
    BT   Duets (Unspecified instruments (2))
Suites (Vibraphone and viola) *(M298)*
    BT   Vibraphone and viola music
Suites (Vibraphone and violin) *(M298)*
    BT   Vibraphone and violin music
Suites (Viol and continuo)
    BT   Viol and continuo music
Suites (Viola) *(M45-47)*
    BT   Viola music
Suites (Viola and harpsichord) *(M224-6)*
    BT   Suites (Viola and piano)
          Viola and harpsichord music
Suites (Viola and harpsichord), Arranged
    (M227-8)
Suites (Viola and mandolin) *(M294-295)*
    BT   Viola and mandolin music
Suites (Viola and piano) *(M224-6)*
    BT   Viola and piano music
    NT   Suites (Viola and harpsichord)
Suites (Viola and piano), Arranged *(M227-8)*
Suites (Viola and violoncello) *(M286-7)*
    BT   Viola and violoncello music
Suites (Viola), Arranged *(M48-49)*
Suites (Viola da gamba and continuo)
    BT   Viola da gamba and continuo music
Suites (Viola da gamba and harpsichord)
    (M239)
    BT   Viola da gamba and harpsichord music
Suites (Viola da gamba with string orchestra)
    (M1105-6)
    BT   Viola da gamba with string orchestra
Suites (Viola d'amore) *(M59)*
    BT   Viola d'amore music
Suites (Viola pomposa) *(M59)*
    BT   Viola pomposa music
Suites (Viola with chamber orchestra)
    (M1014-1015)
    BT   Viola with chamber orchestra
    —Solo with piano *(M1015)*
         BT   Viola and piano music, Arranged
Suites (Viola with instrumental ensemble)
Suites (Viola with orchestra) *(M1014-1015)*
    BT   Viola with orchestra
    —Solo with piano *(M1015)*
         BT   Viola and piano music, Arranged
Suites (Viola with orchestra), Arranged
    (M1014-1015)
    —Scores *(M1014)*
Suites (Viola with string orchestra)
    (M1105-6)
    BT   Viola with string orchestra
Suites (Viola with string orchestra), Arranged
    (M1105-6)
    —Solo with piano *(M1106)*
         BT   Viola and piano music, Arranged
Suites (Viole da gamba (2)) *(M990)*
    BT   Viola da gamba music (Viole da gamba (2))
Suites (Violin) *(M40-42)*
    BT   Violin music
Suites (Violin and continuo)
    BT   Violin and continuo music

Suites (Violin and guitar) *(M294-5)*
    BT   Violin and guitar music
Suites (Violin and harp) *(M294-5)*
    BT   Violin and harp music
Suites (Violin and harpsichord) *(M220)*
    BT   Suites (Violin and piano)
          Violin and harpsichord music
Suites (Violin and organ) *(M182-186)*
    BT   Violin and organ music
Suites (Violin and piano) *(M220)*
    BT   Violin and piano music
    NT   Suites (Violin and harpsichord)
Suites (Violin and piano), Arranged
    (M222-3)
Suites (Violin and piano with chamber
    orchestra) *(M1040-1041)*
    BT   Violin and piano with chamber
          orchestra
Suites (Violin and piano with instrumental
    ensemble) *(M945-949)*
    BT   Violin and piano with instrumental
          ensemble
Suites (Violin and piano with orchestra)
    (M1040-1041)
    BT   Violin and piano with orchestra
    —Solos with piano *(M1041)*
         BT   Trios (Pianos (2), violin), Arranged
Suites (Violin and viola) *(M286-7)*
    BT   Violin and viola music
Suites (Violin and viola with string orchestra)
    (M1105-6)
    BT   Violin and viola with string orchestra
Suites (Violin and violoncello) *(M286-7)*
    BT   Violin and violoncello music
Suites (Violin and violoncello), Arranged
    (M286-7)
Suites (Violin, lyra viol, continuo) *(M990)*
    BT   Lyra-viol music
Suites (Violin, viola, double bass) *(M349-351)*
    BT   String trios (Violin, viola, double bass)
Suites (Violin, violoncello, double bass)
    (M349-351)
    BT   String trios (Violin, violoncello, double
          bass)
Suites (Violin with chamber orchestra)
    (M1012-1013)
    BT   Violin with chamber orchestra
    —Scores *(M1012)*
Suites (Violin with chamber orchestra),
    Arranged *(M1012-1013)*
    —Solo with piano
         BT   Violin and piano music, Arranged
Suites (Violin with orchestra) *(M1012-1013)*
    BT   Violin with orchestra
    —Solo with piano *(M1013)*
         BT   Violin and piano music, Arranged
Suites (Violin with orchestra), Arranged
    (M1060-1061)
Suites (Violin with string orchestra) *(M1105-6)*
    BT   Violin with string orchestra
    —Scores *(M1105)*
    —Solo with piano *(M1113)*
         BT   Violin and piano music, Arranged

Suites (Violins (2)) *(M286-7)*
　BT　Violin music (Violins (2))
Suites (Violins (2), viola) *(M349-351)*
　BT　String trios (Violins (2), viola)
Suites (Violins (2), viola, violoncello, double bass) *(M550-552)*
　BT　String quintets (Violins (2), viola, violoncello, double bass)
Suites (Violins (2), viola, violoncello, double bass), Arranged *(M553-4)*
Suites (Violins (2), violas (2), violoncello) *(M550-552)*
　BT　String quintets (Violins (2), violas (2), violoncello)
Suites (Violins (2), violas (2), violoncello, double bass) *(M650-652)*
　BT　String sextets (Violins (2), violas (2), violoncello, double bass)
Suites (Violins (2), violas (2), violoncellos (2)) *(M660-662)*
　BT　String sextets (Violins (2), violas (2), violoncellos (2))
Suites (Violins (2), violoncello) *(M349-351)*
　BT　String trios (Violins (2), violoncello)
Suites (Violins (2), violoncello), Arranged *(M352-3)*
Suites (Violins (2), violoncello with string orchestra) *(M1140-1141)*
　BT　Violins (2), violoncello with string orchestra
Suites (Violins (3)) *(M349-351)*
　BT　String trios (Violins (3))
Suites (Violins (3)), Arranged *(M352-3)*
Suites (Violins (3), violoncello) *(M450-M451; M452.4)*
　BT　String quartets (Violins (3), violoncello)
Suites (Violins (4)) *(M450-M451; M452.2)*
　BT　String quartets (Violins (4))
Suites (Violoncello) *(M50-52)*
　BT　Violoncello music
Suites (Violoncello and guitar) *(M294-5)*
　BT　Violoncello and guitar music
Suites (Violoncello and harp) *(M294-5)*
　BT　Violoncello and harp music
Suites (Violoncello and piano) *(M232)*
　BT　Violoncello and piano music
Suites (Violoncello and piano), Arranged *(M235-6)*
Suites (Violoncello), Arranged *(M53-54)*
Suites (Violoncello ensemble) *(M950-954)*
　BT　Violoncello ensembles
Suites (Violoncello with chamber orchestra) *(M1016-1017)*
　BT　Violoncello with chamber orchestra
　—Solo with piano *(M1017)*
　　　BT　Violoncello and piano music, Arranged
Suites (Violoncello with chamber orchestra), Arranged *(M1016-1017)*
Suites (Violoncello with jazz ensemble) *(M1366)*
　BT　Violoncello with jazz ensemble

Suites (Violoncello with orchestra) *(M1016-1017)*
　BT　Violoncello with orchestra
　—Solo with piano
　　　BT　Violoncello and piano music, Arranged
Suites (Violoncello with string orchestra) *(M1105-6)*
　BT　Violoncello with string orchestra
Suites (Violoncello with string orchestra), Arranged *(M1105-6)*
Suites (Violoncellos (2)) *(M286-7)*
　BT　Violoncello music (Violoncellos (2))
Suites (Violoncellos (2)), Arranged *(M286-7)*
Suites (Violoncellos (4)) *(M450-M451; M452.4)*
　BT　String quartets (Violoncellos (4))
Suites (Violoncellos (4)), Arranged *(M453-4)*
Suites (Viols (2)) *(M990)*
　BT　Viol music (Viols (2))
Suites (Viols (3)) *(M990)*
　BT　String trios (Viols (3))
Suites (Viols (4)) *(M990)*
　BT　String quartets (Viols (4))
Suites (Viols (5)) *(M990)*
　BT　String quintets (Viols (5))
Suites (Viols (6)) *(M990)*
　BT　String sextets (Viols (6))
Suites (Wind ensemble) *(M955-7)*
　BT　Wind ensembles
　—Excerpts
Suites (Xylophone with orchestra) *(M1038-1039)*
　BT　Xylophone with orchestra
　—Solo with piano *(M1039)*
　　　BT　Xylophone and piano music, Arranged
Sumerian hymns
　USE　Hymns, Sumerian
Sunday-evening services
　NT　Evening-service music
Sunday-schools [May Subd Geog] *(BV1500-1578)*
　—Hymns *(BV520)*
　　　UF　Music—Sunday-schools
　　　　　Song-books, Sunday-school
　　　　　Sunday-schools—Music
　　　BT　Children's songs
　　　　　Hymns
　—Music
　　　USE　Sunday-schools—Hymns
Suo na
　USE　So na
Super flumina (Music)
　USE　Psalms (Music)—137th Psalm
Surnai
　USE　Shehnai
Suspension (Music)
　BT　Harmony
Swan lake (Ballet)
　BT　Ballets
Swedish folk-songs
　USE　Folk-songs, Swedish
Swedish songs
　USE　Songs, Swedish

Swing, Western (Music)
  USE Western swing (Music)
Swing music
  USE Jazz music
Symbolism in music *(ML3838)*
  BT Music
      Music—Philosophy and aesthetics
      Music—Psychology
  RT Program music
  SA *subdivision* Symbolism *under personal*
      names, e.g. Wagner, Richard,
      1813-1883—Symbolism
  NT Death in music
Symmetrical inversion (Music) *(MT50)*
  UF Inversion, Symmetrical
  BT Composition (Music)
      Harmony
Symphonet
  USE Pipe (Musical instrument)
Symphonic poem *(ML1270.S9)*
Symphonic poems *(M1002)*
          Here are entered symphonic poems for
          orchestra. Symphonic poems composed for
          other media are entered under this heading
          followed by specification of medium,
          e.g.*Symphonic poems (Band)*
  UF Tone poems
  BT Orchestral music
  RT Overtures
Symphonic poems (Band) *(M1202)*
  BT Band music
  Note under Symphonic poems
Symphonic poems (Band), Arranged *(M1254)*
Symphonic poems (Chamber orchestra) *(M1002)*
  BT Chamber-orchestra music
  —Scores *(M1002)*
Symphonic poems (Organ) *(M9)*
  BT Organ music
Symphonic poems (String orchestra) *(M1102)*
  BT String-orchestra music
  —Scores *(M1102)*
Symphonic poems arranged for piano *(M35)*
  BT Piano music, Arranged
Symphonic poems arranged for piano (4
      hands) *(M209)*
  BT Piano music (4 hands), Arranged
Symphonic poems arranged for piano (Pianos
      (2)) *(M215)*
  BT Piano music (Pianos (2)), Arranged
Symphonic poems arranged for piano (Pianos
      (2), 8 hands) *(M216)*
  BT Piano music (Pianos (2), 8 hands),
      Arranged
Symphonic poems arranged for violoncello and
      piano *(M235-6)*
  BT Violoncello and piano music, Arranged
Symphonies *(M1001)*
          Here are entered symphonies for orches-
          tra. Symphonies composed for other
          media are entered under this heading
          followed by specification of medium,
          e.g. *Symphonies (Band); Symphonies*
          (Chamber orchestra)

Symphonies *(M1001)*
  (Continued)
  BT Orchestral music
  Note under Symphony
  —Analysis, appreciation *(MT125; MT130)*
  —Excerpts
  — —Scores
        UF Symphonies—Scores—Excerpts
  — —Vocal scores with piano *(M1001)*
        UF Symphonies—Vocal scores with
            piano—Excerpts
  —Excerpts, Arranged
  —Scores
  — —Excerpts
        USE Symphonies—Excerpts—Scores
  —Thematic catalogs *(MT125; MT130)*
        Example under Music—Thematic
        catalogs
  —Vocal scores with piano
  — —Excerpts
        USE Symphonies—Excerpts—Vocal
        , scores with piano
Symphonies, Arranged
  —Excerpts
  — —Scores
        UF Symphonies, Arranged—Scores—
            Excerpts
  —Scores
  — —Excerpts
        USE Symphonies, Arranged—
            Excerpts—Scores
Symphonies (Band) *(M1201)*
  UF Sonatas (Band)
  BT Band music
  Note under Symphonies
  —Excerpts *(M1203)*
Symphonies (Band), Arranged *(M1254)*
  —Excerpts
  — —Scores
        UF Symphonies (Band), Arranged—
            Scores—Excerpts
  — —Scores and parts
        UF Symphonies (Band), Arranged—
            Scores and parts—Excerpts
  —Scores
  — —Excerpts
        USE Symphonies (Band), Arranged
            —Excerpts—Scores
  —Scores and parts
  — —Excerpts
        USE Symphonies (Band), Arranged
            —Excerpts—Scores and parts
Symphonies (Brass ensemble)
  BT Brass ensembles
Symphonies (Chamber orchestra) *(M1001)*
  BT Chamber-orchestra music
  Note under Symphonies
Symphonies (Chamber orchestra), Arranged
      (M1060)
  —Excerpts *(M1060)*
  — —Scores and parts *(M1060)*
Symphonies (Concrete music) *(M175.C6)*
  BT Concrete music

Symphonies (Electronic music) *(M1473)*
  BT Electronic music
Symphonies (Flute with orchestra)
     (M1020-1021)
  BT Flute with orchestra
Symphonies (Harp with orchestra)
     (M1036-M1037)
  BT Harp with orchestra
Symphonies (Instrumental ensemble)
     (M900-M949; M960-M985)
  BT Instrumental ensembles
Symphonies (Organ)
  BT Organ music
  RT Sonatas (Organ)
Symphonies (Organ with orchestra)
     (M1105-6)
  BT Organ with orchestra
  —Solo with piano *(M1106)*
     BT Piano and organ music, Arranged
Symphonies (Organ with string orchestra)
     (M1108-1109)
  BT Organ with string orchestra
Symphonies (Percussion)
  BT Percussion music
Symphonies (Piano with orchestra)
     (M1010-1011)
  BT Piano with orchestra
Symphonies (Plectral ensemble) *(M1360)*
  BT Plectral ensembles
Symphonies (Saxophone with orchestra)
     (M1034.S4)
  BT Saxophone with orchestra
Symphonies (Saxophones (4) with orchestra)
     (M1034.S4; M1035.S4)
  BT Saxophones (4) with orchestra
Symphonies (String orchestra) *(M1101)*
  BT String-orchestra music
Symphonies (String orchestra), Arranged
     (M1160)
  —Excerpts
  — —Scores
     UF Symphonies (String orchestra),
        Arranged—Scores—Excerpts
  —Scores
  — —Excerpts
     USE Symphonies (String orchestra),
        Arranged—Excerpts—Scores
Symphonies (Trombone with orchestra)
     (M1032-1033)
  BT Trombone with orchestra
  —Solo with piano *(M1033)*
     BT Trombone and piano music, Arranged
Symphonies (Trumpet and piano) *(M260-M261)*
  BT Trumpet and piano music
Symphonies (Viola with orchestra)
     (M1014-M1015)
  BT Viola with orchestra
Symphonies (Violin with chamber orchestra)
     (M1012-M1013)
  BT Violin with chamber orchestra
Symphonies (Violin with orchestra)
     (M1012-M1013)
  BT Violin with orchestra

Symphonies (Violoncello with orchestra)
     (M1016-1017)
  BT Violoncello with orchestra
  —Solo with piano *(M1017)*
     BT Violoncello and piano music,
        Arranged
Symphonies (Wind ensemble) *(M955-7)*
  BT Wind ensembles
Symphonies arranged for bassoon, clarinet,
     flute, horn, oboe *(M558-559)*
  BT Wind quintets (Bassoon, clarinet, flute,
     horn, oboe), Arranged
Symphonies arranged for bassoons (3), clarinets
     (2), horns (2), oboes (2) *(M958-M959)*
  BT Wind nonets (Bassoons (3), clarinets (2),
     horns (2), oboes (2)), Arranged
Symphonies arranged for clarinets (4)
     (M458-459)
  BT Woodwind quartets (Clarinets (4)),
     Arranged
Symphonies arranged for flute, violins (2),
     viola, violoncello *(M563-4)*
  BT Quintets (Flute, violins (2), viola,
     violoncello), Arranged
Symphonies arranged for organ *(M12-13)*
  BT Organ music, Arranged
Symphonies arranged for organ and piano
     (M185-6)
  BT Piano and organ music, Arranged
Symphonies arranged for piano *(M35)*
  BT Piano music, Arranged
  —Excerpts
Symphonies arranged for piano (4 hands)
     (M209)
  BT Piano music (4 hands), Arranged
  —Excerpts
Symphonies arranged for piano (Pianos (2))
     (M215)
  BT Piano music (Pianos (2)), Arranged
  —Excerpts
     BT Piano music (Pianos (2)), Arranged
Symphonies arranged for piano (Pianos (2),
     8 hands) *(M216)*
  BT Piano music (Pianos (2), 8 hands),
     Arranged
Symphonies arranged for piano, clarinet, flute,
     violin, violoncello *(M523-4)*
  BT Quintets (Piano, clarinet, flute,
     violin, violoncello), Arranged
Symphonies arranged for piano, flute, violin,
     violoncello *(M423-4)*
  BT Quartets (Piano, flute, violin,
     violoncello), Arranged
Symphonies arranged for piano trios *(M314)*
  BT Piano trios, Arranged
Symphonies arranged for string quartets
  BT String quartets, Arranged
Symphonies arranged for string quintets
     (M553-4)
  BT String quintets, Arranged
Symphonies arranged for viola and piano
     (M227-228)
  BT Viola and piano music, Arranged

Symphonies arranged for violin and piano
(*M222-3*)
BT Violin and piano music, Arranged
**Symphonies arranged for violins (2),
violoncello** (*M352-3*)
BT String trios (Violins (2), violoncello),
Arranged
Symphonies arranged for violoncello and piano
(*M235-6*)
BT Violoncello and piano music, Arranged
Symphony [May Subd Geog] (*ML1255*)
Here are entered works dealing with the
symphony as a musical form. Music
scores are entered under the heading
Symphonies followed by appropriate
subdivisions.
Example under Instrumental music—History
and criticism
Symphony orchestras [May Subd Geog]
BT Music
Musical groups
Orchestra
Synagogue music [May Subd Geog] (*Services,
M2186-M2187; Songs, M2114.3; Special
texts, M2079.5; M2099.5*)
Here are entered collections of miscel-
laneous sacred Jewish music. Compo-
sitions designed for particular services
are entered under this heading fol-
lowed by appropriate subdivision, *e.g.*
Synagogue music—Memorial services.
UF Jewish liturgical music
Music, Religious
Music, Sacred
Religious music
Sacred music
BT Jews—Music
Judaism—Liturgy
Music—Religious aspects—Judaism
Sacred vocal music
NT Chants (Jewish)
Jewish hymns
Passover music
—Day of Atonement services
—Evening services
BT Evening-service music
—Festival services
—High Holiday services
BT High Holidays
—History and criticism (*ML166; ML3195*)
Note under Sacred vocal music
—Holiday services
—Marriage services (*M2017.6; M2187*)
UF Synagogue music—Wedding services
BT Marriage service (Judaism)
Wedding music
—Memorial services
Note under Synagogue music
—New-Year services
USE Synagogue music—Rosh
ha-Shanah services
—Passover services

Synagogue music [May Subd Geog] (*Services,
M2186-M2187; Songs, M2114.3; Special
texts, M2079.5; M2099.5*)
(*Continued*)
—Pilgrimage Festival services
BT Pilgrimage Festivals (Judaism)
—Rosh ha-Shanah services
UF Rosh ha-Shanah—Music
Synagogue music—New-Year
services
BT New Year music
—Sabbath services
—Selihot services
—Wedding services
USE Synagogue music—Marriage
services
Syncopation
BT Musical meter and rhythm
Synthesizer (Musical instrument) (*ML1092*)
BT Musical instruments, Electronic
NT Electronic keyboard (Synthesizer)
Electronic percussion instruments
Synthesizer and piano music
USE Piano and synthesizer music
Synthesizer music (*M1473*)
BT Electronic music
SA Concertos, Minuets, Sonatas, Suites,
*and similar headings with specification
of instruments; also* Trios [Quartets, etc.]
*followed by specifications which include
synthesizer, and headings beginning with
the words Synthesizer or Synthesizers.*
NT Quartets (Flute, oboe, synthesizer, violin)
Ta ti
USE So na
Taar
USE Tar (Musical instrument)
Tabala
USE Tabla
Tabla (*ML1040*)
UF Tabala
BT Musical instruments—India
Percussion instruments
Tabla and flute music
USE Flute and tabla music
Tabla and santūr music
USE Santūr and tabla music
Tabla and sarangi music
USE Sarangi and tabla music
Tabla and sarod music
USE Sarod and tabla music
Tabla and shehnai music
USE Shehnai and tabla music
Tabla and sitar music
USE Sitar and tabla music
Tabla and vina music
USE Vina and tabla music
Tabla and violin music
USE Violin and tabla music
Tabla music (*M146*)
NT Trios (Flute, sitar, tabla)
Trios (Sitar, tabla, violin)

Tablature (Musical notation) *(History, ML431; Instruction, MT35; Wind instruments, MT538)*
>   BT   Guitar music
>   Lute music
>   Musical notation
>   Organ music
>   SA   *subdivisions* Chord diagrams *under names of chordal instruments and* Fingering charts *under names of wind instruments, e.g.* Piano—Chord diagrams; Clarinet—Fingering charts

Tabor
>   USE   Tambourin

Taegŭm *(ML990.T)*
>   UF   Chŏttae
>   BT   Flute
>   Musical instruments—Korea

Taegŭm music *(M110.T3)*

Taensa songs
>   USE   Songs, Taensa

Tamazight folk-songs
>   USE   Folk-songs, Tamazight

Tambi *(ML1015-1018)*
>   BT   Musical instruments—Sweden
>   —Methods *(MT647)*

Tamboritos
>   BT   Dance music—Panama

Tambou *(ML1040)*
>   BT   Drum

Tambour de Basque
>   USE   Tambourin

Tambour de Provence
>   USE   Tambourin

Tamboura
>   USE   Tambura

Tambourin *(M1035)*
>   UF   Tabor
>   Tambour de Basque
>   Tambour de Provence
>   BT   Drum

Tambourin and galoubet music
>   USE   Galoubet and tambourin music

Tambourine *(ML1035)*
>   BT   Percussion instruments

Tambourine and saxophone music
>   USE   Saxophone and tambourine music

Tambourine music *(M175.T)*
>   SA   Concertos, Minuets, Sonatas, Suites, *and similar headings with specification of instruments; also* Trios [Quartets, etc.] *followed by specifications which include the tambourine; and* Percussion ensembles, Percussion music, *and headings that begin with the words* Tambourine *or* Tambourines

Tambura *(ML1015-1018)*
>   UF   Pandur
>   Tamboura
>   Tamburitza
>   Tanbur

Tambura *(ML1015-1018)*
>   *(Continued)*
>   BT   Balalaika
>   Lute
>   Musical instruments—Yugoslavia
>   —Methods *(MT642)*

Tamburitza
>   USE   Tambura

Tamil ballads
>   USE   Ballads, Tamil

Tamil hymns
>   USE   Hymns, Tamil

Tamil folk-songs
>   USE   Folk-songs, Tamil

Tamil lullabies
>   USE   Lullabies, Tamil

Tamil songs
>   USE   Songs, Tamil

Tamtam *(ML1040; MT720)*
>   UF   Gong

Tanbur
>   USE   Tambura

T'ang music
>   USE   Tōgaku

Tangentenflügel
>   USE   Piano

Tangos
>   BT   Dance music

Tanso *(ML990.T)*
>   BT   Flute
>   Musical instruments—Korea

Tape-recorder music
>   USE   Computer music
>   Concrete music
>   Electronic music

Tar (Musical instrument) *(M1015-1018)*
>   UF   Taar
>   BT   Lute

Tar and piano music, Arranged *(M282.T3; M283.T3)*
>   NT   Concertos (Tar)—Solo with piano

Tar and tunbūk music *(M298)*
>   UF   Tunbūk and tar music

Tar music *(M142.T3)*
>   NT   Concertos (Tar)

Tarantella *(GV1796.T; Effects of music, ML3920)*
>   UF   Tarantula dance
>   BT   Dance therapy
>   Music therapy

Tarantellas
>   BT   Dance music

Tarantula dance
>   USE   Tarantella

Tariff on musical instruments
>   USE   Tariff on stringed instruments
>   Tariff on wind instruments

Tariff on stringed instruments [May Subd Geog]
>   UF   Musical instruments—Tariff
>   Stringed instruments—Tariff
>   Tariff on musical instruments

Tariff on wind instruments [May Subd Geog]
>   UF   Musical instruments—Tariff
>   Tariff on musical instruments
>   Wind instruments—Tariff

Tárogató *(ML990.T)*
  BT Clarinet
      Saxophone
      Shawm
      Woodwind instruments
Tárogató and piano music *(M270.T3;*
      M271.T3)
  UF Piano and tárogató music
Tárogató and piano music, Arranged
      (M270.T3; M271.T3)
  NT Concertos (Tárogató with chamber
      orchestra)—Solo with piano
Tárogató music *(M110.T)*
  NT Woodwind octets (Basset horn,
      clarinets (6), tárogató)
Tárogató with chamber orchestra
      (M1034.T3; M1035.T3)
  RT Concertos (Tárogató with chamber
      orchestra)
Taschengeige
  USE Pochette
Tatar folk-songs
  USE Folk-songs, Tatar
Tatar songs
  USE Songs, Tatar
Te Deum laudamus (Music)
  BT Hymns
Teachers [May Subd Geog] *(Biography,*
      LA2301-2397)
  NT Music teachers
Tealia (Ballet)
  BT Ballets
Technicon *(MT258)*
  BT Piano—Instruction and study
Teda folk-songs
  USE Folk-songs, Teda
Television and music
  UF Music and television
  NT Television broadcasting of music
Television broadcasting [May Subd Geog]
      —Music
  USE Television broadcasting of music
Television broadcasting of music [May Subd Geog]
      (PN1992.8.M87)
  UF Television broadcasting—Music
  BT Television and music
Television music
  BT Music
  RT Music videos
  Note under Television broadcasting
Television operas *(M1527.7)*
  BT Operas
Telugu folk-songs
  USE Folk-songs, Telugu
Telugu Hindu hymns
  USE Hindu hymns, Telugu
Telugu songs
  USE Songs, Telugu
Temperament, Musical
  USE Musical temperament
Temperance *(HV5001-5720)*
      —Songs and music *(M2198-9)*

Tempo (Music) *(MT42)*
  UF Musical time
      Time, Musical
  BT Music—Instruction and study
      Musical meter and rhythm
  NT Metronome
Tenebrae service music
  BT Holy-Week music
  NT Lamentations of Jeremiah (Music)
Tenor violin *(ML760)*
  BT Viola
      Violin
      Violoncello
Tenor violin and continuo music
  UF Continuo and tenor violin music
  NT Sonatas (Tenor violin and continuo)
Tenor violin and recorder music
  USE Recorder and tenor violin music
Tenor violin music *(M59)*
  NT Trios (Harpsichord, tenor violin, viola
      da gamba)
Tewa folk-songs
  USE Folk-songs, Tewa
Thai lullabies
  USE Lullabies, Thai
Theater [May Subd Geog] *(PN2000-PN3299)*
  NT Music in theaters
  —Museums and collections *(PN1620)*
      BT Museums
          Music museums
      NT Theaters—Models
  —Japan
      NT Kabuki
          Kōwaka
          Manzai (Comedy)
          Nō
          Yose
Theaters [May Subd Geog] *(Architecture,*
      NA6820-NA6845)
  UF Opera-houses
  RT Music-halls
  —Stage-setting and scenery *(PN2091.S8)*
      RT Moving-pictures—Setting and scenery
      NT Metals in stage setting
          Operas—Stage guides
Theatrical music
  USE Dramatic music
Thematic catalogs (Music)
  USE Music—Thematic catalogs
      Vocal music—Thematic catalogs
Theme with variations
  USE Variations
Themes, motives
  USE subdivisions Themes, motives under literary
      or art forms or under names of persons
      other than literary authors and Themes,
      motives, Literary under music composi-
      tions for general discussions of the themes,
      etc., occurring or possible in the form or in
      the person's creative work
Theorbo *(ML1015-1018)*
  BT Lute

Theorbo and oboe music
USE Oboe and theorbo music
Theorbo music *(M142.T)*
NT Chaconnes (Theorbo)
Suites (Theorbo, violin, lyra viol)
Theory of music
USE Music—Theory
Therapeutics, Physiological [May Subd Geog]
(RM695-RM931)
NT Music therapy
Third-tones
USE Microtones
Thomas organ music
USE Electronic organ music (Thomas
registration)
Thorough bass *(History, ML442; Instruction*
and study, MT49)
UF Basso continuo
Continuo
Figured bass
Through bass
BT Music—Instruction and study
Music—Theory
Musical accompaniment
RT Harmony
—Realizations *(M36.5)*
UF Harpsichord realizations of thorough
bass
Organ realizations of thorough bass
Piano realizations of thorough bass
Realizations of thorough bass
BT Harpsichord music
Organ music
Piano music
Three flutes with band
USE Flutes (3) with band
Three flutes with string orchestra
USE Flutes (3) with string orchestra
Three harpsichords with string orchestra
USE Harpsichords (3) with string orchestra
Three pianos with orchestra
USE Pianos (3) with orchestra
Three pianos with string orchestra
USE Pianos (3) with string orchestra
Three trumpets with band
USE Trumpets (3) with band
Three violins with orchestra
USE Violins (3) with orchestra
Three violins with string orchestra
USE Violins (3) with string orchestra
Three violoncellos with orchestra
USE Violoncellos (3) with orchestra
Through bass
USE Continuo *used as part of the*
specification of medium in headings,
e.g. Trio-sonatas (Violins (2), continuo)
Thorough bass
Ti-tse
USE Ti tzǔ
Ti tzǔ *(History, ML990.T; Instruction,*
MT358.T5)
UF Ti-tse
BT Flute

Ti tzǔ and p'i p'a music
USE P'i p'a and ti tzǔ music
Ti tzǔ music *(M110.T6)*
Ti tzǔ with chamber orchestra *(M1034.T6)*
RT Concertos (Ti tzǔ with chamber
orchestra)
Ti tzǔ with orchestra *(M1034.T6)*
RT Concertos (Ti tzǔ)
Tibetan folk-songs
USE Folk-songs, Tibetan
Tibetan songs
USE Songs, Tibetan
Tibia (Musical instrument) *(ML169)*
BT Flute
Musical instruments, Ancient—Rome
Woodwind instruments
Timbre (Music)
USE Tone color (Music)
Time, Musical
USE Tempo (Music)
Timpani *(ML1036)*
UF Kettledrum
Tympani
BT Drum
Percussion instruments
Timpani and organ music *(M182-186)*
UF Organ and timpani music
Timpani and piano music *(M284.T5; M285.T5)*
UF Piano and timpani music
NT Sonatas (Timpani and piano)
Timpani and piano music, Arranged
(M284.T5; M285.T5)
NT Concertos (Timpani)—Solo with piano
Timpani and piano with string orchestra
(M1140-1141)
RT Concertos (Timpani and piano with
string orchestra)
Timpani and trumpet music
USE Trumpet and timpani music
Timpani and tuba music
USE Tuba and timpani music
Timpani music *(M146)*
SA Concertos, Minuets, Sonatas, Suites,
and similar headings with
specification of instruments; Trios
[Quartets, etc.] *followed by*
specifications which include timpani;
also Percussion ensembles,
Percussion music, *and headings that*
begin with the word Timpani
Note under Percussion music
Timpani with band *(M1205-M1206; M1257)*
RT Concertos (Timpani with band)
Timpani with brass ensemble
RT Concertos (Timpani with brass ensemble)
Timpani with orchestra *(M1038-1039)*
RT Concertos (Timpani)
Timpani with string ensemble
RT Concertos (Timpani with string ensemble)
Tin whistle
USE Penny whistle
Title-page *(Z242.T6)*
NT Music title-pages

Titles of musical compositions
    UF Musical compositions, Titles of
    BT Music
Titon du Tillet, Évrard, 1677-1762. Parnasse
             françois
    BT Musicians—France—Portraits
Tivi songs
    USE Songs, Tivi
Tlingit folk-songs
    USE Folk-songs, Tlingit
Tō-gaku
    USE Tōgaku
Toccata *(Musical form, ML448;*
         Organ music, ML647)
Toccatas and fugues
    USE Canons, fugues, etc.
Toda songs
    USE Songs, Toda
Tōgaku
    UF T'ang music
          Tō-gaku
    BT Gagaku
Tommy talker
    USE Kazoo
Tonadilla *(ML1747)*
    BT Entr'acte music
Tonadillas *(M1500-1508)*
    UF Operettas
    BT Musical revues, comedies, etc.
          Operas
Tonality
         ML3811 (Acoustics and physics)
         MT46 (Instruction)
    UF Keys (Music theory)
    BT Musical intervals and scales
    RT Harmony
    NT Microtones
Tonarius *(ML3082; History, ML171-ML174)*
    UF Intonarium
    BT Church music—Catholic Church
Tone color (Music) *(ML3807)*
    UF Timbre (Music)
          Tone quality
    BT Music—Acoustics and physics
Tone poems
    USE Symphonic poems
Tone quality
    USE Tone color (Music)
Tone-word system *(MT935)*
    BT Musical notation
          Sight-singing
    RT Tonic sol-fa
Tonette
    BT Recorder (Musical instrument)
    —Methods *(MT801)*
Tonguing (Wind instrument playing)
    BT Music—Performance
          Wind instruments
Toni (African people)
    USE Eton (African people)
Tonic sol-fa *(Instruction, MT30)*
    UF Sol-fa system

Tonic sol-fa *(Instruction, MT30)*
    (Continued)
    BT Musical notation
          Sight-singing
    RT Tone-word system
Tonus peregrinus *(History, ML178; Theory,*
         ML174)
    BT Music—500-1400
          Musical intervals and scales
Top forty radio stations
    USE Popular music radio stations
Topan
    USE Tupan
Topical songs
    BT Songs
    SA *subdivision* Songs and music *under*
         specific subjects, classes or persons,
         names of individuals, institutions,
         societies, etc.
    NT Protest songs
          Safety songs
Town musicians
    USE Stadtpfeifer
          Waits
Town pipers
    USE Stadtpfeifer
Toy orchestras
    USE Rhythm bands and orchestras
T'pan
    USE Tupan
Trade-unions [May Subd Geog] *(HD6350-*
         HD6940.7)
    —Musicians [May Subd Geog]
        BT Musicians
Tragedy *(Collections, PN6111-PN6120; History*
        and criticism, PN1890-PN1899)
    NT Tragedy in music
Tragedy in music *(ML63)*
    BT Music
          Program music
          Tragedy
Transcription (Music)
    USE Arrangement (Music)
Transposition (Music) *(MT68)*
    BT Music
          Music—Instruction and study
          Music—Theory
          Musical accompaniment
Trautonium *(ML1092)*
    BT Musical instruments, Electronic
Trautonium music *(M175.T)*
    BT Trautonium with orchestra
    NT Concertos (Trautonium)
Trautonium with orchestra *(M1039.4.T)*
    BT Orchestral music
    RT Concertos (Trautonium)
    NT Trautonium music
Tremolo
    USE Vibrato
Trinity Sunday music
Trio-sonata

Trio-sonatas *(M312.4)*

> Here are entered miscellaneous collections of trio-sonatas for 2 melody instruments and continuo. Separate trio-sonatas and collections of trio-sonatas for 2 specific melody instruments and continuo are entered under the heading followed by specification of medium, *e.g.* Trio-sonatas (Violins (2), continuo)

> BT   Quartets (Harpsichord, violins (2), violoncello)
>
> Sonatas
>
> Trios

Trio-sonatas (Violins (2), continuo)

> *Example under reference from* Basso continuo; Continuo; Figured bass; Through bass
>
> *Note under* Trio-sonatas

Trios *(M300-386)*

> Here are entered collections of compositions for three instruments belonging to various families and in various combinations; and compositions for three specific instruments belonging to various families, followed by specification of instruments (including the specification: Unspecified instrument(s))
>
> Compositions for three bowed stringed instruments are entered under String trios; for three wind instruments under Wind trios; for three brass instruments under brass trios; for three woodwind instruments under Woodwind trios, with or without specification of instruments in each case.
>
> Compositions for piano, violin and violoncello are entered under Piano trios.
>
> Compositions for three plectral instruments are entered under Plectral ensembles, except those for guitars and /or harps, which are entered under Trios followed by specification of instruments.
>
> Compositions for three percussionists are entered under Percussion ensembles.
>
> Compositions for three solo voices are entered under Sacred trios or Vocal trios.
>
> Headings with specification of instruments are printed below only if specific cross references are needed.

> SA   Suites, Variations, Waltzes, *and similar headings with specification of instruments*
>
> NT   Trio-sonatas
>
> *Notes under* Chamber music; Sonatas

Trios, Arranged

Trios, Brass
  USE Brass trios
Trios, Piano
  USE Piano trios
Trios, Sacred
  USE Sacred trios
Trios, Secular
  USE Vocal trios

Trios, String
  USE String trios
Trios, Vocal
  USE Vocal trios
Trios, Woodwind
  USE Woodwind trios

Trios (Accordion, violin, violoncello) *(M385)*
Trios (Bagpipe, hurdy-gurdy, continuo)
Trios (Bagpipes (2), continuo)
Trios (Basset horn, viola, violoncello) *(M360-364)*

> BT   Basset-horn music

Trios (Bassoon, chalumeau, continuo)
Trios (Bassoon, clarinet, violin) *(M360-362)*
Trios (Bassoon, clarinet, violoncello) *(M360-362)*
Trios (Bassoon, clarinet, violoncello), Arranged *(M363-4)*
Trios (Bassoon, flute, guitar) *(M375-7)*

> NT   Minuets (Bassoon, flute, guitar)

Trios (Bassoon, flute, guitar), Arranged *(M378-9)*
Trios (Bassoon, flute, harp) *(M375-7)*
Trios (Bassoon, flute, viola) *(M360-362)*
Trios (Bassoon, flute, violin) *(M360-362)*
Trios (Bassoon, horn, violin) *(M360-362)*
Trios (Bassoon, oboe, viola) *(M360-362)*
Trios (Bassoon, trumpet, percussion) *(M385)*
Trios (Bassoon, violins (2)) *(M360-364)*

> NT   Bassoon, violins (2) with string orchestra
>
> Concertos (Bassoon, violins (2) with string orchestra)

Trios (Clarinet, flute, harp) *(M375-7)*

> NT   Clarinet, flute, harp with string orchestra
>
> Concertos (Clarinet, flute, harp with string orchestra)
>
> Suites (Clarinet, flute, harp)

Trios (Clarinet, flute, viola) *(M360-362)*
Trios (Clarinet, flute, violin) *(M360-362)*
Trios (Clarinet, flute, violin), Arranged *(M363-4)*
Trios (Clarinet, flute, violoncello) *(M360-362)*
Trios (Clarinet, guitar, double bass)
Trios (Clarinet, guitar, viola) *(M380-382)*

> NT   Variations (Clarinet, guitar, viola)

Trios (Clarinet, harp, celesta) *(M385)*

> NT   Clarinet, harp, celesta with string orchestra
>
> Concertos (Clarinet, harp, celesta with string orchestra)

Trios (Clarinet, harp, violin) *(M380-382)*
Trios (Clarinet, oboe, viola) *(M360-362)*

> NT   Suites (Clarinet, oboe, viola)

Trios (Clarinet, oboe, violin) *(M360-364)*

> NT   Clarinet, oboe, violin with orchestra
>
> Concertos (Clarinet, oboe, violin)

Trios (Clarinet, trombone, percussion) *(M385)*
Trios (Clarinet, viola, violoncello) *(M360-362)*
Trios (Clarinet, violin, violoncello) *(M360-362)*

> NT   Suites (Clarinet, violin, violoncello)

Trios (Cornett, violin, continuo)
Trios (Cornetts (2), continuo)

**Trios (Electronic organ, saxophone,
        violoncello)** *(M300-304)*
Trios (Flute, guitar, marimba) *(M385)*
  BT Marimba music
Trios (Flute, guitar, viola) *(M380-382)*
  NT Potpourris (Flute, guitar, viola)
     Suites (Flute, guitar, viola)
     Variations (Flute, guitar, viola)
Trios (Flute, guitar, viola), Arranged
        (M383-4)
  NT Overtures arranged for flute, guitar,
     viola
Trios (Flute, guitar, violin) *(M380-382)*
  NT Potpourris (Flute, guitar, violin)
     Suites (Flute, guitar, violin)
     Waltzes (Flute, guitar, violin)
Trios (Flute, guitar, violin), Arranged
        (M383-4)
  NT Overtures arranged for flute, guitar,
     violin
Trios (Flute, guitar, violoncello) *(M380-382)*
  NT Suites (Flute, guitar, violoncello)
Trios (Flute, harp, viola) *(M380-382)*
  NT Suites (Flute, harp, viola)
Trios (Flute, harp, viola d'amore)
        (M380-382)
Trios (Flute, harp, violin) *(M380-382)*
  NT Variations (Flute, harp, violin)
Trios (Flute, harp, violoncello) *(M380-382)*
Trios (Flute, horn, double bass) *(M360-362)*
Trios (Flute, horn, harp) *(M375-7)*
  NT Concertos (Flute, horn, harp with string
     orchestra)
     Flute, horn, harp with string orchestra
Trios (Flute, lute, percussion) *(M385)*
Trios (Flute, lyre-guitar, violin) *(M380-382)*
  BT Lyre-guitar music
  NT Suites (Flute, lyre-guitar, violin)
Trios (Flute, marimba, vibraphone) *(M385)*
  BT Marimba music
Trios (Flute, oboe d'amore, percussion)
        (M385)
  BT Oboe d'amore music
Trios (Flute, oboe d'amore, viola d'amore)
        (M360-362)
  NT Concertos (Flute, oboe d'amore, viola
     d'amore with string orchestra)
     Flute, oboe d'amore, viola d'amore with
     string orchestra
Trios (Flute, oboe d'amore, violin) *(M360-364)*
  NT Concertos (Flute, oboe d'amore, violin
     with string orchestra)
     Flute, oboe d'amore, violin with
     string orchestra
Trios (Flute, oboe, viola) *(M360-362)*
Trios (Flute, oboe, violin) *(M360-364)*
  NT Concertos (Flute, oboe, violin with
     string orchestra)
     Flute, oboe, violin with string orchestra
Trios (Flute, saxophone, harp) *(M375-7)*
  NT Concertos (Flute, saxophone, harp with
     string orchestra)
     Flute, saxophone, harp with string orchestra

Trios (Flute, sitar, tabla)
  BT Sitar music
     Tabla music
Trios (Flute, timpani, violin) *(M385)*
  NT Concertos (Flute, timpani, violin with
     string orchestra)
     Flute, timpani, violin with string
     orchestra
Trios (Flute, trumpet, violoncello)
        (M360-362)
Trios (Flute, viola, double bass) *(M360-362)*
Trios (Flute, viola, violoncello) *(M360-362)*
  NT Concertos (Flute, viola, violoncello with
     string orchestra)
     Flute, viola, violoncello with string
     orchestra
Trios (Flute, violin, viola) *(M360-362)*
Trios (Flute, violin, violoncello) *(M360-362)*
  NT Suites (Flute, violin, violoncello)
Trios (Flute, violin, violoncello), Arranged
        (M363-4)
Trios (Flute, violins (2)) *(M360-362)*
  NT Suites (Flute, violins (2))
Trios (Flutes (2), glockenspiel) *(M385)*
  NT Concertos (Flutes (2), glockenspiel with
     string orchestra)
     Flutes (2), glockenspiel with string
     orchestra
Trios (Flutes (2), guitar) *(M375-7)*
  NT Suites (Flutes (2), guitar)
     Variations (Flutes (2), guitar)
Trios (Flutes (2), guitar), Arranged *(M378-9)*
Trios (Flutes (2), marimba) *(M385)*
  NT Concertos (Flutes (2), marimba with
     string orchestra)
     Flutes (2), marimba with string
     orchestra
Trios (Flutes (2), vibraphone) *(M385)*
Trios (Flutes (2), viola) *(M360-362)*
Trios (Flutes (2), viola), Arranged *(M363-4)*
Trios (Flutes (2), viola d'amore) *(M360-362)*
Trios (Flutes (2), violin) *(M360-364)*
  NT Concertos (Flutes (2), violin with
     string orchestra)
     Flutes (2), violin with string
     orchestra
Trios (Flutes (2), violoncello) *(M360-364)*
  NT Concertos (Flutes (2), violoncello with
     string orchestra)
     Flutes (2), violoncello with string
     orchestra
Trios (Guitar, viola, violoncello) *(M370-372)*
Trios (Guitar, violin, viola) *(M370-372)*
  NT Suites (Guitar, violin, viola)
Trios (Guitar, violin, viola), Arranged *(M373-4)*
  NT Overtures arranged for guitar, violin, viola
Trios (Guitar, violin, violoncello) *(M370-372)*
  NT Suites (Guitar, violin, violoncello)
Trios (Guitar, violin, violoncello), Arranged
        (M373-4)
Trios (Guitar, violins (2))
  NT Waltzes (Guitar, violins (2))
Trios (Guitar, violins (2)), Arranged *(M373-4)*

Trios (Guitars (3)) *(M365-7)*
UF Guitar music (Guitars (3))
NT Concertos (Guitars (3) with chamber
orchestra)
Guitars (3) with chamber orchestra
Rondos (Guitars (3))
Trios (Harp, violin, violoncello) *(M370-372)*
NT Concertos (Harp, violin, violoncello)
Harp, violin, violoncello with orchestra
Trios (Harps (3)) *(M365-369)*
UF Harp music (Harps (3))
Trios (Harpsichord, bagpipe, hurdy-gurdy)
M340-M344
Trios (Harpsichord, bagpipes (2))
M315-M319
Trios (Harpsichord, bassoon, clarinet)
(M315-317)
BT Trios (Piano, bassoon, clarinet)
Trios (Harpsichord, bassoon, violin)
(M320-322)
Trios (Harpsichord, flute, harp) *(M335-7)*
BT Trios (Piano, flute, harp)
NT Concertos (Harpsichord, flute, harp
with string orchestra)
Harpsichord, flute, harp with string
orchestra
Trios (Harpsichord, flute, oboe) *(M315-317)*
BT Trios (Piano, flute, oboe)
NT Concertos (Harpsichord, flute, oboe
with string orchestra)
Harpsichord, flute, oboe with string
orchestra
Trios (Harpsichord, flute, oboe d'amore)
(M315-317)
BT Oboe d'amore music
Trios (Harpsichord, flute, recorder)
(M315-317)
BT Trios (Piano, flute, recorder)
Trios (Harpsichord, flute, viola) *(M320-322)*
BT Trios (Piano, flute, viola)
NT Suites (Harpsichord, flute, viola)
Trios (Harpsichord, flute, viola da gamba)
(M320-322)
BT Trios (Piano, flute, violoncello)
NT Suites (Harpsichord, flute, viola da gamba)
Trios (Harpsichord, flute, viola d'amore)
(M315-317)
Trios (Harpsichord, flute, violin) *(M320-322)*
BT Trios (Piano, flute, violin)
NT Concertos (Harpsichord, flute, violin
with string orchestra)
Harpsichord, flute, violin with string
orchestra
Suites (Harpsichord, flute, violin)
Trios (Harpsichord, flute, violoncello) *(M320-322)*
BT Trios (Piano, flute, violoncello)
NT Suites (Harpsichord, flute, violoncello)
Trios (Harpsichord, flutes (2)) *(M315-317)*
BT Trios (Piano, flutes (2))
NT Concertos (Harpsichord, flutes (2) with
string orchestra)
Harpsichord, flutes (2) with string orchestra
Suites (Harpsichord, flutes (2))

Trios (Harpsichord, oboe, recorder) *(M315-317)*
BT Trios (Piano, oboe, recorder)
NT Suites (Harpsichord, oboe, recorder)
Trios (Harpsichord, oboe, viola da gamba)
(M320-322)
BT Trios (Piano, oboe, violoncello)
Trios (Harpsichord, oboe, violin) *(M320-322)*
BT Trios (Piano, oboe, violin)
Trios (Harpsichord, oboe, violoncello)
(M320-322)
Trios (Harpsichord, oboes (2)) *(M315-317)*
BT Trios (Piano, oboes (2))
Trios (Harpsichord, piano, harp) *(M340-344)*
NT Concertos (Harpsichord, piano, harp
with string orchestra)
Harpsichord, piano, harp with string
orchestra
**Trios (Harpsichord, piano, trombone),
Arranged**
NT Concertos (Trombone)—Solo with
harpsichord and piano
Trios (Harpsichord, piano, violin)
(M340-344)
NT Concertos (Harpsichord, piano, violin)
Harpsichord, piano, violin with
orchestra
Trios (Harpsichord, recorder, viola)
(M320-322)
Trios (Harpsichord, recorder, viola da gamba)
(M320-322)
BT Trios (Piano, flute, violoncello)
Trios (Harpsichord, recorders (2)) *(M315-317)*
BT Trios (Piano, flutes (2))
NT Suites (Harpsichord, recorders (2))
**Trios (Harpsichord, tenor violin, viola da
gamba)** *(M310-M311; M312.4;
M313-M314)*
BT Tenor violin music
Trios (Harpsichord, trumpets (2)) *(M315-317)*
RT Trios (Piano, trumpets (2))
Trios (Harpsichord, viola, violoncello)
(M310-M311; M312.4)
BT Trios (Piano, viola, violoncello)
Trios (Harpsichord, violas (2)) *(M310-M311;
M312.4)*
NT Suites (Harpsichord, violas (2))
Trios (Harpsichord, viole da gamba (2))
(M310-312)
BT Trios (Piano, viole da gamba (2))
Trios (Harpsichord, viole d'amore (2))
BT Trios (Piano, viole d'amore (2))
NT Suites (Harpsichord, viole d'amore (2))
Trios (Harpsichord, violin, viola) *(M310-M311;
M312.4)*
BT Trios (Piano, violin, viola)
Trios (Harpsichord, violin, viola), Arranged
(M313-314)
Trios (Harpsichord, violin, viola da gamba)
(M310-312)
BT Piano trios
NT Suites (Harpsichord, violin, viola da gamba)
Variations (Harpsichord, violin, viola da
gamba)

Trios (Harpsichord, violin, violoncello)
  (M310-312)
  BT Piano trios
  NT Concertos (Harpsichord, violin,
       violoncello with string orchestra)
     Harpsichord, violin, violoncello with
       string orchestra
     Suites (Harpsichord, violin, violoncello)
**Trios (Harpsichord, violin, violoncello),
  Arranged** *(M313-314)*
Trios (Harpsichord, violins (2)) *(M310-M311;
  M312.4)*
  BT Trios (Piano, violins (2))
  NT Suites (Harpsichord, violins (2))
Trios (Harpsichord, violins (2)), Arranged
  (M313-314)
Trios (Harpsichord, violoncellos (2))
  (M310-M311; M312.4)
  BT Trios (Piano, violoncellos (2))
Trios (Harpsichord, viols (2)) *(M310-M311;
  M312.4; M990)*
  BT Trios (Piano, viols (2))
     Viol music
  NT Suites (Harpsichord, viols (2))
Trios (Horn, violin, violoncello) *(M360-362)*
  NT Suites (Horn, violin, violoncello)
Trios (Horns (2), violoncello) *(M360-362)*
Trios (Hurdy-gurdies (2), continuo)
Trios (Lute, violin, violoncello) *(M370-372)*
Trios (Lute, violin, violoncello), Arranged
  (M373-4)
Trios (Oboe, harp, viola) *(M380-382)*
Trios (Oboe, viola, violoncello) *(M360-362)*
  NT Suites (Oboe, viola, violoncello)
Trios (Oboe, violin, viola) *(M360-362)*
  NT Suites (Oboe, violin, viola)
Trios (Oboe, violin, violoncello) *(M360-362)*
  NT Concertos (Oboe, violin, violoncello)
     Concertos (Oboe, violin, violoncello
       with string orchestra)
     Oboe, violin, violoncello with orchestra
     Oboe, violin, violoncello with string
       orchestra
Trios (Oboes (2), percussion) *(M385)*
Trios (Ondes Martenot (2), percussion)
  (M385)
  BT Ondes Martenot music
Trios (Ondes Martenot (3)) *(M385)*
  UF Ondes Martenot music (Ondes
       Martenot (3))
Trios (Organ, flute, violoncello) *(M300-302)*
Trios (Organ, harp, timpani) *(M385)*
  NT Concertos (Organ, harp, timpani with
       string orchestra)
     Organ, harp, timpani with string
       orchestra
Trios (Organ, harp, violin) *(M300-302)*
Trios (Organ, oboe, violin) *(M300-302)*
Trios (Organ, oboes (2)) *(M300-302)*
Trios (Organ, piano, violin) *(M301-2)*
Trios (Organ, trumpets (2)) *(M300-302)*
Trios (Organ, trumpets (2)), Arranged
  (M303-4)

Trios (Organ, violin, viola) *(M300-302)*
  NT Suites (Organ, violin, viola)
Trios (Organ, violin, viola da gamba)
  (M300-302)
  NT Canons, fugues, etc. (Organ, violin,
       viola da gamba)
     Suites (Organ, violin, viola da gamba)
Trios (Organ, violin, violoncello) *(M300-302)*
Trios (Organ, violins (2)) *(M300-302)*
Trios (Percussion, piano (4 hands))
  USE Trios (Piano (4 hands), percussion)
Trios (Percussion, violin, viola) *(M385)*
Trios (Percussion, violoncellos (2)) *(M385)*
  BT Violoncello music (Violoncellos (2))
Trios (Piano (4 hands), percussion)
  (M340-344)
  UF Trios (Percussion, piano (4 hands))
  BT Percussion and piano music
Trios (Piano (4 hands), trombone)
  (M340-344)
  UF Trios (Trombone, piano (4 hands))
  BT Trombone and piano music
Trios (Piano (4 hands), violin) *(M312.4)*
  UF Trios (Violin, piano (4 hands))
  BT Violin and piano music
Trios (Piano, accordion, violin) *(M385)*
Trios (Piano, basset horn, clarinet)
  (M315-319)
Trios (Piano, bassoon, clarinet) *(M315-317)*
  NT Trios (Harpsichord, bassoon, clarinet)
Trios (Piano, bassoon, clarinet), Arranged
  (M318-319)
  NT Bassoon and clarinet with string
       orchestra—Solos with piano
     Concertos (Bassoon and clarinet)—
       Solos with piano
Trios (Piano, bassoon, flute) *(M315-317)*
Trios (Piano, bassoon, oboe) *(M315-317)*
  NT Suites (Piano, bassoon, oboe)
Trios (Piano, bassoon, oboe), Arranged
  (M318-319)
  NT Concertos (Bassoon and oboe with
       string orchestra)—Solos with piano
Trios (Piano, bassoon, trumpet), Arranged
  (M318-319)
  NT Concertos (Bassoon and trumpet with
       string orchestra)—Solos with piano
Trios (Piano, bassoon, viola) *(M320-322)*
Trios (Piano, bassoon, violin) *(M320-322)*
Trios (Piano, bassoon, violin), Arranged
  (M323-4)
  NT Concertos (Bassoon and violin with
       string orchestra)—Solos with piano
Trios (Piano, bassoon, violoncello)
  (M320-322)
Trios (Piano, bassoons (2))
  (M315-319)
Trios (Piano, bassoons (2)), Arranged
  (M318-319)
  NT Concertos (Bassoons (2) with
       string orchestra)—Solos with piano
Trios (Piano, clarinet, double bass)
  (M320-322)

Trios (Piano, clarinet, English horn)
  (M315-319)

Trios (Piano, clarinet, English horn),
  Arranged *(M318-319)*
  NT Concertos (Clarinet and English
    horn)—Solos with piano

Trios (Piano, clarinet, flute) *(M315-317)*
  NT Suites (Piano, clarinet, flute)

Trios (Piano, clarinet, flute), Arranged
  (M318-319)
  NT Clarinet and flute with orchestra—
    Solos with piano

Trios (Piano, clarinet, glockenspiel) *(M340-342)*
  BT Glockenspiel music

Trios (Piano, clarinet, horn) *(M315-317)*
  NT Suites (Piano, clarinet, horn)

Trios (Piano, clarinet, oboe) *(M315-317)*

Trios (Piano, clarinet, percussion) *(M340-342)*

Trios (Piano, clarinet, trombone) *(M315-317)*

Trios (Piano, clarinet, trumpet) *(M315-317)*

Trios (Piano, clarinet, trumpet), Arranged
  (M318-319)
  NT Concertos (Clarinet and trumpet with
    band)—Solos with piano

Trios (Piano, clarinet, viola) *(M320-324)*

Trios (Piano, clarinet, viola), Arranged
  (M323-324)
  NT Concertos (Clarinet and viola)—Solos
    with piano

Trios (Piano, clarinet, violin) *(M320-322)*
  NT Suites (Piano, clarinet, violin)
    Variations (Piano, clarinet, violin)

Trios (Piano, clarinet, violin), Arranged
  (M323-4)
  NT Concertos (Clarinet and violin)—Solos
    with piano
    Concertos (Clarinet and violin with
      string orchestra)—Solos with piano

Trios (Piano, clarinet, violoncello) *(M320-322)*
  Note under Piano trios

Trios (Piano, clarinet, violoncello), Arranged
  (M323-4)
  NT Concertos (Clarinet and violoncello)—
    Solos with piano

Trios (Piano, clarinet, xylophone) *(M340-342)*

Trios (Piano, clarinets (2)) *(M315-317)*

Trios (Piano, clarinets (2)), Arranged *(M318-319)*
  NT Concertos (Clarinets (2) with string
    orchestra)—Solos with piano

Trios (Piano, cornet, flute) *(M315-317)*

Trios (Piano, double basses (2)) *(M310-M311;*
  M312.4; M313-M314)

Trios (Piano, double basses (2)), Arranged
  (M313-314)
  NT Concertos (Double basses (2))—Solos
    with piano

Trios (Piano, English horn, flute) *(M315-317)*

Trios (Piano, English horn, flute), Arranged
  (M318-319)
  NT Concertos (English horn and flute with
    string orchestra)—Solos with piano

Trios (Piano, English horn, trumpet)
  (M315-317)

Trios (Piano, English horn, trumpet),
  Arranged *(M318-319)*
  NT English horn and trumpet with string
    orchestra—Solos with piano

Trios (Piano, flute, double bass) *(M320-322)*

Trios (Piano, flute, guitar) *(M335-7)*

Trios (Piano, flute, guitar), Arranged
  (M338-9)
  NT Overtures arranged for piano, flute,
    guitar

Trios (Piano, flute, harp) *(M335-7)*
  NT Trios (Harpsichord, flute, harp)
    Variations (Piano, flute, harp)

Trios (Piano, flute, harp), Arranged
  (M338-9)
  NT Concertos (Flute and harp)—Solos with
    piano

Trios (Piano, flute, horn) *(M320-322)*
  NT Concertos (Piano, flute, horn with
    string orchestra)
    Piano, flute, horn with string orchestra

Trios (Piano, flute, horn), Arranged
  (M323-4)
  NT Concertos (Flute and horn with string
    orchestra)—Solos with piano

Trios (Piano, flute, oboe) *(M315-317)*
  NT Suites (Piano, flute, oboe)
    Trios (Harpsichord, flute, oboe)
    Variations (Piano, flute, oboe)

Trios (Piano, flute, oboe), Arranged
  (M318-319)
  NT Concertos (Flute and oboe)—Solos with
    piano
    Flute and oboe with orchestra—Solos
      with piano
    Flute and oboe with string orchestra—Solos
      with piano

Trios (Piano, flute, recorder) *(M315-317)*
  NT Trios (Harpsichord, flute, recorder)

Trios (Piano, flute, viola) *(M320-322)*
  NT Concertos (Piano, flute, viola with
    string orchestra)
    Piano, flute, viola with string orchestra
    Trios (Harpsichord, flute, viola)

Trios (Piano, flute, viola), Arranged
  (M323-4)

Trios (Piano, flute, viola d'amore)
  (M320-322)

Trios (Piano, flute, viola d'amore), Arranged
  (M323-4)
  NT Concertos (Flute and viola d'amore
    with string orchestra), Arranged—
    Solos with piano

Trios (Piano, flute, violin) *(M320-322)*
  NT Concertos (Piano, flute, violin with
    instrumental ensemble)
    Concertos (Piano, flute, violin with
      string orchestra)
    Piano, flute, violin with instrumental
      ensemble
    Piano, flute, violin with string orchestra
    Suites (Piano, flute, violin)
    Trios (Harpsichord, flute, violin)

Trios (Piano, flute, violin), Arranged
    (M323-4)
    NT Concertos (Flute and violin)—Solos
         with piano
        Flute and violin with orchestra—Solos
         with piano
        Suites (Flute and violin with string
         orchestra)—Solos with piano
Trios (Piano, flute, violoncello) *(M320-322)*
    NT Trios (Harpsichord, flute, viola da
         gamba)
        Trios (Harpsichord, flute, violoncello)
        Trios (Harpsichord, recorder, viola da
         gamba)
Trios (Piano, flute, violoncello), Arranged
    (M323-4)
Trios (Piano, flutes (2)) *(M315-317)*
    NT Polkas (Piano, flutes (2))
        Suites (Piano, flutes (2))
        Trios (Harpsichord, flutes (2))
        Trios (Harpsichord, recorders (2))
Trios (Piano, flutes (2)), Arranged
    (M318-319)
    NT Concertos (Flutes (2))—Solos
         with piano
        Concertos (Flutes (2) with string
         orchestra)—Solos with piano
        Flutes (2) with orchestra—Solos
         with piano
        Suites (Flutes (2) with string orchestra),
         Arranged—Solo with piano
Trios (Piano, guitars (2))
    (M325-M329)
Trios (Piano, guitars (2)), Arranged
    (M328-M329)
    NT Concertos (Guitars (2))—Solos with piano
Trios (Piano, harp, viola) *(M330-332)*
Trios (Piano, harp, viola), Arranged
    (M333-4)
    NT Viola and harp with string orchestra—
         Solos with piano
Trios (Piano, harp, violin) *(M330-332)*
Trios (Piano, harp, violin), Arranged
    (M333-334)
    NT Violin and harp with orchestra—Solos
         with piano
Trios (Piano, horn, harp) *(M335-7)*
Trios (Piano, horn, tuba) *(M315-317)*
Trios (Piano, horn, violin) *(M320-322)*
    NT Variations (Piano, horn, violin)
        Piano, horn, violin with orchestra
        Variations (Piano, horn, violin)
Trios (Piano, horn, violoncello) *(M320-322)*
Trios (Piano, horns (2)) *(M315-317)*
Trios (Piano, horns (2)), Arranged *(M318-319)*
    NT Concertos (Horns (2))—Solos with
         piano
        Concertos (Horns (2) with string
         orchestra)—Solos with piano
Trios (Piano, mandolins (2)) *(M325-7)*
Trios (Piano, mandolins (2)), Arranged *(M328-9)*
    NT Concertos (Mandolins (2) with string
         orchestra)—Solos with piano

Trios (Piano, oboe, harp) *(M335-7)*
Trios (Piano, oboe, percussion) *(M385)*
Trios (Piano, oboe, recorder) *(M315-317)*
    NT Trios (Harpsichord, oboe, recorder)
Trios (Piano, oboe, viola) *(M320-322)*
Trios (Piano, oboe, violin) *(M320-322)*
    NT Trios (Harpsichord, oboe, violin)
Trios (Piano, oboe, violin), Arranged
    (M323-324)
    NT Concertos (Oboe and violin with string
         orchestra)—Solos with piano
Trios (Piano, oboe, violoncello) *(M320-322)*
    NT Trios (Harpsichord, oboe, viola da
         gamba)
Trios (Piano, oboes (2)) *(M315-317)*
    NT Trios (Harpsichord, oboes (2))
Trios (Piano, oboes (2)), Arranged
    (M318-319)
    NT Concertos (Oboes (2) with string
         orchestra)—Solos with piano
Trios (Piano, ondes Martenot, percussion)
    (M385)
    BT Ondes Martenot music
Trios (Piano, percussion) *(M340-344)*
    NT Variations (Piano, percussion)
Trios (Piano, percussion), Arranged
    (M343-344)
    NT Variations (Percussion with orchestra)
         —Solos with piano
Trios (Piano, percussion, double bass)
    (M385)
Trios (Piano, percussion, viola) *(M340-342)*
Trios (Piano, percussion, violin) *(M340-342)*
    NT Suites (Piano, percussion, violin)
Trios (Piano, recorder, viola da gamba)
    (M320-322)
Trios (Piano, recorder, viola da gamba),
    Arranged *(M323-4)*
    NT Concertos (Recorder and viola da
         gamba with string orchestra)—Solos
         with piano
Trios (Piano, recorder, violin) *(M320-322)*
Trios (Piano, recorder, violin), Arranged
    (M323-4)
    NT Concertos (Recorder and violin with
         string orchestra)—Solos with piano
Trios (Piano, recorders (2)) *(M315-317)*
Trios (Piano, recorders (2)), Arranged
    (M318-319)
    NT Concertos (Recorders (2))—Solos with
         piano
        Concertos (Recorders (2) with string
         orchestra)—Solos with piano
Trios (Piano, recorders (2)), Juvenile
    (M1413-1417)
Trios (Piano, san hsien, erh hu)
    BT Erh hu music
        San hsien music
Trios (Piano, saxophone, violin) *(M320-322)*
Trios (Piano, saxophone, trumpet)
    (M315-317)
Trios (Piano, saxophone, viola d'amore)
    (M320-322)

Trios (Piano, trombone, trumpet)
    (M315-317)
    NT Suites (Piano, trombone, trumpet)
Trios (Piano, trombone, trumpet), Arranged
    (M318-319)
    NT Concertos (Trombone and trumpet)—
            Solos with piano
        Concertos (Trombone and trumpet with
            string orchestra)—Solos with piano
Trios (Piano, trumpet, drum) *(M385)*
Trios (Piano, trumpet, drum), Arranged
    (M385)
    NT Trumpet and drum with band—Solos
            with piano
Trios (Piano, trumpet, guitar) *(M335-7)*
Trios (Piano, trumpet, viola) *(M320-322)*
    NT Concertos (Piano, trumpet, viola)
        Piano, trumpet, viola with orchestra
Trios (Piano, trumpets (2)) *(M315-317)*
    RT Trios (Harpsichord, trumpets (2))
    NT Piano, trumpets (2) with string
            orchestra
Trios (Piano, trumpets (2)), Arranged
    (M318-319)
    NT Concertos (Trumpets (2) with string
            orchestra)—Solos with piano
        Suites (Trumpets (2) with string
            orchestra)—Solos with piano
        Trumpets (2) with string orchestra—
            Solos with piano
Trios (Piano, tuba, violin) *(M320-322)*
Trios (Piano, viola, violoncello) *(M310-M311;*
    M312.4)
    NT Trios (Harpsichord, viola, violoncello)
Trios (Piano, violas (2)) *(M310-M311; M312.4;*
    M313-M314)
Trios (Piano, violas (2)), Arranged *(M313-314)*
    NT Concertos (Violas (2) with string
            orchestra)—Solos with piano
Trios (Piano, viole da gamba (2)) *(M310-312)*
    NT Trios (Harpsichord, viole da gamba (2))
Trios (Piano, viole d'amore (2)) *(M310-M311;*
    M312.4)
    NT Suites (Piano, viole d'amore (2))
        Trios (Harpsichord, viole d'amore (2))
Trios (Piano, violin, double bass) *(M310-M311;*
    M312.4; M313-M314)
Trios (Piano, violin, double bass), Arranged
    (M313-314)
    NT Concertos (Violin and double bass)—
            Solos with piano
        Violin and double bass with
            instrumental ensemble—Solos with piano
Trios (Piano, violin, viola) *(M310-M311; M312.4)*
    NT Trios (Harpsichord, violin, viola)
        Waltzes (Piano, violin, viola)
Trios (Piano, violin, viola), Arranged *(M313-314)*
    NT Concertos (Violin and viola)—
            Solos with piano
        Concertos (Violin and viola with
            chamber orchestra)—Solos with piano
        Violin and viola with orchestra—Solos
            with piano

Trios (Piano, violin, viola da gamba) *(M310-312)*
Trios (Piano, violin, violoncello)
    USE Piano trios
Trios (Piano, violins (2)) *(M310-M311; M312.4)*
    NT Canons, fugues, etc. (Piano, violins (2))
        Concertos (Piano, violins (2) with string
            orchestra)
        Piano, violins (2) with string orchestra
        Suites (Piano, violins (2))
        Trios (Harpsichord, violins (2))
    Note under Piano trios
Trios (Piano, violins (2)), Arranged *(M313-314)*
    NT Concertos (Violins (2))—Solos with
            piano
        Concertos (Violins (2) with string
            orchestra)—Solos with piano
        Concertos (Violins (2) with string
            orchestra), Arranged—Solos with
            piano
        Violins (2) with orchestra—Solos
            with piano
Trios (Piano, violins (2)), Juvenile *(M1413-1417)*
Trios (Piano, violoncello, double bass)
    (M310-M311; M312.4; M313-M314)
Trios (Piano, violoncello, double bass),
    Arranged *(M313-314)*
    NT Violoncello and double bass with
            orchestra—Solos with piano
Trios (Piano, violoncellos (2)) *(M310-M311;*
    M312.4)
    NT Suites (Piano, violoncellos (2))
        Trios (Harpsichord, violoncellos (2))
Trios (Piano, violoncellos (2)), Arranged
    (M313-314)
    NT Concertos (Violoncellos (2) with string
            orchestra)—Solos with piano
        Violoncellos (2) with orchestra—Solos
            with piano
Trios (Piano, viols (2)) *(M310-M311; M312.4;*
    M990)
    BT Viol music
    NT Trios (Harpsichord, viols (2))
Trios (Piano, wind instruments (2))
    (M315-317)
Trios (Piano, wind instruments (2)), Arranged
    (M318-319)
Trios (Piano, xylophones (2)) *(M340-342)*
    BT Xylophone music
Trios (Piano, xylophones (2)), Arranged
    (M343-4)
Trios (Pianos (2), percussion) *(M340-342)*
Trios (Pianos (2), percussion), Arranged
    (M343-344)
    NT Percussion with orchestra—Solo with
            pianos (2)
Trios (Pianos (2), trumpet) *(M340-342)*
Trios (Pianos (2), trumpet), Arranged *(M343-4)*
    NT Concertos (Trumpet and piano with
            string orchestra)—Solos with piano
Trios (Pianos (2), viola) *(M340-344)*
Trios (Pianos (2), viola), Arranged *(M343-344)*
    NT Concertos (Viola and piano)—Solos
            with piano

Trios (Pianos (2), violin), Arranged
   NT Concertos (Violin and piano)—Solos
        with piano
        Concertos (Violin and piano with
          chamber orchestra)—Solos with piano
        Concertos (Violin and piano with string
          orchestra)—Solos with piano
        Suites (Violin and piano with orchestra)
          —Solos with piano
Trios (Recorder, guitar, violoncello) *(M380-382)*
   NT Suites (Recorder, guitar, violoncello)
Trios (Recorder, lute, viol) *(M380-382)*
   BT Viol music
Trios (Recorder, violin, viola) *(M360-362)*
   NT Suites (Recorder, violin, viola)
Trios (Recorder, violin, violoncello)
      (M360-362)
   NT Canons, fugues, etc. (Recorder, violin,
        violoncello)
Trios (Recorders (2), guitar) *(M375-7)*
   NT Suites (Recorders (2), guitar)
Trios (Recorders (2), lute) *(M375-7)*
Trios (Recorders (2), violin) *(M360-362)*
Trios (Reed-organ, harps (2)) *(M305-309)*
   BT Reed-organ music
Trios (Sarod, sitar, tabla)
Trios (Sitar, tabla, violin)
   BT Sitar music
      Tabla music
Trios (Trombone, percussion, violoncello)
      (M385)
Trios (Trombone, piano (4 hands))
  USE Trios (Piano (4 hands), trombone)
Trios (Trombone, viola, violoncello)
      (M360-362)
   NT Suites (Trombone, viola, violoncello)
Trios (Trumpet, harp, chimes) *(M385)*
   NT Concertos (Trumpet, harp, chimes with
        string orchestra)
      Trumpet, harp, chimes with string
        orchestra
Trios (Vina, percussion, violin)
   BT Vina music
Trios (Violin, piano (4 hands))
  USE Trios (Piano (4 hands), violin)
Tromba marina
  USE Sea-trumpet
Trombone *(ML965-8)*
   BT Brass instruments
   RT Baritone (Musical instrument)
      Euphonium
   NT Bass trombone
      Sackbut
  —Methods
  ——Self-instruction *(MT468)*
     UF Trombone—Self-instruction
  —Orchestra studies *(MT466)*
     BT Trombone—Studies and exercises
  —Self-instruction
     USE Trombone—Methods—
         Self-instruction
  —Studies and exercises *(MT465)*
     NT Trombone—Orchestra studies

Trombone and clarinet music
  USE Clarinet and trombone music
Trombone and continuo music
   UF Continuo and trombone music
Trombone and double-bass music *(M290-291)*
   UF Double-bass and trombone music
Trombone and English horn music
  USE English horn and trombone music
Trombone and flute music
  USE Flute and trombone music
Trombone and horn music
  USE Horn and trombone music
Trombone and oboe music
  USE Oboe and trombone music
Trombone and organ music *(M182-6)*
   UF Organ and trombone music
   NT Chorale preludes (Trombone and organ)
      Sonatas (Trombone and organ)
Trombone and percussion music *(M298)*
   UF Percussion and trombone music
Trombone and piano music *(M262-3)*
   UF Piano and trombone music
   NT Marches (Trombone and piano)
      Sonatas (Trombone and piano)
      Suites (Trombone and piano)
      Trios (Piano (4 hands), trombone)
      Variations (Trombone and piano)
      Waltzes (Trombone and piano)
Trombone and piano music, Arranged *(M262-3)*
   NT Concertos (Trombone)—Solo with piano
      Concertos (Trombone with band)—Solo
        with piano
      Concertos (Trombone with brass band)
        —Solo with piano
      Concertos (Trombone with chamber
        orchestra)—Solo with piano
      Concertos (Trombone with string
        orchestra)—Solo with piano
      Symphonies (Trombone with orchestra)
        —Solo with piano
      Trombone with band—Solo with piano
      Trombone with chamber orchestra—
        Solo with piano
      Trombone with instrumental ensemble
        —Solo with piano
      Trombone with orchestra—Solo with piano
      Trombone with string orchestra—Solo
        with piano
Trombone and timpani with string orchestra
      (M1140-1141)
   RT Concertos (Trombone and timpani with
        string orchestra)
   NT Suites (Trombone and timpani with
        string orchestra)
Trombone and trumpet music *(M288-9)*
   UF Trumpet and trombone music
   NT Concertos (Trombone and trumpet with
        band)
      Concertos (Trombone and trumpet with
        string orchestra)
      Trombone and trumpet with band
      Trombone and trumpet with string orchestra
      Variations (Trombone and trumpet)

Trombone and trumpet with band *(M1205-6)*
  BT Trombone and trumpet music
  RT Concertos (Trombone and trumpet with band)
  NT Suites (Trombone and trumpet with band)
  —Scores *(M1205)*
Trombone and trumpet with brass band *(M1205; M1257)*
  RT Concertos (Trombone and trumpet with brass band)
Trombone and trumpet with orchestra *(M1040-1041)*
  RT Concertos (Trombone and trumpet)
Trombone and trumpet with string orchestra *(M1105-6)*
  BT Trombone and trumpet music
  RT Concertos (Trombone and trumpet with string orchestra)
  —Scores *(M1105-6)*
Trombone ensembles *(M955-M956; M957.4; M958-M959)*
Trombone music *(M90-94)*
  SA Concertos, Minuets, Sonatas, Suites, *and similar headings with specification of instruments;* Brass trios [quartets, etc.], Trios [Quartets, etc.], *and* Wind trios [quartets, etc.] *followed by specifications which include the trombone; also* Brass ensembles, Wind ensembles, *and headings that begin with the words trombone or trombones*
Trombone music (Trombones 2)) *(M288-9)*
  NT Canons, fugues, etc. (Trombones (2))
      Sonatas (Trombones (2))
Trombone music (Trombones (3))
  USE Brass trios (Trombones (3))
Trombone music (Trombones (4))
  USE Brass quartets (Trombones (4))
Trombone music (Trombones (5))
  USE Brass quintets (Trombones (5))
Trombone music (Trombones (7))
  USE Brass septets (Trombones (7))
Trombone music (Trombones (8))
  USE Brass octets (Trombones (8))
Trombone with band *(M1205)*
  BT Band music
  RT Concertos (Trombone with band)
  —Solo with piano *(M1206)*
      BT Trombone and piano music, Arranged
Trombone with band, Arranged *(M1257)*
Trombone with brass band *(M1205-1206)*
  RT Concertos (Trombone with brass band)
Trombone with brass ensemble
Trombone with chamber orchestra *(M1032-3)*
  RT Concertos (Trombone with chamber orchestra)
  —Solo with piano *(M1033)*
      BT Trombone and piano music, Arranged

Trombone with instrumental ensemble
  RT Concertos (Trombone with instrumental ensemble)
  —Solo with piano *(M262-263)*
      BT Trombone and piano music, Arranged
Trombone with orchestra *(M1032-3)*
  BT Orchestral music
  RT Concertos (Trombone)
  NT Symphonies (Trombone with orchestra)
  —Solo with piano *(M1033)*
      BT Trombone and piano music, Arranged
Trombone with string ensemble
  RT Concertos (Trombone with string ensemble)
  NT Variations (Trombone with string ensemble)
Trombone with string orchestra *(M1105-6)*
  RT Concertos (Trombone with string orchestra)
  NT Variations (Trombone with string orchestra)
  —Solo with piano *(M1133)*
      BT Trombone and piano music, Arranged
Trombones (2) with string orchestra *(M1132-1133)*
  RT Concertos (Trombones (2) with string orchestra)
Trombones (3), trumpets (3) with band *(M1205-6)*
  BT Brass sextets (Trombones (3), trumpets (3))
  RT Concertos (Trombones (3), trumpets (3) with band)
Trombones (3) with band *(M1205-6)*
  BT Brass trios (Trombones (3))
  RT Concertos (Trombones (3) with band)
  —Solos with piano *(M1206)*
      BT Quartets (Piano, trombones (3)), Arranged
Trombones (4) with band *(M1205)*
  BT Brass quartets (Trombones (4))
  RT Concertos (Trombones (4) with band)
Tropes (Music)
  UF Verbetas
  RT Sequences (Music)
Troubadours [May Subd Geog] *(General, PC3304-PC3330; Manners and customs, GT3650; Music, ML182)*
  UF Jongleurs
  BT Bards and bardism
      Minstrels
  RT Minnesingers
      Trouvères
Trouvères [May Subd Geog] *(French literature, PQ199; Music, ML182)*
  UF Jongleurs
  BT Bards and bardism
      Minstrels
  RT Minnesingers
      Troubadours

Trumpet (*History and construction,*
      ML960-ML963; Manners and customs,
      GT5020)
  UF Natural trumpet
        Valve trumpet
  BT Brass instruments
        Bugle
  RT Cornet
  NT Siwa (Musical instrument)
  —Methods
  — —Self-instruction (*MT448*)
     UF Trumpet—Self-instruction
  —Methods (Jazz) (*MT442*)
  —Orchestra studies (*MT446*)
     BT Trumpet—Studies and exercises
  —Self-instruction
     USE Trumpet—Methods—
          Self-instruction
  —Studies and exercises (*MT445*)
     NT Trumpet—Orchestra studies
  —Studies and exercises (Jazz)
Trumpet and bassoon music
  USE Bassoon and trumpet music
Trumpet and chimes with string orchestra
      (*M1140-1141*)
  RT Concertos (Trumpet and chimes with
        string orchestra)
Trumpet and clarinet music
  USE Clarinet and trumpet music
Trumpet and continuo music
  UF Continuo and trumpet music
  NT Sonatas (Trumpet and continuo)
        Suites (Trumpet and continuo)
Trumpet and cornet music
  USE Cornet and trumpet music
Trumpet and double-bass music (*M290-M291*)
  UF Double-bass and trumpet music
Trumpet and drum music (*M298*)
  UF Drum and trumpet music
  NT Trumpet and drum with band
Trumpet and drum with band (*M1205*)
  BT Trumpet and drum music
  —Solos with piano (*M1257*)
     BT Trios (Piano, trumpet, drum),
         Arranged
Trumpet and English horn music
  USE English horn and trumpet music
Trumpet and flute music
  USE Flute and trumpet music
Trumpet and guitar music (*M296-297*)
  UF Guitar and trumpet music
Trumpet and harp music (*M296-297*)
  UF Harp and trumpet music
  NT Variations (Trumpet and harp)
Trumpet and harpsichord music (*M260-261*)
  UF Harpsichord and trumpet music
  NT Sonatas (Trumpet and harpsichord)
Trumpet and harpsichord music, Arranged
      (*M260-261*)
  NT Trumpet with string orchestra—Solo
        with harpsichord
Trumpet and horn music
  USE Horn and trumpet music

Trumpet and marimba music (*M298*)
  UF Marimba and trumpet music
  NT Suites (Trumpet and marimba)
Trumpet and oboe music
  USE Oboe and trumpet music
Trumpet and organ music (*M182-4*)
  UF Organ and trumpet music
  NT Canons, fugues, etc. (Trumpet and organ)
        Chorale preludes (Trumpet and organ)
        Marches (Trumpet and organ)
        Sonatas (Trumpet and organ)
        Suites (Trumpet and organ)
        Variations (Trumpet and organ)
Trumpet and organ music, Arranged
      (*M185-6*)
Trumpet and percussion music (*M298*)
  UF Percussion and trumpet music
Trumpet and piano music (*M260-261*)
  UF Piano and trumpet music
  NT Concertos (Trumpet and piano)
        Concertos (Trumpet and piano with
          string orchestra)
        Marches (Trumpet and piano)
        Polkas (Trumpet and piano)
        Rondos (Trumpet and piano)
        Sonatas (Trumpet and piano)
        Suites (Trumpet and piano)
        Symphonies (Trumpet and piano)
        Trumpet and piano with orchestra
        Trumpet and piano with string
          orchestra
        Variations (Trumpet and piano)
        Waltzes (Trumpet and piano)
Trumpet and piano music, Arranged
      (*M260-261*)
  NT Concertos (Trumpet)—Solo with piano
        Concertos (Trumpet with band)—Solo
          with piano
        Concertos (Trumpet with chamber
          orchestra)—Solo with piano
        Concertos (Trumpet with string
          ensemble)—Solo with piano
        Concertos (Trumpet with string
          orchestra)—Solo with piano
        Suites (Trumpet with orchestra)—Solo
          with piano
        Suites (Trumpet with string orchestra)
          —Solo with piano
        Trumpet with orchestra—Solo
          with piano
        Trumpet with string orchestra—Solo
          with piano
        Variations (Trumpet with string
          orchestra)—Solo with piano
Trumpet and piano with chamber orchestra
      (*M1040-1041*)
  RT Concertos (Trumpet and piano with
        chamber orchestra)
Trumpet and piano with orchestra
      (*M1040-1041*)
  BT Orchestral music
        Trumpet and piano music
  RT Concertos (Trumpet and piano)

Trumpet and piano with string orchestra
    (M1105-6)
  BT String-orchestra music
       Trumpet and piano music
  RT Concertos (Trumpet and piano with
       string orchestra)
Trumpet and recorder music
  USE Recorder and trumpet music
Trumpet and saxophone music
  USE Saxophone and trumpet music
Trumpet and timpani music *(M298)*
  UF Timpani and trumpet music
Trumpet and timpani with orchestra
    (M1040-M1041)
  NT Concertos (Trumpet and timpani)
Trumpet and trombone music
  USE Trombone and trumpet music
Trumpet and tuba music *(M288-289)*
  UF Tuba and trumpet music
Trumpet and tuba with brass ensemble
  RT Concertos (Trumpet and tuba with
       brass ensemble)
Trumpet and tuba with instrumental ensemble
  RT Concertos (Trumpet and tuba with
       instrumental ensemble)
Trumpet and vibraphone music *(M298)*
  UF Vibraphone and trumpet music
Trumpet and violin music *(M290-291)*
  UF Violin and trumpet music
  NT Concertos (Trumpet and violin with
       string orchestra)
       Trumpet and violin with string
       orchestra
Trumpet and violin with string orchestra
    (M1105-6)
  BT Trumpet and violin music
  RT Concertos (Trumpet and violin with
       string orchestra)
Trumpet and violoncello music *(M290-291)*
  UF Violoncello and trumpet music
Trumpet-calls *(M1270; Military, UH40-45)*
  BT Military music
       Signals and signaling
  RT Bugle-calls
       Fanfares
       Hunting music
       Military calls
Trumpet ensembles *(M955-M956; M957.4; M958-M959)*
       Here are entered compositions for ten or
       more trumpets and collections of com-
       positions for a varying number of
       trumpets.
Trumpet, harp, chimes with string orchestra
    (M1105-6)
  BT Trios (Trumpet, harp, chimes)
  RT Concertos (Trumpet, harp, chimes with
       string orchestra)
  —Scores *(M1105)*
Trumpet music *(M85-89)*
  SA Concertos, Minuets, Sonatas, Suites,
       and similar headings with
       specification of instruments; Brass

Trumpet music *(M85-89)*
  (Continued)
  SA trios [quartets, etc.], Trios [Quartets,
       etc.], *and* Wind trios [quartets, etc.]
       followed by specifications which
       include the trumpet; also Brass
       ensembles, Wind ensembles, *and*
       headings that begin with the words
       trumpet or trumpets
  NT Bugle and drum music
       Marches (Trumpet)
       Recorded accompaniments (Trumpet)
       Variations (Trumpet)
Trumpet music, Arranged *(M88-9)*
Trumpet music (Jazz) *(M85-89)*
  NT Trumpet with jazz ensemble
Trumpet music (Trumpets (2)) *(M288-9)*
  NT Concertos (Trumpets (2) with string
       orchestra)
       Suites (Trumpets (2))
       Trumpets (2) with orchestra
       Trumpets (2) with string orchestra
Trumpet music (Trumpets (2)), Arranged
    (M288-9)
Trumpet music (Trumpets (3))
  USE Brass trios (Trumpets (3))
Trumpet music (Trumpets (4))
  USE Brass quartets (Trumpets (4))
Trumpet music (Trumpets (5))
  USE Brass quintets (Trumpets (5))
Trumpet music (Trumpets (6))
  USE Brass sextets (Trumpets (6))
Trumpet music (Trumpets (7))
  USE Brass septets (Trumpets (7))
Trumpet music (Trumpets (8))
  USE Brass octets (Trumpets (8))
Trumpet players [May Subd Geog]
  UF Trumpeters
  BT Musicians
Trumpet with band *(M1205)*
  RT Concertos (Trumpet with band)
  NT Variations (Trumpet with band)
       Waltzes (Trumpet with band)
Trumpet with brass band *(M1205; M1257)*
  RT Concertos (Trumpet with brass band)
Trumpet with brass ensemble
Trumpet with chamber orchestra *(M1030-1031)*
  RT Concertos (Trumpet with chamber
       orchestra)
Trumpet with dance orchestra *(M1353)*
  BT Dance-orchestra music
  RT Concertos (Trumpet with dance orchestra)
Trumpet with instrumental ensemble
  RT Concertos (Trumpet with instrumental
       ensemble)
Trumpet with jazz ensemble *(M1366)*
  BT Trumpet music (Jazz)
Trumpet with orchestra *(M1030-1031)*
  RT Concertos (Trumpet)
  NT Rondos (Trumpet with orchestra)
       Suites (Trumpet with orchestra)
  —Solo with piano *(M1031)*
      BT Trumpet and piano music, Arranged

Trumpet with orchestra, Arranged
   (M1030-1031)
Trumpet with percussion ensemble
   RT Concertos (Trumpet with percussion
        ensemble)
Trumpet with string ensemble
   RT Concertos (Trumpet with string
        ensemble)
Trumpet with string orchestra *(M1105-6)*
   RT Concertos (Trumpet with string
        orchestra)
   NT Canons, fugues, etc. (Trumpet with
        string orchestra)
        Overtures (Trumpet with string orchestra)
        Suites (Trumpet with string orchestra)
        Variations (Trumpet with string
        orchestra)
   —Solo with harpsichord *(M1131)*
        BT Trumpet and harpsichord music,
Arranged
   —Solo with piano *(M1106)*
        BT Trumpet and piano music, Arranged
Trumpet with string orchestra, Arranged
   (M1105-6)
   —Scores *(M1105)*
Trumpet with wind ensemble
   RT Concertos (Trumpet with wind
        ensemble)
Trumpets (2) with band *(M1205-M1206;*
   M1257)
   RT Concertos (Trumpets (2) with band)
Trumpets (2) with instrumental ensemble
   RT Concertos (Trumpets (2) with
        instrumental ensemble)
Trumpets (2) with orchestra *(M1030-1031)*
   BT Trumpet music (Trumpets (2))
   RT Concertos (Trumpets (2))
Trumpets (2) with orchestra, Arranged
   (M1030-1031)
Trumpets (2) with string orchestra
   (M1105-6)
   BT String-orchestra music
        Trumpet music (Trumpets (2))
   RT Concertos (Trumpets (2) with string
        orchestra)
   NT Suites (Trumpets (2) with string
        orchestra)
   —Solos with piano *(M1131)*
        BT Trios (Piano, trumpets (2)),
        Arranged
Trumpets (3) with band *(M1205-M1206; M1257)*
   BT Brass trios (Trumpets (3))
   RT Concertos (Trumpets (3) with band)
   —Solos with piano *(M1206)*
        BT Quartets (Piano, trumpets (3)),
        Arranged
Trumpets (3) with orchestra *(M1030-1031)*
   BT Brass trios (Trumpets (3))
   RT Concertos (Trumpets (3))
Trumpets (3) with string orchestra *(M1130-1131)*
   BT Brass trios (Trumpets (3))
   RT Concertos (Trumpets (3) with string
        orchestra)

Trumpets (4) with string orchestra *(M1130-1131)*
   BT Brass quartets (Trumpets (4))
   RT Concertos (Trumpets (4) with string
        orchestra)
Trumpets (5), percussion with string orchestra
   (M1140-1141)
   BT Octets (Trumpets (5), percussion)
        Sextets (Trumpets (5), percussion)
   RT Concertos (Trumpets (5), percussion
        with string orchestra)
Trumpets (8) with string orchestra *(M1130-1131)*
   BT Brass octets (Trumpets (8))
   RT Concertos (Trumpets (8) with string
        orchestra)
Tsogo songs
   USE Songs, Tsogo
Tsonga folk-songs
   USE Folk-songs, Tsonga
Tswana folk-songs
   USE Folk-songs, Tswana
Tswana hymns
   USE Hymns, Tswana
Tuba *(ML970-973)*
   UF Bass horn
        Bombardon
        Helicon bass
        Pelittone
        Sousaphone
   BT Brass instruments
   RT Horn (Musical instrument)
   NT Ophicleide
   —Orchestra studies *(MT486)*
        BT Tuba—Studies and exercises
   —Studies and exercises *(MT485)*
        NT Tuba—Orchestra studies
Tuba and bassoon music
   USE Bassoon and tuba music
Tuba and clarinet music
   USE Clarinet and tuba music
Tuba and euphonium music
   USE Euphonium and tuba music
Tuba and percussion music *(M297-298)*
   UF Percussion and tuba music
   NT Canons, fugues, etc. (Tuba and
        percussion)
Tuba and piano music *(M264-5)*
   UF Piano and tuba music
   NT Chaconnes (Tuba and piano)
        Sonatas (Tuba and piano)
        Suites (Tuba and piano)
        Variations (Tuba and piano)
        Waltzes (Tuba and piano)
Tuba and piano music, Arranged *(M264-5)*
   NT Concertos (Tuba)—Solo with piano
        Concertos (Tuba with band)—Solo with
        piano
        Concertos (Tuba with brass band)—
        Solo with piano
        Concertos (Tuba with string orchestra)
        —Solo with piano
        Tuba with band—Solo with piano
        Waltzes (Tuba with wind ensemble)—
        Solo with piano

Tuba and saxophone music
  USE Saxophone and tuba music
Tuba and timpani music *(M298)*
  UF Timpani and tuba music
Tuba and trumpet music
  USE Trumpet and tuba music
Tuba and vibraphone music *(M298)*
  UF Vibraphone and tuba music
Tuba ensembles *(M955-M956; M957.4;*
      M958-M959)
      Here are entered compositions for ten or
        more tubas and collections of composi-
        tions for a varying number of tubas.
      Note under Brass ensembles
Tuba language
  USE Tuvinian language
Tuba music *(M95-99)*
  SA Concertos, Minuets, Sonatas, Suites,
        and similar headings with
        specification of instruments; Brass
        trios [quartets, etc.], Trios [Quartets,
        etc.], *and* Wind trios [quartets, etc.]
        followed by specifications which
        include the tuba; also Brass
        ensembles, Wind ensembles, *and*
        headings that begin with the words
        tuba or tubas
  NT Suites (Tuba)
Tuba music (Jazz)
      M95-M99
Tuba music (Tubas (2))
      (M288-M289)
  NT Canons, fugues, etc. (Tubas (2))
      Marches (Tubas (2))
Tuba music (Tubas (4))
  USE Brass quartets (Tubas (4))
Tuba music (Tubas (6))
  USE Brass sextets (Tubas (6))
Tuba with band *(M1205-1206)*
  RT Concertos (Tuba with band)
  —Solo with piano *(M1206)*
      BT Tuba and piano music, Arranged
Tuba with band, Arranged *(M1257)*
Tuba with brass band *(M1205-M1206; M1257)*
  RT Concertos (Tuba with brass band)
Tuba with brass ensemble
  RT Concertos (Tuba with brass ensemble)
  NT Variations (Tuba with brass ensemble)
Tuba with instrumental ensemble
  RT Concertos (Tuba with instrumental
      ensemble)
  NT Marches (Tuba with instrumental
      ensemble)
Tuba with orchestra *(M1034-5)*
  RT Concertos (Tuba)
Tuba with percussion ensemble
  RT Concertos (Tuba with percussion
      ensemble)
Tuba with string ensemble
  RT Concertos (Tuba with string ensemble)
  BT Concertos (Tuba with string ensemble)
Tuba with string orchestra *(M1105-6)*
  RT Concertos (Tuba with string orchestra)

Tuba with wind ensemble
  RT Concertos (Tuba with wind ensemble)
  NT Waltzes (Tuba with wind ensemble)
Tunbūk *(ML1040)*
  UF Dombäck
      Dombak
  BT Musical instruments—Iran
Tunbūk and tar music
  USE Tar and tunbūk music
Tunbūk music *(M146)*
Tune-books
      Here are entered collections of hymn
        tunes without words, or with single
        stanzas of text. Works about tunes are
        entered under the heading Hymn
        tunes.
  BT Hymn tunes
  RT Hymn tunes
  NT Chorales
      Note under Hymn tunes
Tuning *(History, ML3809; Instruction,*
      MT165)
  BT Musical instruments
      Stringed instruments
      Stringed instruments, Bowed
  SA *subdivision* Tuning *under specific*
      instruments and types of
      instruments, e.g. Piano—Tuning;
      Brass instruments—Tuning
  NT Musical pitch
      Musical temperament
  —Electronic equipment
Tupan
  UF Topan
      T'pan
  BT Drum
Turkic songs
  USE Songs, Turkic
Turkmen music
  USE Music, Turkmen
Turks in opera
  BT Opera
Tuvinian folk-songs
  USE Folk-songs, Tuvinian
Twelve-note system
  USE Twelve-tone system
Twelve-tone system
  UF Serial composition
      Twelve-note system
      Twelve-tone technique
  BT Harmony
      Music—Theory
      Musical intervals and scales
Twelve-tone technique
  USE Twelve-tone system
Twi ballads
  USE Ballads, Twi
Two clarinets with orchestra
  USE Clarinets (2) with orchestra
Two flutes and glockenspiel with string
      orchestra
  USE Flutes (2), glockenspiel with string
      orchestra

Two flutes, harpsichord with string orchestra
  USE Harpsichord, flutes (2) with string
        orchestra
Two flutes, marimba with string orchestra
  USE Flutes (2), marimba with string
        orchestra
Two flutes with chamber orchestra
  USE Flutes (2) with chamber orchestra
Two flutes with orchestra
  USE Flutes (2) with orchestra
Two flutes with string orchestra
  USE Flutes (2) with string orchestra
Two guitars with chamber orchestra
  USE Guitars (2) with chamber orchestra
Two harpsichords with orchestra
  USE Harpsichords (2) with orchestra
Two harpsichords with string orchestra
  USE Harpsichords (2) with string orchestra
Two horns with orchestra
  USE Horns (2) with orchestra
Two horns with string orchestra
  USE Horns (2) with string orchestra
Two hurdy-gurdies with orchestra
  USE Hurdy-gurdies (2) with orchestra
Two pianos with instrumental ensemble
  USE Pianos (2) with instrumental ensemble
Two pianos with orchestra
  USE Pianos (2) with orchestra
Two recorders with orchestra
  USE Recorders (2) with orchestra
Two recorders with string orchestra
  USE Recorders (2) with string orchestra
Two violins, piano with string orchestra
  USE Piano, violins (2) with string orchestra
Two violins, viola with chamber orchestra
  USE Violins (2), viola with chamber
        orchestra
Two violins, viola with orchestra
  USE Violins (2), viola with orchestra
Two violins with orchestra
  USE Violins (2) with orchestra
Two violins with string orchestra
  USE Violins (2) with string orchestra
Two violoncellos with chamber orchestra
  USE Violoncellos (2) with chamber orchestra
Two violoncellos with orchestra
  USE Violoncellos (2) with orchestra
Two violoncellos with string orchestra
  USE Violoncellos (2) with string orchestra
Txistu
  USE Galoubet
Tympani
  USE Timpani
Type and type-founding [May Subd Geog]
        (Z250-251)
  —Music-type
    USE Music printing
'Ud
  USE Oud
Ukrainian folk-songs
  USE Folk-songs, Ukrainian
Ukrainian hymns
  USE Hymns, Ukrainian

Ukulele *(ML1015-1018)*
  UF Yukelele
  BT Guitar
  —Methods *(MT645)*
  — —Self-instruction *(MT645)*
    UF Ukulele—Self-instruction
  —Self-instruction
    BT Ukulele—Methods— Self-instruction
Ukulele and piano music *(M282-3)*
  UF Piano and ukulele music
  NT Marches (Ukulele and piano)
Ukulele band
  USE Plectral ensembles
Ukulele music *(M142.U5)*
  NT Plectral ensembles
Union Jack (Ballet)
  BT Ballets
United Nations [May Subd Geog]
  —Music
    USE United Nations—Songs and music
  —Songs and music *(M1627; M1627.15)*
    UF United Nations—Music
United States
  —History *(E178)*
  — —Revolution, 1775-1783 *(E201-298)*
  — —Music
    USE United States—History—
          Revolution, 1775-1783—
          Songs and music
  — — —Songs and music *(Music, M1631)*
    UF United States—History—
          Revolution, 1775-1783—Music
United States. Army
  —Bandmasters *(U43)*
    UF Bandmasters
    BT Bands (Music)
  —Music
    USE United States. Army—Songs
          and music
  —Songs and music *(M1629-1630)*
    UF United States. Army—Music
    Example under Military music; National
          music
United States. Navy
  —Music
    USE United States. Navy—Songs
          and music
  —Songs and music *(M1629-1630)*
    UF United States. Navy—Music
    Example under National music
Universities and colleges [May Subd Geog]
        (LB2300-2411; United States,
        LA225-LA228; Other countries,
        LA410-LA2270; Individual institutions,
        LD-LG)
  NT Music in universities and colleges
Unspecified instrument music
  USE *Unspecified instrument* used as part of
        the specification of medium in
        headings, e.g. *Sextets (Unspecified*
        instruments (6)); Suites (Piano,
        unspecified instruments (2)); also,
        Duets, with instrumental specification

Unspecified instrument music
  (Continued)
    USE Brass instrument music
         Solo instrument music
         String instrument music
         Wind instrument music
         Woodwind instrument music
Urdu lullabies
  USE Lullabies, Urdu
Usquequo, Domine (Music)
  USE Psalms (Music)—13th Psalm
Ut quid, Deus (Music)
  USE Psalms (Music)—74th Psalm
Utai [May Subd Geog]
  UF Yōkyoku
  BT Nō
       Nō music
       Nō plays
       Vocal music—Japan
  NT Hōshō school
       Kanze school
       Umewaka school
Uzbek songs
  USE Songs, Uzbek
Valve trumpet
  USE Trumpet
Variation (Music) *(ML3845)*
  UF Musical variation
       Partita
  RT Embellishment (Music)
  NT Ground bass
Variations
       Here are entered collections of variation
         music for various mediums. Individual
         variations and collections of variations
         for a specific medium are entered under
         the heading followed by specification of
         medium.
  UF Theme with variations
  NT Folias (Music)
Variations (Bagpipe) *(M145)*
  NT Pibroch
       Pibrochs
Variations (Band) *(M1203)*
  BT Band music
Variations (Band), Arranged *(M1254)*
  —Scores and parts *(M1254)*
Variations (Bassoon, clarinet, flute, horn,
       oboe) *(M555-7)*
  BT Wind quintets (Bassoon, clarinet, flute,
       horn, oboe)
Variations (Bassoon, clarinet, flute, horn,
       oboe), Arranged *(M558-9)*
Variations (Bassoon, clarinet, flute, horn,
       violins (2), viola, violoncello)
       (M860-862)
  BT Octets (Bassoon, clarinet, flute, horn,
       violins (2), viola, violoncello)
Variations (Bassoon, clarinet, flute, horn,
       violins (2), viola, violoncello, double
       bass) *(M960-962)*
  BT Nonets (Bassoon, clarinet, flute, horn,
       violins (2), viola, violoncello, double bass)

Variations (Bassoon, clarinet, flute, oboe with
       chamber orchestra) *(M1040-1041)*
  BT Bassoon, clarinet, flute, oboe with
       chamber orchestra
  —Scores *(M1040)*
Variations (Bassoon with orchestra) *(M1026-1027)*
  BT Bassoon with orchestra
  —Solo with piano *(M1027)*
    BT Bassoon and piano music, Arranged
Variations (Chamber orchestra) *(M1003)*
  BT Chamber-orchestra music
Variations (Clarinet and flute) *(M288-9)*
  BT Clarinet and flute music
Variations (Clarinet and harp) *(M296-297)*
  BT Clarinet and harp music
Variations (Clarinet and horn) *(M288-9)*
  BT Clarinet and horn music
Variations (Clarinet and koto) *(M296-297)*
  BT Clarinet and koto music
Variations (Clarinet and piano) *(M248-250)*
  BT Clarinet and piano music
Variations (Clarinet and piano), Arranged
       (M251-2)
Variations (Clarinet, flute, violin, violoncello)
       (M460-462)
  BT Quartets (Clarinet, flute, violin,
       violoncello)
Variations (Clarinet, guitar, viola) *(M380-382)*
  BT Trios (Clarinet, guitar, viola)
Variations (Clarinet, violins (2), viola,
       violoncello) *(M560-562)*
  BT Quintets (Clarinet, violins (2), viola,
       violoncello)
Variations (Clarinet with band)
       (M1205-M1206; M1257)
  BT Clarinet with band
Variations (Clarinet with orchestra) *(M1024-5)*
  BT Clarinet with orchestra
  —Solo with piano *(M1025)*
    BT Clarinet and piano music, Arranged
Variations (Clarinet with string ensemble)
  BT Clarinet with string ensemble
  —Solo with piano *(M251-252)*
    BT Clarinet and piano music, Arranged
Variations (Clarinet with string orchestra)
       (M1105-6)
  BT Clarinet with string orchestra
Variations (Concrete music)
  BT Concrete music
Variations (Cornet with band) *(M1205-1206)*
  BT Cornet with band
Variations (Dance orchestra) *(M1356)*
  BT Dance orchestra music
  —Scores *(M1356)*
Variations (Double bass) *(M55-7)*
  BT Double-bass music
Variations (Double bass and piano)
  BT Double-bass and piano music
Variations (Double bass with string orchestra)
       (M1105-6)
  BT Double bass with string orchestra
  —Solo with piano *(M1106)*
    BT Double-bass and piano music, Arranged

Variations (Euphonium and piano)
  M270-M271
  BT Euphonium and piano music
Variations (Flute) *(M60-62)*
  BT Flute music
Variations (Flute and continuo)
  BT Flute and continuo music
Variations (Flute and guitar) *(M296-7)*
  BT Flute and guitar music
Variations (Flute and harp) *(M296-7)*
  BT Flute and harp music
Variations (Flute and harp), Arranged *(M297)*
Variations (Flute and harpsichord) *(M240-242)*
  BT Flute and harpsichord music
Variations (Flute and horn with string
      orchestra) *(M1105-6)*
  BT Flute and horn with string orchestra
Variations (Flute and oboe with string
      orchestra) *(M1140-1141)*
  BT Flute and oboe with string orchestra
Variations (Flute and organ) *(M182-4)*
  BT Flute and organ music
Variations (Flute and piano) *(M240-242)*
  BT Flute and piano music
Variations (Flute and piano), Arranged *(M244)*
Variations (Flute and violin) *(M290-291)*
  BT Flute and violin music
Variations (Flute, guitar, viola) *(M380-382)*
  BT Trios (Flute, guitar, viola)
Variations (Flute, harp, violin) *(M380-382)*
  BT Trios (Flute, harp, violin)
Variations (Flute, violins (2), viola,
      violoncello) *(M560-562)*
  BT Quintets (Flute, violins (2), viola,
        violoncello)
Variations (Flute, violins (2), violoncello)
      (M460-462)
  BT Quartets (Flute, violins (2), violoncello)
Variations (Flute with chamber orchestra)
      (M1020-1021)
  BT Flute with chamber orchestra
Variations (Flute with instrumental ensemble)
  BT Flute with instrumental ensemble
Variations (Flute with orchestra) *(M1020-1021)*
  BT Flute with orchestra
  —Solo with piano *(M1021)*
      BT Flute and piano music, Arranged
Variations (Flute with string orchestra)
      (M1120-1121)
  BT Flute with string orchestra
Variations (Flutes (2))
  BT Flute music (Flutes (2))
Variations (Flutes (2), guitar) *(M375-7)*
  BT Trios (Flutes (2), guitar)
Variations (Guitar) *(M125-7)*
  BT Guitar music
Variations (Guitar and piano) *(M276-7)*
  BT Guitar and piano music
Variations (Guitar with orchestra) *(M1037.4.G8)*
  BT Guitar with orchestra
Variations (Guitar with string orchestra)
      (M1137.4.G8)
  BT Guitar with string orchestra

Variations (Guitars (2)) *(M292-3)*
  BT Guitar music (Guitars (2))
Variations (Guitars (2)), Arranged *(M292-3)*
Variations (Harp) *(M115-117)*
  BT Harp music
Variations (Harp and piano) *(M272-3)*
  BT Harp and piano music
Variations (Harp), Arranged *(M118-119)*
Variations (Harp with brass ensemble)
  BT Harp with brass ensemble
Variations (Harp with chamber orchestra)
      (M1036-7)
  BT Harp with chamber orchestra
Variations (Harp with orchestra) *(M1036-7)*
  BT Harp with orchestra
  —Scores *(M1036)*
Variations (Harpsichord) *(M27)*
  BT Harpsichord music
Variations (Harpsichord, bassoon, violin)
      (M320-322)
Variations (Harpsichord, reed-organ, celesta,
      vibraphone, violins (2), viola,
      violoncello) *(M805-809)*
  BT Reed-organ music
Variations (Harpsichord, violin, viola da
      gamba) *(M310-312)*
  BT Trios (Harpsichord, violin, viola da
        gamba)
      Variations (Piano trio)
Variations (Harpsichord with string orchestra)
      (M1110-1111)
  BT Harpsichord with string orchestra
  —2-piano scores *(M1111)*
      BT Harpsichord and piano music,
            Arranged
Variations (Harpsichords (4)) *(M216)*
  BT Harpsichord music (Harpsichords (4))
Variations (Horn and organ) *(M182-186)*
  BT Horn and organ music
Variations (Horn and piano) *(M255-7)*
  BT Horn and piano music
Variations (Horn, trombone, trumpets (2),
      tuba with instrumental ensemble)
  BT Horn, trombone, trumpets (2), tuba
        with instrumental ensemble
Variations (Horn with orchestra) *(M1028-9)*
  BT Horn with orchestra
  —Solo with piano *(M1029)*
      BT Horn and piano music, Arranged
Variations (Instrumental ensemble) *(M900-985)*
  BT Instrumental ensembles
Variations (Oboe and continuo)
  BT Oboe and continuo music
Variations (Oboe and guitar) *(M296-M297)*
  BT Oboe and guitar music
Variations (Oboe and harpsichord) *(M245-M247)*
  BT Oboe and harpsichord music
Variations (Oboe and organ) *(M182-4)*
  BT Oboe and organ music
Variations (Oboe and piano) *(M245-6)*
  BT Oboe and piano music
Variations (Oboe and violoncello) *(M290-291)*
  BT Oboe and violoncello music

Variations (Oboe, violin, viola, violoncello)
   (M460-462)
  BT Quartets (Oboe, violin, viola,
       violoncello)
Variations (Oboe with band) *(M1205-6)*
  BT Oboe with band
  —Solo with piano *(M1206)*
     BT Oboe and piano music, Arranged
Variations (Oboe with chamber orchestra)
   (M1022-1023)
  BT Oboe with chamber orchestra
Variations (Oboe with orchestra)
   (M1022-1023)
  BT Oboe with orchestra
Variations (Oboe with string orchestra)
   (M1105-6)
  BT Oboe with string orchestra
Variations (Orchestra) *(M1003)*
  BT Orchestral music
Variations (Orchestra), Arranged *(M1060)*
Variations (Organ) *(M9)*
  BT Organ music
Variations (Organ, 4 hands) *(M180-181)*
  BT Organ music (4 hands)
Variations (Organ with string orchestra)
   (M1108-1109)
  BT Organ with string orchestra
Variations (Percussion and piano) *(M284-5)*
  BT Percussion and piano music
**Variations (Percussion and piano with
    instrumental ensemble)**
  BT Percussion and piano with instrumental
     ensemble
Variations (Percussion and viola) *(M298)*
  BT Percussion and viola music
Variations (Percussion with orchestra)
   (M1038-9)
  BT Percussion with orchestra
  —Solos with piano *(M1039)*
     BT Trios (Piano, percussion), Arranged
Variations (Piano) *(M27)*
  BT Piano music
Variations (Piano, 1 hand, with orchestra)
   (M1010-1011)
  BT Piano (1 hand) with orchestra
  —2-piano scores *(M1011)*
     BT Piano music (Pianos (2)), Arranged
Variations (Piano, 3 hands) *(M205)*
  BT Piano music (3 hands)
Variations (Piano, 4 hands) *(M200-M201;*
   M204)
  BT Piano music (4 hands)
Variations (Piano, 4 hands), Arranged
   (M207-211)
Variations (Piano and organ) *(M182-4)*
  BT Piano and organ music
Variations (Piano), Arranged
**Variations (Piano, bassoons (2), flute, horn,
    oboe, violin, violoncello, double
    bass)** *(M922)*
  BT Nonets (Piano, bassoons (2), flute,
     horn, oboe, violin, violoncello,
     double bass)

Variations (Piano, clarinet, violin)
   (M320-322)
  BT Trios (Piano, clarinet, violin)
Variations (Piano, cornets (3)) *(M415-417)*
  BT Quartets (Piano, cornets (3))
Variations (Piano, cornets (3)), Arranged
   (M418-419)
Variations (Piano, flute, harp) *(M335-7)*
  BT Trios (Piano, flute, harp)
Variations (Piano, flute, oboe) *(M315-317)*
  BT Trios (Piano, flute, oboe)
**Variations (Piano, flute, percussion,
    violoncello)** *(M545-7)*
  BT Quintets (Piano, flute, percussion,
     violoncello)
Variations (Piano, flute, violin, violoncello)
   (M420-422)
  BT Quartets (Piano, flute, violin, violoncello)
Variations (Piano, horn, violin) *(M320-322)*
  BT Trios (Piano, horn, violin)
Variations (Piano, percussion)
  BT Trios (Piano, percussion)
Variations (Piano quartet) *(M410-412)*
  BT Piano quartets
Variations (Piano quintet) *(M510-512)*
  BT Piano quintets
**Variations (Piano, recorders (3), violins (2),
    viola, violoncello)** *(M820-822)*
  BT Octets (Piano, recorders (3), violins (2),
     viola, violoncello)
**Variations (Piano, saxophone, percussion,
    double bass with orchestra)**
   (M1040-1041)
  BT Piano, saxophone, percussion, double
     bass with orchestra
Variations (Piano trio) *(M310-312)*
  BT Piano trios
  NT Variations (Harpsichord, violin, viola
     da gamba)
Variations (Piano with band) *(M1205-6)*
  BT Piano with band
Variations (Piano with chamber orchestra)
   (M1010-1011)
  BT Piano with chamber orchestra
**Variations (Piano with chamber orchestra),
    Arranged** *(M1010-1011)*
  —2-piano scores *(M1011)*
     BT Piano music (Pianos (2)), Arranged
Variations (Piano with clarinet choir) *(M1205-1206)*
  BT Piano with clarinet choir
Variations (Piano with orchestra) *(M1010-1011)*
  BT Piano with orchestra
  —2-piano scores *(M1011)*
     BT Piano music (Pianos (2)), Arranged
Variations (Piano with orchestra), Arranged
   (M1010-1011)
  —Scores
Variations (Piano with string orchestra) *(M1105-6)*
  BT Piano with string orchestra
  —2-piano scores *(M1106)*
     BT Piano music (Pianos (2)), Arranged
Variations (Pianos (2)) *(M214)*
  BT Piano music (Pianos (2))

Variations (Pianos (2), 8 hands) *(M216)*
  BT Piano music (Pianos (2), 8 hands)
Variations (Pianos (2)), Arranged *(M215)*
Variations (Pianos (2) with dance orchestra)
      (M1353)
  BT Pianos (2) with dance orchestra
Variations (Pianos (2) with orchestra)
      (M1010-1011)
  BT Pianos (2) with orchestra
  —Scores *(M1010)*
Variations (Pipes (4)) *(M455-459)*
  BT Pipe music
Variations (Recorder) *(M60-62)*
  BT Recorder music
Variations (Recorder and continuo)
  BT Recorder and continuo music
Variations (Recorder and harpsichord)
      (M240-242)
  BT Recorder and harpsichord music
Variations (Recorder and harpsichord),
      Arranged *(M243-4)*
Variations (Recorder and piano) *(M240-242)*
  BT Recorder and piano music
Variations (Recorder, percussion, double bass)
      (M885)
  BT Octets (Recorder, percussion, double
      bass)
Variations (Recorders (2)) *(M288-9)*
  BT Recorder music (Recorders (2))
Variations (Saxhorn and piano) *(M266-7)*
  BT Saxhorn and piano music
Variations (String orchestra) *(M1103)*
  BT String-orchestra music
Variations (String orchestra), Arranged
      (M1160)
Variations (String quartet) *(M450-452)*
  BT String quartets
Variations (String quartet with string
      orchestra) *(M1105-6)*
  BT String quartet with string orchestra
Variations (String trio) *(M349-351)*
  BT String trios
Variations (Trombone and piano) *(M262-3)*
  BT Trombone and piano music
Variations (Trombone and trumpet)
      (M288-289)
  BT Trombone and trumpet music
Variations (Trombone with string ensemble)
  BT Trombone with string ensemble
Variations (Trombone with string orchestra)
      (M1132-1133)
  BT Trombone with string orchestra
Variations (Trumpet) *(M85-87)*
  BT Trumpet music
Variations (Trumpet and harp) *(M296-297)*
  BT Trumpet and harp music
Variations (Trumpet and organ) *(M182-186)*
  BT Trumpet and organ music
Variations (Trumpet and piano) *(M260-261)*
  BT Trumpet and piano music
Variations (Trumpet with band)
      (M1205-1206)
  BT Trumpet with band

Variations (Trumpet with string orchestra)
      (M1105-6)
  BT Trumpet with string orchestra
  —Scores *(M1105)*
  —Solo with piano *(M1106)*
      BT Trumpet and piano music, Arranged
Variations (Tuba and piano) *(M264-5)*
  BT Tuba and piano music
Variations (Tuba with brass ensemble)
  BT Tuba with brass ensemble
Variations (Unspecified instrument and piano)
      (M285.5-285.6)
  BT Duets (Unspecified instrument and
      piano)
Variations (Viola) *(M45-49)*
Variations (Viola and harpsichord) *(M224-6)*
  BT Variations (Viola and piano)
      Viola and harpsichord music
Variations (Viola and organ) *(M183-4)*
  BT Viola and organ music
Variations (Viola and piano) *(M224-6)*
  BT Viola and piano music
  NT Variations (Viola and harpsichord)
Variations (Viola and violoncello) *(M286-7)*
  BT Viola and violoncello music
Variations (Viola da gamba and continuo)
  BT Viola da gamba and continuo music
Variations (Viola with orchestra)
      (M1014-1015)
  BT Viola with orchestra
  —Solo with piano *(M1015)*
      BT Viola and piano music, Arranged
Variations (Violas (2)) *(M286-7)*
  BT Viola music (Violas (2))
Variations (Violas (4) with orchestra)
      (M1014-1015)
  BT Violas (4) with orchestra
Variations (Violin) *(M40-42)*
  BT Violin music
Variations (Violin and accordion) *(M298)*
  BT Violin and accordion music
Variations (Violin and continuo)
  BT Violin and continuo music
Variations (Violin and guitar) *(M294-5)*
  BT Violin and guitar music
Variations (Violin and harp) *(M294-295)*
  BT Violin and harp music
Variations (Violin and harpsichord)
      (M217-M218; M221)
  BT Variations (Violin and piano)
      Violin and harpsichord music
Variations (Violin and harpsichord), Arranged
      (M222-3)
Variations (Violin and piano) *(M217-M218;*
      M221)
  BT Violin and piano music
  NT Variations (Violin and harpsichord)
Variations (Violin and piano), Arranged
      (M222-3)
Variations (Violin and viola) *(M286-7)*
  BT Violin and viola music
Variations (Violin and violoncello) *(M288-9)*
  BT Violin and violoncello music

Variations (Violin and violoncello with string orchestra) *(M1105-6)*
    BT Violin and violoncello with string orchestra
Variations (Violin and violoncello with string orchestra), Arranged *(M1105-6)*
    —Scores *(M1105)*
Variations (Violin with orchestra) *(M1012-1013)*
    BT Violin with orchestra
    —Solo with piano *(M1013)*
        BT Violin and piano music, Arranged
Variations (Violin with string orchestra) *(M1105-6)*
    BT Violin with string orchestra
Variations (Violin with string orchestra), Arranged *(M1105)*
    —Scores
Variations (Violins (2)) *(M286-7)*
    BT Violin music (Violins (2))
Variations (Violins (2), viola, violoncellos (2))
    BT String quintets (Violins (2), viola, violoncellos (2))
Variations (Violins (2), violas (2), violoncello) *(M550-552)*
    BT String quintets (Violins (2), violas (2), violoncello)
Variations (Violins (2), violas (2), violoncello), Arranged *(M553-4)*
Variations (Violins (2), violoncello) *(M349-351)*
    BT String trios (Violins (2), violoncello)
Variations (Violins (2), violoncello with string orchestra) *(M1140-1141)*
    BT Violins (2), violoncello with string orchestra
Variations (Violins (3), viola, violoncello) *(M550-552)*
    BT String quintets (Violins (3), viola, violoncello)
Variations (Violins (3), violoncello) *(M450-M451; M452.4)*
    BT String quartets (Violins (3), violoncello)
Variations (Violoncello)
    BT Violoncello music
Variations (Violoncello and continuo)
    BT Violoncello and continuo music
Variations (Violoncello and piano) *(M229-M230; M233)*
    BT Violoncello and piano music
Variations (Violoncello and piano), Arranged *(M235-6)*
Variations (Violoncello with chamber orchestra) *(M1016-1017)*
    BT Violoncello with chamber orchestra
    —Solo with piano *(M1017)*
        BT Violoncello and piano music, Arranged
Variations (Violoncello with orchestra) *(M1016-1017)*
    BT Violoncello with orchestra
    —Solo with piano *(M1017)*
        BT Violoncello and piano music, Arranged

Variations (Violoncello with string orchestra) *(M1105-6)*
    BT Violoncello with string orchestra
    —Solo with piano *(M1106)*
        BT Violoncello and piano music, Arranged
Variations (Violoncellos (2)) *(M286-7)*
    BT Violoncello music (Violoncellos (2))
Variations (Violoncellos (4)) *(M450-M451; M452.4)*
    BT String quartets (Violoncellos (4))
Variations (Vocal)
    BT Vocal music
Variety shows (Theater)
    USE Music-halls (Variety-theaters, cabarets, etc.)
        Vaudeville
Variety-theaters
    USE Music-halls (Variety-theaters, cabarets, etc.)
        Vaudeville
Vaudeville [May Subd Geog] *(Collections, PN6120.V3; History and criticism, PN1960-PN1969)*
    RT Music-halls (Variety-theaters, cabarets, etc.)
    NT Pantomime (Christmas entertainment)
    —United States
        NT Minstrel shows
Vedas *(PK3000-PK3581; Hinduism, BL1115)*
    —Recitation
        BT Music—India
Veni Creator Spiritus (Music)
Venite, exultemus Domino (Music)
    USE Psalms (Music)—95th Psalm
Vespers (Music)
    RT Evening-service music
Vibraharp
    USE Vibraphone
Vibraharp music
    USE Vibraphone music
Vibraphone *(ML1040)*
    UF Vibraharp
    BT Percussion instruments
    RT Marimba
        Xylophone
Vibraphone and accordion music *(M298)*
    UF Accordion and vibraphone music
Vibraphone and bassoon music
    USE Bassoon and vibraphone music
Vibraphone and clarinet music
    USE Clarinet and vibraphone music
Vibraphone and flute music
    USE Flute and vibraphone music
Vibraphone and harp music
    USE Harp and vibraphone music
Vibraphone and piano music *(M284-5)*
    UF Piano and vibraphone music
Vibraphone and piano music, Arranged (Jazz)
    USE Vibraphone and piano music (Jazz)
Vibraphone and piano music (Jazz) *(M284-5)*
    UF Vibraphone and piano music, Arranged (Jazz)

Vibraphone and trumpet music
　USE　Trumpet and vibraphone music
Vibraphone and tuba music
　USE　Tuba and vibraphone music
Vibraphone and viola music *(M298)*
　UF　Viola and vibraphone music
　NT　Suites (Vibraphone and viola)
Vibraphone and violin music *(M298)*
　UF　Violin and vibraphone music
　NT　Suites (Vibraphone and violin)
Vibraphone music *(M175.X6)*
　UF　Vibraharp music
　SA　Concertos, Minuets, Sonatas, Suites,
　　　and similar headings with
　　　specification of instruments; Trios
　　　[Quartets, etc.] *followed by*
　　　specifications which include the
　　　vibraphone; also Percussion
　　　ensembles, Percussion music, *and*
　　　headings that begin with the words
　　　vibraphone or vibraphones
　NT　Xylophone music
Vibraphone music (4 hands) *(M298)*
Vibraphone with jazz ensemble *(M1366)*
Vibraphone with orchestra *(M1039.4.X9)*
　RT　Concertos (Vibraphone)
Vibraphone with percussion ensemble
　RT　Concertos (Vibraphone with percussion
　　　ensemble)
Vibrato *(ML3817; Violin, MT271; Voice,*
　　　MT882)
　UF　Tremolo
　BT　Music
Vibrator (for bowed instruments) *(ML755)*
　BT　Stringed instruments, Bowed
Videocassettes
　UF　Video cassettes
　　　Videocassette recordings
　　　Videocassette tapes
　　　Videotape cassettes
　BT　Video tapes
Videocassettes for children [May Subd Geog]
　BT　Children's mass media
Vielle
　USE　Hurdy-gurdy
　　　Viol
Vietnamese folk-songs
　USE　Folk-songs, Vietnamese
Vietnamese hymns
　USE　Hymns, Vietnamese
Vietnamese songs
　USE　Songs, Vietnamese
Vihuela *(ML1010)*
　RT　Guitar
　　　Lute
Vihuela and cithern music
　USE　Cithern and vihuela music
Vihuela music *(M142.V53)*
　NT　Canons, fugues, etc. (Vihuela)
Vihuela music (Vihuelas (2)) *(M292-293)*
Vilancetes (Music)
　USE　Villancicos (Music)

Villancicos (Music)
　　　Here are entered collections of villan-
　　　cicos and separately published villan-
　　　cicos, sacred or secular, regardless of
　　　period of composition, style or
　　　medium of performance. The heading
　　　is used only as a second heading, *e.g.*
　　　1. Part-songs, Spanish. 2. Villancicos
　　　(Music)
　UF　Vilancetes (Music)
Villanellas
　USE　Villanelle (Part-songs)
Villanelle (Part-songs)
　UF　Arie napolitane (Part-songs)
　　　Canzone napolitane (Part-songs)
　　　Canzona villanesche
　　　Canzoni alla napolitana (Part-songs)
　　　Villanellas
　　　Villanesche
　BT　Part-songs, Italian
Vina *(Music of India, ML338; Musical*
　　　instruments, ML1015)
　UF　Bîn
Vina and mridanga music
　UF　Mridanga and vina music
Vina and tabla music
　UF　Tabla and vina music
Vina music *(M142.V55)*
　NT　Trios (Vina, percussion, violin)
Viol *(History and construction, ML760)*
　UF　Vielle
　NT　Baryton
　　　Viola da gamba
　　　Viola d'amore
　　　Violone
Viol, Bass
　USE　Viola da gamba
Viol and continuo music
　UF　Continuo and viol music
　NT　Suites (Viol and continuo)
Viol and hurdy-gurdy music
　USE　Hurdy-gurdy and viol music
Viol and lute music *(M990)*
　UF　Lute and viol music
Viol ensembles *(M990)*
　　　Here are entered compositions for ten or
　　　more viols and collections of composi-
　　　tions for a varying number of viols.
　　　Example under reference from Ensembles
　　　(Music)
　　　Notes under Instrumental ensembles; String
　　　ensembles
Viol music *(M59)*
　SA　Concertos, Minuets, Sonatas, Suites,
　　　and similar headings with
　　　specification of instruments; String
　　　trios [quartets, etc.] *and* Trios
　　　[Quartets, etc.] *followed by*
　　　specifications which include the viol;
　　　also String ensembles *and headings*
　　　that begin with the words viol or viols
　NT　Quintets (Harpsichord, violins (2), viols (2))

Viol music *(M59)*
(Continued)
NT Quintets (Harpsichord, viols (2), viola
d'amore, viola da gamba)
Quintets (Organ, violin, viols (3))
Quintets (Organ, violins (2), viols (2))
Quintets (Piano, violins (2), viols (2))
String trios (Viol, viola d'amore, viola
da gamba)
String trios (Viols (3))
Trios (Harpsichord, viols (2))
Trios (Piano, viols (2))
Trios (Recorder, lute, viol)
Viola da gamba music
Viola d'amore music
Violone music
Viol music (Viols (2) *(M990)*
NT Canons, fugues, etc. (Viols (2))
Quintets (Harpsichord, flute, viols (2),
violoncello)
Suites (Viols (2))
Viol music (Viols (3))
USE String trios (Viols (3))
Viol music (Viols (4))
USE String quartets (Viols (4))
Viol music (Viols (5))
USE String quintets (Viols (5))
Viol music (Viols (7))
USE String septets (Viols (7))
Viol players [May Subd Geog]
UF Gamba players
Gambists
Viola da gamba players
BT Musicians
Violists
Viol with instrumental ensemble
RT Concertos (Viol with instrumental
ensemble)
Viola *(ML900-905)*
NT Tenor violin
Viola pomposa
Example under Stringed instruments, Bowed
—Orchestra studies *(MT286)*
BT Viola—Studies and exercises
—Studies and exercises *(MT285)*
NT Viola—Orchestra studies
Viola and bassoon music
USE Bassoon and viola music
Viola and clarinet music
USE Clarinet and viola music
Viola and continuo music
UF Continuo and viola music
NT Sonatas (Viola and continuo)
Viola and double-bass music *(M286-7)*
UF Double-bass and viola music
NT Concertos (Viola and double bass)
Rondos (Viola and double bass)
Sonatas (Viola and double bass)
Viola and double bass with orchestra
Viola and double-bass with orchestra
(M1040-1041)
BT Viola and double-bass music
RT Concertos (Viola and double bass)

Viola and flute music
USE Flute and viola music
Viola and guitar music *(M294-5)*
UF Guitar and viola music
NT Sonatas (Viola and guitar)
Waltzes (Viola and guitar)
Viola and guitar music, Arranged *(M294-5)*
Viola and harp music *(M294-295)*
UF Harp and viola music
NT Concertos (Viola and harp with string
orchestra)
Viola and harp with string orchestra
Viola and harp with string orchestra
(M1140-1141)
BT Viola and harp music
RT Concertos (Viola and harp with string
orchestra)
—Solos with piano *(M1141)*
BT Trios (Piano, harp, viola), Arranged
Viola and harpsichord music *(M224-6)*
UF Harpsichord and viola music
BT Viola and piano music
NT Concertos (Viola and harpsichord with
string orchestra)
Sonatas (Viola and harpsichord)
Suites (Viola and harpsichord)
Variations (Viola and harpsichord)
Viola and harpsichord with string
orchestra
Viola and harpsichord with string orchestra
(M1105-6)
BT Viola and harpsichord music
RT Concertos (Viola and harpsichord with
string orchestra)
Viola and mandolin music
UF Mandolin and viola music
NT Suites (Viola and mandolin)
Viola and oboe music
USE Oboe and viola music
Viola and organ music *(M182-4)*
UF Organ and viola music
NT Chorale preludes (Viola and organ)
Concertos (Viola and organ with string
orchestra)
Sonatas (Viola and organ)
Variations (Viola and organ)
Viola and organ with string orchestra
Viola and organ music, Arranged *(M185-6)*
Viola and organ with string orchestra
(M1105-6)
BT Viola and organ music
RT Concertos (Viola and organ with string
orchestra)
Viola and percussion music
USE Percussion and viola music
Viola and piano music *(M224-6)*
UF Piano and viola music
NT Chaconnes (Viola and piano)
Concertos (Viola and piano)
Concertos (Viola and piano with band)
Concertos (Viola and piano with string
orchestra)
Rondos (Viola and piano)

Viola and piano music *(M224-6)*
(Continued)
NT Sonatas (Viola and piano)
Suites (Viola and piano)
Variations (Viola and piano)
Viola and harpsichord music
Viola and piano with band
Viola and piano with orchestra
Viola and piano with string orchestra
Waltzes (Viola and piano)
Viola and piano music, Arranged *(M227-8)*
NT Concertos (Viola)—Solo with piano
Concertos (Viola), Arranged—Solo with
piano
Concertos (Viola with chamber
orchestra)—Solo with piano
Concertos (Viola with string orchestra)
—Solo with piano
Concertos (Viola with string orchestra),
Arranged—Solo with piano
Rondos (Viola with orchestra)—Solo with
piano
Suites (Viola with chamber orchestra)—
Solo with piano
Suites (Viola with orchestra)—Solo with
piano
Suites (Viola with string orchestra),
Arranged—Solo with piano
Symphonies arranged for viola and
piano
Variations (Viola with orchestra)—Solo
with piano
Viola with chamber orchestra—Solo
with piano
Viola with orchestra—Solo with piano
Viola with string ensemble—Solo with
piano
Viola with string orchestra—Solo with
piano
Viola with wind ensemble—Solo with
piano
Viola and piano with band *(M1205-6)*
BT Viola and piano music
RT Concertos (Viola and piano with band)
Viola and piano with orchestra
(M1040-1041)
BT Viola and piano music
RT Concertos (Viola and piano)
—Scores *(M1040-1041)*
Viola and piano with string orchestra
BT Viola and piano music
RT Concertos (Viola and piano with string
orchestra)
Viola and recorder music
USE Recorder and viola music
Viola and vibraphone music
USE Vibraphone and viola music
Viola and viola d'amore music *(M286-287)*
UF Viola d'amore and viola music
NT Sonatas (Viola and viola d'amore)
Viola and violin music
USE Violin and viola music

Viola and violoncello music *(M286-7)*
UF Violoncello and viola music
NT Sonatas (Viola and violoncello)
Suites (Viola and violoncello)
Variations (Viola and violoncello)
Viola and violoncello with orchestra
(M1040-1041)
RT Concertos (Viola and violoncello)
Viola and violoncello with string orchestra
RT Concertos (Viola and violoncello with
string orchestra)
Viola and violone music *(M286-7)*
UF Violone and viola music
Viola bastarda
USE Lyra viol
Viola da gamba *(ML760)*
UF Bass viol
Viol, Bass
BT Viol
Violoncello
NT Baryton
Lyra viol
Viola da gamba and continuo music
UF Continuo and viola da gamba music
NT Chaconnes (Viola da gamba and
continuo)
Sonatas (Viola da gamba and continuo)
Suites (Viola da gamba and continuo)
Variations (Viola da gamba and
continuo)
Viola da gamba and harpsichord music
(M239)
UF Harpsichord and viola da gamba music
BT Violoncello and piano music
NT Sonatas (Viola da gamba and
harpsichord)
Suites (Viola da gamba and
harpsichord)
Viola da gamba and lute music *(M294-5)*
UF Lute and viola da gamba music
NT Sonatas (Viola da gamba and lute)
Viola da gamba and organ music *(M184)*
UF Organ and viola da gamba music
NT Chorale preludes (Viola da gamba and
organ)
Sonatas (Viola da gamba and organ)
Viola da gamba and piano music *(M239)*
UF Piano and viola da gamba music
Viola da gamba and piano music, Arranged
(M239)
NT Concertos (Viola da gamba with string
orchestra)—Solo with piano
Viola da gamba and recorder music
USE Recorder and viola da gamba music
Viola da gamba and viola d'amore music
USE Viola d'amore and viola da gamba
music
Viola da gamba and violin music
USE Violin and viola da gamba music
Viola da gamba music *(M59)*
BT Viol music
Violoncello music

Viola da gamba music *(M59)*
(Continued)
  SA Concertos, Minuets, Sonatas, Suites,
       and similar headings with
       specification of instruments; String
       trios [quartets, etc.] *and* Trios
       [Quartets, etc.] *followed by*
       specifications which include the viola
       da gamba; also String ensembles *and*
       headings that begin with the words
       viola da gamba or viole da gamba

Viola da gamba music (Viole da gamba (2))
    (M286-7)
  NT Sonatas (Viole da gamba (2))
       Suites (Viole da gamba (2))

Viola da gamba music (Viole da gamba (5))
  USE String quintets (Viole da gamba (5))

Viola da gamba players
  USE Viol players

Viola da gamba with orchestra *(M1019)*
  BT Orchestral music
  RT Concertos (Viola da gamba)

Viola da gamba with string orchestra
    (M1105-6)
  RT Concertos (Viola da gamba with string
       orchestra)
  NT Suites (Viola da gamba with string
       orchestra)

Viola d'amore *(History and criticism,*
    ML760)
  BT Viol

Viola d'amore and continuo music
  UF Continuo and viola d'amore music
  NT Sonatas (Viola d'amore and continuo)

Viola d'amore and double-bass music
    (M286-7)
  UF Double-bass and viola d'amore music
  NT Sonatas (Viola d'amore and double
       bass)

Viola d'amore and flute music
  USE Flute and viola d'amore music

Viola d'amore and guitar music *(M294-5)*
  UF Guitar and viola d'amore music
  NT Concertos (Viola d'amore and guitar
       with string orchestra)
       Sonatas (Viola d'amore and guitar)
       Viola d'amore and guitar with string
       orchestra

Viola d'amore and guitar with string orchestra
    (M1140-1141)
  BT Viola d'amore and guitar music
  RT Concertos (Viola d'amore and guitar
       with string orchestra)

Viola d'amore and harpsichord music *(M239)*
  UF Harpsichord and viola d'amore music
  NT Sonatas (Viola d'amore and harpsichord)

Viola d'amore and lute music *(M294-5)*
  UF Lute and viola d'amore music
  NT Concertos (Viola d'amore and lute
       with string orchestra)
       Viola d'amore and lute with string
       orchestra

Viola d'amore and lute with string orchestra
    (M1105-6)
  BT Viola d'amore and lute music
  RT Concertos (Viola d'amore and lute with
       string orchestra)

Viola d'amore and organ music *(M182-6)*
  UF Organ and viola d'amore music

Viola d'amore and piano music *(M239)*
  UF Piano and viola d'amore music
  NT Sonatas (Viola d'amore and piano)

Viola d'amore and piano music, Arranged
    (M239)
  NT Concertos (Viola d'amore)—Solo with
       piano
       Concertos (Viola d'amore with
       string orchestra)—Solo with piano

Viola d'amore and viola da gamba music
  UF Viola da gamba and viola d'amore
       music
  NT Sonatas (Viola d'amore and viola da
       gamba)

Viola d'amore and viola music
  USE Viola and viola d'amore music

Viola d'amore and violin music
  USE Violin and viola d'amore music

Viola d'amore music *(M59)*
  BT Viol music
  SA Concertos, Minuets, Sonatas, Suites,
       and similar headings with
       specification of instruments; String
       trios [quartets, etc.] *and* Trios
       [Quartets, etc.] *followed by*
       specifications which include the viola
       d'amore; also String ensembles *and*
       headings that begin with the words
       viola d'amore or viole d'amore
  NT Suites (Viola d'amore)

Viola d'amore with chamber orchestra
    (M1019)
  BT Chamber-orchestra music
  RT Concertos (Viola d'amore with chamber
       orchestra)

Viola d'amore with orchestra *(M1019)*
  BT Orchestral music
  RT Concertos (Viola d'amore)

Viola d'amore with string orchestra
    (M1105-6)
  BT String-orchestra music
  RT Concertos (Viola d'amore with string
       orchestra)

Viola d'amore with string orchestra, Arranged
    (M1105-6)
  —Scores *(M1105)*

Viola di bordone
  USE Baryton

Viola music *(M45-49)*
  SA Concertos, Minuets, Sonatas, Suites,
       and similar headings with
       specification of instruments; String
       trios [quartets, etc.] *and* Trios
       [Quartets, etc.] *followed by*
       specifications which include the

Viola music *(M45-49)*
(Continued)
 SA *viola;* String quartets *and* String trios
   without specifications; also Piano
   quartets, Piano quintets, String
   ensembles *and headings that begin*
   with the words viola or violas
 NT Canons, fugues, etc. (Viola)
   Passacaglias (Viola)
   Piano quartets
   Piano quintets
   Recorded accompaniments (Viola)
   Sonatas (Viola)
   Suites (Viola)
Viola music (Violas (2)) *(M286-7)*
 NT Canons, fugues, etc. (Violas (2))
   Concertos (Violas (2) with string orchestra)
   Sonatas (Violas (2))
   Variations (Violas (2))
   Violas (2) with string orchestra
Viola music (Violas (2)), Arranged *(M286-7)*
Viola music (Violas (3))
 USE String trios (Violas (3))
Viola music (Violas (4))
 USE String quartets (Violas (4))
Viola paredon
 USE Baryton
Viola players
 USE Violists
Viola pomposa
 BT Viola
   Violoncello
 NT Violoncello piccolo
Viola pomposa and harpsichord music *(M239)*
 UF Harpsichord and viola pomposa music
 NT Sonatas (Viola pomposa and harpsichord)
Viola pomposa music *(M59)*
 NT Suites (Viola pomposa)
   Violoncello piccolo music
Viola pomposa with string orchestra *(M1119)*
 RT Concertos (Viola pomposa with string
   orchestra)
Viola, violins (2) with orchestra
 USE Violins (2), viola with orchestra
Viola with band *(M1205-6)*
 NT Concertos (Viola with band)
Viola with chamber orchestra *(M1014-1015)*
 RT Concertos (Viola with chamber
   orchestra)
 NT Suites (Viola with chamber orchestra)
 —Solo with piano *(M1015)*
   BT Viola and piano music, Arranged
Viola with instrumental ensemble
 RT Concertos (Viola with instrumental
   ensemble)
Viola with orchestra *(M1014-1015)*
 RT Concertos (Viola)
 NT Rondos (Viola with orchestra)
   Suites (Viola with orchestra)
   Symphonies (Viola with orchestra)
   Variations (Viola with orchestra)
 —Solo with piano *(M1015)*
   BT Viola and piano music, Arranged

Viola with orchestra, Arranged
 (M1014-1015)
 —Scores *(M1014)*
Viola with string ensemble
 RT Concertos (Viola with string ensemble)
 —Solo with piano
   BT Viola and piano music, Arranged
Viola with string orchestra *(M1105-6)*
 RT Concertos (Viola with string orchestra)
 NT Potpourris (Viola with string orchestra)
   Suites (Viola with string orchestra)
 —Scores *(M1105)*
 —Solo with piano *(M1115)*
   BT Viola and piano music, Arranged
Viola with string orchestra, Arranged
 (M1105-6)
Viola with wind ensemble
 RT Concertos (Viola with wind ensemble)
 —Solo with piano
   BT Viola and piano music, Arranged
Violano-virtuoso *(ML1055)*
 BT Musical instruments (Mechanical)
Violano-virtuoso music *(M175.V5)*
Violas (2) with string orchestra
 (M1114-1115)
 BT Viola music (Violas (2))
 RT Concertos (Violas (2) with string
   orchestra)
Violas (4) with orchestra *(M1014-1015)*
 BT String quartets (Violas (4))
 RT Concertos (Violas (4))
 NT Variations (Violas (4) with orchestra)
Violin *(ML800-897)*
 UF Fiddle
 NT Fiddling
   Hardanger fiddle
   Pochette
   Tenor violin
 Example under Stringed instruments, Bowed;
   and under reference from Melody in-
   struments
 —Bow
   USE Stringed instruments, Bowed—
    Bow
 —Construction
 —Group instruction
   USE Violin—Methods—Group
    instruction
 —Instruction and study *(MT260-279)*
   NT Violin music—Teaching pieces
 ——Bowing *(MT260-MT262)*
   UF Bowing (String instruments)
 ——Positions *(MT268)*
   UF Positions (Violin playing)
 —Labels *(ML845)*
   BT Labels
 —Methods *(MT262)*
 ——Group instruction *(MT262)*
   UF Violin—Group instruction
 ——Juvenile *(MT761)*
 ——Self-instruction *(MT278)*
   UF Violin—Self-instruction
 —Methods (Jazz) *(MT262)*

Violin *(ML800-897)*
 (Continued)
 —Orchestra studies *(MT266)*
  BT Violin—Studies and exercises
 —Performance *(ML850-892)*
  UF Violin playing
  BT Music—Performance
    Violin music—Interpretation
    (Phrasing, dynamics, etc.)
 —Self-instruction
  USE Violin—Methods—Self-instruction
 —Studies and exercises *(MT265; MT267-MT271)*
  NT Violin—Orchestra studies
 — —Juvenile *(MT775)*
 —Studies and exercises (Jazz) *(MT265)*
Violin and accordion music *(M298)*
 UF Accordion and violin music
 NT Variations (Violin and accordion)
Violin and bassoon music
 USE Bassoon and violin music
Violin and celesta music *(M298)*
 UF Celesta and violin music
Violin and cimbalom music *(M298)*
 UF Cimbalom and violin music
Violin and clarinet music
 USE Clarinet and violin music
Violin and continuo music *(M217-223)*
 UF Continuo and violin music
 NT Chaconnes (Violin and continuo)
  Marches (Violin and continuo)
  Minuets (Violin and continuo)
  Rondos (Violin and continuo)
  Sonatas (Violin and continuo)
  Suites (Violin and continuo)
  Variations (Violin and continuo)
Violin and double-bass music *(M286-7)*
 UF Double-bass and violin music
 NT Concertos (Violin and double bass
  with string orchestra)
  Sonatas (Violin and double bass)
  Violin and double bass with string
  orchestra
Violin and double bass with instrumental
  ensemble
 RT Concertos (Violin and double bass with
  instrumental ensemble)
 —Solos with piano *(M313-314)*
  BT Trios (Piano, violin, double bass),
  Arranged
Violin and double bass with orchestra
  (M1040-1041)
 RT Concertos (Violin and double bass)
Violin and double bass with string orchestra
  (M1140-1141)
 BT Violin and double-bass music
 RT Concertos (Violin and double bass with
  string orchestra)
Violin and English horn music
 USE English horn and violin music
Violin and flageolet music
 USE Flageolet and violin music
Violin and flute music
 USE Flute and violin music

Violin and guitar music *(M294-5)*
 UF Guitar and violin music
 NT Potpourris (Violin and guitar)
  Sonatas (Violin and guitar)
  Suites (Violin and guitar)
  Variations (Violin and guitar)
Violin and guitar music, Arranged *(M294-5)*
Violin and harp music *(M294-5)*
 UF Harp and violin music
 NT Concertos (Violin and harp)
  Sonatas (Violin and harp)
  Suites (Violin and harp)
  Variations (Violin and harp)
  Violin and harp with orchestra
Violin and harp with orchestra
  (M1040-1041)
 BT Violin and harp music
 RT Concertos (Violin and harp)
 —Solos with piano *(M1041)*
  BT Trios (Piano, harp, violin), Arranged
 Example under reference from Solos with piano
Violin and harpsichord music *(M217-M218;
  M221)*
 UF Harpsichord and violin music
 BT Violin and piano music
 NT Canons, fugues, etc. (Violin and
  harpsichord)
  Chaconnes (Violin and harpsichord)
  Concertos (Violin and harpsichord)
  Concertos (Violin and harpsichord with
  string orchestra)
  Marches (Violin and harpsichord)
  Polonaises (Violin and harpsichord)
  Sonatas (Violin and harpsichord)
  Suites (Violin and harpsichord)
  Variations (Violin and harpsichord)
  Violin and harpsichord with orchestra
  Violin and harpsichord with string
  orchestra
Violin and harpsichord with orchestra
  (M1040-1041)
 BT Orchestral music
  Violin and harpsichord music
 RT Concertos (Violin and harpsichord)
Violin and harpsichord with string orchestra
  (M1105-6)
 BT Violin and harpsichord music
 RT Concertos (Violin and harpsichord with
  string orchestra)
Violin and horn music
 USE Horn and violin music
Violin and hurdy-gurdy music
 USE Hurdy-gurdy and violin music
Violin and keyboard instrument music
  (M217-M218; M221)
 UF Keyboard instrument and violin music
Violin and lute music *(M294-295)*
 UF Lute and violin music
 NT Sonatas (Violin and lute)
Violin and mridanga music
 UF Mridanga and violin music
Violin and oboe music
 USE Oboe and violin music

Violin and organ music *(M182-4)*
> UF Organ and violin music
> NT Canons, fugues, etc. (Violin and organ)
>> Chaconnes (Violin and organ)
>> Chorale preludes (Violin and organ)
>> Concertos (Violin and organ with string orchestra)
>> Sonatas (Violin and organ)
>> Suites (Violin and organ)
>> Violin and organ with string orchestra

Violin and organ music, Arranged *(M185-6)*

Violin and organ with string orchestra *(M1105-6)*
> BT Violin and organ music
> RT Concertos (Violin and organ with string orchestra)

Violin and percussion music
> USE Percussion and violin music

Violin and piano music *(M217-M218; M221)*
> UF Piano and violin music
> NT Canons, fugues, etc. (Violin and piano)
>> Chaconnes (Violin and piano)
>> Chorale preludes (Violin and piano)
>> Concertos (Violin and piano)
>> Concertos (Violin and piano with chamber orchestra)
>> Concertos (Violin and piano with string orchestra)
>> Marches (Violin and piano)
>> Minuets (Violin and piano)
>> Polkas (Violin and piano)
>> Polonaises (Violin and piano)
>> Potpourris (Violin and piano)
>> Rondos (Violin and piano)
>> Sonatas (Violin and piano)
>> Suites (Violin and piano)
>> Trios (Piano (4 hands), violin)
>> Variations (Violin and piano)
>> Violin and harpsichord music
>> Violin and piano with chamber orchestra
>> Violin and piano with instrumental ensemble
>> Violin and piano with orchestra
>> Violin and piano with string orchestra
>> Waltzes (Violin and piano)
> *Note under* Dance music

Violin and piano music, Arranged *(M222-3)*
> NT Concertos (Violin)—Excerpts—Solo with piano
>> Concertos (Violin)—Solo with piano
>> Concertos (Violin), Arranged—Solo with piano
>> Concertos (Violin with chamber orchestra)—Solo with piano
>> Concertos (Violin with string orchestra)—Solo with piano
>> Concertos (Violin with string orchestra), Arranged—Solo with piano
>> Operas arranged for violin and piano
>> Overtures arranged for violin and piano

Violin and piano music, Arranged *(M222-3)*
> *(Continued)*
> NT Potpourris (Violin with orchestra)—Solo with piano
>> Rondos (Violin with chamber orchestra)—Solo with piano
>> Rondos (Violin with orchestra)—Solo with piano
>> Rondos (Violin with string orchestra)—Solo with piano
>> Suites (Violin with chamber orchestra), Arranged—Solo with piano
>> Suites (Violin with orchestra)—Solo with piano
>> Suites (Violin with string orchestra)—Solo with piano
>> Symphonies arranged for violin and piano
>> Variations (Violin with orchestra)—Solo with piano
>> Violin with band—Solo with piano
>> Violin with chamber orchestra—Solo with piano
>> Violin with orchestra—Solo with piano
>> Violin with string orchestra—Solo with piano

Violin and piano with chamber orchestra *(M1040-1041)*
> BT Chamber-orchestra music
>> Violin and piano music
> RT Concertos (Violin and piano with chamber orchestra)
> NT Suites (Violin and piano with chamber orchestra)

Violin and piano with instrumental ensemble *(M945-949)*
> BT Instrumental ensembles
>> Violin and piano music
> NT Suites (Violin and piano with instrumental ensemble)

Violin and piano with orchestra *(M1040-1041)*
> BT Orchestral music
>> Violin and piano music
> RT Concertos (Violin and piano)
> NT Suites (Violin and piano with orchestra)

Violin and piano with string ensemble
> RT Concertos (Violin and piano with string ensemble)

Violin and piano with string orchestra *(M1105-6)*
> BT Violin and piano music
> RT Concertos (Violin and piano with string orchestra)

Violin and piano with wind ensemble
> NT Concertos (Violin and piano with wind ensemble)

Violin and recorder music
> USE Recorder and violin music

Violin and shehnai music
> USE Shehnai and violin music

Violin and sitar music
> UF Sitar and violin music

Violin and tabla music
   UF   Tabla and violin music
Violin and trumpet music
   USE   Trumpet and violin music
Violin and vibraphone music
   USE   Vibraphone and violin music
Violin and viola da gamba music *(M286-7)*
   UF   Viola da gamba and violin music
   BT   Violin and violoncello music
   NT   Sonatas (Violin and viola da gamba)
Violin and viola d'amore music *(M286-287)*
   UF   Viola d'amore and violin music
   NT   Sonatas (Violin and viola d'amore)
Violin and viola music *(M286-7)*
   UF   Viola and violin music
   NT   Canons, fugues, etc. (Violin and viola)
         Concertos (Violin and viola)
         Concertos (Violin and viola with
            chamber orchestra)
         Concertos (Violin and viola with string
            orchestra)
         Passacaglias (Violin and viola)
         Sonatas (Violin and viola)
         Suites (Violin and viola)
         Variations (Violin and viola)
         Violin and viola with chamber orchestra
         Violin and viola with orchestra
         Violin and viola with string orchestra
   Note under Chamber music
Violin and viola music, Arranged *(M286-7)*
Violin and viola with chamber orchestra
      (M1040-1041)
   BT   Chamber-orchestra music
         Violin and viola music
   RT   Concertos (Violin and viola with
            chamber orchestra)
Violin and viola with instrumental ensemble
   RT   Concertos (Violin and viola with
            instrumental ensemble)
Violin and viola with orchestra
      (M1040-1041)
   BT   Orchestral music
         Violin and viola music
   RT   Concertos (Violin and viola)
   —Solos with piano *(M1041)*
      BT   Trios (Piano, violin, viola), Arranged
Violin and viola with string orchestra
      (M1105-6)
   BT   String-orchestra music
         Violin and viola music
   RT   Concertos (Violin and viola with string
            orchestra)
   NT   Suites (Violin and viola with string
            orchestra)
Violin and violoncello music *(M286-7)*
   UF   Violoncello and violin music
   NT   Canons, fugues, etc. (Violin and
            violoncello)
         Concertos (Violin and violoncello)
         Concertos (Violin and violoncello with
            chamber orchestra)
         Concertos (Violin and violoncello with
            string orchestra)

Violin and violoncello music *(M286-7)*
   (Continued)
   NT   Polonaises (Violin and violoncello)
         Sonatas (Violin and violoncello)
         Suites (Violin and violoncello)
         Variations (Violin and violoncello)
         Violin and viola da gamba music
         Violin and violoncello with chamber
            orchestra
         Violin and violoncello with orchestra
         Violin and violoncello with string orchestra
Violin and violoncello music, Arranged
Violin and violoncello with chamber orchestra
      (M1040-1041)
   BT   Violin and violoncello music
   RT   Concertos (Violin and violoncello with
            chamber orchestra)
**Violin and violoncello with instrumental
   ensemble**
   RT   Concertos (Violin and violoncello with
            instrumental ensemble)
Violin and violoncello with orchestra
      (M1040-1041)
   BT   Violin and violoncello music
   RT   Concertos (Violin and violoncello)
   NT   Potpourris (Violin and violoncello with
            orchestra)
   —Solos with piano *(M1041)*
      BT   Piano trios, Arranged
Violin and violoncello with string orchestra
      (M1105-6)
   BT   Violin and violoncello music
   RT   Concertos (Violin and violoncello with
            string orchestra)
   NT   Variations (Violin and violoncello with
            string orchestra)
Violin duets
   USE   Violin music (Violins (2))
Violin ensembles *(M950-M954)*
         Here are entered compositions for ten or
            more violins and collections of compo-
            sitions for a varying number of violins.
Violin makers [May Subd Geog]
   BT   Stringed instrument makers
Violin music *(M40-44)*
   SA   *Concertos, Minuets, Sonatas, Suites,*
         and similar headings with
         specification of instruments; *String
         trios [quartets, etc.]* and *Trios
         [Quartets, etc.]* followed by
         specifications which include the
         violin; *String quartets* and
         String-trios without specifications;
         also *Piano quartets, Piano quintets,
         Piano trios, String ensembles* and
         headings that begin with the words
         violin or violins
   NT   Canons, fugues, etc. (Violin)
         Chaconnes (Violin)
         Fiddle tunes
         Passacaglias (Violin)
         Piano quartets
         Piano quintets

Violin music *(M40-44)*
 (Continued)
  NT Piano trios
    Recorded accompaniments (Violin)
    Shehnai and violin music
    Sonatas (Violin)
    Suites (Violin)
    Variations (Violin)
 —Analysis, appreciation *(MT140; MT145)*
 —Bibliography
 — —Graded lists *(ML132.V4)*
    UF Violin music—Graded lists
 —Graded lists
    USE Violin music—Bibliography—
      Graded lists
 —History and criticism
 —Instructive editions *(MT275-6)*
 —Interpretation (Phrasing, dynamics, etc.)
    (MT271)
    NT Violin—Performance
 —Teaching pieces *(MT274)*
    BT Violin—Instruction and study
Violin music (Violins (2)) *(M286-7)*
 UF Violin duets
 NT Canons, fugues, etc. (Violins (2))
    Concertos (Violins (2))
    Concertos (Violins (2) with string
      orchestra)
    Potpourris (Violins (2))
    Sonatas (Violins (2))
    Suites (Violins (2))
    Variations (Violins (2))
    Violins (2) with orchestra
    Violins (2) with string orchestra
    Waltzes (Violins (2))
Violin music (Violins (2)), Arranged
    (M286-7)
Violin music (Violins (3))
 USE String trios (Violins (3))
Violin music (Violins (4))
 USE String quartets (Violins (4))
Violin music (Violins (5))
 USE String quintets (Violins (5))
Violin players
 USE Violinists
Violin playing
 USE Violin—Performance
Violin, viola, violoncello, double bass with
    string orchestra *(M1140-1141)*
 BT String quartets (Violin, viola, violoncello,
    double bass)
 RT Concertos (Violin, viola, violoncello,
    double bass with string orchestra)
Violin, violoncellos (2) with string
    orchestra *(M1140-1141)*
 BT String trios (Violin, violoncellos (2))
 RT Concertos (Violin, violoncellos (2) with
    string orchestra)
Violin with band *(M1205-6)*
 RT Concertos (Violin with band)
 —Solo with piano *(M1206)*
    BT Violin and piano music, Arranged

Violin with chamber orchestra *(M1012-1013)*
 RT Concertos (Violin with chamber
    orchestra)
 NT Polonaises (Violin with chamber
    orchestra)
    Rondos (Violin with chamber orchestra)
    Suites (Violin with chamber orchestra)
    Symphonies (Violin with chamber orchestra)
 —Solo with piano *(M1013)*
    BT Violin and piano music, Arranged
Violin with chamber orchestra, Arranged
    (M1012-1013)
Violin with instrumental ensemble
 RT Concertos (Violin with instrumental
    ensemble)
Violin with orchestra *(M1012-1013)*
 RT Concertos (Violin)
 NT Monologues with music
      (Violin with orchestra)
    Overtures (Violin with orchestra)
    Polonaises (Violin with orchestra)
    Potpourris (Violin with orchestra)
    Rondos (Violin with orchestra)
    Suites (Violin with orchestra)
    Symphonies (Violin with orchestra)
    Variations (Violin with orchestra)
    Waltzes (Violin with orchestra)
 —Solo with piano *(M1013)*
    BT Violin and piano music, Arranged
    Example under reference from Solo with piano
Violin with orchestra, Arranged
    (M1012-1013)
Violin with percussion ensemble
 RT Concertos (Violin with percussion
    ensemble)
    Note under Percussion ensembles
Violin with string ensemble
 RT Concertos (Violin with string ensemble)
 NT Rondos (Violin with string ensemble)
Violin with string orchestra *(M1105-6)*
 RT Concertos (Violin with string orchestra)
 NT Chaconnes (Violin with string orchestra)
    Overtures (Violin with string orchestra)
    Polonaises (Violin with string orchestra)
    Rondos (Violin with string orchestra)
    Suites (Violin with string orchestra)
    Variations (Violin with string orchestra)
 —Solo with piano *(M1106)*
    BT Violin and piano music, Arranged
Violin with string orchestra, Arranged *(M1105-6)*
 —Scores *(M1105)*
Violin with wind ensemble
 RT Concertos (Violin with wind ensemble)
Violinists [May Subd Geog]
 UF Violin players
 BT Musicians
 NT Fiddlers
Violins (2), viola with chamber orchestra
    (M1040-1041)
 UF Two violins, viola with chamber orchestra
 BT String trios (Violins (2), viola)
 RT Concertos (Violins (2) and viola with
    chamber orchestra)

Violins (2), viola with orchestra
    (M1040-1041)
  UF Two violins, viola with orchestra
       Viola, violins (2) with orchestra
  BT String trios (Violins (2), viola)
  RT Concertos (Violins (2), viola)
Violins (2), violas (2), violoncello with string
    orchestra *(M1140-1141)*
  BT String quintets (Violins (2), violas (2),
       violoncello)
  RT Concertos (Violins (2), violas (2),
       violoncello with string orchestra)
Violins (2), violas (2) with string orchestra
    (M1140-1141)
  BT String quartets (Violins (2), violas (2))
  RT Concertos (Violins (2), violas (2)
       with string orchestra)
Violins (2), violoncello with string orchestra
    (M1140-1141)
  BT String trios (Violins (2), violoncello)
  RT Concertos (Violins (2), violoncello with
       string orchestra)
  NT Suites (Violins (2), violoncello with
       string orchestra)
       Variations (Violins (2), violoncello with
       string orchestra)
Violins (2), violoncellos (2) with string
    orchestra *(M1140-1141)*
  BT String quartets (Violins (2), violoncellos
       (2))
  RT Concertos (Violins (2), violoncellos (2)
       with string orchestra)
Violins (2) with orchestra *(M1012-1013)*
  UF Two violins with orchestra
  BT Orchestral music
       Violin music (Violins (2))
  RT Concertos (Violins (2))
  —Solos with piano *(M1013)*
      BT Trios (Piano, violins (2)), Arranged
Violins (2) with orchestra, Arranged
    (M1012-1013)
Violins (2) with string ensemble
  RT Concertos (Violins (2) with string
       ensemble)
Violins (2) with string orchestra *(M1105-6)*
  UF Two violins with string orchestra
  BT String-orchestra music
       Violin music (Violins (2))
  RT Concertos (Violins (2) with string
       orchestra)
Violins (2) with string orchestra, Arranged
    (M1105-6)
  —Scores *(M1105)*
Violins (3), viola, violoncello with orchestra
    (M1040-M1041)
  NT Concertos (Violins (3), viola,
       violoncello)
Violins (3), viola, violoncello with string
    orchestra *(M1105-6)*
  BT String quintets (Violins (3), viola,
       violoncello)
  RT Concertos (Violins (3), viola,
       violoncello with string orchestra)

Violins (3) with orchestra *(M1012-1013)*
  UF Three violins with orchestra
  BT String trios (Violins (3))
  RT Concertos (Violins (3))
  —Solos with piano *(M1013)*
      BT Quartets (Piano, violins (3)),
         Arranged
Violins (3) with string orchestra *(M1105-6)*
  UF Three violins with string orchestra
  BT String-orchestra music
       String trios (Violins (3))
  RT Concertos (Violins (3) with string
       orchestra)
Violins (4) with string orchestra *(M1105-6)*
  UF Four violins with string orchestra
  BT String quartets (Violins (4))
  RT Concertos (Violins (4) with string
       orchestra)
Violins (5) with orchestra *(M1012-1013)*
  BT String quintets (Violins (5))
  RT Concertos (Violins (5))
Violists [May Subd Geog]
  UF Viola players
  BT Musicians
  NT Viol players
Violo *(ML927.V6)*
Violoncellists [May Subd Geog]
  UF Cellists
       Cello players
       Violoncello players
  BT Musicians
Violoncello *(ML910-915)*
  UF Cello
  NT Arpeggione
       Tenor violin
       Viola da gamba
       Viola pomposa
       Violoncello piccolo
  —Bow
      USE Stringed instruments, Bowed
           —Bow
  —Orchestra studies *(MT306)*
      BT Violoncello—Studies and exercises
  —Studies and exercises *(MT305; MT307-MT310)*
      NT Violoncello—Orchestra studies
Violoncello and bassoon music
  USE Bassoon and violoncello music
Violoncello and clarinet music
  USE Clarinet and violoncello music
Violoncello and continuo music
  UF Continuo and violoncello music
  NT Sonatas (Violoncello and continuo)
       Variations (Violoncello and continuo)
Violoncello and double-bass music *(M286-287)*
  UF Double-bass and violoncello music
  NT Rondos (Violoncello and double-bass)
       Sonatas (Violoncello and double-bass)
Violoncello and double bass with orchestra
    (M1040-1041)
  RT Concertos (Violoncello and double bass)
  —Solos with piano *(M1041)*
      BT Trios (Piano, violoncello, double
         bass), Arranged

Violoncello and English horn music
  USE English horn and violoncello music
Violoncello and flute music
  USE Flute and violoncello music
Violoncello and guitar music *(M294-5)*
  UF Guitar and violoncello music
  NT Potpourris (Violoncello and guitar)
     Suites (Violoncello and guitar)
Violoncello and harp music *(M294-5)*
  UF Harp and violoncello music
  NT Concertos (Violoncello and harp with
     string orchestra)
     Sonatas (Violoncello and harp)
     Suites (Violoncello and harp)
     Violoncello and harp with string
      orchestra
Violoncello and harp with orchestra
    (M1040-1041)
  RT Concertos (Violoncello and harp)
Violoncello and harp with string orchestra
    (M1105-6)
  BT Violoncello and harp music
  RT Concertos (Violoncello and harp with
     string orchestra)
  —Scores *(M1105)*
Violoncello and harp with string orchestra,
    Arranged *(M1105-6)*
  —Scores *(M1105)*
Violoncello and harpsichord music
    (M229-M230; M233)
  UF Harpsichord and violoncello music
  BT Instrumental music
     Violoncello and piano music
  NT Sonatas (Violoncello and harpsichord)
Violoncello and harpsichord music, Arranged
    (M235-6)
Violoncello and horn music
  USE Horn and violoncello music
Violoncello and organ music *(M182-6)*
  UF Organ and violoncello music
  NT Chorale preludes (Violoncello and organ)
     Sonatas (Violoncello and organ)
Violoncello and percussion music
  USE Percussion and violoncello music
Violoncello and piano music *(M229-M230;*
    M233)
  UF Piano and violoncello music
  NT Canons, fugues, etc. (Violoncello and
     piano)
     Chaconnes (Violoncello and piano)
     Chorale preludes (Violoncello and
      piano)
     Minuets (Violoncello and piano)
     Passacaglias (Violoncello and piano)
     Polonaises (Violoncello and piano)
     Potpourris (Violoncello and piano)
     Rondos (Violoncello and piano)
     Sonatas (Violoncello and piano)
     Suites (Violoncello and piano)
     Variations (Violoncello and piano)
     Viola da gamba and harpsichord music
     Violoncello and harpsichord music
     Waltzes (Violoncello and piano)

Violoncello and piano music, Arranged *(M235-6)*
  NT Chaconnes (Violoncello with chamber
     orchestra)—Solo with piano
     Concertos (Violoncello)—Excerpts—
      Solo with piano
     Concertos (Violoncello)—Solo with piano
     Concertos (Violoncello), Arranged—
      Solo with piano
     Concertos (Violoncello with chamber
      orchestra)—Solo with piano
     Concertos (Violoncello with instrumental
      ensemble)—Solo with piano
     Concertos (Violoncello with string
      orchestra)—Solo with piano
     Concertos (Violoncello with string
      orchestra), Arranged—Solo with piano
     Potpourris (Violoncello with orchestra)
      —Solo with piano
     Suites (Violoncello with chamber
      orchestra)—Solo with piano
     Suites (Violoncello with orchestra)
      —Solo with piano
     Symphonic poems arranged for
      violoncello and piano
     Symphonies (Violoncello with
      orchestra)—Solo with piano
     Symphonies arranged for violoncello
      and piano
     Variations (Violoncello with chamber
      orchestra)—Solo with piano
     Variations (Violoncello with orchestra)
      —Solo with piano
     Variations (Violoncello with string
      orchestra)—Solo with piano
     Violoncello with band—Solo with piano
     Violoncello with brass band—Solo with
      piano
     Violoncello with chamber orchestra—
      Solo with piano
     Violoncello with orchestra—Solo with
      piano
     Violoncello with string orchestra—Solo
      with piano
Violoncello and piano with orchestra
    (M1040-1041)
  RT Concertos (Violoncello and piano)
Violoncello and recorder music
  USE Recorder and violoncello music
Violoncello and saxophone music
  USE Saxophone and violoncello music
Violoncello and trumpet music
  USE Trumpet and violoncello music
Violoncello and viola music
  USE Viola and violoncello music
Violoncello and violin music
  USE Violin and violoncello music
Violoncello ensembles *(M950-M954)*
    Here are entered compositions for ten or
     more violoncellos and collections of
     compositions for a varying number of
     violoncellos.
  NT Suites (Violoncello ensemble)
  Note under String ensembles

Violoncello music *(M50-54)*
  SA Concertos, Minuets, Sonatas, Suites,
        and similar headings with
        specification of instruments; String
        trios [quartets, etc.] *and* Trios
        [Quartets, etc.] *followed by*
        specifications which include the
        violoncello; String quartets *and*
        String trios *without specifications;*
        also Piano quartets, Piano quintets,
        Piano trios, String ensembles, *and*
        headings that begin with the words
        Violoncello *or* Violoncellos
  NT Piano quartets
        Piano quintets
        Piano trios
        Recorded accompaniments
          (Violoncello)
        Sonatas (Violoncello)
        Suites (Violoncello)
        Variations (Violoncello)
        Viola da gamba music
  —History and criticism *(ML915)*
Violoncello music (Violoncellos (2))
        (M286-7)
  NT Canons, fugues, etc. (Violoncellos (2))
        Concertos (Violoncellos (2))
        Concertos (Violoncellos (2) with string
          orchestra)
        Passacaglias (Violoncellos (2))
        Sonatas (Violoncellos (2))
        Suites (Violoncellos (2))
        Trios (Percussion, violoncellos (2))
        Variations (Violoncellos (2))
        Violoncellos (2) with chamber orchestra
        Violoncellos (2) with orchestra
        Violoncellos (2) with string orchestra
Violoncello music (Violoncellos (2)), Arranged
        (M286-7)
Violoncello music (Violoncellos (4))
  USE String quartets (Violoncellos (4))
Violoncello music (Violoncellos (6))
  USE String sextets (Violoncellos (6))
Violoncello music (Violoncellos (7))
  USE String septets (Violoncellos (7))
Violoncello music (Violoncellos (8))
  USE String octets (Violoncellos (8))
Violoncello piccolo *(ML760)*
  BT Viola pomposa
        Violoncello
Violoncello piccolo music *(M57)*
  BT Viola pomposa music
  NT Concertos (Violoncello piccolo with
          string orchestra)
        Violoncello piccolo with string
          orchestra
Violoncello piccolo with string orchestra
        (M1105-6)
  BT Violoncello piccolo music
  RT Concertos (Violoncello piccolo with
          string orchestra)
Violoncello players
  USE Violoncellists

Violoncello with band *(M1205-6)*
  RT Concertos (Violoncello with band)
  NT Canons, fugues, etc. (Violoncello with
          band)
  —Solo with piano *(M1206)*
        BT Violoncello and piano music,
              Arranged
Violoncello with brass band *(M1205;M1257)*
  RT Concertos (Violoncello with brass band)
  —Solo with piano *(M1206)*
        BT Violoncello and piano music,
              Arranged
Violoncello with chamber orchestra
        (M1016-1017)
  RT Concertos (Violoncello with chamber
          orchestra)
  NT Chaconnes (Violoncello with chamber
          orchestra)
        Suites (Violoncello with chamber
          orchestra)
        Variations (Violoncello with chamber
          orchestra)
  —Solo with piano *(M1017)*
        BT Violoncello and piano music,
              Arranged
Violoncello with chamber orchestra, Arranged
        (M1016-1017)
  —Scores *(M1016)*
Violoncello with instrumental ensemble
  RT Concertos (Violoncello with
          instrumental ensemble)
Violoncello with jazz ensemble *(M1366)*
  NT Suites (Violoncello with jazz ensemble)
Violoncello with orchestra *(M1016-1017)*
  RT Concertos (Violoncello)
  NT Potpourris (Violoncello with orchestra)
        Rondos (Violoncello with orchestra)
        Suites (Violoncello with orchestra)
        Symphonies (Violoncello with
          orchestra)
        Variations (Violoncello with orchestra)
  —Solo with piano *(M1017)*
        BT Violoncello and piano music,
              Arranged
Violoncello with orchestra, Arranged
        (M1016-1017)
  —Scores *(M1016)*
Violoncello with string ensemble
  RT Concertos (Violoncello with string
          ensemble)
Violoncello with string orchestra *(M1105-6)*
  BT String-orchestra music
  RT Concertos (Violoncello with string
          orchestra)
  NT Suites (Violoncello with string
          orchestra)
        Variations (Violoncello with string
          orchestra)
  —Solo with piano *(M1117)*
        BT Violoncello and piano music,
              Arranged
Violoncello with string orchestra, Arranged
        (M1105-6)

Violoncello with wind ensemble
    RT Concertos (Violoncello with wind
        ensemble)
Violoncellos (2) with chamber orchestra
      (M1016-1017)
    UF Two violoncellos with chamber
        orchestra
    BT Concertos (Violoncellos (2))
        Violoncello music (Violoncellos (2)
    RT Concertos (Violoncellos (2) with
        chamber orchestra)
    —Scores*(M1016)*
Violoncellos (2) with instrumental ensemble
    RT Concertos (Violoncellos (2) with
        instrumental ensemble)
Violoncellos (2) with orchestra
      (M1016-1017)
    UF Two violoncellos with orchestra
    BT Violoncello music (Violoncellos (2))
    RT Concertos (Violoncellos (2))
    —Solos with piano *(M1017)*
        BT Trios (Piano, violoncellos (2)),
           Arranged
Violoncellos (2) with string orchestra *(M1105-6)*
    UF Two violoncellos with string orchestra
    BT String-orchestra music
        Violoncello music (Violoncellos (2))
    RT Concertos (Violoncellos (2) with string
        orchestra)
Violoncellos (3) with orchestra *(M1016-1017)*
    UF Three violoncellos with orchestra
    BT String trios (Violoncellos (3))
    RT Concertos (Violoncellos (3))
    —Solos with piano *(M1017)*
        BT Quartets (Piano, violoncellos (3)),
           Arranged
Violone *(ML927.V63)*
    UF Contre-bass de viol
        Double-bass viol
    BT Viol
Violone and double bass music *(M286-287)*
    UF Double bass and violone music
Violone and harpsichord music *(M239)*
    UF Harpsichord and violone music
    NT Sonatas (Violone and harpsichord)
Violone and viola music
    USE Viola and violone music
Violone music *(M59)*
    BT Viol music
    SA Concertos, Minuets, Sonatas, Suites,
        and similar headings with
        specification of instruments; String
        trios [quartets, etc.] *and* Trios
        [Quartets, etc.] *followed by*
        specifications which include the
        violone; also String ensembles *and*
        headings that begin with the words
        Violone *or* Violones
Virginal
    USE Harpsichord
Virginal music
    USE Harpsichord music

Virtuosity in music *(Interpretation, ML3853)*
    BT Music
        Music—Instruction and study
        Music—Performance
Vispārējie latviešu dziesmu svētki
    USE Latvian Song Festival
Visually handicapped [May Subd Geog]
    NT Music for the visually handicapped
Vocal culture
    USE Singing
        Voice culture
Vocal duets
    BT Choruses, Secular
        Vocal music
    RT Sacred duets
    NT Madrigals (Music)
        Part-songs
Vocal duets, Unaccompanied
Vocal duets with chamber orchestra
    —Vocal scores with piano
        BT Vocal duets with piano
Vocal duets with continuo *(M1549.2;*
      M1550.2; M1551.2)
Vocal duets with electronic music *(M1528-1529)*
Vocal duets with guitar
Vocal duets with harp
Vocal duets with harpsichord
    BT Vocal duets with piano
Vocal duets with instrumental ensemble
      (M1528-1529)
    NT Monologues with music (Vocal duet
        with instrumental ensemble)
Vocal duets with keyboard instruments
Vocal duets with lute
Vocal duets with orchestra
    —Vocal scores with piano
        BT Vocal duets with piano
Vocal duets with piano
    NT Vocal duets with chamber orchestra—
        Vocal scores with piano
        Vocal duets with harpsichord
        Vocal duets with orchestra—Vocal
        scores with piano
        Vocal duets with string orchestra—
        Vocal scores with piano
Vocal duets with pianos (2)
Vocal duets with string orchestra *(M1528-9)*
    —Vocal scores with piano *(M1529)*
        BT Vocal duets with piano
Vocal duets with vibraphone
Vocal ensembles
    UF Ensembles (Music)
    RT Ensemble singing
    NT Madrigals (Music)
        Part-songs
        Sacred vocal ensembles
Vocal ensembles, Unaccompanied *(M1529.4;*
      M1529.5)
Vocal ensembles with band *(M1528-1529)*
    BT Band music
Vocal ensembles with continuo

Vocal ensembles with instrumental ensemble
    (M1528-1529)
    BT Instrumental ensembles
Vocal ensembles with orchestra
    BT Orchestral music
Vocal folds
    USE Vocal cords
Vocal music [May Subd Geog] *(M1495-2199)*
    UF Music, Vocal
    BT Music
    NT Ballads
         Canons, fugues, etc. (Vocal)
         Choruses
         Folk-songs
         Glees, catches, rounds, etc.
         Madrigals
         Part-songs
         Rondos (Vocal)
         Sacred vocal music
         Songs
         Variations (Vocal)
         Vocal duets
         Vocal nonets
         Vocal octets
         Vocal quartets
         Vocal quintets
         Vocal septets
         Vocal sextets
         Vocal trios
         Vocalises
    —Bibliography *(ML128.V7)*
    — —Graded lists *(ML132.V7)*
         UF Vocal music—Graded lists
    —Cadenzas *(M1497)*
    —Graded lists
        USE Vocal music—Bibliography—
               Graded lists
    —History and criticism *(ML1400-3270)*
        SA *various forms of vocal music, e.g.*
             Cantata, Opera
        NT Choral music
            Embellishment (Vocal music)
            Parody (Music)
    —Thematic catalogs *(ML128.V7)*
        UF Thematic catalogs (Music)
    —India
        NT Khyāl (Musical form)
    —Japan
        NT Utai
Vocal music, Popular
    USE Popular music
Vocal music, Sacred
    USE Sacred vocal music
Vocal nonets
    UF Nonets, Secular
         Nonets, Vocal
    BT Choruses, Secular
         Vocal music
    RT Sacred nonets
    NT Madrigals (Music)
         Part-songs
    Note under Nonets

Vocal octets
    UF Octets, Secular
         Octets, Vocal
    BT Choruses, Secular
         Vocal music
    RT Sacred octets
    NT Madrigals (Music)
         Part-songs
    Note under Octets
Vocal octets, Unaccompanied
Vocal octets with instrumental ensemble
    (M1528-1529)
Vocal octets with orchestra *(M1528-9)*
Vocal pouch
    USE Vocal sac
Vocal quartets
    UF Quartets, Secular
         Quartets, Vocal
    BT Choruses, Secular
         Vocal music
    RT Sacred quartets
    NT Madrigals (Music)
         Part-songs
    Note under Quartets
Vocal quartets, Unaccompanied
    NT Barbershop quartets
Vocal quartets with chamber orchestra
    (M1528-9)
    —Vocal scores with piano *(M1529)*
        BT Vocal quartets with piano
Vocal quartets with continuo
Vocal quartets with dance orchestra *(M1353)*
Vocal quartets with electronic music
    (M1528)
    BT Electronic music
Vocal quartets with harpsichord
    RT Vocal quartets with piano
Vocal quartets with instrumental ensemble
    NT Monologues with music (Vocal quartet
         with instrumental ensemble)
Vocal quartets with orchestra *(M1528-9)*
    —Vocal scores with piano *(M1529)*
        BT Vocal quartets with piano
Vocal quartets with percussion *(M1528)*
Vocal quartets with piano
    RT Vocal quartets with harpsichord
    NT Vocal quartets with chamber orchestra
         —Vocal scores with piano
         Vocal quartets with orchestra—Vocal
          scores with piano
Vocal quartets with piano, 4 hands
    NT Waltzes (Vocal quartets with piano,
         4 hands)
Vocal quintets
    UF Quintets, Secular
         Quintets, Vocal
    BT Choruses, Secular
         Vocal music
    RT Sacred quintets
    NT Madrigals (Music)
         Part-songs
    Note under Quintets

Vocal quintets, Unaccompanied
Vocal quintets with instrumental ensemble
    (M1528-1529)
Vocal quintets with organ
Vocal registers
  UF Registers, Vocal
      Singing registers
      Voice registers
  BT Music—Physiological aspects
      Register (Linguistics)
      Singing
      Voice
Vocal sac
  UF Vocal pouch
  BT Sound production by animals
      Vocal cords
Vocal septets
  UF Septets, Secular
      Septets, Vocal
  BT Choruses, Secular
      Vocal music
  RT Sacred septets
  NT Madrigals (Music)
      Part-songs
  Note under Septets
Vocal septets, Unaccompanied
Vocal septets with orchestra *(M1528-9)*
  —Scores *(M1528)*
Vocal sextets
  UF Sextets, Secular
      Sextets, Vocal
  BT Choruses, Secular
      Vocal music
  RT Sacred sextets
  NT Madrigals (Music)
      Part-songs
  Note under Sextets
Vocal sextets, Unaccompanied
Vocal sextets with instrumental ensemble
    (M1528)
Vocal sextets with orchestra *(M1528-9)*
  —Vocal scores with piano *(M1529)*
    BT Vocal sextets with piano
Vocal sextets with piano
  NT Vocal sextets with orchestra—Vocal
      scores with piano
Vocal trios
  UF Trios, Secular
      Trios, Vocal
  BT Choruses, Secular
      Vocal music
  RT Sacred trios
  NT Madrigals (Music)
      Part-songs
  Note under Trios
Vocal trios, Unaccompanied
Vocal trios with chamber orchestra
    (M1528-9)
  —Scores *(M1528)*
  —Vocal scores with piano *(M1529)*
    BT Vocal trios with piano
Vocal trios with continuo

Vocal trios with guitar
Vocal trios with harpsichord
  BT Vocal trios with piano
Vocal trios with instrumental ensemble
    (M1528-1529)
Vocal trios with lute
Vocal trios with orchestra *(M1528-9)*
  NT Monologues with music (Vocal trio
      with orchestra)
  —Scores *(M1528)*
Vocal trios with piano
  NT Vocal trios with chamber orchestra—
      Vocal scores with piano
      Vocal trios with harpsichord
Vocal trios with piano (4 hands)
Vocal trios with pianos (2)
Vocalion
  USE Reed-organ
Vocalion, Aeolian
  USE Aeolian-vocalion
Vocalises
    Here are entered works for one or
    two voices without texts. The heading
    is qualified as appropriate by number of
    voices or voice range and specification
    of accompaniment, *e.g.* Vocalises (Voices
    (2)) with piano; Vocalises (High voice)
    with flute; Vocalises (Medium voice),
    Unaccompanied.
  BT Songs
      Vocal music
  RT Singing—Studies and exercises
Vocalises (2 voices) with piano
Vocalises (High voice) with chamber orchestra
    (M1613.3)
  —Scores *(M1613.3)*
Vocalises (High voice) with clarinet
Vocalises (High voice) with electronic organ
Vocalises (High voice) with flute
Vocalises (High voice) with harpsichord *(MT885)*
  BT Vocalises (High voice) with piano
Vocalises (High voice) with instrumental
    ensemble *(M1613.3)*
Vocalises (High voice) with jazz ensemble
    (M1611; M1613.3)
  BT Jazz ensembles
Vocalises (High voice) with orchestra
    (M1613; M1617)
Vocalises (High voice) with piano
  NT Vocalises (High voice) with harpsichord
Vocalises (High voice) with viola *(M1623.8;*
    M1624.8)
Vocalises (Low voice) with piano
Vocalises (Medium voice), Unaccompanied
    (M1497)
Vocalises (Medium voice) with chamber
    orchestra *(M1613.3; M1614)*
  —Scores *(M1613.3)*
Vocalises (Medium voice) with instrumental
    ensemble *(M1613.3)*
Vocalises (Medium voice) with orchestra
    (M1613; M1617)

Vocalises (Medium voice) with piano *(MT885)*

Vocalises (Medium voice) with string orchestra *(M1613.3; M1614)*

Vocalises (Voices (2)), Unaccompanied

Vocalises (Voices (2)) with piano
  Note under Vocalises

Vocalises with instrumental ensemble *(M1613.3)*

Vocalises with piano *(MT885)*

Vocalists
  USE Singers

Vocals, Jazz
  USE Jazz vocals

Voce mea ad Dominum clamavi, voce mea ad
          Dominum deprecatus sum (Music)
  USE Psalms (Music)—142d Psalm

Voice *(Physiology, QP306; Sound production
          in animals, QL765)*
  BT Music
      Music—Physiological aspects
  RT Singing
  NT Vocal registers
  —Care and hygiene *(MT821)*
      NT Voice culture—Exercises

Voice culture *(PN4162)*
  UF Vocal culture
  RT Singing
  NT Respiration
  —Exercises
      BT Singing—Studies and exercises
          Voice—Care and hygiene

Volshebnaia fleîta (Ballet)
  USE Magic flute (Ballet)

Wa wa erh
  USE So na

Wagner, Richard, 1813-1883
  —Aesthetics
  —Allegory and symbolism
      USE Wagner, Richard, 1813-1833—
          Symbolism
  —Anecdotes *(ML410.W19)*
  —**Anniversaries, etc.**
  —**Anniversaries, etc., [date]**
  —**Chronology**
  —**Dictionaries, indexes, etc.**
  —**Discography** *(ML156.7.W3)*
  —Drama
      USE Wagner, Richard, 1813-1883, in
          fiction, drama, poetry, etc.
  —**Dramaturgy**
  —**Exhibitions** *(ML141)*
  —Fiction
      USE Wagner, Richard, 1813-1883, in
          fiction, drama, poetry, etc.
  —**Friends and associates**
  —**Harmony**
  —**Homes and haunts** [May Subd Geog]
  —Iconography
      USE Wagner, Richard, 1813-1883—
          Pictorial works
  —**Influence**
  —**Language**
  —**Manuscripts**
  — —**Facsimiles**

Wagner, Richard, 1813-1883
  (Continued)
  —**Museums, relics, etc.** [May Subd Geog]
      UF Wagner, Richard, 1813-1883—
          Relics
  —**Parodies, imitations, etc.**
      UF Wagner, Richard, 1813-1883—
          Parodies, travesties, etc.
  —Parodies, travesties, etc.
      USE Wagner, Richard, 1813-1883—
          Parodies, imitations, etc.
  —**Performances** [May Subd Geog]
  —**Performers**
  —**Pictorial works**
      UF Wagner, Richard, 1813-1883—
          Iconography
  —Poetry
      USE Wagner, Richard, 1813-1883, in
          fiction, drama, poetry, etc.
  —**Political and social views**
  —Relics
      USE Wagner, Richard, 1813-1883—
          Museums, relics, etc.
  —**Stories of operas**
  —**Symbolism**
      UF Wagner, Richard, 1813-1883—
          Allegory and symbolism
  —**Thematic catalogs**

**Wagner, Richard, 1813-1883, in
fiction, drama, poetry, etc.**
  UF Wagner, Richard, 1813-1883—Drama
      Wagner, Richard, 1813-1883—Fiction
          Wagner, Richard, 1813-1883—Poetry
  BT Musical fiction

Waits *(Music in England, ML286)*
  UF Musicians, Town
      Town musicians
  BT Musicians—Great Britain
  RT Stadtpfeifer

Walloon folk-songs
  USE Folk-songs, Walloon

Waltzes
      Here are entered collections of waltz mu-
      sic for various mediums. Individual
      waltzes and collections of waltzes for a
      specific medium are entered under the
      heading followed by specification of
      medium.
  BT Dance music
  NT Ländler
  Note under Dance music

Waltzes (Accordion) *(M175.A4)*
  BT Accordion music

Waltzes (Accordion ensemble) *(M1362)*
  BT Accordion ensembles

Waltzes (Balalaika and piano) *(M282-3)*
  BT Balalaika and piano music

Waltzes (Band) *(M1249; M1266)*
  BT Band music

Waltzes (Chamber orchestra) *(M1049;
  M1060)*
  BT Chamber-orchestra music
  —Scores

Waltzes (Chorus with orchestra)
  BT Choruses with orchestra
  —Scores
Waltzes (Chorus with piano)
  BT Choruses, Secular, with piano
Waltzes (Chorus with piano, 4 hands)
  BT Choruses, Secular, with piano, 4 hands
Waltzes (Clarinet and piano) *(M248-252)*
  BT Clarinet and piano music
Waltzes (Dance orchestra)
  BT Dance-orchestra music
Waltzes (Double bass and piano)
      (M237-238)
  BT Double-bass and piano music
Waltzes (Flute and piano) *(M240-244)*
  BT Flute and piano music
Waltzes (Flute, guitar, violin) *(M380-384)*
  BT Trios (Flute, guitar, violin)
Waltzes (Flute, violins (2), violoncello)
      (M463-4)
  BT Quartets (Flute, violins (2), violoncello)
Waltzes (Guitar) *(M125-9)*
  BT Guitar music
Waltzes (Guitar and piano) *(M276-7)*
  BT Guitar and piano music
Waltzes (Guitar, violins (2)) *(M370-374)*
  BT Trios (Guitar, violins (2))
Waltzes (Guitars (2)) *(M292-3)*
  BT Guitar music (Guitars (2))
Waltzes (Harmonica ensemble)
  BT Harmonica ensembles
Waltzes (Harp) *(M115-119)*
  BT Harp music
Waltzes (Horn and piano) *(M255-259)*
  BT Horn and piano music
Waltzes (Orchestra) *(M1049; M1060)*
  BT Orchestral music
Waltzes (Percussion and piano)
  BT Percussion and piano music
Waltzes (Piano) *(M32)*
  BT Piano music
Waltzes (Piano, 1 hand) *(Left hand, M26;*
      Right hand, M26.2)
  BT Piano music (1 hand)
Waltzes (Piano, 4 hands) *(M200-M201; M204;*
      M207; M209)
  BT Piano music (4 hands)
Waltzes (Piano (4 hands), violin, violoncello)
      (M310-314)
  BT Quartets (Piano (4 hands), violin,
      violoncello)
Waltzes (Piano, cornets (3)) *(M415-419)*
  BT Quartets (Piano, cornets (3))
Waltzes (Piano, violin, viola) *(M310-314)*
  BT Trios (Piano, violin, viola)
Waltzes (Piano, violins (2), violoncello) *(M410-414)*
  BT Quartets (Piano, violins (2), violoncello)
Waltzes (Piano with orchestra)
      (M1010-1011)
  BT Piano with orchestra
  —2-piano scores *(M1011)*
      BT Piano music (Pianos (2)), Arranged
  —Scores *(M1010)*

Waltzes (Pianos (2)) *(M214-215)*
  BT Piano music (Pianos (2))
Waltzes (Salon orchestra) *(M1350)*
  BT Salon-orchestra music
  —Scores and parts *(M1350)*
Waltzes (String ensemble)
  BT String ensembles
Waltzes (String orchestra) *(M1145; M1160)*
  BT String-orchestra music
Waltzes (String quartet) *(M450-454)*
  BT String quartets
Waltzes (Trombone and piano) *(M262-3)*
  BT Trombone and piano music
Waltzes (Trumpet and piano) *(M260-261)*
  BT Trumpet and piano music
Waltzes (Trumpet with band) *(M1205-6)*
  BT Trumpet with band
  —Scores and parts *(M1205)*
Waltzes (Tuba and piano) *(M264-5)*
  BT Tuba and piano music
Waltzes (Tuba and piano), Arranged
      (M264-265)
  NT Waltzes (Tuba with wind ensemble)—
      Solo with piano
Waltzes (Tuba with wind ensemble)
  BT Tuba with wind ensemble
  —Solo with piano *(M264-265)*
      BT Tuba and piano music, Arranged
          Waltzes (Tuba and piano), Arranged
Waltzes (Viola and guitar) *(M294-5)*
  BT Viola and guitar music
Waltzes (Viola and piano) *(M224-8)*
  BT Viola and piano music
Waltzes (Violin and piano) *(M217-M218;*
      M221-M223)
  BT Violin and piano music
Waltzes (Violin with orchestra)
      (M1012-1013)
  BT Violin with orchestra
Waltzes (Violins (2)) *(M286-7)*
  BT Violin music (Violins (2))
Waltzes (Violins (2), viola, violoncello, double
      bass) *(M550-554)*
  BT String quintets (Violins (2), viola,
      violoncello, double bass)
Waltzes (Violins (3), viola, double bass)
      (M550-554)
  BT String quintets (Violins (3), viola,
      double bass)
Waltzes (Violoncello and piano) *(M229-236)*
  BT Violoncello and piano music
Waltzes (Vocal quartet with piano, 4 hands)
  BT Vocal quartets with piano, 4 hands
Waltzes (Voice with chamber orchestra)
  BT Songs with chamber orchestra
  —Scores
Waltzes (Voice with orchestra)
  BT Songs with orchestra
  —Scores
Waltzes (Voice with piano)
  BT Songs with piano
Waltzes (Zither) *(M135-9)*
  BT Zither music

War and music
   USE Music and war
War poetry *(American literature, PS595.H5;*
         English literature, PR1195.H5;
         General collections, PN6110.W28)
   RT War-songs
   SA *subdivision* Poetry *under names of*
         wars, e.g. World War, 1939-1945—Poetry
War-songs [May Subd Geog]
   UF Armies—Music
         Battle-songs
         Soldiers' songs
   BT Military music
         National songs
         Songs
   RT Music in the army
         War poetry
   SA *subdivision* Songs and music *under*
         armies, navies, specific wars, veteran
         organizations, etc.
   NT Jody calls
         Revolutionary ballads and songs
         Soldiers—Hymns
Wave-motion, Theory of *(QA927)*
   NT Music and color
Wedding music
   UF Wedding songs
   BT Church music
         Music
         Sacred vocal music
   NT Synagogue music—Marriage services
Wedding songs
   USE Epithalamia
         Wedding music
Welsh folk-songs
   USE Folk-songs, Welsh
Welte-Lichtton-Orgel
   BT Electronic organ
         Organ
Western swing (Music) [May Subd Geog] *(ML3541)*
   UF Swing, Western (Music)
   BT Country music
         Jazz music
Whistle
   USE Penny whistle
Wiener Konzerthaus (Vienna, Austria)
   UF Konzerthaus (Vienna, Austria)
   BT Auditoriums—Austria
         Music-halls—Austria
Wind ensembles *(M955-959)*
         Here are entered compositions for ten or
         more solo wind (i.e. brass and wood-
         wind) instruments, also collections of
         compositions for a varying number or
         combination of solo wind instruments.
         Compositions for ensembles of brass or
         woodwind instruments only are en-
         tered under Brass ensembles and
         Woodwind ensembles respectively.
         When used in conjunction with specific
         solo instrument(s), the qualifier wind
         ensemble may stand for any number or
         combination of solo wind instruments.

Wind ensembles *(M955-959)*
   (Continued)
   UF Ensembles (Music)
   BT Band music
         Harpsichord and piano with wind
         ensemble
   SA Concertos ([Solo instrument(s)] with
         wind ensemble); [Solo instrument(s)]
         with wind ensemble; Suites
         Variations, Waltzes, *and similar*
         headings with specification of
         instruments which include the
         specification Wind ensemble
   NT Brass ensembles
         Canons, fugues, etc. (Wind ensemble)
         Marches (Wind ensemble)
         Overtures (Wind ensemble)
         Suites (Wind ensemble)
         Symphonies (Wind ensemble)
         Woodwind ensembles
   Note under Instrumental ensembles
Wind instrument and piano music
   UF Piano and wind instrument music
Wind instrument and piano music, Arranged
Wind instrument and piano music, Arranged
         (Jazz)
   USE Wind instrument and piano music (Jazz)
Wind instrument and piano music (Jazz)
   UF Wind instrument and piano music,
         Arranged (Jazz)
Wind instrument makers [May Subd Geog]
   UF Wind instruments—Makers
   BT Musical instrument makers
   NT Brass instrument makers
         Woodwind instrument makers
Wind instrument music *(M111)*
         Here are entered musical compositions
         for an unspecified solo wind instru-
         ment. Works for a specified instrument
         are entered under Bassoon music,
         Clarinet music, and similar headings.
   UF Melody instrument music
         Unspecified instrument music
   BT Solo instrument music
   NT Brass instrument music
         Woodwind instrument music
Wind instrument music (Wind instruments (2))
   (M288-289)
Wind instrument with instrumental ensemble
   RT Concertos (Wind instrument with
         instrumental ensemble)
Wind instruments *(History and construction,*
   ML930-ML980)
   RT Bands (Music)
   NT Alboka
         Brass instruments
         Hsüan (Musical instrument)
         Instrumentation and orchestration
         (Band)
         Mirliton
         Tonguing (Wind instrument playing)
         Woodwind instruments
   Example under Musical instruments

Wind instruments *(History and construction,*
    ML930-ML980)
  (Continued)
—Construction *(ML930)*
—Makers
    USE Wind instrument makers
—Methods *(MT339)*
—Methods (Jazz) *(MT339)*
    Example under Jazz music
—Studies and exercises *(MT339)*
—Studies and exercises (Jazz) *(MT339)*
—Tariff
    USE Tariff on wind instruments
—Tuning *(ML930)*
Wind nonets *(M955-959)*
    Collections of compositions for various
      combinations of nine wind (i.e. brass
      and woodwind) instruments are en-
      tered under this heading without
      specification of instruments. Separate
      compositions and collections of com-
      positions for nine specific wind instru-
      ments are entered under this heading
      followed by specification of instru-
      ments in alphabetical order.
    Compositions for nine brass instruments
      are entered under Brass nonets; com-
      positions for nine woodwind instru-
      ments are entered under Woodwind
      nonets.
    Headings with specification of instru-
      ments are printed below only if spe-
      cific cross references are needed.
  UF Nonets, Wind
  SA Suites, Variations, Waltzes, *and similar*
      headings with specification of
      instruments
  Note under Nonets
Wind nonets (Bassoons (3), clarinets (2),
    horns (2), oboes (2)) *(M955-M959)*
Wind nonets (Bassoons (3), clarinets (2),
    horns (2), oboes (2)), Arranged
    (M958-M959)
  NT Overtures arranged for bassoons (3),
      clarinets (2), horns (2), oboes (2)
      Symphonies arranged for bassoons (3),
      clarinets (2), horns (2), oboes (2)
Wind octets *(M855-859)*
    Collections of compositions for various
      combinations of eight wind (i.e. brass
      and woodwind) instruments are en-
      tered under this heading without
      specification of instruments. Separate
      compositions and collections of com-
      positions for eight specific wind instru-
      ments are entered under this heading
      followed by specification of instru-
      ments in alphabetical order.
    Compositions for eight brass instruments
      are entered under Brass octets; com-
      positions for eight woodwind instru-
      ments are entered under Woodwind
      octets.

Wind octets *(M855-859)*
  (Continued)
    Headings with specification of instru-
      ments are printed below only if spe-
      cific cross references are needed.
  UF Octets, Wind
  SA Suites, Variations, Waltzes, *and similar*
      headings with specification of
      instruments
  Note under Octets
Wind octets (Bassoons (2), English horns (2),
    horns (2), oboes (2)), Arranged
    (M858-9)
Wind quartets *(M455-459)*
    Collections of compositions for various
      combinations of four wind (i.e. brass
      and woodwind) instruments are en-
      tered under this heading without
      specification of instruments. Separate
      compositions and collections of com-
      positions for four specific wind instru-
      ments are entered under this heading
      followed by specification of instru-
      ments in alphabetical order.
    Compositions for four brass instruments
      are entered under Brass quartets; com-
      positions for four woodwind instru-
      ments are entered under Woodwind
      quartets.
    Headings with specification of instru-
      ments are printed below only if spe-
      cific cross references are needed.
  UF Quartets, Wind
  SA Suites, Variations, Waltzes, *and similar*
      headings with specification of
      instruments
  Note under Quartets
Wind quartets (Bassoon, clarinet, flute, horn)
    (M455-459)
  NT Bassoon, clarinet, flute, horn with
      orchestra
      Concertos (Bassoon, clarinet, flute,
      horn)
Wind quartets (Bassoon, clarinet, flute,
    trumpet) *(M455-459)*
  NT Bassoon, clarinet, flute, trumpet with
      string orchestra
      Concertos (Bassoon, clarinet, flute,
      trumpet with string orchestra)
Wind quartets (Bassoon, clarinet, horn, oboe)
    (M455-459)
  NT Bassoon, clarinet, horn, oboe with
      orchestra
      Bassoon, clarinet, horn, oboe with
      string orchestra
      Concertos (Bassoon, clarinet, horn,
      oboe)
      Concertos (Bassoon, clarinet, horn,
      oboe with string orchestra)
Wind quartets (Bassoon, flute, horn, oboe)
    (M455-9)
  NT Bassoon, flute, horn, oboe with
      chamber orchestra

Wind quartets (Bassoon, flute, horn, oboe)
   (M455-9)
   (Continued)
   NT   Bassoon, flute, horn, oboe with
         orchestra
         Bassoon, flute, horn, oboe with string
         orchestra
         Concertos (Bassoon, flute, horn, oboe)
         Concertos (Bassoon, flute, horn, oboe
         with chamber orchestra)
         Concertos (Bassoon, flute, horn, oboe
         with string orchestra)
Wind quartets (Horns (2), oboes (2))
   (M455-459)
   NT   Concertos (Horns (2), oboes (2) with
         string orchestra)
         Horns (2), oboes (2) with string
         orchestra
Wind quintets *(M555-559)*
         Collections of compositions for various
         combinations of five wind (i.e. brass
         and woodwind) instruments are en-
         tered under this heading without
         specification of instruments. Separate
         compositions and collections of com-
         positions for five specific wind instru-
         ments are entered under this heading
         followed by specification of instru-
         ments in alphabetical order.
         Compositions for five brass instruments
         are entered under Brass quintets; com-
         positions for five woodwind instru-
         ments are entered under Woodwind
         quintets.
         Headings with specification of instru-
         ments are printed below only if spe-
         cific cross references are needed.
   UF   Quintets, Wind
   SA   Suites, Variations, Waltzes, *and similar*
         headings with specification of
         instruments
   Note under Quintets
Wind quintets, Arranged *(M558-9)*
Wind quintets (Bassoon, clarinet, flute, horn,
   oboe) *(M555-559)*
   NT   Bassoon, clarinet, flute, horn, oboe with
         band
         Bassoon, clarinet, flute, horn, oboe with
         chamber orchestra
         Bassoon, clarinet, flute, horn, oboe with
         orchestra
         Bassoon, clarinet, flute, horn, oboe with
         string orchestra
         Concertos (Bassoon, clarinet, flute,
         horn, oboe)
         Concertos (Bassoon, clarinet, flute,
         horn, oboe with band)
         Concertos (Bassoon, clarinet, flute,
         horn, oboe with chamber orchestra)
         Concertos (Bassoon, clarinet, flute,
         horn, oboe with string orchestra)
         Variations (Bassoon, clarinet, flute,
         horn, oboe)

Wind quintets (Bassoon, clarinet, flute, horn,
   oboe), Arranged *(M558-559)*
   NT   Symphonies arranged for bassoon,
         clarinet, flute, horn, oboe
Wind quintets (Bassoon, flute, horn, oboe,
   trumpet) *(M555-559)*
   NT   Bassoon, flute, horn, oboe, trumpet
         with string orchestra
         Concertos (Bassoon, flute, horn, oboe,
         trumpet with string orchestra)
Wind screens
   USE   Windscreens
Wind septets *(M755-759)*
         Collections of compositions for various
         combinations of seven wind (i.e. brass
         and woodwind) instruments are en-
         tered under this heading without
         specification of instruments. Separate
         compositions and collections of com-
         positions for seven specific wind instru-
         ments are entered under this heading
         followed by specification of instru-
         ments in alphabetical order.
         Compositions for seven brass instruments
         are entered under Brass septets; com-
         positions for seven woodwind instru-
         ments are entered under Woodwind
         septets.
         Headings with specification of instru-
         ments are printed below only if spe-
         cific cross references are needed.
   UF   Septets, Wind
   SA   Suites, Variations, Waltzes, *and similar*
         headings with specification of
         instruments
   Note under Septets
Wind sextets *(M655-659)*
         Collections of compositions for various
         combinations of six wind (i.e. brass
         and woodwind) instruments are en-
         tered under this heading without
         specification of instruments. Separate
         compositions and collections of com-
         positions for six specific wind instru-
         ments are entered under this heading
         followed by specification of instru-
         ments in alphabetical order.
         Compositions for six brass instruments
         are entered under Brass sextets; com-
         positions for six woodwind instru-
         ments are entered under Woodwind
         sextets.
         Headings with specification of instru-
         ments are printed below only if spe-
         cific cross references are needed.
   UF   Sextets, Wind
   SA   Suites, Variations, Waltzes, *and similar*
         headings with specification of instruments
   Note under Sextets
Wind sextets (Bassoon, clarinets (2), flute,
   horn, oboe) *(M655-7)*
Wind sextets (Bassoon, clarinets (2), flute,
   horn, oboe), Arranged *(M658-9)*

Wind sextets (Bassoons (2), clarinets (2), horns (2)) *(M655-7)*
Wind sextets (Bassoons (2), horns (2), oboes (2)) *(M655-7)*
Wind trios *(M355-359)*

    Collections of compositions for various combinations of three wind (i.e. brass and woodwind) instruments are entered under this heading without specification of instruments. Separate compositions and collections of compositions for three specific wind instruments are entered under this heading followed by specification of instruments in alphabetical order.

    Compositions for three brass instruments are entered under Brass trios; compositions for three woodwind instruments are entered under Woodwind trios.

    Headings with specification of instruments are printed below only if specific cross references are needed.

  SA Suites, Variations, Waltzes, *and similar headings with specification of instruments*

Wind trios (Bassoon, clarinet, trumpet) *(M355-359)*
  NT Bassoon, clarinet, trumpet with orchestra
       Bassoon, clarinet, trumpet with string orchestra
       Concertos (Bassoon, clarinet, trumpet)
       Concertos (Bassoon, clarinet, trumpet with string orchestra)

Wind trios (Bassoon, oboe, trumpet) *(M355-359)*
  NT Bassoon, oboe, trumpet with string orchestra
       Concertos (Bassoon, oboe, trumpet with string orchestra)

Wind trios (Clarinet, flute, trumpet) *(M355-359)*
  NT Clarinet, flute, trumpet with string orchestra
       Concertos (Clarinet, flute, trumpet with string orchestra)

Wind trios (Clarinet, trombone, trumpet) *(M355-359)*
  NT Clarinet, trombone, trumpet with string orchestra
       Concertos (Clarinet, trombone, trumpet with string orchestra)

Wind trios (Flute, oboe, trumpet) *(M355-359)*
  NT Concertos (Flute, oboe, trumpet with string orchestra)
       Flute, oboe, trumpet with string orchestra

Wind trios (Oboes (2), trumpet) *(M355-7)*
  NT Concertos (Oboes (2), trumpet with string orchestra)
       Oboes (2), trumpet with string orchestra

Wit and humor, Musical

    Here are entered musical compositions of humorous effect, achieved through the setting of humorous texts, parody of musical styles, devices imitative of non-musical sounds and other phenomena. Used only for additional entries, *e.g.* 1. Orchestral music. 2. Wit and humor, Musical.

  UF Musical parodies
       Musical wit and humor
       Parodies (Music)
  SA Subdivision Parodies, imitations, etc. under names of individual composers
  NT Humorous songs

Wives [May Subd Geog]
  NT Musicians' wives

Women as composers
  USE Women composers

Women composers [May Subd Geog]
  UF Composers, Women
       Women as composers
  BT Composers
       Women musicians

Women composers, Afro-American
  USE Afro-American women composers

Women hymn writers [May Subd Geog] *(BV325)*
  BT Hymn writers
       Women poets

Women in opera

    Here are entered works which discuss the portrayal of women in opera.

  BT Opera

Women jazz musicians [May Subd Geog]
  BT Jazz musicians
       Women musicians

Women musicians [May Subd Geog]
  UF Musicians, Women
       Women as musicians
  BT Musicians
  NT Women composers
       Women jazz musicians
  —Japan
      NT Goze

Women musicians, Afro-American
  USE Afro-American women musicians

Woodland Opera House Site (Woodland, Calif.)
  BT California—Antiquities

Woodwind ensembles *(M955-M959)*

    Here are entered compositions for ten or more different solo woodwind instruments, and collections of compositions for a varying number or combination of different solo woodwind instruments. Compositions for ten or more like woodwind instruments and collections of compositions for a varying number of like woodwind instruments are entered under Flute ensembles, Recorder ensembles, and similar headings.

    When used in conjunction with specific solo instrument(s), the qualifier woodwind

Woodwind ensembles *(M955-M959)*

(Continued)

ensemble may stand for any number or
combination of solo woodwind
instruments.

BT Wind ensembles

SA Concertos ([Solo instrument(s)] with
woodwind ensemble); [Solo
instrument(s)] with woodwind
ensemble; Suites, Variations,
Waltzes, *and similar headings with
specification of instruments which
include the specification:* Woodwind
ensemble

Notes under Instrumental ensemble; Wind ensembles

Woodwind instrument makers

BT Wind instrument makers

NT Flute makers

Woodwind instrument music *(M111)*

Here are entered musical compositions
for an unspecified solo woodwind instrument. Works for a specified instrument are entered under Bassoon music, Clarinet music, and similar headings.

UF Melody instrument music
Unspecified instrument music

BT Solo instrument music
Wind instrument music

Woodwind instruments *(History and
construction, ML931; Instruction,
MT339)*

UF Wood-wind instruments

BT Wind instruments

NT Aulos
Bagpipe
Basset horn
Bassoon
Chalumeau (Single-reed musical
instrument)
Clarinet
Crumhorn
Dulzaina
English horn
Fife
Flageolet
Flute
Galoubet
Oboe
Ocarina
Panpipes
P'illyul
Pipe (Musical instrument)
Pommer
Racket (Musical instrument)
Recorder (Musical instrument)
Saxophone
Shakuhachi
Shawm
Tárogató
Tibia (Musical instrument)
Zumari

Woodwind instruments *(History and construction,
ML931; Instruction, MT339)*

(Continued)

—Reeds

Example under Reeds (Music)

—Tuning

Woodwind nonets *(M955-M959)*

Here are entered collections of compositions for various combinations
of nine woodwind instruments.
Separate compositions and collections of compositions for nine
specific woodwind instruments are
entered under this heading followed
by specification of instruments in
alphabetical order.

UF Nonets, Woodwind

SA Suites, Variations, Waltzes, *and similar
headings with specification of
instruments*

Note under Wind nonets

Woodwind nonets (Clarinets (9)) *(M955-M956;
M957.2; M958-M959)*

UF Clarinet music (Clarinets (9))

Woodwind nonets (Flutes (9)) *(M955-M956;
M957.2; M958-959)*

UF Flute music (Flutes (9))

Woodwind octets *(M855-M859)*

Here are entered collections of
compositions for various combinations of eight woodwind
instruments. Separate compositions
and collections of compositions for
eight specific woodwind instruments
are entered under this heading followed
by specification of instruments in
alphabetical order.

UF Octets, Woodwind

SA Suites, Variations, Waltzes, *and similar
headings with specification of instruments*

Note under Wind octets

**Woodwind octets (Basset horn, clarinets (6),
tárogató)** *(M855-M856; M857.2;
M858-M859)*

BT Tárogató music

Woodwind octets (Clarinets (8)) *(M855-M856;
M857.2; M858-M859)*

UF Clarinet music (Clarinets (8))

Woodwind octets (Flutes (8)) *(M855-M856;
M857.2; M858-M859)*

UF Flute music (Flutes (8))

Woodwind octets (Recorders (8))
(M855-M856; M857.2; M858-M859)

UF Recorder music (Recorders (8))

Woodwind quartets *(M455-M459)*

Here are entered collections of
compositions for various combinations of
four woodwind instruments.Separate
compositions and collections of composi
tions for four specific woodwind instru
ments are entered under this heading
followed by specification of instruments in
alphabetical order.

Woodwind quartets *(M455-M459)*
  (Continued)
  UF Quartets, Woodwind
  SA Suites, Variations, Waltzes, *and similar*
      headings with specification of instruments
  Note under Wind quartets
Woodwind quartets (Basset horn, clarinets
      (3)) *(M455-M456; M457.2;*
      M458-M459)
Woodwind quartets (Basset horns (2),
      bassoon, English horn) *(M455-456;*
      M457.2; M458-459)
Woodwind quartets (Bassoon, clarinet, English
      horn, flute) *(M455-M456; M457.2;*
      M458-M459)
  NT Bassoon, clarinet, English horn, flute
      with orchestra
      Concertos (Bassoon, clarinet, English
      horn, flute)
Woodwind quartets (Bassoon, clarinet, flute,
      oboe) *(M455-M456; M457.2;*
      M458-M459)
  NT Bassoon, clarinet, flute, oboe with
      chamber orchestra
      Bassoon, clarinet, flute, oboe with
      orchestra
      Bassoon, clarinet, flute, oboe with string
      orchestra
      Concertos (Bassoon, clarinet, flute, oboe)
      Concertos (Bassoon, clarinet, flute,
      oboe with chamber orchestra)
      Concertos (Bassoon, clarinet, flute,
      oboe with string orchestra)
Woodwind quartets (Bassoon, clarinets (2),
      oboe) *(M455-M456; M457.2;*
      M458-M459)
  NT Bassoon, clarinets (2), oboe with
      orchestra
      Concertos (Bassoon, clarinets (2), oboe)
Woodwind quartets (Bassoons (4))
      (M455-M456; M457.2; M458-M459)
  UF Bassoon music (Bassoons (4))
Woodwind quartets (Clarinet, English horn,
      flute, oboe) *(M455-M456; M457.2;*
      M458-M459)
  NT Clarinet, English horn, flute, oboe with
      string orchestra
      Concertos (Clarinet, English horn, flute,
      oboe with string orchestra)
Woodwind quartets (Clarinets (2), oboes (2))
      (M455-M456; M457.2; M458-M459)
  NT Clarinets (2), oboes (2) with string
      orchestra
      Concertos (Clarinets (2), oboes (2) with
      string orchestra)
Woodwind quartets (Clarinets (4))
      (M455-M456; M457.4; M458-M459)
  UF Clarinet music (Clarinets (4))
  NT Clarinets (4) with orchestra
      Clarinets (4) with string orchestra
      Concertos (Clarinets (4))
      Concertos (Clarinets (4) with string
      orchestra)

Woodwind quartets (Clarinets (4)), Arranged
      (M458-459)
  NT Symphonies arranged for clarinets (4)
Woodwind quartets (Crumhorns (4)) *(M990)*
  BT Crumhorn music
Woodwind quartets (English horn,
      heckelphone, oboe, oboe d'amore)
      (M455-M456; M457.2; M458-M459)
  BT Heckelphone music
Woodwind quartets (Flutes (4)) *(M455-M456;*
      M457.2; M458-M459)
  UF Flute music (Flutes (4))
  NT Concertos (Flutes (4) with band)
      Concertos (Flutes (4) with chamber
      orchestra)
      Flutes (4) with band
      Flutes (4) with chamber orchestra
Woodwind quartets (Flutes (4)), Arranged
      (M458-459)
  NT Overtures arranged for flutes (4)
Woodwind quartets (Oboes (4)) *(M455-M456;*
      M457.2; M458-M459)
  UF Oboe music (Oboes (4))
  NT Concertos (Oboes (4) with string
      orchestra)
      Oboes (4) with string orchestra
Woodwind quartets (Pipes (4)) *(M455-459)*
  BT Pipe music
Woodwind quartets (Recorders (4)) *(M455-M456;*
      M457.2; M458-M459)
  UF Recorder music (Recorders (4))
  NT Concertos (Recorders (4) with string
      orchestra)
      Recorders (4) with string orchestra
Woodwind quartets (Saxophones (4))
      (M455-M456; M457.2; M458-M459)
  UF Saxophone music (Saxophones (4))
  NT Concertos (Saxophones (4))
      Concertos (Saxophones (4) with band)
      Concertos (Saxophones (4) with
      chamber orchestra)
      Concertos (Saxophones (4) with string
      orchestra)
      Saxophones (4) with band
      Saxophones (4) with chamber orchestra
      Saxophones (4) with orchestra
      Saxophones (4) with string orchestra
Woodwind quintets *(M555-M556; M557.2;*
      M558-M559)
      Collections of compositions for various
      combinations of five woodwind instru-
      ments are entered under this head-
      ing without specification of instru-
      ments. Separate compositions and col-
      lections of compositions for five spe-
      cific woodwind instruments are
      entered under this heading followed by
      specification of instruments in alpha-
      betical order.
      Headings with specification of instru-
      ments are printed below only if spe-
      cific cross references are needed.

Woodwind quintets *(M555-M556; M557.2;*
       M558-M559)
   (Continued)
   UF   Quintets, Woodwind
   SA   Suites, Variations, Waltzes, *and similar*
          headings with specification of
          instruments
   Note under Wind quintets
Woodwind quintets (Clarinets (5))
       (M555-M556; M557.2; M558-M559)
   UF   Clarinet music (Clarinets (5))
Woodwind quintets (Flutes (5)) *(M555-M556;*
       M557.2; M558-M559)
   UF   Flute music (Flutes (5))
Woodwind quintets (Recorders (5))
       (M555-M556; M557.2; M558-M559)
   UF   Recorder music (Recorders (5))
   NT   Overtures (Recorders (5))
Woodwind septets *(M755-M759)*
       Here are entered collections of compo-
       sitions for various combinations of
       seven woodwind instruments. Separate
       compositions and collections of comp-
       ositions for seven specific woodwind
       instruments are entered under this
       heading followed by specification of
       instruments in alphabetical order.
   UF   Septets, Woodwind
   SA   Suites, Variations, Waltzes, *and similar*
          headings with specification of
          instruments
   Note under Wind septets
Woodwind septets (Clarinets (7))
       (M755-M756; M757.2; M758-M759)
   UF   Clarinet music (Clarinets (7))
Woodwind septets (Flutes (7)) *(M755-M756;*
       M757.2; M758-M759)
   UF   Flute music (Flutes (7))
Woodwind septets (Recorders (7))
       (M755-M756; M757.2; M758-M759)
   UF   Recorder music (Recorders (7))
Woodwind sextets *(M655-M659)*
       Here are entered collections of compo-
       sitions for various combinations of
       six woodwind instruments. Separate
       compositions and collections of com-
       positions for six specific woodwind
       instruments are entered under this
       heading followed by specification of
       instruments in alphabetical order.
   UF   Sextets, Woodwind
   SA   Suites, Variations, Waltzes, *and similar*
          headings with specification of
          instruments
   Note under Wind sextets
Woodwind sextets (Clarinets (6))
       (M655-M656; M657.2; M658-M659)
   UF   Clarinet music (Clarinets (6))
   NT   Clarinets (6) with band
          Concertos (Clarinets (6) with band)
Woodwind sextets (Flutes (6)) *(M655-M656;*
       M657.2; M658-M659)
   UF   Flute music (Flutes (6))

Woodwind sextets (Recorders (6))
       (M655-M656; M657.2; M658-M659)
   UF   Recorder music (Recorders (6))
   NT   Concertos (Recorders (6) with string
          orchestra)
          Recorders (6) with string orchestra
Woodwind trios *(M355-M359)*
       Here are entered collections of compo-
       sitions for various combinations of
       three woodwind instruments. Separate
       compositions and collections of com-
       positions for three specific woodwind
       instruments are entered under this
       heading followed by specification of
       instruments in alphabetical order.
   UF   Trios, Woodwind
   SA   Suites, Variations, Waltzes, *and similar*
          headings with specification of instruments
   Notes under Chamber music; Wind trios
Woodwind trios (Bass clarinet, clarinets (2))
       (M355-M356; M357.2; M358-M359)
Woodwind trios (Basset horns (2), bassoon)
       (M355-M356; M357.2; M358-M359)
Woodwind trios (Bassoon, clarinet, flute)
       (M355-M356; M357.2; M358-M359)
   NT   Bassoon, clarinet, flute with string
          orchestra
          Concertos (Bassoon, clarinet, flute with
          string orchestra)
Woodwind trios (Bassoon, clarinet, oboe)
       (M355-M356; M357.2; M358-M359)
   NT   Bassoon, clarinet, oboe with string
          orchestra
          Concertos (Bassoon, clarinet, oboe with
          string orchestra)
Woodwind trios (Bassoon, flute, oboe)
       (M355-M356; M357.2; M358-M359)
   NT   Bassoon, flute, oboe with orchestra
          Concertos (Bassoon, flute, oboe)
Woodwind trios (Bassoon, flutes (2))
       (M355-M356; M357.2; M358-M359)
   NT   Bassoon, flutes (2) with string orchestra
          Concertos (Bassoon, flutes (2) with
          string orchestra)
Woodwind trios (Clarinet, flute, oboe)
       (M355-M356; M357.2; M358-M359)
   NT   Clarinet, flute, oboe with instrumental
          ensemble
          Clarinet, flute, oboe with string
          orchestra
          Concertos (Clarinet, flute, oboe with
          instrumental ensemble)
          Concertos (Clarinet, flute, oboe with
          string orchestra)
Woodwind trios (Clarinets (3)) *(M355-M356;*
       M357.2; M358-M359)
   UF   Clarinet music (Clarinets (3))
   NT   Clarinets (3) with string orchestra
          Concertos (Clarinets (3) with string
          orchestra)
Woodwind trios (English horn, heckelphone,
       oboe) *(M355-M356; M357.2; M358-M359)*
   BT   Heckelphone music

Woodwind trios (Flutes (3)) *(M355-M356;*
  M357.2; M358-M359)
  UF Flute music (Flutes (3))
  NT Concertos (Flutes (3) with band)
    Concertos (Flutes (3) with string
      orchestra)
    Flutes (3) with band
    Flutes (3) with string orchestra
Woodwind trios (Oboes (3)) *(M355-M356;*
  M357.2; M358-M359)
  UF Oboe music (Oboes (3))
  NT Concertos (Oboes (3) with string
      orchestra)
    Oboes (3) with string orchestra
Woodwind trios (Recorders (3)) *(M355-M356;*
  M357.2; M358-M359)
  UF Recorder music (Recorders (3))
  NT Concertos (Recorders (3) with string
      orchestra)
    Recorders (3) with string orchestra
Woodwind trios (Saxophones (3))
    (M355-M356; M357.2; M358-M359)
  UF Saxophone music (Saxophones (3))
Work-songs [May Subd Geog] *(History and criticism,*
    ML3780; Music collections, M1977.L3;
    Music separate works, M1978.L3)
  BT Folk-songs
    Songs
  RT Labor and laboring classes—Songs and
      music
  NT Rice—Planting—Songs and music
World War, 1939-1945 [May Subd Geog]
    (D731-838)
  —Music
    USE World War, 1939-1945—Songs
        and music
  —Music and the war *(D810.E8)*
    RT World War, 1939-1945—Songs and
        music
      Example under Music and war
  —Songs and music
    UF World War, 1939-1945—Music
    RT World War, 1939-1945—Music and
        the war
      Example under Military music; Music
        and the war
Wu li wa
  USE So na
Wurlitzer organ *(ML597)*
  BT Electronic organ
    Organ
Xhosa hymns
  USE Hymns, Xhosa
Xylophone *(ML1040)*
  UF Song bells
    Straw fiddle
  BT Percussion instruments
  RT Marimba
    Menzan
    Vibraphone
  NT Angklung
    Balo

Xylophone and piano music *(M284-5)*
  UF Piano and xylophone music
Xylophone and piano music, Arranged
    (M284.X9; M285.X9)
  NT Concertos (Xylophone)—Solo with
      piano
    Suites (Xylophone with orchestra)—
      Solo with piano
    Xylophone with orchestra—Solo with
      piano
Xylophone and piano music, Arranged (Jazz)
  USE Xylophone and piano music (Jazz)
Xylophone and piano music (Jazz) *(M284-5)*
  UF Xylophone and piano music, Arranged
      (Jazz)
Xylophone music *(M175.X6)*
  BT Vibraphone music
  SA Concertos, Minuets, Sonatas, Suites,
      and similar headings with
      specification of instruments; Trios
      [Quartets, etc.] *followed by*
      specifications which include the
      xylophone; also Percussion
      ensembles, Percussion music *and*
      headings that begin with the words
      xylophone or xylophones
  NT Quintets (Piano, trombone, trumpet,
      xylophone, violin)
    Sonatas (Xylophone)
    Trios (Piano, xylophones (2))
  Note under Percussion music
Xylophone with orchestra *(M1038-9)*
  RT Concertos (Xylophone)
  NT Suites (Xylophone with orchestra)
  —Solo with piano *(M1039)*
    BT Xylophone and piano music,
        Arranged
Zarzuelas
    M1500-M1508
  UF Operettas
  BT Operas
  —Excerpts, Arranged
Zydeco music [May Subd Geog]
  BT Popular music—Louisiana